TAGUCHI METHODS®

TAGUCHI METHODS®

A HANDS-ON APPROACH

Glen Stuart Peace

ADDISON-WESLEY PUBLISHING COMPANY

Reading, Massachusetts • Menlo Park, California • New York • Don Mills, Ontario
Wokingham, England • Amsterdam • Bonn • Paris • Milan • Madrid
Sydney • Singapore • Tokyo • Seoul • Taipei • Mexico City • San Juan

The publisher offers discounts on this book when ordered in quantity for special sales. For more information, please contact:

Corporate & Professional Publishing Group
Addison-Wesley Publishing Company
One Jacob Way
Reading, Massachusetts 01867

Library of Congress Cataloging-in-Publication Data

Peace, Glen Stuart.
Taguchi methods: a hands-on approach / Glen Stuart Peace.
p. cm.
ISBN 0-201-56311-8
1. Taguchi methods (Quality control) I. Title.
TS156.P33 1993
658.5′62—dc20 92-14442
CIP

Cover design by Simone R. Payment
Text design by Wilson Graphics & Design (Kenneth J. Wilson)
Set in 10 point Palatino by J.M. Post Graphics, Corp.

ISBN 0-201-56311-8

2 3 4 5 6 7 8 9 10 11 MU 9796959493
Second printing June 1993

To Patricia
my most devout supporter,
my best critic,
my top reviewer,
and my wife.

And to Gretchen, Donovan, and Gavin,
my patient little editors.

Contents

Foreword xvii

Preface xix

Acknowledgments xxv

Chapter 1 **CONCEPTUAL BACKGROUND** 1

1.1 HISTORY 1

1.2 CONTRIBUTIONS TO QUALITY 3

1.2.1 The Loss Function 3

1.2.2 Orthogonal Arrays and Linear Graphs 4

1.2.3 Robustness 5

1.3 QUALITY ENGINEERING 6

1.3.1 On-line Quality Control 7

1.3.2 Off-line Quality Control 7

1.4 USING EXPERIMENTATION 9

1.4.1 Experiment Design Comparisons 9

1.4.2 Experiment Design Phases 10

Chapter 2 **FORMING THE EXPERIMENTATION TEAM** 13

2.1 ESTABLISHING GOALS 14

2.2 DETERMINING WHO CAN BEST IMPACT THE GOAL 16

2.2.1 Who Is Capable of Understanding the Goal? 16

2.2.2 Whom Does the Goal Impact? 17

2.2.3 Who Is Involved in the Process? 18

2.2.4 Who Understands the Process? 19

2.2.5 Who Supports the Process? 20

2.3 SELECTION OF THE TEAM LEADER 21

Chapter 3 **DETERMINING THE OBJECTIVES** 23

3.1 EXAMINING THE PROCESS AND PRODUCT 24

3.1.1 Brainstorming 25

3.1.2 The Pareto Chart 27

3.1.3 The Process Flow Diagram 31

3.1.4 The Cause-and-Effect Diagram 36

3.1.5 Fault Tree Analysis 39

3.1.6 Failure Mode and Effect Analysis (FMEA) 41

3.2 DEFINING THE QUALITY CHARACTERISTIC 44

3.2.1 Measurable Characteristics 46

3.2.2 Attribute Characteristics 47

3.2.3 Dynamic Characteristics 49

3.2.4 Comparison of Quality Characteristic Types 51

Chapter 4 **MEASUREMENT CONSIDERATIONS** 55

4.1 MEASUREMENT PLANNING 56

4.2 INSTRUMENT AVAILABILITY 57

4.3 INSTRUMENT RESOLUTION 58

4.4 INSTRUMENT ACCURACY/REPEATABILITY 58

4.5 TEST OPERATOR/INSPECTOR 62

4.6 MEASUREMENT ENVIRONMENT 63

4.7 CLASSIFIED ATTRIBUTE MEASUREMENTS 64

4.8 SAMPLING REQUIREMENTS 66

Chapter 5 **SELECTING THE INDEPENDENT VARIABLES** 70

5.1 LISTING THE VARIABLES OF INTEREST 70

5.2 SCREENING THE LIST OF VARIABLES 72

5.3 CLASSIFYING THE VARIABLES 74

5.4 SPECIFYING PARAMETER SETTINGS 79

5.4.1 Control Factors 80

5.4.2 Noise Factors 82

5.5 POTENTIAL INTERACTION CONCERNS 85
5.6 WHITE POWDER CASE STUDY 90

Chapter 6 **EXPERIMENTAL STRATEGY** 97
6.1 SINGLE EXPERIMENTS 98
6.1.1 Single Experiment Example 100
6.2 CONTINUOUS EXPERIMENTS 101
6.2.1 Continuous Experiment Example 104
6.3 SCREENING EXPERIMENTS 104
6.3.1 Screening Experiment Example 106
6.4 FOCUSING EXPERIMENTS 107
6.4.1 Focusing Experiment Example 109
6.5 SEQUENTIAL EXPERIMENTS 110
6.5.1 Sequential Experiment Example 112

Chapter 7 **ORTHOGONAL ARRAYS** 114
7.1 ORTHOGONALITY 114
7.2 TERMINOLOGY 118
7.3 ANALYSIS 119
7.4 INTERACTIONS 119
7.5 ORTHOGONAL ARRAY SERIES 122
7.5.1 2^n Series Orthogonal Arrays 123
7.5.2 3^n Series Orthogonal Arrays 125

Chapter 8 **DEGREES OF FREEDOM** 129
8.1 CONCEPTS 129
8.2 CALCULATIONS 131
8.2.1 Factors or Main Effects 132
8.2.2 Interactions 132
8.2.3 Orthogonal Arrays 134

Chapter 9 **LINEAR GRAPHS** 138
9.1 CONCEPTS 138

9.2 ASSIGNING FACTORS TO LINEAR GRAPHS 141

9.3 STANDARD LINEAR GRAPHS 142

9.3.1 L_4 (2^3) Linear Graph 142

9.3.2 L_8 (2^7) Linear Graphs 142

9.3.3 L_{16} (2^{15}) Linear Graphs 143

9.3.4 L_9 (3^4) Linear Graph 143

9.3.5 L_{18} ($2^1 \times 3^7$) Linear Graph 143

9.3.6 L_{27} (3^{13}) Linear Graphs 145

9.4 STANDARD LINEAR GRAPH PROBLEMS 146

9.4.1 Example Number 1 146

9.4.2 Example Number 2 147

9.4.3 Example Number 3 150

9.4.4 Example Number 4 152

9.5 MODIFYING STANDARD LINEAR GRAPHS 154

9.6 MODIFIED LINEAR GRAPH PROBLEMS 157

9.6.1 Example Number 1 157

9.6.2 Example Number 2 160

9.6.3 Example Number 3 164

Chapter 10 **THE OUTER ARRAY** 167

10.1 NO NOISE FACTORS 167

10.2 NOISE FACTORS 169

10.3 DYNAMIC CHARACTERISTICS 172

Chapter 11 **REMOVING EXPERIMENTAL BIAS** 175

11.1 EXPERIMENTAL ERROR 175

11.2 RANDOMIZATION 178

11.3 REPETITION 180

11.4 REPLICATION 182

11.5 RANDOMIZATION GUIDELINES 183

Chapter 12 **TEST PLAN DEVELOPMENT** 188

12.1 TEST PLAN STRUCTURE 188

12.1.1 Statement of Purpose 189

12.1.2 Experiment Objectives 189

12.1.3 Experiment Description 190

12.1.4 Testing/Inspection Procedures 190

12.1.5 Data Worksheet 191

12.1.6 Analysis Techniques 191

12.2 SAMPLING GUIDELINES 192

12.3 SAMPLE SELECTION 193

12.4 SAMPLE PREPARATION 196

12.5 SAMPLE IDENTIFICATION 196

12.6 SAMPLE ORDERING 197

12.7 DATA WORKSHEET 197

12.7.1 Surface Mount Data Sheet 199

12.7.2 Wavesolder Data Sheet 199

12.8 CRACKED CAPACITOR TEST PLAN EXAMPLE 199

12.8.1 Statement of Purpose 202

12.8.2 Experiment Objectives 202

12.8.3 Experiment Description 202

12.8.4 Testing/Inspection Procedures 205

12.8.5 Data Worksheet 207

12.8.6 Analysis Techniques 207

Chapter 13 **PREPARING THE EXPERIMENT** 208

13.1 SELECTING MATERIAL AND EQUIPMENT 208

13.1.1 Material 208

13.1.2 Equipment 210

13.2 ACQUIRING MATERIAL AND EQUIPMENT 211

13.2.1 Material 211

13.2.2 Equipment 212

13.3 SCREENING MATERIAL 213
13.4 IDENTIFYING AND RANDOMIZING TEST SAMPLES 213
13.5 OPERATOR PREPARATION 214
13.6 INSPECTION GUIDELINES 215
13.7 SCHEDULING EQUIPMENT 217

Chapter 14 **CONDUCTING THE EXPERIMENT** 218
14.1 EXPERIMENTAL RUN COORDINATION 219
14.2 EXPERIMENTAL RUN SHEETS 220
14.2.1 Measurable Characteristic Run Sheet 220
14.2.2 Classified Attribute Run Sheet 224
14.2.3 Dynamic Characteristic Run Sheet 228
14.3 TIME CONSTRAINTS AND OTHER CONSIDERATIONS 228
14.4 DOCUMENTATION OF EXPERIMENT 233

Chapter 15 **LEVEL AVERAGE ANALYSIS** 236
15.1 CONCEPTS 236
15.2 DIGITAL CIRCUIT (LARGER-THE-BETTER) CASE STUDY 240
15.3 CONTROL DEVICE "TIME OUT" (SMALLER-THE-BETTER) CASE STUDY 249

Chapter 16 **CLASSIFIED ATTRIBUTE ANALYSIS** 256
16.1 CONCEPTS 256
16.2 CASING PAINT STUDY 264

Chapter 17 **ANALYSIS: SMALLER-THE-BETTER** 273
17.1 SIGNAL-TO-NOISE RATIO 274
17.2 ANALYSIS TECHNIQUES 276
17.3 ELECTRONIC CIRCUIT "TIME OUT" CASE STUDY 281

Chapter 18 **ANALYSIS: LARGER-THE-BETTER** 292

18.1 SIGNAL-TO-NOISE RATIO 294

18.2 ANALYSIS TECHNIQUES 295

18.3 WIRE CONNECTOR ASSEMBLY CASE STUDY 299

Chapter 19 **ANALYSIS: NOMINAL-THE-BEST** 312

19.1 CONCEPTS 312

19.1.1 Nominal-the-Best Equations 315

19.2 YARDSTICK CASE STUDY 318

19.3 MODEM SUBCIRCUIT CASE STUDY 331

Chapter 20 **ANALYSIS: DYNAMIC CHARACTERISTICS** 338

20.1 APPLICATIONS 338

20.1.1 Measurement Systems 339

20.1.2 Manufacturing Systems 339

20.1.3 Design Systems 340

20.2 CRITERIA 340

20.2.1 Sensitivity 341

20.2.2 Linearity 341

20.2.3 Variability 342

20.3 SIGNAL FACTOR CLASSIFICATIONS 343

20.3.1 True Value Known 343

20.3.2 Intervals between Factor Levels Known 343

20.3.3 Factor Level Ratios Known 344

20.3.4 Factor Level Values Vague 344

20.4 SIGNAL-TO-NOISE RATIO EQUATIONS 345

20.4.1 Zero Point Proportional Equation 346

20.4.2 Reference Point Proportional Equation 346

20.4.3 Linear Equation 348

20.4.4 Slope Calibration 349

20.4.5 No Calibration 349

20.5 ZERO POINT PROPORTIONAL EQUATION 350
20.6 REFERENCE POINT PROPORTIONAL EQUATION 353
20.7 LINEAR EQUATION 357
20.8 CIRCUIT DESIGN EXAMPLE 360

Chapter 21 **SPECIAL DESIGN TECHNIQUES** 364
21.1 MULTILEVEL ARRANGEMENTS 364
21.1.1 Four-Level Factor 365
21.1.2 Eight-Level Factor 367
21.1.3 Other Applications 372
21.1.4 Interactions Involving Multilevel Factors 372
21.2 DUMMY TREATMENT 373
21.2.1 Treating Two-Level Factors in $L_3{}^n$ Orthogonal Arrays 373
21.2.2 Combining Dummy Treatment with Multilevel Arrangements 375
21.3 COMBINATION DESIGNS 378
21.3.1 Two Two-Level Factors 379
21.3.2 Multiple Factors 381
21.4 SLIDING LEVELS 382
21.4.1 Wavesolder Experiment 383
21.4.2 Plastic Injection Molding Experiment 384
21.5 NESTED FACTOR DESIGN 385
21.6 IDLE COLUMN METHOD 391

Chapter 22 **MULTIPLE CHARACTERISTICS** 400
22.1 MEASURABLE CHARACTERISTICS 401
22.1.1 Measurable Characteristic Example 403
22.2 ATTRIBUTE CHARACTERISTICS 407
22.2.1 Attribute Characteristic Example 408
22.3 MEASURABLE AND ATTRIBUTE CHARACTERISTICS 412
22.3.1 Nominal-the-Best and Attribute Characteristics 413

22.3.2 Smaller-the-Better and Attribute Characteristics 414
22.3.3 Larger-the-Better and Attribute Characteristics 416
22.4 OPERATING WINDOW 418
22.4.1 Wavesolder Example 418

Chapter 23 **MISSING AND INFEASIBLE DATA** 423
23.1 MISSING DATA 424
23.1.1 Estimation Techniques 424
23.1.2 Missing Data Example 426
23.2 INFEASIBLE DATA 430
23.2.1 Smaller-the-Better Characteristic 431
23.2.2 Larger-the-Better Characteristic 433
23.2.3 Nominal-the-Best Characteristic 435
23.3 IDEAL DATA, INFEASIBLE CALCULATIONS 437

Bibliography 439
Appendix A: ORTHOGONAL ARRAYS 442
Appendix B: LINEAR GRAPHS 463
Appendix C: INTERACTIONS BETWEEN TWO COLUMNS TABLES 507
Index 515

Foreword

There are three important aspects in product, process and manufacturing engineering activities:

Precedency
Universality
Reproducibility

The first leads to technology readiness, which is an absolute necessity for leading the market. The second tunes a product or process to ensure that it satisfies diversified customer requirements. The third assures that the designed system, product, or process functions as it is supposed to through continual use in varied environments. In order for a company to be world-class, all three aspects must be mastered. In the United States most companies are at least equal to their Japanese counterparts in precedency and universality. American engineers are now striving to achieve the same high standards in reproducibility.

Dr. Genichi Taguchi has emphasized two engineering strategies for improving reproducibility and overall quality. One is to use a new set of technical considerations to determine what should be accepted as valid data. A function must be continuously improved in order to eliminate troublesome symptoms, but engineers tend to measure the *symptoms* of variability instead of collecting data that reflect the performance of the function itself. Taguchi strongly recommends taking the dynamic or nominally best characteristic as the true measure of a process, thus avoiding measuring the symptoms. The other crucial strategy is to take noise factors into account to ensure robustness at downstream conditions. Noise factors are uncontrollable variables that can cause significant functional variability. Robustness is desirable since it means that the system functions as it is supposed to in the face of various noise factors. Learning and using Design of Experiments (DOE) can help engineers assess where their methods currently stand and uncover the practical, realistic improvements they need to make.

This book focuses on Taguchi's DOE methodologies. DOE has been used by almost all major Japanese manufacturing companies since the 1950s and 1960s. Nippon Denso Company, an automotive electrical and electronics subsystem supplier in Japan, reports that their engineers conduct more than 4000 experiments every year. One hundred engineers from Toyota Motor Company take a full 120-hour training course in the design of experiments every year. Clearly, this technique provides documented, profound knowledge to engineers—and a straightforward path to improvement.

American companies did not truly become quality conscious until the 1980s, when it became apparent that good quality sells, reduces costs, and increases profits. They also discovered that improving quality without increasing unit manufacturing costs will lead to opportunities to reduce costs proactively. As the quality revolution began to gain momentum, DOE and Taguchi methods became recognized as powerful tools for improvement. In 1985 Ford Motor Company decided to require suppliers to practice DOE, and in 1988 the Department of Defense highlighted the importance of DOE methods in their report on the **Variability Reduction Program.**

I frequently see people facing difficulties in managing experiments due to lack of experience. In addition to the well-selected subjects, the most splendid aspect of this practical new book is the author's insight into planning and running experiments. Readers will learn how to avoid the common traps and pitfalls of applying DOE. In today's competitive manufacturing environment, engineers practicing the ideas outlined in this book will take a big step toward improving their own design and manufacturing methods.

Shin Taguchi
September 1991

Preface

The intention of this book is to provide a basic guide for solving and gaining insight into the everyday quality problems and processes for which the reader is either responsible or which he or she has a duty to support. The focused audience is the supervisor, the engineer, the technician, or any other person who is on the front line and must handle quality problems. This is not an advanced text on statistics. This is meant to be a basic step-by-step guide of simple techniques related in down-to-earth language.

This book is based on the teachings of Dr. Genichi Taguchi, who refers to these techniques as "quality engineering." In line with this philosophy, this book has taken an engineering approach to understanding process information as opposed to a purely statistical approach, although some statistical applications are used.

A controversy does exist concerning these methods. Many in academia complain that Dr. Taguchi does not faithfully follow all applicable statistical rules. Many engineers on the other hand prefer Dr. Taguchi's approach, which uses statistics as a foundation but emphasizes engineering judgment. My experience has been that engineers and other applied users tend to find these techniques more practical and easier to implement in the industrial workplace. At the same time they provide lasting solutions to complex problems and accelerate learning within new technology.

Amid the dispute between "Taguchi bashers" and quality engineering purists, my position is neutral. Nor is my role to debate the controversy. Instead, my purpose is to explain those techniques of Dr. Taguchi that I have found useful and to convey an interpretation of their applicability. In line with a focus on the non-technical user, I have decided to limit the scope to the basic tools of Taguchi methodology.

Concerning the explanations behind Dr. Taguchi's concepts, this is an application guide for the "rolled-up sleeves" problem solver. The purpose behind this particular book is to serve as a tool to facilitate and direct the action takers. Numerous examples have been drawn from real life to demonstrate the power and applicability of these techniques and to serve as guides in similar situations.

The format of this text is a systematic approach for guiding the user step-by-step through a design of experiment using Taguchi techniques. Although not a cookbook format, the framework is laid out in a logical order so that the user can understand each phase and insure that every step has been properly completed.

Chapter 1 provides a conceptual overview of Dr. Taguchi's contributions to quality along with a historical background. Also included is an explanation of the four essential phases of performing an experiment.

Planning the Experiment

Chapters 2 through 6 are devoted to the planning aspects of experimentation. Insuring that the appropriate individuals are involved and that sufficient support is provided throughout the experimentation effort is critical to the success of the experiment. Identification of key personnel and solicitating their support is covered in Chapter 2, "Forming the Experimentation Team."

Chapter 3, "Determining the Objectives," discusses the techniques for properly examining the product or process for defining experiment objectives in specific terms. The uses of Pareto analysis, flow charting, cause-and-effect diagrams, fault tree analysis, and failure mode and effect analysis are explained and illustrated. Properly defining the quality characteristic that is the measure of attaining the experiment objective is also addressed. Definitions of the basic types of quality characteristics, measurable, attribute, and dynamic, are given along with explanations of the differences between each type.

Chapter 4, "Measurement Considerations," is devoted to proper planning for fulfilling measurement requirements. Instrumentation issues covered include availability, precision, accuracy, and repeatability. Test operator and inspection concerns are addressed along with environmental issues. Sampling requirements and guidelines for making subjective readings are also covered.

Chapter 5, "Selecting the Independent Variables," takes the experimenter step-by-step through the selection of factors to incorporate into the study, and specifies meaningful values or settings for these factors. Rules for effective brainstorming are covered for creating a list of potential factors of interest. Instructions for screening the list, classifying the factors, and specifying factor settings are given along with explanations of the logic behind the steps. The concept of interactions is addressed, and methods of dealing with potential interactions are explained.

Chapter 6, "Experimental Strategy," discusses alternative approaches for performing the experiment based on team objectives. The number of factor levels and specific factor settings are contingent on the selected strategy, and their determination is explained. Specific strategies discussed include single experiments, continuous experimentation, screening experiments, focusing studies, and sequential experimentation.

Designing the Experiment

Chapter 7, "Orthogonal Arrays," defines orthogonality and discusses the use of orthogonal arrays for meaningful and cost-effective experimental designs. Terminology is explained, and the most common arrays are reviewed and discussed. Analyses of factors and associated interactions are also covered to provide a further understanding of how orthogonal arrays work.

Chapter 8, "Degrees of Freedom," explains the computations for determining the appropriate orthogonal arrays and discusses the concepts behind them.

Chapter 9, "Linear Graphs," outlines the techniques for assigning factors and interactions to the orthogonal array and provides numerous examples.

Chapter 10, "The Outer Array," explains how noise factors are incorporated into the experiment. The chapter also deals with the design of experiments involving dynamic quality characteristics.

Chapter 11, "Removing Experimental Bias," addresses experimental error. The application of randomization is discussed as it applies to parameter design including where it is appropriate and where it is not essential. Repetition and replication are explained and illustrated, and guidelines for selecting them are presented.

Conducting the Experiment

Chapter 12, "Test Plan Development," covers the requirements for developing a set of written instructions for conducting the experiment. Included is an itemized list of the essential components that comprise a basic test plan structure. Sampling guidelines are also covered including sample selection, preparation, and identification. Suggestions for developing an appropriate data sheet are also given along with examples.

Chapter 13, "Preparing the Experiments," discusses the preliminary work and coordination efforts that must be accomplished to insure smooth conducting of the experiment. Advice on selection and acquisition of material and equipment is given. Recommendations for screening of raw material and identification and randomization of test samples are explained. Operator preparation and inspection guidelines are discussed as well. Equipment scheduling is also addressed.

Chapter 14, "Conducting the Experiment," covers the actual execution of the experimental runs. Topics include coordination of experimental runs, time constraints and related issues, and effective documentation of results and observations. Examples of run sheets to insure correct factor setting for each experimental run are given for each type of quality characteristic.

Analyzing the Experiment

Chapter 15, "Level Average Analysis," provides step-by-step guidelines for interpreting the results for continuously measurable data when an outer array is not present. Generation and interpretation of response tables and graphs are covered. Interaction considerations include development of interaction matrices and graphs and the explanation of their interpretation. Guidelines for identifying strong effects and recommending the most appropriate settings are given. Construction of the prediction equation is explained. The importance of conducting confirmation runs and their evaluation is also addressed. Comprehensive examples are given.

Chapter 16, "Classified Attribute Analysis," covers the step-by-step guidelines for analyzing the results for classified attribute data. The construction and interpretation of response tables and graphs are covered from the perspective of classified attribute data. Interaction matrices and graphs are similarly handled. The omega transformation is explained, and its importance in determining a realistic prediction of optimal results is discussed. Confirmation run analysis is also covered. A case study is included.

Chapter 17, "Analysis: Smaller-the-Better," and Chapter 18, "Analysis: Larger-the-Better," explain the concepts behind the signal-to-noise ratio (S/N) and present the corresponding formulas. Guidelines for constructing and analyzing response tables and graphs based on the S/N are given. The effect of interactions is also covered. The S/N prediction equation, the confirmation run, and their comparison are presented. Examples are provided in each chapter with complete analysis.

Chapter 19, "Analysis: Nominal-the-Best," explains the concepts and strategy behind analyzing nominal-the-best data. Development of means and S/N response tables and graphs and their interpretation are covered including interaction considerations. Prediction equations and confirmation run analysis are also covered. Comprehensive examples with thorough explanations are given.

Chapter 20, "Analysis: Dynamic Characteristics," explains the concepts behind the dynamic S/N computations for measurement, manufacturing, and design systems. Criteria for determining significant factors are covered. The basic types of signal factors and their respective S/N equations are addressed. Working examples for each case are given.

Chapter 21, "Special Design Techniques," provides step-by-step instructions for modifying the experimental design to handle special case factors. Techniques include multilevel arrangements, dummy treatment, combination designs, sliding levels, nested factor design, and the idle column method. Analysis where different from standard practices is also explained. Examples are provided for each technique.

Chapter 22, "Multiple Characteristics," deals with analyzing experiments involving more than one quality characteristic. Examples and explanations are provided for a diverse variety of response type combinations including multiple measurable characteristics of the same type, multiple measurable characteristics of different types, more than one classified attribute, and an assortment of measurable and classified attribute characteristics.

Chapter 23, "Missing and Infeasible Data," addresses those situations in which experimental data either are missing or produce results that are unmeasurable. Specific methods are given for estimating missing raw data and calculating the S/N for smaller-the-better, larger-the-better, and nominal-the-best characteristics. The handling of ideal nominal-the-best data when all responses for a specific experimental run are the same is also covered.

Acknowledgments

I would like to express my appreciation to those persons who guided the development of my understanding of the subject matter and helped shape my perspective on quality engineering. I was fortunate in learning many of the more technical aspects of Taguchi methods from Professor Yuin Wu of the American Supplier Institute, whose knowledge of the subject I hold in the highest esteem. I would also wish to express my gratitude to Shin Taguchi, who has been helpful both as a friend and as a mentor in providing suggestions of topics to cover in the book.

As senior statistical specialist for formerly Texas Instruments Industrial Automation, Richard Wetherell, quality assurance manager, selected me to become the "Taguchi expert" for the business and to introduce the methodology into design disciplines and manufacturing operations. I am extremely appreciative of the faith he entrusted in me and the opportunities afforded me by this decision.

I was also privileged by the close and warm association with my counterparts in the associated Texas Instruments divisions. I am especially appreciative of the assistance and the providing of reference material by Lisa Reagan, Eric Shield, and their colleagues from the Texas Instruments Digital Systems Equipment Group.

I would also like to thank the reviewers for their efforts and for the comments and suggestions which have served to deliver the best possible book for the intent and targeted audience. A special thank you goes to Andy Ferguson and Roger Helm who reviewed specific sections at my request and helped me insure that I was communicating the desired message. A round of applause and a big hug go to my wife, Patricia, who reviewed every page of the manuscript with me for typographical and grammatical errors.

In obtaining the hands-on skills and experience essential for writing such a book, I was involved with many associates on various experiments and related quality improvement efforts which produced many of the ideas on which the examples in the book are based. I would like to give special recognition to John Broadwater, who was involved in numerous projects from which many of these same examples are derived. His assistance was greatly appreciated, and I hold a deep respect for his talents and achievements, which are not recognized enough.

I would like to recognize all of the other associates with whom I have had the good fortune to work and who contributed in some way to the development of the material within *Taguchi Methods: A Hands-On Approach.* I apologize for any oversights resulting in deserving persons' being accidentally left off the list. I would like to thank and recognize the following:

Art Cambique	Bob Russell	Hayes Blackwell
Bob Mininger	Marcus Post	Shaliesh Patel
John Murray	Myrtle Banks	Greg Asztalos
Pete Rainwater	Chris Foran	Harold Licht
Bob Palermo	Mack Marshall	

Chapter 1

CONCEPTUAL BACKGROUND

To compete effectively in today's marketplace, companies must find ways to improve the quality of their products while lowering the cost of production. They must also bring products to market quicker and at minimal research and development costs. Although there are many tools available for increasing productivity and solving problems, Dr. Genichi Taguchi has developed a set of techniques based on statistical principles and utilizing engineering knowledge. By recognizing the importance of associating quality with the financial loss imparted by poor quality, Dr. Taguchi has developed a methodology that makes quality decisions based on cost effectiveness.

1.1 HISTORY

Dr. Genichi Taguchi's methods are a product of the Japanese post–World War II era. When resources were scarce and financial support was at best minimal, the demands for reconstruction of Japanese industry were enormous. This period in Japanese history required accelerated learning and giant strides in improvement while being restrained by inferior raw material and lack of capital. From an engineering background, Dr. Taguchi converted his study of statistics and advanced mathematics into a system merging statistical techniques and engineering expertise.

Dr. Taguchi was born on January 1, 1924. His advanced formal training was directed toward textile engineering at Kiryu Technical College, but he devoted extensive personal study to statistics. After World War II, he was hired by the Japanese Ministry of Public Health and Welfare to deploy the country's first national study on health and nutrition. His associations there led him to become involved with Morinaga Pharmaceutical, where efficient experimentation techniques were critical to developing methods for producing penicillin. The realities of deadlines and production limitations helped to shape his approach to applying experimentation techniques to actual design and production situations. This fostered a growing appreciation for taking assumptions from engineering knowledge to reduce the size of experiments and thereby speed up the experimentation process. Productivity was reported to have increased tenfold annually during his efforts there.[1]

His continued research took him in the direction of the study of random noise and its effect on variability. He adapted the use of the orthogonal array as an effective experimental design tool for greatly reducing the size of experiments while still achieving new insights and improving product designs and process productivity. Previously, most experimental studies had been performed using the classical full factorial approach. Whereas the orthogonal array had previously been used to reduce experimental bias, he adapted it for determining the influence of each variable under study on both the mean result and the variation from that result.[2] The understanding of real-life limitations, particularly during postwar Japan, helped Dr. Taguchi to focus his studies on minimizing the effect of the causes of variation instead of removing the problems themselves. By inserting a second orthogonal array into the experiment, he added the capability of determining those combinations of controllable factors that minimize the effect of the sources of experimentation variability. He went on to define this ability as *robustness.*

These concepts were applied at Morinaga Sieka, which produced candies, and resulted in an improved caramel formula which significantly impeded melting at room temperature. Another success story, often more publicized, relates to his next position at the Electrical Communications Laboratories of the Nippon Telephone and Telegraph Company. Both Electrical Communications Laboratories and Bell Laboratories from the United States were developing similar cross-bar telephone exchange systems. In addition to facing Bell's greater resources, the Japanese were limited to inferior materials. Despite all the adversity, the new cross-bar system from Japan was rated superior and at a much lower cost to produce. The effect was so dramatic that Western Electric stopped production and began importing the systems from Japan.[3]

Other Japanese companies learned from these lessons and adopted Dr. Taguchi's techniques as well. Toyota, Fuji Film, and other Japanese firms have followed suit and become both quality and price leaders.[4]

From the adage, "If you can't beat 'em, join 'em," American companies began efforts to learn about these techniques and how to use them. AT&T Bell Laboratories, Xerox, and Ford Motor Company were among the first American firms to embrace Taguchi methodology.[5] Many additional companies have since adopted these techniques and have reaped the benefits of improved customer satisfaction and decreased cost of operations.

1.2 CONTRIBUTIONS TO QUALITY

In order to present an overview of the evolution of Dr. Taguchi's techniques, we must explain his fundamental philosophy and review his most notable contributions to quality improvement. The emphasis of the methodology is on functional variation, which can be measured in terms of product performance such as strength, pressure, shrinkage, response time, taste, and mean time between failures. Viewed as the enemy of the producer and its customer, functional variation can relate to the performance of the end product or to the process that manufactures the end result. The purpose of experimentation using Taguchi methodology is to identify those key factors that have the greatest contribution to variation and to ascertain those settings or values that result in the least variability.

In developing methods to understand better the influences upon the functionality of products and associated processes, Dr. Taguchi has been particularly recognized for three major contributions to the field of quality:

1. the loss function
2. orthogonal arrays and linear graphs
3. robustness.

1.2.1 The Loss Function

The idea of developing and using systematic approaches to obtain a better understanding of the unknown is not new. However, Dr. Taguchi realized the

Figure 1-1 Quadratic Loss Function

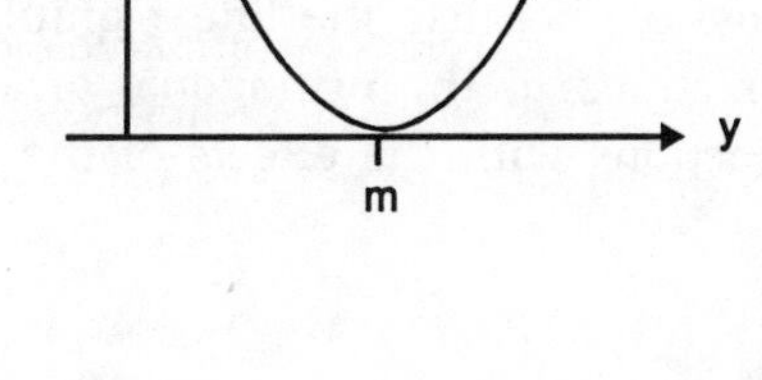

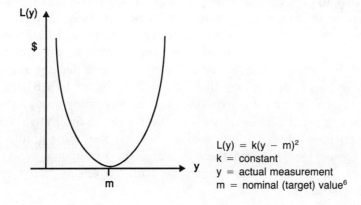

$L(y) = k(y - m)^2$
k = constant
y = actual measurement
m = nominal (target) value[6]

importance of cost in postwar Japan and made the direct link that exists between quality and corporate profitability. Although many other approaches developed by academia were valid and statistically correct, the real world of profitability and loss was not considered. This unique approach belongs to Taguchi methodology.

Using the Taylor Expansion Series, Dr. Taguchi has developed a mathematical model in which loss is a quadratic function of the deviation of the quality of interest from its target value (see Figure 1-1). Based on this concept, sound management decisions can now be made on the true worth of quality improvement efforts. Decisions can be made based not on rhetoric or emotions, but on facts pulled from data.

1.2.2 Orthogonal Arrays and Linear Graphs

A second major contribution is the adaptation of orthogonal arrays for designing efficient experiments and analyzing experimental data. Orthogonal arrays were originally developed in England by R. A. Fisher for controlling experimental error.[7] Dr. Taguchi has since used the orthogonal array not only to measure the effect of a factor on the average result, but to determine the variation from the mean as well. A primary advantage of orthogonal arrays is the relationship among the factors under investigation. For each level of any one factor, all levels of the other factors occur an equal number of times. This constitutes a balanced experiment and permits the effect of one factor under study to be separable from the effects of other factors. The result is that the findings of the experiment are reproducible.

An additional advantage of orthogonal arrays is their cost efficiency. Although balanced, the design of an orthogonal array does not require that all combinations of all factors be tested. Therefore, the experimental matrix can be smaller without losing any vital information. The result is an experiment that is cost effective to perform. For example, an L_8 orthogonal array can incorporate seven different factors while requiring only eight experimental runs.

An enhancement that Dr. Taguchi incorporated to add flexibility to the orthogonal array is the linear graph. The linear graph is a graphical representation of the orthogonal array for assigning factors under investigation and corresponding interactions among these factors (see Figure 1-2). By using these specially designed graphs, the experimenter can effectively study interactions between experimental factors as well as the effects of the individual factors (main effects) themselves. This is possible because the linear graphs provide a logical scheme for assigning interactions to the orthogonal array without confounding the effects of the interactions with the effects of the individual factors being studied.

Figure 1-2 L_8 Orthogonal Array and Linear Graphs

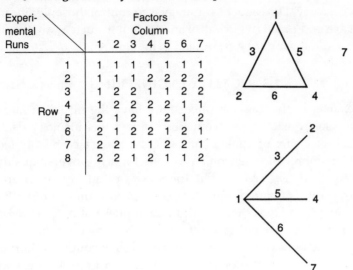

Experimental Runs \ Factors Column	1	2	3	4	5	6	7
Row 1	1	1	1	1	1	1	1
2	1	1	1	2	2	2	2
3	1	2	2	1	1	2	2
4	1	2	2	2	2	1	1
5	2	1	2	1	2	1	2
6	2	1	2	2	1	2	1
7	2	2	1	1	2	2	1
8	2	2	1	2	1	1	2

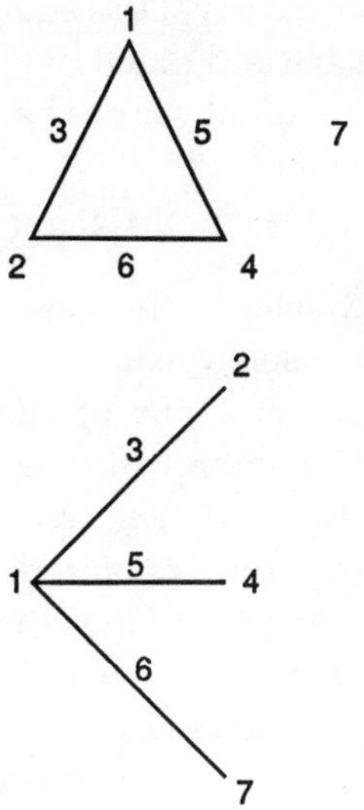

Using engineering knowledge and experience, the experimenter can incorporate into the experiment those interactions that have the most likely chance of having a strong effect on the product and/or process. The end result is that the experimental matrix remains highly efficient and cost effective while the conclusions are consistently reproducible.

1.2.3 Robustness

A third major contribution is the concept of *robustness.* We can define robustness from both a product- and a process-related standpoint as follows:

Product: The ability of the product to perform consistently as designed with minimal effect from changes in uncontrollable operating influences.

Process: The ability of the process to produce consistently good product with minimal effect from changes in uncontrollable manufacturing influences.

This departure from classical experimentation recognizes that we cannot always control some of the things that create variation within the process or the product. For example, many aspects of our environment, such as weather, are factors that we cannot regulate. Control of some influences may be possible but not practical or maybe just too expensive. Sole sourcing of raw material could fall into this category. Dr. Taguchi's strategy is to control those significant factors that are feasible and practical to control and to do it in such a way that the effect of those factors that cannot be controlled is minimized.

1.3 QUALITY ENGINEERING

Many newcomers to the Taguchi philosophy have the mistaken idea that his methods deal solely with experimentation. In fact, his ideology deals with a much broader spectrum of quality concerns and associated quality techniques and tools. The umbrella that encompasses Dr. Taguchi's overall quality philosophy is called *quality engineering.* The framework of quality engineering interrelates with the roles of both design engineering and manufacturing. It contains the quality control activities that constitute each phase of product research and development, process design, production, and customer satisfaction. The role of each of these activities is to support overall goals of continued improvement, accelerated discovery, rapid problem solving, and cost effectiveness while sustaining quality gains. To support these goals, quality engineering can be divided into two categories: (1) on-line quality control and (2) off-line quality control (Figure 1-3).

Figure 1-3 Quality Engineering

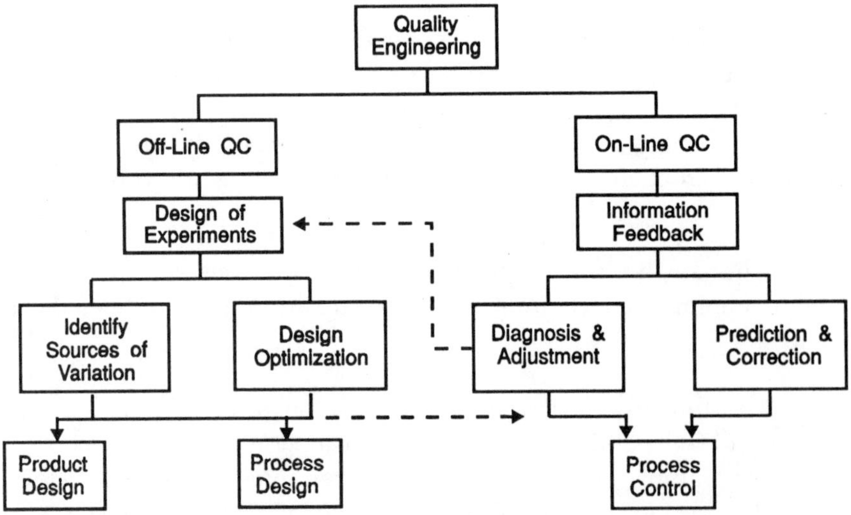

1.3.1 On-line Quality Control

Efforts toward on-line quality control involve the actual production of the product. These are the techniques that monitor production, measure ongoing quality, provide signals of potential problems, and direct corrective action. Information feedback systems are the foundation for notifying the operator and the manufacturing supervisor of process performance. Data obtained from critical process points report the real-time status of production.

Although recording raw data is fundamentally important, more is needed. This is where diagnosis and adjustment come into play. The information must be analyzed to determine if process settings are being properly maintained. This means that production data must be compared to some desired targets and that the desired targets are known.

If the analysis indicates that current conditions are not acceptable, then adjustments must be made to bring the process back within an acceptable range. The prediction and correction functions support and react to the diagnosis inputs and adjustments. Based on historical data and capability studies, predicted targets provide the reference for determining if current process status is acceptable or if adjustment is required. In addition, the magnitude of adjustments can be determined for making corrections.

Other considerations within on-line quality control include preventive maintenance, calibration of sensor devices, and economic inspection. Each of these functions contributes to and results in cost-effective process control.

1.3.2 Off-line Quality Control

The purpose of off-line quality control is to optimize product and process design in support of on-line quality control. Design of experiment is the fundamental tool of off-line quality control and serves as the focus of this book. Some of these efforts may be purely research and development activities. If process related, they may be accomplished on prototype lines that simulate actual production, or they could be performed on the actual manufacturing process prior to production, on off shifts, or during production shutdown.

Experimentation techniques play two key roles: (1) identifying sources of variation and (2) determining design and process optimization. Identifying the principal contributors to overall variation can focus attention on the most important factors that affect functional variation and divert efforts from those factors that have minimal impact on the overall quality of the outgoing product. The determination of the best levels of these critical factors establishes the target values for on-line quality control activities and provides solutions to problems identified in production.

In addition to being described from a functional standpoint, off-line quality control can also be viewed as three sequential stages for optimizing a product or process. These are: (1) system design, (2) parameter design, and (3) tolerance design.[8] To understand how the techniques covered within this book fit into the overall concept of quality engineering, we shall explain each of these three phases of off-line quality control activities.

1.3.2.1 System Design

The conceptual stage of any new product development or process innovation is system design. This is the "idea" stage where something revolutionary or perhaps an offshoot of previous developments is conceived and tested. The concepts may be based on past experience, scientific/engineering knowledge, a new revelation, or any combination of the three. The strategy behind system design is to take these new ideas and convert them into something that can work.

For example, we can look at the Wright Brothers' airplane flown at Kitty Hawk. Their accomplishments were achieved based on their prior experience and technical know-how with engines and bicycles. Although their invention flew under a certain set of wind conditions, this did not mean that the plane could operate in diverse weather. Neither did this prove that all aircraft that they could construct with the same design would perform successfully. This only meant that the airplane could operate satisfactorily under the right conditions. In the manufacturing or design environment, this typically relates to nominal conditions or the center of specifications. Making products and processes that can operate consistently well is the subject of the next design stage.

1.3.2.2 Parameter Design

The objective of parameter design is to take the innovation which has been proven to work in System Design and enhance it so that it will consistently function as intended. A major portion of Dr. Taguchi's focus has been on making the product and the process robust against the uncontrollable influences that can prevent proper functioning. In later chapters, we will refer to these undesirable factors as *noise*.

The tool for achieving parameter design objectives is the design of experiment. The strategy behind parameter design experiments is based on cost considerations. Efforts should be directed toward determining the best design at the least cost. To achieve this goal, studies should begin with the lowest-cost components or ingredients.[9] The idea is to make the "best" with the "least." In the area of electronic design, this could refer to the use of 10% resistors instead of 1% parts. In other areas, it may relate to lower-cost materials or a cheaper grade. The idea is not to value cost over quality, but to get the most quality for the cost.

Secondly, the focus is on reducing variability without adding cost. Instead of eliminating causes of variation, which could be very expensive to achieve, the strategy is to minimize the effect of these causes.[10] By determining the best settings or values of those factors that are inexpensive to change or control, quality can be improved without adding cost. For example, instead of adding humidity controls to the operating floor, parameter design is concerned with determining those ingredients that are least sensitive to humidity changes.

1.3.2.3 Tolerance Design

The objective of tolerance design is to determine the acceptable range of variability around the nominal settings determined in parameter design. Again, design of experiments is used to study the product or process, while analysis of variance (ANOVA) provides interpretation of the experimental data. Wide toleranced parts and cheap grade raw material whose values were determined in parameter design are used.[11]

The strategy is to determine which tolerances and grades of material have the greatest effect on variability. Tolerances can be tightened and materials upgraded based on tradeoffs between the cost of higher-grade parts or ingredients and the reduction in product/process variation.[12]

1.4 USING EXPERIMENTATION

Now that we have presented an overview of quality engineering, you should have a clearer understanding of the role of parameter design and its relationship to on-line quality control and the other design stages. The emphasis of this book is on explaining the importance of parameter design in improving quality and the steps required to perform a parameter design experiment.

1.4.1 Experiment Design Comparisons

In the past, "firefighting" has been a common practice for tackling critical problems. Quite often the solution has only a "Band-Aid" effect with the problem recurring or the situation becoming worse. Changing one factor at a time is more systematic, but suffers from several pitfalls. For one, studying a single factor at a time is a slow process, which translates into long delays without solutions and into expensive studies. Since only one factor is changed at a time, interactions between factors are ignored, and reproducibility of the experimental conclusions is often disappointing.

A full factorial experiment considers potential interactions, and the conclusions are highly reproducible. However, the full factorial requires the testing of all combinations of the factor levels under study. This can be extremely time consuming and expensive. A study involving 13 factors at 3 levels each would require 1,594,323 experimental runs! A more efficient classical experimentation approach is the use of fractional factorials. Although less time consuming, these require statistical expertise which is often not possessed by the engineers or other persons faced with a need for increasing product/process knowledge.

The orthogonal array produces smaller, less costly experiments that have high rates of reproducibility. Using the appropriate orthogonal array, a study involving 13 factors at 3 levels can be conducted with only 27 experimental runs. Besides being efficient, the procedures for using orthogonal arrays are straightforward and easy to use.

1.4.2 Experiment Design Phases

To achieve a successful experiment and obtain reproducible results calls for a well-organized and executed effort, requiring careful planning and faithful execution to the plan. The essential steps for properly performing an experiment can be categorized into four distinct phases, outlined in Figure 1-4:

1. planning the experiment
2. designing the experiment
3. conducting the experiment
4. analyzing the experiment

Effective experiment planning relates to those efforts required up front to lay the groundwork for the other three phases. Included are organizational issues such as involvement of the appropriate personnel and obtaining management support, as well as developing a precise statement of the team objective. Conscientious planning also involves careful attention to identifying the quality characteristic, determining measurement requirements, selecting factors for study and associated settings, and laying experimentation strategy.

Designing the experiment involves the construction of the experiment layout and includes selection of the most efficient experimental matrix to provide meaningful results and contain all of the required information. This phase also involves the proper assignment of the factors and interactions of interest to the appropriate locations within the experimental matrix.

Conducting the experiment includes execution of the experiment as developed in the planning and design phases. In addition to the actual running of the experiment, this phase also includes development of the test plan and the

Figure 1-4 Experimentation steps

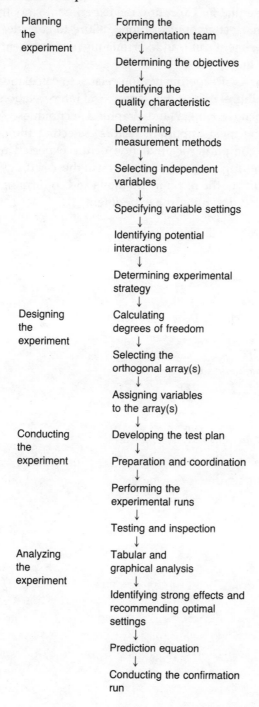

Planning the experiment	Forming the experimentation team
	↓
	Determining the objectives
	↓
	Identifying the quality characteristic
	↓
	Determining measurement methods
	↓
	Selecting independent variables
	↓
	Specifying variable settings
	↓
	Identifying potential interactions
	↓
	Determining experimental strategy
	↓
Designing the experiment	Calculating degrees of freedom
	↓
	Selecting the orthogonal array(s)
	↓
	Assigning variables to the array(s)
	↓
Conducting the experiment	Developing the test plan
	↓
	Preparation and coordination
	↓
	Performing the experimental runs
	↓
	Testing and inspection
	↓
Analyzing the experiment	Tabular and graphical analysis
	↓
	Identifying strong effects and recommending optimal settings
	↓
	Prediction equation
	↓
	Conducting the confirmation run

preparations and coordination essential for conducting the study. These preliminary efforts are essential for executing the experiment smoothly with the least effort and in the shortest amount of time. Failure to consider these aspects of conducting an experiment can lead to erroneous measurements, biased results, or even no data at all.

The analysis phase of experimentation relates to calculations for converting raw data into meaningful information and to the interpretation of those results. Analysis should include tabular and graphical techniques. Analysis includes determination of the most important factors, selecting the optimal levels for those factors, and computing a prediction of the expected results at the recommended factor settings. A confirmation run at these settings is vital for checking the reproducibility of the recommendations and confirming the assumptions used in planning and designing the experiment.

Notes

1. Ealey, Lance A., *Quality by Design,* pp. 102–108.
2. Ibid., pp. 113–114.
3. Ibid., pp. 116, 120.
4. *Introduction to Quality Engineering.*
5. Ibid.
6. Ibid., pp. 2–16.
7. Ealey, p. 110.
8. *Introduction to Quality Engineering,* pp. 3–5.
9. Ibid., pp. 3–7.
10. Ibid.
11. Ibid., pp. 3–10.
12. Ibid.

Chapter 2

FORMING THE EXPERIMENTATION TEAM

Unfortunately, many well-intended efforts at experimentation go awry not because of lack of technical knowledge, misuse of statistical formulas or errant calculations, but because of improper planning. In a hurry to give management a quick solution, we may cut short the fundamental phases of experimentation.

First, effective planning is brushed aside. Process variables are hastily thrown together into an experimental design to assure managers and affected customers that proper actions are taking place in a timely manner. After a convenient number of factors have been identified, other potentially important variables are deleted to keep the experiment small enough so that production will consent to scheduling the experiment without a lot of squawking. The reality is that some significant factors are omitted, while other factors less likely to be important are included.

The experiment is then conducted by uninvolved operators who, not understanding the reasoning behind experimentation, feel that these efforts are a total waste of time and resources. Therefore, test runs are performed as fast as possible, often with little regard for insuring that process variables are properly set and maintained.

After experimental runs have been completed, measurements are taken. In many cases, inexperienced personnel may be called upon to obtain the readings as more experienced persons work elsewhere to insure that production quotas are met. Other situations may involve the use of numerous operators or inspectors in taking the measurements, where one operator takes some of the readings and another finishes the task. Finally, the time to analyze the data arrives. However, the conclusions either don't make sense or recommended process settings do not give the desired results.

How often does this situation occur in real life? How often is the blame placed on misapplication of the methodology? "These techniques just don't work in our type of industry!" A principle feature of this book is to address the issues raised by the fiasco described above and to guide and direct efforts to avoid these pitfalls. In this chapter, we shall discuss the importance of forming an effective experimentation team, an essential ingredient for performing a successful experiment. To prepare properly for an experiment, it is helpful to think of an experiment in terms of the four distinct and essential phases, which we can refer to as the PDCA Cycle[1]: planning the experiment, designing the experiment, conducting the experiment, and analyzing the experiment.

Too often in the past, the emphasis has been on analyzing the data with little regard for how the data was obtained or for insuring that the information is meaningful. A well-intentioned but uneducated manager might say, "Hurry up and get me some data, and we will have the statisticians tell us what it means." Instead of spending most of the effort trying to abstract knowledge from the data, the real emphasis should be placed on the planning phase. Without diligent attention to planning, the other three phases are at risk.

If effective planning is the cornerstone for successfully performing an experiment, the experimentation team must be put together at the start of the project. Formation of the team should begin as soon as possible so that the selection of team members will include anyone with an input to the initial issues of the planning phase.

2.1 ESTABLISHING GOALS

In formulating a coordinated effort, we should first address the need for performing an experiment. What is it that we are trying to accomplish? Are we trying to solve a major quality problem? Are we being called upon to assist with setting up a new production line by helping to accelerate the learning curve? Answers to these questions help us to prepare for the planning efforts and to insure that the essential management support and contributions by affected work groups are there when needed (see Table 2-1).

Management support is vital not just for obtaining the necessary material and for allocating sufficient production downtime. It is also key for soliciting support from each of the work groups that may have knowledge that is essential for effective planning or that will later play a vital role in any of the other phases of experimentation. If management demonstrates that this is an important project and that they expect it to succeed, it is more likely that the necessary support will be there.

The ensuing question is, "How do you get this support?" Management typically talks and listens in terms of dollars and cents. Therefore the request for management support must be translated into this same language. A simple initial approach is to determine existing scrap and rework costs. By projecting the estimated savings from completing the study, the attention of upper-level man-

Table 2-1 Initial Experimentation Team Meeting Agenda

I.	Project goal
II.	Project scope
III.	Management commentary
IV.	Team leader selection
V.	Taguchi methods overview
VI.	Determining objectives
VII.	Team research/data gathering requirements
VIII.	Summary

agement is received. A projected reduction in quality costs of only 50% is often enough to obtain the necessary support. More sophisticated cost analysis is usually not needed at this time. Our initial purpose is just to get the appropriate personnel into a room together. More concise cost analysis can come later when we propose approval for running the experiment.

Once the initial approval has been given at least for planning the experiment, the next step is to coordinate a joint meeting of the essential players. Although deceptively simple, the task of setting up such a meeting and insuring that all key personnel attend requires interpersonal skills and tactics. For the experienced coordinator, these steps may be obvious. For the inexperienced such as the newly graduated engineer, I have seen good intentions wrecked by failing to pay proper attention to management protocol and by lack of communication.

A good common practice is to insure that all key personnel are properly notified by sending a memo to each individual that you wish to attend. Verbal invitations and face-to-face conversations on the purpose of the meetings are fine for generating interest, but back up these efforts with written announcements. Make sure that the managers of those invited are copied. I have found this approach quite helpful in insuring that lukewarm supporters show up. To insure continued support of those actively participating, send out communiqués of what was covered at each meeting, who participated, and who did not attend. This gesture will give recognition where due, get the attention of those not participating and induce their involvement, and keep management abreast of the project status.

It is also a good idea to invite managers at least to the introductory portion of the first meeting. Their appearance can go a long way in encouraging the involvement of others. If they have previously indicated strong support for the project, ask them to say a few words. Their short speech can add leverage to your effort to obtain the involvement of their subordinates. If you plan on asking managers to comment at the meeting, let them know beforehand what you would like their role to be. This step may sound elementary, but it is sound business etiquette. You need this person's support, so don't accidentally antagonize him or her.

Also, it will be helpful to communicate the fundamental goal that you are trying to achieve, in order to determine who should be involved as participants on the team. This action is not to be confused with determining the experiment objectives, which is covered in Chapter 3. The purpose of setting a fundamental goal is to give a general direction and is not meant to replace more specific experiment objectives. After being formed, the experimentation team will determine the objectives during the planning process. Examples of basic goals include:

1. reducing solder defects on the modem circuit assembly,
2. minimizing scrap in the cheese packaging process, and
3. maximizing pressure value performance.

Just as it is important to determine a primary goal and to define the scope of the project as you initially see it, it is important to communicate this determination to the prospective team members. Within the memo calling the first meeting, state the proposed goals and the scope of the projected effort required. At the first and each subsequent session, have an agenda prepared to help make the sessions more productive and reduce the potential for discussions drifting off into the weeds.

2.2 DETERMINING WHO CAN BEST IMPACT THE GOAL

Management of course has the most impact, which is why their support is essential. Their commitment spreads downward to involve those who work for them. Whereas their role consists of promoting the participation of subordinates and providing budgetary support, others will make their impact felt as a result of direct contributions. It is important that each of these potential contributors be involved at the earliest point. It is far better to include some that will not actually be involved than to omit anyone who could have a vital role. I have never had a problem in thanking people who attended but who, upon understanding the scope of the project, dismissed themselves from further involvement.

2.2.1 Who Is Capable of Understanding the Goal?

At least one member of the team should have a solid understanding of Taguchi methodology. Either a Taguchi expert, a statistician, or a design-of-experiment specialist can play this fundamental role. Their function is to insure that the team's efforts conform to basic methodology concepts and are theoretically sound. They can provide guidance on how to obtain the most knowledge most effectively from the least amount of data. When it is time to design the experiment itself, they can be called upon to review the structure to insure it is sound. Their help in dealing with unique factors within the experiment and addressing outside textbook type problems can greatly enhance the team effort.

Because of the straightforwardness of basic Taguchi methodology, many more participants are likely to understand the techniques and how they can help achieve team goals. For those involved who have had neither a course in nor an overview of Taguchi methodology, it is recommended that a brief introductory overview be presented. This presentation should include the basic concepts and potential benefits and how they relate specifically to participants' support of the project.

2.2.2 Whom Does the Goal Impact?

Besides insuring the participation of those who may be able to contribute key information to the planning of the experiment, it is also important to include those whom the experiment and its ramifications affect. If one makes them feel that they are indeed a part of the effort, they are most apt to contribute to the success of the experiment. The following are just a few examples of how and why those impacted by the experiment may need to be involved (see Table 2-2).

Marketing personnel: Although not usually thought of as a normal part of an experimentation team, marketing personnel may have important inputs concerning the objectives and the crucial quality characteristics. This input can be particularly important if the experimentation efforts are a result of customer dissatisfaction. Marketing may have insight on what the customer truly cares about.

Manufacturing supervisor: The people responsible for getting the production out the door may or may not have the technical expertise for understanding pertinent variables, but they certainly need to be involved. For one thing, they have ownership of the process being studied. Second, if you want to conduct an experiment on their production line, you had better have their commitment to the project, or you are going to have a difficult time getting those experimental runs scheduled. Not just their support, but their active participation is crucial to the success of the experiment.

Table 2-2 Potential Experimentation Team Members

Management (opening session)
Customer (determining objectives & defining quality characteristics)
Marketing (determining objectives & defining quality characteristics)
Process engineer
Product/manufacturing engineer
Manufacturing supervisor
Quality engineer/supervisor
Quality/statistical/experimentation expert
Design engineer
Operator (selecting variables & levels)
Inspector (selecting variables & levels)
Industry-specific engineer:
Aeronautical
Agricultural
Chemical
Metallurgical
Technician:
Machine set-up
Repair/maintenance
Product repair/troubleshoot

Customer: Too often we forget about who this effort is for in the first place. Why not include the customers? After all, it is their priorities that we really need to be concerned with. As far as divulging trade secrets is concerned, if you are truly trying to create a long-term trusting relationship, this aspect should not be an issue.

2.2.3 Who Is Involved in the Process?

In the example on what not to do at the start of this chapter, we talked about operators running the process per special experimental run instructions and not understanding why. Imagine yourself as an experienced operator of long standing on "your" machine. You know how it is supposed to run and how to control it. You know all of the proper dial settings and when to make adjustments. Now, someone who has never spent one hour operating this machine that you know so well is telling you to adjust the settings to readings that you know cannot work. Under these conditions, what kind of support would you give? Would you perhaps not even change the settings to those requested?

The problems here are twofold. For one, there is a lack of understanding on what is being done and why. The second issue is ownership. This was not the operator's experiment. This was someone else's idea. It is for these reasons that the involvement of the machine operators is critical and presenting an overview of Taguchi methodology and explaining the project goals are important. I have found that by soliciting the involvement of the hourly production personnel and educating them, not to be Taguchi experts but to understand what we are trying to do and the basic premise of how it works, they will provide total support. The issue of commitment works as well. By actively seeking their ideas and inputs in planning the experiment, the engineer no longer has sole ownership of the project. It is **their experiment.** They will insure doubly that all experimental runs are conducted correctly and all process variables are set at the levels that *they decided on* in the planning phase.

Operator: As stated above, operators are often overlooked when it comes to process knowledge. However, they spend more time with the machinery than anyone else and know all of the peculiarities of the process that no one else is aware of. Concerning their role in process planning, instead of asking them to be present for the entire planning process, solicit each operator's participation for a specific period of time. You still get their inputs and make them feel part of the team without creating excessive line shutdown. I have seen this technique be particularly successful when an experiment included multi-step processes where a different operator was responsible for each step. For example, Operator #1 was called in when we discussed his machine, and we dismissed him afterwards. Then, Operator #2 was brought into the session as we began discussing her operation, and she left after her inputs were made, etc.

Inspector: If you are not at the point of self-inspection, inspectors can be vital sources of information not found elsewhere. The inspector may be aware of problems that are perhaps glossed over or that are corrected so quickly that no one else is aware of them.

2.2.4 Who Understands the Process?

Process engineers: They are referred to as process experts. They have the theoretical background and the technical expertise for understanding the complexity of the process, how it is supposed to operate, how it actually runs, and what is normally needed to insure it runs as it is supposed to.

Product/manufacturing engineers: These engineers' expertise is more related to the product being built than the process itself. Their knowledge of raw material and the subassemblies that make up the end product can be valuable in determining the critical product parameters that contribute to the manufacturability of the product.

Design engineers: Design engineers are the experts on the product itself. The importance of their role will depend on the newness of the product. If it is just going into production, their importance to the team will be critical. If this is an older sustaining product, they may not need to be included.

Quality engineers/supervisors: These are typically "the" Champions of Quality within the work group, although everyone should really be an advocate of quality. They or their subordinates are likely to have vital historical information and data analysis readily available, which can provide key insight into determining team objectives, identifying quality characteristics, and selecting factors and settings to study.

Other engineers/experts: Depending on the type of industry and specific application, a wide range of engineering disciplines may need to be considered. In the electronics industry, component engineers have in-depth knowledge concerning the parts and subassemblies that comprise the end product. In other applications, it may be the metallurgical engineer, the mechanical engineer, the chemist, the agricultural engineer, or the biologist. The list could become almost endless. The purpose of mentioning so many possibilities is not to create a team requiring a football stadium to contain it, but simply to stress the importance of an open mind for considering those who may be able to contribute to a better understanding of the process and/or product that is being examined.

2.2.5 Who Supports the Process?

Some additional considerations relate to others who may not need to be members of the experimentation team, but who can have an influence just the same on the success or failure of the effort. Schedulers and planners need to be informed of what you are trying to do and of your timetable. You need to let them know how much production time is needed and how much raw material is required. Purchasing agents need to be informed of parts and materials that need to be ordered, particularly special order items. Lead times and availability are information that is critical to conducting the experiment effectively. These individuals do not need to be brought into the project at the onset, because the team does not know yet what the requirements are going to be. However, as soon as material and scheduling requirements are determined, they should be brought into the project.

2.3 SELECTION OF THE TEAM LEADER

To insure that the experimentation team has direction and proceeds toward its directed goal, the team needs to select a leader or facilitator. The team leader should be capable of understanding the technical issues related to the experiment and have a vested interest in the success of the project. Good organizational abilities for coordinating the efforts of the team plus the talent for getting others to cooperate and support team efforts are also valued assets for selection. The team leader should be selected as early in the planning process as possible, preferably near the start of the initial planning session. It may well be the person who originally called the meeting. The duties of the team leader include organizing the team meetings, the logistics of which include room arrangements, sending meeting notices, and developing the agendas.

Documentation is also a vital part of the leader's role. He or she should be responsible for minutes of the meetings and for maintaining a list of action items including who, what, and when. Since the team leader will be busy enough orchestrating the planning sessions, it is highly recommended that someone else be delegated to record the minutes of each meeting. At the end of a meeting, the leader can then take the information and use it for preparing status reports and related documentation. Reports and presentations including project results would also come under the leader's responsibility and direction.

The leader may also be called on to assist fellow team members in accomplishing team tasks by helping to remove barriers or obstacles. Therefore, an ideal team leader should possess some amount of authority, either actual or perceived. The ability to develop and sustain communications with other work groups for effective support is also important. The leader is the hub for inter-

Table 2-3 Typical Electronic Assembly Experimentation Team

Manufacturing supervisor
Process engineer
Product engineer
Quality assurance supervisor
Taguchi advisor/expert
Component engineer
Product technician
Set-up technician
Machine maintenance technician
Operator

Table 2-4 Typical Plastics Industry Experimentation Team

Process engineer
Equipment maintenance engineer
Automation engineer
Line supervisor
Quality manager
Taguchi specialist/advisor
Set-up technician
Machine operator

Table 2-5 Typical Food Industry Experimentation Team

Controls engineer
Production supervisor
Quality assurance supervisor
Quality assurance inspector
(Laboratory specialist)
Process engineer
Tooling engineer
Operators
Taguchi consultant

facing with project-related tasks performed by non-team members. Not that he or she has to make all of the contacts, but the leader should have the ability to assist fellow team members when they run into problems. For typical team structures, see Tables 2-3, 2-4, and 2-5.

Notes

1. Melder, Melissa, *et al.*, *Taguchi Training Manual*, p. 3-1.

Chapter 3

DETERMINING THE OBJECTIVES

Once the experimentation team has been assembled, the fundamental goal is understood, and team members have become acquainted with the basic concepts, the group is ready to determine the objectives. A pitfall that many groups tend to fall into is to rush through this part of the planning phase and select what appears to be the most obvious desired end result as the objective. However, this goal may not lead to the greatest gain in process/product knowledge. If a chronic quality problem precipitated the creation of the team, this lack of dedication can prevent finding the ultimate long-term cure. In order effectively to pursue actions that will result in the most significant benefit, some research can be well spent up front that will in turn provide dividends down the road.

For example, a team from an electronics assembly operation has gotten together because of a high frequency of defects. They hurriedly decide that their objective is "to reduce defects." Although this is certainly something that they want to do and must accomplish, this vague resolution fails to provide focus, to promote a real gain in process/product knowledge, and to allow for a system to measure success or failure. A more definitive statement would be "to insure a consistent solder volume of 2 milligrams per solder pad." This enhanced objective focuses the attention on a specific desired result. By striving to achieve a target value of 2 mgs and minimizing the variation around that target, the team is setting their sights on an objective that encourages a gain in new understanding. The inclusion of a quantifiable desired result allows for a standard by which to measure success.

Another important consideration in determining the objectives is not to try to solve all of the world's problems in one experiment. Focus on a specific attainable goal; "take one bite out of the apple at a time." By taking one attainable step at a time, each success paves the way for other opportunities. Doubting Thomases become champions, and lukewarm supporters become zealots. On the other hand, an initial failure can close the door for further applications. Barriers to implementation, which once appeared to be ten feet tall, have now grown to be a hundred. Therefore, it is essential to make your first effort successful.

3.1 EXAMINING THE PROCESS AND PRODUCT

Obtaining a basic understanding of the process and/or product under study is essential for effective planning of the experiment. Some of this vital knowledge can be obtained through the interchange of ideas within team meetings. Uncontrolled discussions can make a meeting unproductive, and conversations can drift into topics not directly related to the goals of the project. However, a regulated format for effectively controlling the focus of comments and extracting vital information from team members can minimize the occurrence of these unproductive situations. Brainstorming has proven to be an effective tool for guiding team discussions and encouraging the efficient acquisition of knowledge and understanding.

Developing a meaningful objective may require research on the part of the experimentation team. Retrieval of historical data may be needed. Special tests or extra production runs may be necessary in order to obtain additional understanding prior to finalizing the team objective. Data analysis using such tools as the Pareto principle[1] can help provide focus for the team's efforts. A better understanding of the process under study can make the entire planning phase run more smoothly and effectively. Developing a process flow chart can provide key insights into the scope of what needs to be investigated in the study. Cause-and-effect diagrams[2] (Ishikawa diagrams) are also effective tools for obtaining a wealth of information concerning the process.

Understanding that additional information is required, specific research activities may need to be delegated within the team. If more information, such as performance, is needed concerning the end product, the product engineer may volunteer or be assigned to lead efforts to obtain this knowledge prior to the next meeting. Developing a flow chart to understand the process better may be an assignment for the process engineer and manufacturing supervisor to perform. The construction of cause-and-effect diagrams can be led by the quality supervisor or engineer, the process engineer, the product engineer, or the manufacturing supervisor. My experience has been that in most cases the quality supervisor has the best expertise for cause-and-effect studies.

As discussed in the previous paragraphs, planning an experiment is not an activity that can be performed in one brief meeting. The direction set within the initial session will probably lead to the demand for additional information resulting in a list of action items that will need to be performed prior to determining the objective, defining an appropriate quality characteristic, and selecting process/product variables for study.

3.1.1 Brainstorming

Brainstorming can be very helpful in producing a list of viable alternative objectives for the experiment. The team can then choose the most appropriate candidate(s) from this list. Brainstorming promotes creativity by drawing from the participants ideas that are free from bias and restrained mind sets. By fostering an atmosphere of open-mindedness within the group, effective brainstorming is likely to help members expand the horizons of their thinking and to help particularly quiet members of the team to make a larger contribution. Besides spurring enthusiasm and encouraging everyone's involvement, the techniques will produce a more complete list and often lead to novel or unique ideas that would not have been thought of or considered otherwise. These original ideas are what lead to discoveries and trade secrets.

Besides facilitating the determination of the experiment objective(s), brainstorming can also be used to define alternative quality characteristics, identify means of measuring the selected quality characteristics (Chapter 4), and direct the listing and selecting of factors (Chapter 5) to incorporate into the experiment. Brainstorming can be effective when the entire team is assembled or on a smaller scale with a subgroup of the team performing specific research.

When applied to other quality tools used for facilitating process understanding, brainstorming objective(s) can enhance their value and increase the likelihood that all essential aspects are considered. This applies to defining the categories used in Pareto analysis, to the process steps in flow charting, to potential causes in cause-and-effect diagrams, to failures in fault tree analysis, and to each of the segments of failure mode and effect analysis (FMEA). Each of these combinations can provide the team with very powerful and effective tools for understanding the process and associated products.

When using brainstorming, it is always a good practice to have more than one work session. Individuals may be in a different frame of mind from one meeting to another; their thinking may be focused in one direction one day, generating one type of idea, and may be different the next day, resulting in a totally new set of ideas. The period after the first brainstorming session allows individuals to contemplate their responses and those of fellow team members. This time can help generate additional ideas that can be written down and saved for the next meeting.

Before beginning the brainstorming exercise, it is wise to state the rules you will be following. Emphasize that in the initial phase that there is no such thing as a bad or wrong idea. I have seen numerous occasions where well-intentioned team members have quickly asserted that someone's idea was not good: "Charlie, those injectors don't have any effect on the process results." Once this has been said, the damage has been done, and Charlie may become withdrawn and shy away from making other suggestions. Therefore, it is best to state up front the ground rules. Also, no discussion of the ideas should be made during the brainstorming. Discussion will come later. Encourage the team to be creative and contribute unusual suggestions along with obvious ones. Highlight the advantage of building onto the ideas of others.

In the process of acquiring this information, be sure that these new ideas are being written down. A flip chart is one good way to record the information. After filling up a sheet, detach it and post it on the wall so that everyone can still see the previous ideas and perhaps continue to build off these suggestions. If enough blackboard space is available around the room, it may be sufficient. However, there is always the potential for running out of room and having to erase some of the information. Also, after the session, you can't take the board with you. It is also highly probable that between the initial and follow-up sessions, someone will need the board for other purposes. You can take the flip chart sheets with you and simply post them up again at the next meeting.

For conducting an effective brainstorming session, the following steps have been proven as sound rules to follow and should be reviewed with the team prior to proceeding with the brainstorming exercise.

1. Go in rotation. One idea per person in each turn. Going clockwise around the table is a good standard method.

2. Encourage everyone to be free in bringing up any idea that comes to mind. Promote spontaneity. Ideas breed other ideas. Emphasize quantity over quality.

3. Forbid discussion and criticism at this stage. Even groans or other subtle expressions of disapproval including gestures are to be disallowed. Positive reinforcement such as applauding is acceptable, however, and may encourage additional good ideas.

4. If a participant cannot think of anything on their turn, it is perfectly acceptable for them to pass. As you continue to go around the table, they will have other opportunities. The ideas of others may also spur them to think of related ideas.

5. Promote stretching of the imagination. One of the major reasons for an unsuccessful experiment is failure to incorporate a significant factor that no one thought was important.

6. Laugh! Good-natured humor can loosen up the group and make the timid members more comfortable and the atmosphere more conducive for creative thinking.

7. Continue to go around the table until all ideas have been exhausted and all team members have passed.

3.1.2 The Pareto Chart

Pareto charts are useful tools for determining where the specific focus of problem solving should be directed. The charts are based on the Pareto principle, which basically says, "Most occurrences of any quality problem can be grouped into as few as one, two, or three classifications." Quite often, no more than three categories will represent at least 80% of the occurrences of the problem. Quality improvement efforts are thus directed more efficiently toward fixing the vital few instead of spending an inordinate amount of energy on the trivial many.[3] The chart's contribution as a problem-solving or prevention tool is to improve the process/product in regard to those few issues that are the most important instead of trying to optimize the process/product in light of all concerns.

The first step is to obtain the total number of occurrences of the problem that are being investigated. Second, define the problem in terms of some type of classification system. Third, categorize the total number of occurrences among these classes. Fourth, calculate the frequency of occurrence. Fifth, sort the categories in order of frequency of occurrence from largest to smallest. Sixth, calculate the cumulative frequency for each classification from largest to smallest. Seventh, construct a bar graph representing each category as a bar and plot a line graph above the bars showing cumulative frequencies. See Figure 3-1.

The principle can be applied to a single set of classifications or to a multitude of groupings. After performing Pareto analysis on a primary classification, the techniques can be applied further to subcategories. For example in Table 3-1, we see the calculations for the Pareto analysis of defects within an electronic assembly process. A study of defects was made according to both circuit board type and type of defect. Since the 5011 unit had so many defects, defect information for this product was dissected further according to defect type. The Pareto charts for these calculations are shown in Figure 3-2.

Figure 3-1 Pareto Chart Steps

1. Determine total number of occurrences.
2. Define classifications (defect type, product type, etc.).
3. Categorize occurrences according to classification.
4. Calculate frequency of occurrence for each classification.
5. Sort classifications by frequency of occurrence.
6. Calculate cumulative frequency of occurrence by classifications in descending order of occurrence.
7. Construct bar graph for individual frequencies by classification.
8. Plot line graph of cumulative frequencies.

Table 3-1 Electronic Assembly Pareto Analysis

Pareto Analysis by Circuit Board Type

Circuit board	Defects	Percent of All Defects: This category	Percent of All Defects: Cumulative
5011	113	34.8	34.8
5001	67	20.6	55.4
5055	50	15.4	70.8
5037	33	10.2	81.0
5056	23	7.1	88.1
5035	19	5.8	93.9
5010	8	2.5	96.4
5020	6	1.8	98.2
5007	6	1.8	100.0
Total	325		

Pareto Analysis by Defect Type
(All Circuit Board Types)

Defect type	Defects	Percent of All Defects: This category	Percent of All Defects: Cumulative
Insufficient solder	170	52.3	52.3
Solder on connector	73	22.5	74.8
Missing component	37	11.4	86.2
Leads not thru	33	10.2	96.3
Excess solder	7	2.2	98.5
Lead out	5	1.5	100.0
Total	325		

Pareto Analysis by Defect Type
(Circuit Board 5011)

Defect type	Defects	Percent of All Defects: This category	Percent of All Defects: Cumulative
Insufficient solder	38	33.6	33.6
Solder on connector	31	27.4	61.0
Missing component	20	17.7	78.7
Leads not thru	19	16.8	95.5
Lead out	3	2.7	98.2
Excess solder	2	1.8	100.0
Total	113		

Figure 3-2 Electronic Assembly Pareto Analysis

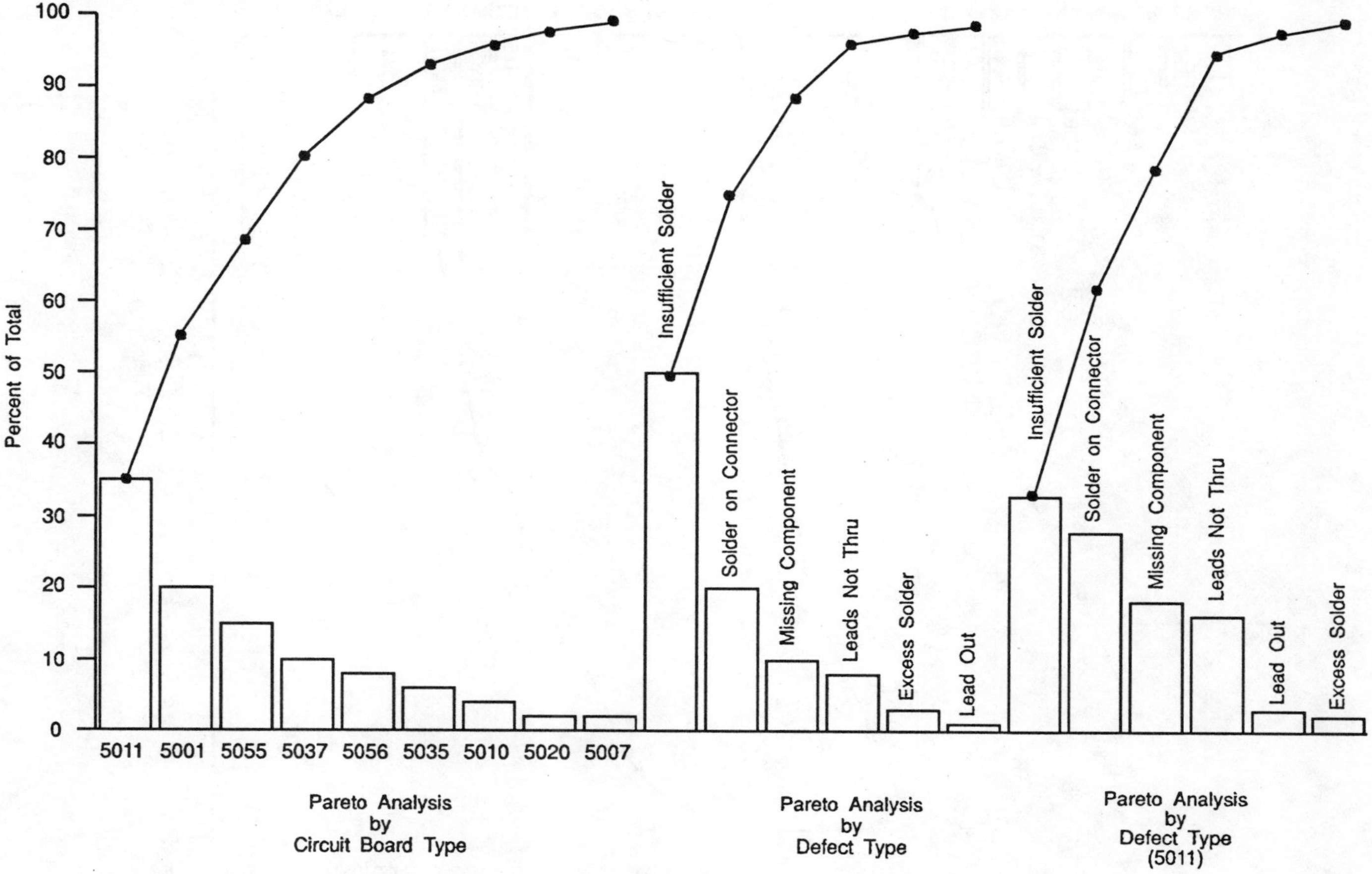

Figure 3-3 Semiconductor Slice Scrap and Rework Paneto Analysis

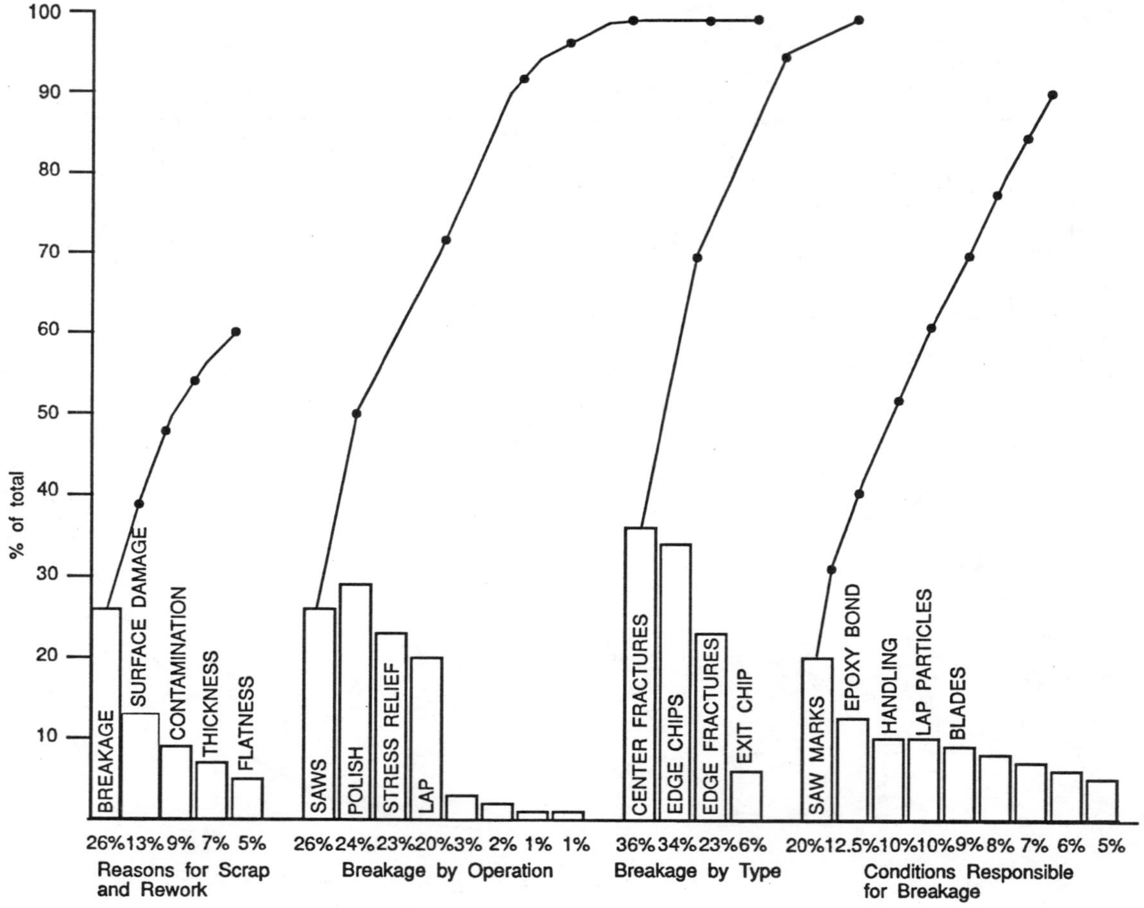

An additional example is shown in Figure 3-3. Defects within a semiconductor slicing operation were first analyzed according to the reasons for scrap and rework. The number one reason, which was breakage, was studied further. The units affected by breakage were than categorized according to where the breakage occurred (operation), type of breakage, and conditions attributed to the breakage. Although the preceding explanation used frequency of occurrence as the unit of measure, the costs associated with defects and repair could be applied instead. In fact, the applicability of this principle is broad, and the technique can be applied to any type of process or product. Although the principle is understood by many, surprisingly few remember its potential role in experiment planning. There are numerous texts with additional material on the use of Pareto charts including *Guide to Quality Control* by Dr. Kaoru Ishikara and *Quality Control Handbook* by J. M. Juran.

3.1.3 The Process Flow Diagram

The purpose of the flow chart is to help understand the sequence of events that leads to the finished product. By gaining a better insight into the individual components of the process from a common perspective, members of the team can more easily discuss what to do, where to do it, and when to do it. Figures 3-4, 3-5, and 3-6 give examples of process flow diagrams.

Besides educating the team on the sequence of production steps, the flow chart can also show the interdependencies between stages. Also potentially important are data collection points and test station locations. These can help isolate and track problem origins. In the event that the process is too immense or complex to include all variables of interest in one experiment, the flow chart can help determine the most appropriate dividing line between experiment segments. The knowledge may also be useful in deleting process stages from the study that are found unrelated to the team objective.

However, the main contribution of developing the flow chart is to understand the actual process flow. Process engineers and manufacturing supervisors, who may feel that they have a full understanding of the process, frequently become surprised when they learned that their interpretations were quite different. In fact, the only ones who correctly knew the process flow were the production operators.

The actual effort in developing the flow chart will require not only some of the team members but input from others as well. Besides the process engineer, line supervisor, and product engineer, the line leader, operators, test operators, inspectors, and line technicians can all play vital roles in insuring that the flow chart generated is authentic and up-to-date. Remember, when it comes to how the product is built, they are the experts. They are the ones who spend the most time with the process.

Figure 3-4 Electronic Manufacturing Process Flow Diagram

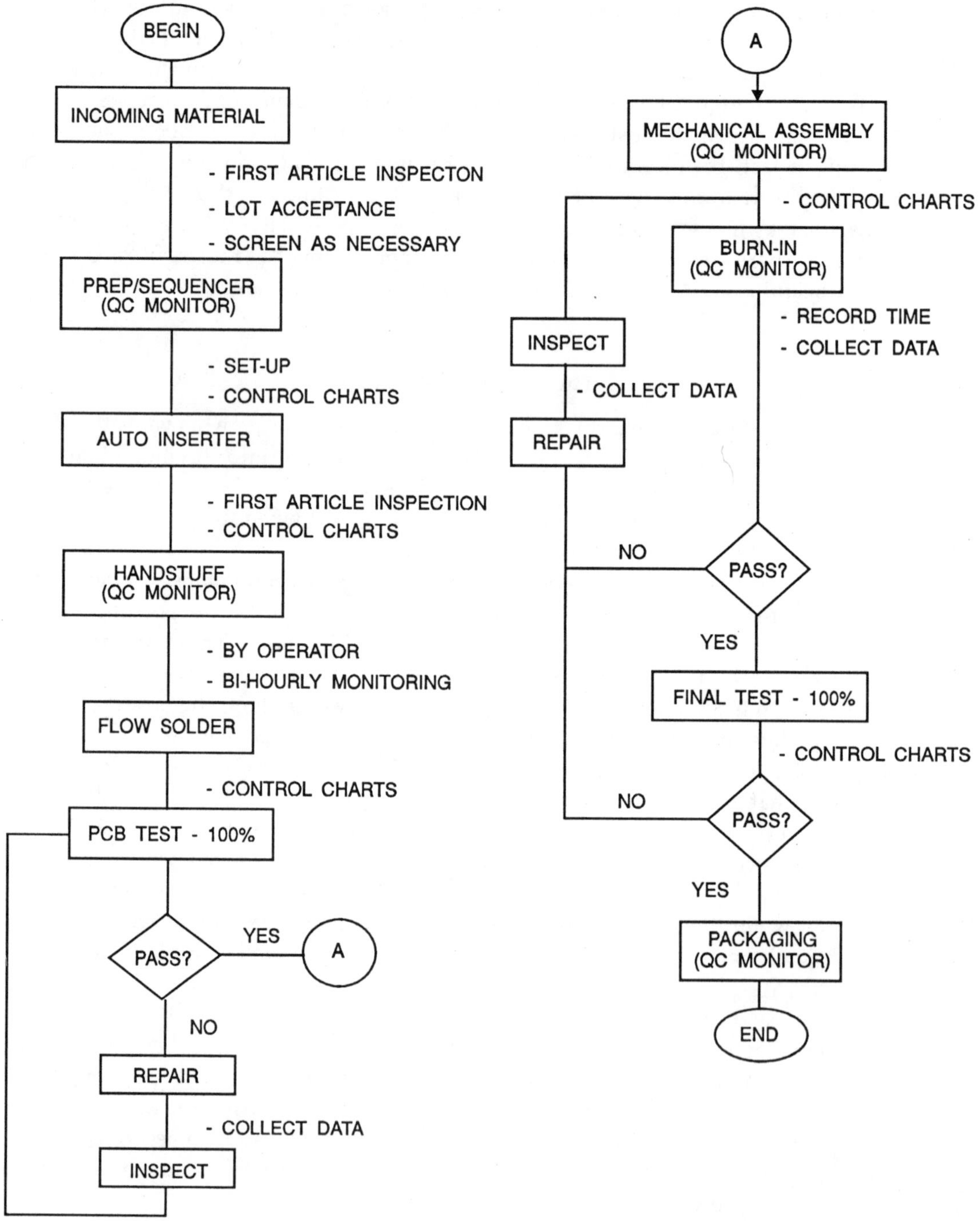

Figure 3-5 Control Device Final Assembly Detailed Process Flow Diagram

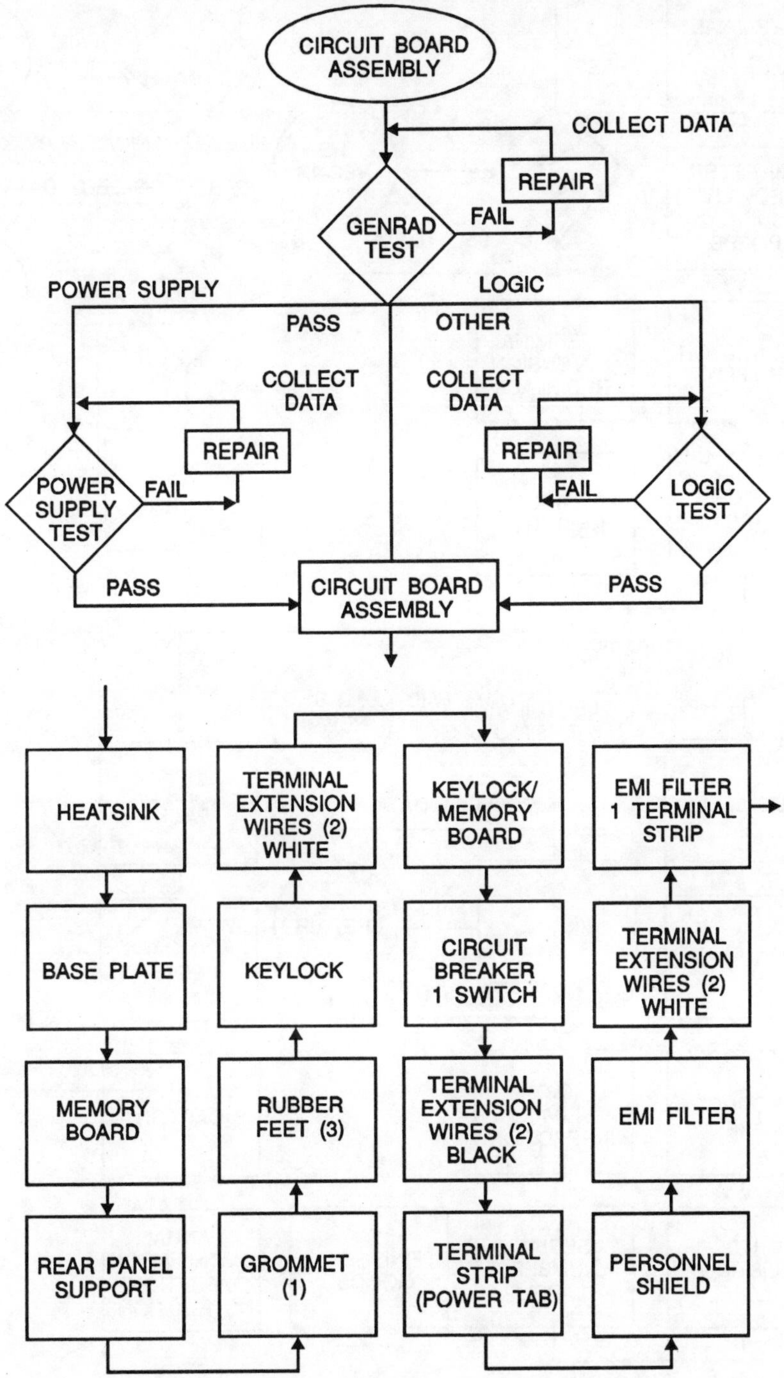

Figure 3-5 Continued

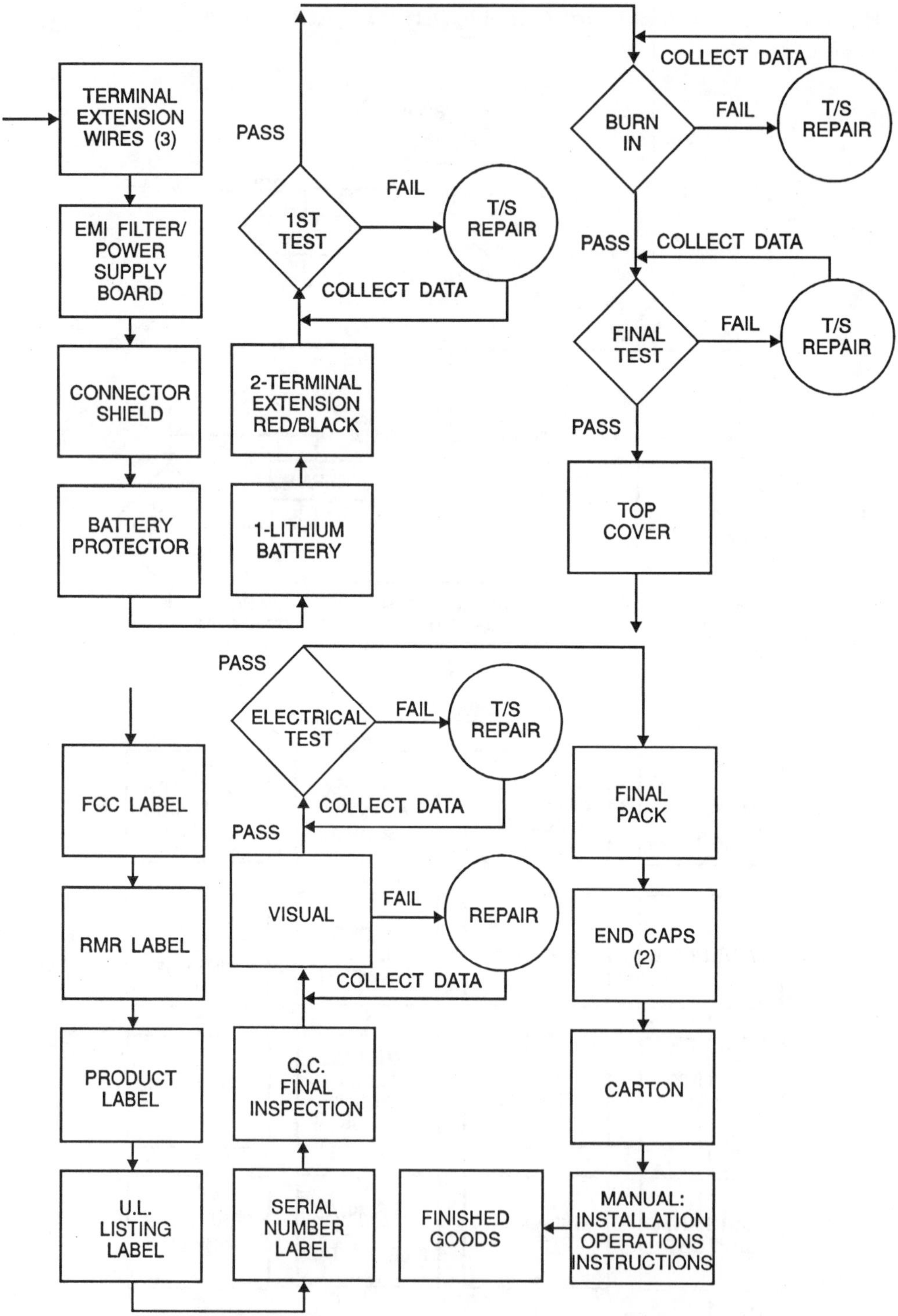

Figure 3-6 Plastic Injection Molding Process Flow Diagram

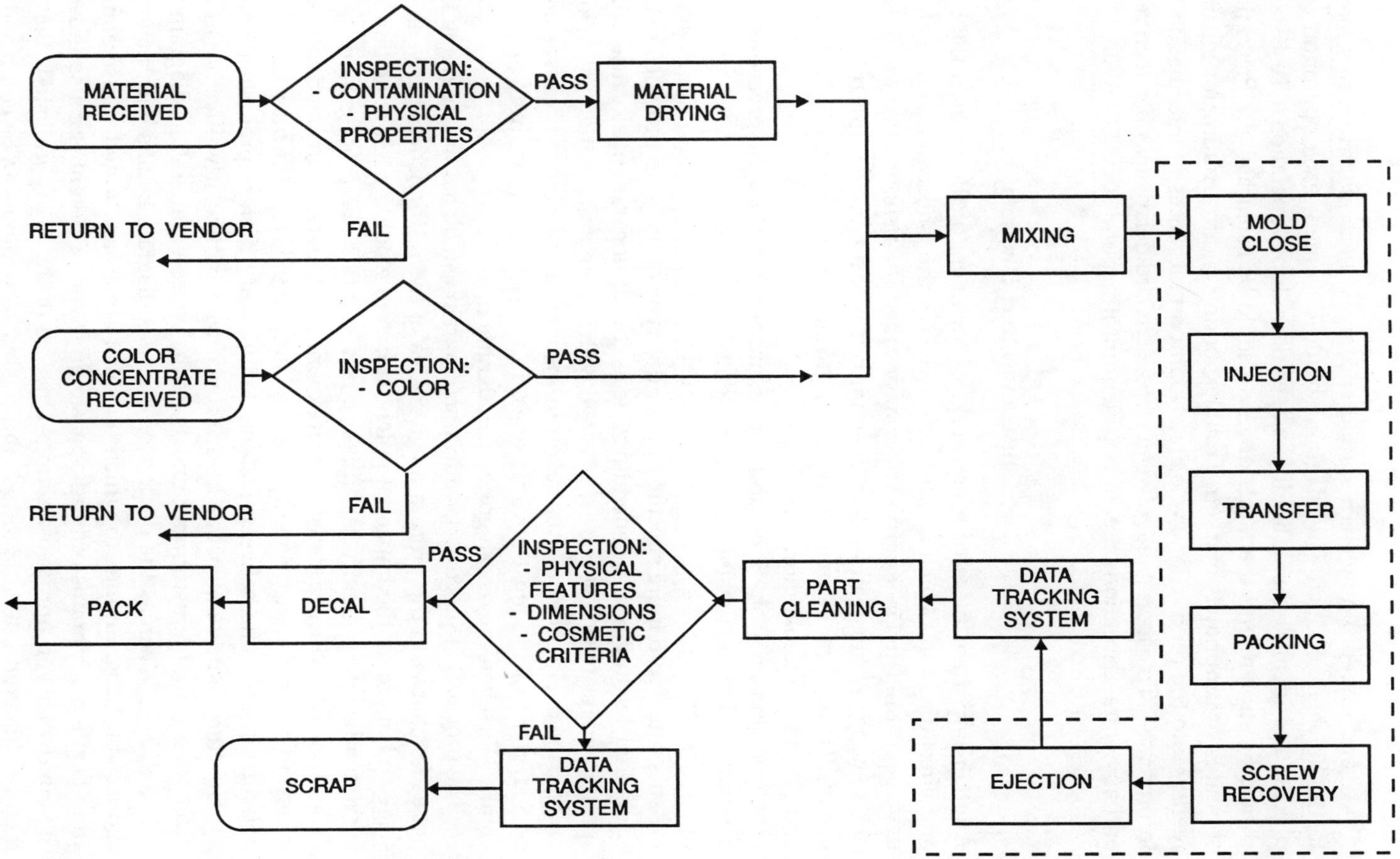

A good in-depth flow chart should encompass each step from raw material to the finished product. The diagram should document each operation of the process and identify the individual stages of multiple operations. Test stations should be shown, and the kinds of tests should be listed as well. Pass and fail should be appropriately marked. Troubleshooting and the routing for repair and reentry into the production cycle are also important pieces of information to be incorporated. Transportation between steps, standard delay times between points, and any storage locations are all pertinent information.

3.1.4 The Cause-and-Effect Diagram

Another important piece of homework for members of the team is the cause-and-effect diagram, which is often referred to as the Ishikawa diagram after its developer, the late Dr. Kaoru Ishikawa, or called the fishbone diagram because of its shape. A cause-and-effect diagram can be categorized into one of three groups: (1) dispersion analysis type, (2) production process classification type, and (3) cause enumeration type.[5]

Dispersion analysis is helpful for organizing the thought process and for developing the relationships among potential causes. By first developing major categories of potential causes and then breaking these down into subgroups and the subgroups into more specific causes, this type of diagram provides a simple structured technique for generating ideas concerning potential causes of the specific end result that you are concerned with and organizing them into a logical order. However, care must be taken to insure that all potential causes are included, not just the most obvious ones. In the dispersion analysis diagram in Figure 3-7, seven major categories are identified.

The production process classification diagram can be helpful in giving those not as familiar with the process a better idea of the relationships between each stage and of where the impact of potential factors would be felt. One limitation is the tendency to identify repetitive causes at difference process steps, a tendency that, when incorporated into an experiment, can result in an unnecessarily large and expensive experiment. A second limitation is the difficulty in detecting potential interactions between factors identified at different process steps.

The third type, which has been proven as a particularly effective tool for promoting team brainstorming efforts, is the cause enumeration diagram (Figures 3-8, 3-9). Whereas the dispersion analysis diagram begins with major categories and subgroupings to which potential causes are added, cause enumeration begins with brainstorming open to any type of potential cause linked to the effect that you are investigating. Once all of the ideas are listed, they can then be clustered into subgroups, and related subgroups can be combined into

Figure 3-7 Dispersion Analysis Diagram Surface Mount Technology

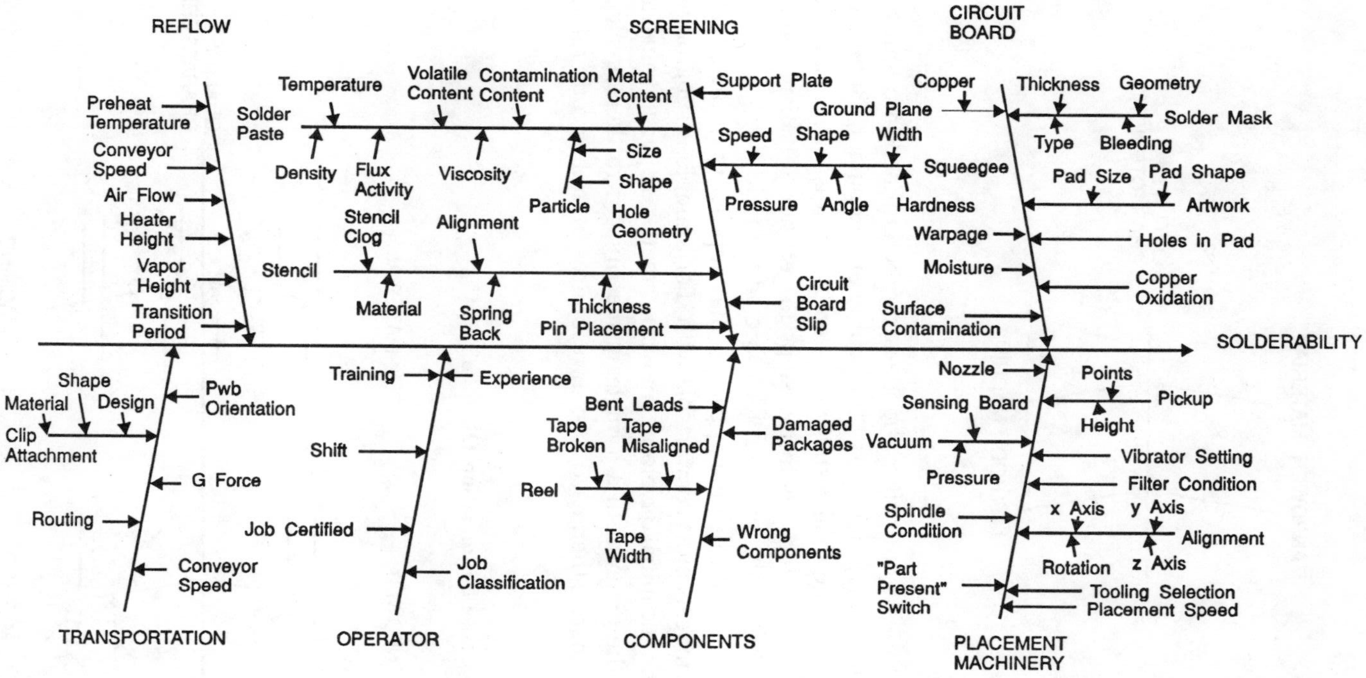

Figure 3-8 Cause Enumeration Diagram

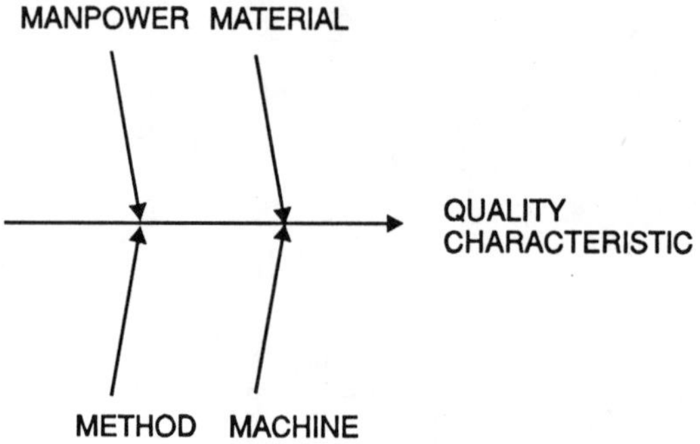

major categories. Quite often the ideas can be grouped into four major classifications such as: (1) materials, (2) machine or equipment, (3) methods, and (4) measurement.[6] The final result will resemble the dispersion analysis diagram. However, the difference is in the steps to get there. In dispersion analysis, a structure is first built, and then ideas are added to it.

The team should use the approach that appears to fit the situation best or that the team feels most comfortable with. For example, a subgroup of the team may perform the initial development work, create a dispersion analysis diagram, and bring the diagram to a joint team meeting for further development. The unfinished chart is then used to spur responses from the group for adding more

Figure 3-9 Cause Enumeration Diagram

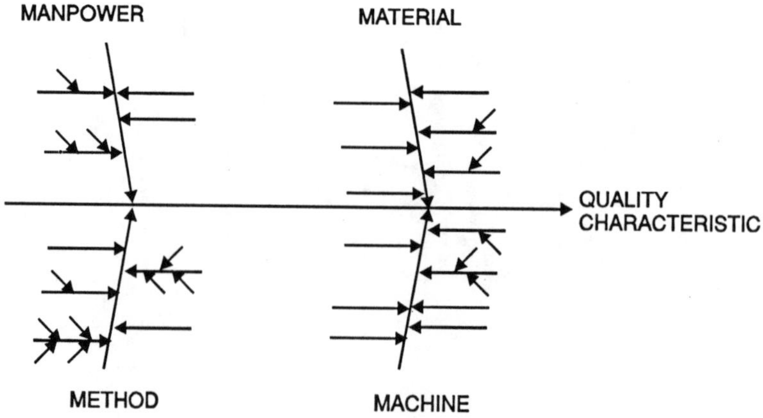

potential factors (causes) to the existing list. A second technique using cause enumeration is to begin the brainstorming (see Chapter 5) at a joint session. Draw as many ideas as possible from the group and list them. From the list, logical groupings can be developed for designing the cause-and-effect diagram.

3.1.4.1 Developing a Cause-and-Effect Diagram

In relation to Pareto analysis and the process flow chart, the cause-and-effect diagram (Figure 3-10) would typically follow after determination of the project objective. Based on this desired result, the diagram would evolve as the team develops a list of those factors that may have an impact. This activity may be the work of a subgroup of the team, team brainstorming, or a combination of both. The following are a few guidelines for constructing a cause-and-effect diagram.

1. Construct a straight horizontal line with an arrow facing outward on its right end.
2. Write the quality characteristic to the right of the arrow.
3. Draw 45-degree angle lines from the horizontal line to designate the major cause categories (usually four). Write in these major classifications.
4. Add possible causes by drawing lines with arrows connected to major category lines and parallel to the main horizontal line.
5. Add more detailed potential causes by connecting 45-degree lines to the primary causes. Even more detailed possibilities can be added by constructing lines at angles to these related potential causes.

3.1.5 Fault Tree Analysis

Initially used to detect potential safety and reliability problems, fault tree analysis provides a highly structured and formal tool for facilitating the planning of experiments. The technique involves first listing key customer concerns or potential problem areas. For each concern or potential problem, the conditions are identified which could either result in the problem's occurring or contribute to its effect. Lines can be drawn from the stated problem to each of these possible causes. The listing of potential problems at the top of the diagram and the spreading out of lines down to the various causes associated with each problem gives the pictorial effect of a tree (Figure 3-11).[7]

Once the tree has been created, closer scrutiny can be given to each of the causes or conditions included in the tree. The resulting clearer vision of what your specific objective should be can serve as a guide in defining what you will

Figure 3-10 Construction of Cause-and-Effect Diagram

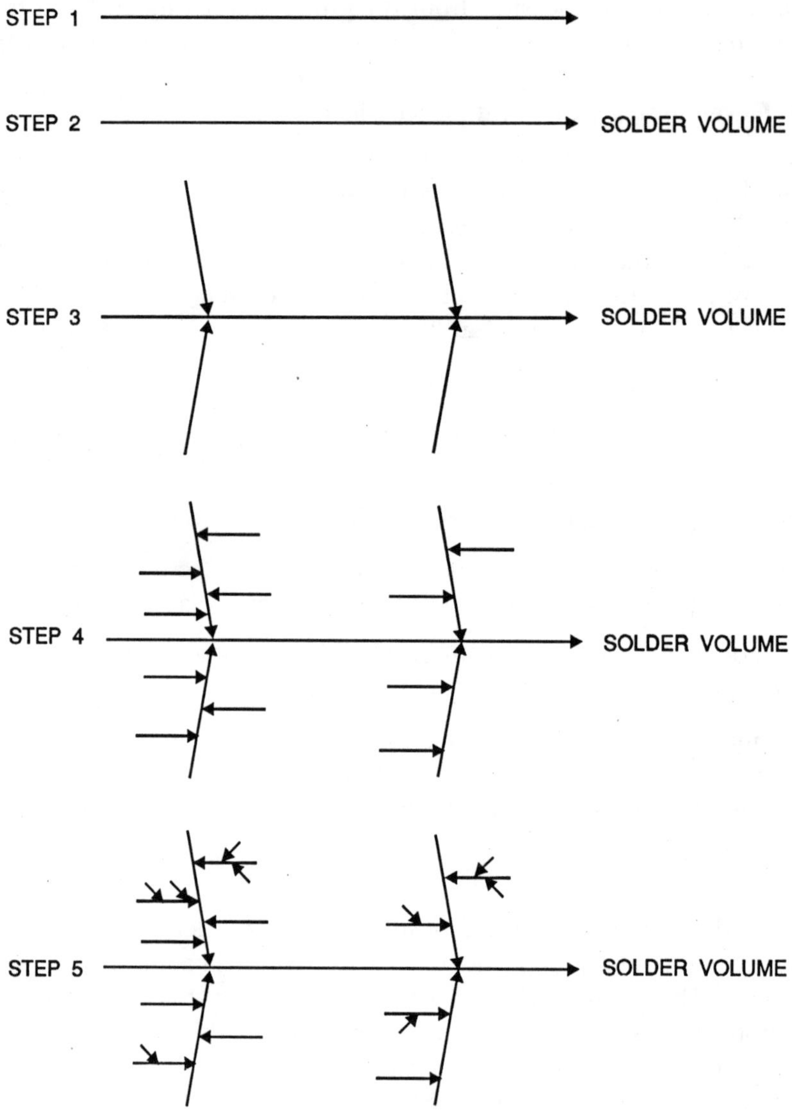

be measuring within the experiment as well. In addition to a clearer and more precise statement of the objective or a more direct and meaningful measurement criterion, the decision tree can also help identify those factors that should be incorporated within the study and included in the experimental matrix. Determining whether to eliminate a condition or reduce its effect on the primary

Figure 3-11 Television Fault Tree Analysis*

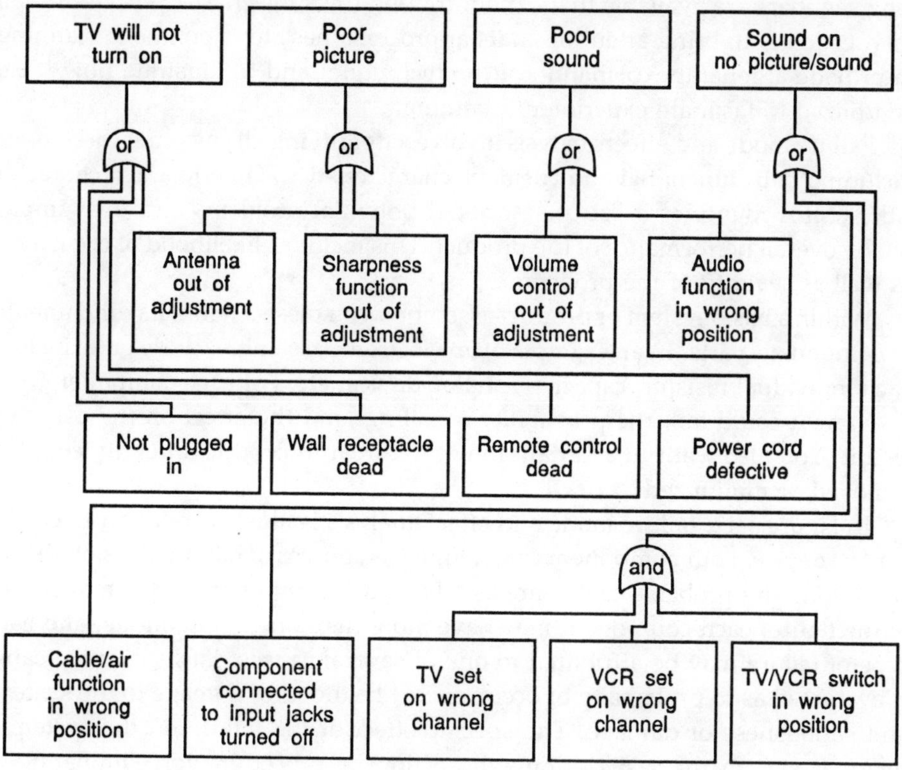

*Adapted from RCA Color Television Owner's Manual. (Indianapolis: Thomson Consumer Electronics, 1990), p. 34.

problem will also assist you later in classifying factors as control factors or noise factors (Chapter 5).

The most obvious application of fault tree analysis is within the design environment. "What can go wrong?" and "What will cause it not to operate?" are typical questions asked by the designer. Extending this approach to the manufacturing disciplines, we can translate the typical design questions into "What process steps or operations within a step can cause the final product not to function as required?"

3.1.6 Failure Mode and Effect Analysis (FMEA)

Another technique for formalizing up front analysis of the product or process design is failure mode and effect analysis. In the recent acceleration of quality awareness and growth in industrial appetites for effective quality tools, FMEA has increasingly become an important tool for obtaining greater design and producibility understanding. Although the topic will be covered only briefly here, there are numerous sources that go into greater detail, and various week-long seminars are available that expound upon the subject. The purpose within this section is to bring attention to its appropriateness to experiment planning, to provide a general explanation of the technique, and to illustrate how it can be utilized to facilitate experiment planning.

Failure mode and effect analysis involves identifying all customer care-abouts including both functional and cosmetic characteristics. Then for each characteristic, FMEA identifies a list of associated potential problems and their impact on the overall performance of the product. This includes likelihood of occurrence as well as severity of the problem.

Within a basic system or product assembly, you dissect it into its fundamental or component parts. In an example of an electronic assembly, these parts include each individual resistor, capacitor, analog device, etc. For each component, you ask how it could fail, the probability of failing, and the effect on the complete circuit. You also want to ascertain how the threat to product integrity could be removed or minimized.

In Figure 3-12, failure mode and effect analysis is illustrated for an electronic control device. Four components are defined as sources of failure. Possible failure conditions and probable causes are listed for each component. As demonstrated in the figure, each component may have more than one failure mode, and each type of failure may be attributed to one of several causes. Each potential cause is evaluated as to probability of occurrence, likelihood of damage to the system, and seriousness of damage. The specific effect of the failure on the system is defined, and in the last column, the action or procedure for eliminating or reducing the probability of occurrence is identified.

This systematic approach to identifying potential product problems and assessing their importance can prevent the common pitfall within defining the experiment objective of trying to solve all your problems in one broad stroke. FMEA also reduces the risk of forgetting potentially critical problem areas which could be easily overlooked amid a mass of more visible care-abouts. This has the greatest likelihood within a complex and sophisticated product. Careful attention to the most critical and likely-to-occur problems will result in a more clearly defined focus that can maximize the benefits achieved from a well thought-out experiment and insure solutions to the truly important problems.

Besides helping to reach a meaningful objective, FMEA can also serve to identify the means of measurement within the experiment. Once you have determined from this analysis technique the most potentially critical concerns, the types of failure associated with the specific problem may provide the guidelines for setting measurement criteria. When you proceed later with the selection of experiment factors (Chapter 5), the severity and probability of failure assessed

Figure 3-12 CPU/Power Supply Failure Mode and Effect Analysis

Component	Possible Failure	Cause of Failure	P	D	S	Effect of Failure on the System	How Can Failure Be Eliminated or Reduced?
Status LEDs	Will not illuminate.	Infant mortality.	2	1	1	Cannot report CPU status.	Increase burn in time to catch infant mortality.
		Wear out.	1	1	1		Change to higher grade LEDs.
Communication port	Will not communicate.	ESD damage to driver/receiver IC.	2	1	2	Cannot edit or monitor user program.	Add clamping diodes.
		Cable loose.	2	1	2		Provide screw terminals to secure cable to port.
		Cable miswired.	3	2	2		Sell cable so user does not have to build his own.
Power supply	Out of regulation.	Component value variability causes regulator to be out of desired range.	1	1	3	Stops executing program, turns off all outputs.	Change to tighter tolerance and components.
	Drops to 0 volts.	Switching transistors blown.	2	2	3		Change to higher power transistors.
Ram	Scrambles user memory.	Ram manufacturing defect.	1	1	3	Stops executing program and turns off all outputs.	Change to higher grade rams.

Legend: P = probability of occurrence
D = likelihood of damage to system
S = seriousness of damage to system
Evaluation scale: 1 = low
2 = moderate
3 = high[8]

during FMEA can be used as a decision tool in determining which components or subsystem considerations are to be incorporated into the experiment.

Although this thoroughness reduces the potential for leaving out potentially critical problem areas, there can also be a high cost associated with this effort. Dividing a large, complex system into its many parts and performing an intensive failure analysis on each element including probability, severity, and solution to each problem can be extremely time consuming. Like an overloaded plane, the experiment may never get off the ground. Therefore engineering judgment is particularly important in the use of failure mode and effect analysis for determining the proper level of depth required.

3.2 DEFINING THE QUALITY CHARACTERISTIC

By forming a foundation for understanding the process through the use of the techniques described in the first section of this chapter, the team can more intelligently come to agreement on the objectives of the study and determine a relevant and meaningful quality characteristic for measuring success. This is really the first milestone in an experiment and should not be hurriedly passed through. Often, a well-meaning group will select the most obvious concern as the standard measure of success and proceed without understanding the consequences. Such shortcuts can result in lost opportunities, add to the complexity of the experiment, or even create misleading results. Therefore, it is essential that the team evaluate the task of defining the quality characteristic with the respect that it deserves.

In arriving at an objective and at the definition of the quality characteristic, certain guidelines should be followed to insure effective team coordination and prevent unnecessary misunderstanding. These basic rules are:

1. clearly define the objectives in terms that everyone on the team can understand;
2. insure that all team members agree on and can support the objectives selected by the majority of the team;
3. attain mutual agreement on the criteria for measuring the ability to achieve the objectives;
4. put into place communication safeguards to insure that all affected personnel become aware of any changes in the objective or quality characteristic;
5. provide the opportunity to respond to any changes so as to assure continued agreement and support by all team members.[9]

The administering and coordination of these efforts should belong to the team leader unless otherwise delegated.

In selecting an appropriate quality characteristic, several considerations should be covered. The study will be more meaningful if the quality characteristic is defined in terms that are clear and measurable. A key issue concerns the units of measurement of the quality characteristic. The objectives, "to prevent defects" and "to accelerate production ramp up," have noble implications, but how you measure them is a more substantial yardstick for determining success. More meaningful objectives would include "reduce solder paste volume variability" and "increase mean time between failures," which incorporate the measures of dimensions and time, respectively, and are therefore better evaluators of success and failure.

In selecting these units, you need to consider the conditions and environment under which measurements will be taken. If you are measuring moisture content, will the humidity within the testing area change the readings? More generally, is a controlled environment required to attain accurate readings, and if so, will you be using a controlled environment? If the answer to the first question is yes and the response to the second no, perhaps this quality characteristic is not appropriate for this study. Maybe you need to select an alternate characteristic that can be more accurately and consistently measured.

Measurement instrumentation is also a consideration. Is the proper equipment available? I remember one experiment in which a very precise quality characteristic was suggested, but research had not been sufficiently conducted to discover that the necessary test equipment was not available. So be careful in recommending theoretically sound characteristics that are impractical. If measuring devices are available, what is their accuracy? Instruments with accuracy of + or − .005 inches will be useless if the characteristic of interest involves a dimension in which changes of .001 inches may be significant.

When considering an unfamiliar quality characteristic, it may also be helpful to take trial samples prior to proceeding to the next step. This can demonstrate the applicability of the measure to the experiment objectives, provide understanding of the relationship of the characteristic to the process, and indicate the capability of obtaining measurement repeatability.

Another key consideration for insuring the selection of an appropriate quality characteristic is additivity. What is meant by additivity is that the impact of all significant factors can be combined (added) to determine the total effect of all important factors. For example, unit increases in conveyor speed decrease circuit board (top side) temperature by 5 degrees, unit increases in the preheaters raise the temperature by 60 degrees, unit increases in railing height raise temperature by 12 degrees, and unit increases in solder temperature raise the temperature by 4 degrees. In this demonstration, the effect of each factor can be combined with the effect of the other factors. Therefore, circuit board (top side) temperature is a good quality characteristic because it has additivity.

Let's look at this example again, but use solder defects as the quality characteristic. Increases in conveyor speed increase solder opens (not enough solder); an increase in preheater settings decreases solder opens, but too high temperatures can increase solder shorts (too much solder); an increase in railing height can also decrease solder opens, but may increase solder shorts if set too high. Based on this information, let's say that the process factors are set to reduce solder opens and therefore minimize the number of solder defects. However, the end result is just the opposite. The number of solder defects actually increases from the process level changes as a consequence of a dramatic increase in solder shorts. Therefore, in this case, solder defects has poor additivity and is thus a poor quality characteristic.

To guide you in determining appropriate quality characteristics, it may be helpful to think of them as falling into one of three categories:

1. measurable characteristics,
2. attribute characteristics, and
3. dynamic characteristics.

3.2.1 Measurable Characteristics

Measurable characteristics are those end results or care-abouts that can be measured on a continuous scale.[10] Examples include dimensions, weight, pressure, and clearance. Within the framework of measurable characteristics, we can subdivide this classification further into nominal-the-best, smaller-the-better, and larger-the-better characteristics.

3.2.1.1 Nominal-the-Best

This term refers to a characteristic with a specific numerical goal or target value.[11] Dimensions typically fall within this category. Specific examples include:

height	pressure	top-side board temperature
length	density	percent moisture
width	viscosity	PH
thickness	time	overrun (dairy)
diameter	alignment	voltage
area	frequency	current
volume	timing	capacitance
clearance		

3.2.1.2 Smaller-the-Better

A smaller-the-better characteristic is one in which the desired goal is to obtain a measure of zero.[12] A common example is percent shrinkage. Other examples include:

machine wear
residue
percent contamination
lines of computer code
warpage
loudness
braking
product deterioration
access time
response time
power dissipation
heat dissipation
impact damage

Defects are not typically defined as measurable characteristics since they are discrete in nature. However, if enough variability or a large enough sample is used, the number of defects can approach being continuous and be defined as a smaller-the-best measurable characteristic. *But be forewarned and extremely cautious;* defects in themselves exhibit poor additivity as a rule and should be defined very carefully and within a narrow framework.

3.2.1.3 Larger-the-Better

Just the opposite of smaller-the-better, the goal of larger-the-better characteristics is to achieve the highest value possible. Infinity is the ultimate objective.[13] Examples of this type of characteristic are:

strength
pull strength
miles/gallon
shelf life
flash point
ignition temperature
mean time between failures
EMI
operating temperature range
melting point
corrosion resistance
vibration

3.2.2 Attribute Characteristics

Attribute characteristics cannot be measured on a continuous scale. Instead, they consist of classes into which the end results can be grouped.[14] For example, eggs are grouped into Grade A small, Grade A medium, Grade A large, Grade A extra large, and Grade A jumbo. The simplest form of attribute data is Go / No Go or Pass / fail data. In a production run in a paint operation, castings are inspected prior to shipping. Those that meet all coating specifications are considered "good" and packed. Those that are evaluated as "bad" are sent back for

Table 3-2 Suggested Sample Size per Experimental Run

	High >30%	Medium	Low <3%
Measurable	1–2	2–5	6–20
Classified attribute	1–5	5–20	20–100
Go/no go	5–20	20–200	200–2000

From *System of Experimental Design,* by permission of American Supplier Institute, a non-profit organization dedicated to improving the competitive position of U.S. industry.

rework or touch-up. Therefore, the reject rate is an example of Go / No Go attribute data. Scrap rate and yield are two other examples commonly used to measure quality. Number of defects, which provides more specific information, is still another example of attribute data. That is, the measure is in terms of whether something is acceptable or not acceptable and is therefore discrete in nature.

A major disadvantage of quality characteristics such as yields and reject rate is the much larger number of samples required to obtain the same relative amount of information as that received from a smaller data base for a measurable characteristic. This problem is illustrated in Table 3-2 in which the sampling of equivalent information is based on the incremental cost of producing additional units for each experimental run. For example, the cost of producing additional units is rated high if the cost of each additional unit is more than 30% of the combined cost of set-up and building the first unit at predetermined process settings. If the cost of producing additional units is less than 3% of set-up costs and the expense of building the first unit, then the cost of producing additional units is rated low. If the percent is between 3% and 30%, that incremental cost can be rated as medium.

As can be seen from the table, a measurable quality characteristic provides more efficient information than Go / No Go data. However, when the experimenter is unable to define the objective in terms of a measurable characteristic, a classified attribute quality characteristic is far superior over simply using Go / No Go criteria.

The reason that classified attribute characteristics provide more information than Go / No Go is that instead of just determining whether the units are good or bad, one evaluates the units in terms of degree of goodness or badness. For example, in electronics assembly, bleedover is defined as the tendency of solder to run from one circuit pad to another. We could say that we either have bleedover (fail—No Go) or do not have bleedover (pass—Go). However, a more meaningful descriptor would be to classify bleedover as follows:

Rating	Description
0	No bleedover
1	Bleedover up to 25% to adjacent pad
2	Bleedover between 25% and 50% to adjacent pad
3	Bleedover between 50% and 75% to adjacent pad
4	Bleedover over 75% to adjacent pad

As can be seen, the placing of a rating on the degree of goodness or badness provides considerably more insight. Other examples of classified attributes and their classifications are given in Table 3-3.

If the team does agree on using a classified attribute quality characteristic, an additional consideration must be made. If the results are dependent on subjective assignment of classifications, then the criteria for this selection must be well defined and documented. If the characteristic is cosmetic in nature, visual aids such as photographs, diagrams, and even actual examples should be provided. Good examples would include samples that are borderline cases, appropriately labeled as to their classification. This documentation should also be thoroughly reviewed with the one who will be doing the inspecting and classification.

3.2.3 Dynamic Characteristics

The idea of dynamic characteristics is the most complex and difficult to understand of the three principle groups, and the concepts have not been readily practiced within the United States although they are widely used in Japan.

Table 3-3 Classified Attributes

	Class 1	Class 2	Class 3
Percent contamination	0%	0%< <50%	>50%
Percent oxidation	0%< <10%	10%< <50%	>50%
Percent damaged parts	0%	0%< <40%	>40%
Degree of damaged parts	No defect	Minor	Critical
Sunburn	First	Second	Third
Magnitude of cosmetic defects	None	Mild	Severe
Surface scratches	None	Thin	Wide & deep
Classification of taste	Sweet	Bland	Sour

However, this tool can be powerfully effective and efficient for facilitating process knowledge once the concepts have been understood. A dynamic characteristic (see examples, Table 3-4) is a functional representation of the process being studied. Within the mind set of a dynamic characteristic, the process is viewed as a dynamic system described by a signal or input and by the resulting output or end result that is a result of this signal. Another way to think of a dynamic characteristic is to view the process as a system involving energy transfer from the input to the end result.

A basic example of a dynamic characteristic is the temperature control for a room. The thermostat (system) can be adjusted to a range of temperatures (input signal), and the resulting room temperature (output) will be a result of this thermostat setting combined with exterior influences such as outside weather and the number of people in the room (Figure 3-13).

Another example is the steering system of your car (Figure 3-14). While you are driving on the road, you may notice the distance between the tires on the car and the edge of the road. When entering a curve, you turn the steering

Table 3-4 Dynamic Characteristic Examples

System/Subsystem	*M*: Input Signal	*y*: Output
Measurement system	True value	Measured value
Sensing system	True state	Signal sent out
Photographic system	True image	Photographic image
Control system	Control given	Resulting control
Adjustment system	Adjustment made	Resulting change
Communication system	Signal to be sent	Signal transmitted
Radar	True position	Measured position
Radar	True image	Received image
Microscope	True image	Received image
Copying function	Original contrast	Copied contrast
Paper feeder	Roller rotation	Paper travel distance
Automatic transmission	Engine RPM	Change of gear
Molding	Die dimension	Molded dimension
Shower water temperature	Adjustment	Resulting temperature
Steering function	Steering wheel angle	Vehicle turning radius
Digital communication	Zero/one	Zero/one
Thermostat	Temperature	On/off

From "Dynamic System Optimization: An Introduction to Dynamic Characteristics," by permission of American Supplier Institute, a non-profit organization dedicated to improving the competitive position of U.S. industry.

Figure 3-13 Dynamic Temperature Control System

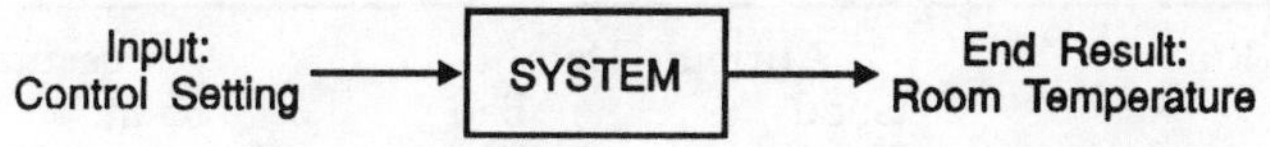

wheel (input signal) to compensate for the change in the road and to insure that you remain a safe distance from the edge. The actual distance between the car and the side of the road is the resulting output.

3.2.4 Comparison of Quality Characteristic Types

Classified attribute characteristics are often selected over measurable and dynamic characteristics because they are so obvious and easy for everyone to relate to. Data collection is simple and straightforward as well. However, as is often the case, you get what you pay for.

As previously mentioned within this chapter, a serious problem with attribute characteristics is additivity of results. Since various effects may result in a reject or defect, the impact of one factor may affect one cause while another factor has a bearing on a totally different contributor. For example, factor A can cause 1 reject. Factor B can also cause 1 reject. If both occur together (1 + 1), we have 1 reject (1 + 1 = 1). As demonstrated in the inequality, this type of characteristic does not have good additivity. The reason that this is so important is that you want to be able to repeat the predicted results of the optimal conditions determined from your analysis. If the selected quality characteristic does not have additivity, repeatability cannot be assured.

Another disadvantage of attribute data is that it does not provide as much insight into the process or design being studied. For example, observe the data from Figure 3-15.

Figure 3-14 Dynamic Car Steering System

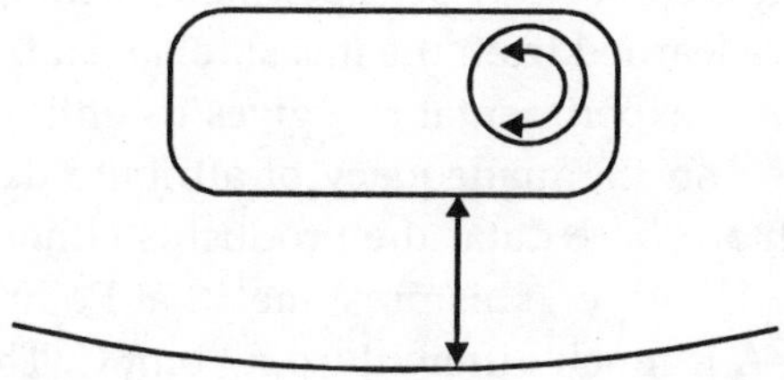

Figure 3-15 Manufacture of Yardsticks

Experimental Run	Attribute Data		Measurable Data
	Good	Bad	35 in. 37 in.
1	9	1	X XXX X XXXXX
2	9	1	XX XXX XXXX X
3	9	1	XX XXX XXXX X
4	9	1	X X XX X XXXXX
5	9	1	X X X X X X X X X X

Based on the attribute data, it appears that each of the experimental runs and consequently each combination of experiment factors produces the same results. However, as we learned from the measurable data, this would be a false assumption. In fact, each experimental run gives us entirely different results.

Another perspective on the inadequacy of attribute data can be illustrated from Figure 3-16. With attribute data, the product is either within specification or out of specification. However, this presumes that Point A is just as good as Point B and that Point A is much different from Point C. This is essentially how

Figure 3-16 Attribute Quality Characteristic Interpretation of Data

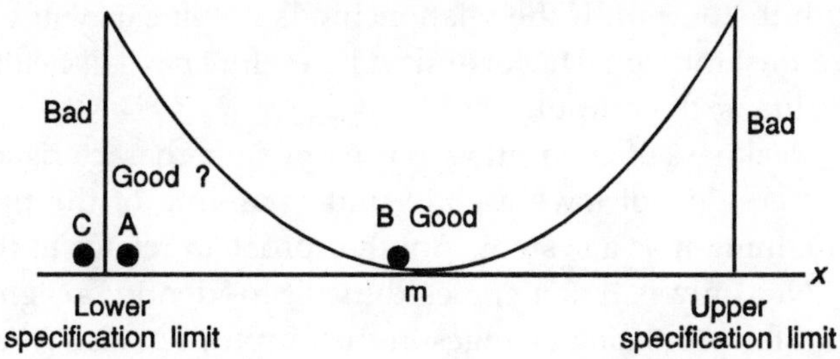

an attribute quality characteristic interprets the data. But if we view the center or nominal value (Point *m*) as the ideal or most desired result, then Point B is considerably superior to Point A, and there is actually little difference between Point A and Point C. This perspective can also be visualized with the use of the parabolic curve passing through the nominal value (Point *m*). If we consider the vertical distance from the *x*-axis as a measure of customer dissatisfaction or quality cost, then the farther the value is from the target value, the greater the customer dissatisfaction and quality loss. Consequently, the farther the point or measurement is from the target, the less desirable is that unit. This type of understanding can be achieved only with measurable data. This limitation is another important reason for avoiding the use of attribute quality characteristics if at all possible.

Just as classified attribute characteristics are relatively inefficient measures as compared to continuous variables, dynamic characteristics are extremely powerful tools for obtaining process knowledge. By viewing the process as a system, the experimenter can obtain a better understanding of the relationship between components of the process and the end result. After defining the process and determining the output of interest, an input signal must be identified that produces changes in the output as the signal is varied. From studying the impact of the input signal on the system and its relationship with the output, the experimenter obtains more than just an understanding concerning the process and its effect on the output, which is basically the scope of knowledge obtained from continuous measurable characteristics. In addition, an understanding of the relationship between the input signal and the output gives the experimenter the ability to achieve the desired output through adjusting the signal factor while considering the effects of the system. This approach is certainly more powerful as far as process tuning capability and desired output maintenance is concerned.

However, there are certain requirements that must be met to use a dynamic characteristic effectively. It is essential that enough initial understanding of the process exists to define the system, the output, and an input signal properly.

This means, first, that the output should be defined in terms of energy or a measure produced by energy. Second, the input signal must have a linear relationship with the output. If the relationship is not linear, you will not be able accurately to adjust the signal factor and will therefore have difficulty in obtaining the desired value of the output.

A serious weakness of attempting to use dynamic characteristics is that often the experimenters do not have a good understanding of the process or have difficulty in defining it as a system. Another problem relates to the selection of input signal. Not only is it sometimes difficult to identify a signal that can be easily adjusted for producing changes in the output, but also it can be tough to know beforehand if the relationship is in fact linear or not. Therefore, if you have good insight into the process, can characterize the output as energy, and can identify an easily adjustable factor that has a linear relationship with the output of interest, the dynamic characteristic is the most effective type of characteristic to use. However, we do not always possess this knowledge. In those cases, a continuously measurable characteristic would be more appropriate.

Notes

1. Horner, Stan, *Statistical Process Control,* pp. V2–1 to V2–2.
2. Ishikawa, Kaoru, *Guide to Quality Control,* p. 18.
3. Juran, Joseph M., *Quality Control Handbook,* pp. 2–16 to 2–17.
4. Horner, pp. V2–3 to V2–4.
5. Ishikawa, p. 22.
6. Ibid., p. 19.
7. Juran, Joseph M., *Juran on Quality Improvement,* pp. 12–12 to 12–13.
8. Juran, *Quality Control Handbook,* pp. 8–21 to 8–23.
9. Melder, Melissa, *et al., Taguchi Training Manual,* pp. 4–6 to 4–7.
10. *Introduction to Quality Engineering,* pp. 2–3.
11. Ibid., p. 2–3.
12. Ibid., p. 2–3.
13. Ibid., p. 2–3.
14. Ibid., p. 2–3.
15. Ibid., p. 2–3.

Chapter 4

MEASUREMENT CONSIDERATIONS

An integral part of experiment planning is determining how the results will be measured. Failure to cover measurement considerations adequately can create havoc during the conducting of the experiment. Such issues as what to measure, where to measure, when to measure, how to measure, and who to measure are all essential questions that need to be responded to during the planning phase of the experiment. Failure to address these issues properly can lead to confusion and even frustration by the persons performing the experiment and obtaining the test data.

Gaps within measurement planning can also result in experiment delays and lost time if appropriate measuring and test equipment are unavailable or awaiting arrival. Lost opportunities in acquiring new process understanding and technological breakthroughs may result when so much effort has to be exerted to resolve measurement problems. Team members are so busy trying to get data that they overlook what is happening with the process. Improper equipment can lead to erroneous conclusions as well. Excessive measurement variability can lead to incorrect deductions and result in the inability to detect significant factors. An inexperienced or uninformed test operator or inspector can contribute just as much to measurement error as unreliable test equipment or gauges. If attribute data is being obtained, judgmental bias can greatly affect the data unless proper instructions with explicit explanations are provided.

The purpose of this chapter is to provide the experimenter with some guidelines to avoid the pitfalls that come from lack of measurement planning. This chapter will cover instrument selection and tie it to the experiment objective(s) and related quality characteristic(s). Specifically addressing the measurement device during the planning phase can help to reveal bad or inappropriate quality characteristics. If the problem does exist, exposing it up front allows the team to redefine the quality characteristic before going any further and perhaps having to delay the conducting of the experiment. The chapter will also touch on accuracy and repeatability. Excessive variability within the measurement device can reduce the sensitivity of the experiment and result in failure to recognize significant factors. We will also discuss essential issues related to the test operator or inspector. The testing environment can create measurement problems of its own, and alternative techniques for minimizing its effect will be explained. Guidelines for handling judgments associated with classified attribute data will also be presented. Finally, we will discuss sampling requirements and provide some hints on how to determine appropriate sample sizes.

4.1 MEASUREMENT PLANNING

Measurement considerations need to be covered within the framework of the team planning meetings. This stipulation does not mean that everyone needs to be involved in all the groundwork. Specific research issues such as equipment availability, measurement accuracy, operator status, and sampling costs and procedures can be delegated to appropriate team members who can report their findings at a later meeting. For the specific topic of measuring equipment, you may want to invite the test engineer or test engineering manager to the meeting. He can give on-the-spot answers to the team's questions and perhaps even provide suggestions for making the measurement activities easier. The manufacturing or quality control supervisor can follow up on test operator or inspector capability.

Based on this information, the team can then decide on the appropriateness of available equipment, selection of test personnel, and sample size. If the proper equipment is not accessible, the team may also at this point redefine the quality characteristic in terms of something more easily measured. If the team has decided on a classified attribute quality characteristic, this would be the time for the team to develop specific guidelines for categorizing the results.

Measurement planning is particularly important either when a new process is being studied or when a new quality characteristic previously unmeasured is selected. Running trial samples prior to the experiment may be desirable and can provide several benefits. First, it may indicate how good a relationship there is between what is being measured and the objective that you are trying to achieve. Through observations or measuring other characteristics, the comparisons can give you an understanding of the relationship between the chosen characteristic and actual product or process performance. Second, taking readings before conducting the experiment allows you to determine up front if the characteristic is practical to measure, the data is easy to obtain, and the measuring device possesses accuracy. Third, running trial samples provides you with an indication of the measurement sensitivity to extraneous factors. You may need, for instance, to control the environment during the measurement activity by performing the tests in a laboratory. Fourth, taking sample test measurements with process settings held constant and comparing the readings can provide an indication of the repeatability of the process and the measuring system. If this variability is too great, it will mask the effect of any factor being studied. If the variability is a measurement system issue, you will want to look for a more dependable testing method or redefine the quality characteristic in terms of something that can be reliably measured. If the cause of the variability is inherent within the process, additional process variables need to be controlled during the production of the units and therefore should be considered for incorporation into the experiment.

4.2 INSTRUMENT AVAILABILITY

Does the appropriate test equipment exist and is it available? This question typically enters the mind first when it comes to measurement selection. Along with these concerns, you should also ask what it is that the test equipment or measuring device actually measures. What are the units of measure? Do they in fact relate to the experiment objectives, and are they a true indicator of the quality characteristic of interest? If the response to any of these questions is no, you may need to look elsewhere for the right piece of equipment. If the equipment is just not available, you may want to consider two alternate courses of action. One would be to develop and construct your own testing or measurement device. If the characteristic requires a sophisticated testing device, this course may not be economically practical, or time requirements might be too long; in either case, it would be more prudent to re-analyze the quality characteristic and redefine a new measurement still in keeping with the experiment objective. A second alternative is to pull out the Pareto analysis and quality cost data again to justify and obtain approval for getting the appropriate equipment built; this course is advisable when measurements require special calipers or a custom fabricated fixture.

Pulling measurement considerations up into the planning stage as early as possible certainly helps to avoid scheduling delays caused by any fabrication needs. This approach becomes even more critical when it is discovered that the equipment needs to be ordered. Therefore, the question of how to measure the quality characteristic of interest should be addressed during the early planning stages. As a matter of fact, this question should be part of the discussion and a major consideration in the selection of the quality characteristic. Considering measurements up front will prevent having to repeat some of the planning steps such as tying factors to a new characteristic. As an additional thought, insure that what you are measuring is tied to the experiment objectives and product or process performance. Don't just select something to measure because it is easily accessible. Get something worthwhile out of your efforts.

4.3 INSTRUMENT RESOLUTION

Once you have located or obtained the test equipment, you need to evaluate the ability to indicate small increments of variation of the measured dimension from a reference value. What is the smallest fraction indicated on the calipers? How many decimal places are available in the measuring device readout? For gauges with indicators, this measure is often referred to as *sensitivity*. For digital devices, it is commonly called *resolution*.[1] To determine if the equipment is adequate for the task, the level of resolution of the equipment must be compared to that required for the experiment.

You may need some background information to judge whether the resolution is adequate or not. Product or customer specifications can prove to be an effective yardstick. Historical data can give you an idea of what the needs should be. Information pulled from technical journals on the latest developments can provide indices on how small the increments of the measurement readings ought to be for acquiring new knowledge and facilitating technological development. It does little good to have an instrument measuring a critical dimension in .01 inches when industry standards and customer guidelines are set in .0001 inches. The test equipment must have sensitivity that corresponds to specification requirements and needs.

4.4 INSTRUMENT ACCURACY/REPEATABILITY

The number of decimal places on the readout has little meaning if the reading is incorrect. Therefore, instrument accuracy and repeatability are extremely important issues. By accuracy, we mean the closeness of the measured value to the accepted reference value.[2] This amount can be mathematically expressed as the deviation between the measured value and the reference value, divided by the reference value. Whereas accuracy relates to an individual measurement, repeatability relates to the consistency from one measurement to the next. How close is one reading to the next of the same part at the same place? By insuring that the selected instrument has both accuracy and repeatability, experiment data can be confidently analyzed.

Calibration is a good safeguard to insure accuracy. You should check on how often calibration is performed and when the equipment was last calibrated.[3] You should also investigate whether the calibration procedures are clearly defined and if they are adequate for insuring the accuracy that you need for the experiment. If not, new procedures may need to be developed and institutionalized. The reason to make procedures permanent is that, in the event that the equipment is needed again for a similar effort, you will not have to experience the same headaches.

How is the equipment calibrated? Is it checked against a more accurate piece of equipment or just a similar unit that has had a history of being consistent? You may want to consider checking the equipment by measuring standard units that have been verified in accordance with the National Bureau of Standards. Who calibrates the equipment? How do they perform their check and what techniques do they employ? Often it has been discovered that equipment that was thought to be maintained at the tightest accuracy possible was merely receiving a token calibration sticker after an inaccurate check that meant little. If in-house calibration appears suspect, you may want an outside calibration service to check out the equipment. For a long-term solution that will prevent similar occurrences, you may want to promote training of designated personnel who will be responsible for all calibration or propose a maintenance contract with a specialist in this area. The reason for including these long-term solutions is not only to assist with the current experiment but also to make succeeding studies easier as well.

Along with accuracy comes the need for repeatability. The measuring device must be accurate over time, not just today. In terms of the experiment, the instrument must be capable of accurately measuring each and every unit, not just the first piece or some of the units. Several approaches can be taken to ascertain repeatability. One technique is to take readings of the same units at the same location and calculate the variability associated with measurement error. Taking repeated readings at various locations on more than two or three units will help prevent recollection of the previous readings and minimize measurement bias.

A second technique is to construct measurement error control charts. Plotting control charts based on repeating measurements on the same unit at the same location can provide an understanding of the reproducibility of the measurement process. Reproducibility can be defined as measurement consistency, which can be broken down into accuracy, which relates to average results, and precision, which translates to variability.[4] By the use of the x chart, x-bar chart, or moving average chart in association with the range chart, s chart, or moving range chart, whichever is appropriate, we can obtain an understanding of the accuracy and repeatability of the measuring device. Control charts for the characteristic you are interested in measuring can help tell you how sporadic or consistent the device is over time and the degree of inaccuracy when measurements vary.

For example, an experimentation team was studying a surface mount technology process. The quality characteristic was solder paste height. Their concern was that the measurement probe might give inconsistent results depending on the strength and sensitivity of the operator's hand in turning the wheel that pressed the end of the probe into the solder paste. Measurements were made at the same location on each of 30 circuit board assemblies. This first set of measurements was labeled "measurement A." A second set of data was also collected by remeasuring these 30 units in the same order as before and using the same operator and probe. These were labeled "measurement B." The two sets of measurements were then logged together, and the average and range for each pair of measurements were calculated. An x-bar and R chart was then constructed and analyzed (Table 4-1).[5]

The procedures for analyzing measurement control charts are the same as for regular control charts. However, the interpretation is different. The R chart in this application represents the magnitude of measurement error.[6] In examining the R chart in Figure 4-1, we find several points out of control, signifying that measurements are not consistent. The x-bar chart provides the ability to

Table 4-1 Surface Mount Technology Repeatability Study

Solder Paste Height (mils)

circuit assembly	#1	#2	#3	#4	#5	#6	#7	#8	#9	#10
measurement A	7.4	7.8	6.6	6.4	9.5	8.2	9.3	5.9	7.4	8.4
measurement B	6.6	9.5	7.3	13.6	8.0	10.0	10.5	8.6	8.4	9.1
$\bar{x}$	7.0	8.65	6.95	10.0	8.75	9.1	9.9	7.25	7.9	8.75
R	0.8	1.7	0.7	7.2	1.5	1.8	1.2	2.7	1.0	0.7

circuit assembly	#11	#12	#13	#14	#15	#16	#17	#18	#19	#20
measurement A	8.3	8.1	7.6	8.8	7.7	8.9	9.1	7.4	10.3	8.2
measurement B	8.4	8.5	7.8	5.0	7.1	5.7	9.2	6.6	8.5	7.4
$\bar{x}$	8.35	8.3	7.7	6.9	7.4	7.3	9.15	7.0	9.4	7.8
R	0.1	0.4	0.2	3.8	0.6	3.2	0.1	0.8	1.8	0.8

circuit assembly	#21	#22	#23	#24	#25	#26	#27	#28	#29	#30
measurement A	7.5	7.6	6.4	8.3	8.4	10.7	13.5	14.1	7.4	13.3
measurement B	9.2	7.6	9.6	7.2	8.2	8.4	6.6	6.5	9.1	6.3
$\bar{x}$	8.35	7.6	8.0	7.75	8.3	9.55	10.05	10.3	8.25	9.8
R	1.7	0.0	3.2	1.1	0.2	2.3	6.9	7.6	1.7	7.0

Figure 4-1 Surface Mount Technology Solder Paste Height Measurement Error Control Chart

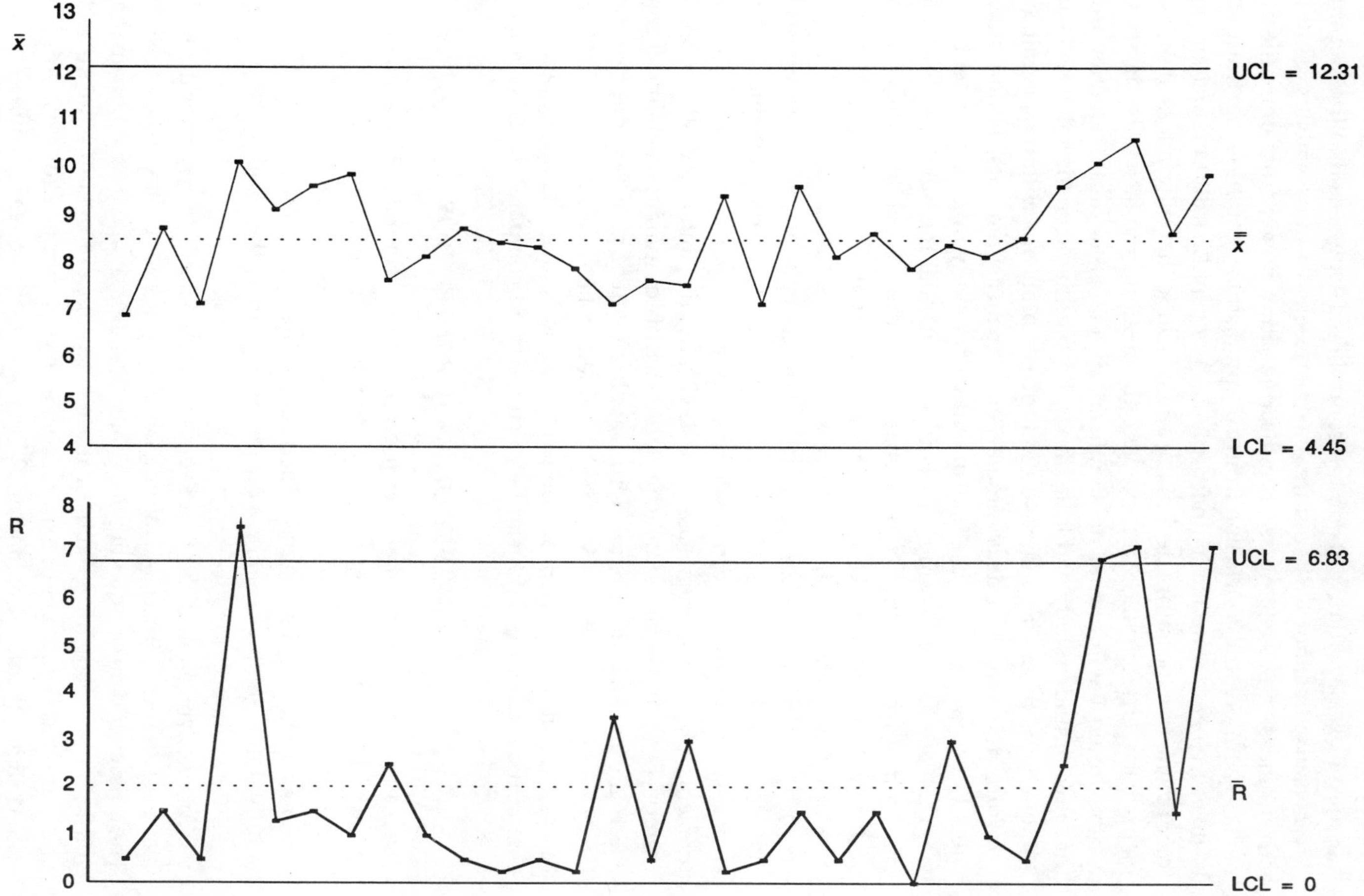

differentiate between one measured unit and the next. That no points on the x-bar chart in Table 4–1 are outside the control limits suggests that the measuring device as used cannot tell the difference between circuit assemblies. Thus, the current measuring system has little discriminating power from one unit to the next.[7] Therefore, the conclusion from examining these graphs is that the method of measurement examined is unacceptable. We could hardly conduct an experiment using this measuring technique and conclude that differences in measurements between experimental runs were the result of the factors being studied. Neither could we infer that no significant difference in measurements proved that a factor under study had little impact on the characteristic being measured. Although this particular demonstration reveals problems with the magnitude of error and the ability to discriminate between measurements, either situation should discourage use of the instrument under study in an experiment.

Another source for gaining insight into potential measurement error problems comes from existing control charts. If a prior capability study has been performed, this information can provide valuable insight into the instrument's measuring performance. If the process is not in statistical control, the reason could be related to measurement error. For example, if the comments section of the control chart reports that out-of-control points are related to measurement error instead of actual defective situations, you have an indication of equipment problems. Similar comments associated with trends, shifts, and other unnatural patterns can provide you with insight into lack of equipment reliability. If control charts are unavailable, a short-term capability study in which the test device measures standard units of consistent value can be performed. The average of the test readings can then be compared to the actual average value, and the standard deviation for both can be calculated and compared to each other.

4.5 TEST OPERATOR/INSPECTOR

Once you have insured that the appropriate test equipment is available, the required resolution is obtainable, calibration is current, and accuracy and repeatability have been verified, problems with measurement can still arise. The equipment will only be as good or accurate as the operator using it unless testing is fully automated. Therefore, you need to address the proficiency of the test operator or inspector as well.

For one, you should *always* utilize the same operator or inspector throughout the measurement process. Training on the equipment should be considered. The most experienced and knowledgeable operator should be used. Even though you have obtained the services of the most proficient operators or inspectors, find out what their level of expertise is. Are they certified for this work? If so, who certified them? How long ago? Do they need a refresher course? You may find out that no one is truly qualified. In that case, insure that adequate training is provided so that they can properly support the experiment.

Concerning the measurements that will be taken during the experiment, are specific procedures clearly defined? All of the training and experience in the world will be wasted if the specific procedures for taking the measurements in the experiment have not been explained to the operator. Besides reviewing the steps with the operator until he or she feels confident with the procedures, instructions should be placed in writing. This precaution prevents misunderstanding and provides a reference for potential questions. It can also serve as a guide and insure consistency if, for one reason or another, the initial test person has to be replaced midway through data collection.

What about potential bias? This refers to readings being consistently different from the actual value. For example, let's say that a weight scale over time continually indicates weights 4 pounds greater than the actual amount for each person who steps onto the scale. We can calculate measurement bias as the difference between the average of the observed measurements and the true value of the characteristic being measured. Sometimes personal prejudices can result in the data's coming closer to reflecting the feelings of the measurer than to representing the actual situation: "I know what the answer is!" The measurements become part of a self-fulfilling prophecy. With probes or calipers that require an amount of pressure to use, the measurement may depend upon the strength of the user's grip.

Each of these concerns needs to be addressed. Too much effort has gone into determining what to study and insuring the availability of proper measurement devices to permit lack of homework in assuring proficient test/inspection personnel to spoil the experiment.

4.6 MEASUREMENT ENVIRONMENT

The environment in which measurements are made can contribute to deviations in the readings from actual values just as much as uncalibrated test equipment and untrained personnel. In Chapter 5 we will discuss external forces, called outer noises, and their impact in causing deviations of the quality characteristic from desired values. The influence of outer noises can apply to measurement devices as well. Instead of causing end product performance to miss a desired target, the noises in this application can cause each measurement to read differently from the actual value. The noise factors may cause readings to be consistently high or low or sporadically different from actual values.

Understanding which factors constitute the measurement noises will go a long way in minimizing their effect and reducing measurement error. Typical examples of measurement noise include temperature and relative humidity. If probes or related measuring devices are heat sensitive, the surrounding temperature can cause readings to be consistently high or low. Conducted and radiated electrical noise can also impact test equipment. An arc welding system operating in the area can cause erroneous readings. Increases or decreases in line voltage caused by the starting or shutdown of large equipment can also result in sporadic changes of varying magnitude in voltage and current readings. So if the characteristic is defined in terms of an electrically related variable such as current or voltage, a sudden start-up of a large motor may create erroneous results in the test readings. If various motors of different size are operating in the same area, the potential for misleading data will increase with the higher frequency of start-ups and shutdowns, and the magnitude of each deviation can vary based on which motor or combination of motors is contributing to the deviation at the time.

Several strategies can be used to compensate for these noises. In the examples of the welding operation and the motors, knowledge of when welding is planned or when motors will typically be put on-line or off-line can facilitate scheduling around them. If ambient temperature is a concern and room temperature will remain at a high temperature for a sufficient period of time, take all your measurements at the same time and record the temperature on the data sheet. Since the noise in this type of situation is close to the same level for each reading, the influence is relatively the same for each reading, and deviations from the actual values will be approximately the same for each piece of data. With the same base line, shifted from the real average, measurements can be compared to one another, and conclusions can be determined especially with regard to control factor induced variation.

The ideal situation for dealing with measurement noise is to have measurements taken in a controlled environment. This may be particularly applicable in the petrochemical and food industries where pilot plants and laboratories are utilized to perform special studies and analysis. However, in many situations such controlled environments are not available. In those situations, timing can be an effective tool for avoiding the full impact of these measurement noises. Experienced operators can help deal with these factors and have often developed techniques for minimizing their effect during production. It is still a good idea to record the readings of these factors, if available, for later scrutiny of the data analysis.

4.7 CLASSIFIED ATTRIBUTE MEASUREMENTS (SUBJECTIVE READINGS)

Although operator bias, along with equipment and environmental effects can play a major role in affecting measurement error in measurable quality characteristics, the inspector has an even greater influence when it comes to classified attribute data. The inspector determines whether the unit is good or bad and the degree of badness. Let's say that the quality characteristic relates to the color of cheese. Cheese color is divided into five color classifications: (1) white, (2) slightly yellow, (3) light yellow, (4) yellow, and (5) dark yellow. The inspector's frame of reference regarding what is yellow will influence how every measurement will be defined.

Careful selection of the inspector can help reduce the possibility of misclassification of the experiment results. Ascertaining who is the most experienced and knowledgeable and acquiring that person's participation in performing the inspection can help assure the most reliable data set. If employing the same test operator to prevent measurement bias is essential, using just one inspector to classify the attribute results is absolutely critical. Let's look at an example with sheet metal involving surface scratches as the criteria and the classifications of good, moderately bad, and severe. Inspector number one has a frame of reference that minute indentions are bad and anything greater is severe. Inspector number two considers a unit bad only if his fingernail cannot move smoothly across the mark. He considers the scratch severe if the scratch is of certain width and depth. Based on these two different perspectives, there will very likely be a greater difference between their findings than between the results associated with any of the factors under study. Therefore, it is essential to use the most capable inspector and *only* that inspector.

To facilitate inspector decision making in regard both to a correct evaluation and to consistent classification from one unit to another, visual aids should be provided. They should provide a reference for determining what falls into one category and what falls into another. Photographs, drawings, illustrations, and actual examples of each type of classification can serve as guides for determining the appropriate category. My preference is to provide actual production units that depict each of the available classifications. The use of real examples will be

Figure 4-2 Cheese Color Classifications

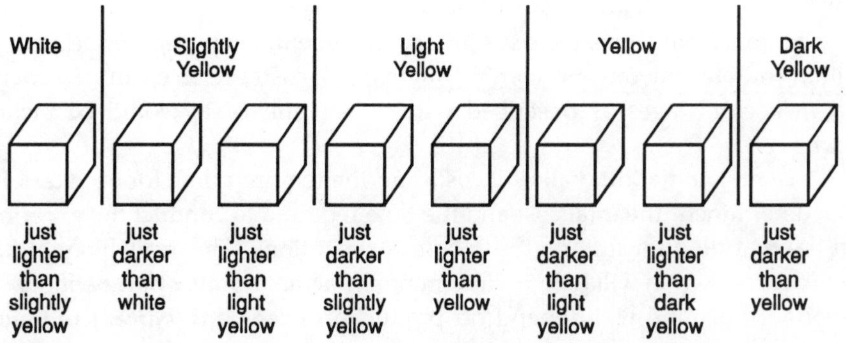

of greatest benefit if the units reflect the extremes of each classification. Using the cheese example again, samples are selected (Figure 4-2) to reflect the borderline conditions of each category. By comparing actual blocks of cheese to the samples, the inspector can deduce that each piece is better or worse than given samples and thereby can accurately assign the cheese to the appropriate classification. It can also be of help if you review the samples, photographs, illustrations, or whatever is used as an aid with the person who will be doing the evaluations. This will insure that he or she understands what is expected and can prevent any unforeseen problems with the visual aids.

4.8 SAMPLING REQUIREMENTS

The number of samples will depend on several factors including cost, time, type of characteristic, and desired confidence. Cost is a major consideration for any decision involving the use of Taguchi methodology. Before determining the number of repetitions or replications for each experimental run, some cost accounting homework should be performed up front.

Costs for conducting an experiment can be divided into two categories: first unit costs and additional unit costs. As can be seen in Table 4-2, first unit costs consist of those expenses required for running a single unit for each experimental run or combination of factor settings. First unit costs comprise any fixed costs and those variable costs associated with building just one unit. Setup costs, which include the labor of the technicians and operating support, are those expenses incurred to change factor level settings between experimental runs; they are a part of first unit costs, as are costs associated with any equipment programming changes. The time involved with each of these setup tasks should be noted as well for calculating labor costs and for reconciling with scheduling constraints. The purchase of test equipment would be another first unit fixed cost. The material required to produce a finished unit would be part of the first unit variable costs. The labor associated with production and testing, such as operator and inspector labor rates multiplied by hours worked, are also first unit variable costs; additional research and assistance from the team will determine how much time is required for these specific tasks.

Additional unit costs consist of those incremental expenses associated with building and testing one more unit. Unit material costs are an example. Operator and inspector wages as described within first unit costs would be included as well.

Once first and additional unit costs and the required time for each task have been determined, the total cost and the time required to conduct the experiment can be computed for different numbers of repetitions. The availability of funds for experimentation will help to determine the actual number of repetitions. The importance of time will depend on production needs and current production

Table 4-2 Experiment Cost Estimation

(A) First Unit Costs			First unit costs
Materials:	raw		
	equipment		
	other		
		Time (hrs) × Rate	
Labor:	engineer		
	technician		
	operator		
	inspector		
	other		
		Total first unit costs =	______

(B) Additional Unit Costs		Incremental cost	Units	Additional unit costs
Materials:	raw			
	other			
		Time (hrs) × Rate		
Labor:	engineer			
	technician			
	operator			
	inspector			
	other			
		Total additional unit costs =		______
		Total experimentation costs =		______

status. For example, time considerations would not be as major an issue for a one-shift operation as they would be for a three-shift operation working seven days a week. In the first situation, experiment costs would likely be the deciding factor. Time to conduct the experiment would be the most important consideration in the second case.

A third factor is the type of quality characteristic. As discussed in Chapter 3, process understanding requires more data with classified attribute data than with continuously measurable data. By calculating the ratio of additional unit cost to first unit cost and by considering the type of quality characteristic, Table

Table 4-3 Suggested Sample Size per Experimental Run

	High >30%	Medium	Low <3%
Measurable	1–2	2–5	6–20
Classified attribute	1–5	5–20	20–100
Go/No go	5–20	20–200	200–2000

From *System of Experimental Design,* by permission of American Supplier Institute, a non-profit organization dedicated to improving the competitive position of U.S. industry.

4-3 can provide a useful guide for determining the number of repetitions. Also in using the table, the suggested number of samples reflect the total number of units to be produced at each combination of control factors. As you study designing experiments with noise factors, you will discover that each combination of control factors will be run at least once for each combination of noise factors. Therefore, if the table recommends 6 to 20 samples per experimental run and you have 4 combinations of noise factors, you would plan for 5 samples for each experimental run to be conducted for each set of noise levels (5 samples × 4 sets of noise factor levels = 20 repetitions).

The more data you are able to obtain, the greater confidence you can have in discovering the key factors, determining the best settings for the factors, and calculating the predicted results under the best settings. For measurable data, the result will be an estimate of the value of the quality characteristic. For classified attribute data, it will be a prediction of the percent of units that will fall within the category you are most concerned with. For sample size determination, Table 4-3 should give sufficient guidelines in determining a reasonable number of samples. For those wishing to calculate specific prediction intervals, there are numerous sources explaining those calculations that are outside the scope of this text.

Other sampling considerations include how samples will be taken and recorded. The labeling of units or batches, depending on the type of process, will be explained in detail in Chapter 12. Randomization of test samples may also become an issue and will be covered in Chapter 11.

NOTES

1. Farago, Francis T, *Handbook of Dimensional Measurement,* p. 4.
2. American Society for Quality Control, Statistics Division, Glossary and Tables for Statistical Quality Control, p. 1.

3. Melder, Melissa, *et al.*, *Taguchi Training Manual*, p. 4–15.
4. Grant, Eugene L., and Richard S. Leavenworth, *Statistical Quality Control*, p. 335.
5. Handbook Committee, Statistical Quality Control Handbook, pp. 84–86.
6. Ibid., p. 87.
7. Ibid.

Chapter 5

SELECTING THE INDEPENDENT VARIABLES

After determining the team objective and defining the quality characteristic by which we will measure the ability to achieve our objective, we need to select the independent variables that may have a significant impact on this measurement. We can think of the quality characteristic as the dependent variable, and each of the influences that affect it as an independent variable. Dr. Taguchi and others adopting his methodology typically use the term *factors* instead of independent variables, and we will generally conform to this convention.

In discussing the determination of an appropriate quality characteristic, it was emphasized that this decision should not be taken lightly and that considerable thought should be put forth. For the development and selection of factors to be tested for their influence on the quality characteristic, the same attention must be exerted. Typically, the tasks of selecting process variables (factors) and assigning appropriate factor level settings are the most time consuming and mentally exhausting part of experiment planning. However, disciplining yourself to performing a thorough investigation of potential factors that can affect the selected quality characteristic will pay off in the long run. Careful selection of process and product factors will help to uncover those effects that have a significant influence on the end result that you care about. On the other hand, short cuts can lead to false conclusions and require studies to be repeated. As a matter of fact, when experiments result in unsatisfactory results, the cause is usually traced back to this area. But by obeying certain rules and following some standard procedures, the potential to omit critical factors from the experiment can be greatly reduced.

5.1 LISTING THE VARIABLES OF INTEREST

In generating the list of potentially strong factors, the use of brainstorming is extremely valuable. In association with the other tools discussed in Chapter 3 for gaining process understanding and specifically for defining the experiment objective(s), brainstorming is just as applicable for identifying factors for consideration and for determining which ones to include within the experiment. Although Chapter 3 does not provide an inclusive list, understanding the use of each of the tools mentioned can give the experimentation team a versatile arsenal from which to choose. You don't have to use all of them, just those that the team feels are appropriate.

In developing a list of factors, several approaches utilizing these tools may be considered. For example, the cause-and-effect diagram may be selected because it provides a systematic structure for creating the list of factors and is easy to use and understand. Let's say that an initial cause-and-effect diagram is developed by a subgroup of the team between the initial and follow-up sessions. The construction of the chart can be based on grouping factors within the major types of factors (dispersion analysis) or relating factors to specific locations on the process flow diagram (production process classification). The team would brainstorm to add additional ideas to the list. The potentially negative aspect of this approach is that it may induce team members to limit the scope of their thinking and prevent the generating of original ideas and the including of unique factors and thus defeat the main purpose of brainstorming.

A second and often more effective approach is to have the team develop the list of factors through brainstorming, and then have specific members of the team develop the cause-and-effect diagram (cause enumeration) from the list for the following meeting. At the next session, the subgroup presents the diagram showing the factors arranged in an organized and logical manner. The diagram is then used to promote additional ideas and to add to the factor list.

Concerning team participation, those members who have the process and related material expertise must be there for this part of the experiment planning. However, operators who are needed in production may not be able to attend all the brainstorming sessions. A way to deal with this situation is to look at each specific step of the process one at a time. When you get to a step where an operator has specific knowledge, have that person come to that segment and return to his or her duties after making inputs.

In developing a list of factors that may impact the selected quality characteristic, here are some further suggestions specifically applicable to experiment planning. Have the team objectives posted where everyone can see them. Since you are working to generate a list of factors that affect a specific result, this quality characteristic too should be posted as a constant reminder and frame of reference. To focus on the specific area of interest, display a flow diagram of the area of interest. If this is a follow-up session, you may want to exhibit a cause-and-effect diagram produced from the ideas generated from the previous brainstorming sessions.

Table 5-1 Plastic Injection Molding

Brainstorming		
Barrel heater no. 1	Barrel set time	Shift
Barrel heater no. 2	Cure time	Operator
Barrel heater no. 3	Ejector time	Day of week
Barrel heater no. 4	Injection speed	Time of day
Suck back time	Chill water	Polypropylene
Injection pressure	Hydraulic oil pressure	Raw material
Hold pressure	Hydraulic water pressure	Color concentrate
Hold time	Injection time	Contamination
Clamp tonnage	Nozzle pressure	Physical properties
Load time	Pack time	Mixing ratio
Pack pressure	Viscosity	Shot size
Pull back time	Wall thickness	Transfer position
Unload time	Shift	
Velocity	Back pressure	
Mold close time	Recovery time	

These are the basic rules for applying brainstorming to generating the list of potential factors that may have an effect on the selected quality characteristic. Additional steps will be discussed as we proceed with refining the list.

An example of a brainstorming list of variables is given in Table 5-1, where, in a plastic injection mold operation, the experimentation team has a problem with the end products not having complete fills. As a quality characteristic, the team defines weight as a viable measure of whether each piece is completely filled out. A unit that is completed and without any flash (excess material) has been determined to weigh 30 grams. The ideas are listed in the order in which they were generated.

5.2 SCREENING THE LIST OF VARIABLES

Once brainstorming has been completed, the next step is to review each suggested factor and determine which factors should be incorporated into the study and which should be left for later consideration. I did not say to delete the other factors; if it later appears that you have left out a significant variable in the original experimentation, you should have an information base to fall back on. Also if you participate in a future experiment involving the same process, this same library of information can be drawn upon for generating the new list of factors. Those factors that are not pertinent to the current quality characteristic may be important in the study of the next one.

In discussing the list of factors, it is suggested that the team member who originally thought of the idea discuss it first. Others can add to his or her comments. Within this phase, comments can be negative as well as positive. Team members should pay particular attention to redundancy, logical groupings of similar ideas, and factors that are actually a subset of another factor.

Once the discussion of all ideas has been completed, have the team vote on the different factors. Within this preliminary vote, members can vote as many times as they wish. The purpose of this preliminary screening is to delete the obviously redundant and inapplicable items. From the smaller list, continue the discussions on each of the remaining factors. Then hold another vote with the same rules as before. This list becomes your screening list. (In traditional brainstorming, the rule for the second vote is usually one choice per person. However, in this application, the team is trying to narrow down to a group of ideas or factors, not just one.) For the plastic injection molding example, Table 5-2 gives the screening list items in boldface.

Additional considerations in screening the list of potential factors relate to the handling of the possible debates between team members over what should

Table 5-2 Plastic Injection Molding

List of Variables		
Barrel heater no. 1	Barrel set time	Shift
Barrel heater no. 2	Cure time	**Operator**
Barrel heater no. 3	Ejector time	Day of week
Barrel heater no. 4	Injection speed	Time of day
Suck back time	Chill water	Polypropylene
Injection pressure	Hydraulic oil pressure	**Raw material**
Hold pressure	Hydraulic water pressure	**Color concentrate**
Hold time	Injection time	Contamination
Clamp tonnage	Nozzle pressure	Physical properties
Load time	**Pack time**	Mixing ratio
Pack pressure	Viscosity	Shot size
Pull back time	Wall thickness	Transfer position
Unload time	Shift	
Velocity	**Back pressure**	
Mold close time	**Recovery time**	

Retained Factors
Deleted Factors

and should not be included in the study. This area calls for effective control of the discussions by the team leader. Obviously, some persons are more vocal and more assertive than others. When it appears that one person is trying to dominate and force their viewpoint, the team leader should take a majority vote to neutralize the vocal member's impact in relation to more timid participants. Concerning the quieter members, try to draw them out. When the subject relates to an area where they may have an in-depth knowledge, ask them for their opinion.

In finalizing the screening list, strive to obtain agreement from all team members so that each will fully support the experiment composed of the factors on the final list. This suggestion does not mean that everyone must be totally in agreement and feel that all included factors are important and all deleted ones insignificant. It just means that all can support the team consensus and none is adamantly opposed to the final list. I would like to mention one additional concern with regard to consensus and deleting factors from the list. If one team member feels very strongly that a factor should be included while others consider it irrelevant, I would really hesitate to remove this factor from the list. It is better to include too many items than too few. After all, the main purpose of performing the experiment is to determine which factors influence the end result that you care about and which ones don't.

5.3 CLASSIFYING THE VARIABLES

Once the team has narrowed down the list of potential factors, the next step is to classify them. The remaining factors on the list should be grouped into "control" factors and "noise" factors. Reviewing the concepts from Chapter 1, we find a process is basically a system that takes certain inputs and transforms them into desirable outputs. The mechanisms for performing this conversion are control factors. However, additional influences on this system make the end results different from one another. If the impact of these influences becomes too great, the differences between one final unit and the next may be too great for the product to be acceptable.

The reason for the differences among each of the final units can be explained in this way. As discussed earlier, we typically think of the finished product in terms of functional and descriptive characteristics. When I speak of functional characteristics, I am referring to product performance and characteristics that affect performance, such as tire wear, percent shrinkage, output voltage, and moisture content. Descriptive characteristics include dimensions, weight, and other visual features. So when we or our customers evaluate the product, it is compared to some ideal or desired value based on a scale associated with the characteristic of interest. Goodness is measured in terms of consistency with and closeness to this target. But why is each unit not at or near the desired value, and why are the units inconsistent from one to another?

The answer is that certain effects, which we can refer to as noises, cause deviations within the functional and descriptive characteristics. The greater the effect of the noise, the greater the inconsistency from one unit to another and the greater the difference between actual and desired results. Examples of noise are given in Table 5-3.

Table 5-3 Typical Noise Examples

General	
Weather	Shift
Ambient temperature	Operator
Humidity	Operating environment
Vibration	User
Raw material	
Material constraints	Material properties
Moisture content	Percent regrind
Supplier	Lot number
Date code	
Mechanical	
Machine type	Machine number
Machine age	Tool wear
Tool die	Tool fixture design
Cleanliness	
Electronics	
Motor interference	Component density
Electrical isolation	Component type
Oxidation	Circuit board thickness
Circuit board fabrication	
Water temperature	Wait time between tanks
Plastics	
Moisture content	Percent regrind
Metal stamping	
Material hardness	Material thickness
Oil level	

We can classify these noises into three types, pictured in Figure 5-1:

1. outer noise
2. inner noise
3. between product noise[1]

Outer noise refers to variation created by external forces. Within the manufacturing process, we can think of room temperature, relative humidity, and dust as typical examples of outer noise that can affect the end product. Beyond the production of the unit, we can also relate the application of outer noise to the environment in which the product will be used. The tires of a car, for example, may be exposed to a variety of weather and road conditions that affects their performance, ranging from the blistering heat on a highway along the Mojave Desert in the peak of summer to a frozen and icy roadway in the north central United States in the dead of winter. The tires must provide a smooth ride and responsive stopping whether being used on a concrete paved interstate or a gravel or dirt side road. All of these elements constitute outer noise factors.

Whereas outer noises are sources of deviation from outside the system that produces the product, inner noise relates to those causes of variation that are a consequence of those elements constituting the product itself. More specifically, inner noise consists of those causes of functional and descriptive deviation that are a result of the nature of the ingredients making up the finished product. The tendency of the material that makes up the product to decompose is an example of inner noise. Within electronic equipment, deterioration of subassemblies, individual electronic components, or mechanical parts is a source of inner noise.

Figure 5-1 Effect of Noise Factors

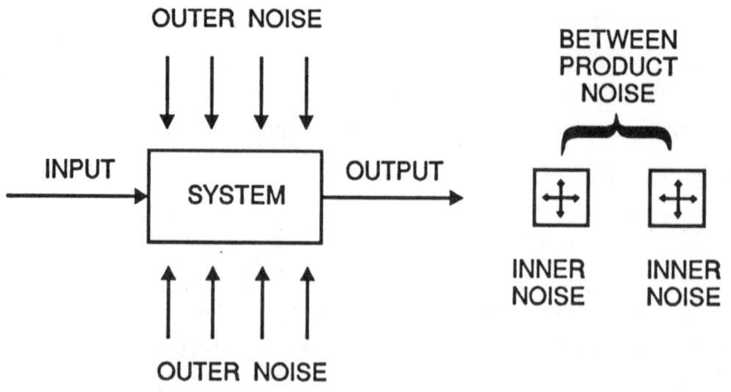

Between product noise refers to the differences between one completed unit and another. These differences tend to come about as a result of manufacturing imperfections and are often referred to as piece-to-piece variation. For example, serial number 000001 does not exactly operate or look like serial number 999999. Lot number, date produced, and location within a batch are all examples of between product noise. If you were examining a coil of wire or a reel of tape, the consistency between the front and the end of the coil or reel would also be considered between product noise.

Realizing that noise factors exist and acknowledging the types of noise factors that can occur help us to understand better how to deal with their influence on the quality characteristics that concern us. Within the framework of parameter design, we want to minimize the effect of these noise factors. Getting rid of them may be neither possible nor practical, but we wish to desensitize the process or the end product to them. This is what Dr. Taguchi refers to as *robustness.* The process or resulting product exhibits robustness towards these outer noises, inner noises, and between product noises so that they have little effect on the quality characteristics of interest.[2]

Let's look at some examples. In an electronic assembly operation, the soldering operation produces consistently good solder joints despite changes in relative humidity. The soldering system is robust to relative humidity. The tires described earlier in this chapter display a long life and provide a smooth ride and the required amount of traction despite their use in diverse weather conditions and on a wide variety of road conditions. The ability of the tires to provide consistent (minimal deviation) performance (the functional characteristic) at expected levels (target value) is an example of product robustness.

Now that we have established that the objective of parameter design is robustness against the effects of noise factors, how do we achieve it? The answer is in the selection of the settings of those factors that we can control, called *control factors.* By determining the control factor levels by which the quality characteristics of interest stay consistent despite changes in the noise factors, we have effectively minimized the impact of noise and made the process robust against the noise factors.

With the understanding of the relationship between control factors and noise factors, let's discuss in more detail how we actually determine into which category to assign a variable under consideration. A control factor is:

a factor whose value can be set and maintained

and

a factor whose value we want to set and maintain.[3]

Therefore, any factors within the process or going into the process that we can and want to control are classified as control factors.

We have discussed in detail the different classes of noise factors and given examples as well. Let's go one step further and look at a definition which should help with classifying factors under study. A noise factor is:

a factor whose value *cannot* be set and maintained

or

a factor whose value we *do not* wish to be set and/or maintained.[4]

In some instances, it is either impractical or impossible to control the factor. For example, one stamping machine is better than the others. However, production requirements and delivery commitments are too high to allow all products to be built on that machine. Therefore, machine selection is impossible to control and is a noise factor. In other cases, it may be possible to control a specific factor, but the cost is too high or the inconvenience is too great. For example, relative humidity within the production area can be regulated if $1.5 million is spent to encase the operation in a plastic bubble-like controlled environment. In this case, relative humidity is a noise factor due to the preference not to control it.

Table 5-4 Plastic Injection Molding

Classifying the Variables into Control and Noise Factors

Barrel heater no. 1	**Operator**
Barrel heater no. 2	Raw material
Barrel heater no. 3	Color concentrate
Barrel heater no. 4	Pack time
Injection pressure	Back pressure
Load time	Recovery time
Pack pressure	
Pull back time	
Unload time	
Mold close time	

Control Factor
Noise Factor

Based on this understanding, let's continue with the plastic injection molding example. In the last step, we deleted some factors because they either lacked potential importance or were not relevant to the specific quality characteristic being measured. Redundant factors were eliminated as well, and similar factors were combined. With the resulting list, we now want to classify the remaining factors as those that we can and want to control (control factors) or those that either cannot or will not be controlled (noise factors), as in Table 5-4, where noise factors are in boldface.

5.4 SPECIFYING PARAMETER SETTINGS

After separating factors of interest into control factors and noise factors, the next step is to decide on the number of levels of each factor and to specify the settings or values for each level. The exercise of establishing settings can in itself be a learning experience. In defining appropriate levels for a particular control factor, you may learn that these values cannot in fact be controlled. Therefore, the factor needs to be redefined as a noise factor. You may learn that the value or setting for another factor is held constant. In this case, the factor could be eliminated from further consideration in this particular study. Therefore, the process of screening the factors, classifying them as either control or noise fac-

Figure 5-2 Screening, Classifying, and Specifying Settings

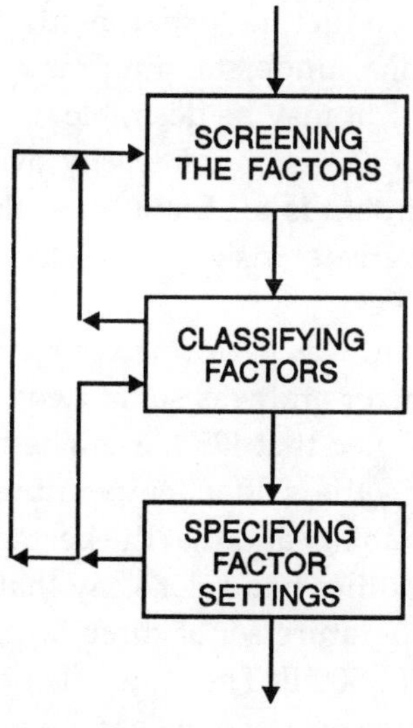

tors, and assigning values is actually an iterative process, as shown in Figure 5-2.

5.4.1 Control Factors

Before setting values for the control factors, you must first determine the desired number of levels. The way that we handle this issue will change depending on whether the factor is a continuously measurable factor or a discrete factor. The appropriate number of levels for a discrete factor will usually be clear from the experiment objectives and the understanding of the factor itself. If you wish to determine the best vendor for a particular raw material, the number of levels would be equal to the number of available suppliers. In studying tooling dies, the number of levels could be determined based on the number of available dies.

Choosing the appropriate number of levels for a continuously measurable factor is a much harder task and requires additional considerations. The experiment objective provides some direction. If the purpose of the experiment is exploratory, two levels set at the extreme boundaries of the feasible operating range may be sufficient in determining if in fact this factor is of any importance. Two levels are usually adequate for screening designs in which your immediate concern is not to determine optimal factor values, but to ascertain which factors are important and need to be included in more in-depth studies. If your basic concern is what needs to be monitored and controlled, two levels are also usually sufficient.

Although three levels will likely cost more in terms of experiment size, raw material required, time to conduct the experiment, and time to inspect and/or perform testing, the additional understanding may far outweigh the cost. If a new process is being studied, it may be desirable to run three levels for each of the continuous variables to evaluate nonlinearity over the experimental range. If the purpose of the experiment is for fine tuning the process, more than two levels will provide you with greater insight into selecting better levels for achieving your experiment objectives.

For example an experiment was performed to reduce solder defects in which solder temperature was a factor and was set at two levels, a low of 495°F and a high of 505°F. The study revealed that 495°F was a better temperature. Therefore, we know that by decreasing the solder temperature below 505°F and toward 495°F we can improve solderability and that the best temperature setting is closer to 495°F than 505°F. On the other hand, let's say that the same experiment was conducted with solder temperature set at three levels, the same low and high values plus a middle value of 500°F. The study also revealed that 495°F was the better temperature. In this case we not only learned which was the better setting, we also discovered that the ideal value was not only closer to 495°F than 505°F, it was also less than 500°F. For continuous fine tuning, this is a significant increase in process understanding.

In some cases, more than three levels may be desired, particularly when a discrete type factor is composed of four or more unrelated alternatives, and we wish to determine which alternative is the best. The specific handling of these special cases will be addressed in Chapter 21.

Besides obtaining agreement on the number of levels for each factor, we must also address the range of values. Assuming a linear relationship, the wider the range between the lowest value and the highest value, the more likely that you will be successful in discovering the real effect of that variable on the quality characteristic. However, expanding the range of the factor settings may make the assumption of linearity less reasonable.[5] This difficulty is an additional reason for using three levels where economically feasible. Three levels helps to pick up indications of nonlinearity. The width of the range also depends on whether the purpose of the experiment is exploration over a broad region or fine tuning to achieve optimum conditions. If the purpose is to gain new insight, it is particularly important to be bold in setting factor levels, with discrete factors as well as with continuous variables. I have seen trade secrets result from experiments because different and unique types of tooling were incorporated within the study and proved to be superior to traditional methods.

Setting should also be wide enough to represent the actual process adequately. A major reason for experiment failure is not setting factor levels wide enough. If the experiment levels are closer than normal operating conditions, the study can incorrectly indicate that the factor does not have a significant impact on the quality characteristic of interest. Then when the process is optimized based on the other factors considered important, the result is different than predicted because the "insignificant" factor is at a value that does affect the result of interest.

For example, conveyor speed typically operates as low as 4 ft/min and as high as 8 ft/min. For the purpose of the experiment, conveyor speed is set at a low of 5 ft/min and at a high of 7 ft/min. Analysis indicates that conveyor speed is not significant within this range, and so we remove it from consideration for control. The process is then operated without controlling conveyor speed. As the value approaches 8 ft/min, which we said was within the operating window, the process suddenly begins building bad product despite our prediction to the contrary because we did not consider performance beyond 7 ft/min.

Another major consideration in determining factor settings is that factor levels should be within physical constraints. If one of two factor settings is set so low that bad product will likely result, and the other factor setting is set so high that bad product will also likely result, then little knowledge has been gained. Aside from destroying good raw material and using up valuable production time, little has been learned about optimal factor settings except the identification of extreme values that should be avoided.

Besides staying away from factor levels outside physical boundaries, you should also be on guard against the possibility of specific experimental runs incorporating a combination of factor settings that result in an infeasible operating condition. This is especially true in chemical related processes. In the event that you experience an infeasible combination of settings later while conducting an experiment, appropriate techniques for handling them are explained in Chapter 23.

5.4.2 Noise Factors

The purposes of setting noise factor levels are to simulate current variability in the noise factors and consequently to ensure robustness to this current variability. Effectively, you want to widen the range of noise factor variability at which the quality characteristic has minimal change. Therefore, you should select those levels that are at the extremes of the typical ranges. In most cases involving continuous variables, a lower and upper boundary setting will be sufficient for ensuring robustness. For discrete noise factors, the number of levels may be larger. For example, if the shifts in a 24-hour operation are the noise factor, you may wish to use three levels (first, second, and third shift). If you were trying to insure consistent packaging of different salad dressings in individual packets, each of the types of dressing could be defined as a level.

Let's look at some additional points concerning the selection of noise factors which may be more apparent during the specification of noise factor settings. Since the goal of setting noise factors is to simulate worst case conditions that could realistically occur, not all potential noise factors need to be incorporated on an individual basis. It is more important to include the potentially strongest noise factors. Normally, if a process or product is made robust to the most important noise factors, it will be robust to the lesser ones as well. Studying the noise levels may also help make the weaker factors more apparent and facilitate elimination of them from consideration. Defining a general noise factor that encompasses several weaker noise factors within its scope is also an effective way of ensuring robustness while minimizing the size of the experiment and thereby holding down the cost of experimentation.

Another method of insuring economies of scale without losing any valuable information concerning robustness is *compounding noise factors*.[6] Since the idea behind parameter design is to make the process robust to any of the typical noise factor values, this method inherently suggests robustness to any combination of typical noise factor values as well. If we perform the experiment with the best combination and the worst combination of noise level settings and are able to make the process robust to these two extremes, then the process will be robust to any combination of noise factor settings in between. This result is the logic behind compounding noise factors.

Let's look at an example of compounding noise levels and how it can reduce the size of an experiment. In studying a wavesolder process, we have three noise factors:

1. bake time
2. set out time
3. relative humidity

Three noise factors require four experiments for each combination of control factors being run. Therefore, if 16 combinations of control factors are required, the total number of experiments will be 16 × 4 = 64. If we look at the individual noise factor settings, we have:

(1)	bake time	0 hr	4 hr
(2)	set out time	0–1 hr	6–8 hr
(3)	relative humidity	low	high

We can also identify which level for each factor is the best and the worst case.

		worst	best
(1)	bake time	0 hr	4 hr
(2)	set out time	6–8 hr	0–1 hr
(3)	relative humidity	high	low

We can now redefine these three noise factors as one—moisture conditions—with two levels of worst combined noise conditions and best combined noise conditions. Only two experiments are required for each combination of control factors, and the total number of experiments in the above example is now 16 × 2 = 32. Therefore, the size of the experiment has been cut in half without compromising the loss of any process understanding.

As mentioned at the beginning of this section, one of the purposes of setting noise factor levels is to simulate current variability. However, by definition a noise factor is a variable that you cannot or do not want to control. So what do you do for experimenting purposes? In the case of noise factors that you can control but prefer not to, simply maintain selected levels during the conducting of the experiment or schedule experiment runs to coincide with specific levels.

For example, raw material is a noise factor comprising two levels. Schedule the use of material A and run the first half of the experiment. Then schedule material B and run the second half. In another example, shifts are the noise factor. Schedule the first shift to run the initial third of the experiment. When the second shift reports for work, begin the next third. When the third shift reports, have them complete the remainder of the runs. Another option, which would reduce the number of switches from production to special tests and back, is to have the third shift perform their part at the end of their shift, the first shift conduct their third at the first of their shift, and the second shift run their units at the most convenient time. The point of elaborating on these alternatives is that you may have to schedule experimental runs to coincide with desired noise level settings, and some thought should go into the process for attaining experiment efficiency.

So far we have discussed discrete noise factors and how either to set them or to plan the experiment so as to achieve desired levels. As with control factors, continuous noise factors are more difficult to handle. Some can be controlled, and specific levels can be maintained for short periods of time, particularly if

Table 5-5 Plastic Injection Molding Specifying Parameter Settings

Control Factor	Level 1	Level 2
Barrel heater no. 1	350°F	360°F
Barrel heater no. 2	365°F	375°F
Barrel heater no. 3	380°F	390°F
Barrel heater no. 4	390°F	400°F
Injection pressure	20,000 psi	25,000 psi
Pack pressure	480 psi	520 psi
Pull back time	2 sec.	2.5 sec.
Mold close time	4 sec.	5 sec.
Raw material	Vendor A	Vendor B
Color concentrate	Supplier X	Supplier Y
Pack time	10 sec.	15 sec.
Back pressure	50 psi	60 psi
Recovery time	15 sec.	20 sec.
Noise Factor	**Level 1**	**Level 2**
Load/unload times	10/15 sec.	20/5 sec.
Operator	Gavin Stuart	Grant Brown

laboratory conditions can be imposed. Other noise factors cannot be handled so easily. The best solution in these cases is to schedule experimental runs so that desired noise factor settings are approached and to take measurements of the noise factor during the experiment and label appropriately. For example, relative humidity is a noise factor with levels of low humidity and high humidity. Based on projected weather conditions, half the experiment is conducted during rainy days and the other half during a dry period. Readings are taking during the experiment and reviewed for understanding the humidity range for which we can achieve robustness.

In Table 5-5 we look again at the plastic injection molding example. Since the initial study was to determine if the control factors under study were in fact important enough to monitor and maintain control charts, two levels per control factor were considered adequate. Level settings were selected based on the extreme observed low and high values. Two levels for each noise factor were also selected. Let's say that this was an insert molding operation with manual loading and unloading. In this type of operation, consistency in load and unload times is the greatest concern. Since the extreme combinations of these two noise factors produce a low time for one and a longer time for the other, we can compound load and unload times into one factor with the two extreme combinations as the two levels. This reduces the effective number of noise factors from three to two.

5.5 POTENTIAL INTERACTION CONCERNS

An interaction occurs when two or more factors acting together have a different effect on the quality characteristic than the effect of each factor acting individually. Let's look at some examples. A patient takes a pink pill to lower her blood pressure. A yellow pill relieves insomnia. However if the patient takes both pills, the patient fails to wake up at all. The end result from taking both pills is clearly different from the result anticipated if either one of the pills is taken by itself. This is an interaction. In a petroleum study, 2 ml of additive A is added to a gallon of gasoline, increasing the mileage from 24 miles per gallon to 28 miles per gallon. Using the same gasoline, adding 2 ml of additive B will increase the mileage from 24 miles per gallon to 30 miles per gallon. However, if 1 ml of additive A and 1 ml of additive B are added to a container of gasoline and the mileage rises to 37.5 miles per gallon, an interaction is clearly present.

The concept of interaction is an important consideration in effectively planning an experiment. Failure to recognize the presence of an interaction can lead to misinterpretation of the data and failure to include important considerations in optimizing the process. Not all interactions are bad. Besides gaining insight into possible sources of problems, you also want to take advantage of an interaction that is working in your favor, as in the gasoline example.

The strength of interactions can be studied most effectively through the use of graphs, as illustrated in Figures 5-3, 5-4, and 5-5. Let's say that we are examining the interaction between factor x and factor y. When the quality characteristic increases or decreases at the same rate as the value of x changes for different levels of y, an interaction graph (Figure 5-3) will show parallel lines, meaning that the interaction does not exist. When the quality characteristic increases or decreases at slightly different rates as x varies at different levels of y, the graph (Figure 5-4) will show lines that are not parallel and, although not converging, appear to intersect at some point outside the area graphed: a weak to mild interaction. When the quality characteristic changes at dramatically different rates for different levels of factor y, the lines on the graph will intersect. In the classic situation, the quality characteristic increases as x increases for one level of y, and the quality characteristic decreases as x increases for the other level of y. These are examples of a strong interaction and need to be included for consideration in optimizing the process.

To be able to understand the impact of an interaction, you must specifically design the interaction into the experiment. Otherwise, its effect will be intermixed or confounded with the effects of the other factors. Therefore, consideration of interactions is an essential part of planning an experiment.

Concerning the treatment of interactions within an experiment, there are several trains of thought. Dr. Taguchi stresses the importance of focusing on main effects (the individual effects of each factor by itself) and selecting quality characteristics with good additivity so that the effects of interactions between control factors are minimized (though not eliminated) and therefore need not be considered in the study.

An effective way to insure good additivity is to select an energy-related quality characteristic. A good example is heat. In an electronics application, topside circuit board temperature has much greater additivity and minimizes the effect of potential interactions more than, say, solder defects. The same can be said in a food industry process. The temperature inside the vat of ingredients

Figure 5-3 No Interaction

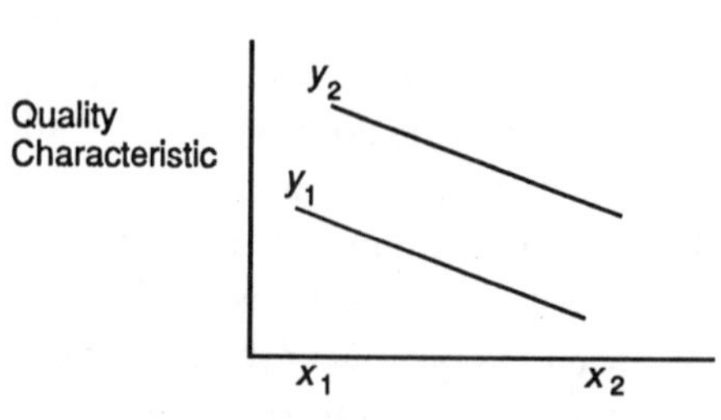

Figure 5-4 Weak or Mild Interaction

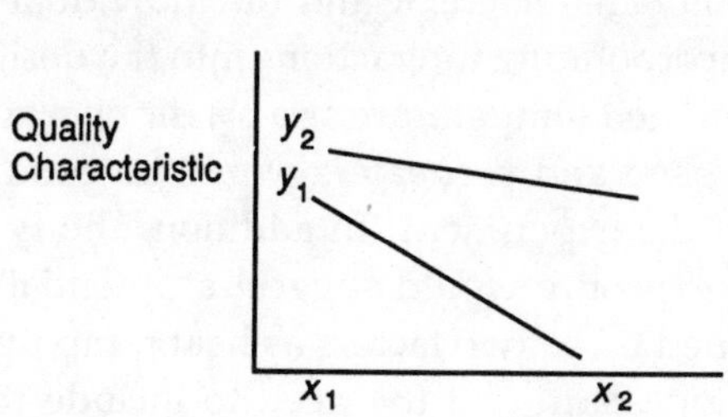

will be a far more efficient energy-related characteristic than the number of cookies that are burnt or uncooked. Just as minimizing the effects of interactions between control factors is desirable, the detection of interactions between control factors and noise factors is valuable knowledge for achieving robustness. However, these types of interactions do not have to be specially designed into the experiment.

The opposing viewpoint to Dr. Taguchi's method of treating interactions is to incorporate any and all interactions of possible interest. Proponents say that valuable insight into the process may be lost by ignoring the effects of interactions. My perspective is somewhere between the two opposing views, but closer to Dr. Taguchi's. To include interactions blindly in an experiment is very costly and an inefficient use of time. A retired statistician who held a doctorate in statistics related to me that he had seen a total of only five significant three-way interactions in his lifetime of performing experiments. Everything else consisted of two-way interactions. So to incorporate multiple-term interactions is just too expensive in light of the unlikely possibility of catching that rare exception. In the event that such a case exists, performing a confirmation run on the process at the predicted optimal settings will reveal whether any of your assumptions are incorrect.

Figure 5-5 Strong Interaction

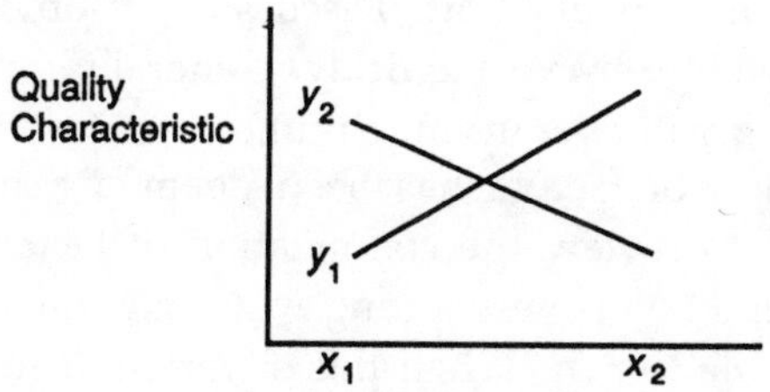

Concerning two-way interactions, Dr. Taguchi's recommendations for carefully defining the quality characteristic and the individual factors can eliminate a lot of the need for incorporating interactions into the design of the experiment. For example, we mentioned temperature as a classic energy-related quality characteristic. Conveyor speed and preheaters would be good candidates for being included as factors in the experiment. In addition, the typical relationship between heat and heat exposure would suggest a potentially strong interaction. However if we redefined these two factors as heat ramp up rate, the two factors would be defined as one term and the need to include this interaction would no longer exist. Redefining the factors results in fewer terms and therefore a more efficient and less expensive study although we have not actually deleted any potential effects from consideration.

Thus, in considering interactions within an experiment, the approach of selecting an energy-related quality characteristic and carefully defining factors of interest can help eliminate the need to include interactions. However, there may be times in which you do not have the expertise or ability to define the quality characteristic or factors so that interaction effects are insignificant. In those cases, include the suspect interactions within the design of the experiment. It is far better to include an interaction that is not important than to have to redo the experiment because the confirmation run was unsuccessful as a result of failing to include an important interaction. Therefore, avoid the use of interactions whenever possible, but do not be afraid to add them to the experiment if they seem appropriate.

In considering which potential interactions to include in the experiment, those team members who know the process best should be able to suggest which factors are most likely to interact with each other. Depending on the nature of the industry, process engineers, chemists, etc. are likely to have the best understanding for making recommendations. In assuring that no potentially important interactions are omitted from investigation, I tend to take one combination of two factors at a time and have the team discuss the likelihood of a strong interaction. If the opinion is positive, it is added to the list of factors to be included. If not, the combination is deleted from consideration. Then, discussion turns to the next combination. This process may sound tedious, but the planning phase really is the most important part of an experiment and should involve the greatest amount of effort. Discussion of obviously weak or nonexistent interactions will go by very quickly. Generally, only the combinations really worth discussing will take up much time.

Once a combination of factors has been deemed a potentially important interaction, you need to review the combination of factor settings within the interaction. If the interaction is very strong, you may uncover a combination of settings that is infeasible to run. When this situation arises, a technique called

Figure 5-6 Sliding Levels

Heater Temperature	Standard Level Settings Conveyor Speed 5 ft/min	 7 ft/min	Heater Temperature	Sliding Value Settings Conveyor Speed 5 ft/min	 7 ft/min
1200 F	data	insufficient heat	low	1200 F	1300 F
1600 F	burned parts	data	high	1500 F	1600 F

sliding levels may be appropriate. Sliding levels refers to setting the levels of one factor based on the levels of another factor. For example, Figure 5-6 shows a combination of conveyer and heater settings. Our resident metallurgist tells us that the combination of low speed and high temperature will create too much heat and damage the product. He also informs us that the combination of high

Table 5-6 Plastic Injection Molding

Identifying Potential Interactions

Control Factor	Level 1	Level 2
Barrel heater no. 1	350°F	360°F
Barrel heater no. 2	365°F	375°F
Barrel heater no. 3	380°F	390°F
Barrel heater no. 4	390°F	400°F
→Injection pressure	20,000 psi	40,000 psi
Pack pressure	480 psi	520 psi
→Pull back time	10 sec.	100 sec.
Mold close time	4 sec.	5 sec.
Raw material	Vendor A	Vendor B
Color concentrate	Supplier X	Supplier Y
Pack time	30 sec.	180 sec.
Back pressure	300 psi	500 psi
Recovery time	30 sec.	180 sec.
Noise Factor	**Level 1**	**Level 2**
Load/unload times	5/100 sec.	30/5 sec.
Operator	Gavin Stuart	Grant Brown

speed and low temperature will lead to insufficient heat and result in faulty product. However if we establish specific low and high heating-element settings that will "slide" up as conveyor speed is raised, each combination of factor settings will give us experimental runs with meaningful data. An additional benefit of sliding levels is that the shifting of the settings of the second factor as the level of the factor paired with it changes reduces the effect of the interaction between them. Thus, the interaction no longer needs to be designed into the experiment. Selection of optimal settings will depend on the best conveyor speed and the best corresponding heater settings.

In examining each pair of control factors for the example of plastic injection molding, the process experts on the team recommended the study of the interaction between injection pressure and pull back time. Further investigation of the combination of factor levels for the two control factors (Table 5-6) did not suggest any infeasible combinations of experimental runs. Therefore, sliding level techniques were not used.

5.6 WHITE POWDER CASE STUDY

A team was put together to study the causes contributing to a white powder residue occurring on circuit boards during the wavesoldering process.

Objective: eliminate white powder residue.

Quality characteristic: percent residue on board surface.

1. **Listing the variables of interest:** After reviewing flowcharts of the board fabrication and soldering processes and constructing cause-and-effect diagrams, the team used brainstorming techniques to generate the list of factors for consideration (Table 5-7).

2. **Screening the list of variables:** Through discussion and the use of the voting techniques described in brainstorming, the team narrowed the list of factors that would be used in the study (Table 5-8).

3. **Classifying the variables:** The team next categorized the remaining factors into control factors and noise factors (Table 5-9).

4. **Specifying parameter settings:** Since the team was trying to induce conditions to cause the appearance of residue, values were selected which were on the edge of the feasible operating ranges. Since the team would be dealing with low

Table 5-7 White Powder

List of Variables	
Laminate:	**Pre-bake:**
material	time
Tin Strip:	
conveyor speed	percent solution
temperature	
Pre-clean:	
anti-tarnish %	scrub pressure
brush condition	
Solder Mask:	
cure type	cure time
cure temperature	screen type
hardener	filler
dwell time	
Hot Air Leveling:	
acid concentration	acid exposure
microetch (volume)	microetch (time)
microetch (temperature)	flux type
flux specific gravity	flux pH
flux temperature	preheater temperature
solder temperature	solder contamination
hot air leveling temp.	post clean dwell time
post clean temperature	post clean flow rate
brush condition	scrub pressure
water flow rate	conveyor speed
Silk Screen:	
ink	cure type
cure time	cure temperature
Circuit Board Bake Process:	
time	stacking method
Wavesolder:	
flux density	conveyor speed
preheater temperature	solder temperature
Water Wash:	
water temperature	conveyor speed
direct nozzle flow	recirculating nozzle flow
IR heater temperature	

Table 5-8 White Powder

Screened List of Variables	
Laminate:	**Pre-bake:**
material	time
Tin Strip:	
conveyor speed	percent solution
temperature	
Pre-clean:	
anti-tarnish %*	scrub pressure*
brush condition*	
Solder Mask:	
cure type	cure time
cure temperature	screen type
hardener	filler*
dwell time	
Hot Air Leveling:	
acid concentration	acid exposure
microetch (volume)	microetch (time)
microetch (temperature)	flux type
flux specific gravity	flux pH
flux temperature	preheater temperature
solder temperature*	solder contamination
hot air leveling temp.	post clean dwell time
post clean temperature	post clean flow rate
brush condition*	scrub pressure*
water flow rate*	conveyor speed*
Silk Screen:	
ink*	cure type
cure time	cure temperature
Circuit Board Bake Process:	
time	stacking method*
Wavesolder:	
flux density*	conveyor speed
preheater temperature	solder temperature*
Water Wash:	
water temperature	conveyor speed
direct nozzle flow*	recirculating nozzle flow*
IR heater temperature*	

*deleted factors

Table 5-9 White Powder

Control and **Noise** Factors

Laminate:	Pre-bake:
material	time
Tin Strip:	
conveyor speed	percent solution
temperature	
Solder Mask:	
cure type	cure time
cure temperature	screen type
hardener	dwell time
Hot Air Leveling:	
acid concentration	acid exposure
microetch (volume)	microetch (time)
microetch (temperature)	flux type
flux specific gravity	flux pH
flux temperature	preheater temperature
solder contamination	hot air leveling temperature
post clean dwell time	post clean temperature
post clean flow rate	
Silk Screen:	
cure type	cure time
cure temperature	
Circuit Board Bake Process:	
time	
Wavesolder:	
conveyor speed	**preheater temperature**
Water Wash:	
water temperature	**conveyor speed**

Control Factor
Noise Factor

Table 5-10 White Powder

	Parameter Settings	
Control Factors	Level 1	Level 2
Laminate		
material	NVF	Polyclad
Pre-bake		
time	0 hr	4 hr
Tin Strip		
conveyor speed	2 ft/min	12 ft/min
percent solution	10%	100%
temperature	ambient	80°F
Solder Mask		
cure type	oven	IR
cure time (oven)	45 min	60 min
cure temp. (oven)	265°F	300°F
screen type	157 mesh	111 mesh
hardener	low spec.	high spec.
dwell time	4 hr	16 hr
Hot Air Leveling		
acid conc.	10%	15%
acid exposure	15 sec	30 sec
microetch (volume)	minimum	1%
microetch (time)	30 sec	60 sec
microetch (temp.)	70°F	90°F
flux type	Gyrex	Ardox
flux specific gravity	low	high
flux pH	low	high
flux temp.	low	high
preheater temp.	low	high
solder contamination	fresh solder	max contamination
hot air level temp.	low	high
post clean dwell time	8 sec	9 min
post clean temp.	low	high
post clean flow rate	low	high

Table 5-10 White Powder

Parameter Settings		
Control Factors	**Level 1**	**Level 2**
Silk screen		
cure type	oven	IR
cure time (oven)	10 min	20 min
cure temp. (oven)	175°F	300°F
Noise Factors	**Level 1**	**Level 2**
bake time wavesolder conveyor speed preheater temp. water temp. water wash conveyor speed	(worst combination of noise conditions)	(best combination of noise conditions)

and high extremes, two levels would be sufficient for each control factor under consideration. This approach was also carried over to treatment of the five noise factors. These factors were incorporated into one noise factor with one level defined as the combination of best noise conditions and the second level defined as the combination of worst conditions.

5. **Identifying potential interactions:** The team paired each control factor under consideration with the other control factors and discussed where potentially strong interactions might be present. Those considered most likely were designed into the experiment. These were:

solder mask: cure time × cure temperature

hot air leveling: acid concentration × acid exposure

post clean temp. × post clean flow rate

silk screen: cure time × cure temperature

In the event that the study of the interactions would require a larger sized experiment (this will be further explained in chapters 7 and 8), the team further agreed on additional settings for cure temperature as cure time changed. By using sliding level techniques, the team was able to minimize the effect of these potential interactions without increasing the size of the experiment.

	Solder Mask		Silk Screen	
Cure temperature	265°F	300°F	175°F	300°F
Cure time low	45 min	30 min	15 min	10 min
Cure time high	60 min	45 min	25 min	20 min

Notes

1. *Introduction to Quality Engineering,* p. 1-4 to 1-5.
2. Ibid., p. 1-4.
3. Ibid., p. 6-1.
4. Ibid., p. 6-1
5. Melder, Melissa, *et al., Taguchi Training Manual,* p. 4-14.
6. Introduction to Quality Engineering, p. 6-5.
7. Wu, Yuin, and Dr. Wilhe Hobbs Moore, *Quality Engineering: Product & Process Optimization,* pp. 116–117.

Chapter 6

EXPERIMENTAL STRATEGY

As the experiment objective establishes the goal of the team and sets the focus of the team efforts, you also need to consider the path to reach this goal. Knowing where you want to go without formulating the strategy for getting there can be just as bad as setting your sights on the wrong destination. Often an experimenter will decide on a worthwhile objective but will spend an inordinate amount of time in the planning stage due to a lack of understanding of how to go about achieving the team's objective. A lot of the discussion and confusion over which factors to include, the number of factor levels, and the most appropriate factor settings would be reduced if the team understood the best strategy to help them achieve their objectives.

The vast majority of reasons for wanting to perform an experiment can be categorized into five major classifications.

1. Single experiment: You want to obtain a better understanding of how the process works. You want to know the important factors in a process. What causes changes in the end product?

2. Continuous experiment: You are striving for continuous improvement. This effort may fall into two subcategories depending on your current knowledge of the process. If you have an understanding of the variation within the process, you may be trying to reduce this variation by a specific amount or down to a predetermined level. This situation may be the result of an unacceptable capability study, a low Cpk, or control chart limits being too wide. If you do not know how much the existing variation is, but you do know that it is unacceptable, perhaps due to excessive rework or scrap, you may be trying to begin actions to reduce this variation. Initially, you would like to drive it dramatically downward. For the future, you want to pave the road for sustaining these efforts and for making further experimentation efforts easier to foster.

3. Screening experiment: This process may have just been installed or may still be in the stages of being built. A large or complicated process in which there is little current understanding would probably also fall into this category. More than likely, the process is sophisticated or very complex with many variables of potential importance. You are interested in refining the list of process factors down to a more manageable number in order to perform further experimentation to determine optimal settings for the most significant parameters.

4. Focusing experiment: The experiment objective is specifically targeted toward solving a problem. The purpose of the study is to determine the culprit or culprits by studying simultaneous changes in the process and product variables. The advantage of using this technique over other cause-and-effect tools occurs when the problem is sporadic and frequency of occurrence suggests that the problem is more likely to occur under a yet undetermined unique combination of process factor values.

5. Sequential experiment: Sequential experiments are applicable where the process consists of many steps with numerous factors at each stage. The incorporation of all factors of interest into one experiment would result in a study too large to conduct practically. But by segmenting the process, a study of the first section can be performed first, followed by a second study involving only the final portion of the process. Specific applications include problem solving where the process is too involved to study all at once and a new process that you are trying to optimize a section at a time.

By determining which strategy best applies to your particular situation, you will be more capable of properly planning the experiment and reducing the time needed to do so. Most important, the appropriate strategy will make the road smoother and easier and insure that you are able to achieve the team objective.

6.1 SINGLE EXPERIMENTS

In the basic situation that most of us think of when we consider experimentation, there is a specific objective we wish to achieve, which can be accomplished through the completion of one experiment. The circumstances may be such that we are trying to improve the individual quality and overall consistency of the outgoing product. Another applicable situation is a problem-solving study in which one is striving to correct a chronic and persistent quality problem. In each case, the aim is to achieve the goal of the team in a single experiment.

Within the context of a single experiment strategy, you will obtain a better understanding of the process and be able to reduce variability more effectively if you choose a measurable or dynamic quality characteristic. In an optimization effort, selecting an attribute characteristic will limit the magnitude of improvement that can be gained. In a problem-solving experiment, selection of an attribute characteristic limits the sights of the team to improving quality to meet specifications. A continuously measurable characteristic will take you beyond these constraints to a process where the quality is not just acceptable but superior to customer guidelines.

For example, a wavesolder operation experiences a dramatically large number of rejects, and rework costs are extremely high. It would be very easy for the team to define the quality characteristic as solder defects. However, a successful experiment within this context would only insure that the conditions that create solder defects are controlled to the thresholds that contribute to the rejects. If the evaluation of the defects is judgmental, improvements only insure that quality is borderline acceptable. By defining what is a continuously measurable variable, such as circuit board top side temperature, the process can be optimized at factor settings that are better than the threshold values beyond which defects result. Normal variability within the process factors would then be less likely to cause unacceptable results such as solder voids or solder shorts. In the latter case, optimizing the measurable characteristic to provide quality improvement opportunities would lead to the product's exceeding criteria requirements. Defects such as excessive solder would be reduced as solder volume became more consistently closer to the target level.

Concerning the number of levels for the control factors, more levels will give you a greater choice of settings for improving the process. In the case of continuous factors, the use of three levels as opposed to two settings will allow you to detect nonlinear relationships between the factors and the quality characteristic. Even if a nonlinear effect does not exist, you have a more descriptive understanding of the relationship between a factor and the characteristic of interest. If you determine that the factor does in fact have a significant effect on the output, you will be able to select among low, middle, and high values instead of just between low and high. The center of the operating range may be superior to either the lower or upper operating boundaries.

The level settings within a single experiment strategy will be based on team knowledge and the specific objectives of the study. If this is a problem solving project, typically you would select a low at the bottom of the normal operating range, a high at the top of the normal operating range, and a middle value either at the center of the total range or at the typical operating setting. The success of the experiment will be measured by two criteria:

1. How close the predicted results from the analysis come to the target value of the quality characteristic. The predicted results are based on the weighted impact of the factors, which are determined to have a significant effect on the quality characteristic.

2. How well the confirmation run validates the prediction equation. The confirmation run consists of operating the process with the significant factors set and maintained at the levels deemed optimal in the analysis and used in the prediction equation.

6.1.1. Single Experiment Example

In an electronic assembly operation, solder defects have become chronic. A team is put together whose intention is obviously to reduce or eliminate defects. Based on his expertise, the process engineer recommends that top side board temperature is a more definitive measure for insuring solder quality. He also reports that his prior studies and research show 250°F to be the optimal temperature. The team agrees on the objective and the quality characteristic based on these recommendations.

Objective: reduce solder defects by maintaining recommended top side board temperature.

Quality characteristic: top side board temperature.

Control Factors	Level 1	Level 2	Level 3
board orientation	forward	backward	
circuit board vendor	Acme	Bravo	
conveyor speed	5 ft/min	6 ft/min	7 ft/min
flux density	.898	.899	.900
pre-heater #1 temperature	low	medium	high
pre-heater #2 temperature	low	medium	high
solder temperature	480°F	490°F	500°F
Noise Factors	**Level 1**	**Level 2**	**Level 3**
relative humidity	low	high	
set out time	0 hrs	4–6 hrs	

Note: sliding values were used to minimize the effect of the interactions between conveyor speed and pre-heater #1 and #2. By minimizing the effect of the two interactions, they did not need to be included in the experiment. A smaller experiment was thus required and meant a more cost efficient study. The specific pre-heater levels were recommended by the process engineer based on experience and prior thermal studies.

	Conveyor Speed		
Pre-heater #1	5 ft/min	6 ft/min	7 ft/min
low	1000°F	1100°F	1200°F
medium	1100°F	1200°F	1300°F
high	1200°F	1300°F	1400°F
Pre-heater #2	5 ft/min	6 ft/min	7 ft/min
low	1000°F	1200°F	1400°F
medium	1200°F	1400°F	1600°F
high	1400°F	1600°F	1800°F

6.2 CONTINUOUS EXPERIMENTS

As mentioned previously, the theme behind continuous experiments is continuous improvement. Whereas the single experiment strategy is aimed at a one-time study either to solve a problem or to determine process settings that will be acceptable over the long-term, the purpose of the continuous experiment strategy is either to establish the framework for further process tuning or to take the key factors ascertained perhaps from a screening experiment and continue to get closer to the ideal optimal factor setting. The philosophy is one of perpetual experimentation—which does not mean that a full-time experimenter or team of experts does nothing but work on improving this specific process. A more realistic situation would involve improvement on the process associated with the greatest quality cost. As the process variation is sufficiently reduced, efforts are directed toward the next highest priority and so on. When the variation of other processes is reduced so that the first area now has the greatest variation, then the team reforms to improve this process further.

To illustrate how this strategy systematically fine-tunes the process settings, let's look at Figure 6-1 and Figure 6-2. In a solder paste screening process, a squeegee presses solder paste through the holes of a stencil onto the pads of the circuit board underneath it. The team agrees that squeegee pressure is one of the variables to study in the optimization of screening solder paste. Squeegee pressure is initially set at three levels:

1. low end of the manufacturer's specification
2. middle of specification range
3. high end of the manufacturer's specification

Figure 6-1 Surface Mount Solder Paste Screening Operation

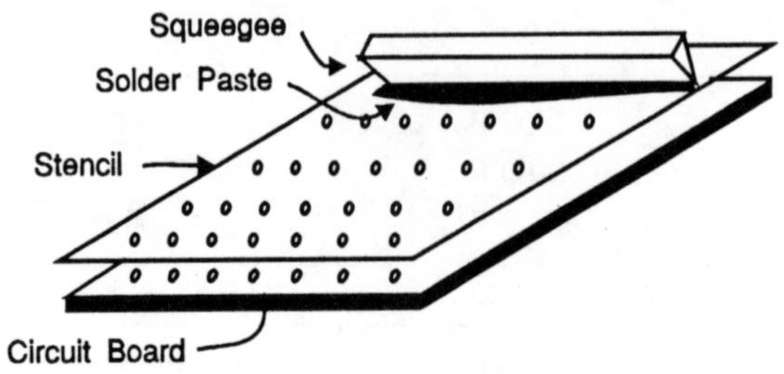

The initial study shows that squeegee pressure has a major impact on the amount and consistency of solder paste placed on circuit pads. Analysis also shows that the middle value is the best of the three settings. In a follow-up study, squeegee pressure is again set at three levels, but closer around the middle of the specification range:

1. halfway between the low end and middle of specification
2. middle of specification range
3. halfway between the high end and middle of specification

Figure 6-2 Continuous Experimentation Squeegee Pressure Example

Low 10 psi		Medium 40 psi		High 70 psi
		best setting		
	low 25 psi	medium 40 psi	high 55 psi	
	best setting			
low 20 psi	medium 25 psi	high 30 psi		

Again, squeegee pressure has a significant effect on solder paste. This time, the lower value of the three settings results in the best results. If an additional experiment is performed, appropriate squeegee pressure settings could be as follows:

1. slightly below the new level 2
2. halfway between the low end and middle of specification
3. slightly above the new level 2

This process can continue until the change in settings has no significant effect on solder paste. The low and high would then be the optimal operating window for squeegee pressure. By no longer including factors that have been narrowed down to a range in which changes have little effect on the end result, subsequent experiments will become smaller and thus quicker and less expensive to perform.

Although defining the quality characteristic in terms of a continuously measurable variable over an attribute characteristic is always recommended, this approach is even more important within the strategy of continuous experimentation. Classified attributes just do not allow you to improve beyond marginal acceptability. The number of level settings for continuously measurable factors should almost always be at least three. Besides allowing detection of potential nonlinear effects, having three levels gives direction, as shown in Figure 6-2, for continuing to refine the process. Discrete factors take on the number of levels associated with the number of choices. However, once an initial experiment has been performed and the best setting for the discrete factor has been determined, this setting should be maintained for succeeding studies. Therefore, it is not likely that discrete factors would need to be incorporated into the later studies unless a new discrete factor was inserted. With this likelihood in mind, most continuous experiments will tend to be composed of continuous factors only and to consist of three levels each.

The measure of success within continuous experimentation is dependent on continuous reduction in the process variation and on getting closer to long-term goals. If the characteristic is nominal-the-best, smaller variation around the target value is the goal. In a smaller-the-better characteristic such as percent shrinkage, a continuing decrease in average shrinkage is the desired result. In a larger-the-better characteristic such as the breaking pressure on a connector, a predicted increase in the pressure that a part can withstand is the objective. After the predicted results based on the analysis indicate improvement, the true measure of success is the ability of the confirmation run, with control factors set at the recommended settings, to produce the predicted results.

6.2.1 Continuous Experiment Example

In a surface mount screen printing operating, the work group is continuing to refine the process and enhance the consistency of screening solder paste onto the circuit board pads. The most appropriate measure of consistent solder paste is paste height which is measured with a metal probe.

Objective: improve consistency in screening solder paste onto circuit pads by reducing solder paste variability.

Quality characteristic: solder paste height.

Control Factors	Level 1	Level 2	Level 3
paste volume	150 gm	325 gm	500 gm
solder viscosity	720 k	800 k	880 k
squeegee pressure	10 psi	40 psi	70 psi
squeegee speed	50 mm/sec	200 mm/sec	350 mm/sec
Noise Factors	**Level 1**	**Level 2**	**Level 3**
paste exposure to air	0–2 hr	6–8 hr	
humidity	low	high	

6.3 SCREENING EXPERIMENTS

In either starting efforts to understand a new process or beginning to experiment on an existing operation for the first time, you may find that there are too many factors to study at once. The size of the experiment would be too large to be manageable. Therefore, you may want to perform an initial experiment or a set of preliminary studies to eliminate those factors that have little to no effect on the output of interest. Next, a more comprehensive study encompassing the more important factors can be conducted. A follow-up experiment such as that described within the context of continuous experimentation could be employed.

Therefore, the purpose of the screening design is not so much to better the process as to determine which factors are essential for making improvements. The knowledge gained from these studies can also be used to identify those factors that should be monitored through on-line quality control activities such as control charts. The determinations from these studies can help to justify the cost of purchasing measuring equipment and probes for monitoring these parameters and conducting capability studies necessary for setting up process control. Subsequently, more in-depth experiments can be utilized to pinpoint optimal values at which the control charts will monitor and can help serve to maintain parameters.

The objectives within the screening design strategy can be divided into short term and long term. The short-term objective not only is complementary to the latter, but also paves the way for its success. The long-term goal is to reduce process variability by optimizing the significant process variables. To get there, the short-term intent is to identify which factors should be optimized.

Let's look at an example of a complex operation comprising many potentially important parameters. A new SMT (surface mount technology) vapor phase soldering system is being installed, and process learning must be accelerated to facilitate a quick ramp up of production. Due to the enormous number of potential factors, a single experiment would be too large to be practical for conducting and determining optimal factor settings. Therefore a screening strategy is adopted to narrow the number of factors under investigation down to a more manageable group by eliminating those that do not have an impact. Once this step is accomplished, a study looking more critically at specific settings of the remaining factors can be performed to minimize solder variability.

The number of levels for the continuous factors do not need to be more than two at this point. All that you are trying to do is to determine if the factor has an impact on the quality characteristic within its operating range. Discrete factors would still have the same number of levels as associated with the number of alternate selections. An exception would occur if team knowledge suggests that specific alternatives describe the range of this particular factor. For example, in a cheese processing operation, five vendors supply raw cheese. The most important concern is the water content of the cheese. Contented Cow Company historically supplies cheese with the lowest percent water, whereas Bovine Dairy produces the highest water content. Therefore, instead of having five levels of raw cheese in the screening experiment, Contented Cow and Bovine were selected as the two levels for determining if raw cheese supplier (percent water–raw cheese) was a significant factor.

The level settings for the continuous factors should depict either the normal operating range or the feasible operating boundaries if the factors are sometimes operated beyond their typical values. The measure of success in this type of experimentation can be interpreted according to discrete and variable factors. With discrete factors, success is the ability to determine which setting improves the process. For continuously measurable factors, the goal is to identify those that are significant. After analysis, the predicted results are calculated based on the best discrete level settings and the better of each pair of measurable factors. If the results from the confirmation run compare favorably with this prediction, the conclusions made during the analysis are judged correct.

Just as nonlinear effects are not considered in a screening design, interactions are not investigated at this time. Interactions can be studied if deemed necessary in the follow-up experiments. Again, careful defining of the quality characteristic and the factors under study should decrease the need for studying interactions anyway.

6.3.1 Screening Experiment Example

In a new SMT vapor phase operation, the team wishes to identify the key factors and the optimal settings for those factors for producing consistently good solderability. Due to the complexity of the process, an experiment incorporating all of the factors of interest would be too large to manage at one time. Therefore, a screening design is conducted first:

1. to determine the best levels of the discrete factors;
2. to identify the continuous factors that require further study.

Objective: to achieve consistently good solderability.

Quality characteristic: top side board temperature.

Control Factors	Level 1	Level 2
solder mask registration	0 mils	6 mils
squeegee pressure	10 psi	70 psi
squeegee angle	45°	60°
squeegee hardness	70	90
squeegee speed	50 mm/sec	350 mm/sec
stencil hole geometry	78%	100%
copper weight	1 oz.	2 oz.
pwb moisture	baked	not baked
solder mask thickness	2 mils	4 mils
solder paste	Super Paste	A One
placement tooling	die 36-57	die 42-43
pwb orientation	front first	back first
pre-heater #1	180°F	260°F
pre-heater #2	200°F	300°F
pre-heater #3	220°F	340°F
conveyor speed	5 ft/min	7 ft/min
chain pre-heater	80°F	250°F

Noise Factors	Level 1	Level 2
pwb type	low density	high density
delay between screening and vapor phase	0–2 hr	6–8 hr

6.4 FOCUSING EXPERIMENTS

The name of this type of strategy stems from the fact that the team is focusing attention on a specific problem and its solution. The specific application of this strategy is related to the type of problem that occurs infrequently, but has major ramifications when it does occur. The process produces acceptable product consistently until, all of a sudden, quality degradation occurs. Either all or most of the units built within this time frame must be reworked or scrapped. Unexplained, the problem goes away, and the process once again steadily produces good output. Then after a period of time, the process once again unexpectedly produces the same type of defects and at about the same magnitude. Again, the problem disappears without explanation. Over time, this continuing cycle of good and bad continues without any explanation of the cause.

Whereas the previous experimental strategies were directed toward reducing variation so as to improve quality and prevent defects, the purpose of this type of study is to duplicate the conditions that have previously caused excessive variation and consequently resulted in unacceptable product. By determining the factors or combination of factors that contribute to catastrophic yet rarely occurring failures, you can then determine factor settings that will insure that this sporadic problem will be prevented permanently. This does not mean that we are deviating from any of the major premises of Taguchi methodology. A fundamental concept of quality engineering is the philosophy of minimizing the effect of a cause as opposed to the possible high cost of removing or fixing the cause. Within the focusing strategy, we are not necessarily trying to determine the cause of the problem so as to eliminate it. By discovering the basis for the problem and the associated factors and settings that contribute to its duplication, we can ascertain the process settings that can prevent its recurrence. This strategy again is minimizing the effect, not eliminating the cause.

For example, in the electronics industry, numerous companies have experienced a white powder residue forming on circuit boards after wavesolder operations. The cause is unknown, but just as suddenly as it occurs, the problem quickly disappears, preventing investigative effort from determining the culprit. Perhaps six months later, the problem recurs and then quickly vanishes.

Although the problem appears for only a short interval, the loss in terms of scrap and/or rework can be substantial. This is a classic example of a situation in which the focusing experiment strategy would be appropriate.

The objective of a focusing experiment is straightforward. You have a problem, and you want to stop it from ever occurring again. You must therefore duplicate the conditions that have caused it in the past. By learning which set of conditions can cause the problem, you have solved the mystery that is essential for determining how to prevent the problem from recurring in the future. This goal requires that you define the quality characteristic in terms that relate to the problem itself. The most obvious selection would be to define experiment results in terms of rejects or defects and count the number of bad parts or incidences of the unacceptable conditions. As discussed in the previous section on the selection of type of quality characteristic, attribute data such as good/bad are inefficient measurers of quality and fail to indicate the magnitude of badness. By defining the quality characteristic in terms of a continuous measure, you would not only possess the ability to record the frequency of the problem occurring within the experiment, but also have a measure of the magnitude of each occurrence. In the event that you are unable to obtain an accurate measure of the problem, a compromise between a continuous measure and merely defining the results as good or bad would be to set up categories or degrees of badness. You would then classify the units produced in the experiment according to the appropriate group. To obtain the most meaning from the data, you should define as many classifications as can be practically differentiated. Looking at the white powder example, let's say you cannot obtain an accurate measure of the amount of residue. Although you are unable to calculate the exact percent of the circuit board surface covered by the residue, you can classify the magnitude of contamination as:

1. no contamination
2. less than 25% of surface covered
3. between 25% and 50% of surface covered
4. between 50% and 75% of surface covered
5. greater than 75% of surface covered

This classification enables you to have a much clearer picture of the relationship between the factor settings that contribute to the occurrence of the problem being studied and the problem itself.

In determining the appropriate number of factor levels, the primary consideration is the effort to duplicate an uncommon event. Since this consideration suggests that the factor or factors that contributed to the problem were beyond the usual settings, the logical selections of experiment settings are the extreme values just inside the feasible operating boundaries. Therefore, two levels should normally suffice for continuous factors. Discrete factors should be selected based on the settings deemed by the team most likely to result in reproducing the problem. The number of levels will depend on how many of these alternative settings are chosen by the team.

The success of the experiment is dependent on the ability of the study to reproduce the problem. By determining which factor settings contribute to the occurrences, we consequently know those settings that minimize the likelihood of those occurrences. The confirmation test of the experiment is the production of units with the pertinent factors set at those settings least likely to result in the defects of interest. If no defects occur in the confirmation run, we can assume that our hypothesis is correct.

6.4.1 Focusing Experiment Example

In a wavesoldering process, a white powder residue appears during the water wash stage. This is the final step after soldering. Its purpose is to remove any contaminants from the circuit board and components which resulted either as flux was applied to the assembly prior to soldering or from contaminants contained within the solder. To complicate prevention measures, the condition occurs infrequently, but is chronic when it does appear. The residue suddenly appears, and then mysteriously vanishes just as quickly. After a lengthy period of inactivity, the problem recurs. Over time, the cycle continues.

Objective: to determine the factors and corresponding levels for producing white powder residue.

Quality characteristic: percent of board covered by white powder residue.

Control Factors	Level 1	Level 2
material	NVF	POLYCLAD
pre-bake time	0 hr	4 hr
conveyor speed	2 ft/min	12 ft/min
percent solution	10%	100%
temperature	ambient	80°F
cure time	45 min	60 min
cure temperature	265°F	300°F
screen type	157 mesh	111 mesh

Control Factors	Level 1	Level 2
hardener	low spec.	high spec.
dwell time	4 hr	16 hr
acid concentration	10%	15%
acid exposure	15 sec	30 sec
microetch (volume)	minimum	1%
microetch (time)	30 sec	60 sec
microetch (temperature)	70°F	90°F
flux type	GYREX	ARDOX
flux specific gravity	low spec.	high spec.
flux pH	low spec.	high spec.
flux temperature	low spec.	high spec.
pre-heater temperature	low spec.	high spec.
solder contamination	fresh solder	maximum
hot air level temperature	low spec.	high spec.
post clean dwell time	8 sec	9 min
post clean temperature	low spec.	high spec.
post clean flow rate	low spec.	high spec.
silk screen cure type	oven	IR
silk screen cure time (oven)	10 min	20 min
silk screen cure temperature (oven)	175°F	300°F
Noise Factors	**Level 1**	**Level 2**
bake time	worst	best
wavesolder conveyor speed	combina-	combina-
wavesolder pre-heater temp.	tion	tion
water wash conveyor speed		

6.5 SEQUENTIAL EXPERIMENTS

Like screening designs, sequential experiments facilitate the study of processes too extensive to incorporate all of the variables of interest in one in-depth experiment. The difference between the two strategies is the approach for making the factors more manageable to study. Screening experiments typically contain all factors of interest and are used to determine which variables are significant enough to merit further investigation. More in-depth studies are then performed and optimization is determined based on the best settings of these significant variables. Within sequential experimentation, the process is divided into logical groupings, and smaller in-depth experiments are performed within each segment. Each process stage is optimized individually. The sequence of experimentation begins at the head of the process and proceeds to the end.

This strategy is applicable to new complex processes where there is little existing knowledge as well as to problem solving involving existing multi-step operations. Let's take the start-up of a new electronics assembly operation utilizing surface mount technology (see Figure 6-3). The basic process steps are:

1. solder paste is applied to the circuit board
2. electronic components are placed on the circuit board
3. solder paste is converted to solder

The first stage of the sequence is to optimize step 1, then step 2, and finally step 3. Since the quality of the solderability results from step 3 may be dependent on solder paste volume, assemblies from step 1 can be categorized according to solder paste volume (small, medium, and large) and considered as one of the factors within the third sequence of the experimentation.

Concerning the application to problem solving, I am reminded of another example related to a surface mount electronic assembly process. Cracked components were resulting from the process, and fingers were being pointed by the suppliers, process engineers, and equipment manufacturers at one another. The process was split into the soldering and routing operations (Figure 6-4). The soldering experiment was conducted first, and "good" units from this phase were used to perform the routing study. The analysis produced identification of the source of the problem and the factor settings for practically eliminating cracked capacitors.

Just as a single experiment can serve to help reduce variation or minimize the number of undesirable results, the objectives of sequential experimentation can be defined in the same manner. The one difference is that each phase may have its own distinctive quality characteristic. The number of factor levels and the

Figure 6-3 New SMT Electronic Assembly Operation

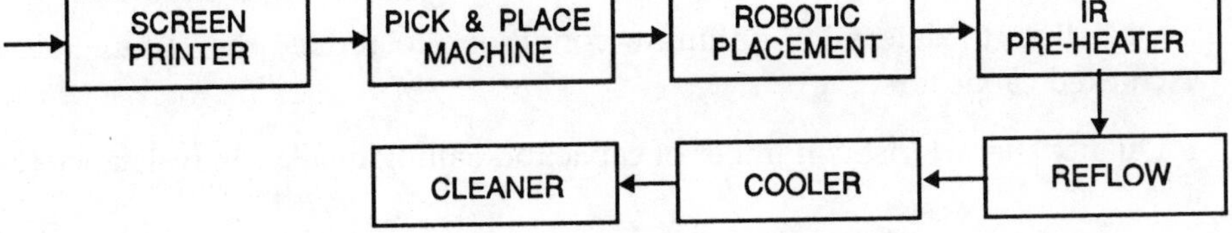

Figure 6-4 Cracked Capacitor Operation

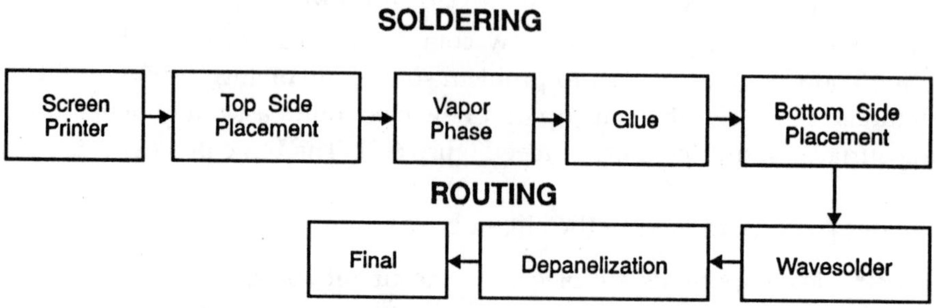

values of the settings will depend on the experiment objectives. If the objective is optimization, three levels should be appropriate for the continuous factors. If the goal is problem solving and identification of where the problem is occurring, the selecting of two levels near the ends of the feasible operating range would probably best serve the interests of the study.

The measure of success within sequential experimentation is the ability of the confirmation run to validate the predicted results determined from the analysis. If the objective is more related to variation reduction than problem solving, there should be a confirmation run for each sequential study and a final validation study incorporating the entire process. If the emphasis is on problem solving, a confirmation run encompassing each of the process segments would be the most effective test for determining if the problem has been resolved.

6.5.1 Sequential Experiment Example

From a surface mount electronic assembly operation, a large percentage of the completed units failed to function due to cracked ceramic capacitors. Testing of parts prior to placement on the circuit boards indicated that the components were not flawed prior to assembly. Experimentation was divided into two phases:

1. screen printing through soldering
2. depanelization.[1]

Objective: to determine optimum conditions to reduce the failure rate of cracked capacitors.

Quality characteristic: number of capacitors failing insulation resistance test.

Phase I—Screen Printing through Reflow

Control Factors	Level 1	Level 2	Level 3
stencil paste thickness	4 mils	7 mils	
cooling rate	1	2	3
heating rate	1	2	3
reflow	VP1	VP2	VP3
pwb thickness	.031 in.	.062 in.	.062 in.
pwb material	FR4	CER	FR4
glue assembly	yes	no	no
component supplier	AVX	Kemet	Vitramon

Phase II—Depanelization

Control Factors	Level 1	Level 2
method	router	hand
pwb thickness	.031 in.	.062 in.

Notes

1. Broadwater, John, "Cracked Ceramic Surface Mount Capacitors."

Chapter 7

ORTHOGONAL ARRAYS

After the experimentation team has concluded the planning phase of the experiment, the next activity is setting up the experiment or actually designing the experiment. With clear identification of variables and interactions to incorporate within the experiment, classification of these variables as either control factors or noise factors, and determination of the number of levels for each variable under consideration, the planning phase, if properly performed, should provide all of the essential ingredients for a meaningful experiment. The purpose of the second phase of experimentation is to take these inputs and not only to develop an experimental design that provides data that can result in meaningful conclusions, but also to create the most efficient design for the variables and levels being studied.

Within the scope of designing the experiment, we will discuss orthogonal arrays, degrees of freedom, linear graphs, and the overall experimental matrix structure. Although there are numerous types of experimental designs and a variety of methods for generating them, we will focus our attention first on this one specific type of matrix. Second, we will define degrees of freedom (Chapter 8) and how this measure is used to determine the appropriate orthogonal array. Third, we will explain how to develop linear graphs (Chapter 9), which are a tool for assigning factors and interactions to the orthogonal array. Last, we will show how to put each of the fundamental components of an experimental design together to form a complete experimental matrix (Chapter 10).

7.1 ORTHOGONALITY

The foundation for designing an experiment using Taguchi methodology is the orthogonal array. Although more classical types of designs, such as the full factorial and any of the wide variety of fractional factorials, could be employed, the orthogonal array has traditionally been associated with Taguchi experimentation techniques. We will continue this custom not just because it personifies the nature of experimentation as embraced by Dr. Taguchi and has been the primary tool for experimentation using his techniques, but also the orthogonal array is so efficient in obtaining only a relatively small amount of data and being able to translate it into meaningful and verifiable conclusions. Furthermore, the designs of experiments utilizing orthogonal arrays are basically simple to understand and the guidelines are easy to follow, as we hope to prove within the context of this book.

Concerning the history of the orthogonal array, the origin of the development of the orthogonal array is attributed to Sir R. A. Fisher of England. His early efforts in applying orthogonal arrays were to control error in an experiment.[1] Dr. Taguchi has since adapted the orthogonal array to measure not only the effect of a factor under study on the average result, but also to determine the variation from the average result. In addition, he developed the linear graph for mapping experimentation factors, often called main effects, and their corresponding interactions to the appropriate columns of the array. The result is that the influence of main effects or factors under consideration and any interactions specifically incorporated into the experiment can be separated. Each can be studied and analyzed without the individual effects being contaminated by the impact of other main effects or interactions under study.

Before explaining what an orthogonal array is, it would be best to explain or define what we mean by *orthogonality. Orthogonal* means being balanced and not mixed.[2] In the context of experimental matrices, orthogonal means statistically independent. If we examine a typical orthogonal array (Figure 7-1), we will note that each level has an equal number of occurrences within each column. For each column of the array in Figure 7-1, level 1 occurs four times, and level 2 occurs four times as well. Although different orthogonal arrays may have more than two levels within each column and each array has a different number of columns, the same rule applies. Within each column, you will find an equal number of occurrences for each level.

Figure 7-1 L_8 Orthogonal Array

$L_8\ (2^7)$

No.	1	2	3	4	5	6	7
1	1	1	1	1	1	1	1
2	1	1	1	2	2	2	2
3	1	2	2	1	1	2	2
4	1	2	2	2	2	1	1
5	2	1	2	1	2	1	2
6	2	1	2	2	1	2	1
7	2	2	1	1	2	2	1
8	2	2	1	2	1	1	2

Concerning statistical independence, this idea of balance goes farther than meaning simply an equal number of levels within each column. If we look at the relationship between one column and another, we can discover that for each level within one column, each level within any other column will occur an equal number of times as well. Referencing Figure 7-2, we see that for factor A, which is assigned to column 1, level 1 occurs four times, and level 2 is repeated the same number of times. If we look at column 2, we can see that for A at level 1, factor B is at level 1 twice and at level 2 twice. The same is true for factor A at level 2. If we look at the last column, we will also note the same relationship between factors A and G. No matter which two columns you select, the same will be true.

Figure 7-2 Orthogonality

Orthogonal Array L_8 (2^7)

Number	A 1	B 2	C 3	D 4	E 5	F 6	G 7	Results
1	1	1	1	1	1	1	1	y_1
2	1	1	1	2	2	2	2	y_2
3	1	2	2	1	1	2	2	y_3
4	1	2	2	2	2	1	1	y_4
5	2	1	2	1	2	1	2	y_5
6	2	1	2	2	1	2	1	y_6
7	2	2	1	1	2	2	1	y_7
8	2	2	1	2	1	1	2	y_8

A at level 1, occurs 4 times: B at level 1 occurs 2 times
B at level 2 occurs 2 times
A at level 2, occurs 4 times: B at level 1 occurs 2 times
B at level 2 occurs 2 times

A at level 1, occurs 4 times: G at level 1 occurs 2 times
G at level 2 occurs 2 times
A at level 2, occurs 4 times: G at level 1 occurs 2 times
G at level 2 occurs 2 times[3]

The ramifications of this orthogonality among columns are in the reproducibility of the experimental results.[4] Since each column is orthogonal to the others, if the results associated with one level of a specific factor are much different at another level, it is because changing that factor from one level to the next has a strong impact on the quality characteristic being measured. Because the levels of the other factors are occurring an equal number of times for each level of the strong factor, any effect by these other factors will be cancelled out. Therefore, an estimation of the effect of any one particular factor will tend to be accurate and reproducible because the estimated effect does not include the influence of other factors.

In addition to reproducible results, another advantage of the orthogonal array is cost efficiency. Although balanced, the design of an orthogonal array does not require that all combinations of all factors have to be tested. In the orthogonal array in Figure 7-3, only 16 experimental runs are required to study 15 different factors. A full factorial experiment studying the same number of factors would require 32,768 (2^{15}) experimental runs. More factors and additional levels would necessitate even larger experimental matrices. For example, 13 factors at 3 levels each would require 1,594,323 experimental runs, whereas an orthogonal array with 27 runs could provide the same essential information. Therefore, orthogonal arrays are much more cost effective and can provide more timely information. There are fractional factorials and methods to create specialized experimental designs that can produce much smaller experiments than a full factorial. However, they often require an in-depth understanding of statistical design techniques. The advantage of the orthogonal array is the twofold benefit of both efficiency and simplicity. Efficiency provides an affordable avenue for problem solving and discovery. Simplicity results in a set of tools more easily adopted and embraced by the nonstatistical expert.

Figure 7-3 L_{16} Orthogonal Array

L_{16} (2^{15})

	A	B	C	D	E	F	G	H	I	J	K	L	M	N	O
No.	1	2	3	4	5	6	7	8	9	10	11	12	13	14	15
1	1	1	1	1	1	1	1	1	1	1	1	1	1	1	1
2	1	1	1	1	1	1	1	2	2	2	2	2	2	2	2
3	1	1	1	2	2	2	2	1	1	1	1	2	2	2	2
4	1	1	1	2	2	2	2	2	2	2	2	1	1	1	1
5	1	2	2	1	1	2	2	1	1	2	2	1	1	2	2
6	1	2	2	1	1	2	2	2	2	1	1	2	2	1	1
7	1	2	2	2	2	1	1	1	1	2	2	2	2	1	1
8	1	2	2	2	2	1	1	2	2	1	1	1	1	2	2
9	2	1	2	1	2	1	2	1	2	1	2	1	2	1	2
10	2	1	2	1	2	1	2	2	1	2	1	2	1	2	1
11	2	1	2	2	1	2	1	1	2	1	2	2	1	2	1
12	2	1	2	2	1	2	1	2	1	2	1	1	2	1	2
13	2	2	1	1	2	2	1	1	2	2	1	1	2	2	1
14	2	2	1	1	2	2	1	2	1	1	2	2	1	1	2
15	2	2	1	2	1	1	2	1	2	2	1	2	1	1	2
16	2	2	1	2	1	1	2	2	1	1	2	1	2	2	1

However, one pays a price for the efficiency of the orthogonal array as opposed to the power of the often large full factorial experiment. All interaction combinations can be studied within the full factorial. This is not true of the orthogonal array. However, by using sound engineering judgment during the planning phase, the list of interactions to be incorporated into the experimental matrix can be reduced to those that merit consideration without omitting potentially significant interactions. Through effective planning, this potential weakness can be compensated for.

7.2 TERMINOLOGY

To facilitate the understanding of orthogonal arrays, it is essential to understand the standard nomenclature for describing each orthogonal array. Each array can be identified by the form $L_A(B^C)$ and can be illustrated by the orthogonal array in Figure 7-4. The subscript of L, which is designated by *A*, represents the number of experimental runs or combinations of factors which can be conducted in the experiment. B denotes the number of levels within each column. The letter C, which is shown as the exponent of the base letter B, identifies the number of columns available within the orthogonal array.[5]

In Figure 7-4, the orthogonal array L_{12} (2^{11}) contains 12 experimental runs or combinations of factors to be conducted in the experiment. Within the L_{12} (2^{11}), each column contains 2 levels, meaning each factor under study will possess 2 levels. The superscript 11 represents 11 columns within the array and means that up to 11 factors and interactions can be incorporated into the experiment.

Although the example in Figure 7-4 illustrates an experiment in which all columns (factors) contain the same number of levels, that condition is not nec-

Figure 7-4 L_{12} (2^{11}) Orthogonal Array

No.	1	2	3	4	5	6	7	8	9	10	11
1	1	1	1	1	1	1	1	1	1	1	1
2	1	1	1	1	1	2	2	2	2	2	2
3	1	1	2	2	2	1	1	1	2	2	2
4	1	2	1	2	2	1	2	2	1	1	2
5	1	2	2	1	2	2	1	2	1	2	1
6	1	2	2	2	1	2	2	1	2	1	1
7	2	1	2	2	1	1	2	2	1	2	1
8	2	1	2	1	2	2	2	1	1	1	2
9	2	1	1	2	2	2	1	2	2	1	1
10	2	2	2	1	1	1	1	2	2	1	2
11	2	2	1	2	1	2	1	1	1	2	2
12	2	2	1	1	2	1	2	1	2	2	1

Figure 7-5 L_8 (2^7) **Alternate Level Designations**

	1	2	3	4	5	6	7		1	2	3	4	5	6	7		1	2	3	4	5	6	7
1	O	O	O	O	O	O	O	1	−	−	−	−	−	−	−	1	L	L	L	L	L	L	L
2	O	O	O	X	X	X	X	2	−	−	−	+	+	+	+	2	L	L	L	H	H	H	H
3	O	X	X	O	O	X	X	3	−	+	+	−	−	+	+	3	L	H	H	L	L	H	H
4	O	X	X	X	X	O	O	4	−	+	+	+	+	−	−	4	L	H	H	H	H	L	L
5	X	O	X	O	X	O	X	5	+	−	+	−	+	−	+	5	H	L	H	L	H	L	H
6	X	O	X	X	O	X	O	6	+	−	+	+	−	+	−	6	H	L	H	H	L	H	L
7	X	X	O	O	X	X	O	7	+	+	−	−	+	+	−	7	H	H	L	L	H	H	L
8	X	X	O	X	O	O	X	8	+	+	−	+	−	−	+	8	H	H	L	H	L	L	H

essarily true for all orthogonal arrays. Some can contain columns with different numbers of levels. Take the case of the L_{54} ($2^1 \times 3^{25}$). Within this orthogonal array, 25 columns contain 3 levels, and one unique column has only 2.

Within the examples shown so far and within Appendix A, levels within the orthogonal array columns have been designated by numbers such as 1, 2, 3, etc. However, this designation system is not hard and fast, and you may encounter different nomenclature or actually prefer to use your own method for identifying levels. For example, 0 and X, + and −, L and H are all alternate representations for expressing levels 1 and 2. Within orthogonal arrays containing 3 levels, the symbols −, 0, and + and also the letters L, M, and H can represent the low, middle, and high settings for a factor under study.

7.3 ANALYSIS

Although analysis will be covered in detail in later chapters, a general explanation of how the raw data are converted into meaningful information may be beneficial at this point in order to enhance your understanding of the experiment design.

The analysis is based on combining the data associated with each level for each factor or interaction (column). The difference in the average results for each level is the measure of the effect of that factor. Those factors with the greatest effect or difference are the ones that can be used to improve the process and/or product (Figure 7-6).

7.4 INTERACTIONS

Besides determining the effects of individual factors, the same techniques can be used to understand the impact of interactions as well. Column 3 in Figure 7-6 represents the interaction between factors A and B. If we performed the same calculations as in the previous section:

Figure 7-6 Orthogonal Array Analysis

	A	B	A × B	C	D	E	F	Response
1	1	1	1	1	1	1	1	$y_1 = 12$
2	1	1	1	2	2	2	2	$y_2 = 15$
3	1	2	2	1	1	2	2	$y_3 = 10$
4	1	2	2	2	2	1	1	$y_4 = 14$
5	2	1	2	1	2	1	2	$y_5 = 18$
6	2	1	2	2	1	2	1	$y_6 = 22$
7	2	2	1	1	2	2	1	$y_7 = 20$
8	2	2	1	2	1	1	2	$y_8 = 14$

$$\overline{A_1} = \frac{y_1 + y_2 + y_3 + y_4}{4}$$

$$\overline{A_1} = \frac{12 + 15 + 10 + 14}{4} = 12.75$$

$$\overline{A_2} = \frac{y_5 + y_6 + y_7 + y_8}{4}$$

$$\overline{A_2} = \frac{18 + 22 + 20 + 14}{4} = 18.50$$

$$\text{Effect of A} = |\overline{A_1} - \overline{A_2}| = |12.75 - 18.50| = 5.75$$

$$\overline{A \times B_1} = \frac{y_1 + y_2 + y_7 + y_8}{4} = \frac{12 + 15 + 20 + 14}{4} = 15.25$$

$$\overline{A \times B_2} = \frac{y_3 + y_4 + y_5 + y_6}{4} = \frac{10 + 14 + 18 + 22}{4} = 16.00$$

$$\text{Effect of A} \times \text{B} = |\overline{A \times B_1} - \overline{A \times B_2}| = |15.25 - 16.00| = .75$$

Two questions typically arise in handing interactions. First, how do you set an interaction at level 1 or level 2? Second, how does the orthogonal array determine that an interaction for analysis purposes is at level 1 or level 2? In response to the first question, the settings for an interaction are governed by the levels set for the individual factors. In experimental run no. 3 (row 3) in Figure 7-6, the array assigns level 2 to the interaction A × B. However, A is set at level 1 (column 1), and B is set at level 2 (column 2). No settings are actually based on the levels given for the interaction. As a matter of fact, the levels for the interaction are a result of the levels of the individual factor levels. If we think of the interaction as a cross product of the factors involved (A × B) and define the levels in terms of − and + (Figure 7-7), the determination of interaction levels is quite logical.

Figure 7-7 Interaction Level Assignments

	A	B	A × B	C	D	E	F	Response
1	+	+	+	+	+	+	+	y_1
2	+	+	+	−	−	−	−	y_2
3	+	−	−	+	+	−	−	y_3
4	+	−	−	−	−	+	+	y_4
5	−	+	−	+	−	+	−	y_5
6	−	+	−	−	+	−	+	y_6
7	−	−	+	+	−	−	+	y_7
8	−	−	+	−	+	+	−	y_8

If we look at the analysis of the interaction A × B based on the data in Figure 7-6, we can also achieve a better understanding of how the level assignments relate to plotting interactions as explained in Section 5.5: Potential Interaction Concerns (see Figure 7-8).

$$\text{Point 1:}\quad \overline{A_1 \ B_1} = \frac{y_1 + y_2}{2} = \frac{12 + 15}{2} = 13.5$$

$$\text{Point 2:}\quad \overline{A_1 \ B_2} = \frac{y_3 + y_4}{2} = \frac{10 + 14}{2} = 12.0$$

$$\text{Point 3:}\quad \overline{A_2 \ B_1} = \frac{y_5 + y_6}{2} = \frac{18 + 22}{2} = 20.0$$

$$\text{Point 4:}\quad \overline{A_2 \ B_2} = \frac{y_7 + y_8}{2} = \frac{20 + 14}{2} = 17.0$$

Figure 7-8 Interaction Analysis

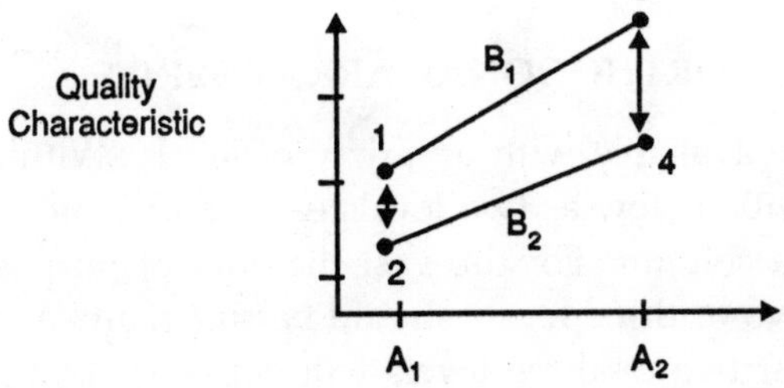

Whether the interaction is weak, mild, or strong depends on whether the two lines are parallel, converging, or intersecting. Mathematically, this corresponds to the difference between the heights associated with the end points of both response lines.

$$\text{If point 1: } A_1\,B_1 = \frac{y_1 + y_2}{2} \text{ and point 2: } A_1\,B_2 = \frac{y_3 + y_4}{2},$$

the height associated with the left end points is

$$H_L = \frac{y_1 + y_2 - y_3 - y_4}{2}.$$

$$\text{If point 3: } A_2\,B_1 = \frac{y_5 + y_6}{2} \text{ and point 4: } A_2\,B_2 = \frac{y_7 + y_8}{2},$$

the height associated with the right end points is

$$H_R = \frac{y_5 + y_6 - y_7 - y_8}{2}.$$

If we take the difference,

$$H_L - H_R = \frac{y_1 + y_2 - y_3 - y_4}{2} - \frac{y_5 + y_6 - y_7 - y_8}{2},$$

and then we group terms with like signs,

$$H_L - H_R = \frac{y_1 + y_2 + y_7 + y_8}{2} - \frac{y_3 + y_4 + y_5 + y_6}{2},$$

the two groups correspond to level 1 and level 2 in column 3 of the orthogonal array.

7.5 ORTHOGONAL ARRAY SERIES

Orthogonal arrays are available with a variety of levels. Within Appendix A, arrays are provided with as few as two levels each, and some contain as many as five levels within a column. For the vast majority of purposes, orthogonal arrays consisting of two or three levels should be sufficient. Whether to use an array possessing either two or three levels will depend on your objective and corresponding strategy. If developing screening designs or focusing experiments, the selection of two-level orthogonal arrays may be more cost effective in relation to the desired knowledge. For single experiments, continuous experimentation, and sequential studies, three-level orthogonal arrays may prove more appropriate for the desired understanding.

7.5.1 2^n Series Orthogonal Arrays

Arrays in which all of the columns contain two levels are referred to as the 2^n Series. The most commonly used two-level arrays are the L_4 (2^3), L_8 (2^7), L_{12} (2^{11}), and L_{16} (2^{15}). Larger 2^n arrays exist, but their size makes experimentation logistics cumbersome. This can create problems for experimentation scheduling. Even more seriously, it can cause confusion in running the experiment and result in either faulty data or incorrect experimental run settings. For purposes of simulation studies, this confusion may not present a problem.

The L_4 (2^3) (Figure 7-9) is basically a full factorial comprising two factors and the interaction between them. If engineering judgment considers the interaction weak, a third factor can be assigned to the third column.

The L_8 (2^7) (Figure 7-10) is a very flexible array for investigating interactions along with the factors (main effects). A combination of up to seven factors (main effects) and interactions can be incorporated into the array.

The L_{12} (2^{11}) (Figure 7-11) is a unique orthogonal array in that the effects of interactions are consistently spread across all columns. This trait minimizes the potential for the confounding of the effects of the factors and interactions. On the other hand, interactions cannot be incorporated into the L_{12} (2^{11}). If the size of the L_{12} (2^{11}) is appropriate for your design, but you wish to incorporate interactions, the L_{16} (2^{15}) would be a more appropriate design.

The L_{16} (2^{15}) (Figure 7-12) and the L_{32} (2^{31}) (Figure 7-13) are larger orthogonal arrays and provide wide flexibility for incorporating interactions along with factors (main effects) under consideration. Combinations of up to 15 and 31 factors and interactions, respectively, can be studied.

Figure 7-9 L_4 (2^3)

No.	1	2	3
1	1	1	1
2	1	2	2
3	2	1	2
4	2	2	1

Figure 7-10 L_8 (2^7)

No.	1	2	3	4	5	6	7
1	1	1	1	1	1	1	1
2	1	1	1	2	2	2	2
3	1	2	2	1	1	2	2
4	1	2	2	2	2	1	1
5	2	1	2	1	2	1	2
6	2	1	2	2	1	2	1
7	2	2	1	1	2	2	1
8	2	2	1	2	1	1	2

Figure 7-11 L_{12} (2^{11})

No.	1	2	3	4	5	6	7	8	9	10	11
1	1	1	1	1	1	1	1	1	1	1	1
2	1	1	1	1	1	2	2	2	2	2	2
3	1	1	2	2	2	1	1	1	2	2	2
4	1	2	1	2	2	1	2	2	1	1	2
5	1	2	2	1	2	2	1	2	1	2	1
6	1	2	2	2	1	2	2	1	2	1	1
7	2	1	2	2	1	1	2	2	1	2	1
8	2	1	2	1	2	2	2	1	1	1	2
9	2	1	1	2	2	2	1	2	2	1	1
10	2	2	2	1	1	1	1	2	2	1	2
11	2	2	1	2	1	2	1	1	1	2	2
12	2	2	1	1	2	1	2	1	2	2	1

Figure 7-12 L_{16} (2^{15})

No.	1	2	3	4	5	6	7	8	9	10	11	12	13	14	15
1	1	1	1	1	1	1	1	1	1	1	1	1	1	1	1
2	1	1	1	1	1	1	1	2	2	2	2	2	2	2	2
3	1	1	1	2	2	2	2	1	1	1	1	2	2	2	2
4	1	1	1	2	2	2	2	2	2	2	2	1	1	1	1
5	1	2	2	1	1	2	2	1	1	2	2	1	1	2	2
6	1	2	2	1	1	2	2	2	2	1	1	2	2	1	1
7	1	2	2	2	2	1	1	1	1	2	2	2	2	1	1
8	1	2	2	2	2	1	1	2	2	1	1	1	1	2	2
9	2	1	2	1	2	1	2	1	2	1	2	1	2	1	2
10	2	1	2	1	2	1	2	2	1	2	1	2	1	2	1
11	2	1	2	2	1	2	1	1	2	1	2	2	1	2	1
12	2	1	2	2	1	2	1	2	1	2	1	1	2	1	2
13	2	2	1	1	2	2	1	1	2	2	1	1	2	2	1
14	2	2	1	1	2	2	1	2	1	1	2	2	1	1	2
15	2	2	1	2	1	1	2	1	2	2	1	2	1	1	2
16	2	2	1	2	1	1	2	2	1	1	2	1	2	2	1

Figure 7-13 $L_{32}(2^{31})$

No.	1	2	3	4	5	6	7	8	9	10	11	12	13	14	15	16	17	18	19	20	21	22	23	24	25	26	27	28	29	30	31
1	1	1	1	1	1	1	1	1	1	1	1	1	1	1	1	1	1	1	1	1	1	1	1	1	1	1	1	1	1	1	1
2	1	1	1	1	1	1	1	1	1	1	1	1	1	1	1	2	2	2	2	2	2	2	2	2	2	2	2	2	2	2	2
3	1	1	1	1	1	1	1	2	2	2	2	2	2	2	2	1	1	1	1	1	1	1	1	2	2	2	2	2	2	2	2
4	1	1	1	1	1	1	1	2	2	2	2	2	2	2	2	2	2	2	2	2	2	2	2	1	1	1	1	1	1	1	1
5	1	1	1	2	2	2	2	1	1	1	1	2	2	2	2	1	1	1	1	2	2	2	2	1	1	1	1	2	2	2	2
6	1	1	1	2	2	2	2	1	1	1	1	2	2	2	2	2	2	2	2	1	1	1	1	2	2	2	2	1	1	1	1
7	1	1	1	2	2	2	2	2	2	2	2	1	1	1	1	1	1	1	1	2	2	2	2	2	2	2	2	1	1	1	1
8	1	1	1	2	2	2	2	2	2	2	2	1	1	1	1	2	2	2	2	1	1	1	1	1	1	1	1	2	2	2	2
9	1	2	2	1	1	2	2	1	1	2	2	1	1	2	2	1	1	2	2	1	1	2	2	1	1	2	2	1	1	2	2
10	1	2	2	1	1	2	2	1	1	2	2	1	1	2	2	2	2	1	1	2	2	1	1	2	2	1	1	2	2	1	1
11	1	2	2	1	1	2	2	2	2	1	1	2	2	1	1	1	1	2	2	1	1	2	2	2	2	1	1	2	2	1	1
12	1	2	2	1	1	2	2	2	2	1	1	2	2	1	1	2	2	1	1	2	2	1	1	1	1	2	2	1	1	2	2
13	1	2	2	2	2	1	1	1	1	2	2	2	2	1	1	1	1	2	2	2	2	1	1	1	1	2	2	2	2	1	1
14	1	2	2	2	2	1	1	1	1	2	2	2	2	1	1	2	2	1	1	1	1	2	2	2	2	1	1	1	1	2	2
15	1	2	2	2	2	1	1	2	2	1	1	1	1	2	2	1	1	2	2	2	2	1	1	2	2	1	1	1	1	2	2
16	1	2	2	2	2	1	1	2	2	1	1	1	1	2	2	2	2	1	1	1	1	2	2	1	1	2	2	2	2	1	1
17	2	1	2	1	2	1	2	1	2	1	2	1	2	1	2	1	2	1	2	1	2	1	2	1	2	1	2	1	2	1	2
18	2	1	2	1	2	1	2	1	2	1	2	1	2	1	2	2	1	2	1	2	1	2	1	2	1	2	1	2	1	2	1
19	2	1	2	1	2	1	2	2	1	2	1	2	1	2	1	1	2	1	2	1	2	1	2	2	1	2	1	2	1	2	1
20	2	1	2	1	2	1	2	2	1	2	1	2	1	2	1	2	1	2	1	2	1	2	1	1	2	1	2	1	2	1	2
21	2	1	2	2	1	2	1	1	2	1	2	2	1	2	1	1	2	1	2	2	1	2	1	1	2	1	2	2	1	2	1
22	2	1	2	2	1	2	1	1	2	1	2	2	1	2	1	2	1	2	1	1	2	1	2	2	1	2	1	1	2	1	2
23	2	1	2	2	1	2	1	2	1	2	1	1	2	1	2	1	2	1	2	2	1	2	1	2	1	2	1	1	2	1	2
24	2	1	2	2	1	2	1	2	1	2	1	1	2	1	2	2	1	2	1	1	2	1	2	1	2	1	2	2	1	2	1
25	2	2	1	1	2	2	1	1	2	2	1	1	2	2	1	1	2	2	1	1	2	2	1	1	2	2	1	1	2	2	1
26	2	2	1	1	2	2	1	1	2	2	1	1	2	2	1	2	1	1	2	2	1	1	2	2	1	1	2	2	1	1	2
27	2	2	1	1	2	2	1	2	1	1	2	2	1	1	2	1	2	2	1	1	2	2	1	2	1	1	2	2	1	1	2
28	2	2	1	1	2	2	1	2	1	1	2	2	1	1	2	2	1	1	2	2	1	1	2	1	2	2	1	1	2	2	1
29	2	2	1	2	1	1	2	1	2	2	1	2	1	1	2	1	2	2	1	2	1	1	2	1	2	2	1	2	1	1	2
30	2	2	1	2	1	1	2	1	2	2	1	2	1	1	2	2	1	1	2	1	2	2	1	2	1	1	2	1	2	2	1
31	2	2	1	2	1	1	2	2	1	1	2	1	2	2	1	1	2	2	1	2	1	1	2	2	1	1	2	1	2	2	1
32	2	2	1	2	1	1	2	2	1	1	2	1	2	2	1	2	1	1	2	1	2	2	1	1	2	2	1	2	1	1	2

7.5.2 3^n Series Orthogonal Arrays

Arrays in which the columns predominantly contain three levels are referred to as the 3^n Series. The most commonly used 3^n arrays are the L_9 (3^4), L_{18} ($2^1 \times 3^7$), and L_{27} (3^{13}). Again, larger arrays exist, but their size makes experimentation logistics difficult. However, the larger arrays, such as the L_{54} ($2^1 \times 3^{25}$) and the L_{81} (3^{40}) may be appropriate for a large simulation study, as in the design of an electronic circuit. This distinction would be applicable to mechanical designs as well.

Figure 7-14 L_9 (3^4)

No.	1	2	3	4
1	1	1	1	1
2	1	2	2	2
3	1	3	3	3
4	2	1	2	2
5	2	2	3	1
6	2	3	1	2
7	3	1	3	2
8	3	2	1	3
9	3	3	2	1

The L_9 (3^4) (Figure 7-14) is a simple orthogonal array designed for investigating up to four factors, or two factors and one interaction. In Chapter 8, "Degrees of Freedom," we will discuss why adding one interaction in this case reduces the number of factors (main effects) that can be studied down to two.

The L_{18} ($2^1 \times 3^7$) (Figure 7-15) is unique on several counts. For one, the first column contains two levels whereas the other seven columns contain three

Figure 7-15 L_{18} ($2^1 \times 3^7$)

No.	1	2	3	4	5	6	7	8
1	1	1	1	1	1	1	1	1
2	1	1	2	2	2	2	2	2
3	1	1	3	3	3	3	3	3
4	1	2	1	1	2	2	3	3
5	1	2	2	2	3	3	1	1
6	1	2	3	3	1	1	2	2
7	1	3	1	2	1	3	2	3
8	1	3	2	3	2	1	3	1
9	1	3	3	1	3	2	1	2
10	2	1	1	3	3	2	2	1
11	2	1	2	1	1	3	3	2
12	2	1	3	2	2	1	1	3
13	2	2	1	2	3	1	3	2
14	2	2	2	3	1	2	1	3
15	2	2	3	1	2	3	2	1
16	2	3	1	3	2	3	1	2
17	2	3	2	1	3	1	2	3
18	2	3	3	2	1	2	3	1

levels. Second, the L_{18} ($2^1 \times 3^7$) is similar to the L_{12} (2^{11}) in that the effects of interactions are evenly distributed among the columns with the exception of the relationship between columns 1 and 2. Third, a special relationship exists between column 1 and column 2. Because of the layout of these two columns, the interaction between the factors assigned to column 1 and to column 2 can be studied without sacrificing additional columns. This analysis can be accomplished by developing a 2 × 3 Response Table and inserting the average results for each combination of the two factors.

The L_{27} (3^{13}) (Figure 7-16) is a more conventional 3^n Series Orthogonal Array and contains three levels in each of its 13 columns. A maximum of 13 three-level factors can be incorporated into the L_{27} (3^{13}). As many as three interactions can be assigned within the array. But as more interactions are included, fewer factors (main effects) can be considered.

Figure 7-16 L_{27} (3^{13})

No.	1	2	3	4	5	6	7	8	9	10	11	12	13
1	1	1	1	1	1	1	1	1	1	1	1	1	1
2	1	1	1	1	2	2	2	2	2	2	2	2	2
3	1	1	1	1	3	3	3	3	3	3	3	3	3
4	1	2	2	2	1	1	1	2	2	2	3	3	3
5	1	2	2	2	2	2	2	3	3	3	1	1	1
6	1	2	2	2	3	3	3	1	1	1	2	2	2
7	1	3	3	3	1	1	1	3	3	3	2	2	2
8	1	3	3	3	2	2	2	1	1	1	3	3	3
9	1	3	3	3	3	3	3	2	2	2	1	1	1
10	2	1	2	3	1	2	3	1	2	3	1	2	3
11	2	1	2	3	2	3	1	2	3	1	2	3	1
12	2	1	2	3	3	1	2	3	1	2	3	1	2
13	2	2	3	1	1	2	3	2	3	1	3	1	2
14	2	2	3	1	2	3	1	3	1	2	1	2	3
15	2	2	3	1	3	1	2	1	2	3	2	3	1
16	2	3	1	2	1	2	3	3	1	2	2	3	1
17	2	3	1	2	2	3	1	1	2	3	3	1	2
18	2	3	1	2	3	1	2	2	3	1	1	2	3
19	3	1	3	2	1	3	2	1	3	2	1	3	2
20	3	1	3	2	2	1	3	2	1	3	2	1	3
21	3	1	3	2	3	2	1	3	2	1	3	2	1
22	3	2	1	3	1	3	2	2	1	3	3	2	1
23	3	2	1	3	2	1	3	3	2	1	1	3	2
24	3	2	1	3	3	2	1	1	3	2	2	1	3
25	3	3	2	1	1	3	2	3	2	1	2	1	3
26	3	3	2	1	2	1	3	1	3	2	3	2	1
27	3	3	2	1	3	2	1	2	1	3	1	3	2

Notes

1. Ealey, Lance A., *Quality by Design*, pp. 109–111.
2. Wu, Yuin, and Dr. Willie Hobbs Moore, *Quality Engineering: Product & Process Design Optimization*, p. 123.
3. *Introduction To Quality Engineering*, pp. 4-10–4-11.
4. Ibid., p. 4-10.
5. Ibid., p. 4-24.

Chapter 8

DEGREES OF FREEDOM

The experiment objective and corresponding strategy will direct you toward a family of orthogonal arrays from which to select. Whether you have narrowed the selection down to a 2^n Series or a 3^n Series array, you still have different arrays from which to make your selection. Typically, efficiency and cost are major concerns, and you will wish to use the smallest possible orthogonal array that can still provide enough information for comprehensive analysis and valid conclusions. To ascertain within an orthogonal array family which is the smallest array that can provide the necessary information requires the calculation of the required degrees of freedom.

8.1 CONCEPTS

Degrees of freedom is a measure of the amount of information concerning an item of interest that can be obtained. A general definition is "the number of comparisons that need to be made without being redundant to derive a conclusion." Within the scope of experimentation, this definition translates into "the number of comparisons between factor (main effect) or interaction levels that need to be made to determine which level is better and specifically how much better it is."

If we look at Figure 8-1, we can see the comparison between the size of two basketball players. One is 7 feet tall while the other is 6 feet in height. To understand how much bigger the one on the left is than the player on the right, we need to make only one comparison. That comparison tells us that Number 14 is 12 inches taller than Number 25.

If we expand the comparison to include a third basketball player (Figure 8-2), we only need two comparisons to obtain an understanding of the size relationship between all three athletes. The comparison between Number 14 and Number 25 tells us that the second player is 12 inches shorter than the first. If we make a second comparison between Number 14 and the player on the right who is 6 feet 4 inches tall, we learn that Number 36 is 8 inches shorter than the taller player. From these two comparisons, it is inherent that the middle player

Figure 8-1 One Degree of Freedom

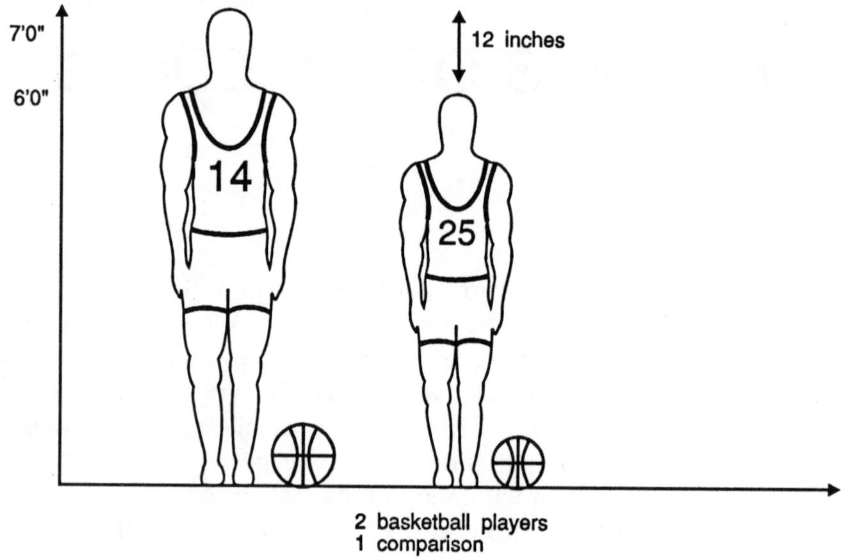

Figure 8-2 Two Degrees of Freedom

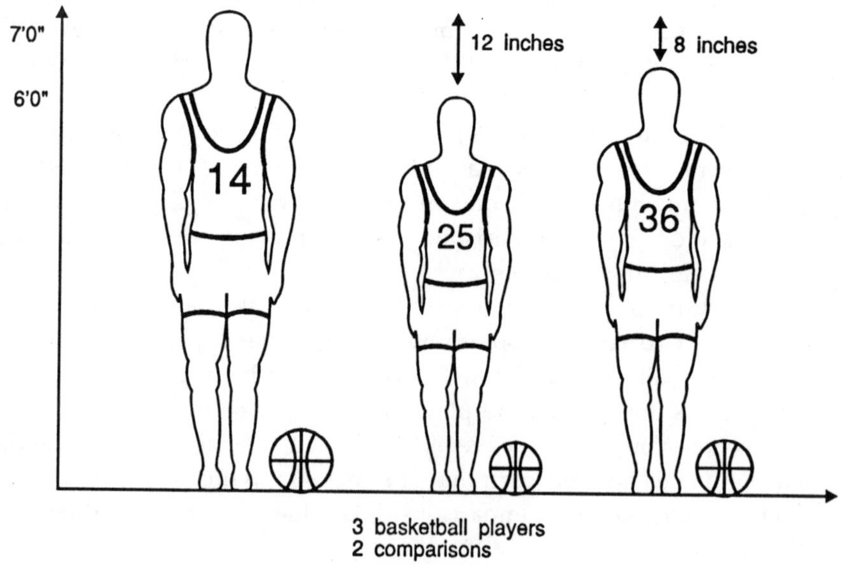

(Number 25) is 4 inches shorter than Number 36. Therefore, two comparisons provide us with sufficient information to obtain an understanding of the size relationship among all three. In other words, *two* degrees of freedom are required to ascertain the relationship among the *three* basketball players. If we were to expand this analogy to include more players, the number of comparisons or degrees of freedom would continue to equal one fewer than the number of persons being studied. If a fourth athlete were added, we would need three comparisons or degrees of freedom. If we performed a study of the entire team of 12 players, 11 comparisons or degrees of freedom would allow us to obtain an understanding of the relationship among the sizes of all members of the team.

This same analogy can be applied to process factors or product components within an experiment. To achieve an understanding concerning the relationship between an experimental factor and the quality characteristic of interest, we need to make comparisons between values of the quality characteristic at different levels or settings of the factor under study. These comparisons tell us if the factor has a major impact on the characteristic of interest and which level or setting gives us a more desirable result.

These comparisons translate mathematically into degrees of freedom. If a process variable is studied at two levels, this means one comparison or degree of freedom is required. If an experiment involves three different values of a particular ingredient used in a food processing operation, two comparisons or degrees of freedom are required to determine the effect of changing the quantity of this ingredient on the end product.

In an experiment, numerous factors are studied simultaneously with each other with settings or levels for each factor changed concurrently. Because each factor requires its own set of comparisons or degrees of freedom, the total number of comparisons or degrees of freedom required equals the sum of the comparisons or degrees of freedom required for each individual factor under study.

The importance of understanding how many degrees of freedom are required to study a factor of interest is important in determining which orthogonal array to use for designing the experiment. Each orthogonal array has available a specific number of degrees of freedom within its structure. If we understand how many degrees of freedom we need, we can properly select an array that can provide us with a sufficient number of comparisons or degrees of freedom for obtaining this knowledge.

8.2 CALCULATIONS

By applying some simple rules and basic formulas, we can determine the degrees of freedom that are required for factors or main effects and interactions and that are available within each orthogonal array under consideration. By comparing the number of degrees of freedom required to the number of degrees available among the arrays within the appropriate array series, we can select the smallest orthogonal array that can still provide us with all of the essential information to make a comprehensive study of the quality characteristic of interest and the impact upon it by the factors under investigation.

8.2.1 Factors or Main Effects

The degrees of freedom required to study a factor or main effect is equal to one fewer than the number of levels or settings to be changed within the experiment. As in the previous example of the basketball players, the comparison of two players required one degree of freedom, and the relationship between the size of three players required two degrees of freedom. If we translate players to process variables or product components or ingredients, two settings for a factor require one degree of freedom. Likewise, three settings for a variable under investigation dictate two degrees of freedom needed.

$$\text{Degrees of freedom: factor (main effect)} = \text{number of levels} - 1$$

$$2 \text{ levels} = 1 \text{ degree of freedom}$$

$$3 \text{ levels} = 2 \text{ degrees of freedom}$$

$$4 \text{ levels} = 3 \text{ degrees of freedom}$$

$$\cdots\cdots\cdots\cdots\cdots\cdots$$

$$n \text{ levels} = n - 1 \text{ degrees of freedom}$$

8.2.2 Interactions

If we think of an interaction as a cross product (A × B) of the two factors (A and B) that make up the combined effect, we can perceive the logic by which the degrees of freedom associated with an interaction is equal to the product of the degrees of freedom of the individual factors composing the interaction.

$$\text{Degrees of freedom: interaction (A} \times \text{B)} = (\text{Number of levels for factor A} - 1) \times (\text{Number of levels for factor B} - 1)$$

Another way to obtain an understanding of the calculation for the degrees of freedom of an interaction is graphically. If we look at Figure 8-3, we see two

Figure 8-3 2 × 2 Levels Interaction

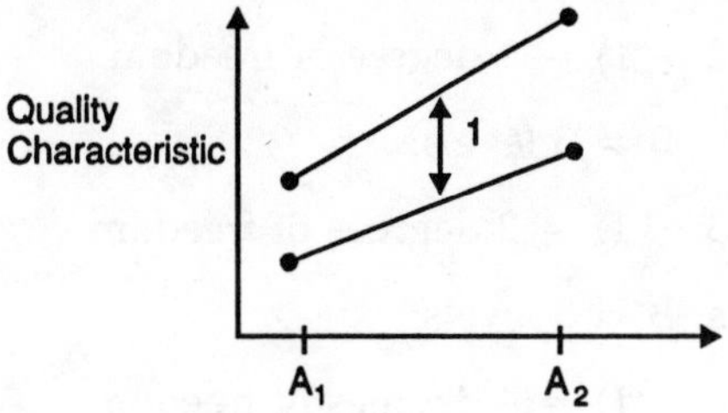

lines which represent the relationship of the interaction between factors A and B. Only one comparison between the two lines is needed to ascertain if the two lines are parallel, converging or intersecting. This determination will tell us whether the interaction is weak, mild, or strong, respectively. If we perform the corresponding calculations,

Degrees of freedom of factor A	(2 − 1)
×	×
Degrees of freedom of factor B =	(2 − 1) =
Degrees of freedom of interaction A × B	1

we see that both analogies give us the same answer.

Let's look at a more complex example. Both factor A and factor B possess three levels. If we look at Figure 8-4, we see three sets of lines, one for each level of factor B. Within each line, there exist two line segments. For us to determine graphically the relationship between factors A and B, we must make

Figure 8-4 3 × 3 Levels Interaction

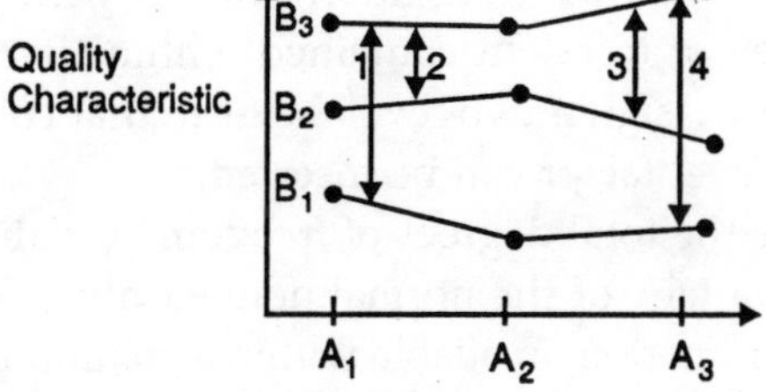

Table 8-1 Degrees of Freedom Calculations for Interactions

A = 2 levels, B = 2 levels:

$(2 - 1) \times (2 - 1) = 1$ degree of freedom

A = 2 levels, B = 3 levels:

$(2 - 1) \times (3 - 1) = 2$ degrees of freedom

A = 3 levels, B = 3 levels:

$(3 - 1) \times (3 - 1) = 4$ degrees of freedom

A = 4 levels, B = 2 levels:

$(4 - 1) \times (2 - 1) = 3$ degrees of freedom

A = m levels, B = n levels:

$(m - 1) \times (n - 1) = mn - m - n + 1$ degrees of freedom

comparisons of the three leftmost line segments (3 − 1 degrees of freedom or 2 comparisons) and then the three far right line segments (3 − 1 degrees of freedom or 2 comparisons). If we use the same formula as before,

Degrees of freedom of factor A	$(3 - 1)$
×	×
Degrees of freedom of factor B =	$(3 - 1) =$
Degrees of freedom of interaction A × B	4,

we again obtain the same answer.

8.2.3 Orthogonal Arrays

The degrees of freedom available within an orthogonal array relate to the number of levels available in each column. Just as we equated two levels of a factor to one degree of freedom, we can translate two levels within an orthogonal array column as one degree of freedom contained within that column. If a column has two levels, we can assign a two-level factor to that column. If a column has three levels, a three-level factor can be inserted.

For us to calculate the total degrees of freedom available within an entire array, we can take advantage of the normal nomenclature for describing each array. As the degrees of freedom available within a column is equal to the number of levels within the column minus one, the total degrees of freedom for the entire array is equal to the sum of the individual degrees of freedom for each column. Therefore, if we use the standard mathematical convention of L_A (B^C) for describing an orthogonal array, the total degrees of freedom for the array can be calculated by:

Degrees of freedom per column	(B − 1)
×	×
Number of columns	C

For example, the degrees of freedom for an L_8 (2^7) would be computed as follows:

Degrees of freedom per column	(2 − 1)
×	×
Number of columns	7
	7 df

For the L_9 (3^4), we could calculate the degrees of freedom in a similar manner and obtain the results as follows:

Degrees of freedom per column	(3 − 1)
×	×
Number of columns	4
	8 df

The L_{18} $(2^1 \times 3^7)$ poses a unique situation for calculating the degrees of freedom it contains.

Figure 8-5 L_8 (2^7) Degrees of Freedom

No.	1	2	3	4	5	6	7	
1	1	1	1	1	1	1	1	
2	1	1	1	2	2	2	2	
3	1	2	2	1	1	2	2	
4	1	2	2	2	2	1	1	
5	2	1	2	1	2	1	2	
6	2	1	2	2	1	2	1	
7	2	2	1	1	2	2	1	
8	2	2	1	2	1	1	2	
	1 +	1 +	1 +	1 +	1 +	1 +	1	= 7

Figure 8-6 L_9 (3^4) Degrees of Freedom

No.	1	2	3	4
1	1	1	1	1
2	1	2	2	2
3	1	3	3	3
4	2	1	2	3
5	2	2	3	1
6	2	3	1	2
7	3	1	3	2
8	3	2	1	3
9	3	3	2	1
	2 +	2 +	2 +	2 = 8

Figure 8-7 L_{27} (3^{13}) with Interaction

	A	B	A × B	A × B	C	D	E	F	G	H	I	J	K
No.	1	2	3	4	5	6	7	8	9	10	11	12	13
1	1	1	1	1	1	1	1	1	1	1	1	1	1
2	1	1	1	1	2	2	2	2	2	2	2	2	2
3	1	1	1	1	3	3	3	3	3	3	3	3	3
4	1	2	2	2	1	1	1	2	2	2	3	3	3
5	1	2	2	2	2	2	2	3	3	3	1	1	1
6	1	2	2	2	3	3	3	1	1	1	2	2	2
7	1	3	3	3	1	1	1	3	3	3	2	2	2
8	1	3	3	3	2	2	2	1	1	1	3	3	3
9	1	3	3	3	3	3	3	2	2	2	1	1	1
10	2	1	2	3	1	2	3	1	2	3	1	2	3
11	2	1	2	3	2	3	1	2	3	1	2	3	1
12	2	1	2	3	3	1	2	3	1	2	3	1	2
13	2	2	3	1	1	2	3	2	3	1	3	1	2
14	2	2	3	1	2	3	1	3	1	2	1	2	3
15	2	2	3	1	3	1	2	1	2	3	2	3	1
16	2	3	1	2	1	2	3	3	1	2	2	3	1
17	2	3	1	2	2	3	1	1	2	3	3	1	2
18	2	3	1	2	3	1	2	2	3	1	1	2	3
19	3	1	3	2	1	3	2	1	3	2	1	3	2
20	3	1	3	2	2	1	3	2	1	3	2	1	3
21	3	1	3	2	3	2	1	3	2	1	3	2	1
22	3	2	1	3	1	3	2	2	1	3	3	2	1
23	3	2	1	3	2	1	3	3	2	1	1	3	2
24	3	2	1	3	3	2	1	1	3	2	2	1	3
25	3	3	2	1	1	3	2	3	2	1	2	1	3
26	3	3	2	1	2	1	3	1	3	2	3	2	1
27	3	3	2	1	3	2	1	2	1	3	1	3	2

Degrees of freedom for one 2-level column:	$(2 - 1)$
Degrees of freedom for seven 3-level columns:	$7 \times (3 - 1)$
Degrees of freedom for inherent interaction between column 1 and column 2:	$\underline{(2 - 1) \times (3 - 1)}$
	17 df

In the assignment of factors to columns of an array, generally the task is simply matching a factor with a column containing the same number of levels. For interactions, a different type of situation may arise. For an experiment involving three-level factors, a 3^n Series orthogonal array would be appropriate. Within each column, two degrees of freedom would be available. If an interaction between two of the factors under consideration was to be incorporated into the array, four degrees of freedom ([3 − 1] × [3 − 1]) would be required. Since each column contains only two degrees of freedom, insertion of the interaction into the array would require the use of two columns (2 df × 2 columns = 4 df). To incorporate an interaction into an L_9 (3^4) or an L_{27} (3^{13}) would absorb two columns and reduce by two the number of factors or main effects that could be assigned to a column within the array (Figure 8-7). Identification of specific column assignments will be covered in Chapter 9, "Linear Graphs."

Chapter 9

LINEAR GRAPHS

Up to this point in the context of designing the experiment, we have described orthogonal arrays and explained degrees of freedom. From these topics we have shown how to select the most appropriate and efficient orthogonal array for factors and settings being investigated. The purpose of this chapter is to provide you with a tool for assigning factors (main effects) and interactions to appropriate columns so as to achieve reproducible results.

9.1 CONCEPTS

Assigning interactions at random to any available column within the orthogonal array can lead to incorrect analysis and faulty conclusions. To prevent the occurrence of these experimental design errors, Dr. Taguchi has developed a system for mapping interactions to the appropriate columns of the array. By setting up a graphical representation of the relationships among factors and the interactions between them, the experimenter can systematically assign factors (main effects) and interactions to columns within the orthogonal array without fear of confounding the effects of factors and their interactions. These graphical representations are called *linear graphs.* A comprehensive compilation of linear graphs is contained in Appendix B.

Linear graphs are constructed of interconnecting dots or circles. Each dot or circle within a linear graph represents a column within the orthogonal array in which a factor (main effect) can be assigned. The connecting line represents the interaction between the two factors represented by the dots (circles) at each end of the line segment. The number accompanying the line segment represents the column within the array to which the interaction should be assigned.

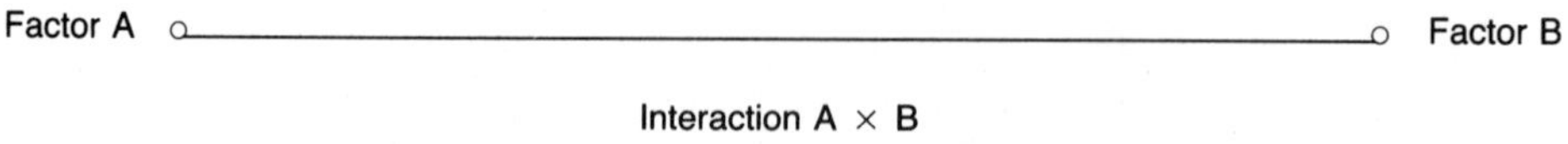

Depending on the size of the orthogonal array, linear graphs vary in complexity. From a simple line segment for the L_4 (2^3) shown in Figure 9-1 to the intricate

Figure 9-1 L_4 (2^3) Linear Graph

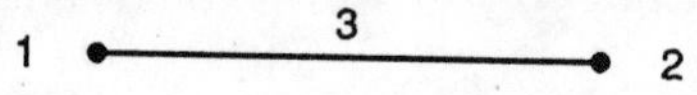

pattern of the linear graph in Figure 9-2 for the L_{64} (2^{63}), linear graphs come in a variety of diverse patterns ranging from the simple to the complicated.

Also depending on the size of the orthogonal array, there may be only one or a multitude of linear graphs available for any one specific linear graph. The L_4 (2^3) has only one linear graph, shown in Figure 9-1. On the other hand, an assortment of linear graphs is available for the L_{16} (2^{15}) as demonstrated in Figure 9-3.

An additional feature that is available for larger orthogonal arrays is alternate mapping for the same linear graph. Looking at Figure 9-4, you will observe three linear graphs with identical shapes, but the columns associated with each dot (circle) and line segment are different. The advantage of having this flexibility is related to the realization that not all factors are equal in terms of set-up time and associated cost. The most cost effective experiment would be one in which

Figure 9-2 L_{64} (2^{63}) Linear Graph

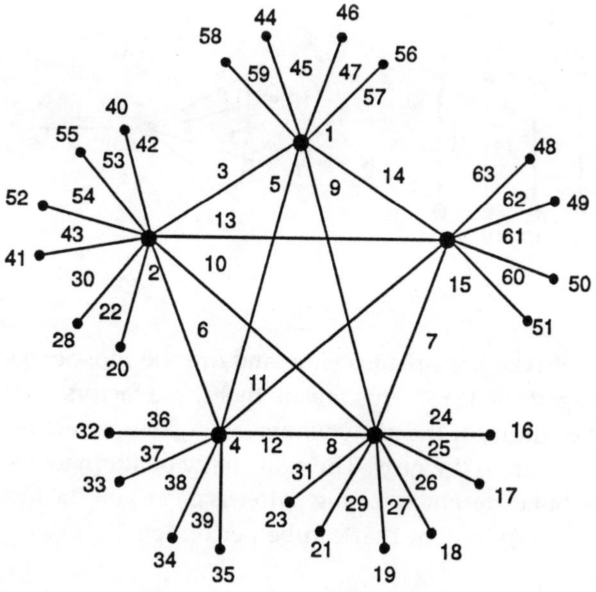

Figure 9-3 L_{16} (2^{15}) Linear Graphs

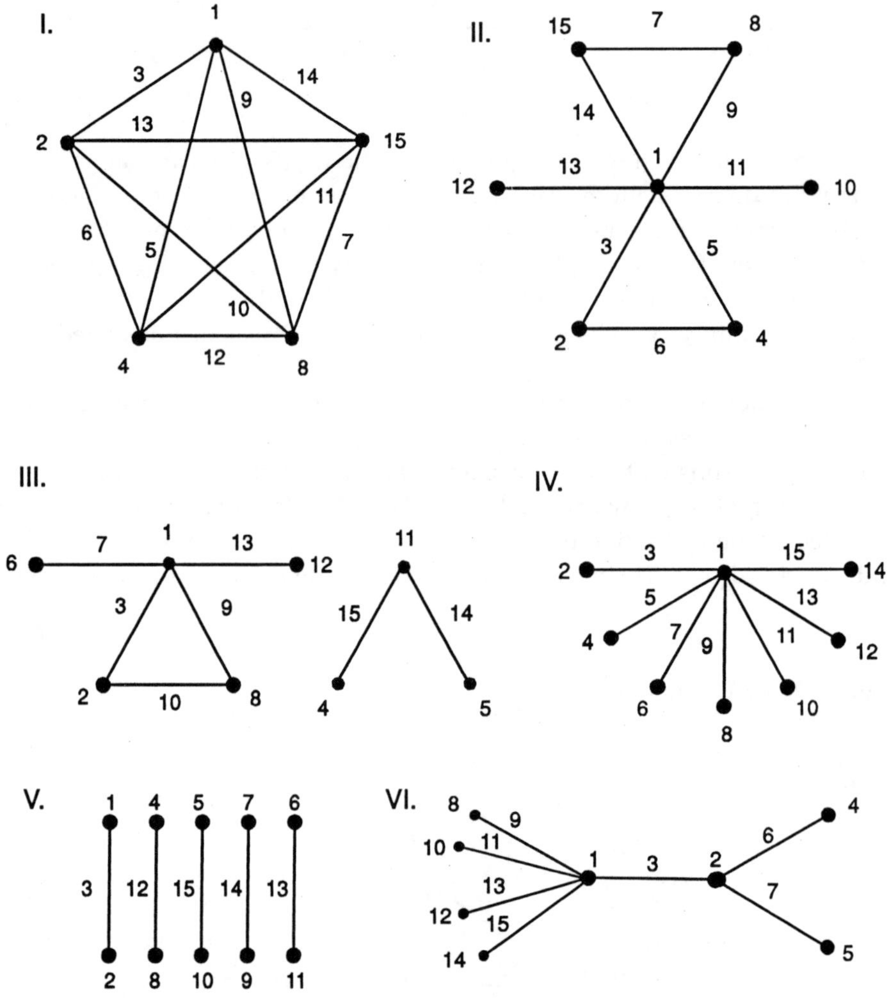

those factors that take the greatest time and are the most expensive to change have to be changed the least. This means that these factors need to be assigned to the leftmost columns of the array where factor changes are less frequent from one experimental run to the next. The availability of alternate linear graphs with the same shape but different mapping patterns gives you the flexibility to design the most efficient experiment that can be performed.

Figure 9-4 L_{16} (2^{15}) Alternate Mapping

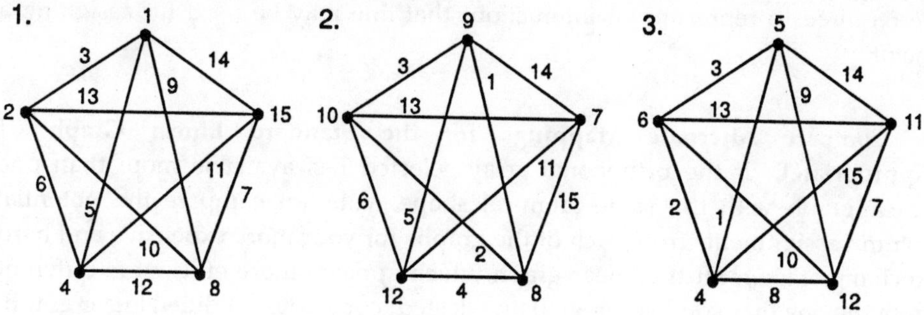

9.2 ASSIGNING FACTORS TO LINEAR GRAPHS

The designing of the experiment can be most easily accomplished in the following sequence of steps. We will first list these procedures and then proceed through some examples to obtain a working understanding.

1. Select the Orthogonal Array. This step requires first calculating the total degrees of freedom needed for studying the factors (main effects) and interactions of interest. The degrees of freedom required are then matched against the degrees of freedom of the orthogonal arrays within the appropriate array series (2^n or 3^n). The smallest array with at least as many degrees of freedom as required is selected.

2. Draw the Required Linear Graph. Based on the factors (main effects) and interactions identified for study in the planning phase, construct a linear graph. Use dots or circles to represent factors, and connect the dots with straight lines where interactions have been planned into the experiment.

3. Match the Required Graph to a Standard Linear Graph. Using Appendix B, compare the graph drawn in step 2 to the alternate shapes available for the orthogonal array selected. Select the standard linear graph that most closely resembles the graph which you drew earlier.

4. Redraw the Required Linear Graph. Based on the standard linear graph selected in step 3, modify the required graph to resemble the preferred graph from the appendix.

5. Assign Factors and Interactions. Mark each factor and interaction beside the appropriate dot or line segment. If a line segment of the linear graph will not be required to represent an interaction, that line may be used for assigning a factor.

6. Compare Alternate Mappings for the Standard Linear Graph (if Appropriate). If the orthogonal array selected has available more than one linear graph with the same identical shape, you can compare the potential column assignments from each of the graphs for your more expensive and hard to change factors. If the linear graph which appears more efficient is different from the one that you had previously selected, copy your modified linear graph, and renumber the dots (circles) and line segments as shown in the preferred linear graph pattern.

9.3 STANDARD LINEAR GRAPHS

As an aid to designing your experiments, it may prove helpful at this point to examine the standard linear graphs for the most frequently used orthogonal arrays. In studying these graphs, we will highlight graph peculiarities and add comments to enhance your understanding of specific linear graphs. We will also point out useful hints for helping you to match your required linear graph with the most appropriate standard linear graph.

9.3.1 L_4 (2^3) Linear Graph

Within the L_4 (2^3) (Figure 9-5), only one linear graph is available. Assignment of only a single interaction is possible and is limited to the third column of the array.

9.3.2 L_8 (2^7) Linear Graphs

Two linear graphs are available for the L_8 (2^7) (Figure 9-6). If all interactions of interest involve a common factor, the graph on the right would be the most appropriate. If the design requires the study of three interactions involving the same three factors (A $\times$ B, B $\times$ C, and A $\times$ C), the graph on the left should be selected. For an experiment involving two interactions with a common factor, either linear graph could be used. If you require the investigation of two inter-

Figure 9-5 L_4 (2^3) Linear Graph

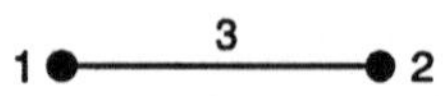

Figure 9-6 L_8 (2^7) Linear Graphs

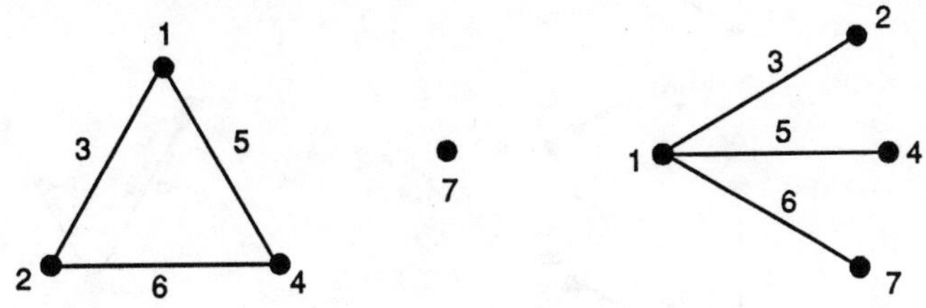

actions without a common factor, the required graph cannot be modified to fit either of the two available standard linear graphs. In this special case, you would have to move up to the next larger array.

9.3.3 L_{16} (2^{15}) Linear Graphs

Six different linear graph shapes are available for the L_{16} (2^{15}) (Figure 9-7). For each shape, there are also three different mapping schemes. Linear graph I may prove appropriate when numerous interactions are being considered which have interacting factors. An example would be A × B, B × C, and A × C. Linear graph II would be a better choice if you were investigating one factor interacting with many other factors and if one or two of these factors interacted with each other. Type III would be selected over linear graph II if some of the factors under study interacted with each other but not with the most common interacting factor. Type IV represents the situation where all interactions of interest involve the same common factor. If the graph is to include interactions in which each factor is tied to only one other factor, then Type V would be the preferred choice. Type VI is similar to linear graph III, but would be preferred where desirable to look at two factors interacting with numerous factors as well as with each other.

9.3.4 L_9 (3^4) Linear Graph

The L_9 (3^4) (Figure 9-8) is similar to the L_4 (2^3) in that only one linear shape and mapping scheme is available and only one interaction can be incorporated. The one difference between the two graphs is that the L_9 (3^4) interaction uses up two columns instead of one because of the degrees of freedom required.

9.3.5 L_{18} ($2^1 \times 3^7$) Linear Graph

If the L_{18} ($2^1 \times 3^7$) has been selected as the appropriate orthogonal array, the assignment of factors is straightforward as indicated by the linear graph (Figure

Figure 9-7 L_{16} (2^{15}) Linear Graphs

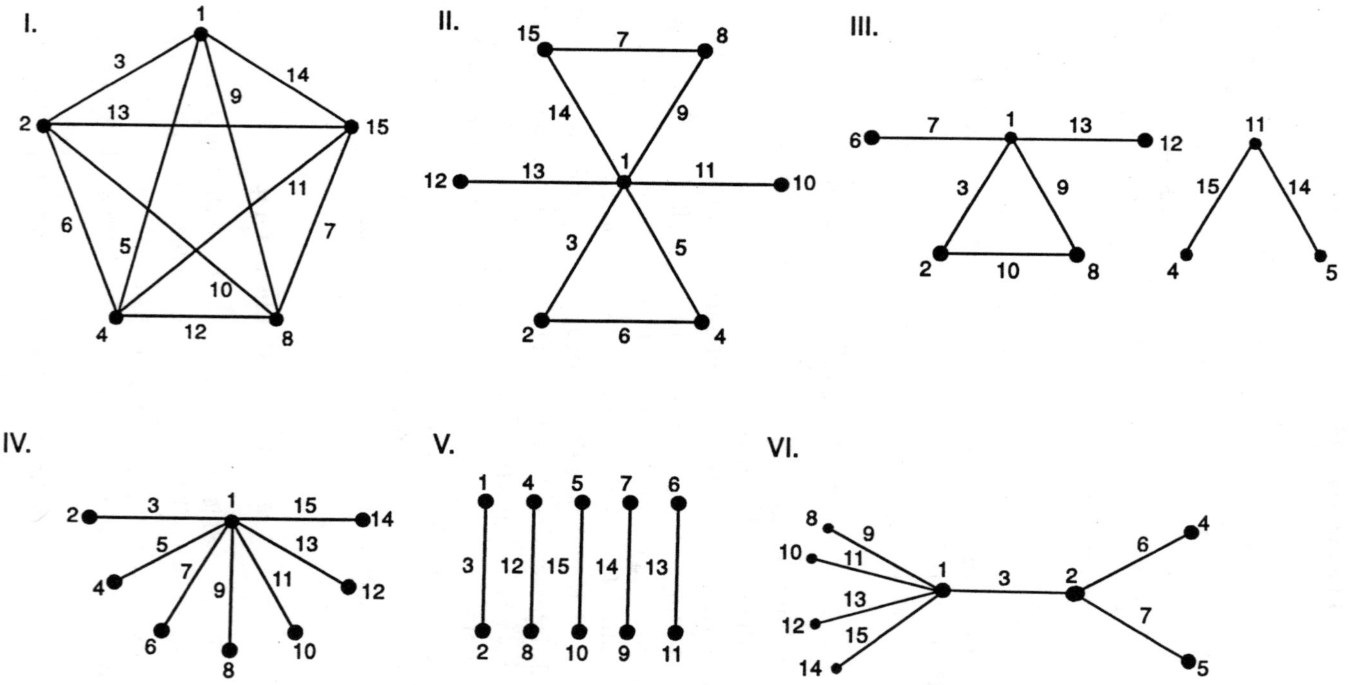

Figure 9-8 L_9 (3^4) Linear Graph

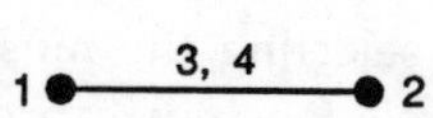

Figure 9-9 L_{18} ($2^1 \times 3^7$) Linear Graph

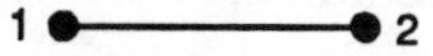

9-9). The two-level factor has to be assigned to column 1, and the three-level factor, which is a component of the interaction identified for study, is assigned to column 2. *No* columns have to be set aside for the interaction.

9.3.6 L_{27} (3^{13}) Linear Graphs

Two linear graphs are available for the L_{27} (3^{13}). Two separate mapping schemes exist for the second linear graph, whereas only one is available for the far left pattern shown in Figure 9-10. If one common factor is present in each interaction of interest, either the middle or far right graph should be used. If the experimental design is to incorporate three jointly interacting factors (A × B, B × C, and A × C), the far left linear graph should be chosen. If designing an experiment with only one interaction or with two interactions involving a common factor, the experimenter can choose according to individual preference. Each interaction identified will require *both* columns called for in the linear graph.

More diverse linear graphs exist for the larger 2^n Series and 3^n Series orthogonal arrays. The techniques of looking for commonalities between the required linear graph and available standard graphs will still apply. Characteristics such as the dominating factor interacting with many other factors (shape of a wheel with a spoke), several dominating factors tied to a number of other factors (multiple wheels with more than one spoke), and sets of three interrelated factors (triangular shapes) are common among the linear graphs of the larger orthogonal

Figure 9-10 L_{27} (3^{13}) Linear Graphs

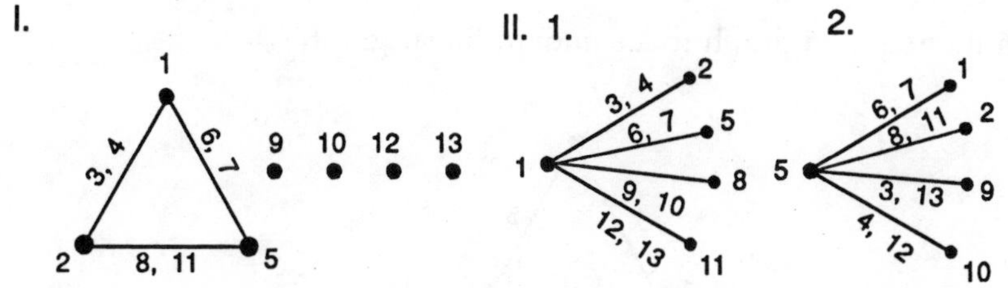

arrays. Recognizing these shapes when they occur within the required linear graph will help guide you in selecting the most appropriate standard linear graph. Understanding which relationships can create these patterns will also aid you in drawing the required linear graph so that it can be more easily matched with a standard graph.

9.4 STANDARD LINEAR GRAPH PROBLEMS

9.4.1 Example Number 1

Two-level factors: A, B, C
Interactions: A × B, B × C, A × C

1. Select the orthogonal array.

A. Calculate the total degrees of freedom required.

Factors: $3 \times (2 - 1) = 3$

Interactions: $3 \times (2 - 1) \times (2 - 1) = 3$

6 df

B. Calculate the degrees of freedom for the most appropriate orthogonal arrays.

$L_4\ (2^3)$: $3 \times (2 - 1) = 3$ df   **$L_8\ (2^7)$: $7 \times (2 - 1) = 7$ df**

C. Select the smallest array that contains the required number of degrees of freedom (boldfaced).

2. Draw the required linear graph.

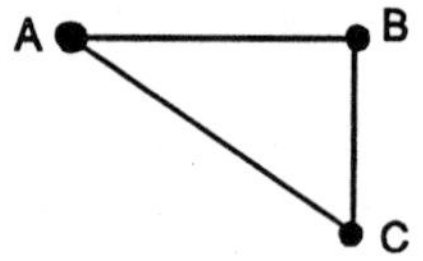

3. Match the required graph to a standard linear graph.

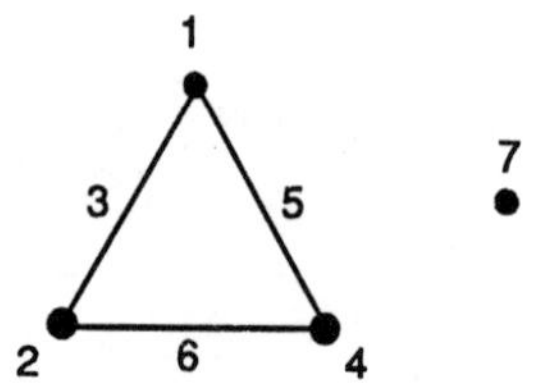

4. Redraw the required linear graph.

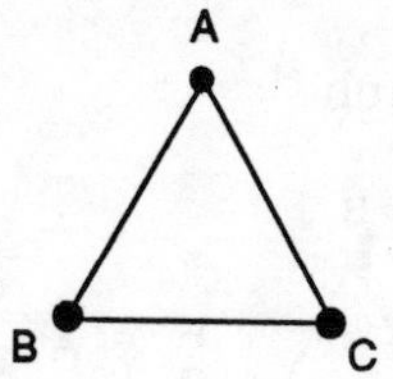

5. Assign factors and interactions.

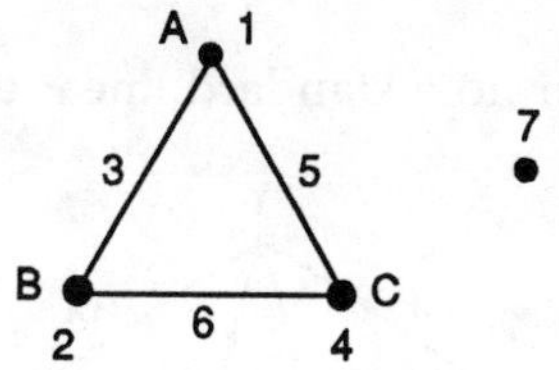

Since column 7 is unassigned, it can be used as a measure of experimental error, or an additional factor can be added to the study without increasing the size of the experiment.

9.4.2 Example Number 2

Two-level factors: A, B, C, D, E, F, G, H
Interactions: B × C, B × D, B × E, C × D, D × E, D × F, E × F

1. Select the orthogonal array.

A. Calculate the total degrees of freedom required.

Factors:	$8 \times (2 - 1)$	$= 8$
Interactions:	$7 \times (2 - 1) \times (2 - 1)$	$= 7$
		15 df

B. Calculate the degrees of freedom for the most appropriate orthogonal arrays.

$$L_4\ (2^3)\text{: } 3 \times (2 - 1) = 3 \text{ df}$$

$$L_8\ (2^7)\text{: } 7 \times (2 - 1) = 7 \text{ df}$$

$$L_{16}\ (2^{15})\text{: } 15 \times (2 - 1) = 15 \text{ df}$$

C. Select the smallest array that contains the required number of degrees of freedom (boldfaced).

2. Draw the required linear graph.

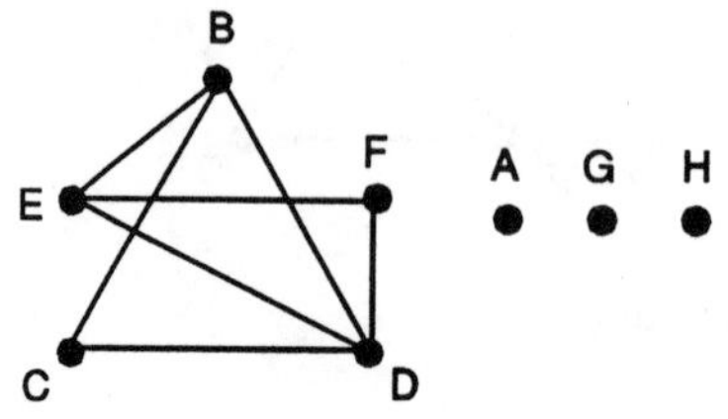

3. Match the required graph to a standard linear graph.

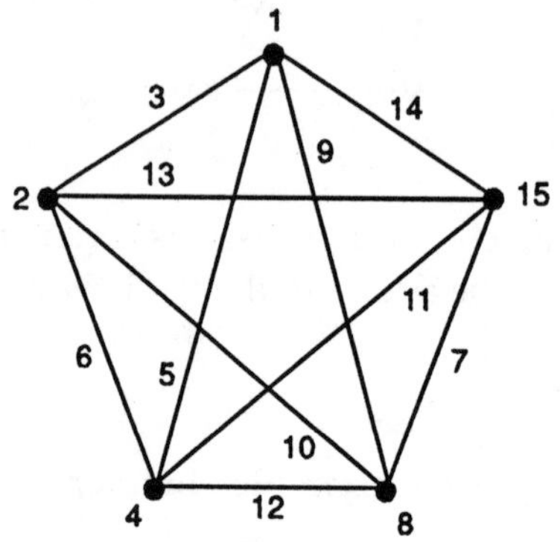

In trying to determine the most suitable linear graph, the best strategy might be to eliminate the obviously inappropriate ones first. Since not all other factors interact with one common factor, Type IV can be eliminated. A pattern of interconnecting factors forming triangles removes Types V and VI from further consideration. This narrows the choices down to three patterns. Since the required linear graph is composed of a series of enclosed triangles, the Type I linear graph appears to be the best alternative among the remaining options.

4. Redraw the required linear graph.

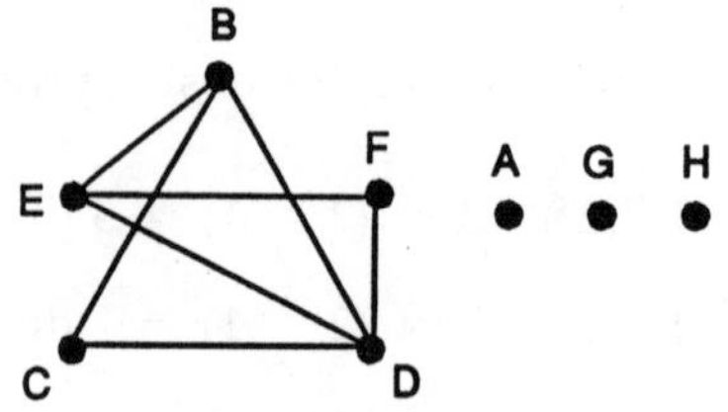

5. Assign factors and interactions.

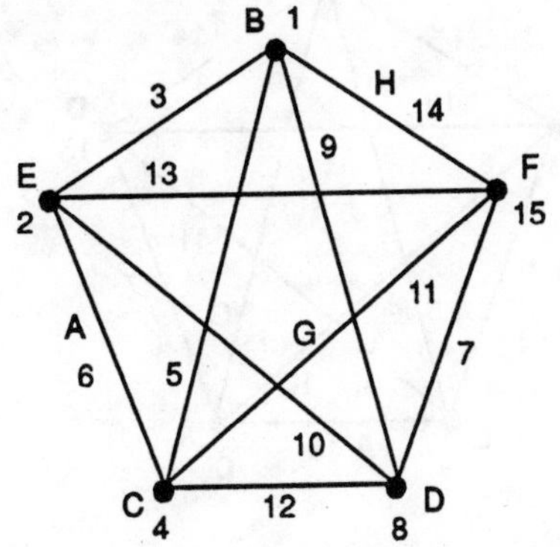

6. Compare alternate mappings for the standard linear graph (if appropriate).

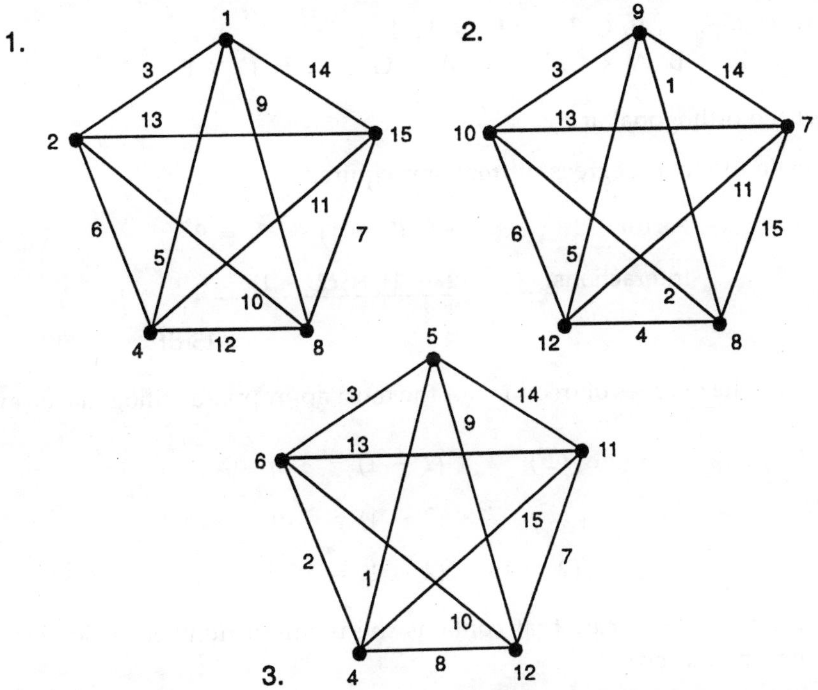

Because the L_{16} (2^{15}) is one of those orthogonal arrays that has optional mapping schemes for each linear graph, you can choose from three different sets of column assignments. Pattern #1 is typically preferred because it provides the most columns to the left for factors (columns 1, 2, and 4), which translates to fewer changes for those expensive-to-switch factor levels. If in the example above, factor F was considerably more difficult to alter than factor B, we could rotate the factors around the pentagon as shown below.

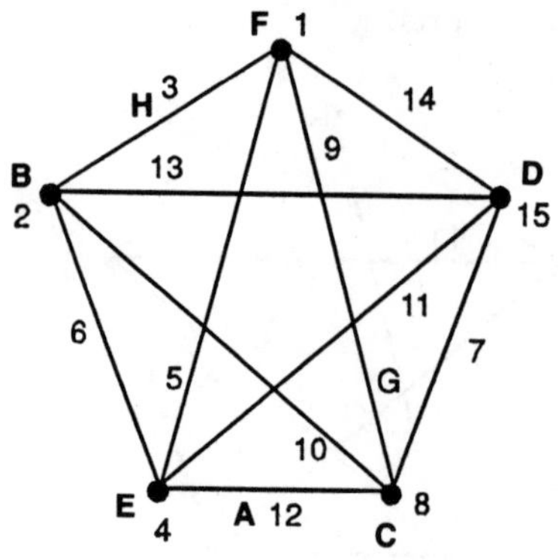

9.4.3 Example Number 3

Two-level factors: A, B, C, D, E, F, G, H, I
Interactions: A × B, A × C, B × C, A × G, D × E, D × F

1. Select the orthogonal array.

A. Calculate the total degrees of freedom required.

Factors:	$9 \times (2-1)$	$= 9$
Interactions:	$6 \times (2-1) \times (2-1)$	$= 6$
		15 df

B. Calculate the degrees of freedom for the most appropriate orthogonal arrays.

$L_4\ (2^3)$: $3 \times (2-1) = 3$ df

$L_8\ (2^7)$: $7 \times (2-1) = 7$ df

$L_{16}\ (2^{15})$: $15 \times (2-1) = 15$ df

C. Select the smallest array that contains the required number of degrees of freedom (boldfaced).

2. Draw the required linear graph.

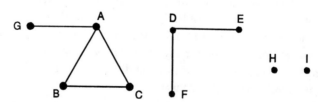

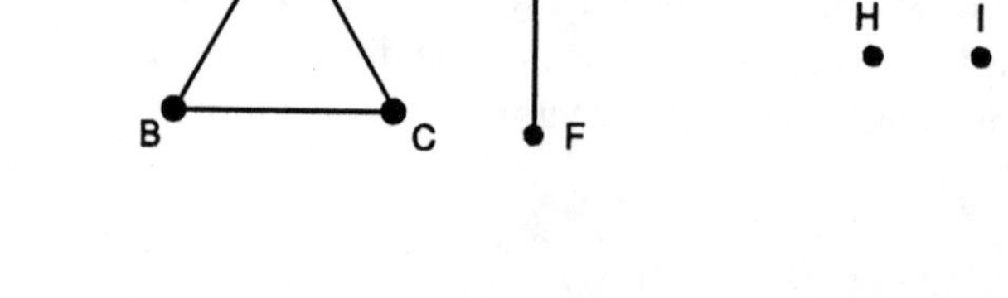

3. Match the required graph to a standard linear graph.

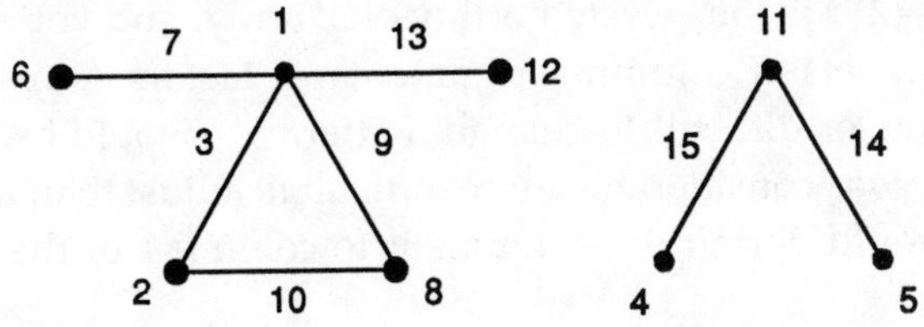

In selecting the most suitable linear graph, we will again eliminate the obviously inappropriate ones first. Because the interactions A × B, A × C, and B × C form a triangle, we can eliminate Graphs IV, V, and VI. Since one and only one triangle is present in the required linear graph, the Type III Graph appears to be the most likely to provide a good match. Although in this example our first inclination was correct, it may not always be true. You may need to try several graphs before finding an appropriate shape. In other instances, there may be more than one, perhaps even several different standard graphs that can match the required linear graph. As a matter of fact, the required linear graph that you would draw for a specific set of factors and interactions might look entirely different from that constructed by someone else, yet both could be correct. Therefore, you may think of drawing linear graphs as more of an art than a science, in that there can be more than one right answer.

4. Redraw the required linear graph.

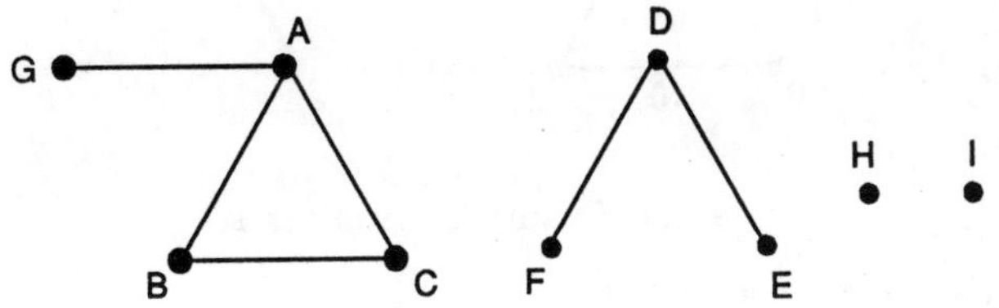

5. Assign factors and interactions.

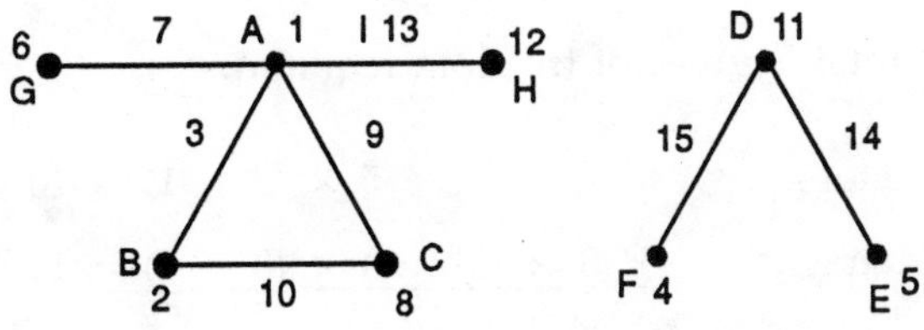

6. Compare alternate mappings for the standard linear graph (if appropriate).

Again the L_{16} (2^{15}) is the selected orthogonal array, and you can choose from three different sets of column assignments. If factors A and B or C are the most expensive or difficult to change, Pattern #1 would be the best choice. If factor E or F was considerably more difficult to adjust than the other factors, Pattern #3 would permit its assignment to column 1 of the array.

1.

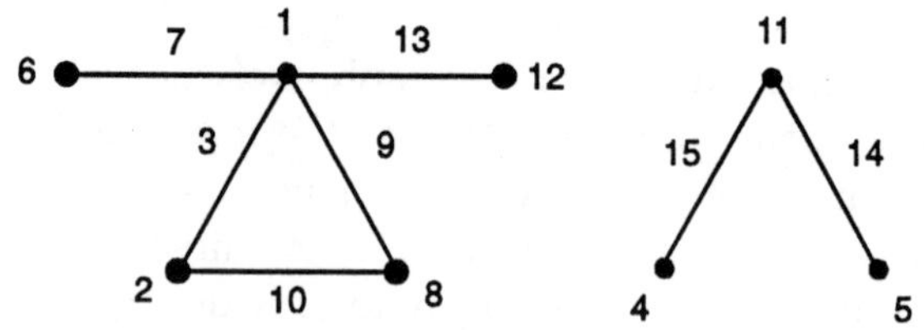

2.

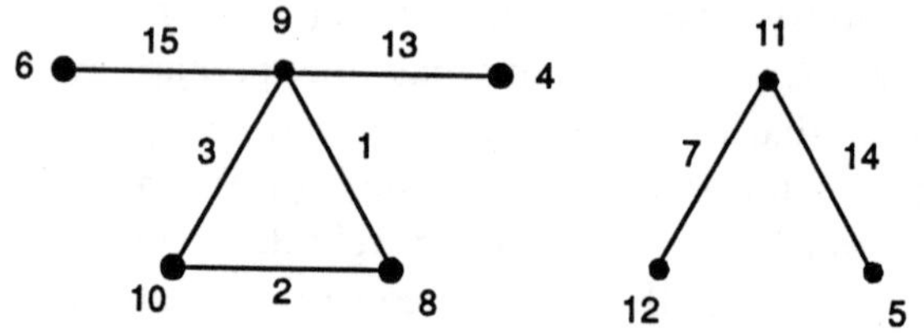

3.

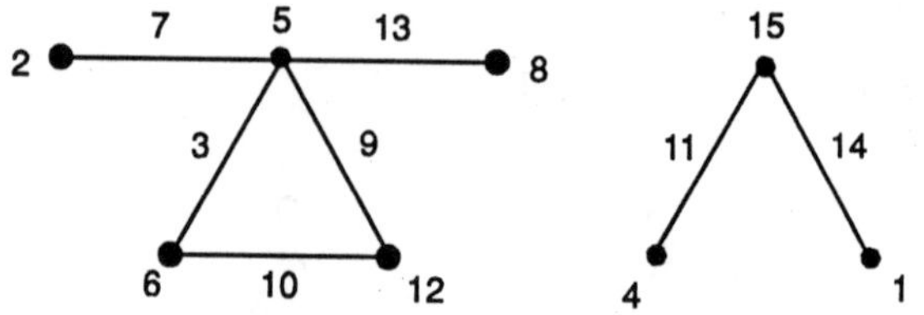

9.4.4 Example Number 4

Three-level factors: A, B, C, D, E
Interactions: A × B, A × C, A × E

1. Select the orthogonal array.

A. Calculate the total degrees of freedom required.

Factors:	$5 \times (3 - 1) = 10$
Interactions:	$3 \times (3 - 1) \times (3 - 1) = 12$
	22 df

B. Calculate the degrees of freedom for the most appropriate orthogonal arrays.

$$L_9\ (3^4):\ 4 \times (3 - 1) = 8 \text{ df}$$

$$L_{27}\ (3^{13}):\ 13 \times (3 - 1) = 26 \text{ df}$$

C. Select the smallest array that contains the required number of degrees of freedom (boldfaced).

2. Draw the required linear graph.

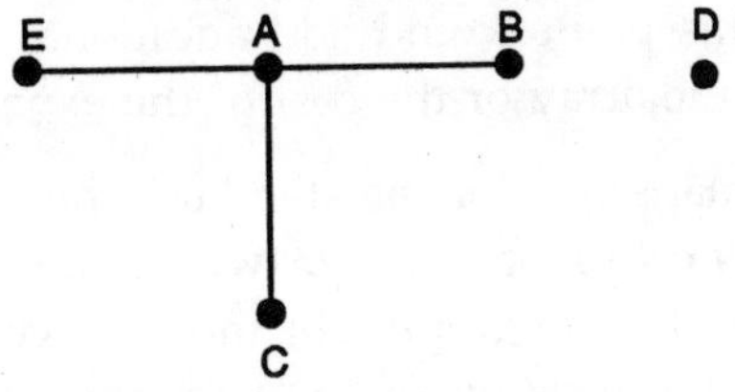

3. Match the required graph to a standard linear graph.

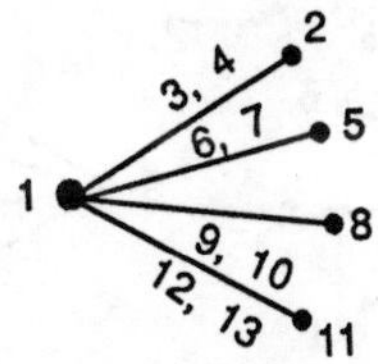

Since there exist three interactions of interest possessing a common factor, the Type II linear graph must be chosen.

4. Redraw the required linear graph.

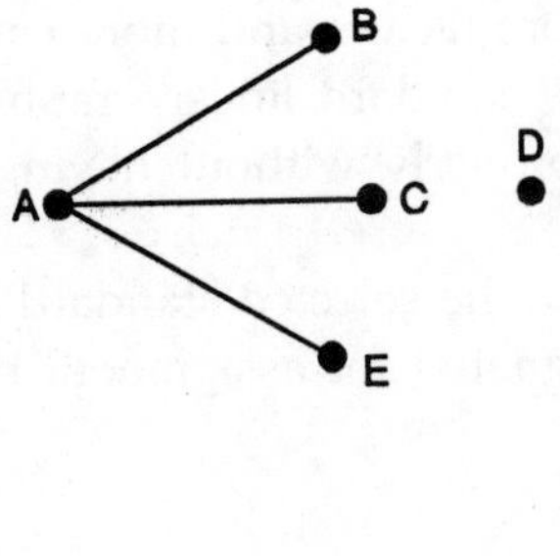

5. Assign factors and interactions.

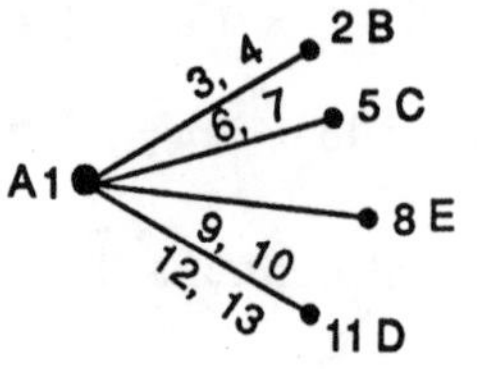

Since columns 12 and 13 are vacant, they could be used to look at the interaction between factor A and factor D. Although not considered potentially important enough to be initially designed into the experiment, adding this interaction at this point would add additional knowledge without increasing the size of the array or the cost of the experiment.

6. Compare alternate mappings for the standard linear graph (if appropriate).

   With the L_{27} (3^{13}) orthogonal array, two separate mapping schemes are available for the Type II linear graph. The most noticeable difference between the two patterns is the location of the common interacting factor. If this common factor is difficult or expensive to change, Pattern #1 (common factor in column 1) should be selected. If one of the other factors is more difficult to adjust (common factor in column 5), Pattern #2 may be preferable.

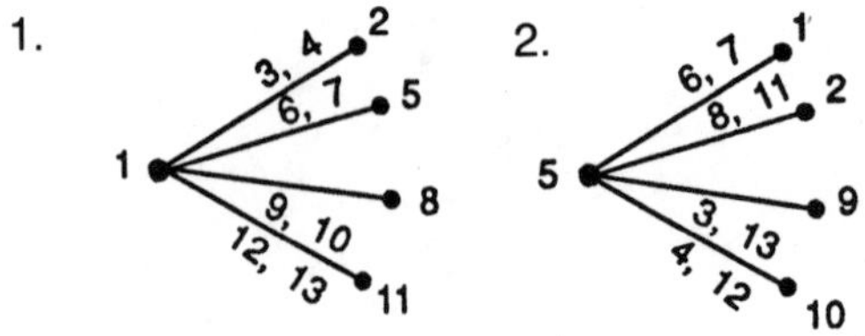

9.5 MODIFYING STANDARD LINEAR GRAPHS

In the examples covered in the previous sections of this chapter, we were always able to match the required linear graph to an available standard graph. However, this match may not always take place. In some special cases, you have to move up to the next larger array. In most situations, particularly involving the L_{16} (2^{15}) and larger arrays with more factors and more complex linear graphs, we can make modifications of the standard linear graph that will allow us to assign factors and interactions properly without having to increase the size of the experimental matrix.

To make the changes to the selected standard linear graph requires remapping of the columns designated for assignment of interactions. Special tables called "Interactions between Two Columns" (Appendix C) have been developed to give the appropriate column for assigning an interaction for every possible combination of factor assignments within the array. This quick reference table can help prevent confusion and simplify the design effort while insuring that the effects of factors and interactions will not be confounded. The resulting effect is to speed up the process of modifying the linear graph and insuring the development of a reproducible experiment.

Let's look at the "Interactions between Two Columns" table in Figure 9-11. The table is triangular in shape, and each column and row represents a column within the orthogonal array that has been assigned a factor. The corresponding column number within the matrix represents the appropriate location to assign the corresponding interaction. For example, factor A is assigned to column 3, and factor B is to be placed in column 9. If we move across row 3 and down column 9 of the table, we will find that column 10 is the proper column to assign the interaction A × B.

In Figure 9-12, we have an interaction table for the L_{27} (3^{13}), which is a 3^n Series array. Within the table, each row and every column consists of two column assignments instead of one. That characteristic relates back to the degrees of freedom required by interactions of three level factors (2 × 2 = 4 df) and the subsequent need for two columns within the orthogonal array. Let's illustrate the use of the table through an example. Factor A is assigned to column 4, and factor B is to be located in column 12. If we move across row 4 and down column 12 of the table, we will find that columns 5 and 10 are the proper columns to assign the interaction A × B.

Figure 9-11 L_{16} (2^{15}) Interactions between Two Columns

	1	2	3	4	5	6	7	8	**9**	10	11	12	13	14	15
	(1)	3	2	5	4	7	6	9	8	11	10	13	12	15	14
		(2)	1	6	7	4	5	10	11	8	9	14	15	12	13
			(3)	7	6	5	4	11	**10**	9	8	15	14	13	12
				(4)	1	2	3	12	13	14	15	8	9	10	11
					(5)	3	2	13	12	15	14	9	8	11	10
						(6)	1	14	15	12	13	10	11	8	9
							(7)	15	14	13	12	11	10	9	8
								(8)	1	2	3	4	5	6	7
									(9)	3	2	5	4	7	6
										(10)	1	6	7	4	5
											(11)	7	6	5	4
												(12)	1	2	3
													(13)	3	2
														(14)	1

Figure 9-12 L_{27} (3^{13}) Interactions between Two Columns

	1	2	3	4	5	6	7	8	9	10	11	12	13
	(1)	3 4	2 4	2 3	6 7	5 7	5 6	9 10	8 10	8 9	12 13	11 13	11 12
		(2)	1 4	1 3	8 11	9 12	10 13	5 11	6 12	7 13	5 8	6 9	7 10
			(3)	1 2	9 13	10 11	8 12	7 12	5 13	6 11	6 10	7 8	5 9
				(4)	10 12	8 13	9 11	6 13	7 11	5 12	7 9	5 10	6 8
					(5)	1 7	1 6	2 11	3 13	4 12	2 8	4 10	3 9
						(6)	1 5	4 13	2 12	3 11	3 10	2 9	4 8
							(7)	3 12	4 11	2 13	4 9	3 8	2 10
								(8)	1 10	1 9	2 5	3 7	4 6
									(9)	1 8	4 7	2 6	3 5
										(10)	3 6	4 5	2 7
											(11)	1 13	1 12
												(12)	1 11

With the additional tool for modifying standard graphs where needed, we can restate the steps for designing the experiment as follows:

1. Select the orthogonal array.

A. Calculate the total degrees of freedom required.

B. Calculate the degrees of freedom for the most appropriate orthogonal arrays.

C. Select the smallest array that contains the required number of degrees of freedom.

2. Draw the required linear graph.

3. Match the required graph to a standard linear graph.

4. Redraw the required linear graph.

5. Assign factors and interactions.
   If all interactions can be properly assigned, go to step 8.

6. Use the appropriate "Interactions between Two Columns" table to designate location(s) for unassigned interaction(s).

7a. If the column is unoccupied, assign the interaction to the column.

7b. If the column is already filled, redraw the required graph so that either one or more factors are assigned to different columns. Return to step 6.[1]

8. Compare alternate mappings based on the original standard linear graph (if appropriate).

I would like to make one additional suggestion at this point. If in the initial assignment of factors and interactions, you are unable to assign more than two of your interactions, you have probably selected an inappropriate linear graph. In that case, it would be best to select another linear graph and perform the assigning of factors and interactions again.

9.6 MODIFIED LINEAR GRAPH PROBLEMS

9.6.1 Example Number 1

Two-level factors: A, B, C, D, E, F, G, H
Interactions: A × B, A × C, A × D, A × E, B × F, B × G, C × F

1. Select the orthogonal array.
A. Calculate the total degrees of freedom required.

Factors:	$8 \times (2 - 1) =$	8
Interactions:	$7 \times (2 - 1) \times (2 - 1) =$	7
		15 df

B. Calculate the degrees of freedom for the most appropriate orthogonal arrays.

$$L_4\ (2^3):\ 3 \times (2 - 1) = 3 \text{ df}$$

$$L_8\ (2^7):\ 7 \times (2 - 1) = 7 \text{ df}$$

$$L_{16}\ (2^{15}):\ 15 \times (2 - 1) = 15 \text{ df}$$

C. Select the smallest array that contains the required number of degrees of freedom (boldfaced).

2. Draw the required linear graph.

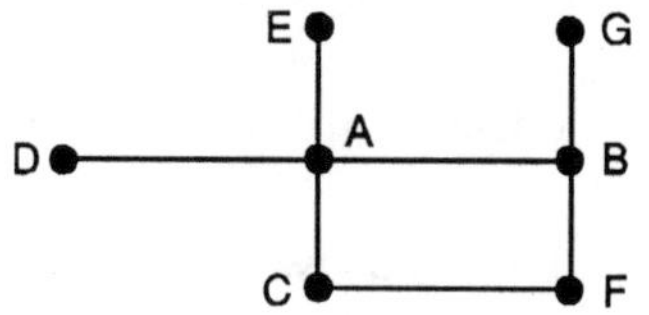

3. Match the required graph to a standard linear graph.

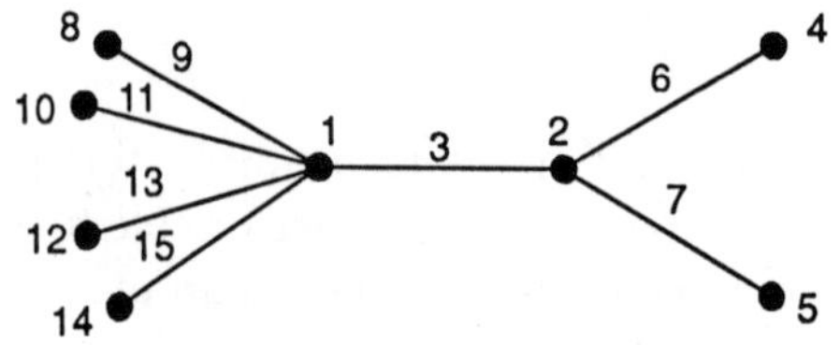

Since no triangular shapes are present, linear graph types I, II, and III appear to be inappropriate. Because the required graph does not have one common factor, Type IV is ruled out. Factors interacting with more than one factor cause Type V to be eliminated. Type VI does not exactly fit, but we must find the standard linear graph that comes the closest to the required graph. In reviewing the choices, Type VI appears to be the closest in appearance.

4. Redraw the required linear graph.

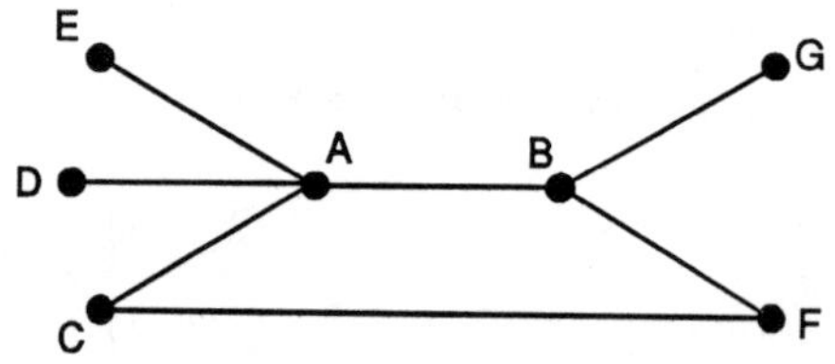

5. Assign factors and interactions.
If all interactions can be properly assigned, go to step 8.

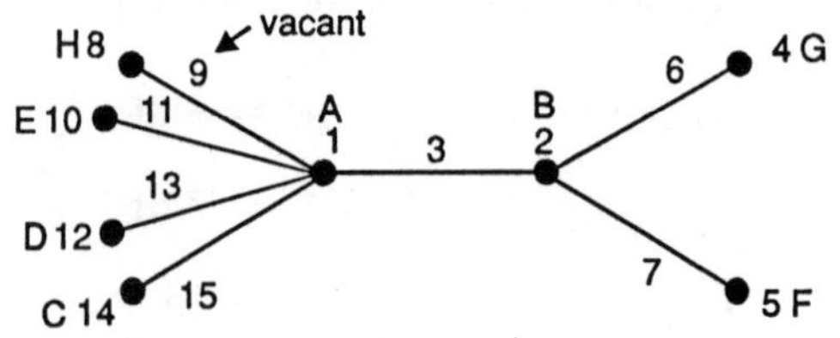

Since one interaction has still not been assigned, we will need to continue to step 6.

6. Use the appropriate "Interactions between Two Columns" table to designate location(s) for unassigned interaction(s).

L_{16} (2^{15}) Interactions between Two Columns

	1	2	3	4	5	6	7	8	9	10	11	**12**	13	**14**	15
	(1)	3	2	5	4	7	6	9	8	11	10	13	12	15	14
		(2)	1	6	7	4	5	10	11	8	9	14	15	12	13
			(3)	7	6	5	4	11	10	9	8	15	14	13	12
				(4)	1	2	3	12	13	14	15	8	9	10	11
					(5)	3	2	13	12	15	14	**9**	8	**11**	10
						(6)	1	14	15	12	13	10	11	8	9
							(7)	15	14	13	12	11	10	9	8
								(8)	1	2	3	4	5	6	7
									(9)	3	2	5	4	7	6
										(10)	1	6	7	4	5
											(11)	7	6	5	4
												(12)	1	2	3
													(13)	3	2
														(14)	1

By going across row 5 and down column 14 in the table, we can determine that column 11 of the orthogonal array is the appropriate location for assigning the interaction C × F.

7a. If the column is unoccupied, assign the interaction to the column.
Since column 11 is already occupied by the interaction A × E, we must go to step 7b.

7b. If the column is already filled, redraw the required graph so that either one or more factors are assigned to different columns. Return to step 6.

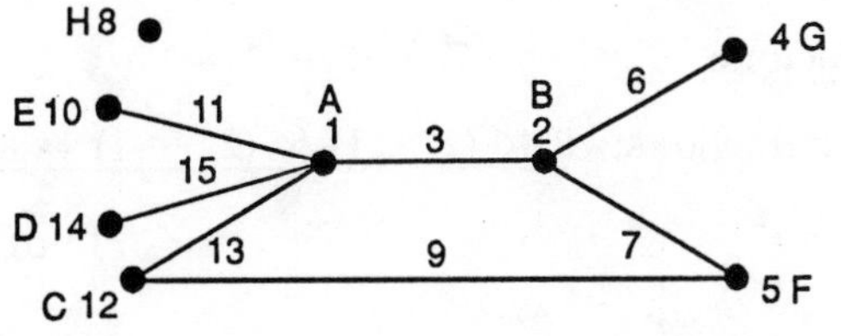

By switching the column assignments for factors C and D, C now moves to column 12. From the interaction table, we observe that the interaction column associated with factors in columns 5 and 12 is column 9, which is vacant.

8. Compare alternate mappings based on the original standard linear graph (if appropriate).

Since the orthogonal array being used is the L_{16} (2^{15}), three mapping patterns are available. Instead of modifying the first pattern, we could have changed either of the other two with similar results. For pattern #2, the interaction C × F would have been assigned to column 1. In pattern #3, the assignment would have been to column 9.

#2

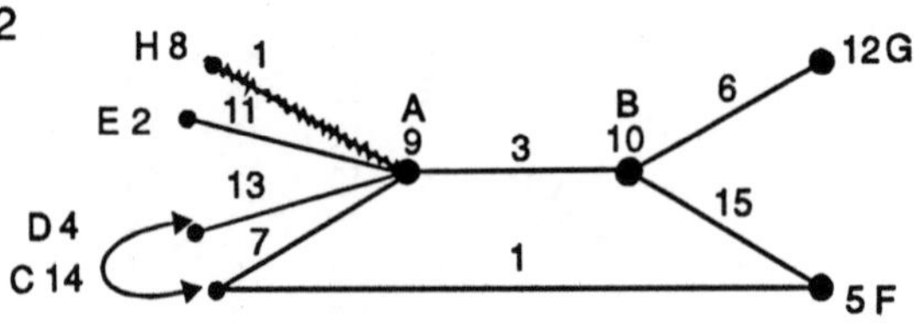

#3

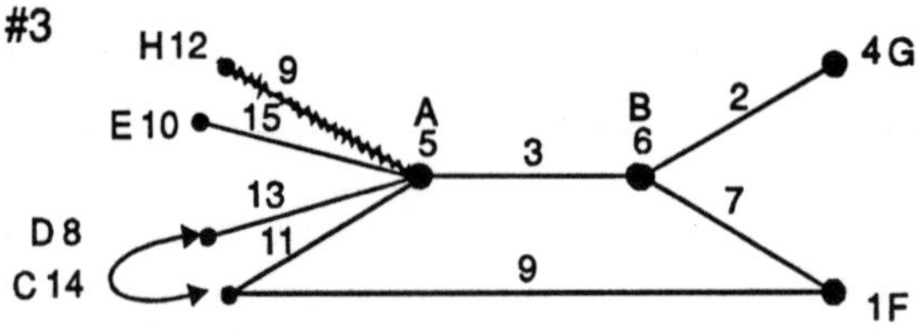

9.6.2 Example Number 2 (Hourglass Problem)

Two-level factors: A, B, C, D, E, F, G
Interactions: A × B, A × C, A × D, A × E, A × F, C × D, D × E, F × G

1. Select the orthogonal array.
A. Calculate the total degrees of freedom required.

Factors:	$7 \times (2 - 1) = 7$
Interactions:	$\underline{8 \times (2 - 1) \times (2 - 1) = 8}$
	15 df

B. Calculate the degrees of freedom for the most appropriate orthogonal arrays.

$$L_4\ (2^3):\ 3 \times (2 - 1) = 3 \text{ df}$$

$$L_8\ (2^7):\ 7 \times (2 - 1) = 7 \text{ df}$$

$$\mathbf{L_{16}\ (2^{15})}:\ 15 \times (2 - 1) = 15 \text{ df}$$

C. Select the smallest array that contains the required number of degrees of freedom (boldfaced).

2. Draw the required linear graph.

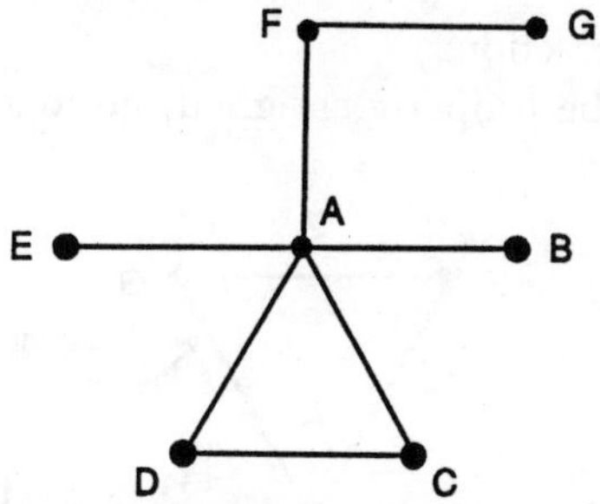

3. Match the required graph to a standard linear graph.

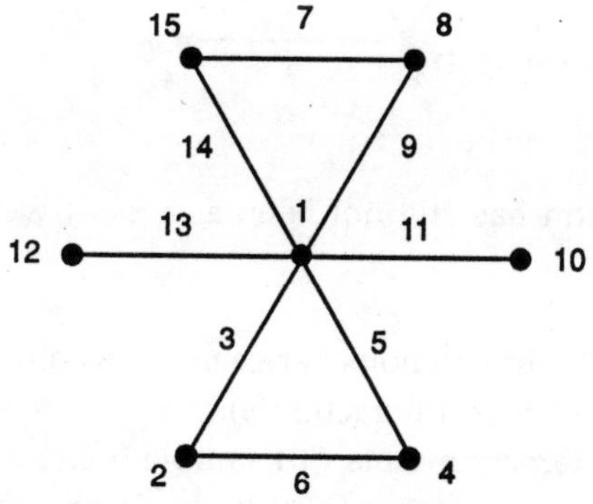

As in the case of the previous example, no standard linear graph makes an exact match. Therefore, we must find the standard linear graph that comes the closest to satisfying our needs. The Type II, or hourglass shape, provides a close likeness to our required graph.

4. Redraw the required linear graph.

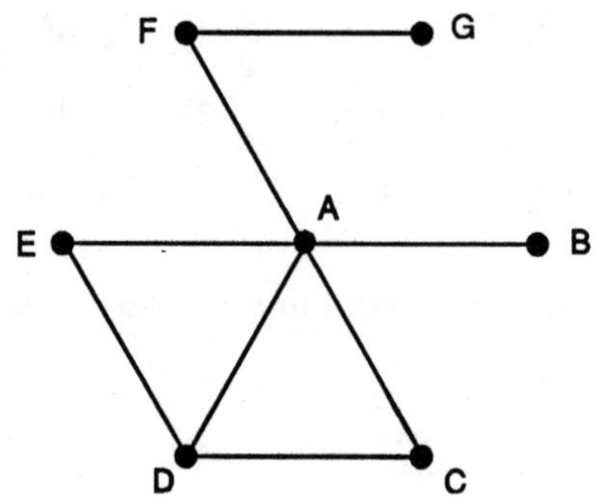

5. Assign factors and interactions.
   If all interactions can be properly assigned, go to step 8.

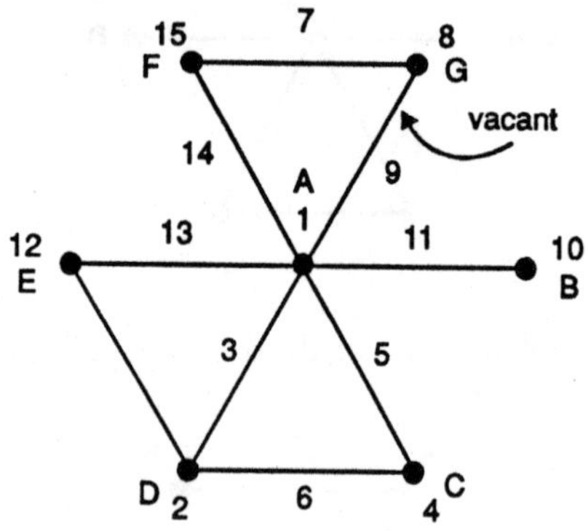

Since one interaction has still not been assigned, we will need to continue to step 6.

6. Use the appropriate "Interactions between Two Columns" table to designate location(s) for unassigned interaction(s).

   Referencing the interaction table in Example 9.6.1, the appropriate column for the interaction between factor D (column 2) and factor E (column 12) is column 14.

7a. If the column is unoccupied, assign the interaction to the column.

   Since column 14 is already occupied by the interaction A × F, we must go to step 7b.

7b. If the column(s) is already filled, redraw the required graph so that either one or more factors are assigned to different columns. Return to step 6.

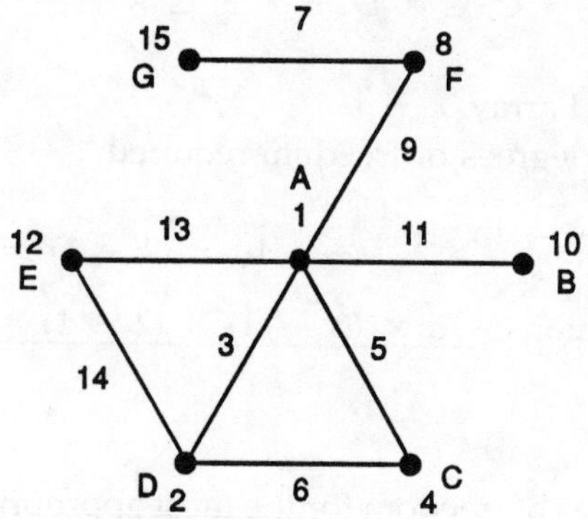

By switching factors F and G, the interaction A × F moves to column 9, and column 14 now becomes vacant. The interaction D × E can now be inserted in column 14.

8. Compare alternate mappings based on the original standard linear graph (if appropriate).

Again, three mapping patterns are available. The interaction D × E would be assigned to column 14 in all three patterns.

#2

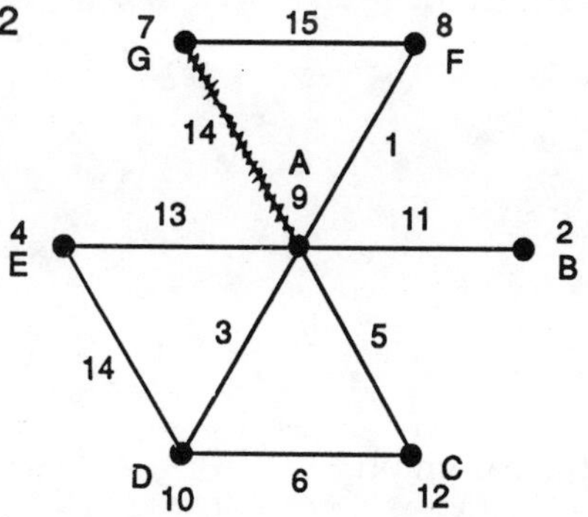

#3

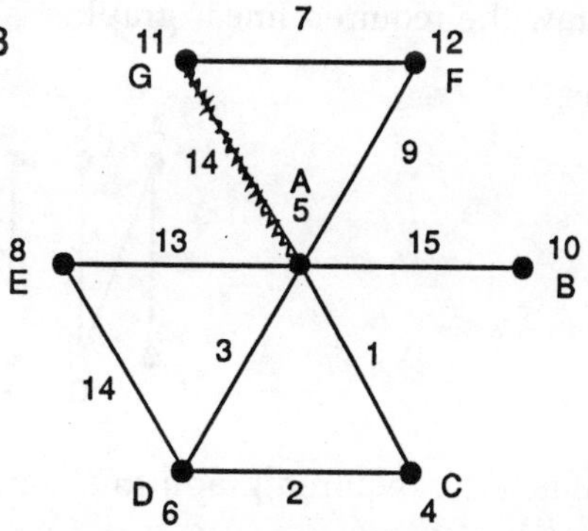

It should also be pointed out that due to the symmetry of the Type II linear graph, this particular graph is very easy to modify. The factors for the upper left and right dots can be switched without posing a problem as well as those assigned to the lower left and right dots and the ones assigned to the far left and far right dots.

9.6.3 Example Number 3 (Parallel Lines)

Two-level factors: A, B, C, D, E, F, G, H, I, J
Interactions: A × B, A × C, C × D, E × F, G × H

1. Select the orthogonal array.
A. Calculate the total degrees of freedom required.

Factors:	$10 \times (2 - 1)$	$= 10$
Interactions:	$5 \times (2 - 1) \times (2 - 1)$	$= 5$
		15 df

B. Calculate the degrees of freedom for the most appropriate orthogonal arrays.

$L_4\ (2^3)$: $3 \times (2 - 1) = 3$ df

$L_8\ (2^7)$: $7 \times (2 - 1) = 7$ df

$L_{16}\ (2^{15})$: $15 \times (2 - 1) = 15$ df

C. Select the smallest array that contains the required number of degrees of freedom (boldfaced).

2. Draw the required linear graph.

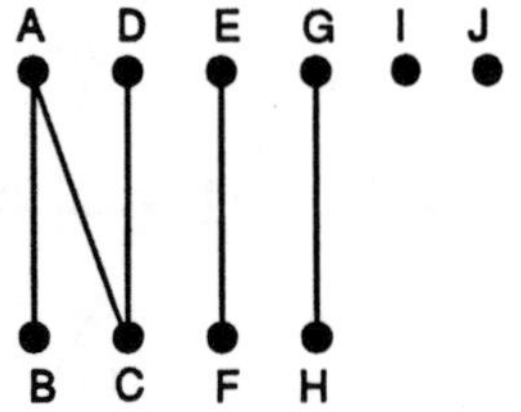

3. Match the required graph to a standard linear graph.

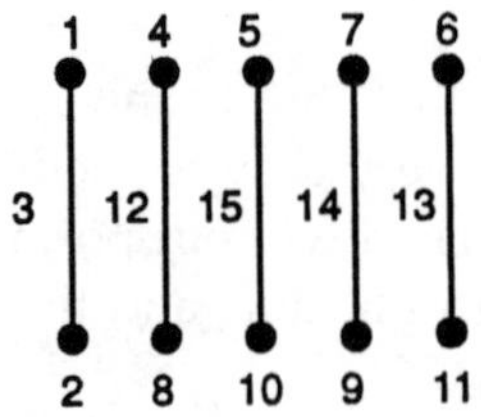

Although not an ideal match with any of the six standard linear graphs, the required linear graph resembles Type V except for the interaction between factors A and C. Based on this similarity, we will choose Type V.

4. Redraw the required linear graph.

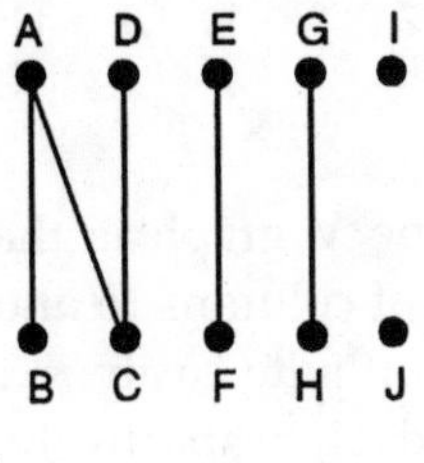

5. Assign factors and interactions.
   If all interactions can be properly assigned, go to step 8.

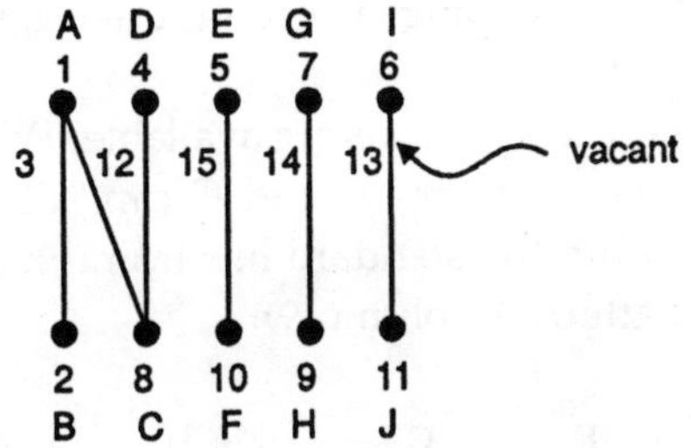

Since the A × C interaction cannot be assigned without modifying the standard linear graph, we will need to continue to step 6.

6. Use the appropriate "Interactions between Two Columns" table to designate location(s) for unassigned interaction(s).
   By referring to the interaction table, the appropriate column for the interaction between factor A (column 1) and factor C (column 8) is column 9.

7a. If the column is unoccupied, assign the interaction to the column.
   Since column 9 is already occupied by factor H, we must go to step 7b.

7b. If the column is already filled, redraw the required graph so that either one or more factors are assigned to different columns. Return to step 6.

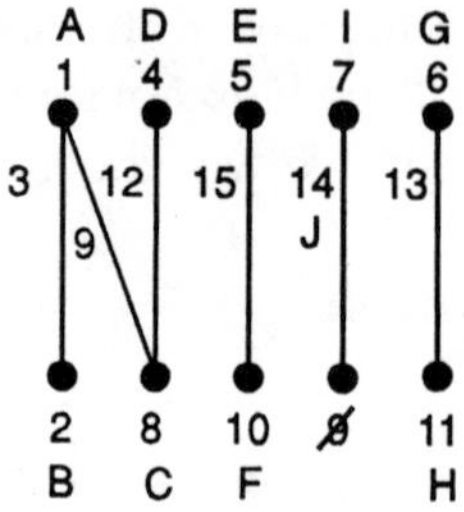

An advantage of using the Type V graph is that it permits the switching of interacting factors from one set of columns to another. Although column 9 was filled in the initial graph, we can quite easily redraw the graph with factors G and H moved to columns 6 and 11, respectively. Then, factors I and J can be switched to columns 7 and 14, accordingly. This leaves column 9 vacant, and it can then be used for assigning the interaction A × C.

8. Compare alternate mappings based on the original standard linear graph (if appropriate).

   Again, three mapping patterns are available. Whichever pattern is preferred, the interaction between factors A and C can still be assigned from the same physical location within the standard linear graph (Pattern 1: column 9, Pattern 2: column 1, and Pattern 3: column 9).

#2

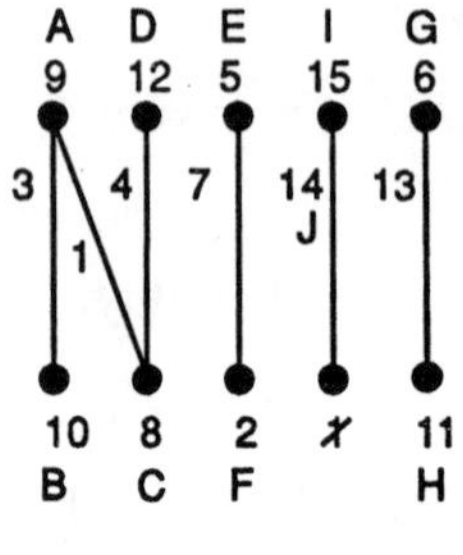

#3

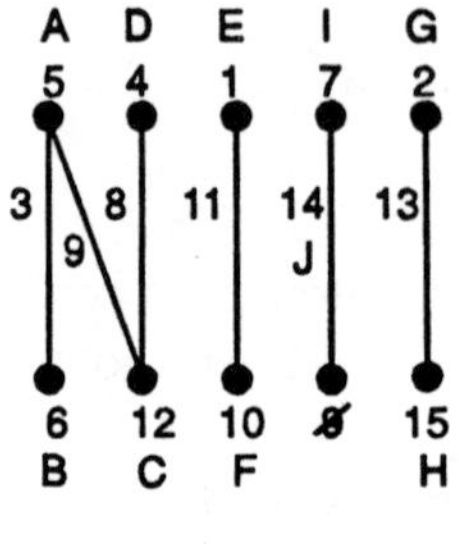

Notes

1. *Introduction to Quality Engineering,* p. 4-42.

Chapter 10

THE OUTER ARRAY

With the selection of the most efficient orthogonal array and the assignment of the control factors and selected interactions, we are nearly ready for the conducting of the experiment. However, we still need a few details to complete the entire experimental matrix. Although we have carefully inserted the control factors and any selected interactions between them into an orthogonal array, we still need to incorporate any noise factors into the design. In the case of a dynamic characteristic, we must also consider the signal factor.

In constructing a matrix for the noise factors, we can follow the same procedures as in selecting an orthogonal array for the control factors, by assigning the factors to columns within the matrix. The orthogonal array containing the control factors is often called the *inner array,* and we can position it to the left side in the experiment structure (Figure 10-1). The array for the noise factors is often referred to as the *outer array* because it is typically placed to the right and above the array containing the control factors. If you will also notice, the control factor settings for a specific experimental run are read across the row of the inner array, whereas the levels for the noise factors are read from the bottom to the top of the column. The turning of the outer array 90° in relation to the inner array permits a unique combination of control and noise factor levels for each experiment data point.

10.1 NO NOISE FACTORS

If we have limited our study to control factors only, the design of an outer array is not necessary. However, we still need to address the issue of how to handle repetitions or replications (if desired) within the design of the experiment. The specific structure will differ depending on whether the quality characteristic is continuously measurable or a classified attribute.

For the continuously measurable characteristic, the design is simply an inner array with sufficient columns for the number of repetitions or replications defined in the planning phase (Figure 10-2). If only a single measurement is to be obtained per experimental run, level average analysis (Chapter 15) will be per-

Figure 10-1 Inner and Outer Arrays

			Noise Factors
		k	• • • •
		•	• • • •
		•	• • • •
Experi-		O	1 • • •
mental	Control Factors & Interactions	N	1 • • •
Run #	A B C • • • i	M	1 • • •
1	1 1 1 • • • • • • • • • • • • • • •		experiment data
2	• • • • • • • • • • • • • • • • • •		
3	• • • • • • • • • • • • • • • • • •		
•	• • • • • • • • • • • • • • • • • •		
•	• • • • • • • • • • • • • • • • • •		
•	• • • • • • • • • • • • • • • • • •		
j	• • • • • • • • • • • • • • • • • •		

formed. For multiple data, the signal-to-noise ratio can be calculated for each experimental run, and the results can be interpreted using the appropriate chapters on S/N ratio analysis (Chapters 17-19).

For the classified attribute experiment, the data column can be divided according to the classifications previously identified in the planning phase of the experiment (Figure 10-3). After performing the experiment, the data can then be analyzed using the techniques spelled out in Chapter 16, "Classified Attribute Analysis."

Figure 10-2 Experimental Matrix: Continuously Measurable Characteristic, No Noise Factors

Experi-mental Run #	A	B	C	D	E	F	G	H	I	J	K	Repetitions 1 2 ... k
1	1	1	1	1	1	1	1	1	1	1	1	experiment data
2	1	1	1	1	1	2	2	2	2	2	2	
3	1	1	2	2	2	1	1	1	2	2	2	
4	1	2	1	2	2	1	2	2	1	1	2	
5	1	2	2	1	2	2	1	2	1	2	1	
6	1	2	2	2	1	2	2	1	2	1	1	
7	2	1	2	2	1	1	2	2	1	2	1	
8	2	1	2	1	2	2	2	1	1	1	2	
9	2	1	1	2	2	2	1	2	2	1	1	
10	2	2	2	1	1	1	1	2	2	1	2	
11	2	2	1	2	1	2	1	1	1	2	2	
12	2	2	1	1	2	1	2	1	2	2	1	

(Column header spanning A–K: Control Factors)

Figure 10-3 Experimental Matrix: Classified Attribute Characteristic

Experi-mental	Control Factors											Classifications		
Run #	A	B	C	D	E	F	G	H	I	J	K	Poor	Fair	Good
1	1	1	1	1	1	1	1	1	1	1	1			
2	1	1	1	1	1	2	2	2	2	2	2			
3	1	1	2	2	2	1	1	1	2	2	2			
4	1	2	1	2	2	1	2	2	1	1	2			
5	1	2	2	1	2	2	1	2	1	2	1			
6	1	2	2	2	1	2	2	1	2	1	1			
7	2	1	2	2	1	1	2	2	1	2	1			
8	2	1	2	1	2	2	2	1	1	1	2			
9	2	1	1	2	2	2	1	2	2	1	1			
10	2	2	2	1	1	1	1	2	2	1	2			
11	2	2	1	2	1	2	1	1	1	2	2			
12	2	2	1	1	2	1	2	1	2	2	1			

10.2 NOISE FACTORS

The insertion of noise factors into the experiment necessitates an outer array. This array may or may not require the selection of an appropriate orthogonal array and the corresponding assignment of noise factors to the columns. Since the purpose of parameter design is to make the process and/or product robust against noise, the aim of the outer array is to reflect the broadest spectrum of potential noise conditions under which the process must operate or the product must function. This effort to duplicate extreme noise conditions only requires us to include the strongest noise factors. This approach is different from the need of the inner array to incorporate any control factors which *may* have a strong effect on the quality characteristic of interest. By emphasizing strong noise factors, the outer array is typically smaller than the inner array. Using the method of compounding noise factors discussed in Section 5.4.2, the outer array can be reduced even further. It would not be rare to see the outer array reduced to two levels (Figure 10-4) representing either one major noise factor or the best combination (noise level 1) and the worst combination (noise level 2) of multiple noise conditions. If we were to identify two noise factors of two levels each instead of the single noise factor, the outer design would expand from two columns to four columns representing every combination of the two factors (Figure 10-5).

Figure 10-4 Parameter Design: One Noise Factor—Two Levels

Experi-mental Run #	Control Factors A	B	C	D	E	F	G	H	Noise Factor Level 1	Level 2
1	1	1	1	1	1	1	1	1		
2	1	1	2	2	2	2	2	2		
3	1	1	3	3	3	3	3	3		
4	1	2	1	1	2	2	3	3		
5	1	2	2	2	3	3	1	1		
6	1	2	3	3	1	1	2	2		
7	1	3	1	2	1	3	2	3		
8	1	3	2	3	2	1	3	1		
9	1	3	3	1	3	2	1	2		
10	2	1	1	3	3	2	2	1		
11	2	1	2	1	1	3	3	2		
12	2	1	3	2	2	1	1	3		
13	2	2	1	2	3	1	3	2		
14	2	2	2	3	1	2	1	3		
15	2	2	3	1	2	3	2	1		
16	2	3	1	3	2	3	1	2		
17	2	3	2	1	3	1	2	3		
18	2	3	3	2	1	2	3	1		

Figure 10-5 Parameter Design: Two Noise Factors—Two Levels

Experi-mental	Control Factors								Noise Factors M_1		M_2	
Run #	A	B	C	D	E	F	G	H	N_1	N_2	N_1	N_2
1	1	1	1	1	1	1	1	1				
2	1	1	2	2	2	2	2	2				
3	1	1	3	3	3	3	3	3				
4	1	2	1	1	2	2	3	3				
5	1	2	2	2	3	3	1	1				
6	1	2	3	3	1	1	2	2				
7	1	3	1	2	1	3	2	3				
8	1	3	2	3	2	1	3	1				
9	1	3	3	1	3	2	1	2				
10	2	1	1	3	3	2	2	1				
11	2	1	2	1	1	3	3	2				
12	2	1	3	2	2	1	1	3				
13	2	2	1	2	3	1	3	2				
14	2	2	2	3	1	2	1	3				
15	2	2	3	1	2	3	2	1				
16	2	3	1	3	2	3	1	2				
17	2	3	2	1	3	1	2	3				
18	2	3	3	2	1	2	3	1				

Although it is easy to get locked into the mind set that two levels are sufficient for all noise factors, two may not be enough to reflect the real environment satisfactorily or to achieve the experiment objectives when a discrete noise factor is involved. For example, let's look at a salad dressing packaging operation. The objective of the experiment is to improve the process so that packaging is consistent and scrap is minimized for all types of dressing produced. Since the type of salad dressing is the one major element that we do not have control over, the outer array will consist of the one factor with sufficient levels to represent each type of dressing produced (Figure 10-6).

Although we have mentioned the term *outer array,* all that we have used to represent noise so far has been all or selected levels of one factor or all combinations of two factors. The purpose is to reflect actual situations and demonstrate options for designing cost effective and meaningful experiments. However, there will frequently be situations when three and even more noise factors need to be incorporated into the experiment. When this situation occurs, the orthogonal array is the most efficient tool for designing the noise factors into the experiment. Since typically we are looking at extremes, the array will most often consist of noise factors with two levels. Therefore, 2^n Series orthogonal arrays are the norm for the outer array, instead of 3^n Series arrays. The orthogonal array used quite frequently for the outer array is the L_4 (2^3). As shown in Figure 10-7, the array is turned so that each combination of noise factor levels or settings reflects a column in the experimental matrix. In simulation studies, however, experimentation logistics may not be as critical and noise factor considerations can be more complex, resulting in much larger outer arrays.

Figure 10-6 One Noise Factor—Multiple Levels

Experimental Run #	Control Factors							Noise Factor—Salad Dressing Types				
	A	B	C	D	E	F	G	French	Italian	Russian	1000 Island	Ranch
1	1	1	1	1	1	1	1	y_{11}	y_{12}	y_{13}	y_{14}	y_{15}
2	1	1	1	2	2	2	2	•••	•••	•••	•••	•••
3	1	2	2	1	1	2	2	•••	•••	•••	•••	•••
4	1	2	2	2	2	1	1	•••	•••	•••	•••	•••
5	2	1	2	1	2	1	2	•••	•••	•••	•••	•••
6	2	1	2	2	1	2	1	•••	•••	•••	•••	•••
7	2	2	1	1	2	2	1	•••	•••	•••	•••	•••
8	2	2	1	2	1	1	2	•••	•••	•••	•••	•••

Figure 10-7 Parameter Design: Three Noise Factors—Two Levels

Experi-mental Run #	Inner Array Control Factors								Outer Array				
									O	1	2	2	1
									N	1	2	1	2
	A	B	C	D	E	F	G	H	M	1	1	2	2
1	1	1	1	1	1	1	1	1					
2	1	1	2	2	2	2	2	2					
3	1	1	3	3	3	3	3	3					
4	1	2	1	1	2	2	3	3					
5	1	2	2	2	3	3	1	1					
6	1	2	3	3	1	1	2	2					
7	1	3	1	2	1	3	2	3					
8	1	3	2	3	2	1	3	1					
9	1	3	3	1	3	2	1	2					
10	2	1	1	3	3	2	2	1					
11	2	1	2	1	1	3	3	2					
12	2	1	3	2	2	1	1	3					
13	2	2	1	2	3	1	3	2					
14	2	2	2	3	1	2	1	3					
15	2	2	3	1	2	3	2	1					
16	2	3	1	3	2	3	1	2					
17	2	3	2	1	3	1	2	3					
18	2	3	3	2	1	2	3	1					

10.3 DYNAMIC CHARACTERISTICS

If the quality characteristic happens to be a dynamic characteristic, the outer array becomes more involved. For each noise factor level (single noise factor) or combination of noise factor settings (multiple noise factors), the experiment is run for each level of the signal factor. For an experiment involving an L_8 (2^7) inner array, an L_4 (2^3) outer array, and a signal factor possessing three levels, the total number of experiment combinations that would need to be performed would be 96 ($8 \times 4 \times 3$).

A straightforward approach to designing an experiment incorporating a signal factor is to set up an appropriate inner array and outer array structure based on the previous section. After setting up the outer array, duplicate the outer array or combination of noise factor levels for each setting of the signal factor. After conducting the experiment and collecting the data, you can perform analysis based on the guidelines in Chapter 20, Analysis: Dynamic Characteristics.

The format for labeling the signal factors settings may vary depending on the nature of the signal factor measurements. In most instances, the signal factor values will reflect true or actual values, and settings can be presented by "M_n" as shown in Figure 10-8. If the range of the signal factor settings for the exper-

Figure 10-8 Dynamic Quality Characteristic
Three Noise Factors—Two Levels
Complete Experiment Design

Experimental Run #	A	B	C	D	E	F	G	H	I	J	K	M_1				M_2				M_3			
P												1	2	2	1	1	2	2	1	1	2	2	1
O												1	2	1	2	1	2	1	2	1	2	1	2
N												1	1	2	2	1	1	2	2	1	1	2	2
1	1	1	1	1	1	1	1	1	1	1	1												
2	1	1	1	1	1	2	2	2	2	2	2												
3	1	1	2	2	2	1	1	1	2	2	2												
4	1	2	1	2	2	1	2	2	1	1	2												
5	1	2	2	1	2	2	1	2	1	2	1												
6	1	2	2	2	1	2	2	1	2	1	1												
7	2	1	2	2	1	1	2	2	1	2	1												
8	2	1	2	1	2	2	2	1	1	1	2												
9	2	1	1	2	2	2	1	2	2	1	1												
10	2	2	2	1	1	1	1	2	2	1	2												
11	2	2	1	2	1	2	1	1	1	2	2												
12	2	2	1	1	2	1	2	1	2	2	1												

(Control Factors: A–K)

Figure 10-9 Dynamic Quality Characteristic, Reference Point Proportional
Two Noise Factors—Two Levels
Complete Experiment Design

Experimental Run #	A	B	C	D	E	F	G	H	I	J	K	$M_1 - M_s$				$M_2 - M_s$				$M_3 - M_s$			
												O_1		O_2		O_1		O_2		O_1		O_2	
												N_1	N_2	N_1	N_2	N_1	N_2	N_1	N_2	N_1	N_2	N_1	N_2
1	1	1	1	1	1	1	1	1	1	1	1												
2	1	1	1	1	1	2	2	2	2	2	2												
3	1	1	2	2	2	1	1	1	2	2	2												
4	1	2	1	2	2	1	2	2	1	1	2												
5	1	2	2	1	2	2	1	2	1	2	1												
6	1	2	2	2	1	2	2	1	2	1	1												
7	2	1	2	2	1	1	2	2	1	2	1												
8	2	1	2	1	2	2	2	1	1	1	2												
9	2	1	1	2	2	2	1	2	2	1	1												
10	2	2	2	1	1	1	1	2	2	1	2												
11	2	2	1	2	1	2	1	1	1	2	2												
12	2	2	1	1	2	1	2	1	2	2	1												

(Control Factors: A–K)

iment is wide, and none of the values is in proximity to zero, the reference point proportional approach would apply[1] (see Chapter 20). When this approach is to be used, the signal factor settings should be modified in the form "$M_n - M_s$" where M_s designates some predetermined reference standard[2] (Figure 10-9). An example would be an experiment determining the accuracy and reliability of a voltmeter where using a given reference point instead of the value of zero would tend to reduce error associated with equipment calibration.

Notes

1. *Quality Engineering: Dynamic Characteristics and Measurement Engineering*, p. 4-3.
2. Ibid., p. 5-6.

Chapter 11

REMOVING EXPERIMENTAL BIAS

In analyzing the data from an experiment, a serious concern can be experimental bias. If extraneous forces induce data to be different from the results that would occur without their interference, faulty conclusions can be derived from the analysis. Funds may be appropriated to measure and control variables that do not have a significant effect upon the quality characteristic of interest. This can certainly be considered a loss to the company since this money could be better spent elsewhere. A more extreme case would exist where the variable is indeed important, but experimental error results in the wrong setting's being selected as optimal. Besides false identification either of significant factors or factor settings, experimental error can be so large that it actually masks the effect of the really significant factors. Thus, an opportunity for gaining process understanding is lost, and a primary element for improving the process is overlooked.

The purpose of this chapter is to address those forces that can cause the types of problems mentioned in the previous paragraph. By identifying the types of extraneous effects that can create experimental bias and obtaining an understanding of the alternate methods of minimizing the effects of these factors, we can minimize their impact and create a more accurate representation of the process being studied. Then, we can detect the truly significant process variables and successfully determine the most effective process settings.

11.1 EXPERIMENTAL ERROR

Bias within an experiment can normally be attributed to two types of experimental error:

1. primary error (e_1)
2. secondary error (e_2).

Primary error is often called "between experiment error", and is the error that can be produced as you change from one experimental run to the next.[1] Variation generated by set-up changes is a typical cause and often a main contributor to primary error. The resulting variation created by these process adjustments between experimental runs may result in excessive, dramatic changes in recorded readings (Figure 11-1). These changes in measurements may be misjudged as significant effects of the factors under study instead of difficulty in realigning the process after changing process settings. Or if the process continues to shift with every new setup, fluctuations can hide any significant changes that result from the factors under study themselves. Another contributor to primary error is the effect of external factors that may not have existed during prior experimental runs but entered the experiment with the next set of process settings. The frequency of occurrence and the magnitude of effect tend to increase as the time lapse between experimental runs lengthens.

One use of primary error is in determining the significance of the factors under study. Let's say that a column in the orthogonal array is unfilled. Either we did not have as many factors to study as columns within the orthogonal array were available, or we did not feel a need to use that column or columns to study a specific interaction. In this case, the column or columns can be used as a measure of experimental error. The differences among the average results for each of the error levels can then be used as a reference for determining the significance of the effects assigned to the other columns.

In Figure 11-2, the average result is calculated for each level setting of each factor and transposed to a response table for making relative comparisons. For the error column, the measurements associated with level 1 are totaled and averaged, and the same is performed for those values associated with level 2. The difference between levels 1 and 2 for the error column indicates the amount of "between experiment error." Since the difference in average values between levels for factors B, C, and E is less than that attributed to primary error, we

Figure 11-1 Primary Error

Experimental Runs	1	2	3	4	
1	15.2	20.6	18.9	16.4 }	
2	15.6	14.5	20.2	17.5 }	
3	17.5	18.5	20.5	17.0 }	
4	20.5	22.0	24.0	23.5 }	e_1
5	17.5	18.0	18.5	18.2 }	
6	22.1	22.5	24.0	23.0 }	
7	21.5	21.5	22.4	23.0 }	
8	15.4	16.5	16.0	16.5 }	

Figure 11-2 Determining Significance with Primary Error

Response Table

Level	A	B	C	D	E	F	e
				Factors			
1	23.5	24.0	23.4	22.8	24.6	27.2	23.8
2	25.5	25.0	25.6	26.2	24.4	21.8	25.2
	2.0	1.0	**2.2**	**3.4**	0.2	**5.4**	**1.4**

can judge that these factors are not significant. More sophisticated techniques using analysis of variance (ANOVA) can provide a more quantifiable analysis, but the conclusions should remain the same.

Secondary error is often referred to as "within experiment error." Variability associated with sampling and measurement error are the most common contributors.[2] If secondary error is excessive, individual readings can distort the understanding of the real impact of specific factor level combinations (Figure 11-3). Errant readings can throw off the analysis and make specific factor settings appear better or worse than they really are. If secondary error exists throughout the sampling or measuring of data, large differences may result unnaturally between measurements, which may tend to make the effects of any significant factors appear relatively minor and hence unnoticed. Instead of leading to misinterpretation of which factors are significant and which factor settings are optimal, secondary error in this latter case is more likely to make significant factors appear unimportant.

An effective step to minimize the effect of within experiment error is to evaluate the measurement process prior to conducting the experiment and to insure that sampling procedures are understood. If the accuracy or precision of the measurement device is suspect, the ability of the equipment to perform as

Figure 11-3 Secondary Error

Experimental Runs	1	2	3	4
1	15.2	20.6	18.9	16.4
2	15.6	14.5	20.2	17.5
3	17.5	18.5	20.5	17.0
4	20.5	22.0	24.0	23.5
5	17.5	18.0	18.5	18.2
6	22.1	22.5	24.0	23.0
7	21.5	21.5	22.4	23.0
8	15.4	16.5	16.0	16.5

e_2

required should be addressed prior to conducting the experiment. As covered in Chapter 4, a repeatability study of the measuring instrument may be necessary. To prevent error attributed to sampling, procedures should be well defined and fully documented so that everyone understands them.

11.2 RANDOMIZATION

Randomization is the mixing or shuffling of the order in which events occur so that each event has an equal chance of being selected or happening next. Within the context of experimentation, randomization can mean the sequence in which experimental runs are conducted, samples are made, or measurements are taken. The purpose of randomization during experimentation is twofold:

1. to guard against systematic bias that could be caused through the creation and collection of the data;
2. to reduce the effect of irrelevant factors and other influences not being considered within the scope of the experiment.

The application of randomization can be appropriate anywhere within an experiment where there is a potential for bias. The sequence in which experimental runs are conducted can lead to bias being induced into the experimental data if not properly planned for. Let's say that the material supplier is a factor within the experiment and that as part of the experiment we are comparing Vendor A and Vendor B along with other process factors under consideration. Half of the experiment with Vendor A supplying the raw material is conducted on Monday. The second half using material from Vendor B is performed on Friday. If the results were better on Friday, does this support the premise that Vendor B supplies better material? Or were extraneous conditions not considered within the experiment more favorable for producing good product on Friday than on Monday? If the series of experimental runs had been randomized so that materials from both suppliers were used on both days, the issue could have been avoided altogether. If the analysis supported Vendor B as the superior supplier, there would have been no question concerning the validity of the data.

Preparation of test samples is another area where randomization should be considered. By randomizing the numbering or labeling of the samples, we can deter the influence of any presupposed notions by the test analyst or assayer as to which experimental conditions should produce the best or worst results. Since the person performing the tests or reading the results cannot tell which samples go with which experimental conditions, his or her overt or subconscious bias cannot be injected into the results.

Testing may be another area in which randomization is appropriate. Variability that exists within test equipment can affect the experiment results. Perhaps the variability becomes more pronounced as more experimental units are tested. There may also be time-related influences that cause test readings to be artificially high or low as these effects become stronger. If any of these conditions can occur, then test bias is a possibility, and randomization of the testing of units should be seriously considered.

The taking of measurements is another area open to operator bias. As the operator proceeds with the measurements, fatigue may set in. If a set of calipers is the measuring tool, perhaps the operator presses the ends of the calipers harder against the surfaces of edges of the units being measured as he or she goes from one unit to the next. If this happens, the later readings may tend to have higher readings than the first. If the units produced in the experiment are not randomized, the factor settings employed for the earlier tested units may appear to produce shorter pieces than the settings used in the production of the latter units, a conclusion that may not be the case.

Inspection that requires the interpretation of what is good or bad and the classification of the units produced into classes such as varying degrees of badness can result in significant operator bias. If the operator has a preconceived notion that certain process settings give worse results than others, he or she may be more critical regarding what is acceptable when inspecting these units. Conversely, units manufactured under assumed ideal conditions may be checked more leniently. Therefore, when determination of good, bad, and degrees of badness is required, inspection should be so arranged that the inspector does not know which units were produced by which settings. Another consideration of attribute inspection is fatigue. If the eyes begin to tire, perhaps the inspector begins to miss defects or downgrade the relative levels of badness. In other cases, maybe the inspector begins to become overly critical. Thus, judgment on the last units is not consistent with that of the earlier ones. In either case, randomization of units should be utilized to minimize inspector bias.

Various methods, both sophisticated and simple, have been used to randomize the order of selecting samples or determining the occurrence of specific actions. Shuffling numbered cards and drawing numbers out of a hat or a well-shaken bag are examples of simple techniques for performing randomization. Many reference books have random number tables that can be used to randomize a group of units. Many computers and calculators have random number-generating capability as well. Any of these techniques can serve the purpose.

On the other hand, be leery of systematic methods of ordering units; they can unintentionally induce bias. For example, closing your eyes and pulling a unit out of a box may appear random when in fact it is not. Since the length of your arm is constant, you will always select units within the same radius from the center of your body first. Samples farther away will be selected last. And if you continue to replace the units selected in the box with the latest units built, these too will in all likelihood be chosen before the older units. Thus parts built with the initial factor settings will tend to be inspected or tested together at the end while those later units will tend to be grouped and checked first.

As stated previously, one of the purposes of randomization is to reduce the effect of influences not being considered within the scope of the experiment, including factors that are not controllable. In classical experimentation, this goal is critical. Within the framework of Taguchi methodology, factors that either cannot or will not be controlled are called noise factors. These considerations can be grouped into the outer array of the experiment design. The experiment is then performed for the purpose of selecting the best control factor settings at which the process is robust against the effect of these noise factors. If extraneous noise factors can cause different results from one day to another, these effects can be collectively represented in the outer array by day of the week. Reflecting back on the previous example in this section, let's say that level one is Monday and level two is Friday. Each combination of control factor settings within the inner array is run on Monday and again on Friday. This means that the raw material used on both days is evenly divided between Vendor A and Vendor B. If Vendor B appears to be the best source, it is because the results with Vendor B material were consistently better from Monday to Friday, not because of superior conditions when it was used. By using the outer array approach, not only is the process optimized while considering uncontrollable influences, but randomization is no longer necessary. Because of this technique of including extraneous forces in the outer array, randomization is not nearly as important in parameter designed experiments as it is in the classical approaches. As long as each of these outside influences is considered within the design of the experiment, randomization of the experimental runs is not critical for minimizing potential experimental bias.

11.3 REPETITION

Repetition is the type of randomization in which groups of data are mixed so that each group of data has an equal chance of being selected. When a group is selected, each unit or data point within that group is automatically selected as part of that group.

For example, 10 boxes containing 20 parts each are randomized using repetition. Each box has an equal chance of being selected. When a container is chosen, the 20 parts within the carton are examined one after the other. After checking all 20 pieces, a new box is selected.

Experimental runs can be randomized using repetition as well. Let's look at an L_8 orthogonal array with five repetitions. Five units will be produced or five measurements taken for each experimental run (each unique combination of factors being studied). The order of experimental runs is randomly determined. When a specific run is selected, the appropriate factor levels are set, and five units are built or five samples taken. Then another experimental run is selected, and the next set of five is generated.

As illustrated by the example in Figure 11-4, randomization can be applied wherever there exist logical groupings of data. The sampling and/or testing of batches of samples and sets of assembled units can be treated in this manner. Once the experimental runs have been completed, repetition can again be used to randomize sampling, inspection, and testing to prevent bias between the data from one experimental run and another. Although the advantages of repetition in randomizing experimental runs may be more obvious, the techniques can also be used to reduce error when it is appropriate to sample or test units in groups.

When used in conducting an experiment, repetition is effective in reducing experimental error while minimizing the number of required setup changes. However, excessive variation between experimental runs, caused by setup changes, can result in misleading data and erroneous analysis. Therefore, you should have a good feel for the effects of setup changes prior to using repetition. An initial repeatability study may be worthwhile.

An additional benefit of repetitions is the ability to calculate both the primary (e_1—between experiment) error and the secondary (e_2—within experiment) error. The calculations for the two types of error will not be explained within this text. However, we feel that it is pertinent to point out this capability since so many Taguchi software packages can automatically calculate both.

Figure 11-4 L_8 Experiment: Repetition

Experimental Run	Factors A	B	C	D	E	F	G	Measurements				
1	1	1	1	1	1	1	1	y_{11}	y_{12}	y_{13}	y_{14}	y_{15}
2	1	1	1	2	2	2	2	y_{21}	y_{22}	y_{23}	y_{24}	y_{25}
3	1	2	2	1	1	2	2	y_{31}	y_{32}	y_{33}	y_{34}	y_{35}
4	1	2	2	2	2	1	1	y_{41}	y_{42}	y_{43}	y_{44}	y_{45}
5	2	1	2	1	2	1	2	y_{51}	y_{52}	y_{53}	y_{54}	y_{55}
6	2	1	2	2	1	2	1	y_{61}	y_{62}	y_{63}	y_{64}	y_{65}
7	2	2	1	1	2	2	1	y_{71}	y_{72}	y_{73}	y_{74}	y_{75}
8	2	2	1	2	1	1	2	y_{81}	y_{82}	y_{83}	y_{84}	y_{85}

Randomized Order by Repetition

y_{21}	y_{22}	y_{23}	y_{24}	y_{25}
y_{11}	y_{12}	y_{13}	y_{14}	y_{15}
y_{51}	y_{52}	y_{53}	y_{54}	y_{55}
y_{71}	y_{72}	y_{73}	y_{74}	y_{75}
y_{31}	y_{32}	y_{33}	y_{34}	y_{35}
y_{81}	y_{82}	y_{83}	y_{84}	y_{85}
y_{41}	y_{42}	y_{43}	y_{44}	y_{45}
y_{61}	y_{62}	y_{63}	y_{64}	y_{65}

11.4 REPLICATION

Replication is the type of randomization in which all observations or pieces of data are mixed so that every individual unit has an equal chance of being chosen. Each data point, regardless of the specific grouping from which it comes, has the same probability of selection.

For example, 10 boxes containing 20 parts each are randomized using replication. All 200 components have an equal chance of being selected. When a specific piece is picked, only that one unit is examined. Then the next component is randomly selected. Since all parts have an equal chance of being selected, the next unit may come either from the same box or a different carton.

Experimental runs may be randomized using replication as well. Let's look at the L_8 orthogonal array used as an illustration in Section 11.3 and reshown in Figure 11-5. The experiment consists of 8 experimental runs that are repeated 5 times each. All 40 measurements are randomized. When a specific experimental run (combination of factor settings) is selected, the factor levels associated with that particular run are set, and one unit is built or one sample is taken, depending on which is appropriate. Then another run is randomly chosen, and the next unit or sample is generated. This next unit may require a change in experimental run settings. The sample within the same experimental run may also be chosen consecutively with the luck of the draw.

By observing in Figure 11-5 the total number of experiment setup changes, we see that replication can result in a substantial increase in the time to conduct

Figure 11-5 L_8 Experiment Replication

Experimental Run	Factors A	B	C	D	E	F	G	Measurements				
1	1	1	1	1	1	1	1	y_{11}	y_{12}	y_{13}	y_{14}	y_{15}
2	1	1	1	2	2	2	2	y_{21}	y_{22}	y_{23}	y_{24}	y_{25}
3	1	2	2	1	1	2	2	y_{31}	y_{32}	y_{33}	y_{34}	y_{35}
4	1	2	2	2	2	1	1	y_{41}	y_{42}	y_{43}	y_{44}	y_{45}
5	2	1	2	1	2	1	2	y_{51}	y_{52}	y_{53}	y_{54}	y_{55}
6	2	1	2	2	1	2	1	y_{61}	y_{62}	y_{63}	y_{64}	y_{65}
7	2	2	1	1	2	2	1	y_{71}	y_{72}	y_{73}	y_{74}	y_{75}
8	2	2	1	2	1	1	2	y_{81}	y_{82}	y_{83}	y_{84}	y_{85}

Randomized Order by Replication

y_{81}	y_{21}	y_{11}	y_{22}	y_{41}
y_{23}	y_{51}	y_{12}	y_{31}	y_{61}
y_{32}	y_{33}	y_{13}	y_{52}	y_{71}
y_{14}	y_{82}	y_{62}	y_{24}	y_{72}
y_{53}	y_{54}	y_{63}	y_{73}	y_{42}
y_{15}	y_{83}	y_{64}	y_{43}	y_{34}
y_{84}	y_{65}	y_{44}	y_{45}	y_{25}
y_{55}	y_{74}	y_{85}	y_{75}	y_{35}

an experiment. If specific factors are difficult to change, the increased time requirements not only can increase the labor costs, but can create scheduling problems as well. This may force the experiment to be performed in segments, which could induce outside factors to contaminate the experiment results and affect the analysis. If the increase in time requirements becomes excessive, the ability to schedule the experiment may be jeopardized altogether. Also, if some factor levels are defined in terms of types of material or by supplier, the cost of changing from one material or supplier to another may induce additional expenses. If the material is expensive, replication may lead to exorbitant material costs. On the other side, replication completely randomizes the experiment, protecting against bias from both between experiment and within experiment error. Any error associated with setup changes will be more or less evenly distributed between the various data points. The critical issue is whether the cost of replication in terms of time and money justifies its use.

Besides its use in determining the sequence of experimental runs, replication can also be used in setting up a sampling plan or the order of the units to be inspected or tested. Unlike the additional costs associated with replicating experimental runs, the cost of randomizing the samples with replication is usually quite small. Typically, the only cost effect of replication is the increase in time to identify the order of the units for testing or inspection. The advantage of replication is that testing or inspector bias is more effectively treated. If repetition is used, the inspector might unconsciously insure that all repeats of the same experimental run obtain the same or similar evaluations. If the test equipment accuracy changes slowly, measurement error might be small between units within an experimental run, but artificially greater between units of different experimental runs. Replication serves to safeguard against these types of error.

11.5 RANDOMIZATION GUIDELINES

Classical experimentation purists tend to recommend complete randomization of the experimental runs. In the opposite corner, Taguchi fundamentalists may cite the incorporation of noise factors into the experiment will supersede the need for randomization. Although both have valid arguments from their perspectives, a middle ground based on cost and practical considerations should provide the guidelines for determining the use of randomization. Instead of full randomization, partial randomization may provide a compromise for minimizing experimental bias while preventing excessive costs and logistical problems.

The following is a list of considerations for what type of randomization to use and how to apply it to your particular experiment:

Are noise factors incorporated within the experiment?

What is the cost associated with changing factor levels?

What is the setup time between experimental runs?

Is setup error potentially large?

Is the quality characteristic continuously measurable or discrete in nature?

Is inspector bias a possible factor?

If the experimental design incorporates noise factors which include extraneous influences, randomization is not critical. Within the context of parameter design, optimal control factor settings will be derived based on the ability to build consistently good and reliable products that are robust against these external forces. Therefore, it is essential within the planning and design of the experiment to consider the potential effects of these noises. If properly considered, randomization need be utilized only where costs and total experiment time will not be substantially increased.

If full randomization is not considered a workable approach, strategic assignment of factors to appropriate columns in the orthogonal array may provide a feasible alternative. The levels within an orthogonal array change less frequently in the leftmost columns than in those to the right. Therefore, those factors that are the most difficult or expensive to change can be assigned to the leftmost columns of the orthogonal array. The factors that are easier to manipulate are assigned to the columns to the right. As noted in the standard L_{16} orthogonal array in Figure 11-6, column 1 requires that the factor assigned to it be changed only once. Columns 2 and 3 require only three and two changes, respectively. However, the columns to the right require more. Column 8 requires a change in level for each change in experimental runs for a total of 15 changes. Therefore, if you were to run a straight experiment with no randomization, the hardest-to-change factor should be assigned to column 1. The next two most difficult could be fitted to columns 2 and 3. The easier-to-change factors could be placed in the remaining columns. Setup time and expense is controlled, and the more flexible factors are changed from one experimental run to another, treating at least a portion of the potential bias.

Up to this point, we have only discussed randomization with regard to control factors. What about noise factors? By definition, we have described noise factors as factors that are difficult to control. Since cost and feasibility are considerations for randomization decisions, the rule of thumb is to run all of the combinations of control factors for one combination of noise factor settings and then proceed to another. Depending on the ability to control noise factor settings in the short term, the noise factor combinations may be randomized or you may have to run at these settings as they are available. This situation is particularly true if one of the noises is related to weather such as room temperature or humidity.

Figure 11-6 L_{16} Orthogonal Array: Column Level Changes

Experimental Run	$L_{16}(2^{15})$														
	1	2	3	4	5	6	7	8	9	10	11	12	13	14	15
1	1	1	1	1	1	1	1	1	1	1	1	1	1	1	1
2	1	1	1	1	1	1	1	**2**	2	2	2	2	2	2	2
3	1	1	1	2	2	2	2	1	1	1	1	2	2	2	2
4	1	1	1	2	2	2	2	**2**	2	2	2	1	1	1	1
5	1	**2**	**2**	1	1	2	2	1	1	2	2	1	1	2	2
6	1	**2**	**2**	1	1	2	2	**2**	2	1	1	2	2	1	1
7	1	**2**	**2**	2	2	1	1	1	1	2	2	2	2	1	1
8	1	**2**	**2**	2	2	1	1	**2**	2	1	1	1	1	2	2
9	**2**	1	**2**	1	2	1	2	1	2	1	2	1	2	1	2
10	**2**	1	**2**	1	2	1	2	**2**	1	2	1	2	1	2	1
11	**2**	1	**2**	2	1	2	1	1	2	1	2	2	1	2	1
12	**2**	1	**2**	2	1	2	1	**2**	1	2	1	1	2	1	2
13	**2**	**2**	1	1	2	2	1	1	2	2	1	1	2	2	1
14	**2**	**2**	1	1	2	2	1	**2**	1	1	2	2	1	1	2
15	**2**	**2**	1	2	1	1	2	1	2	2	1	2	1	1	2
16	**2**	**2**	1	2	1	1	2	**2**	1	1	2	1	2	2	1

If, on the other hand, the experiment design involves only an inner array, randomization becomes much more critical. Failure to randomize can result in misleading data and faulty conclusions. The preferred method of handling this potential bias is to define an outer array that will consider these perhaps unknown influences. After all, the purpose of parameter design is to determine the best control factor levels at which the forces you are not controlling have a minimal effect. Randomization can minimize experimental bias, but it won't result in a robust process design by itself.

In randomizing experimental runs, repetition is more cost efficient than replication and is typically the preferred method. Besides reducing the number of setups, repetition can help obtain estimates of between experiment error and within experiment error. This information can be very useful in viewing the significance of differences in factor level changes as compared to experimental error. If setup error is a concern, an initial run of a few units before and after setup changes can disclose whether the concern is valid. If variation between setup changes appears excessive, replication should be used over repetition.

In deciding between full and partial randomization, you may not find all factors created equal. The settings for some factors can be changed with the turn of a knob. Conveyor speed is a typical example of a factor that can be easily and quickly changed. The changing of other factor levels may be very time consuming and result in high costs. Raw material is a factor that may fall into

Figure 11-7 Partial Randomization: SMT Primary Fluid Experiment

	Inner Array								Outer Array			
Runs	Primary Fluid	Conveyor Speed	Chain Speed	Heat #1	Heat #2	Cool Down Rate	Solder Vol.	Pwb Humidity	1 1	1 2	2 1	2 2
1	1	1	1	1	1	1	1		$2y_{11}$	$2y_{12}$	$2y_{13}$	$2y_{14}$
2	1	1	1	2	2	2	2		$2y_{21}$	$2y_{22}$	$2y_{23}$	$2y_{24}$
3	1	2	2	1	1	2	2		$2y_{31}$	$2y_{32}$	$2y_{33}$	$2y_{34}$
4	1	2	2	2	2	1	1		$2y_{41}$	$2y_{42}$	$2y_{43}$	$2y_{44}$
5	2	1	2	1	2	1	2		$2y_{51}$	$2y_{52}$	$2y_{53}$	$2y_{54}$
6	2	1	2	2	1	2	1		$2y_{61}$	$2y_{62}$	$2y_{63}$	$2y_{64}$
7	2	2	1	1	2	2	1		$2y_{71}$	$2y_{72}$	$2y_{73}$	$2y_{74}$
8	2	2	1	2	1	1	2		$2y_{81}$	$2y_{82}$	$2y_{83}$	$2y_{84}$

this category. If the raw material is fed into the process from a large vat, the entire batch may have to be depleted or discarded before changing to an alternate supplier. This can be extremely expensive and very time consuming. In the case of two suppliers of raw material, a more efficient experiment would be first to conduct all of the experimental runs at which Vendor A is the raw material level (the first half). Then after changing to Vendor B, the experimental runs associated with the latter raw material would be conducted (the second half). Within each half of the experiment, the runs associated with that portion could be randomized. Figure 11-7, from the following case study, provides a demonstration of partial randomization.

Randomization Case Study

An experiment was designed to study the feasibility of changing the type of primary fluid used in a surface mount vapor phase operation. Numerous other process factors were also incorporated into the experiment. Changing the fluid from one type to the other would require a full day of purging the system and adding the replacement chemical. In addition, the existing fluid, which is very expensive, would have to be scrapped. The design of the experiment resulted in an L_8 inner array and a four-column outer array. All other factors were relatively easy to change. To minimize the cost and time in changing the fluid, the primary fluid was assigned to column 1. The other factors were assigned to the remaining columns. Partial randomization was used to order the experimental runs within each half of the experiment. Two repetitions were run for each combination of control and noise factors.

On day 1 (May 5), the humidity was low. Both types of circuit boards were available. Therefore, columns 1 and 3 of the outer array were run. Circuit board #1 was run first since the process was already set up for its production.

On day 2 (May 7), the humidity was higher. (Note: day 1 and day 2 were not consecutive days because the team had to wait 2 days for the humidity to rise.) Again, both types of circuit boards were available. Columns 2 and 4 of the outer array were run. Since the process was still set up for the manufacture of circuit board #2, we began day 2 with that product.

At the halfway mark, the primary fluid was replaced.

On day 3 (May 8), the humidity remained high. Therefore, columns 2 and 4 of the outer array were run. The process was already set up for circuit board #1.

On day 4 (May 11), the humidity decreased. (Note: the humidity was high the previous 2 days.) Columns 1 and 3 of the outer array were run. The process was already set up for circuit board #1.

The experimental runs are listed in the order in which they were conducted. As you will note, on each day, the order of running the two sets of circuit boards was randomized.

Day 1: $2y_{41}$, $2y_{11}$, $2y_{21}$, $2y_{31}$, $2y_{33}$, $2y_{23}$, $2y_{13}$, $2y_{43}$

Day 2: $2y_{14}$, $2y_{44}$, $2y_{24}$, $2y_{34}$, $2y_{22}$, $2y_{42}$, $2y_{12}$, $2y_{32}$

Day 3: $2y_{72}$, $2y_{82}$, $2y_{62}$, $2y_{52}$, $2y_{84}$, $2y_{64}$, $2y_{54}$, $2y_{74}$

Day 4: $2y_{61}$, $2y_{71}$, $2y_{81}$, $2y_{51}$, $2y_{83}$, $2y_{53}$, $2y_{63}$, $2y_{73}$

Once the runs have been conducted and the samples or units built during the experiment have been collected, the next experimental bias concern is measurement error. If the samples or units are to undergo physical or functional testing, full randomization as in replication can minimize test bias. In the event that the quality characteristic is a classified attribute and the inspection is required, randomization of the samples or units is considerably more critical. Prior to submitting the pieces for inspection, the units should be fully randomized so that the inspector will evaluate each independently of the other samples and without knowing which experiment settings are associated with that unit.

Notes

1. Wu, Yuin, and Dr. Willie Hobbs Moore, *Quality Engineering: Product and Process Design Optimization,* p. 149.
2. Ibid.

Chapter 12

TEST PLAN DEVELOPMENT

The greatest potential for failure during the conducting of the experiment, which is the third portion of the experimentation cycle, stems from failure to understand what needs to be done and why it needs to be done. The experimentation team may carefully develop an experiment that will enable the team to achieve its objectives. But if it fails to document and relay this information accurately to those who will actually conduct the experiment and test or inspect the resulting samples, the efforts exerted in effectively planning and efficiently designing the experiment will be wasted. This vital information includes the reasons for planning and designing the experiment in the first place, the way the experiment will be conducted, procedures for sampling and testing, and the methodology for analyzing the data obtained. Developing a comprehensive yet concise test plan prior to conducting the experiment can reduce misunderstanding going into the actual conducting of the experiment and prevent the creation of faulty or misleading results. The specified components that constitute the framework of an effective test plan will be covered within this chapter:

1. Test plan structure
2. Sampling guidelines
3. Sample selection
4. Sample preparation
5. Sample identification
6. Sampling sequence
7. Data worksheets

12.1 TEST PLAN STRUCTURE

Too often, the experimentation team takes for granted that its objective and its plan to achieve the objective should be obvious to everyone. In some instances, in an effort to shorten the time between planning and designing the experiment and running the experiment, team members fail to document their progress and the procedures to which they have mutually agreed. In other cases, it is assumed that verbal instructions are sufficient.

Each of these assumptions or failings can create confusion, misunderstanding, and frustration. A well laid-out and documented test plan will reiterate the objectives and strategies that have been determined, to insure that there is no difference between what each member thought he or she was agreeing to and what will be done. This effort of documentation also prevents the occasional task of having to remember forgotten details or reconvening to make decisions on minor points all over again. For the operators, testers, and inspectors, the test plan gives them a reference for understanding why this effort is being put forth. It also provides direction for what they should do and for whom to call if specific steps are unclear. The test plan also serves to promote feedback. By highlighting key points and explaining complex procedures, this step may bring to surface questions that otherwise might not be addressed until too late—during the middle of the experimental runs or after the test units have all been built.

To address these concerns, the test plan needs to include the following segments:

1. Statement of purpose
2. Experiment objectives
3. Experiment description
4. Testing/inspection procedures
5. Data worksheet
6. Analysis techniques

The length of the test plan will depend on the complexity and depth of the study. In addition, there may be other sections that you may wish to include in addition to the six basic ones listed here.

12.1.1 Statement of Purpose

The statement of purpose is a clear and precise definition of the intention of the experiment. In many cases, the statement would be an explanation of a specific problem that brought the experimentation team together.

12.1.2 Experiment Objectives

The experiment objectives respond to how the experimentation team plans to fulfill its purpose. This plan may relate to continuous improvement, discovery within new areas, or identification of a specific problem being attacked. If more than one objective is desired, they should be identified in order of importance. Each objective should be defined in quantifiable terms if possible, with the desired or targeted results identified.

12.1.3 Experiment Description

The experiment description is a summary of the information developed during the planning phase and of the experimental matrix as constructed in the design phase. With this knowledge, those who either have a hand in the running of the experiment or actually perform the testing or inspection can gain insight into why they are being called upon to perform specific tasks related to the experiment. For the operators, it provides a schedule for insuring that the right number of units are built or samples are taken at the appropriate setting levels and in the desired order. Specific information that should be incorporated in the experiment description includes:

- definition of quality characteristic
- target value (if nominal-the-best)
- selection of control factors and settings
- selection of interactions (if appropriate)
- identification of noise factors and levels
- identification of signal factor (if dynamic characteristic)
- selection of orthogonal array(s)
- column assignment
- number of measurements or units per experimental run
- type of randomization
- order of experimental runs[1]

12.1.4 Testing/Inspection Procedures

This section explains how the experiment will be performed, the scope to which the study is limited, how measurements will be taken, and inspection criteria if appropriate. Specific information that should be incorporated in the experiment description includes:

identification of test equipment

explanation of test procedures (schematic or drawing if appropriate)

explanation of inspection criteria (drawings or illustrations if appropriate)

identification of inspector

sampling techniques

sample identification/labeling

12.1.5 Data Worksheet

The data worksheet is the log for recording pertinent experiment information. The worksheet may be specifically designed to record process variable readings, end product dimensions, test data, or inspection findings, depending on the nature of the quality characteristic of interest. The worksheet is also an appropriate place to record any deviations from the test plan itself. Besides providing a log for this information, this section should also explain the procedures for recording the information onto the sheet. Typical information requested on a data worksheet includes:

date and time

operator/inspector

experimental run number

measurement readings

  test equipment name/serial number

  test equipment calibration date

inspection findings

  locations

  degree of goodness/badness

The data worksheet will be discussed further in Section 12.7.

12.1.6 Analysis Techniques

The analysis techniques section should provide a brief explanation of how the data (readings, measurements, or inspection findings) obtained in the experiment will be used in the analysis. This explanation enlightens those contributing to running the experiment and obtaining the data as to the importance of their role and of the information they help to obtain.

12.2 SAMPLING GUIDELINES

The procedure for sampling should be incorporated within the test plan. Specific guidelines include the manner of establishing the order of selection, type of randomization if used, and method of applying randomization if applicable. Listing the order of sample selection spells out the sequence of events for the operator or tester, which (a) simplifies the instructions so that the operator can more easily adhere to the intent of the test plan, and (b) insures that the experiment is conducted as determined during experiment planning. The written orders prevent miscommunication, and the simplification of the instructions limits potential frustration from the operator or tester's trying to interpret someone else's explanation of how to support the experiment. The operator may already be uncomfortable either from having to perform unfamiliar tasks or just from having to alter normal routines. Complicating the operator's involvement further can only increase anxiety. Minimizing potential problems in interpreting the plan enables operators to focus their attention elsewhere in insuring that samples are collected correctly and according to the test plan. Describing the method of sample selection and where it is to be applied helps everyone involved in the experimentation effort understand the sampling guidelines, and insures that the sampling will be performed according to the experimentation team consensus. In addition, this documentation provides a check to ascertain if any essential sampling requirements have been overlooked.

Concerning the scope of the sampling guidelines, the test plan should be more than just a list of sampling instructions. The plan should be a formal written plan for conducting the experiment. Any portion of the experiment in which sampling is applied should be incorporated into the test plan, ranging from selection of raw material for running the experiment to the collection of finished product samples from a batch process. Experiment setup applications could include the mixing and combining of chemicals or ingredients such as required in the petrochemical and food industries, respectively.

The guidelines may include special instructions. These may be industry specific or pertain to a unique type of operation. Sampling may need to be performed under controlled conditions, particularly if you are trying to recreate or simulate maximum variability within specified noise factors. The operator or tester may have to wait until certain conditions are met or have been reached. Other factors may need to be held constant during the testing. Perhaps a given period of time must be observed before or during testing. Maybe a minimum quantity of the finished product is required in the sample for sufficient testing.

Figure 12-1 Electronic Circuit Board Assembly: Sampling Guidelines

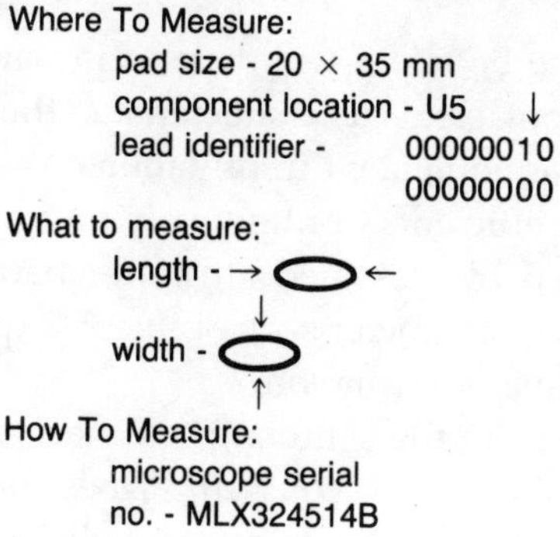

Sampling instructions should also contain more information than just the number of units required for testing. Guidelines should include specifically where, what, and how to measure. In an example of electronic surface mount assemblies (Figure 12-1), the units contained circuit pads of varying sizes located across the top side surface. To obtain a representative picture of assembly quality, the sampling guidelines identified specific pad sizes and locations across the top surface. Data collection and analysis for determining variability in solder quality based on circuit pad size and pad location could then be done without having to measure each of the more than 300 pads on each unit. In addition to the explanation of measurement procedures, instruction on recording the data and filling out the data sheets should be included. After all, the intent of conducting the experiment is to obtain meaningful information that can be analyzed for the purpose of producing reproducible conclusions.

12.3 SAMPLE SELECTION

In determining how to select your sample, several considerations need to be taken into account. These are:

- quality characteristic type
- appropriateness
- difficulty

- time
- cost

The number of samples to be taken will depend in part on the type of quality characteristic. The more powerful the characteristic, the fewer samples that will be needed for the same or equivalent information. An energy-related dynamic characteristic is the most efficient. Continuously measurable characteristics are next in strength, followed by classified attribute characteristics and the even more inefficient Go/No Go characteristics. Table 3-2 (page 48) lists equivalent sample sizes for comparable information.

Appropriateness relates to the sampling selection supporting the objectives of the experiment. You should ask yourself, "Does the sampling insure that I will obtain information to help increase my knowledge of the process?" A primary function of parameter design is to study the variability of the process under investigation. This study may require inducing variability to determine the relationships between the control factors and the quality characteristic of interest and the effect of noise on the control factors. In that case, you may want to select samples that reflect the conditions creating the greatest variation. In other situations, you may need to define your sampling so as to incorporate each type of variation that is pertinent to your objectives. You can think of four primary sources of variation:

- within piece variation
- piece-to-piece variation
- time-to-time variation
- line-to-line variation[2]

In defining your sample selection, you may wish to consider a plan that incorporates one or all of these variation types. In a batch process, you may wish to select samples from different parts of the vat to gain a picture of within piece variation. If you are striving to make the process robust from one batch to another, you may determine a need to take samples from consecutive batches. This sampling will reflect piece-to-piece variation. If consistency over time is an objective, then a sampling strategy that will reveal time-to-time variation may be needed. If determining which is the better of two process lines or machines is the goal, then sampling should reflect the difference of these factors with all other factors equal. This will provide an understanding of line-to-line variation.

A third consideration in making your sample selections is difficulty. Sampling should not be based on pure convenience alone. However, what if the complexity of procuring the desired information creates confusion or the method for obtaining data is a long drawn-out process potentially creating delays in the process that can affect the experimental results? In these cases, a compromise between convenience or simplification and the ideal sampling plan may provide a more realistic approach and result in more accurate and consistent data.

Time is another factor in determining sample selection. Time may be associated with the difficulty of obtaining data or may be related to the actual number of samples that will be taken. Obviously, more samples collected will improve the ability to draw accurate inferences from the data. However, as the time to obtain samples expands, the labor required also increases, meaning additional costs.

Last on our list but certainly not least important, cost is a major factor in determining factor selection. Cost may be a consideration on its own merit, such as the expenses involved in obtaining and installing probes or purchasing measurement devices or test equipment. Cost may also be a consequence of measurement difficulty or of the labor rates for acquiring the data. In determining sample size, the previously cited Table 3-2 provides a guide for considering both cost and type of quality characteristic.

In a printed circuit board experiment (Figure 12-2), we wished to study the variability of solder paste volume between circuit pads. However, measuring

Figure 12-2 Printed Circuit Board: Sample Selection

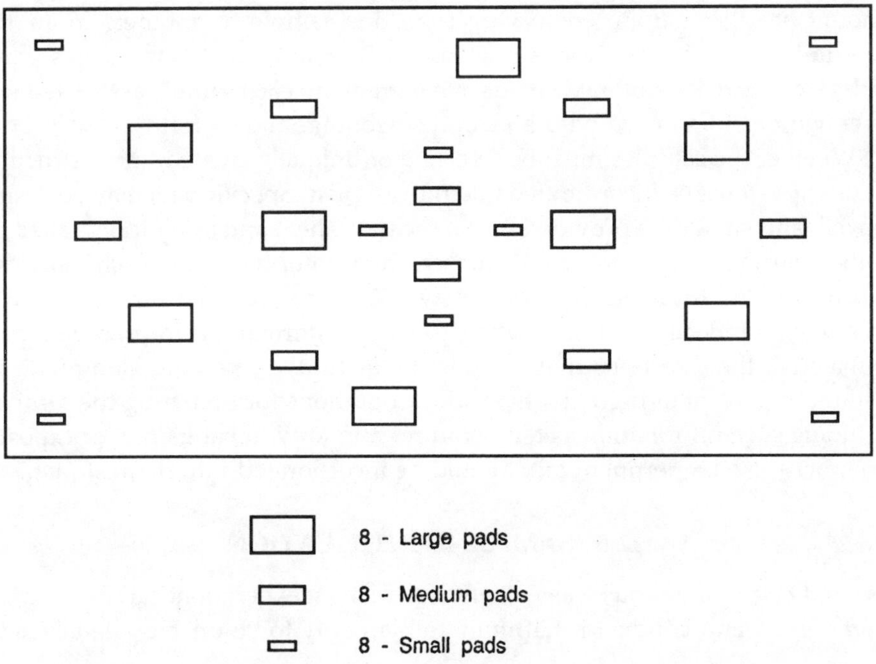

the volume at every pad across an entire board would have required an exorbitant amount of measurement time and subsequently raised the cost of performing the experiment. In addition the increased time requirements would have delayed the conclusions to the experiment, which were sorely needed to facilitate startup of the new production line. Therefore, a sampling plan was devised to study all three sizes of pads and to consider paste volume across the entire circuit board surface. Eight pads of each size were identified at strategic locations.

12.4 SAMPLE PREPARATION

In certain experiments, the items or samples that are to be measured or tested must be specially prepared. In some cases, this preparation may mean simply screening raw material with specific characteristics from the remainder of the lot. In other situations, the samples must be specially prepared. This is often true in experiments related to chemical process or even in food processing. Although the most obvious applications are in the petrochemical and pharmaceutical industries, other examples frequently occur in other types of operations.

In a chemical process, perhaps one of the control factors is the percentage of a specific compound to be included in the material. Another example could include a factor defined as solution strength. Both cases require special preparation prior to the experiment. Besides varying the percentages of various chemicals, one may need to add different substances for different samples in the experiment. The same type of examples apply in the food industry. Perhaps the amount of salt is supposed to vary from one sample to another. In another experiment, a control factor is seasoning. Therefore, each sample associated with level one of seasoning contains one ingredient; each sample associated with level two must be mixed with a second seasoning, and so forth.

Whether the samples must be screened or uniquely created, the instructions for doing so must be incorporated into the test plan. Specific data may be desired as well, and should be provided for on the data sheet and specifically called out in the instructions. If parts are being screened, information on each individual part may be useful later. Such data may include the manufacturer, date code, lot number, and other differentiating pieces of information. In preparing parts or material, the directions may include the quantity to prepare along with the amount or percent of ingredients to add. Conditions for preparing the samples, including such information as temperature, humidity, mixing time, or exposure time, may also be pertinent and should be incorporated into the test plan.

12.5 SAMPLE IDENTIFICATION

It would be a tremendous waste of effort to plan an experiment carefully, design it efficiently, and conduct it faithfully to plan only to be unable to analyze the data because no one knows which samples match which experimental runs. It is essential to identify each sample clearly. This marking of each unit or batch serves two essential purposes:

1. Matching samples with experimental runs. This step insures that the operator understands which sample or piece of raw material is associated with each experimental run and associated set of process settings. It helps to guarantee that each end unit is produced or built as designed in the experiment.

2. Correlating produced units with corresponding location in the experimental matrix. A potential problem especially with numerous repetitions is proper sorting and assignment of completed units to their respective row and column of the experimental matrix. By proper identification of the sample, measurements can be correctly recorded in the proper location.

Experimental units may be marked with indelible pens, or identification can be etched into the parts by scribes. The emphasis here is on a method that provides for clear identification and markings that cannot be easily removed. In some situations, such as chemical or food samples, the sample number or name cannot be placed on the sample itself. In these situations, a label may need to be prepared and affixed to the sample container—a label on a test tube or beaker or a sticker on a tray.[3] Tying an identification tag to the sample holder may be appropriate as well. The system that is to be used should be noted and explained in the test plan.

12.6 SAMPLE ORDERING

In those cases where the raw samples for the experiment must be specially prepared, the order of preparation must be based on the sequence agreed to in the planning phase and defined in the design stage. Randomization of the order of processing these samples should be spelled out in the test plan. Whether involving replication, repetition, partial randomization, or going in order from first to last of the corresponding rows and columns of the orthogonal arrays, the order should be specifically defined in the test plan instead of left to the discretion of the individual preparing the samples.

12.7 DATA WORKSHEET

As mentioned in Section 12.1, the data worksheet is the log for recording data and documenting events that occur during the conducting of the experiment. The data sheet should be designed not only to facilitate the recording of the desired information, but also to provide the flexibility to record unforeseen events and additional data not considered during the planning phase. In one experiment, four quality characteristics were identified, and the data sheet was specifically designed to record this information. However, during the inspection of the product built in the study, a fifth concern was exposed that had not previously been considered important. The effect of the variability in this new characteristic proved significant after all. Since spare columns for recording data for each sample had been designed into the sheets, the new information was easily added and analyzed along with the previously defined outputs of interest.

Concerning basic information that relates to each experimental run and each unit produced during the conducting of the experiment, do not assume that you will remember everything that may be of importance later in the analysis. Provide for this potential need even if the information may not appear to be essential. The serial number of the measuring device may not seem important, but if readings appear consistently off, research may reveal that this instrument has a history of inaccurate readings. Failure to record the serial number may prevent this discovery and result in incorrect conclusions from the analysis. Specific information could include:

- the quality characteristic definition
- space to record the readings or results of the inspection
- tester/inspector
- instrumentation, including
  - type
  - name
  - serial number
  - calibration date
- sample identification and associated experimental run number
- special remarks section for unforeseen events/additional information

There is some information that you may wish to omit purposely from the log sheet. It may be wise not to include control and noise factor levels or values on the data sheet. The measurer or inspector may read the settings prior to taking the readings or making the inspection judgments and, knowing that certain settings give better or worse results, may bias the data they obtain.

An additional aid that may be added to the log sheet to facilitate data gathering is a condensed set of data gathering instructions. The purpose is not to replace or duplicate the test plan. The aim is to restate the procedures in just a few words to reinforce the instructions for proper data recording.

12.7.1 Surface Mount Data Sheet

Figure 12-3 shows a log sheet used to record data from an experiment in which two measurements are to be taken and two quality criteria are to be used for inspection. The number of samples per pad size are defined and provided for. At the top of the page, the specific experiment is defined and a place is provided to identify the experimental run. Below the rows for recording measurements and inspection results is a comment section set aside for additional information. This section is essential to any good data sheet. At the bottom of the log is a place for the inspector to write his or her name. Although a simple data sheet, this form provided for all the essential information which was required in the particular experiment in which it was used.

12.7.2 Wavesolder Data Sheet

This particular log as shown in Figure 12-4 is more explicit in asking for information and facilitating the documentation of the results. In this particular experiment, five repetitions were required for each experimental run. The primary quality characteristic was the surface temperature of the top of the circuit board. At the same time, the team was also interested in the number of resulting defects as determined by customer standards. As shown in the figure, temperature and defects are both addressed, and spaces are allocated for recording data related to each. In the case of defects, two inspection aids are provided. An assembly drawing is provided on the data sheet for the inspector to indicate at which specific locations a defect resulted. Secondly, a legend is provided noting the specific types of defects to inspect for and corresponding symbols to facilitate marking the exact locations on the drawing at the top. Instructions have also been incorporated in the lower left section for differentiating the defects occurring from one repetition to another. At the bottom right hand, the essential comment section is provided. On this data sheet, a place has been provided for both operator and inspector. This is normally a good idea. However in this particular experiment, listing both was even more important than usual. The operator recorded the temperature readings, and the inspector was responsible for identifying defects.

12.8 CRACKED CAPACITOR TEST PLAN EXAMPLE

The following is an example of a test plan that you may wish to use for reference in constructing your own plan. Although the difference between your process and that of this example may be great, the basic structure of the format can still be adopted regardless of the diversity in application.

Figure 12-3 **Surface Mount Technology Screening Experiment Data Sheet**

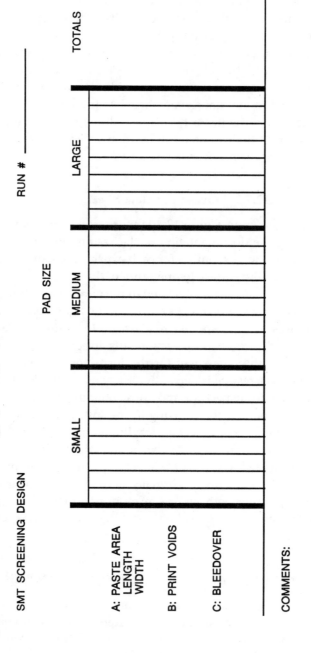

SMT SCREENING DESIGN RUN # ____________

PAD SIZE

	SMALL	MEDIUM	LARGE	TOTALS
A: PASTE AREA LENGTH WIDTH				
B: PRINT VOIDS				
C: BLEEDOVER				

COMMENTS:

INSPECTOR ____________

Figure 12-4 Wavesolder Experiment Data Sheet

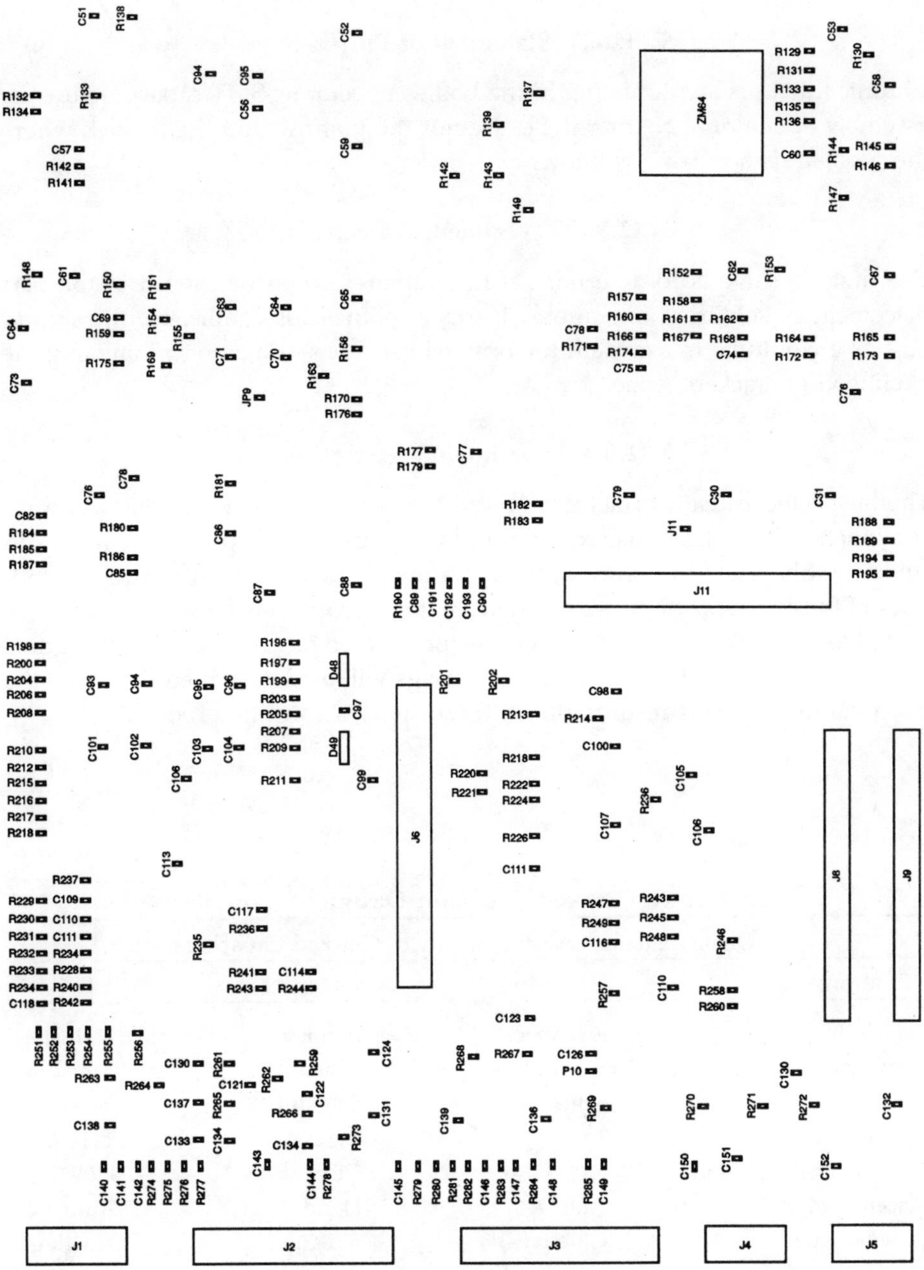

12.8.1 Statement of Purpose

Chronic fractures are occurring in the bodies of ceramic SMT capacitors during assembly operations. Neither the cause nor the point within the process where the problem is occurring is known.

12.8.2 Experiment Objectives

The first objective is to determine if the fractures could be caused in the part placement or soldering operations. If this hypothesis is confirmed, the second objective would be to ascertain the optimal process settings for minimizing the likelihood of cracked capacitors.

12.8.3 Experiment Description

The suspected cause of fractures is stresses, either thermal, mechanical, or a combination of both. This experiment will focus on the part placement and soldering phases of the process. By operating at the extreme operating boundaries of the control factors, we can deduce if the problem is located within these two phases of the process. All major factors related to mechanical and thermal stress are to be investigated. Optimal settings will be determined to reduce the potential for fractures resulting from these steps within the process.

Table 12-1 Cracked Capacitor Design of Experiment

Quality Characteristic: Quantity of Cracked Capacitors

Control factors:	Level 1	Level 2	Level 3
Stencil thickness	low spec.	nominal	high spec.
Cooling rate	Schedule 1	Schedule 2	Schedule 3
Heating rate	Schedule 1	Schedule 2	Schedule 3
Reflow type	Type 1	Type 2	Type 3
Pwb material	FR4	CER	FR4
Placement type	Auto #1	Hand	Auto #2
Glue/no glue	Glue (yes)	No glue	No glue
Capacitor supplier	Supplier 1	Supplier 2	Supplier 3

Cooling Rate Schedule:

Schedule 1	Schedule 2	Schedule 3
nominal − x	nominal	nominal + x

Table 12-1 Cracked Capacitor Design of Experiment

Quality Characteristic: Quantity of Cracked Capacitors

Heating Rate Schedule:

Zone	Schedule 1	Schedule 2	Schedule 3
1	nominal − 100	nominal	nominal + 100
2	nominal − 100	nominal	nominal + 100
3	nominal − 100	nominal	nominal + 100
4	nominal − 100	nominal	nominal + 100
5	nominal − 100	nominal	nominal + 100
6	nominal − 100	nominal	nominal + 100

Orthogonal Array: L_{27} (3^{13})

Orthogonal Array Layout

Run #	Stencil	Cool	Heat	Reflow	Thick	Material	Placement	Glue	Cap
1	low	1	1	Type 1	low	FR4	Auto #1	Yes	1
2	low	1	1	Type 1	nom	FR4	Hand	No	2
3	low	1	1	Type 1	high	CER	Auto #2	No	3
4	low	2	2	Type 2	low	FR4	Auto #1	No	2
5	low	2	2	Type 2	nom	FR4	Hand	No	3
6	low	2	2	Type 2	high	CER	Auto #2	Yes	1
7	low	3	3	Type 3	low	FR4	Auto #1	No	3
8	low	3	3	Type 3	nom	FR4	Hand	Yes	1
9	low	3	3	Type 3	high	CER	Auto #2	No	2
10	nominal	1	2	Type 3	low	FR4	Auto #2	Yes	2
11	nominal	1	2	Type 3	nom	CER	Auto #1	No	3
12	nominal	1	2	Type 3	high	FR4	Hand	No	1
13	nominal	2	3	Type 1	low	FR4	Auto #2	No	3
14	nominal	2	3	Type 1	nom	CER	Auto #1	No	1
15	nominal	2	3	Type 1	high	FR4	Hand	Yes	2
16	nominal	3	1	Type 2	low	FR4	Auto #2	No	1
17	nominal	3	1	Type 2	nom	CER	Auto #1	Yes	2
18	nominal	3	1	Type 2	high	FR4	Hand	No	3
19	high	1	3	Type 2	low	CER	Hand	Yes	3
20	high	1	3	Type 2	nom	FR4	Auto #2	No	1
21	high	1	3	Type 2	high	FR4	Auto #1	No	2
22	high	2	1	Type 3	low	CER	Hand	No	1
23	high	2	1	Type 3	nom	FR4	Auto #2	No	2
24	high	2	1	Type 3	high	FR4	Auto #1	Yes	3
25	high	3	2	Type 1	low	CER	Hand	No	2
26	high	3	2	Type 1	nom	FR4	Auto #2	Yes	3
27	high	3	2	Type 1	high	CER	Auto #1	No	1

Each panel in Figure 12-5 consists of nine circuit boards laid out in a 3 × 3 matrix. Each board assembly is to consist of a total of 24 capacitors consisting of 6 each of the following types:

- .01 uf x0805
- .1 uf x1206
- .1 uf x1210
- .68 uf x1812

Capacitors of each type should be screened so as to obtain an equal number of the oldest and newest date codes (three each). Capacitors should also be inspected to insure no visible damage to the frame or leads.

The panels are to be marked with the number of their corresponding experimental run number on the upper left board in the upper left corner. The marking is to be made with an indelible ink pen. Circuit boards on each panel are to be identified A to I from left to right, top row to bottom row. Capacitors on each circuit board are to be identified from 01 to 24 from top to bottom and from left to right (see Figure 12-5).

Figure 12-5 Capacitor Labeling System

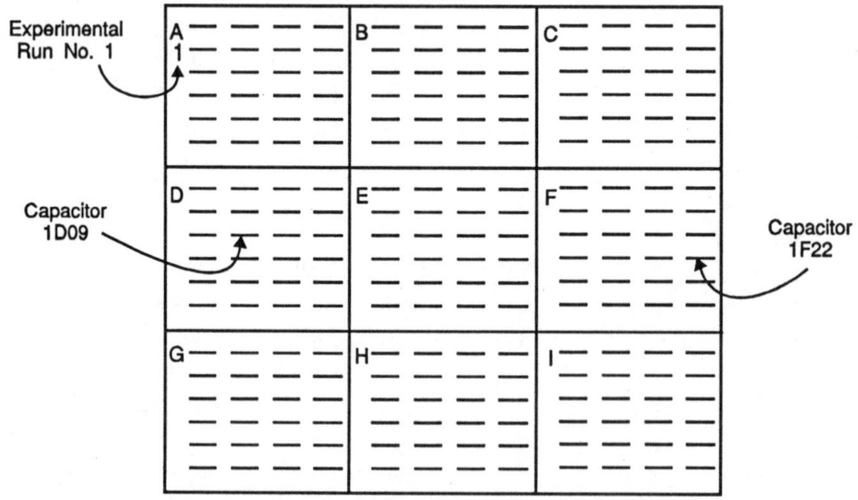

The experimental runs are to be conducted in the order shown (Run #1 first, Run #2 second, and so on).

12.8.4 Testing/Inspection Procedures

After part placement is completed and each panel has passed through the soldering system, each is to be placed in the environmental chamber for 24 hours. Temperature and humidity are to be maintained at 65°C and 85% relative humidity, respectively. After removal from the chamber, the circuits are to be tested by applying 50 Vdc across each capacitor.

Test setup as illustrated in Figure 12-6 will consist of connecting each capacitor concurrently through a series resistor of 100k ohms. Each capacitor will also be connected to ground through a header connector. Testing will be performed as follows:

1. Apply 50 Vdc from P1 to ground.
2. Connect voltmeter from M+ to ground.
3. Measure the voltage across Rs.[4]

If the voltage drop (Vrs) is 50 volts, the value of the insulation resistance of each capacitor in the circuit is 0. If the voltage drop (Vrs) is less than 50 volts, measure the resistance across each individual capacitor in the circuit with an ohmmeter. If any result is less than 100M ohms, identify that capacitor on the data sheet as a failure.

Figure 12-6 Cracked Capacitor Experiment Test Schematic

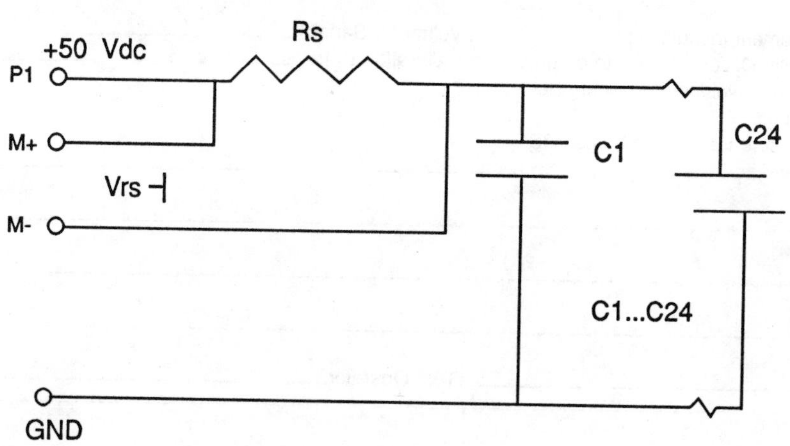

Figure 12-7 Cracked Capacitor Experiment Data Sheet

Date ____________

Experimental Run # ____________ Time ____________

BOARD#	READING	FAILURE	BOARD#	READING	FAILURE	BOARD#	READING	FAILURE
1A01			1B01			1C01		
1A02			1B02			1C02		
1A03			1B03			1C03		
1A04			1B04			1C04		
1A05			1B05			1C05		
1A06			1B06			1C06		
1A07			1B07			1C07		
1A08			1B08			1C08		
1A09			1B09			1C09		
1A10			1B10			1C10		
1A11			1B11			1C11		
1A12			1B12			1C12		
1A13			1B13			1C13		
1A14			1B14			1C14		
1A15			1B15			1C15		
1A16			1B16			1C16		
1A17			1B17			1C17		
1A18			1B18			1C18		
1A19			1B19			1C19		
1A20			1B20			1C20		
1A21			1B21			1C21		
1A22			1B22			1C22		
1A23			1B23			1C23		
1A24			1B24			1C24		

CODE: 1ST DIGIT = EXPERIMENTAL RUN #
LETTER = PWB LOCATION IN PANEL
LAST TWO DIGITS = CAPACITOR LOCATION

Measurement Instructions:

1. Apply 50 Vdc from P1 to ground.
2. Connect voltmeter from M+ to ground.
3. Measure the voltage across RS.

Voltmeter Serial# ____________

Calibration Date ____________

Comments ____________

____________ Test Operator ____________

12.8.5 Data Worksheet

The data sheet should be filled out as indicated on Figure 12-7. Unusual occurrences and deviations from the test plan should be recorded in the comments section.

12.8.6 Analysis Techniques

If the insulation resistance is less than 100M ohms, the capacitor will be considered defective and will be indicated as such on the data sheet. Analysis will then be performed to determine the optimal settings for minimizing capacitor defectives.

Notes

1. Melder, Melissa, *et al.*, *Taguchi Training Manual*, p. 4-21.
2. Horner, Stan, *Statistical Process Control*, p. 1-3.
3. Melder, p. 4-22.
4. Broadwater, John, "Cracked Ceramic Surface Mount Capacitors."

Chapter 13

PREPARING THE EXPERIMENT

Strict observance of the fundamental requirements for effective planning and efficient design of an experiment is essential for insuring that an experiment can be successful and for increasing the likelihood of achieving the desired results. However, attention to detail and careful planning follow over into the actual conducting of the experiment as well. In getting ready for the actual running of the experiment, the process and test equipment, raw material, and participating personnel must be in place and prepared to start and complete this phase of the experiment. Equipment and material must be properly selected, acquired in a timely manner, and screened or prepared for use. Operators must be ready as well, and inspectors must be knowledgeable in their particular functions within the performing of the experiment. Any randomization of test samples should be agreed upon, and the related instructions should be published for the benefit of those who will perform the actual task. Scheduling can be crucial to the coordination of conducting the experiment. The purpose of this chapter is to address each of these issues and to provide guidance into their effective handling.

13.1 SELECTING MATERIAL AND EQUIPMENT

Appropriate material and equipment must be used when conducting the experiment. Otherwise, the integrity of the experiment may be jeopardized and perhaps even violated. Therefore, it is important that the required material and the proper equipment are selected for completing each of the experimental runs. Those on the team most involved with and knowledgeable about the specific material and equipment needs of the experiment objectives must play the primary role of selecting the material and equipment.

13.1.1 Material

The number one consideration in determining the material to use in the experiment is how the selection of material affects and supports the objectives of the experiment. Is the purpose of the experiment to determine the best supplier? If so, each of the alternate suppliers currently being used along with others obtainable on the market or soon to be available should be included in the study. The process experts may be most aware of the available alternatives in the marketplace. Purchasing agents may learn of new alternatives from their associations with vendor representatives. Procurement specialists or incoming quality engineers may have in-depth knowledge of which material would provide the most suitable alternatives for study. Their expertise and close relations with suppliers may also make them aware of new developments that are worthy of study and enable them to gain access to samples for testing.

A different objective would be to obtain better understanding of process variability and the contribution to it by each process variable. In this situation, material must be selected to represent the total range of variability within the material itself. Material can be selected by supplier, by manufacturing site if the supplier has multiple locations, or by date code. The process engineers may have the best insight based on process knowledge into which of these considerations should be used in selecting the material for the experiment. The operators, as the best judges of what causes different results from one batch of raw material to another, may be the most capable of recommending the criteria for selecting the material for the experiment. In a food or petrochemical process, a laboratory analyst may have the clearest understanding based on prior analysis of which traits in the raw material are most likely to induce changes in the process output or end product. This knowledge can then be used to define and select the material to be used in the study.

If the purpose of the experiment is to make the process robust against differences in the incoming material, it is most essential that the material selected represent the full spectrum of material variability. For insuring robustness, only two levels, the opposing extremes, are typically required. In the event that the nature of the material constitutes various features that cannot be cumulated into a best- and worst-case combination or a set of two opposing extremes, additional levels may be required. Again, the process engineers and operators could very well have the best understanding.

Besides appropriateness, availability is another consideration in selecting material. If timeliness is critical, as is often the case, a three-month delay in obtaining a sample with specific characteristics may be unacceptable. In this particular situation, this choice would not be practical. Although not usually a member of the experimentation team, procurement or the associated purchasing agent may be called on to determine availability and lead time to delivery. Based on these findings, the team can then decide which material to select for the experiment.

Cost is always an important consideration in quality engineering, particularly in parameter design experiments. It would do little good to determine that one source or type of material was superior if the increase in the selling price as a consequence of the additional cost of the raw material would be unacceptable to customers. Therefore cost is a very strong factor in selecting type of material. Cost can also influence the amount of material acquired for the experiment. As with availability, procurement or the purchasing agent may be the best source for obtaining this information and feeding it back to the experimentation team for deciding if it should be selected for incorporation within the experiment.

13.1.2 Equipment

As in the case of selecting material, the equipment to be used in conducting the experiment must be appropriate for the intent. Measuring something just to be obtaining data is like traveling without a destination and hoping that the road will take you somewhere meaningful. The primary factor in equipment selection is that it will provide a quantifiable measure tied directly to the objective of the experiment.

The question of which equipment can most appropriately fulfill the needs of the study can probably be best answered by representatives of test engineering. Availability inputs will depend on whether the hardware and related software (if applicable) are currently being used in-house. If sources of the testing apparatus are available internally, test engineers and technicians can help provide the technical expertise and guidance in selecting the most appropriate ones. They can also assist in locating and obtaining the equipment. If internal sources are not available, test engineering can help provide the direction for determining test equipment requirements and locating possible sources. It may then be wise to turn over the external search to the procurement section to obtain specific details on availability, alternate sources, cost, delivery, and other concerns that could affect the conducting of the experiment.

As stated previously, the capability of the test equipment must be tied to the experiment objective; that is, the apparatus must be able effectively to obtain readings or measurements of the quality characteristic of interest. The precision of the instrument must be as good as or better than that desired for insuring a desired level of quality or variability. For example, if a critical dimension on a specific part must have variability down into the microns (10^{-6} meters), the measuring device must be able to measure at least in the microns if not more precisely. Being able to measure no closer than in millimeters would be unsatisfactory. Accuracy and repeatability are critical for obtaining meaningful data and deriving valid conclusions. On internally used instruments, the technicians that use them can best give you an evaluation of their performance. Calibration information either located on the equipment or kept by the repair and maintenance group can also assist the team in determining if internally available apparatus are suitable for the experiment or outside sources need to be investigated. The environment in which the equipment will be used—whether controllable or noncontrollable, including factors such as temperature variations—should also be addressed in selecting the most appropriate equipment. For a more detailed discussion, Chapter 4 includes additional issues and provides further guidance.

In addition to appropriateness, availability is another major concern. For example, if the desired precision is not available in-house, the search will need to continue externally. If this effort also fails, the experimentation team may need to reconvene and redefine the quality characteristic in terms of a measurement for which instrumentation is available. However, locating the right piece of equipment may not be enough in itself. If the lead time to delivery is excessive and delivery would make the results of the experiment untimely, then the team needs to act as if the device could not be found at all.

Some sophisticated and precise equipment is very expensive. If the instrument is not available internally, some capital expenditures may be required. In this event, cost becomes a major consideration in the selection of the equipment. This is an area in which purchasing can play a key role. Purchasing personnel are the most likely to be able to obtain a viable source of equipment that can perform the required functions at an affordable price.

13.2 ACQUIRING MATERIAL AND EQUIPMENT

Once the specific material and equipment that will be used during the conducting of the experiment have been selected, the next step is the actual acquisition. Although availability was one of the criteria for selection, what is apparently obtainable and what can actually be acquired may be completely different. Estimated lead times may turn into false promises. Therefore, the information gathered in making selection decisions does not provide all of the information necessary for acquiring the desired material and equipment. However, it typically provides ample direction to facilitate this effort.

13.2.1 Material

If the material is available in-house, scheduling and planning should be contacted to insure that enough material can be allotted for use in the experiment. *Never assume that there will be sufficient raw resources or parts on hand.* If sufficient material either is in storage or will be based on outstanding orders, go ahead and request the amount required for the experiment. If the material is regularly stocked, but the levels are insufficient to supply the needs of the experiment, get your order into planning as soon as you ascertain the actual amount required. You do not want experiment delays due to material shortage. Such a shortage may cause you to miss an opportunity to use the regular production facilities that may not arise again for weeks. It would also be a good idea to include a small excess amount or a few additional spares as a safety factor. Also as part of the request, include the date and time required. This will help Planning in maintaining adequate but not excessive inventory levels and prevent delays in conducting the experiment due to material not arriving on the manufacturing floor.

Material that is not normally carried in stock may need to be specially ordered. In this event, the appropriate purchasing agent will need to be involved. Again, a small excess should be included in the order. I have seen several occasions where only the exact amount was ordered. Then one damaged part or a small spill resulted in not enough material being available to run the entire experiment. In addition to obtaining a sufficient quantity, place the order early to insure timely arrival. Another concern is partial shipments. *All required material needs to be readily available at the start of the experimental runs.* Half of the necessary amount will not do. If a portion of the experiment is run and then late material delays the remainder of the experiment, the effect of extraneous factors can significantly increase and make the data invalid.

13.2.2 Equipment

Equipment that can be located internally will certainly reduce the overall cost of conducting the experiment. Therefore, it would be wise to exhaust all avenues of search within your operations before going to the outside. Certainly test engineering or the appropriate manufacturing support group may be the most likely source to have the desired equipment. If not, they could still be the best choice for directing you to where the devices are available. The worst case is that the required device or devices cannot be located within the facility. Even in this type of situation, the appropriate manufacturing support group can probably provide you with information on outside sources, the types of apparatus on the market, and their capability.

If the required equipment is located internally, schedule its use early. Don't assume that you are the only one who would ever need this device. Once the unit has been located, check out its capability. Talk to the users and compare the specifications to the needs of the experiment. Check its calibration date. If the date has expired or is close to expiration, insure that it is recalibrated before you need it. It is also a good idea to perform a test run. Measure a few samples and evaluate its performance. Also consider the measuring environment in which you will actually be using it. As an additional safety factor, have a backup unit in reserve if practical. This precaution may prove extremely helpful in the use of commonly available measuring devices such as calipers, voltmeters, and oscilloscopes. This will prevent excessive delays if equipment failure occurs.

In the event that the proper device has to be acquired from the outside, the appropriate purchasing agent should be contacted as early as possible. You should provide the agent with all the relevant information concerning functional requirements, scheduling deadlines, and cost restrictions. You may also wish to get the plant measurement experts involved to help insure that the proper apparatus is selected. Since the unit is being obtained externally, lead time is a critical concern and needs to be considered in the selection process. If the cost is high and future use of the instrument is not anticipated to be very high, you may wish to consider leasing for the period of performing the tests or taking the measurements, which includes the conducting of the experiment and performing the confirmation run.

13.3 SCREENING MATERIAL

Part of the effort in preparing for the conducting of the experiment may relate to the screening of material. This will depend on the relationship between the raw material identified for use in the experiment and the study objectives. If the material is not included as a factor in the experiment, then it needs to be screened so that it is uniform from one experimental run to another. This means that all parts look alike and bulk parts such as flour have the same consistency. If the material is specifically included in the experiment, then the material must be separated according to the distinguishing characteristics defined in the planning phase. In the case of lot variability, components may be screened according to date code. In bulk material examples, perhaps the containers need to be appropriately labeled and separated.

Someone on the team should be assigned the responsibility of insuring that the screening is carried out according to the test plan. They need not physically perform the task themselves, but it is their responsibility to assign the task and to follow up to insure it has been performed as directed. Concerning the timing of the task, just prior to the actual conducting of the experiment should suffice. If the material is sensitive to the environment, the team should be cautious about performing the screening too soon. On the other hand, screening should not be conducted so late as to interfere with the schedule for running the experiment.

13.4 IDENTIFYING AND RANDOMIZING TEST SAMPLES

The method for randomization should have been agreed upon in the planning phase and documented in the test plan. In preparation for obtaining the test samples, the act of randomizing the order should be performed in advance of setting up the first experimental run. Sampling containers should be acquired and appropriately marked so as to make identification clear and easy. As mentioned previously, check to be sure that the identification method cannot be removed or made illegible. Have the system for storing and transferring the samples instituted and clearly defined so that those who will be handling them will be able to carry out the sampling proficiently.

Review the sampling procedures with those who will be taking the samples. It is also a good idea to ask them to explain in their own words what they are supposed to do. This step will provide a safeguard from the situation where the operator feels embarrassed to say that he doesn't understand and responds that he comprehends the instructions when actually he is totally confused.

Special preparations may need to be made of the raw material to be used in the experiment, as in the case of chemical solutions or food ingredients. The same precautions as mentioned for obtaining samples from the experimental runs should apply, including:

randomization

labeling

handling system

operator instruction

As we explained in relation to material screening, prepared samples should also be ready at the start of the experimental runs.

13.5 OPERATOR PREPARATION

In preparing for the experiment, getting the material and equipment ready takes care of two of the three major elements required in conducting an experiment. What about the third piece, operator involvement? Just as the proper material must be selected and prepared, the person or group of persons conducting the experiment needs to be prepared as well. They must understand the purpose of the experiment and why it is important. They need to be aware of what is expected of them and how to perform these tasks.

The best way to achieve operator understanding is to get them involved as early as possible in the planning phase. Besides the tapping of a potentially valuable resource, this up-front activity provides them with an understanding of the experiment objectives and an insight into the importance of the effort. Another significant consequence of this early introduction is a feeling of *ownership* by operators. From this, operators become more receptive to what their role in the experiment should be and take a more proactive role in understanding how they can help.

Careful reviewing of the test plan with the operators can facilitate their understanding of their duties during the experimental runs. However, an even better approach is to get them involved during the writing of the plan. As you construct the sections that specifically relate to them, ask them if the instruction is understandable. Do they follow what is being stated? Does it explain to them in terms that they can relate to what they are expected to do? What are their suggestions? An important rule to remember when writing operator instructions is to keep them simple and on the level of the person who is to read them.

It may prove helpful to give the operator a copy of those parts of the test plan that specify her responsibility and what she is supposed to do. You don't have to print the whole plan for her. *Keep it simple!* Just print those parts that apply to her. Another aid that has proven quite valuable is a printout of the sequence of experimental runs and associated process settings (see Chapter 14). By your spelling out the order in which the operator is to conduct the experiment and the related changes that she is to make to her process, confusion can be reduced, and erroneous factor settings can be prevented.

Just prior to setting up the machinery for the very first experimental run, it would be a good idea to review the experiment with the operators involved. Have the meeting on the production floor or wherever is close to the actual conducting of the experiment. This way, if questions are brought up about specific steps or machinery controls, the answers can be pointed out and demonstrated instead of just given a verbal explanation. In going over the specific tasks, restate why the experiment is being conducted and what the team is striving to achieve. Remember to emphasize "we" and "us." Promote the message that we can all be successful together. Review the specific tasks each of the individuals involved will undertake and areas of responsibility. Ask for questions. If in doubt of operators' understanding of particular tasks or steps, ask them to repeat in their own words what they are supposed to do. However, be careful not to embarrass anyone. If someone appears confused, talk to that person aside from the rest of the group after the meeting breaks up. Most important, at the meeting, reiterate the importance of their roles and acknowledge their full involvement and contribution of ideas.

13.6 INSPECTION GUIDELINES

As in the case of operators, the inspector needs to feel that he is an integral part of the experimentation team and that he has a valued role in the performance of the experiment. He should be able to go into the inspection or testing with the feeling that his performance is important. He should also feel that the inspection tasks and how they will be performed are at least in part based on the inspector's ideas and suggestions.

To achieve this sense of involvement and importance, pull ideas and opinions from the prospective inspector during the writing of testing/inspection procedures. The instructions should be put in the words that the inspector can understand. In the development of the data sheet, combine your ideas of what is important with the inspector's suggestions on making the worksheet easy to use. If inspection is to be performed based on judgmental criteria, discuss with the inspector what type of visual aids will help his decision making. Would the inspector prefer detailed instructions? Are diagrams, pictures, or actual samples depicting each type of situation more helpful? Based on the inspector's recommendations, actions need to be taken to insure that the aids are in place when inspection is to begin. This timely reaction does two things:

1. It provides the tools the inspector needs.
2. It demonstrates that the inspector's ideas are important and will be acted upon.

Both typically increase individual conscientiousness and enthusiasm.

After the test plan has been completed and right before inspection is to be performed, review the procedures with the inspector for performing his tasks. Whether his role is testing, obtaining measurements, or pure inspection, discuss with him how he intends to perform his part. If equipment is involved, insure that he is proficient with the devices that he is about to use. Review labeling of samples so that the correct data is recorded for the corresponding sample or experimental run. Discuss proper handling. It may be a wise idea to have the inspector go through a trial run and see if any problems occur or he has any problems. Also, check that visual aids are in place. Ask the inspector if the aids serve the purpose for which they were intended. If not, take the necessary action to insure that the inspector does obtain the appropriate tools.

Review the data sheet form and discuss the procedures for filling it out. Insure that each inspector understands how to identify each sample and experimental run properly on the data sheet. You do not want information from one run confused with another or data between two samples accidentally reversed. Discuss the comments section, which may prove extremely important during the analysis. You never know when unexpected events or unforeseen results might occur. These little surprises can sometimes have a big impact on the conclusions derived from recorded information.

In completing your discussions with the inspector, reiterate the importance of the experiment. Emphasize the significance of his role and how it affects the success of the experiment. Ask questions. Solicit feedback. Leave him with a sense of importance and enthusiasm for the effort he is about to undertake.

13.7 SCHEDULING EQUIPMENT

The final preparations for conducting the experiment involve scheduling the setup of the appropriate process and test equipment and of the measuring devices. Although the team has already made the appropriate selections and determined where they can be obtained, the work is not yet done. The equipment must be put in place and set up for the function it is to perform.

If the device is to be borrowed from an internal source or leased from a local distributor or dealer, it needs to be scheduled so that there will be sufficient time for the apparatus to be put in place and set up. If the unit is being purchased, close communication with purchasing may be required to follow the expected due date and coordinate setup. Time should be allotted for the operator to become familiar with the device if the unit is complex or requires in-depth knowledge. If this is the case, a trial run or test with the device is a good idea as well.

There are also other scheduling considerations in addition to assuring that the proper equipment is in place at the start of the experiment—or at its completion, if we are referring to test equipment or measuring devices. You need to consider the length of time that the apparatus is needed. In the event that this unit is owned or controlled by the group performing the experiment, time is no problem. However, if the equipment has been borrowed or leased, difficulties could arise if the duration of the loan or lease expires before the end of the period for which it is required. Therefore, an estimation of the length of time from setup of the first experimental run to completion of the last run should be made. The estimate should include the estimated length of each setup change and individual processing times plus a margin of safety. In regard specifically to test equipment and measuring devices, an estimate of the time required to obtain each reading should be calculated. Based on these estimations, loan or lease arrangements where applicable can be arranged more effectively.

Chapter 14

Conducting the Experiment

In preparation for a concert, a symphony orchestra spends countless hours preparing and rehearsing for a one evening performance. The music is carefully selected to match the theme of the concert. The arrangement is meticulously prepared to please the anticipated audience and to utilize fully the strengths of the orchestra. The appropriate musicians and instruments are selected to play each of the parts called for in the arrangement. Each musician practices his part and checks that his particular instrument is functioning properly. The orchestra rehearses together to insure that their efforts merge into a harmonious sound. Each member gains an understanding of his role as well as that of his fellow musicians. Prior to the performance, they insure that the instruments are clean. In tuning their instruments prior to the opening number, they make adjustments so that the sound is neither flat nor sharp.

The college football coaching staff works hours, days, even weeks in preparation for 60 minutes of playing time. Players are selected for particular positions and trained to fill those roles. The necessary protective equipment, such as pads and mouthpieces, is provided. Strategy is developed by the staff for reaching the goal line and preventing the opposition from doing the same. The players are schooled in the various play formations and learn their particular roles. By game time, the team is ready to take the field and win the game. Although what happens on the field determines the success of the game, the efforts put forth prior to the game will dictate the team's actions and affect the eventual outcome.

Both of these examples can be related in their own way to an experiment and the preparation that is required for its successful performance. In each case, whether a concert, game, or experimental run, the planning and preparation take considerably longer time and greater effort than the actual activity itself. In all cases, success cannot occur without careful attention to the steps preceding the actual activity. Another commonality is the leader, who insures that all participants perform their roles in the effort and who facilitates the coordination of these roles. In the concert, this person is the conductor. On the football field, the quarterback leads the team down the field. In conducting an experiment a leader or coordinator is needed to coordinate experimental runs and facilitate the efforts of those who play a role in producing experimental data.

14.1 EXPERIMENTAL RUN COORDINATION

The key person during the actual conducting of the experiment is the experimental runs coordinator. I typically refer to her as the "straw boss." Her main responsibility is to insure that the experiment goes as planned. If an operator or inspector runs into a problem, she is the person who is contacted. She will resolve those issues that are within her capability. As liaison between the operating floor and the experimentation team, she will take issues beyond her capacity to the appropriate member of the team. Interfacing between the associated participants, the coordinator plays the primary role in quickly reacting to problems and obtaining fast responses to resolve them.

A second function of the coordinator is to insure that the experimental runs are ready to begin. She asks if the parts are available and in the area. If applicable, she may check to see if they have been properly screened. Special preparation of samples or the proper processing of the raw material is reviewed. She also insures that each experimental unit is appropriately labeled. The coordinator ascertains that the operator has the equipment ready and the proper settings adjusted for the first experimental run. If the equipment requires special programming, she asks if this has been completed.

As the actual performance of the experiment begins, the coordinator oversees the movement of the material through the pertinent process stages. When setup changes between experimental runs are required, she assists if needed and checks the new settings prior to the run. She monitors the operations as the experiment progresses and insures that any experiment deviations and unusual occurrences are recorded. She also double checks to insure that a data sheet is provided for each experimental sample.

The coordinator continues to follow the units after they have completed production or assembly. She makes sure that each unit or sample is accompanied by the data sheet with the matching experimental run number or other identifying description. Once the data have been entered onto the logs, she collects the forms and places them according to the order in the experimental design matrix. In other words, the log sheet for the run conducted at the factor settings associated with the first row of the orthogonal array is placed first. The sheet for the unit(s) or sample(s) produced at the factor settings associated with the second row of the orthogonal array is placed second, and so forth. This final task of the coordinator is where confusion and problems occur more times than at any other step of the conducting phase. On more than one occasion, an experimenter deep in the analysis has wondered why the results are so different from expected only to realize suddenly that the data were incorrectly assigned to the wrong rows.

14.2 EXPERIMENTAL RUN SHEETS

A valuable tool for the coordinator is the experimental run sheet. This is a printout of the experimental run sequence with the corresponding settings or values for each factor in the experiment. The sheet can assist the coordinator in monitoring the progress of the experimental runs. In addition, the cookbook recipe structure can provide tremendous help in resolving potential confusion on the part of the operators as to what they are supposed to do. The printout can serve as a checklist by which the operators mark off the setting change for each control factor as they go from the setup for one experimental run to the next.

14.2.1 Measurable Characteristic Run Sheet

A typical run sheet for a measurable quality characteristic would include the settings for both the control factors and the noise factors. Such a reference guide would apply to nominal-the-best, smaller-the-better, and larger-the-better characteristics. Since noise factors by definition are those conditions that either cannot be changed or are very difficult to change, it is usually more efficient to divide the printout into sections according to the noise factor combinations. For each combination of noise factor levels, the order of experimental runs with associated control factor settings can be generated.

Each experimental run should have an identifying number or name. If the experiment is being randomized, both the run number or name and the associated row of the inner orthogonal array should be given. Identifying the appropriate row can help assure later during the analysis that the data has been loaded into the right location in the orthogonal array and that the resulting calculations are correct.

In Figure 14-1, an example of a typical run sheet for a parameter design experiment has been reproduced. The study involved a nominal-the-best characteristic, but the same format could be used for a smaller-the-better or larger-the-better characteristic as well.

For brevity, the last portions of the printout are not shown here. The remaining experimental runs would follow in the same format as shown. The fourth and last noise factor combination would match the fourth row of the L_4 outer orthogonal array. The corresponding experimental runs would be identified as #1D through #8D. The control factor settings would follow the same pattern as shown in noise factor combinations #1 and #2.

Figure 14-1 Continuously Measurable Characteristic Experimental Run Sheet

PLASTIC INJECTION EXPERIMENT

NOISE FACTOR COMBINATION: #1

Load Time	–	5 seconds
Unload Time	–	5 seconds
Colorant	–	Blue

Experimental Run: # 1A

Column	Control Factor	Level Setting	Units
1	Injection pressure	20000	PSI
2	Pull back time	10.0	milliseconds
4	Raw material	Vendor A	
5	Barrel heater #1	350	°F
6	Barrel heater #3	380	°F

Experimental Run: # 2A

Column	Control Factor	Level Setting	Units
1	Injection pressure	20000	PSI
2	Pull back time	10.0	milliseconds
4	Raw material	Vendor B	
5	Barrel heater #1	400	°F
6	Barrel heater #3	450	°F

Experimental Run: # 3A

Column	Control Factor	Level Setting	Units
1	Injection pressure	20000	PSI
2	Pull back time	100.0	milliseconds
4	Raw material	Vendor A	
5	Barrel heater #1	350	°F
6	Barrel heater #3	450	°F

Experimental Run: # 4A

Column	Control Factor	Level Setting	Units
1	Injection pressure	20000	PSI
2	Pull back time	100.0	milliseconds
4	Raw material	Vendor B	
5	Barrel heater #1	400	°F
6	Barrel heater #3	380	°F

Figure 14-1 *Continued*

Experimental Run: # 5A

Column	Control Factor	Level Setting	Units
1	Injection pressure	40000	PSI
2	Pull back time	10.0	milliseconds
4	Raw material	Vendor A	
5	Barrel heater #1	400	°F
6	Barrel heater #3	380	°F

Experimental Run: # 6A

Column	Control Factor	Level Setting	Units
1	Injection pressure	40000	PSI
2	Pull back time	10.0	milliseconds
4	Raw material	Vendor B	
5	Barrel heater #1	350	°F
6	Barrel heater #3	450	°F

Experimental Run: # 7A

Column	Control Factor	Level Setting	Units
1	Injection pressure	40000	PSI
2	Pull back time	100.0	milliseconds
4	Raw material	Vendor A	
5	Barrel heater #1	400	°F
6	Barrel heater #3	450	°F

Experimental Run: # 8A

Column	Control Factor	Level Setting	Units
1	Injection pressure	40000	PSI
2	Pull back time	100.0	milliseconds
4	Raw material	Vendor B	
5	Barrel heater #1	350	°F
6	Barrel heater #3	380	°F

NOISE FACTOR COMBINATION: #2

Load Time – 5 seconds
Unload Time – 100 seconds
Colorant – Red

Experimental Run: # 1B

Column	Control Factor	Level Setting	Units
1	Injection pressure	20000	PSI
2	Pull back time	10.0	milliseconds
4	Raw material	Vendor A	
5	Barrel heater #1	350	°F
6	Barrel heater #3	380	°F

Figure 14-1 *Continued*

Experimental Run: # 2B

Column	Control Factor	Level Setting	Units
1	Injection pressure	20000	PSI
2	Pull back time	10.0	milliseconds
4	Raw material	Vendor B	
5	Barrel heater #1	400	°F
6	Barrel heater #3	450	°F

Experimental Run: # 3B

Column	Control Factor	Level Setting	Units
1	Injection pressure	20000	PSI
2	Pull back time	100.0	milliseconds
4	Raw material	Vendor A	
5	Barrel heater #1	350	°F
6	Barrel heater #3	450	°F

Experimental Run: # 4B

Column	Control Factor	Level Setting	Units
1	Injection pressure	20000	PSI
2	Pull back time	100.0	milliseconds
4	Raw material	Vendor B	
5	Barrel heater #1	400	°F
6	Barrel heater #3	380	°F

Experimental Run: # 5B

Column	Control Factor	Level Setting	Units
1	Injection pressure	40000	PSI
2	Pull back time	10.0	milliseconds
4	Raw material	Vendor A	
5	Barrel heater #1	400	°F
6	Barrel heater #3	380	°F

Experimental Run: # 6B

Column	Control Factor	Level Setting	Units
1	Injection pressure	40000	PSI
2	Pull back time	10.0	milliseconds
4	Raw material	Vendor B	
5	Barrel heater #1	350	°F
6	Barrel heater #3	450	°F

Experimental Run: # 7B

Column	Control Factor	Level Setting	Units
1	Injection pressure	40000	PSI
2	Pull back time	100.0	milliseconds
4	Raw material	Vendor A	
5	Barrel heater #1	400	°F
6	Barrel heater #3	450	°F

Figure 14-1 *Continued*

Experimental Run: # 8B

Column	Control Factor	Level Setting	Units
1	Injection pressure	40000	PSI
2	Pull back time	100.0	milliseconds
4	Raw material	Vendor B	
5	Barrel heater #1	350	°F
6	Barrel heater #3	380	°F

NOISE FACTOR COMBINATION: #3

Load Time – 50 seconds
Unload Time – 5 seconds
Colorant – Red

Experimental Run: # 1C

Column	Control Factor	Level Setting	Units
1	Injection pressure	20000	PSI
2	Pull back time	10.0	milliseconds
4	Raw material	Vendor A	
5	Barrel heater #1	350	°F
6	Barrel heater #3	380	°F

14.2.2 Classified Attribute Run Sheet

The run sheet for the classified attribute is similar to that for the continuously measurable quality characteristic except for two differences. Since an attribute experiment does not typically include an outer array, the order of experimental runs only has to be listed once, not a number of times matching the size of the outer array. Secondly, you may want to provide space beside each experimental run indicating the number of repetitions and their associated identification number if applicable.

Figure 14-2 provides an example of an experimental run sheet that could be used in a typical classified attribute experiment. Along with the experimental run number, the number of repetitions required is stated. This helps to insure that the required quantity has been produced for each experimental run.

Figure 14-2 Classified Attribute Characteristic Experimental Run Sheet

METAL CASING PAINT OPERATION EXPERIMENT

Experimental Run: # 1

Column	Control Factor	Number of units: 20 Level Setting
1	Paint method	Manual
2	Handling	No gloves
3	Metal dip	Chromate
4	Dip time	5 minutes
5	Masking procedure	No inspection
6	Primer	Sherwin-Williams
7	Secondary coat	Sherwin-Williams
8	Number of coats	1
9	Texturing	No texturing

Experimental Run: # 2

Column	Control Factor	Number of units: 20 Level Setting
1	Paint method	Manual
2	Handling	No gloves
3	Metal dip	Chromate
4	Dip time	5 minutes
5	Masking procedure	No inspection
6	Primer	Lilly
7	Secondary coat	Lilly
8	Number of coats	2
9	Texturing	Texturing

Experimental Run: # 3

Column	Control Factor	Number of units: 20 Level Setting
1	Paint method	Manual
2	Handling	No gloves
3	Metal dip	Iridite
4	Dip time	30 minutes
5	Masking procedure	Inspection
6	Primer	Sherwin-Williams
7	Secondary coat	Sherwin-Williams
8	Number of coats	1
9	Texturing	Texturing

Experimental Run: # 4

Column	Control Factor	Number of units: 20 Level Setting
1	Paint method	Manual
2	Handling	Gloves
3	Metal dip	Chromate
4	Dip time	30 minutes

Figure 14-2 *Continued*

Experimental Run: # 4 — Number of units: 20

Column	Control Factor	Level Setting
5	Masking procedure	Inspection
6	Primer	Sherwin-Williams
7	Secondary coat	Lilly
8	Number of coats	2
9	Texturing	No texturing

Experimental Run: # 5 — Number of units: 20

Column	Control Factor	Level Setting
1	Paint method	Manual
2	Handling	Gloves
3	Metal dip	Iridite
4	Dip time	5 minutes
5	Masking procedure	Inspection
6	Primer	Lilly
7	Secondary coat	Sherwin-Williams
8	Number of coats	2
9	Texturing	No texturing

Experimental Run: # 6 — Number of units: 20

Column	Control Factor	Level Setting
1	Paint method	Manual
2	Handling	Gloves
3	Metal dip	Iridite
4	Dip time	30 minutes
5	Masking procedure	No inspection
6	Primer	Lilly
7	Secondary coat	Lilly
8	Number of coats	1
9	Texturing	Texturing

Experimental Run: # 7 — Number of units: 20

Column	Control Factor	Level Setting
1	Paint method	Automatic
2	Handling	No gloves
3	Metal dip	Iridite
4	Dip time	30 minutes
5	Masking procedure	No inspection
6	Primer	Sherwin-Williams
7	Secondary coat	Lilly
8	Number of coats	2
9	Texturing	No texturing

Figure 14-2 *Continued*

Experimental Run: # 8 | Number of units: 20

Column	Control Factor	Level Setting
1	Paint method	Automatic
2	Handling	No gloves
3	Metal dip	Iridite
4	Dip time	5 minutes
5	Masking procedure	Inspection
6	Primer	Lilly
7	Secondary coat	Lilly
8	Number of coats	1
9	Texturing	No texturing

Experimental Run: # 9 | Number of units: 20

Column	Control Factor	Level Setting
1	Paint method	Automatic
2	Handling	No gloves
3	Metal dip	Chromate
4	Dip time	30 minutes
5	Masking procedure	Inspection
6	Primer	Lilly
7	Secondary coat	Sherwin-Williams
8	Number of coats	2
9	Texturing	Texturing

Experimental Run: # 10 | Number of units: 20

Column	Control Factor	Level Setting
1	Paint method	Automatic
2	Handling	Gloves
3	Metal dip	Iridite
4	Dip time	5 minutes
5	Masking procedure	No inspection
6	Primer	Sherwin-Williams
7	Secondary coat	Sherwin-Williams
8	Number of coats	2
9	Texturing	Texturing

Experimental Run: # 11 | Number of units: 20

Column	Control Factor	Level Setting
1	Paint method	Automatic
2	Handling	Gloves
3	Metal dip	Chromate
4	Dip time	30 minutes
5	Masking procedure	No inspection
6	Primer	Lilly
7	Secondary coat	Sherwin-Williams
8	Number of coats	1
9	Texturing	No texturing

Figure 14-2 *Continued*

Experimental Run: # 12 | Number of units: 20

Column	Control Factor	Level Setting
1	Paint method	Automatic
2	Handling	Gloves
3	Metal dip	Chromate
4	Dip time	5 minutes
5	Masking procedure	Inspection
6	Primer	Sherwin-Williams
7	Secondary coat	Lilly
8	Number of coats	1
9	Texturing	Texturing

14.2.3 Dynamic Characteristic Run Sheet

The run sheet for a dynamic characteristic can be developed similarly to that of a continuously measurable characteristic. The run sequence can be grouped by the required noise factor setting combinations (outer array columns). Within each group, the sheet lists the experimental runs in order with their respective control factor settings (inner array rows). Since this is a dynamic characteristic, you will also need to consider the signal factor. One effective method of handling this is to set up corresponding columns to the right of the control factor levels.

Figure 14-3 illustrates a run sheet for a study in which the purpose was to increase measurement accuracy within an electronic circuit. The specific quality characteristic was the value of the input resistor, R_{input}. Seven control factors were incorporated into an L_8 inner array. The outer array consisted of one noise factor at two levels. The adjustment factor had three levels.

14.3 TIME CONSTRAINTS AND OTHER CONSIDERATIONS

Acquiring production time to perform an experiment is often difficult. Justifying the interruption of production to run tests can sometimes require a concerted effort. Often, manufacturing supervision does not understand the merit of building product at process settings that are likely to produce unacceptable results. In other cases, customer commitments may strain the production limits as it is. Manufacturing may be unwilling to jeopardize promised delivery dates. Performing an experiment often requires the bridging of such barriers. Time constraints are often one of the biggest barriers to overcome. It is essential to develop appropriate tactics to surmount these obstacles.

Figure 14-3 Dynamic Characteristic Experimental Run Sheet

Quality characteristic = R_{input}

Experimental Run: # 1				10 ohms		200 ohms		2000 ohms	
Column	Control Factor	Level Setting		No Scan	Scan	No Scan	Scan	No Scan	Scan
1	Fixed time	8.2	ms.						
2	Integrate time	16.7	ms.						
3	Cint	.1	μf.						
4	Caz	.01	μf.						
5	Cref	.1	μf.						
6	Supply voltage	−5.0	volts						
7	Rint	125k	ohms						

Experimental Run: # 2				10 ohms		200 ohms		2000 ohms	
Column	Control Factor	Level Setting		No Scan	Scan	No Scan	Scan	No Scan	Scan
1	Fixed time	8.2	ms.						
2	Integrate time	16.7	ms.						
3	Cint	.1	μf.						
4	Caz	.47	μf.						
5	Cref	.2	μf.						
6	Supply voltage	−7.0	volts						
7	Rint	250k	ohms						

Experimental Run: # 3				10 ohms		200 ohms		2000 ohms	
Column	Control Factor	Level Setting		No Scan	Scan	No Scan	Scan	No Scan	Scan
1	Fixed time	8.2	ms.						
2	Integrate time	33.3	ms.						
3	Cint	.2	μf.						
4	Caz	.01	μf.						
5	Cref	.1	μf.						
6	Supply voltage	−7.0	volts						
7	Rint	250k	ohms						

Experimental Run: # 4				10 ohms		200 ohms		2000 ohms	
Column	Control Factor	Level Setting		No Scan	Scan	No Scan	Scan	No Scan	Scan
1	Fixed time	8.2	ms.						
2	Integrate time	33.3	ms.						
3	Cint	.2	μf.						
4	Caz	.47	μf.						
5	Cref	.2	μf.						
6	Supply voltage	−5.0	volts						
7	Rint	125k	ohms						

Figure 14-3 *Continued*

Experimental Run: # 5				10 ohms		200 ohms		2000 ohms	
Column	Control Factor	Level Setting		No Scan	Scan	No Scan	Scan	No Scan	Scan
1	Fixed time	32.8	ms.						
2	Integrate time	16.7	ms.						
3	Cint	.2	μf.						
4	Caz	.01	μf.						
5	Cref	.2	μf.						
6	Supply voltage	−5.0	volts						
7	Rint	250k	ohms						

Experimental Run: # 6				10 ohms		200 ohms		2000 ohms	
Column	Control Factor	Level Setting		No Scan	Scan	No Scan	Scan	No Scan	Scan
1	Fixed time	32.8	ms.						
2	Integrate time	16.7	ms.						
3	Cint	.2	μf.						
4	Caz	.47	μf.						
5	Cref	.1	μf.						
6	Supply voltage	−7.0	volts						
7	Rint	125k	ohms						

Experimental Run: # 7				10 ohms		200 ohms		2000 ohms	
Column	Control Factor	Level Setting		No Scan	Scan	No Scan	Scan	No Scan	Scan
1	Fixed time	32.8	ms.						
2	Integrate time	33.3	ms.						
3	Cint	.1	μf.						
4	Caz	.01	μf.						
5	Cref	.2	μf.						
6	Supply voltage	−7.0	volts						
7	Rint	125k	ohms						

Experimental Run: # 8				10 ohms		200 ohms		2000 ohms	
Column	Control Factor	Level Setting		No Scan	Scan	No Scan	Scan	No Scan	Scan
1	Fixed time	32.8	ms.						
2	Integrate time	33.3	ms.						
3	Cint	.1	μf.						
4	Caz	.47	μf.						
5	Cref	.1	μf.						
6	Supply voltage	−5.0	volts						
7	Rint	250k	ohms						

One tactic to get around busy production schedules is to consider off shifts. This approach can be particularly effective if the affected process is a one-shift operation. The experiment can be conducted either prior to or at the conclusion of the regular work hours. A two-shift operation provides less convenient alternative solutions, but the required experimentation time can still be acquired. The study can be planned for the period prior to first shift or at the conclusion of second shift. If the conducting of the experiment is time consuming, you may need to set up a third shift on a temporary basis.

If the operation consists of three shifts and continues around the clock, a second tactic may need to be used. Schedule the necessary personnel to work Saturday. If Saturdays are being utilized, take advantage of open Sundays. Another tactic is to take advantage of nonproduction time. This refers to those periods in which group meetings are held, training is being conducted, or other nonproduction activities are occurring.

If the process is a continuous seven-days-a-week, twenty-four-hours-a-day operation, the experimental runs will have to supersede time that would normally be allocated for production. This is where management support up front and manufacturing participation in planning the experiment as explained in Chapter 2 pay dividends.

When the experiment is scheduled during regular production hours, the time allotted is not always as much as you would like. However, the available windows may be few and far between. Therefore, the opportunity must be taken advantage of, and the time must be utilized to the fullest. To achieve these aims requires detailed planning, precise scheduling, and effective coordination.

Starting out on the right foot is critical to the efficient use of the time allocated for the experiment. Parts and material must be in place at the start of the experiment. You need to insure that planning has allocated the necessary number of parts and that scheduling has insured that the parts are on the manufacturing floor and conveniently located. Any material screening or preparation should have already been coordinated and be complete.

Along with the material being ready, the appropriate personnel and equipment must be in place and prepared. Part of the critical planning requirements is to determine the type of personnel, the number of personnel, and the length of time each will be needed. This determination will require knowledge of the process including setup time between factor level changes and the time required to produce each experimental unit. A vital consideration in estimating setup times is that not all process factors are created equal. Some take considerably longer to change than others. This difference must be taken into consideration in determining the required process time. Although these determinations will not guarantee that you will receive the ideal amount of time that you desire, this show of attention to detail will increase your probability of ideal time and even at worst will increase the amount of time that you do receive.

Other personnel considerations may include specific technical skills. If sophisticated equipment is involved, a software specialist may have to write a special program for the experimental runs and load the instructions into the computer. This step may take considerable time. To avoid such delays, the specialist needs to be contacted well in advance of running the experiment. In addition, the specialist needs to be educated on the intent of the study and what specifically the machinery must do so that he or she can properly write the appropriate instructions. If special tooling is required, the die maker or machinist may need to be involved. Time is needed not only to make the part, but to design it as well. This requirement must also be provided for in the schedule.

Coordinating the start of the experiment is critical, as is the timely transfer from one process stage to the next. Unless the transfer time is a specific factor being studied in the experiment, the periods between steps should be minimized. This is an area where detailed planning and thorough coordination become most evident. Breakdowns between process stages can disrupt the entire experiment and even affect the outcome of the data. For example, in an electronic assembly operation involving both surface mount and through hole technology, long delays after surface mount soldering will result in excessive oxidation and subsequent poor soldering in the through hole process regardless of the process settings at either stage.

Coordination with testing, measurements, and inspection is important as well. In testing, the equipment, tester, and units need to come together at the same time. The equipment may only be available for a limited time and must be returned. The tester may have other duties which will allow him or her a limited time supporting the project. In some circumstances, the experimental units and the corresponding quality characteristic may be too sensitive to time. Therefore, in these situations, you do not want to wait too long after running the experiment to collect data. Long durations between the actual production of the units and the testing may create changes in the results.

The same can basically be said for taking measurements. Perhaps someone else needs the measuring device and has scheduled its use. Therefore, you need to take advantage of the time that it is in your possession. Just as a tester's time is valuable, so is that of the measurer. Again, you must be careful of product sensitivity to time.

If inspection is required, the coordination of inspector, units to be inspected, and visual aids must be planned together. Failure for the inspection aids to be ready at the time of inspection can affect the results for the same reasons as were explained with testing and measurements. An example of a quality characteristic in electronic assembly that would require inspection and could change over time is percent oxidation. For such a characteristic, you should perform inspection as soon as possible after completing processing.

Starting to test, taking measurements, or inspecting as scheduled with the proper tools is important. Also key is completing the acquisition of data in a timely fashion. Just as delays in getting started can affect time-sensitive quality characteristics, excessive breaks between testing or inspection can create measurement bias. The operator may measure just a little differently on Thursday than he did on Tuesday. Perhaps he holds the calipers a little tighter the second time. Let's say the inspector is not as serious about the task on Friday as he was on Wednesday and he checks for nonconformance with a less critical eye. Subsequently, the units checked on the first day have more defects that those inspected on the last day regardless of which units were actually built under the worse process conditions.

If by definition of factor levels, more than one shift is required in the experiment, scheduling may become more complicated. If at all possible, it is best in this case if the experiment can roll over from the one shift of interest to the next shift of interest. This change helps to minimize the effect of extraneous factors. Because of this concern, it is best to conduct the entire experiment all at one time if at all possible. Consider a choice between conducting an experiment with, let us say, five repetitions across two different intervals and an experiment run at one time with four repetitions. The potential harm from inducing undefined factors to affect the results will probably outweigh the good derived from the additional data points.

14.4 DOCUMENTATION OF EXPERIMENT

Considerable discussion has been put forth on the need for recording information during the conducting of the experiment. In the planning phase, we discussed the importance of determining up front the essential facts that are required to help make value judgments concerning the experimental results. In the chapter on developing test plans, the importance of documenting and publishing those pieces of information that should be recorded during the experiment was emphasized. In line with the current topic of what to do during the actual running of the experiment, it might be wise at this time to review the types of items that should be incorporated and the sequence in which they are likely to appear and will be recorded.

Concerning what should be documented, the test plan itself should be used as a guide to insure that all appropriate information is recorded. The items for consideration can fall into one of the following groups:

Table 14-1 Typical Experiment Documentation

Initial Startup:
- Date and Time
- Operator
- Raw Material—Supplier/Manufacturer
  - Lot Number
  - Date Code
- Equipment—Manufacturer
  - Model Number/Type
  - Serial Number
  - Calibration Date

Experimental Runs:
- Deviations from Test Plan
- Unexpected/Unplanned Events
- Experimental Conditions
- Process Irregularities
- Delays between Process Steps
- Operator Observations
- Process Readings

Completion of Experimental Runs:
- Test Sample Preparation Notes
- Tester/Measurer/Inspector
- Test Equipment—Manufacturer
  - Model Number/Type
  - Serial Number
  - Calibration Date
- Measurement—Measurement Device
  - Manufacturer
  - Serial Number
  - Calibration Date
- Data—Test Results
  - Measurements
  - Inspector Evaluation
- Comments—Tester/Measurer/Inspector

1. experimental conditions
2. deviations from the test plan
3. unexpected and unplanned events
4. experiment irregularities
5. response values/inspection results

Experimental conditions include information on raw material such as supplier name and date code and machinery identification including type and serial number. The operator name and date of the experiment would also follow into this group. Deviations from the test plan would relate to those procedures specifically called for in the written plan which could not be performed and either had to be replaced by alternate steps or had to be dropped altogether. Unexpected and unplanned events are just that: occurrences during the conducting of the experiment which no one on the team anticipated. The team may or may not have been prepared for the particular contingencies. Experiment irregularities are the results or measurements that are either a consequence of deviations from the plan or the result of unexpected or unplanned events. An example is an experiment in which one quality characteristic (thickness) is deemed important and will be measured and a second characteristic (color) is considered unimportant due to relatively little change and will not be monitored. As sample parts are produced, color varies significantly from one experimental run to another. Because of this unexpected result, color evaluations are performed and recorded in the comments section of the log sheet. Response values and inspection results constitute the data that the experimentation team has predetermined in the planning phase that they wish to obtain.

Another way to look at experimental information that should be documented is the order in which it may appear. Table 14-1 summarizes the sequence of events that typically occur during the actual conducting of experimental runs and the associated information.

Chapter 15

LEVEL AVERAGE ANALYSIS

The type of analysis to be performed on the experiment data will be dictated by the design of the experiment. We can categorize the different designs in terms of the type of quality characteristic and the involvement of noise factors. When the quality characteristic has been defined in terms of a continuously measurable variable and no noise factors have been designed into the experiment, level average analysis may be the most appropriate technique for interpreting the data.

15.1 CONCEPTS

Level average analysis gets its name from determining the average response for factor and interaction levels and analyzing the importance of factors and interactions based on these computed values. The goal behind level average analysis is to identify the strongest effects and determine the combination of factors and interactions investigated that can produce the most desired results. The first step within the strategy is to calculate the average experiment result for each level or setting for each factor and interaction (if defined in the experiment). The relative impact of each factor can be determined either tabularly (Figure 15-1) or graphically (Figure 15-2). As a good self check, it is recommended that the analysis be performed both ways. Once the strong effects and desired levels have been ascertained, a calculation of the predicted results is made based on the impact of the important effects on the experiment results. Then a confirmation run is performed using the optimal factor levels identified in the analysis. The results of the confirmation run are compared against the predicted results to verify the analysis and confirm the assumptions made in designing the experiment.

Using the tabular method for analysis, a response table should be constructed displaying the average experiment result for each factor level under study. For each factor, the range in average response values should then be computed. In an experiment involving two level factors, this is merely the difference between the average values of the two settings. However for three levels or more, you must identify the highest average response and the lowest average response.

Figure 15-1 Tabular Method

Run No.	A	B	A × B	Data
1	1	1	1	20
2	1	2	2	40
3	2	1	2	25
4	2	2	1	10

$L_4 (2^3)$

Response Table

Level	A	B	A × B
1	30.0	22.5	15.0
2	17.5	25.0	32.5
	12.5	2.5	**17.5**

(Significant factors in **bold**.)

Be careful in identifying the proper levels for computing the range. The extreme values may not necessarily come from the highest and lowest factor settings. Once the differences have been ascertained, the next step is to separate the strong effects from the mild and weak effects. A sound and consistent approach is to rank the factors in order from the largest difference to the smallest. Then, you will want to move from the largest to the smallest delta looking for a logical breaking point between the strong effects and the mild and weak effects. A rule of thumb is to identify approximately half of the effects as having a significant impact on the quality characteristic.

Figure 15-2 Graphical Method

$L_4 (2^3)$

Run No.	A	B	A × B	Data
1	1	1	1	20
2	1	2	2	40
3	2	1	2	25
4	2	2	1	10

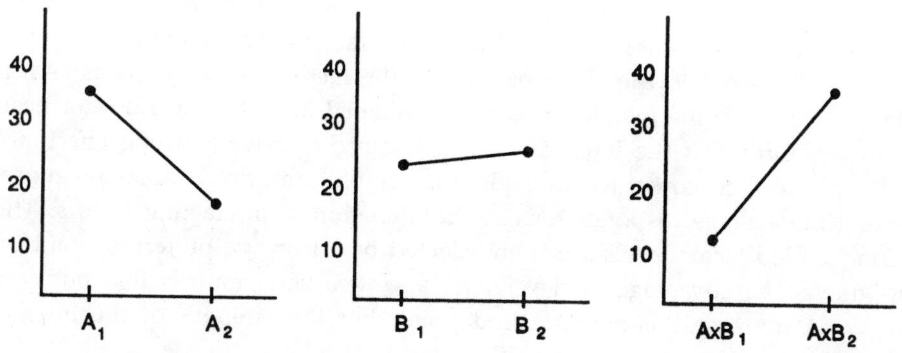

The strongest factors can also be identified graphically. By plotting the average response value for each factor level, we can make relative comparisons of the slopes between points plotted. Again, the factors can be ranked, but based this time on the relative steepness of the slopes. The rule of selecting approximately half of the factors investigated still applies.

Once the strong effects have been identified, a prediction of the expected results with process settings at the preferred settings should be calculated. The prediction is calculated based on the effect of these preferred settings on the average experiment results. Process settings should then be changed to these values, and a confirmation run can be performed. As stated earlier, the purpose of the confirmation run is to validate the conclusions and the assumptions on which the experiment was based. The confirmation run is a set of units run together under the optimal conditions determined from the analysis. These conditions include the best or preferred settings for mild and weak influences as well as for strong effects. However, the less influential factors are not incorporated into the prediction equation. The reasoning is that the differences in the average results may be due to experimental variation and to incorporate their effect could result in an overestimate of the predicted results.[1] This could lead to a disappointing confirmation run when actually the results would have validated the experiment analysis if the predicted results had not been artifically high or low.

If interactions have been incorporated into the design of the experiment, analysis may become more detailed (see Figure 15–3). Using the tabular method of analysis, the range for any interaction under study is similarly compared to the ranges for each of the factors under study. If the interaction is not determined to be important based on the relative comparisons and logical breaking point, analysis of the interaction does not need to go any further. If on the other hand the interaction is deemed important, a matrix of the various combinations of the two factors comprising the interaction should be constructed. The levels of the associated factors can then be selected on the basis of the factor level combination resulting in the most desired experiment result.

Graphical analysis, also in Figure 15-3, can be even more helpful in determining the best combination of interacting factors. The slope of the interaction is compared to the slope of each of the factors or main effects. As in tabular analysis, if the interaction is not considered important, we do not need to go any further. If the interaction is determined to have a strong effect, we will then need to construct an additional graph comprised of points representing the average response for each combination of interacting factors. The recommended factor levels are then selected based on the preferred point on the graph. The advantage of developing an interaction graph is that not only can you determine the most desired point, but the strength of the interac-

Figure 15-3 Interaction Analysis

$L_4 (2^3)$

Run No.	A	B	A × B	Data
1	1	1	1	20
2	1	2	2	40
3	2	1	2	25
4	2	2	1	10

	B_1	B_2
A_1	20.0	40.0
A_2	25.0	10.0

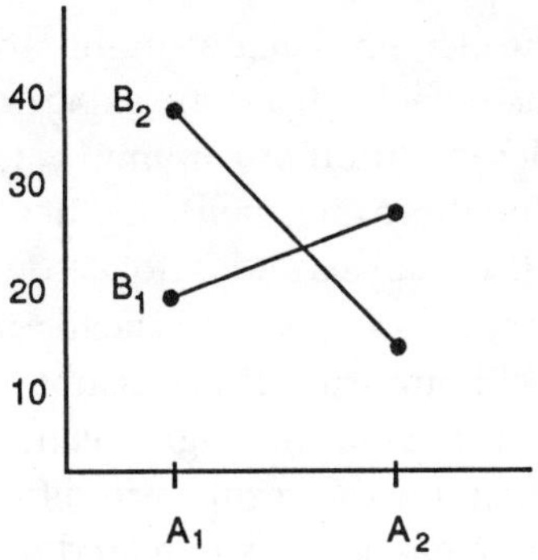

tion is often clearer when shown graphically (see Section 5.5, "Potential Interaction Concerns").

An additional point, which will be reiterated as you continue through the chapters on analysis, concerns factors that are significant both as a main effect and as part of an interaction. The values computed for an interaction matrix and plotted on an interaction graph are a culmination of the individual effects of the factors and their interaction. The best value will be a result of these combined effects. The strongest effects will have the overriding influence on recommended settings. Therefore if an interacting factor is significant by itself, the level chosen from either the interaction matrix or the interaction graph will not be in conflict with the level selected for the strong main effect studied by itself.

The analysis strategy will change depending on the type of quality characteristic. If the output of interest is a larger-the-better characteristic, the emphasis will be on determining which levels result in the highest response. For a smaller-the-better characteristic, the goal is to identify those factor levels that will achieve the lowest expected results. For nominal-the-best quality characteristics, the analysis is more complicated. Moving the average process results closer to the desired or target value is hardly desirable if the variation from one unit or batch to the next increases. Therefore, regular analysis is not recommended for handling nominal-the-best quality characteristics. A preferred approach is to run repetitions for each experimental run and to treat the repetitions as noise factor setting combinations. The data can then be analyzed using the techniques in Chapter 19.

Once the confirmation run has been performed, the actual and predicted results can be compared against each other. If the results are similar, then the experiment can be deemed a success, and the preferred settings should be instituted. For those factors determined to have a weak effect on the result of interest, the easiest or most cost effective levels can be implemented. If the confirmation results are disappointing, the team will need to return to the planning phase to reevaluate the elements that went into the experiment. A possible cause is the omission of a key factor from the experiment. Perhaps a powerful interaction was not considered. Another common cause is the setting of factor levels too close together for the experiment. In these situations, the factor is found insignificant during the analysis and is not accounted for in the validation. During the confirmation run, let's say that this factor operates at a value beyond the experimental values. Although the factor is not a strong effect within the experimental range, moving outside this region causes a significant change in the output of interest. Therefore, the results are different from what was predicted. Another potential problem occurs when randomization is used to conduct the experiment. After performing the experiment with the order of experimental runs scrambled, the team fails to reorder the sequence of the runs for the analysis. This is a simple mistake, but I have seen it happen more than once. An experiment may not always prove a rousing success or a total failure; there can be many gray areas in between. Let's say that the purpose of the experiment is directed toward problem solving. If the confirmation results are not as good as the predicted results, but better than the current production results, you may want to consider implementing the recommended settings temporarily while returning to the planning phase. This at least gives you some improvement until better understanding of the process or product can lead to a better confirmation run and more desirable results.

15.2 DIGITAL CIRCUIT (LARGER-THE-BETTER) CASE STUDY

Problem: A design engineering team is working together to develop a digital circuit that will reliably operate upon receiving the proper input signal (see Figure 15-4).

Objective: To maximize the mean time between failures.

The mean time between failures is to be measured in terms of the number of operations successfully performed prior to receiving a valid input and not operating. Experiment design and data are given in Figure 15-5.

Figure 15-4 Digital Circuit

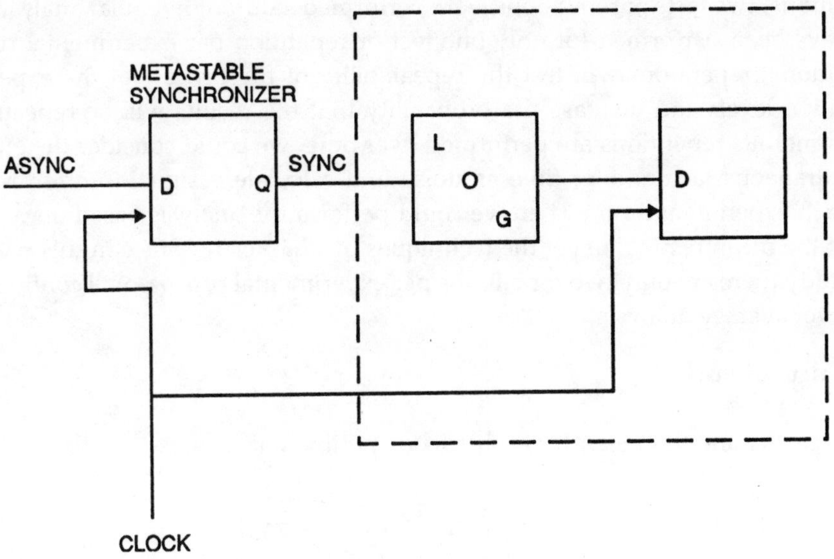

Figure 15-5 Experiment Design and Data

Selected Characteristics
Y = mean time between failures

Control Factors	Level 1	Level 2
A. Input Signal	200 nsec	400 nsec
B. Clock Frequency	10 mhz	25 mhz
C. Flip Flop	LS	AS
D. Synchronizers	1	2
E. Capacitive Loading	15 pf	50 pf

Interactions

input signal × clock frequency
clock frequency × flip flop

	A 1	B 2	A × B 3	C 4	D 5	B × C 6	E 7	Data	
1	1	1	1	1	1	1	1	75	71
2	1	1	1	2	2	2	2	68	65
3	1	2	2	1	1	2	2	18	15
4	1	2	2	2	2	1	1	22	23
5	2	1	2	1	2	1	2	45	47
6	2	1	2	2	1	2	1	12	9
7	2	2	1	1	2	2	1	25	28
8	2	2	1	2	1	1	2	2	3

For each experimental run or combination of circuit designs and operating conditions, two tests or repetitions were performed. Although regular analysis could have been performed for only one test or repetition per experimental run, additional repetitions will test the repeatability of the process at the experimentation levels and increase the probability that the results will be repeatable. If numerous repetitions are performed over time, we could consider the effects of extraneous factors over time as noise and calculate a signal-to-noise ratio for each experimental run. Then we could perform the analysis based on η instead of the mean results, using the techniques in Chapter 18. Since in this particular study there are only two repetitions per experimental run, we will continue with level average analysis.

Calculations:

1. Determine the mean for each row (experimental run).

$$\#1\ \bar{y}_1 = \frac{75 + 71}{2} = 73.0$$

$$\#2\ \bar{y}_2 = \frac{68 + 65}{2} = 66.5$$

....

$$\#8\ \bar{y}_8 = \frac{2 + 3}{2} = 2.5$$

After calculating the mean response for each row, we can set up an additional column alongside the orthogonal array matching the corresponding mean with each combination of factor levels.

Run#	A	B	A × B	C	D	B × C	E	Data		Mean Response $\bar{y}$
1	1	1	1	1	1	1	1	75	71	73.0
2	1	1	1	2	2	2	2	68	65	66.5
3	1	2	2	1	1	2	2	18	15	16.5
4	1	2	2	2	2	1	1	22	23	22.5
5	2	1	2	1	2	1	2	45	47	46.0
6	2	1	2	2	1	2	1	12	9	10.5
7	2	2	1	1	2	2	1	25	28	26.5
8	2	2	1	2	1	1	2	2	3	2.5

2. Calculate the average $\bar{y}$ (mean response) for each factor and interaction level and develop a response table. This is performed by grouping the mean responses by factor level for each column in the array, taking the sum, and dividing by the number of responses. The absolute difference or delta between the two average results (two levels) or the highest and lowest average results (more than two levels) is the effect of the factor or interaction.

For example: The associated values of $\bar{y}$ for A_1 would match those experimental runs at which A was set at level 1 as indicated in bold type in the following graph.

Run#	A	B	A × B	C	D	B × C	E	Data		Mean Response $\bar{y}$
1	**1**	1	1	1	1	1	1	75	71	**73.0**
2	**1**	1	1	2	2	2	2	68	65	**66.5**
3	**1**	2	2	1	1	2	2	18	15	**16.5**
4	**1**	2	2	2	2	1	1	22	23	**22.5**
5	2	1	2	1	2	1	2	45	47	46.0
6	2	1	2	2	1	2	1	12	9	10.5
7	2	2	1	1	2	2	1	25	28	26.5
8	2	2	1	2	1	1	2	2	3	2.5

Then,

$$\overline{A}_1 = \frac{73.0 + 66.5 + 16.5 + 22.5}{4} = 44.625.$$

By the same method,

$$\overline{A}_2 = \frac{46.0 + 10.5 + 26.5 + 2.5}{4} = 21.375$$

$$\text{Effect of A} = |\overline{A}_1 - \overline{A}_2| = |44.625 - 21.375| = 23.250$$

Similarly,

$$\overline{B}_1 = \frac{73.0 + 66.5 + 46.0 + 10.5}{4} = 49.000$$

$$\overline{B}_2 = \frac{16.5 + 22.5 + 26.5 + 2.5}{4} = 17.000$$

$$\text{Effect of B} = |\overline{B}_1 - \overline{B}_2| = |49.000 - 17.000.| = 32.000$$

By performing these calculations for each of the other columns, the following response table is generated:

Response Table

	A	B	A × B	C	D	B × C	E
Level 1	44.625	49.000	42.125	40.500	25.625	36.000	33.125
Level 2	21.375	17.000	23.875	25.500	40.375	30.000	32.875
Delta	23.500	32.000	18.250	15.000	14.750	6.000	.250

3. Based on the average $\overline{y}$ (mean response) computed for each factor and interaction level, construct means response graphs (Figure 15-6).

4. Analyze the means response table and means response graphs. The purpose of the analysis is to determine those factors that have a strong effect on the quality characteristic of interest. In this case study, the primary concern is mean time between failures. A consistent and systematic approach is to identify the strongest effect, then the next largest, and so on. Remembering the one-half rule of thumb, we will want to look for a logical breaking point as we compare each factor or interaction with the next strongest effect. The exact breaking point between the factors identified as strong and those regarded as having a mild or weak influence is based on the relative difference from one effect to another.

Response Table

	A	B	A × B	C	D	B × C	E
Level 1	44.625	49.000	42.125	40.500	25.625	36.000	33.125
Level 2	21.375	17.000	23.875	25.500	40.375	30.000	32.875
Delta	**23.500**	**32.000**	**18.250**	**15.000**	**14.750**	6.000	.250

In this study, factor B (clock frequency) has the greatest effect on mean time between failures. Factor A (input signal) is second with a delta or difference between levels of 23.500. The interaction A × B is next followed by factor C. The

Figure 15-6 Digital Circuit Response Graphs

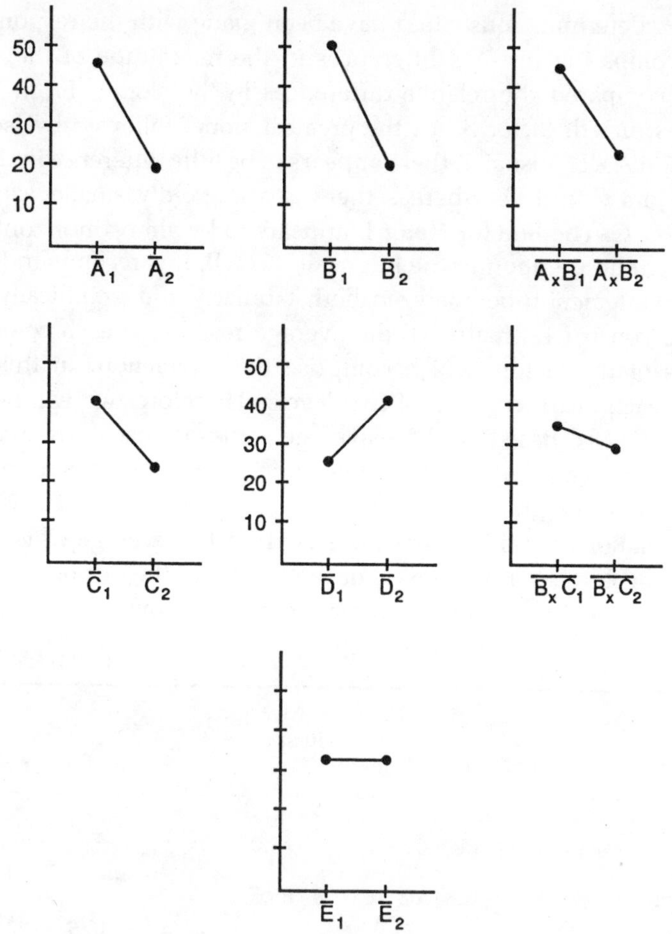

difference between the effects of interaction A × B and factor C is 3.250 (18.250 − 15.000). The drop from factor C to factor D is only .250 (15.000 − 14.750). If we continue farther to the interaction B × C, the difference in effects jumps to 8.750 (14.750 − 6.000). Therefore, we will choose this as our breaking point.

Since by definition our output of interest is a larger-the-better quality characteristic, we will want to choose the level that resulted in the larger average response value. Based on this premise, we would recommend C_1 and D_1. Since the interaction A × B was determined to be a strong effect along with factors A and B, we will need to investigate this interaction in more detail. Since the interaction B × C was deemed a weak effect, we will not study it further. Since factor E was a very weak effect, the recommended level can be based on cost or convenience.

The same determinations could have been made with the response graphs. Instead of comparing relative differences in the magnitude of the effects, we could have compared the relative differences in the slopes. From the graphs that we constructed, factor B has the greatest slope, followed by factor A and the interaction A × B. Visually, there appears to be little difference in the absolute slope of factors C and D, whereas there is a markedly smaller slope for the interaction B × C. The line for factor E appears to be almost horizontal.

Returning our attention to the interaction A × B, it is recommended that the effect of the interaction be analyzed both tabularly and graphically. First, we will need to construct a matrix of the average results for each combination of the settings of the factors which comprise the interaction. In this particular interaction, each factor consists of two levels. Therefore, we will need to construct a 2 × 2 matrix. Based on these average values for each factor combination in the matrix, we can also plot the interaction graph. Each value in the matrix will be a point in the graph.

The calculations for the matrix are based on the average of y (average response) for the corresponding levels of the factors in the orthogonal array. The calculations for the interaction A × B matrix are as follows:

Run#	A	B	A × B	C	D	B × C	E	Data		Mean Response $\bar{y}$	
1	1	1	1	1	1	1	1	75	71	73.0	$\bar{A}_1 \bar{B}_1 = \frac{73.0 + 66.5}{2} = 69.75$
2	1	1	1	2	2	2	2	68	65	66.5	
3	**1**	**2**	2	1	1	2	2	18	15	**16.5**	$\mathbf{\bar{A}_1 \bar{B}_2 = \frac{16.5 + 22.5}{2} = 19.50}$
4	**1**	**2**	2	2	2	1	1	22	23	**22.5**	
5	2	1	2	1	2	1	2	45	47	46.0	$\bar{A}_2 \bar{B}_1 = \frac{46.0 + 10.5}{2} = 28.25$
6	2	1	2	2	1	2	1	12	9	10.5	
7	**2**	**2**	1	1	2	2	1	25	28	**26.5**	$\mathbf{\bar{A}_2 \bar{B}_2 = \frac{26.5 + 2.5}{2} = 14.50}$
8	**2**	**2**	1	2	1	1	2	2	3	**2.5**	

We can then fill the interaction matrix for A × B and plot the corresponding interaction graph.

Interaction Matrix

	B_1	B_2
A_1	69.75	19.50
A_2	28.25	14.50

The converging lines in the interaction graph in Figure 15-7 indicate that the interaction $A \times B$ does have an effect on the response. However, since the two lines do not intersect, this is not an extremely strong interaction. Since our evaluation of the response table ranked this interaction as third in relative importance and close to the fourth and fifth strongest effects, these two conclusions are in harmony. In both the 2×2 matrix and the interaction graph, the recommended levels are A_1 and B_1. This conclusion is in accord with the preferred levels for factors A and B if we were to select them based solely on their individual effect on the response of interest.

Therefore, the recommended factor levels are: A_1, B_1, C_1, D_2, with E based on cost and practicality.

5. Compute an estimate of the predicted response based on the selected levels of the strong effects.

Figure 15-7 Interaction Graph

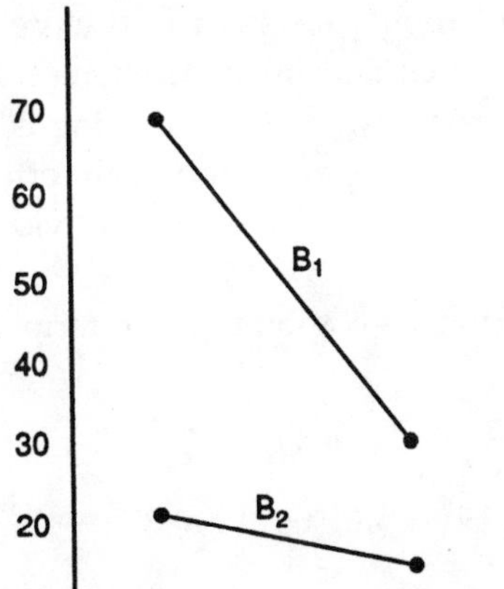

As mentioned earlier, only the strong effects are included in the prediction equation. Based on our analysis, those effects and associated levels are: A_1, B_1, $A \times B$, C_1, D_2.

The calculations are based on the overall average experimental value and the effect that each of the recommended levels of the strong factors and interactions has on the overall average.

If we define the overall experimental average as $\overline{T}$, we will have:

$$\overline{T} = \sum_{i=1}^{n} \frac{y}{n} = \frac{\overline{y}_i + \overline{y} + \ldots + \overline{y}_n}{8}$$

$$\overline{T} = \frac{73.0 + 66.5 + 16.5 + 22.5 + 4.60 + 10.5 + 26.5 + 2.5}{8}$$

$$T = 33.000$$

If we define the prediction average as $\hat{\mu}$ and incorporate the effect on the overall average by each of the strong factors and interactions, the prediction equation will be as follows:

$$\hat{\mu} = \overline{T} + (\overline{A}_1 - \overline{T}) + (\overline{B}_1 - \overline{T}) + [(\overline{A_1B_1} - \overline{T}) - (\overline{A}_1 - \overline{T}) - (\overline{B}_1 - \overline{T})] + (\overline{C}_1 - \overline{T}) + (\overline{D}_2 - \overline{T}).$$

The reason for subtracting the individual effects of factors A and B from the effect of $\overline{A_1B_1}$ is that $\overline{A_1B_1}$ is comprised of the effects of factor A, factor B, and the interaction itself. Unless the effects of the two factors are subtracted, we would be including these strong effects twice. If either factor A or factor B had been insignificant and not included in the prediction equation, we would still have subtracted its effect from $\overline{A_1B_1}$. The reasoning is that failure to deduct its effect would have meant including an insignificant effect that could result in an overestimate. In either case, the effects of the individual factors should be deducted from the combined effect.

If we reduce the equation by combining like terms, we will get:

$$\hat{\mu} = \overline{A_1B_1} + \overline{C}_1 + \overline{D}_2 - 2 \times \overline{T}$$

$$\hat{\mu} = 69.750 + 40.500 + 40.375 - 2(33.000)$$

$$\hat{\mu} = 84.625$$

It should be noted that the combined effect of all of the strong effects resulted in a greater predicted value than any of the experiment results. This is only logical when we consider that the overall predicted result is based on the combined effect of all of the strong factors and interactions' being set at their preferred levels and the assumption of additivity of the effects.

6. Conduct a confirmation run and compare the actual results to the predicted results.

A number of units built according to the recommended levels should be tested with the results compared against the predicted result of 84.625. The number of units will typically be determined by economics and time constraints. If the average result is close to 84.625, the recommended settings can be implemented. If the actual results are disappointingly low, the team will need to return to the planning phase and consider the possible causes.

15.3 CONTROL DEVICE "TIME OUT" (SMALLER-THE-BETTER) CASE STUDY

Problem: For a specific control device, the time required for the circuit to switch from the "On" state to the "Off" state when the L.E.D. (light emitting diode) drive current is removed is critical. The product specification requirement states that the time between changing states can be no more than .005 seconds. However, functional testing of current production reveals a large percentage of the units have not been in compliance with the timing specification.

Objective: Minimize the time required for the device to switch from the "On" state to the "Off" state.

Experiment design and data are given in Figure 15-8.
1. Determine the mean for each row (experimental run).

Since in this particular experiment we have only one data point for each experimental run, the mean response for each row is the single measurement obtained for that combination of experimental factors.

2. Calculate the average $\overline{y}$ (mean response) for each factor and interaction level and develop a response table.

Figure 15-8 Experiment Design and Data

y = Switching time (milliseconds)

Control Factors	Level 1	Level 2
A. Package Type	Type 1	Type 2
B. Burn In	No	Yes
C. Test Delay	No Delay	Delay
D. Component Supplier	Vendor X	Vendor Y

Interactions:

A × B: Package Type × Burn in
B × C: Burn In × Test Delay

Run#	A	B	A × B	C	D	B × C	e	Data (msec.)
1	1	1	1	1	1	1	1	7.98
2	1	1	1	2	2	2	2	6.21
3	1	2	2	1	1	2	2	5.10
4	1	2	2	2	2	1	1	6.27
5	2	1	2	1	2	1	2	4.10
6	2	1	2	2	1	2	1	2.95
7	2	2	1	1	2	2	1	2.40
8	2	2	1	2	1	1	2	3.02

For factor A,

$$\overline{A}_1 = \frac{7.98 + 6.21 + 5.10 + 6.27}{4} = 6.3900$$

$$\overline{A}_2 = \frac{4.10 + 2.95 + 2.40 + 3.02}{4} = 3.1175$$

$$\text{Effect of A} = |\overline{A}_1 - \overline{A}_2| = |6.3900 - 3.1175| = 3.2725$$

Similarly for factor B,

$$\overline{B}_1 = \frac{7.98 + 6.21 + 4.10 + 2.95}{4} = 5.3100$$

$$\overline{B}_2 = \frac{5.10 + 6.27 + 2.40 + 3.02}{4} = 4.1975$$

$$\text{Effect of B} = |\overline{B}_1 - \overline{B}_2| = |5.3100 - 4.1975| = 1.1125$$

The average response and effect for the remaining factors and interactions are calculated in the same fashion producing the following response table.

Response Table

	A	B	A × B	C	D	B × C	error
Level 1	6.3900	5.3100	4.9025	4.8950	4.7625	5.3425	4.9000
Level 2	3.1175	4.1975	4.6050	4.6125	4.7450	4.1650	4.6075
Delta	3.2725	1.1125	.2975	.2825	.0175	1.1775	.2925

3. Based on the average $\overline{y}$ (mean response) computed for each factor and interaction level, construct means response graphs (Figure 15-9).

4. Analyze the means response table and means response graphs.

By identifying the order of the effects from largest to smallest from the response chart or ranking the steepness of the slopes in the response graphs, we find that factor A is the strongest effect. The interaction B × C is second and is closely followed by factor B. By looking for a logical breaking point that includes approximately half of the effects being studied, we find the best split occurs between factor B and the interaction A × B. We also observe that the effect of A × B is close to that of the empty column (error), which also suggests that the effect of A × B (.2975 = .2925) is not significant. The effect in column 7 could be the result of experimental error or the impact of the interaction between factors A and C, which would have been assigned to column 7 if incorporated into the experiment. If the effect from column 7 had been judged as being strong, we would have needed to investigate the reason for the magnitude of this effect further.

Response Table

	A	B	A × B	C	D	B × C	error
Level 1	6.3900	5.3100	4.9025	4.8950	4.7625	5.3425	4.9000
Level 2	3.1175	4.1975	4.6050	4.6125	4.7450	4.1650	4.6075
Delta	**3.2725**	**1.1125**	.2975	.2825	.0175	**1.1775**	.2925

Figure 15-9 Means Response Graphs

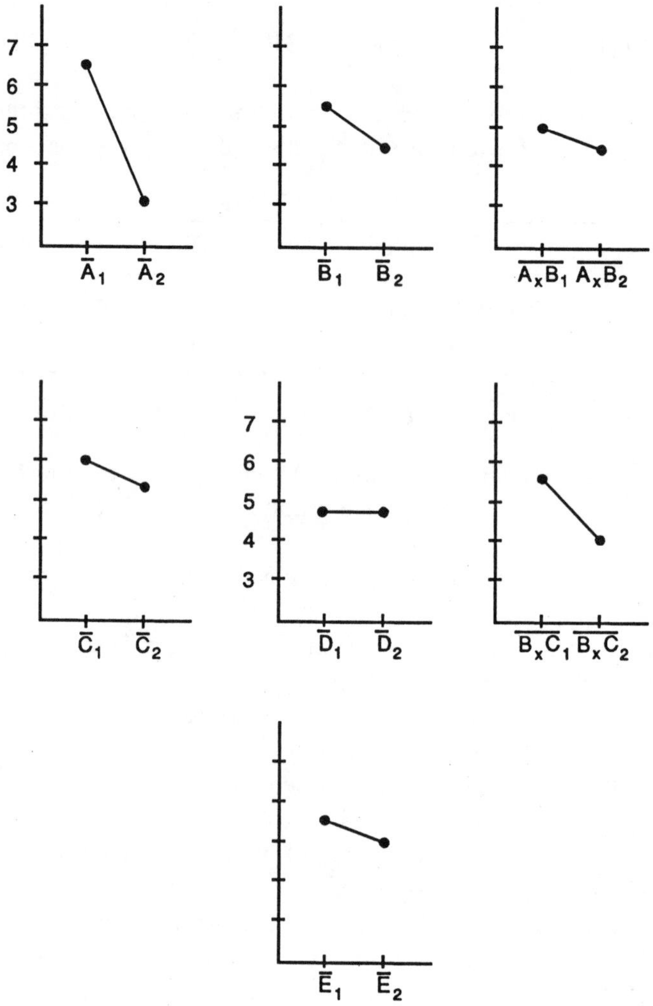

Since our quality characteristic is smaller-the-better, we will want to select the levels from the response table that show the lowest average responses. If we are selecting a level based on a response graph, our decision will be based on the lowest plotted point. Therefore, A_2 is the preferred level for factor A. Before determining the recommended level for factor B, we will need to analyze the interaction $B \times C$. The interaction $A \times B$ was not determined to be a strong effect and will not be addressed further. The calculations for the 2×2 matrix and the data points for the interaction graph for interaction $B \times C$ are as follows:

Run#	A	B	A × B	C	D	B × C	e	Data	Mean Response
1	1	1	1	1	1	1	1	7.98	$\overline{B}_1\,\overline{C}_1 = \frac{7.98 + 4.10}{2} = 6.040$
2	1	**1**	1	**2**	2	2	2	**6.21**	
3	1	**2**	2	1	1	2	2	5.10	$\overline{B}_1\,\overline{C}_2 = \frac{6.21 + 2.95}{2} = 4.580$
4	1	2	2	**2**	2	1	1	**6.27**	
5	2	1	2	1	2	1	2	4.10	$\overline{B}_2\,\overline{C}_1 = \frac{5.10 + 2.40}{2} = 3.750$
6	2	**1**	2	**2**	1	2	1	**2.95**	
7	2	**2**	1	1	2	2	1	2.40	$\overline{B}_2\,\overline{C}_2 = \frac{6.27 + 3.02}{2} = 4.645$
8	2	2	1	**2**	1	1	2	**3.02**	

We can then fill the interaction matrix for B×C and plot the corresponding interaction graph (Figure 15-10).

From the interaction graph, the intersecting lines tell us that this is indeed a strong interaction. Both the matrix and the graph show that the lowest response is at B_2C_1. Referring back to the response table, we find the recommended level for factor B as a strong individual effect concurs with the preferred level in the interaction. Since factor C was a weak effect by itself, its preferred level will be

Figure 15-10 Interaction Graph

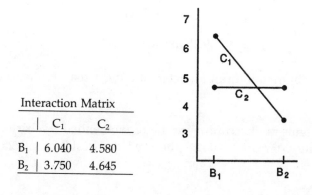

Interaction Matrix

	C_1	C_2
B_1	6.040	4.580
B_2	3.750	4.645

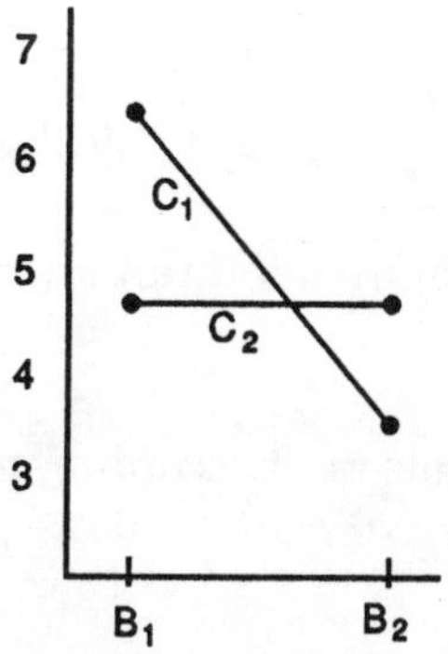

based purely on the interaction B×C. Therefore, level 1 is the recommended level for factor C.

In summary, the recommended levels are: A_2, B_2, C_1. Since changes in factor D (component supplier) had almost no effect, we can selects parts based on cost considerations.

5. Compute an estimate of the predicted response based on the selected levels of the strong effects.

Based on our analysis, the strong effects are: A_2, B_2, B×C.

The overall experimental average ($\overline{T}$) is calculated as follows:

$$\overline{T} = \sum_{i=1}^{n} \frac{\overline{y}_i}{n} = \frac{\overline{y}_1 + \overline{y}_2 + \ldots + \overline{y}_8}{8}$$

$$\overline{T} = \frac{7.98 + 6.21 + 5.10 + 6.27 + 4.10 + 2.95 + 2.40 + 3.02}{8}$$

$$\overline{T} = 4.75375$$

Defining the predicted switching time as $\hat{\mu}$, the prediction equation can be written as:

$$\hat{\mu} = \overline{T} + (\overline{A}_2 - \overline{T}) + (\overline{B}_2 - \overline{T}) + [(\overline{B_2C_1} - \overline{T}) - (\overline{B}_2 - \overline{T}) - (\overline{C}_1 - \overline{T})].$$

Combining like terms reduces the equation to:

$$\hat{\mu} = \overline{A}_2 + \overline{B_2C_1} - \overline{C}_1.$$

Substituting values from the response table and interaction matrix,

$$\hat{\mu} = 3.1175 + 3.7500 - 4.8950$$

$$\hat{\mu} = 1.9725 \text{ msec.}$$

6. Conduct a confirmation run and compare the actual results to the predicted results.

A number of units built according to the recommended levels should be tested with the results compared against the predicted result of 1.9725 msec. If the average result is close to the predicted value, the recommended settings can be implemented. If the actual results are higher, but still lower than the specification limit of 5 msec., the team may still want to implement the changes while studying the problem further.

Notes

1. *Introduction to Quality Engineering,* p. 5-7.

Chapter 16

CLASSIFIED ATTRIBUTE ANALYSIS

Just as level average analysis provides a set of techniques for analyzing experiments involving continuously measurable quality characteristics, classified attribute data require their own special approach for determining strong effects and recommending factor levels. In many ways the analysis for each of the two types of data is either very similar or exactly alike. At the same time, the two approaches require their own unique techniques for addressing certain steps within the analysis.

16.1 CONCEPTS

The procedures and format that are appropriate for continuously measurable data are not entirely applicable to classified attribute results. For one, many more units per experimental run are required for attaining equivalent information. Thus, there are more repetitions to deal with. Second, instead of recording specific measurements, the results of the classified attribute experiment are sorted and totaled for each classification. This step transforms them into separate groups of information like apples and oranges that cannot be combined, whereas the measurable data can be added together and an average response can be obtained. One purpose of this chapter is to identify the similarities and highlight the differences of the two approaches so as to enhance the understanding of each set of techniques. Another purpose, as explained in this portion of the book, is to enumerate and explain a series of logical and systematic steps for effectively handling the analysis of classified attribute data. And within the framework of identifying these essential steps, an additional goal is to provide helpful hints and practical suggestions including results to look for and what to avoid.

As in the application of level average analysis, noise factors are not involved in the design or analysis of the classified attribute study. Analysis is based strictly on the effect of those process parameters and design components that have been defined as potentially important control factors. In level average analysis, the results for an individual factor level were determined by matching the levels of the appropriate column of the orthogonal array with its corresponding data and compiling the data for those experimental runs for which the common factor level was set. In classified attribute analysis, the approach is similar. As in Chapter 15, the results for each level of a factor are compared against each other and the mathematical differences are the measure of the strength of that factor. Importance of a factor is again based on the relative magnitude of the effect in relation to the other factors being studied. The same rule of thumb applies for identifying approximately half of the factors and interactions under investigation as strong effects, as does the determination of a logical breaking point between strong effects and mild and weak influences. Both tabular and graphical means of analyzing the data apply and should complement each other. Interactions that have been identified as strong effects must be examined in more detail. Matrices and interaction graphs showing the results for each combination of levels of the factors that make up the interaction must be generated. The prediction equation is again based on only the strong effects and is important (a) for determining the potential improvement from changing to the recommended levels and (b) for making comparisons to the confirmation run. In the case of all experimental studies, the *confirmation run* is an essential ingredient in performing the analysis and validating the assumptions that were used in designing and conducting the experiment.

Just as the basic strategy and fundamental framework for performing the analysis are similar for level average and classified attribute analysis, innate differences between the two types of data require different approaches to performing the analysis although the steps are similar. With continuously measurable data, an average response is computed for each row (experimental run). For attribute data, each unit produced is assigned to the most appropriate classification, and the totals are tabulated for each category for each row (experimental run) as illustrated in Figure 16-1.

Figure 16-1 Classified Attribute Data

	$L_8\ (2^7)$							
Run No.	A	B	A × B	Class 1	Class 2	Class 3	...	Class *n*
1	1	1	1	y_{11}	y_{12}	y_{13}	...	y_{1n}
2	1	2	2	y_{21}	y_{22}	y_{23}	...	y_{2n}
3	2	1	2	y_{31}	y_{32}	y_{33}	...	y_{3n}
4	2	2	1	y_{41}	y_{42}	y_{43}	...	y_{4n}

Once the number of units has been tabulated for each classification for each row, we can compile the total results for each factor level. Whereas with the continuous data we calculated the average response for each level of the factors under study, the attribute totals are computed for each category for each level of the factors and inserted into the response table as demonstrated in Figure 16-2. With more than one result for each factor level based on the number of classifications, the response table becomes more complex in the classified attribute experiment. As in level average analysis, the effect of a factor or interaction is determined by the difference or delta between the results for each factor. With classified attribute data, the number of differences equals the number of categories instead of just the one delta determined in level average analysis.

Once the response table has been constructed, a decision has to be made concerning how to proceed with the analysis. Based on the experiment objective, one of the classifications is more important than the others. In the example shown in Figure 16-2, complete removal of any imperfections may result in the classification of good being determined as the most critical category. In that case, we would want to determine those factor settings that would maximize the number of units falling into the good category. If minor flaws are easily corrected but more serious defects are totally unacceptable, then the classification of poor is the most important criterion. Correspondingly, our strategy would be to

Figure 16-2 Classified Attribute Response Table

L_8 (27)

Run No.	A	B	A × B	Good	Fair	Poor
1	1	1	1	15	10	35
2	1	2	2	5	35	20
3	2	1	2	30	25	5
4	2	2	1	25	20	15

Response Table

Effect	A			B			A × B		
Class	G	F	P	G	F	P	G	F	P
Level 1	20	45	55	45	35	40	40	30	50
Level 2	55	45	20	30	55	35	35	60	25
Delta	35	0	35	15	20	5	5	30	25

determine those factor settings that minimize the number of units that would be evaluated as of poor quality. Once this decision is made, the determination of strong effects, the identification of recommended levels, and the prediction equation can all be based on the primary category.

The importance of singling out one of the categories is twofold. For one, changes in levels or settings for a particular factor may cause a dramatic increase or decrease in the number of units falling into one category while another category is unaffected. Second, different factor levels may be preferable for maximizing or minimizing different categories. For example, in the response table in Figure 16-2, we can see that factor A had the greatest effect on the quantity of poor units produced, closely followed by the interaction A × B. Factor B had little effect on the number of poor units. If we had focussed our attention on maximizing the number of good units instead, the ranking of the relative importance of the effects would have been different. Although factor A would still be the strongest factor, factor B would be the second most influential effect, and the interaction A × B had a weak effect on the number of units being evaluated as good. From this simple demonstration, it can be deduced that the identification of strong effects and the selection of the recommended levels may very well depend on the selection of the most important attribute classification.

Response graphs can be constructed in one of two ways. A block diagram

Figure 16-3 Response Block Diagram

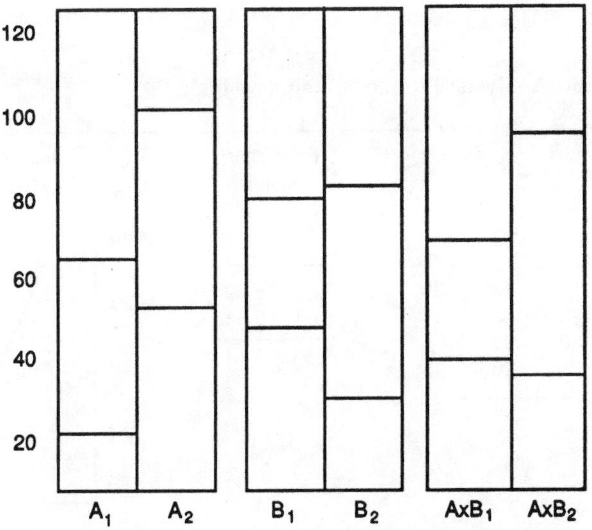

(Figure 16-3) can be developed showing pictorially the relative magnitude of units that fall into each category for each level for all factors and interactions under investigation. The alternative is the standard response graph for each factor and interaction based on the category deemed most critical. The advantage of the block diagram is that comparisons can be made simultaneously of the impact of each factor and interaction on all categories. The disadvantage is that so much information combined into one table can make the table undecipherable and any conclusions unclear. Although the standard response graph does not permit concurrent analysis of more than one category, it can provide an efficient visual tool for determining the strongest effects and recommending the preferred levels after the most critical category has been identified. For a small orthogonal array and only three classifications, the response block diagram will not be overly complex and may be preferred. However, as the number of effects and categories increase, it will become harder to discern the truly important results from trivial information.

When the strength of an interaction justifies additional study, an interaction matrix and an interaction graph can be constructed using the same procedures that were applied to analyzing interactions in level average analysis. The limitation is that classified attribute analysis is best performed on only one category at a time.

Although selection of the strong effects follows the same rules as in level average analysis, determination of the preferred settings for the mild and weak effects is a little different. If changes in settings of a factor have little effect on the most important category, perhaps the factor has a more pronounced influ-

Figure 16-4 Interaction Analysis: Primary Category—Poor

$L_8 (2^7)$

Run No.	A	B	A × B	Good	Fair	Poor
1	1	1	1	15	10	35
2	1	2	2	5	35	20
3	2	1	2	30	25	5
4	2	2	1	25	20	15

Interaction Matrix

	B_1	B_2
A_1	35	20
A_2	5	15

Interaction Graph

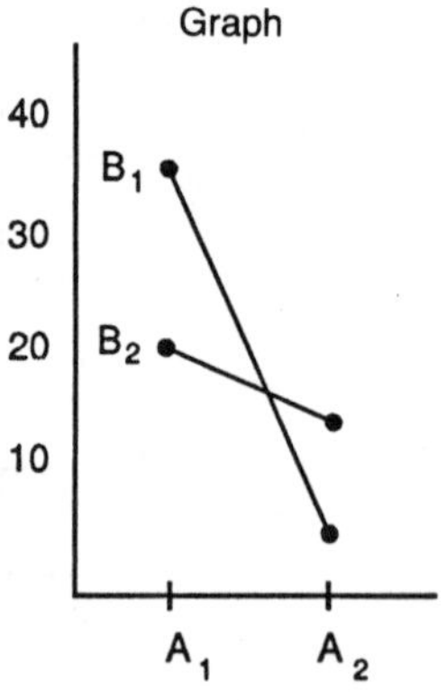

ence on the next most critical category. In the previous example, factor B had little effect on the number of very bad or poor units, but it had a more pronounced effect on the number of good units. Therefore, level 1 was chosen not because it resulted in fewer poor units (actually, it led to five more poor units during the experiment), but because more good units were built at that setting. If a factor does not exhibit a strong effect on any of the categories studied, then cost considerations can be used to determine the most desirable setting. In setting up the prediction equation, only the factors and interactions that had a strong effect on the category for which the prediction is being calculated are included.

Perhaps the most significant difference between level average analysis and classified attribute analysis is in the way that the prediction equation is handled and the projected estimate is obtained. With continuously measurable data, the effects of the strong factors and interactions are combined based on the average response for recommended levels. For attribute data, the approach must be different. In the analysis, we compare the number of units in the most critical category for each level of the factors investigated. Since an equal number of units were run or built for each experimental run, relative comparisons are meaningful. Using an absolute quantity for each of the effects in the prediction equation, however, does not present as clear a picture of the resulting improvements. For example, reducing poor units down to five pieces has little meaning by itself. Does this imply that 5 out of every 10 units built will be of poor quality? This result is hardly acceptable. Does it mean that only 5 out of 1,000,000 are bad? This may be a tremendous improvement. We can see that substituting absolute values into the classified attribute prediction equation will have little meaning.

A more relevant form of the data would be the percentage of units that occur within the category of interest. The resulting prediction would then be calculated in percent. A prediction that 5% of the products built under the recommended factor levels will be poor has relevance and gives us understanding of what to expect from changing the settings.

Although percentages are an improvement over absolute values, they do have one serious drawback. The prediction equation is based on the assumption that the quality characteristic of interest possesses good additivity. In other words, the magnitude of each of the (strong) effects can be summed together resulting in an accurate estimate of the total effect. Percentages do not enjoy this trait. As the value of the percentage nears 0 or 100, additivity becomes worse and worse. Trying to combine the effects of factors where the effects are defined in terms of percentages can result in inaccurate predictions and can even produce meaningless estimates. For example, let's say that we had an experiment where we wanted to minimize the percentage of poor units, with the following percentages for the experiment average and the recommended levels for the strong effects:

$$\overline{T} = 30.0\%,\ \overline{A} = 8.0\%,\ \overline{B} = 5.0\%,\ \overline{C} = 10.0\%.$$

The prediction equation would be as follows:

$$\hat{\mu} = \overline{T} + (\overline{A} - \overline{T}) + (\overline{B} - \overline{T}) + (\overline{C} - \overline{T})$$

$$\hat{\mu} = 30.0 + (8.0 - 30.0) + (5.0 - 30.0) + (10.0 - 30.0)$$

$$\hat{\mu} = 30.0 - 22.0 - 25.0 - 20.0 = -37.0\%$$

A negative 37.0% bad has no realistic meaning. If we had reversed the situation and attempted to obtain a prediction of the percentage of good units, we may have obtained a value greater than 100%, which is just as unrealistic. Therefore, we must convert the percentages into a form that has better additivity.

Dr. Taguchi derived the Omega Transformation for converting these percentages into a form which has better additivity. The Omega Transformation is as follows:

$$\Omega = -10 \log \left| \frac{1}{p} - 1 \right|^{1}$$

where p = percentage of units within the category of interest. Although not derived here, a detailed explanation and the derivation of the formula can be obtained in *System of Experimental Design* by Genichi Taguchi.

If we apply the Omega Transformation to the preceding example, we will get the following results:

$$\overline{T} = 30.0\%,\ A = 8.0\%,\ B = 5.0\%,\ C = 10.0\%$$

$$\overline{T}_{db} = -10 \log \left| \frac{1}{\overline{T}} - 1 \right| = -10 \log \left| \frac{1}{.30} - 1 \right| = -3.680 \text{ db}$$

$$\overline{A}_{db} = -10 \log \left| \frac{1}{\overline{A}} - 1 \right| = -10 \log \left| \frac{1}{.08} - 1 \right| = -10.607 \text{ db}$$

$$\overline{B}_{db} = -10 \log \left| \frac{1}{\overline{B}} - 1 \right| = -10 \log \left| \frac{1}{.05} - 1 \right| = -12.788 \text{ db}$$

$$\overline{C}_{db} = -10 \log \left| \frac{1}{\overline{C}} - 1 \right| = -10 \log \left| \frac{1}{.10} - 1 \right| = -9.542 \text{ db}$$

Note: Since the Omega Transformation is a logarithmic function, the percentages convert into decibels.

$$\hat{\mu}_{db} = \overline{T}_{db} + (\overline{A}_{db} - \overline{T}_{db}) + (\overline{B}_{db} - \overline{T}_{db}) + (\overline{C}_{db} - \overline{T}_{db})$$

$$\hat{\mu}_{db} = \overline{A}_{db} + \overline{B}_{db} + \overline{C}_{db} - 2\times\overline{T}_{db}$$

$$\hat{\mu}_{db} = -10.607 - 12.788 - 9.542 - 2\times(-3.680)$$

$$\hat{\mu}_{db} = -25.5774 \text{ db}$$

If we solve for the cumulative p, we will obtain the predicted response as a percentage.

$$-25.5774 = -10 \log \left|\frac{1}{p} - 1\right|$$

$$2.55774 = \log \left|\frac{1}{p} - 1\right|$$

$$361.193 = \frac{1}{p} - 1$$

$$362.193 = \frac{1}{p}$$

$$p = .002761 = .2761\%$$

This value is much more realistic and meaningful than the -37.0% computed earlier.

What would happen if we were again dealing with an undesired category (poor) and the percentage for one of the recommended levels was 0? If we inserted 0 for p in the transformation, the result would be infinity, and we could not calculate an estimate of the predicted value. A suggested technique is to replace the 0 with a value that is small relative to the percentages of the other effects in the prediction equation. After computing the cumulative percentage, deduct this same amount to obtain an estimate for the prediction. Using 10% of the smallest percentage among the other effects in the prediction equation has been found appropriate.

In performing the confirmation run, the objective is again to confirm the conclusions of the analysis and the assumptions in designing and conducting the experiment. In comparing the prediction to the actual results, the focus is on the primary category. The results for the other categories can be inspected as well for further understanding of the effects of the recommended factor settings. One concern that often arises is how to relate the confirmation to the prediction when the predicted value is extremely small. Let's say the predicted results were 6 defective parts per million and only 100 pieces will be built in the confirmation run. Since one defective would translate to 10,000 defective parts per million, the confirmation would have to result in no defectives occurring for the experiment to be validated.

16.2 CASING PAINT STUDY

Problem: Casings painted by the primary vendor exhibit a large number of orange peels (rough surface usually caused by hardened accumulations of dried paint). After not finding an appropriate continuously measurable characteristic to describe the condition, the team decided to count the number of rejected units and treated the information as classified attribute data. The units would be qualitatively rated and grouped into one of three classes:

1. No orange peels
2. Some orange peels
3. Severe condition

Although a few rough spots on any one unit was not viewed as critical by customers, conditions involving orange peels across the entire unit were unacceptable.

Objective: To minimize the percentage of units exhibiting severe orange peel problems.

Instructions were given for performing inspection of units produced in the experiment, and samples representing each class were provided. Experiment design and data are given in Figure 16-5.

Figure 16-5 Experiment Design and Data

	LEVEL 1	LEVEL 2
A: Paint Method	Manual	Automatic
B: Handling	No Gloves	Gloves
C: Metal Dip	Chromate	Iridite
D: Masking Procedure	No Inspection	Inspection
E: Primer	Brand X	Brand Y
F: Texturing	No Texturing	Texturing
Interaction A × B		

Forty casings were painted at each of the eight combinations of factors.

Run#	A	B	A × B	C	D	E	F	None	Some	Severe	Total
1	1	1	1	1	1	1	1	4	14	22	40
2	1	1	1	2	2	2	2	8	16	16	40
3	1	2	2	1	1	2	2	20	12	8	40
4	1	2	2	2	2	1	1	28	8	4	40
5	2	1	2	1	2	1	2	22	12	6	40
6	2	1	2	2	1	2	1	14	14	12	40
7	2	2	1	1	2	2	1	38	2	0	40
8	2	2	1	2	1	1	2	36	4	0	40

Calculations:

1. Add the number of units across each row of the orthogonal array.

At the right of the data in the matrix above, the total number of units inspected has been tabulated. This step provides a quick check to insure that all of the required samples have been assigned to a column. An additional thought concerns the number of repetitions in the experiment. Although 40 repetitions were conducted for each experimental run, we actually have more comparisons than that for studying the different levels of each factor. The entire experiment consists of 320 units. Since each factor has two levels, we will be comparing the results of 160 units at one level versus another 160 pieces at the second level. Therefore, we have more information available to us than first appears.

2. Compile the total results for each classification for each factor level and develop a response table.

For factor A, level 1:

None:

$A_1 = 4 + 8 + 20 + 28 = 60$

Some:

$A_1 = 14 + 16 + 12 + 8 = 50$

Severe:

$A_1 = 22 + 16 + 8 + 4 = 50$

$\text{Total} = 60 + 50 + 50 = 160$

level 2:

None:
$A_2 = 22 + 14 + 38 + 36 = 110$
Some:
$A_2 = 12 + 14 + 2 + 4 = 32$
Severe:
$A_2 = 6 + 12 + 0 + 0 = 18$
$\text{Total} = 110 + 32 + 18 = 160$

Effect of A:

None: $|60 - 110| = 50$

Some: $|50 - 32| = 18$

Severe: $|50 - 18| = 32$

Similarly for factor B, level 1:

None:
$B_1 = 4 + 8 + 22 + 14 = 48$
Some:
$B_2 = 14 + 16 + 12 + 14 = 56$
Severe:
$B_1 = 22 + 16 + 6 + 12 = 56$
$\text{Total} = 48 + 56 + 56 = 160$

level 2:

None:
$B_2 = 20 + 28 + 38 + 36 = 122$
Some:
$B_2 = 12 + 8 + 2 + 4 = 26$
Severe:
$B_2 = 8 + 4 + 0 + 0 = 12$
$\text{Total} = 122 + 26 + 12 = 160$

Effect of B:

$$\begin{aligned} &\text{None:} && |48 - 122| = 74 \\ &\text{Some:} && |56 - 26| = 30 \\ &\text{Severe:} && |56 - 12| = 44 \end{aligned}$$

By performing these calculations for each of the other factors (and interactions), the classified attribute response table is generated:

3. Construct a response block diagram based on all categories or a response graph based on the primary category.

Since only three categories were involved and the study consisted of just seven effects, it was decided that the response block diagram would not contain too much information to prevent detection of the truly important results. There, it was selected over the primary category response graph.

4. Analyze the response table and response block diagram (or primary category response graph).

Analysis can be based on the response graph, the block diagram, or both. My personal preference is that I can obtain more understanding from evaluating the summary numbers in the classified attribute response table than by looking for distinctly different heights in the block diagram. However, your choice should be based on the tool with which you feel the most comfortable. You may wish to use both.

Focusing on the category of "severe orange peeling," factor B had the strongest effect, with factor A next. Following the one-half rule, factor D would be included as the third strong effect with the logical breaking point separating it from factor F and the interaction A × B. Since the interaction A × B was not regarded as a strong effect and both factors A and B were discovered to be very important, the settings for the two factors would be determined based on the individual effects of the factors alone. Level 2 was the best setting for both factors, as was factor D.

Concerning the mild effects, level 2 for factor F (texturing) would be preferred if texturing was not too expensive. Factor E (paint supplier) had a weak effect on severe peeling, but had a greater influence on "no orange peels," with Brand Y being the better paint. Factor C (metal dip) had little impact on any of the categories. Therefore, the less expensive of the two coatings could be chosen.

Therefore, the recommended factor levels are: A_2, B_2, D_2, E_1, F_2, with C, based on cost considerations.

Classified Attribute Response Table

Class	A			B			A × B			C			D			E			F		
	N	So	Se	N	So	Se	N	So	Se	N	So	Se	N	So	Se	N	So	Se	N	So	Se
Level 1	60	50	50	48	56	56	86	36	38	84	40	36	74	44	42	90	38	32	84	38	38
Level 2	110	32	18	122	26	12	84	46	30	86	42	32	96	38	26	80	44	36	86	44	30
Delta	50	18	**32**	74	30	**44**	2	10	8	2	2	4	22	6	**16**	10	6	4	2	6	8

Strong effects = **Bold**

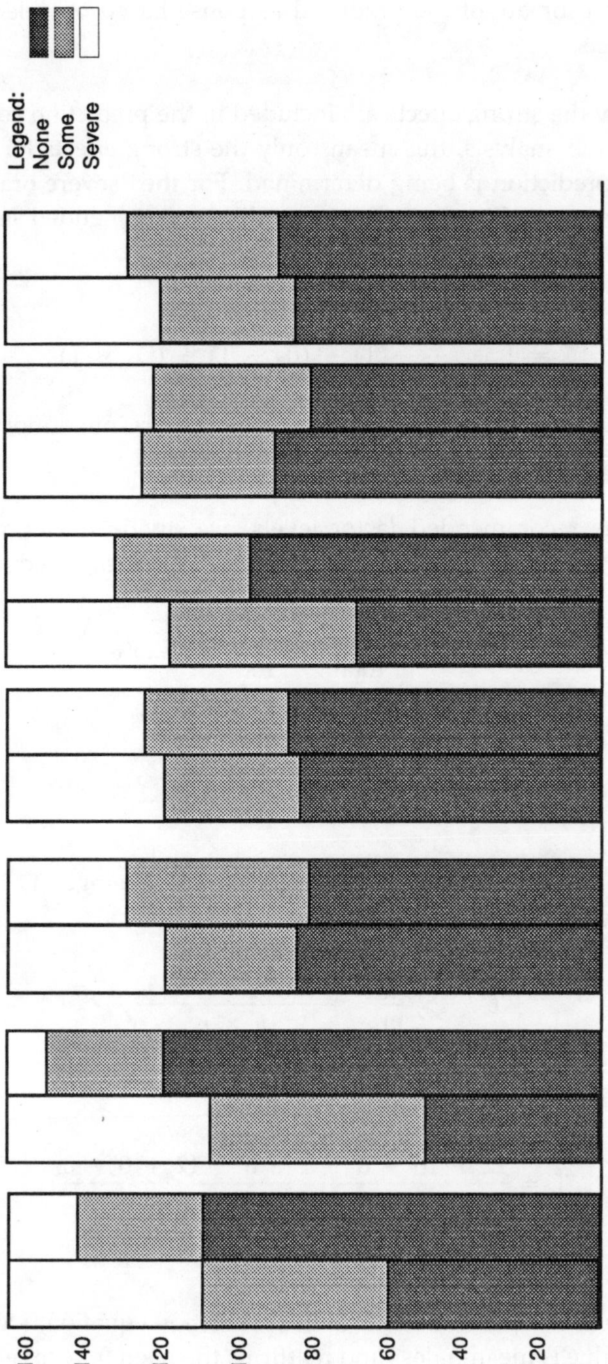
Legend:
None
Some
Severe
160
140
120
100
80
60
40
20
A1
A2
B1
B2
AxB1
AxB2
C1
C2
D1
D2
E1
E2
F1
F2

5. Compute an estimate of the predicted response based on selected levels of the strong effects.

As always, only the strong effects are included in the prediction equation. With classified attribute analysis, this means only the strong effects for the category for which the prediction is being determined. For the "severe orange peeling" category, the strong effects and corresponding recommended levels are: A_2, B_2, D_2.

The prediction equation becomes:

$$\hat{\mu} = \overline{T} + (\overline{A}_2 - \overline{T}) + (\overline{B}_2 - \overline{T}) + (\overline{D}_2 - \overline{T}).$$

5a. Convert the responses for the recommended levels into a more meaningful form (percent of occurrence).

For each of the recommended factor levels, we divide the number of units displaying the severe condition by the number of units sampled at that level.

$$\overline{A}_2\ (\%) = \frac{\text{Severe}}{\text{total}} = \frac{18}{160} = 11.25\%$$

$$\overline{B}_2\ (\%) = \frac{\text{Severe}}{\text{total}} = \frac{12}{160} = 7.50\%$$

$$\overline{D}_2\ (\%) = \frac{\text{Severe}}{\text{total}} = \frac{26}{160} = 16.25\%$$

We will need to calculate the overall experimental average, $\overline{T}$, in terms of a percentage as well.

$$\overline{T} = \sum_{i=1}^{n} \frac{y_i}{nr} = \frac{y_1 + y_2 + \ldots y_8}{n \times r},$$

where r = number of repetitions.

$$\overline{T} = \frac{22 + 16 + 8 + 4 + 6 + 12 + 0 + 0}{8 \times 40}$$

$$\overline{T} = 21.25\%$$

If we insert the above percentages into the prediction equation, we can see that the resulting value is meaningless and reaffirms the need for converting the data into a form that has better additivity.

$$\hat{\mu} = \overline{T} + (\overline{A}_2 - \overline{T}) + (\overline{B}_2 - \overline{T}) + (\overline{D}_2 - \overline{T})$$

$$\hat{\mu} = 21.25 + (11.25 - 21.25) + (7.50 - 21.25) + (16.25 - 21.25)$$

$$\hat{\mu} = 21.25 - 10.00 - 13.75 - 5.00 = -7.50\%$$

5b. Transpose the data using the Omega Transformation, and calculate an estimate for the predicted results.

$$\overline{T} = 21.25\%,\ \overline{A} = 11.25\%,\ \overline{B} = 7.50\%,\ \overline{D} = 16.25\%$$

$$\overline{T}_{db} = -10 \log \left|\frac{1}{\overline{T}} - 1\right| = -10 \log \left|\frac{1}{.2125} - 1\right| = -5.689$$

$$\overline{A}_{db} = -10 \log \frac{1}{\overline{A}} - 1 = -10 \log \left|\frac{1}{.1125} - 1\right| = -8.970$$

$$\overline{B}_{db} = -10 \log \frac{1}{\overline{B}} - 1 = -10 \log \left|\frac{1}{.0750} - 1\right| = -10.911$$

$$\overline{D}_{db} = -10 \log \frac{1}{\overline{D}} - 1 = -10 \log \left|\frac{1}{.1625} - 1\right| = -7.121$$

Substituting these values into the prediction equation,

$$\hat{\mu}_{db} = \overline{T}_{db} + (\overline{A}_{db} - \overline{T}_{db}) + (\overline{B}_{db} - \overline{T}_{db}) + (\overline{D}_{db} - \overline{T}_{db})$$

$$\hat{\mu}_{db} = \overline{A}_{db} + \overline{B}_{db} + \overline{D}_{db} - 2 \times \overline{T}_{db}$$

$$\hat{\mu}_{db} = -8.970 - 10.911 - 7.121 - 2 \times (-5.689)$$

$$\hat{\mu}_{db} = -15.624 \text{ db}$$

If we solve for the cumulative p, we will obtain the predicted response as a percentage.

$$-15.624 = -10 \log \left|\frac{1}{p} - 1\right|$$

$$1.5624 = \log \left|\frac{1}{p} - 1\right|$$

$$36.509 = \left|\frac{1}{p} - 1\right|$$

$$37.509 = \frac{1}{p}$$

$$p = .02666 = 2.666\%$$

6. Conduct a confirmation run and compare the actual results to the predicted results.

The success of the experiment will be judged on whether the percentage of severely bad units in the confirmation run is close to 2.666. Understandably, building more units in the confirmation run will result in a better comparison that can be made to the predicted result and will provide a more accurate picture for understanding the effect of the recommended settings on the process. For a small validation sample, that may mean no units with severe orange peeling. In addition to comparing the actual number of bad units to the predicted result, it would be worthwhile to ascertain the percentage of units without any orange peels in the confirmation run as well. If the actual results compare favorably with the prediction, the recommended levels can be instituted. If the validation results are disappointing, the team should return to the planning phase and investigate further. The same common causes for a failed confirmation run in level average analysis also apply to classified attribute experimentation.

Notes

1. *Introduction to Quality Engineering,* p. 5-35.

Chapter 17

ANALYSIS: SMALLER-THE-BETTER

When noise factors have been incorporated into the study, the experiment allows you to determine not only the key factors and the best settings, but the best factor levels that will consistently result in good performance over time as those elements which are not being controlled change. This is a much more powerful concept than simply identifying the best settings for factors that you can control under specific environmental conditions and forgetting about what may happen if they change. This capability can apply both to the performance of the process in building consistently good product and to the design of products that will perform consistently well within diverse applications and environmental conditions.

In the chapter on level average analysis, we gave examples for the format of the data and how the smaller-the-better quality characteristic can be analyzed. Within level average analysis, there may or may not be more than one piece of data for each experimental run. If two or more repetitions are produced for each experimental run, then an average response is calculated for each row, and the analysis is based on these averages. Therefore, conclusions are based only on the effect on the mean results for the quality characteristic of interest. With signal-to-noise ratio (S/N) analysis, the calculations take into consideration both the mean and the variation from one result to the next. Therefore, we can think of signal-to-noise ratio analysis as being two-dimensional as opposed to regular analysis being only one-dimensional (see Figure 17-1). The strategy of basing the experiment conclusions solely on the signal-to-noise ratio (S/N) is especially applicable to smaller-the-better and larger-the-better (covered in Chapter 18) quality characteristics. From the analysis, we then can ascertain the control factor settings or levels that will not just produce the best results (average response) under the right controlled conditions, but will consistently produce the most desirable outcomes. From the analysis, the conclusions from an experiment involving a smaller-the-better characteristic should give us the best factor settings which will result in the consistently lowest values for the response of interest.

Figure 17-1 Regular and Signal-to-Noise Ratio Format Comparison

Regular Analysis Format									Signal-to-Noise Ratio Analysis Format								
Run No.	A	B	A × B	Data				$\bar{y}$	Run No.	A	B	A × B	Data				S/N
1	1	1	1	y_{11}	y_{12}	y_{13}	y_{14}	$\bar{y}_1$	1	1	1	1	y_{11}	y_{12}	y_{13}	y_{14}	S/N_1
2	1	2	2	y_{21}	y_{22}	y_{23}	y_{24}	$\bar{y}_2$	2	1	2	2	y_{21}	y_{22}	y_{23}	y_{24}	S/N_2
3	2	1	2	y_{31}	y_{32}	y_{33}	y_{34}	$\bar{y}_3$	3	2	1	2	y_{31}	y_{32}	y_{33}	y_{34}	S/N_3
4	2	2	1	y_{41}	y_{42}	y_{43}	y_{44}	$\bar{y}_4$	4	2	2	1	y_{41}	y_{42}	y_{43}	y_{44}	S/N_4

17.1 SIGNAL-TO-NOISE RATIO

The signal-to-noise ratio is one of the major contributions that Dr. Taguchi gave to quality engineering. The signal-to-noise ratio is often written as S/N or represented by the Greek letter η. Both representations are used within this text. As a measurement tool for determining robustness, the signal-to-noise ratio is an essential component of parameter design. As discussed in Chapter 5, noise can denote environmental conditions (outer noise), internal deterioration (inner noise), or variation from unit to unit (between product noise).[1] The relevance of the signal-to-noise ratio equation is tied to interpreting the signal or numerator of the ratio as the ability of the process to build good product, or of the product to perform correctly. By including the impact of the noise factors on the process or product as the denominator, we can then adapt the signal-to-noise ratio as the barometer of the ability of the system (process or product) to perform well in relation to the effect of noise. By successfully applying this concept to experimentation, we can determine the control factor settings that can produce the best performance (high signal) in a process or product while minimizing the effect of those influences we cannot control (low noise).

To obtain a better understanding of how this approach works and what it means, let's discuss a practical example, illustrated in Figure 17-2. If we tune into a radio station on our car radio on the way to work in the morning, this could be considered an example of a signal. If it was a local station, the sound would likely be clear and easy to hear—because we have a strong signal. If we were trying to tune into a station halfway across the country, we would have trouble locating the station although we knew the exact frequency—because the signal is so weak. If, on the other hand, we were trying to listen to any station during a severe thunderstorm, we would have difficulty due to the crackling and static. The reason is the noise induced by the storm which is interfering with the signal from the radio station. The ideal situation is the reception of the strong clear local station on a bright sunny day. And this last description is our

Figure 17-2 Signal-to-Noise Ratio

$$\frac{\text{Signal}}{\text{Noise}} \rightarrow \frac{\text{Radio Signal}}{\text{Storm Interference}}$$

Desirable $$\frac{\text{Strong Signal}}{\text{Little Interference}}$$

Not Desirable $$\frac{\text{Strong Signal}}{\text{Strong Interference}} \qquad \frac{\text{Weak Signal}}{\text{Little Interference}}$$

Least Desirable $$\frac{\text{Weak Signal}}{\text{Strong Interference}}$$

objective in performing the parameter design experiment. We want solid performance from our process and resulting products reflecting the type of output expected from the best noise conditions even when these conditions may be unfavorable (stormy) instead of favorable (sunny).

The actual equation for calculating the signal-to-noise ratio for the smaller-the-better quality characteristic is a logarithmic function based on the mean square deviation. The S/N ratio can be written as:

$$S/N = -10 \log \text{MSD}.$$

The mean square deviation for a smaller-the-better characteristic is:

$$\text{MSD} = \frac{y_1^2 + y_2^2 + \ldots + y_n^2}{n}.$$

We can then rewrite the S/N equation as:

$$S/N = -10 \log \left| \frac{y_1^2 + y_2^2 + \ldots + y_n^2}{n} \right|.$$

From the context of our example on radio stations, we would want the S/N to be as large as possible. To achieve an improvement in the process or product,

Figure 17-3 Smaller-the-Better Signal-to-Noise Ratio

Data Set 1: 10, 14, 16, 20
Data Set 2: 5, 9, 11, 15
Data Set 3: 15, 15, 15, 15
Data Set 4: 10, 10, 10, 10

$$\text{Data Set 1:}\quad S/N = -10 \log \left| \frac{10^2 + 14^2 + 16^2 + 20^2}{4} \right| = -23.77 \text{ db}$$

$$\text{Data Set 2:}\quad S/N = -10 \log \left| \frac{5^2 + 9^2 + 11^2 + 15^2}{4} \right| = -20.53 \text{ db}$$

$$\text{Data Set 3:}\quad S/N = -10 \log \left| \frac{15^2 + 15^2 + 15^2 + 15^2}{4} \right| = -23.52 \text{ db}$$

$$\text{Data Set 4:}\quad S/N = -10 \log \left| \frac{10^2 + 10^2 + 10^2 + 10^2}{4} \right| = -20.00 \text{ db}$$

we would likewise wish to increase its signal-to-noise ratio. For the smaller-the-better characteristic, this could mean reducing the average results or improving the consistency from one unit to the next. Figure 17-3 demonstrates mathematically that either change can lead to a better signal-to-noise radio. In data set 4, we see that a combined reduction in the mean result and the variability will result in the greatest increase in S/N. Translated, this means that our goal in conducting parameter design type experiments involving a smaller-the-better characteristic should be to identify those factor settings that will produce the most consistently small response values.

17.2 ANALYSIS TECHNIQUES

Just as in level average analysis, we will seek out the strong effects and ascertain the best levels or settings for each of the control factors under consideration. Response tables and graphs will again be the primary tools for guiding us to new knowledge. The fundamental difference is that instead of using the mean response as the measure of goodness or badness, we will be using the signal-to-noise ratio.

After collecting the experimental data and referencing each set to the appropriate experimental run (orthogonal array row), we will need to calculate S/N for each row just as we would have calculated $\overline{y}$ for each row in level average

Figure 17-4 Smaller-the-Better S/N Calculations

L_4 (2^3)

Run No.	A	B	A × B	N_1	N_2	S/N
1	1	1	1	20	40	−30.00
2	1	2	2	25	35	−28.89
3	2	1	2	15	25	−23.01
4	2	2	1	10	12	−28.82

$$S/N_1 = -10 \log \left| \frac{20^2 + 40^2}{2} \right| = -30.00$$

$$S/N_2 = -10 \log \left| \frac{25^2 + 35^2}{2} \right| = -28.89$$

$$S/N_3 = -10 \log \left| \frac{15^2 + 25^2}{2} \right| = -23.01$$

$$S/N_4 = -10 \log \left| \frac{10^2 + 12^2}{2} \right| = -28.82$$

analysis (Figure 17-4). After performing the computations, we need to add an additional column alongside the raw data, and the corresponding S/N can be recorded for each row. This step will greatly facilitate the calculation of the average S/N for the S/N response table and response graphs.

The signal-to-noise response table is generated in the same fashion using the S/N values as the mean response table was derived in level average analysis, by combining and averaging the mean response for each factor (and interaction) level. Accordingly, the effect of a factor (or interaction) is equal to the difference between the average S/N for each level (two levels) or the difference between the highest average S/N and the lowest average S/N (more than two levels).

For A_1 in Figure 17-5, the average signal-to-noise ratio will be calculated as follows:

Similarly for A_2, the average signal-to-noise ratio is:

$$S/N = \frac{(-23.01) + (-28.82)}{2} = -25.92.$$

Then,

$$\text{Effect of A} = |\overline{A}_1 - \overline{A}_2| = |(-29.45) - (-25.92)| = 3.53 \text{ db}$$

Figure 17-5 Signal-to-Noise Ratio Response Table

L_4 (2^3)

Run No.	A	B	A × B	N_1	N_2	S/N
1	1	1	1	20	40	−30.00
2	1	2	2	18	35	−28.89
3	2	1	2	12	16	−23.01
4	2	2	1	25	30	−28.82

S/N Response Table

Level	A	B	A × B
1	−29.45	−26.51	−29.41
2	−25.92	−28.86	−25.95
Delta	3.53	2.35	3.46

By following these same calculations, the average S/N for each level of factor B and the interaction A × B can be determined in a like manner and are shown in Figure 17-5.

S/N response graphs can also be drawn in conjunction with the S/N response table (Figure 17-6). Instead of plotting average mean response points, average S/N values are used.

The analysis also follows similar guidelines to that of level average analysis. Continuing the use of the one-half rule and a logical breaking point, both the response table and the response graphs for the simple L_4 (2^3) example indicate that factor A and the interaction A × B are strong effects, whereas factor B has a milder influence. Concerning recommended levels, let's think back to the radio

Figure 17-6 Signal-to-Noise Ratio Response Graphs

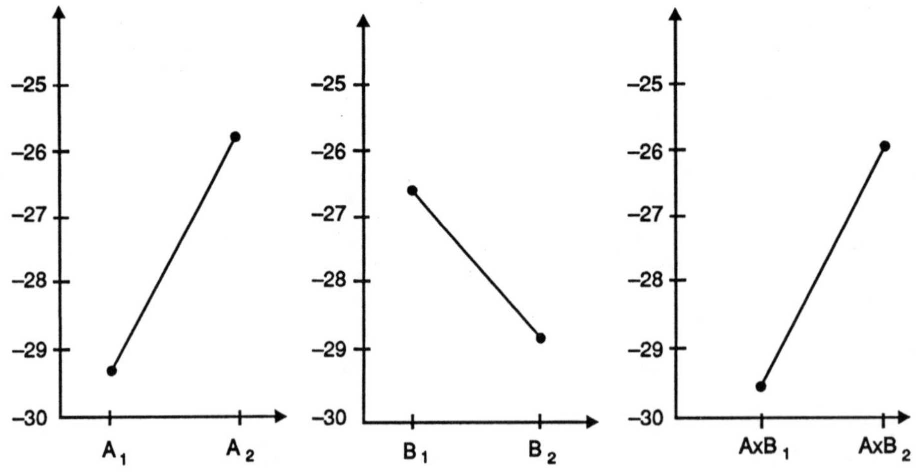

and the impact of the noise was weak. In other words, as in any signal-to-noise analysis, we wanted the greatest signal-to-noise ratio. Therefore, we will need to select the levels with the highest average S/N values. In using the S/N response graphs, this means that we will *always* look for the highest point on the graph. For strong effects, the highest point will indicate the recommended level. The one exception is when multiple levels of a particular factor are being investigated and, although there is diversity in the signal-to-noise ratios across all levels, the best levels are still very close together. In this event, one of these settings would be selected. Concerning mild and weak effects, the higher point will still be preferred if cost considerations are similar.

Returning to the L_4 (2^3) example and factor A, since -25.92 is algebraically larger than -29.45 and also a higher point on the response graph, A_2 is recommended. Factor B is not a strong effect by itself. So, we will proceed with a more in-depth analysis of the interaction $A \times B$, which was determined to be a strong effect by the logical breaking point rule.

Once again we can use the techniques followed in level average analysis. We can develop an interaction matrix and an interaction graph as shown in Figure 17-7.

From the S/N Interaction Graph, the intersecting lines show clearly that the interaction $A \times B$ is a strong effect. If we base factor level selection on the highest point, A_2B_1 is the best combination. The S/N Interaction Matrix will give you the same answer. The identification of A_2B_1 as the best interaction combination is in accord with selection of A_2 on the basis of the effect of factor A by itself.

Figure 17-7 S/N Interaction Analysis

L_4 (2^3)

Run No.	A	B	A × B	N_1	N_2	S/N
1	1	1	1	20	40	−30.00
2	1	2	2	18	35	−28.89
3	2	1	2	12	16	−23.01
4	2	2	1	25	30	−28.82

Interaction Matrix

	B_1	B_2
A_1	−30.00	−28.89
A_2	−23.01	−28.82

Interaction Graph

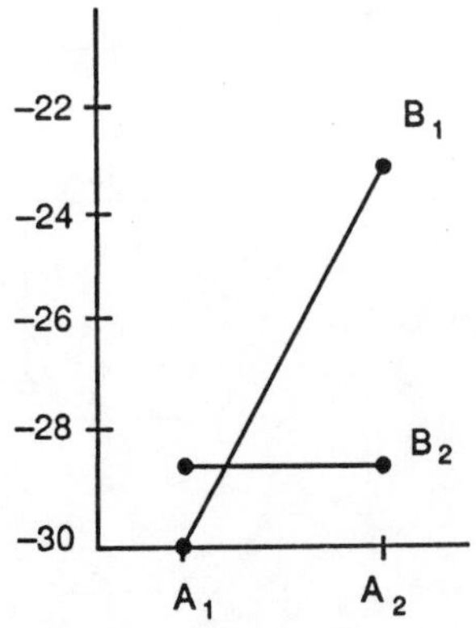

The reason that I emphasize the graphical analysis here is that graphical analysis of interactions seems clearer to me than the tabular method.

An additional consideration for smaller-the-better S/N analysis is the influence of the noise factor(s). Although by definition we have defined noise factors as those factors that we either cannot or will not control, we may want to reconsider our position if the effect of these influences is too great.

By adding the data for each column of the outer array and then calculating the average response as shown in Figure 17-8, we can obtain a relative comparison of the impact of changes in the noise factor(s). If the difference is considered great, efforts may be considered to reduce the variation imposed by the noises. If the noise factor is raw material, a more stringent selection process or tougher vendor requirements may be considered. If the issue is environmental in nature, perhaps controls may be put into place. If the outer array consists of three or more factors, you may wish to consider analyzing the outer array using level average analysis to determine the strongest noise factors. In this application of level average analysis, calculations are based on summing columns and obtaining noise level averages instead of summing rows and calculating control factor level averages.

The prediction equation is generated in the same manner as before except that an estimate of η is calculated instead of μ. The confirmation run is conducted across the range of noise factor settings, and η for the actual results is computed and compared to the predicted η. For discrete noise factors, this may mean producing units at several different times to reproduce the effect of the noise factors and to check the robustness of the recommended control factor settings. The same is true of continuous noise factors. However, you may not have the

Figure 17-8 Noise Factor Analysis

	L_4 (2^3)					
Run No.	A	B	A × B	N_1	N_2	S/N
1	1	1	1	20	40	−30.00
2	1	2	2	18	35	−28.89
3	2	1	2	12	16	−23.01
4	2	2	1	25	30	−28.82
			Totals	75.00	121.00	
			Average	18.75	30.25	
			Delta	11.50		

luxury of waiting for exactly the same values as used in the experiment. As an expedient to timely problem solving, it may be more practical to use values that reflect typical changes in the noise factor values instead of creating a prolonged delay in confirming the analysis by trying to capture the extreme values.

If the confirmation results validate the conclusions from the analysis, the recommended factor settings can be confidently implemented. If the results are disappointing, a return to the planning phase is needed. The same pitfalls that we would have checked for in level average analysis and classified attribute analysis apply to S/N analysis as well.

Concerning the impact of a successful experiment, the signal-to-noise ratio can also provide an estimate of the cost savings associated with instituting the improvements. For every 3-decibel increase in η, the cost of quality is reduced by 50%. We can write this relationship as follows:

$$\text{Cost}_{\text{new}} = \text{Cost}_{\text{existing}} \left| \frac{1}{2} \right|^{\frac{\eta_{\text{new}} - \eta_{\text{existing}}}{3}}$$

$$\text{Cost Savings} = \text{Cost}_{\text{existing}} - \text{Cost}_{\text{new}}$$

As a fundamental applications guide, we will not take the time to derive the relationship here. However, the connection between cost and S/N has proven effective time and again in estimating savings and obtaining management support for corrective actions.

17.3 ELECTRONIC CIRCUIT "TIME OUT" CASE STUDY

Taking a previous study modified for explaining level average analysis, we will now discuss how parameter design using the appropriate signal-to-noise calculations can be used to understand better the operation of the same circuit.

Problem: For a specific control device, the time required for the circuit to switch from the "On" state to the "Off" state when the L.E.D. (light emitting diode) drive current is removed is critical. The product specification requirement states that the time between changing states can be no more than .005 seconds. However, functional testing of current production reveals a large percentage of the units have not been in compliance with the timing specification.

Objective: Minimize the time required for the device to switch from the "On" state to the "Off" state. Experiment design and data are shown in Figure 17-9.

Figure 17-9 Experiment Design and Data

y = Switching time (milliseconds)		
Control Factors	Level 1	Level 2
A. Package Type	Type 1	Type 2
B. Burn in	No	Yes
C. Test Delay	No Delay	Delay
D. Component Supplier	Vendor X	Vendor Y
Interactions:		
A × B: Package Type × Burn in		
B × C: Burn In × Test Delay		
Noise Factors	Level 1	Level 2
M. Moisture	Low	High
N. Drying	Normal	Heat Gun
O. Soldering	Hand Solder	Wave Solder

The team decided to run two repetitions for each combination of control and noise factors.

Run#	A	B	A × B	C	e	B × C	D	O N M	1 1 1	2 2 1	2 1 2	1 2 2
1	1	1	1	1	1	1	1		2.62	2.66	10.00	10.00
									2.56	2.56	8.24	10.00
2	1	1	1	2	2	2	2		2.27	2.29	5.65	6.07
									2.30	2.29	10.00	10.00
3	1	2	2	1	1	2	2		2.30	2.27	3.73	4.19
									2.33	2.33	8.09	10.00
4	1	2	2	2	2	1	1		2.61	2.53	6.36	8.10
									2.61	2.59	10.00	8.14
5	2	1	2	1	2	1	2		2.36	2.29	2.28	4.24
									2.29	2.25	4.22	2.25
6	2	1	2	2	1	2	1		2.54	2.58	6.51	6.33
									2.46	2.47	10.00	6.22
7	2	2	1	1	2	2	1		2.53	2.54	4.40	4.51
									2.51	2.52	6.25	8.12
8	2	2	1	2	1	1	2		2.30	2.27	10.00	4.27
									2.21	2.22	2.20	8.05

In the inner array, factor D was assigned to column 7, and column 5 was left vacant. The reverse could have done as well depending on the preference of the experimenter. The one advantage of leaving column 5 vacant in this experiment is that if the unaccounted-for interaction $A \times C$ was stronger than expected, its effect would show up in column 5. (Refer to the L_8 (2^7) linear graphs in Appendix B.)

1. Determine the S/N for each row (experimental run).

#1 S/N =

$$-10 \log \frac{2.62^2 + 2.66^2 + 10.00^2 + 10.00^2 + 2.56^2 + 2.56^2 + 8.24^2 + 10.00^2}{8}$$

S/N = −16.93 db

#2 S/N =

$$-10 \log \frac{2.27^2 + 2.29^2 + 5.65^2 + 6.07^2 + 2.30^2 + 2.29^2 + 10.00^2 + 10.00^2}{8}$$

S/N = −15.59 db

. . . .

#8 S/N =

$$-10 \log \frac{2.30^2 + 2.27^2 + 10.00^2 + 4.27^2 + 2.21^2 + 2.22^2 + 2.20^2 + 8.05^2}{8}$$

S/N = −14.15 db

After calculating S/N for each row, we can add an additional column to the experimental matrix matching each combination of control factors to its respective signal-to-noise ratio.

			A			B		O	1	2	2	1	
			×			×		N	1	2	1	2	
Run#	A	B	B	C	e	C	D	M	1	1	2	2	S/N
1	1	1	1	1	1	1	1		2.62	2.66	10.00	10.00	−16.93
									2.56	2.56	8.24	10.00	
2	1	1	1	2	2	2	2		2.27	2.29	5.65	6.07	−15.59
									2.30	2.29	10.00	10.00	
3	1	2	2	1	1	2	2		2.30	2.27	3.73	4.19	−14.36
									2.33	2.33	8.09	10.00	

			A			B		O	1	2	2	1	
			×			×		N	1	2	1	2	
Run#	A	B	B	C	e	C	D	M	1	1	2	2	S/N
4	1	2	2	2	2	1	1		2.61	2.53	6.36	8.10	−15.72
									2.61	2.59	10.00	8.14	
5	2	1	2	1	2	1	2		2.36	2.29	2.28	4.24	−9.24
									2.29	2.25	4.22	2.25	
6	2	1	2	2	1	2	1		2.54	2.58	6.51	6.33	−14.88
									2.46	2.47	10.00	6.22	
7	2	2	1	1	2	2	1		2.53	2.54	4.40	4.51	−13.27
									2.51	2.52	6.25	8.12	
8	2	2	1	2	1	1	2		2.30	2.27	10.00	4.27	−14.15
									2.21	2.22	2.20	8.05	

2. Calculate the average S/N for each factor and interaction level and develop a response table.

For factor A,

$$\overline{A}_1 = \frac{(-16.93) + (-15.59) + (-14.36) + (-15.72)}{4} = -15.65$$

$$\overline{A}_2 = \frac{(-9.24) + (-14.88) + (-13.27) + (-14.15)}{4} = -12.89$$

$$\text{Effect of A} = |\overline{A}_1 - \overline{A}_2| = |(-15.65) - (-12.89)| = 2.76$$

Similarly for factor B,

$$\overline{B}_1 = \frac{(-16.93) + (-15.59) + (-9.24) + (-14.88)}{4} = -14.16$$

$$\overline{B}_2 = \frac{(-14.36) + (-15.72) + (-13.27) + (-14.15)}{4} = -14.38$$

$$\text{Effect of B} = |\overline{B}_1 - \overline{B}_2| = |(-14.16) - (-14.38)| = .22$$

The average S/Ns for the remaining factors and interactions are calculated in the same fashion producing the following S/N response table.

S/N Response Table

	A	B	A × B	C	error	B × C	D
Level 1	−15.65	−14.16	−14.99	−13.45	−15.08	−14.01	−15.20
Level 2	−12.89	−14.38	−13.55	−15.09	−13.46	−14.53	−13.33
Delta	2.76	.22	1.44	1.64	1.62	.52	1.87

3. Based on the average S/N computed for each factor and interaction level, construct S/N response graphs (Figure 17-10).

4. Analyze the S/N response table and S/N response graphs.

By identifying the order of the effects from largest to smallest from the S/N response table or ranking the steepness of the slopes in the S/N response graphs, factor A is the strongest effect (delta = 2.76). Factor D is second (delta = 1.87) and is closely followed by factor C (delta = 1.64), vacant column 5 (delta = 1.62), and the interaction A × B. The effects then drop off to the interaction B × C (delta = .51) and factor B (delta = .21).

From the comparative analysis, the strong effects are factors A, D, and C; the interaction A × B; and the effect from column 5. The preferred levels for individual factors that exhibited a strong effect on the quality characteristic, turn-off time, were A_2, D_2, and C_1. Since the interaction A × B was also included in the group, we will need to construct a S/N interaction matrix and a S/N interaction graph.

The calculations for the 2 × 2 matrix and the data points for the interaction graph for the interaction B × C are as follows:

Run#	A	B	A × B	C	e	B × C	D	S/N
1	1	1	1	1	1	1	1	−16.93
2	1	1	1	2	2	2	2	−15.59
3	**1**	**2**	2	1	1	2	2	**−14.36**
4	**1**	**2**	2	2	2	1	1	**−15.72**
5	2	1	2	1	2	1	2	−9.24
6	2	1	2	2	1	2	1	−14.88
7	**2**	**2**	1	1	2	2	1	**−13.27**
8	**2**	**2**	1	2	1	1	2	**−14.15**

$$\bar{A}_1\,\bar{B}_1 = \frac{(-16.93) + (-15.59)}{2} = -16.26$$

$$\bar{A}_1\,\bar{B}_2 = \frac{(-14.36) + (-15.72)}{2} = -15.04$$

$$\bar{A}_2\,\bar{B}_1 = \frac{(-9.24) + (-14.88)}{2} = -12.06$$

$$\bar{A}_2\,\bar{B}_2 = \frac{(-13.27) + (-14.15)}{2} = -13.71$$

Figure 17-10 S/N Response Graphs

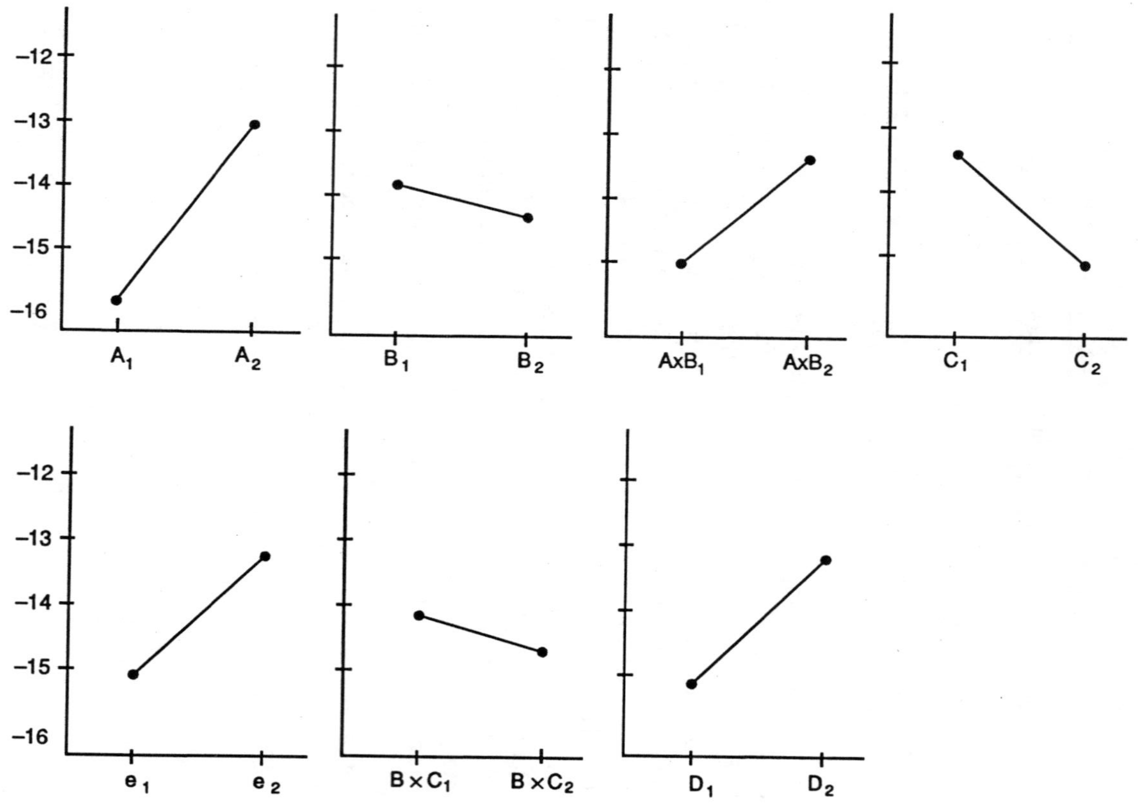

Figure 17-11 Interaction Graph

Interaction Matrix

	B_1	B_2
A_1	−16.26	−15.04
A_2	−12.06	−13.71

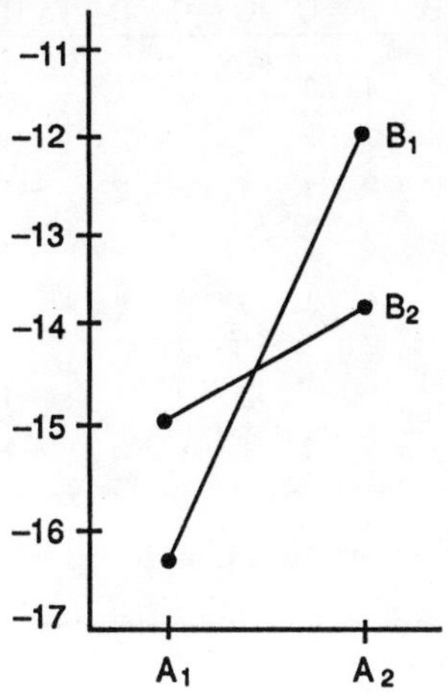

The S/N interaction matrix can then be constructed and the S/N interaction graph plotted as in Figure 17-11.

The intersecting lines in the S/N interaction graph reflect a strong interaction between factors A and B. With $\overline{A}_2\overline{B}_1$ being the highest point on the graph, the diagram denotes A_2B_1 as the best combination of factor settings.

Since the further study of the interaction $A \times B$ suggested that the strong interaction between the two factors and its effect (delta = 1.44) was less than that of column 5 (delta = 1.62), we should also pursue the possibility that the interaction $A \times C$ may have been strong after all. Therefore, let's generate a S/N interaction matrix and a S/N interaction graph (Figure 17-12) to investigate it.

The converging lines from the $A \times C$ interaction graph indicate enough relative strength that we should consider it after all. This is particularly true in this experiment since factor A and the interaction $A \times B$ were incorporated into the group of strong effects, and column 5 demonstrated a stronger effect for the interaction $A \times C$.

Therefore, we can conclude from the analysis of the factors (main effects) and interactions that the strong effects are:

$$A,\ A \times B,\ C,\ A \times C, \text{ and } D.$$

From the S/N response table and S/N response graphs, A_2, C_1, and D_2 are recommended. From the $A \times B$ interaction matrix and interaction graph, A_2B_1

Run#	A	B	A × B	C	A × C	B × C	D	Data	Mean Response
1	1	1	1	1	1	1	1	−16.93	$\bar{A}_1\bar{C}_1 = \frac{(-16.93) + (-14.36)}{2} = -15.65$
2	1	1	1	**2**	2	2	2	−15.**59**	
3	1	2	2	1	1	2	2	−14.36	$\bar{A}_1\bar{C}_2 = \frac{(-15.59) + (-15.72)}{2} = -15.66$
4	1	2	2	**2**	2	1	1	−15.**72**	
5	**2**	1	2	1	2	1	2	**−9**.24	$\bar{A}_2\bar{C}_1 = \frac{(-9.24) + (-13.27)}{2} = -11.26$
6	**2**	1	2	**2**	1	2	1	**−14.88**	
7	**2**	2	1	1	2	2	1	−13.27	$\bar{A}_2\bar{C}_2 = \frac{(-14.88) + (-14.15)}{2} = -14.52$
8	**2**	2	1	**2**	1	1	2	**−14.15**	

Figure 17-12 Interaction Graph

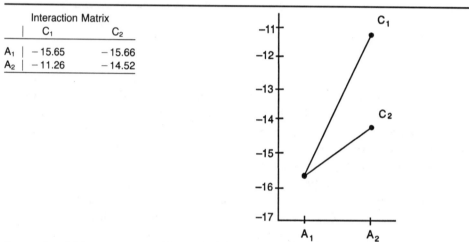

Interaction Matrix

	C_1	C_2
A_1	−15.65	−15.66
A_2	−11.26	−14.52

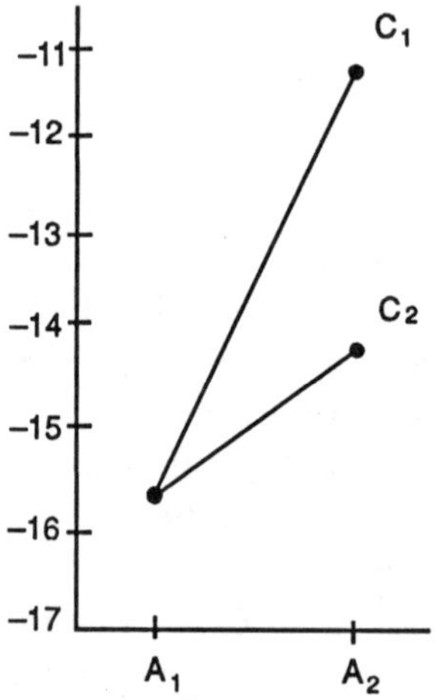

From the S/N response table and S/N response graphs, A_2, C_1, and D_2 are recommended. From the A×B interaction matrix and interaction graph, A_2B_1 was the best combination, which reinforced the selection of A_2 and resulted in the choice of B_1. The A×C interaction matrix and interaction graph indicated A_2C_1 as the preferred combination. This again supported the selection of A_2 as well as reconfirming the selection of C_1 based on its individual effect. In summary, the recommended levels are:

$$A_2,\ B_1,\ C_1,\ D_2.$$

One additional consideration concerning the results from the experiment is the impact of the noise factors (moisture, drying, and soldering) themselves. Can moisture be such a problem that it would warrant installation of humidity controls? Do special drying procedures need to be instituted?

To help address these questions, we need to perform some basic means analysis of the data. First, we need to total the results for each column of the outer array and calculate the average response.

			A × B		A × C	B × C		O / N / M	1 / 1 / 1	2 / 2 / 1	2 / 1 / 2	1 / 2 / 2
Run#	A	B	B	C	C	C	D					
1	1	1	1	1	1	1	1		2.62	2.66	10.00	10.00
									2.56	2.56	8.24	10.00
2	1	1	1	2	2	2	2		2.27	2.29	5.65	6.07
									2.30	2.29	10.00	10.00
3	1	2	2	1	1	2	2		2.30	2.27	3.73	4.19
									2.33	2.33	8.09	10.00
4	1	2	2	2	2	1	1		2.61	2.53	6.36	8.10
									2.61	2.59	10.00	8.14
5	2	1	2	1	2	1	2		2.36	2.29	2.28	4.24
									2.29	2.25	4.22	2.25
6	2	1	2	2	1	2	1		2.54	2.58	6.51	6.33
									2.46	2.47	10.00	6.22
7	2	2	1	1	2	2	1		2.53	2.54	4.40	4.51
									2.51	2.52	6.25	8.12
8	2	2	1	2	1	1	2		2.30	2.27	10.00	4.27
									2.21	2.22	2.20	8.05
			Totals						38.80	38.66	107.93	110.49
			Average						2.43	2.42	6.75	6.91

From the average response for each column, we can match the values to the appropriate noise factor levels and calculate an average response for each noise factor setting.

$$\overline{M}_1 = \frac{2.43 + 2.42}{2} = 2.425 \qquad \overline{M}_2 = \frac{6.75 + 6.91}{2} = 6.830$$

$$\overline{N}_1 = \frac{2.43 + 6.75}{2} = 4.590 \qquad \overline{N}_2 = \frac{2.42 + 6.91}{2} = 4.665$$

$$\overline{O}_1 = \frac{2.43 + 6.91}{2} = 4.670 \qquad \overline{O}_2 = \frac{2.42 + 6.75}{2} = 4.585$$

By inserting the average response value for each noise level into a response table and calculating the difference, we can see that the most dramatic difference is in the effect of humidity. Therefore, if we were to consider a potential area for instituting better control, we may wish to focus on humidity. In conducting the comfirmation run at the optimal control factor settings, we should pay particular attention to the results as the humidity changes.

Response Table

Level	M	N	O
1	2.425	4.590	4.670
2	6.830	4.665	4.585
Delta	**4.405**	.075	.085

5. Compute an estimate of the predicted signal-to-noise ratio based on the selected levels of the strong effects. From our analysis, the strong effects and elements to be included into the prediction equation are:

$$A,\ A\times B,\ C,\ A\times C,\ D.$$

The prediction equation then becomes:

$$\hat{\eta} = \overline{T} + (\overline{A}_2 - \overline{T}) + [(\overline{A_2B_1} - \overline{T}) - (\overline{A}_2 - \overline{T}) - (\overline{B}_1 - \overline{T})] + (\overline{C}_1 - \overline{T})$$
$$+ [(\overline{A_2C_1} - \overline{T}) - (\overline{A}_2 - \overline{T}) - (\overline{C}_1 - \overline{T})] + (\overline{D}_2 - \overline{T})$$

By combining like terms, the equation reduces to:

$$\hat{\eta} = \overline{A_2B_1} - \overline{B}_1 + \overline{A_2C_1} - \overline{A}_2 + \overline{D}_2.$$

Substituting values from the response table and interaction matrices,

$$\hat{\eta} = (-12.06) - (-14.16) + (-11.26) - (-12.89) + (-13.33)$$
$$\hat{\eta} = -9.60 \text{ db}$$

6. Conduct a confirmation run and compare the actual results to the predicted results.

A number of units should be built according to the recommended control factor levels with an equal number assembled against each set of noise factor conditions used in the experiment. After completing the confirmation run, an actual η should be computed and compared to the predicted value of -9.60 decibels. If the actual result is close to the predicted value, the recommended settings can be implemented. If the actual η is lower, but the raw data (delay time) is consistently within the specification limit of 5 milliseconds, the team may want to implement the changes while studying the problem further to look for additional improvement opportunities.

If the confirmation run validates the experiment hypotheses, an estimation of the cost savings from instituting the improvements can be calculated using the following two equations.

$$\text{Cost}_{new} = \text{Cost}_{existing} \left| \frac{1}{2} \right|^{\frac{\eta_{new} - \eta_{existing}}{3}}$$

$$\text{Cost Savings} = \text{Cost}_{existing} - \text{Cost}_{new}$$

The estimate serves three purposes. One, it quantifies the success of the efforts. Two, it helps to insure implementation of the recommended levels. Three, it gathers management support for future projects.

Notes

1. *Introduction to Quality Engineering,* p. 3-1.

Chapter 18

ANALYSIS: LARGER-THE-BETTER

The analysis techniques for a larger-the-better quality characteristic are closely patterned after the procedures used for smaller-the-better characteristics. Since both characteristics involve continuously measurable results, both types of data can be handled in similar manners. With the incorporation of noise factors into an experiment involving a larger-the-better characteristic, you can determine the key factors and the best settings for consistently good performance over time despite changes in uncontrollable influences. As in the case of smaller-the-better characteristics, the concept of parameter design can lead you beyond the mere determination of what works best under nominal environmental conditions. The concept of robustness is just as applicable for the attaining of consistently high larger-the-better responses for process performance and end product functionality.

In Chapter 15, we discussed the use of level average analysis in determining the strong effects and recommended settings for both smaller-the-better and larger-the-better characteristics. Chapter 17 was devoted to taking the basic procedures of Chapter 15, translating and building upon these steps to formulate parameter design methodology, and specifically applying the concepts to the study of smaller-the-better characteristics. The purpose of Chapter 18 is to take the prior knowledge from each of these chapters and construct a set of logical steps for conducting parameter design studies involving larger-the-better characteristics.

The data format of a parameter design experiment for a larger-the-better quality characteristic is identical to that of a smaller-the-better response (Figure 18-1). Both build onto an inner orthogonal array by adding an outer array that may consist of columns either representing each level of a single noise factor or designating noise factor level combinations if numerous noise factors are considered. The experimental matrix also resembles the structure for a study involving only control factors with repetitions and requiring level average analysis. The difference between the level average analysis format and the other two formats is in the transformation of the data for each row of the experimental matrix. In the level average analysis format, the mean response is calculated for

Figure 18-1 Data Format Comparison

Level Average Analysis Data Format

Run No.	A	B	A × B	Data				$\bar{y}$
1	1	1	1	y_{11}	y_{12}	y_{13}	y_{14}	$\bar{y}_1$
2	1	2	2	y_{21}	y_{22}	y_{23}	y_{24}	$\bar{y}_2$
3	2	1	2	y_{31}	y_{32}	y_{33}	y_{34}	$\bar{y}_3$
4	2	2	1	y_{41}	y_{42}	y_{43}	y_{44}	$\bar{y}_4$

Smaller-the-Better Signal-to-Noise Ratio Data Format

Run No.	A	B	A × B	Data				S/N
1	1	1	1	y_{11}	y_{12}	y_{13}	y_{14}	S/N_1
2	1	2	2	y_{21}	y_{22}	y_{23}	y_{24}	S/N_2
3	2	1	2	y_{31}	y_{32}	y_{33}	y_{34}	S/N_3
4	2	2	1	y_{41}	y_{42}	y_{43}	y_{44}	S/N_4

Larger-the-Better Signal-to-Noise Ratio Data Format

Run No.	A	B	A × B	Data				S/N
1	1	1	1	y_{11}	y_{12}	y_{13}	y_{14}	S/N_1
2	1	2	2	y_{21}	y_{22}	y_{23}	y_{24}	S/N_2
3	2	1	2	y_{31}	y_{32}	y_{33}	y_{34}	S/N_3
4	2	2	1	y_{41}	y_{42}	y_{43}	y_{44}	S/N_4

each row, and these averages are then used to generate response tables and graphs. For both larger-the-better and smaller-the-better parameter designs, a signal-to-noise ratio is calculated for each row of the inner array. The results are then used to create S/N response tables and graphs.

In Chapter 15, we saw the analysis of smaller-the-better and larger-the-better data run parallel courses. For each set of responses, we constructed and analyzed response tables and graphs, and we developed prediction equations and estimated the expected results for recommended optimal conditions. In smaller-the-better level average analysis, we selected levels based on the smaller mean response. Conversely, in larger-the-better level average analysis, the larger mean response was chosen. For signal-to-noise ratio analysis, you *always* look for the larger value whether the quality characteristic is smaller-the-better or larger-the-better. The fundamental difference between the two is in how the signal-to-noise ratio is determined.

18.1 SIGNAL-TO-NOISE RATIO

The purpose, again, in the computation and use of the signal-to-noise ratio is to encapsulate the effect of environmental conditions (outer noise), internal deterioration (inner noise), and variation from unit to unit (between product noise)[1] on those factors that can be controlled. In the specific application of the signal-to-noise ratio concept to larger-the-better characteristics, we are looking for those combinations of control factor settings that result in consistently high values. An extremely high readout under ideal environmental conditions will not do if the results are unsatisfactory the remainder of the time. We are looking for consistently high response values.

The formula for the signal-to-noise ratio for the larger-the-better quality characteristic is also a logarithmic function and can be written in exactly the same form as the smaller-the-better S/N formula. We can again write this as:

$$\text{S/N} = -10 \log \text{MSD}$$

The difference in the two computations is in the calculation of the mean square deviation. The equation for the larger-the-better mean square deviation is:

$$\text{MSD} = \frac{1/y_1^2 + 1/y_2^2 + \ . \ . \ . + 1/y_n^2}{n}$$

Instead of taking the square of each data value and adding them together as in smaller-the-better calculations, we are inverting each of the individual squared

Figure 18-2 Larger-the-Better Signal-to-Noise Ratio

Data Set 1: 5, 9, 11, 15
Data Set 2: 10, 14, 16, 20
Data Set 3: 10, 10, 10, 10
Data Set 4: 15, 15, 15, 15

Data Set 1: $S/N = -10 \log \left| \dfrac{1/5^2 + 1/9^2 + 1/11^2 + 1/15^2}{4} \right| = 17.89$ db

Data Set 2: $S/N = -10 \log \left| \dfrac{1/10^2 + 1/14^2 + 1/16^2 + 1/20^2}{4} \right| = 22.69$ db

Data Set 3: $S/N = -10 \log \left| \dfrac{1/10^2 + 1/10^2 + 1/10^2 + 1/10^2}{4} \right| = 20.00$ db

Data Set 4: $S/N = -10 \log \left| \dfrac{1/15^2 + 1/15^2 + 1/15^2 + 1/15^2}{4} \right| = 23.52$ db

terms and then taking the average. We can then rewrite the larger-the-better S/N equation as:

$$S/N = -10 \log \left| \frac{1/y_1^2 + 1/y_2^2 + \ldots + 1/y_n^2}{n} \right|$$

Again, an improvement in the process or resulting product is signified by an increase in the signal-to-noise ratio. With the smaller-the-better characteristic, this meant a decrease in the average results or an improvement in the consistency from one unit to the next. For the larger-the-better characteristic, the S/N increases as the average results increase. Improved consistency or reduced variability between units will again raise the S/N. Figure 18-2 demonstrates mathematically how the calculations are performed and how the effects of changes in the individual values impact the signal-to-noise ratio. In data set 2, we can see the effect of an increase in the average response on the larger-the-better signal-to-noise ratio. The impact of reduced variability is illustrated in data set 3, and the combined effect of larger values and less variability is shown in data set 4. We can conclude from these sample calculations that our goal in conducting parameter design type experiments involving a larger-the-better characteristic should be to identify those factor settings that will produce the most consistently large response values.

18.2 ANALYSIS TECHNIQUES

Following the same procedures prescribed in Chapter 17, we can identify the strong effects and ascertain the best levels or settings for each of the control factors under consideration. S/N response tables and graphs will again form the basis for enhancing our knowledge of the process or product we are studying. The fundamental change is in the calculation of the mean square deviation.

To facilitate understanding of how to perform S/N analysis on larger-the-better type data and how it compares to smaller-the-better analysis, we will proceed step-by-step through an L_4 (2^3) example similar to the one used in Chapter 17. This time, our goal will be to produce consistently larger response values instead of determining factor settings that will reduce the values of the characteristic which we are measuring.

After collecting the experiment data and referencing each set to the appropriate experimental run (orthogonal array row), we will need to calculate S/N for each row using the larger-the-better S/N formula (Figure 18-3). After performing the computations, an additional column should be added alongside the raw data, and the corresponding S/N can be recorded for each row. Organizing the computations in this manner will facilitate the later calculations that will be needed in constructing the S/N response table and plotting the S/N response graphs.

The signal-to-noise response table for the larger-the-better response is generated in the exact same manner as that for the smaller-the-better S/Ns. If we take the signal-to-noise ratios calculated in Figure 18-3, we can develop a response table as shown in Figure 18-4.

Let's review the calculations for determining the effect of a factor (or interaction) and demonstrate how they are used with larger-the-better S/Ns by calculating the effect of factor A.

Figure 18-3 Larger-the-Better S/N Calculations

L_4 (2^3)

Run No.	A	B	A × B	N_1	N_2	S/N
1	1	1	1	10	25	22.37
2	1	2	2	16	32	26.12
3	2	1	2	40	45	32.52
4	2	2	1	20	30	27.43

$$S/N_1 = -10 \log \left| \frac{1/10^2 + 1/25^2}{2} \right| = 22.37$$

$$S/N_2 = -10 \log \left| \frac{1/16^2 + 1/32^2}{2} \right| = 26.12$$

$$S/N_3 = -10 \log \left| \frac{1/40^2 + 1/45^2}{2} \right| = 32.52$$

$$S/N_4 = -10 \log \left| \frac{1/20^2 + 1/30^2}{2} \right| = 27.43$$

Figure 18-4 Larger-the-Better S/N Response Table

L_4 (2^3)

Run No.	A	B	A × B	N_1	N_2	S/N
1	1	1	1	10	25	22.37
2	1	2	2	16	32	26.12
3	2	1	2	40	45	32.52
4	2	2	1	20	30	27.43

S/N Response Table

Level	A	B	A × B
1	24.245	27.445	24.900
2	29.975	26.775	29.320
Delta	5.730	.670	4.420

For $\overline{A}_1$, we would obtain:

$$S/N = \frac{(22.37) + (26.12)}{2} = 24.245.$$

Similarly for $\overline{A}_2$, the average signal-to-noise ratio is:

$$S/N = \frac{(32.52) + (27.43)}{2} = 29.975.$$

Then,

$$\text{Effect of A} = | \overline{A}_1 - \overline{A}_2 | = | 24.245 - 29.975 | = 5.730 \text{ db.}$$

The values for factor B and the interaction A×B to complete the response table can be determined similarly.

The S/N response graphs for the larger-the-better characteristic are also constructed and plotted like those for the smaller-the-better responses. The S/N response graphs for the preceding example are displayed in Figure 18-5.

The analysis also follows the same guidelines. Reading the response table and the response graphs, factor A and the interaction A×B are clearly the strong effects. A_2 is recommended since it is the larger signal-to-noise ratio in the response table and the higher point on the response graph. Consistent with our previous treatment of interactions, strong interactions require construction of the interaction matrix and corresponding interaction graph. The two are demonstrated for the L_4 (2^3) larger-the-better example in Figure 18-6.

As shown in the interaction graph and supported by the interaction matrix. A×B is indeed a strong interaction. A_2B_1 is the highest point on the graph, signifying the best combination of the two factors. Based on the S/N response

Figure 18-5 Larger-the Better S/N Response Graphs

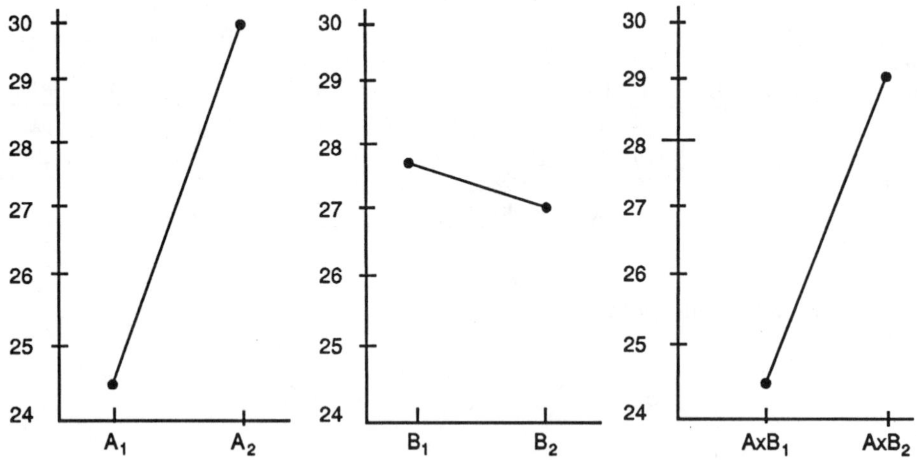

table, the S/N response graphs, the interaction matrix, and the interaction graph, we would recommend the settings of A_2 and B_1.

Just as we could make a relative comparison of the impact of the noise factor(s) on the process or product being investigated in the earlier smaller-the-better examples, the same type of examination can be conducted based on larger-the-better data. From the noise factor analysis in Figure 18-7, we can see that the impact of the noise factor is relatively worse for level 1. As for both smaller-the-better and larger-the-better responses, decisions on whether to respond to these influences will depend on the relative magnitude and the consequence of these effects. Engineering judgment should play a vital role in these decisions.

Like the smaller-the-better parameter design experiment, the prediction equation is set up to calculate an estimate of η at the recommended control factor settings.

Figure 18-6 Larger-the-Better Interaction Analysis

$L_4 (2^3)$

Run No.	A	B	A × B	N_1	N_2	S/N
1	1	1	1	10	25	22.37
2	1	2	2	16	32	26.12
3	2	1	2	40	45	32.52
4	2	2	1	20	30	27.43

Interaction Matrix

	B_1	B_2
A_1	22.37	26.12
A_2	32.52	27.43

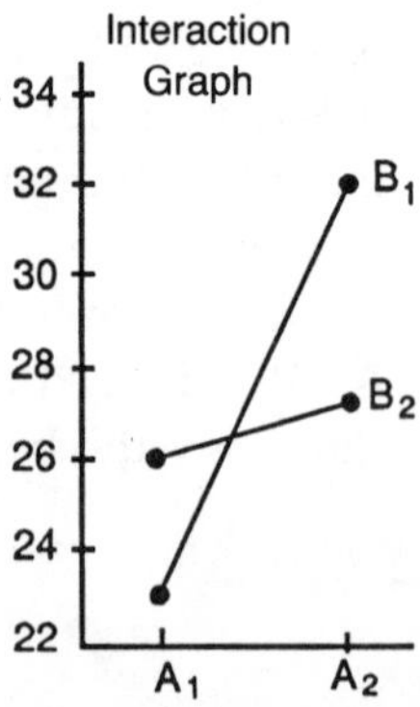

Figure 18-7 Larger-the-Better Noise Factor Analysis

$L_4 (2^3)$

Run No.	A	B	A × B	N_1	N_2	S/N
1	1	1	1	10	25	22.37
2	1	2	2	16	32	26.12
3	2	1	2	40	45	32.52
4	2	2	1	20	30	27.43
			Totals	86.00	132.00	
			Average	21.50	33.00	
			Delta	11.50		

$$\hat{\eta} = \overline{T} + (\overline{A}_2 - \overline{T}) + [(\overline{A_2B_1} - \overline{T}) - (\overline{A}_2 - \overline{T}) - (\overline{B}_1 - \overline{T})]$$

Then, the confirmation run is conducted across the range of noise factor settings with η computed for the actual results and compared to the predicted η. As explained in Chapter 18, time constraints and the ability to control the noise factors for short periods will govern the capability of setting noise factor levels at or close to experimental conditions.

If the confirmation results validate the conclusions from the analysis, the recommended factor settings can be confidently implemented. If the results are disappointing, a return to the planning phase is needed. The same potential causes discussed in the previous types of studies covered will continue to be relevant and should be investigated if the actual results are considerably less than expected.

Concerning the impact of a successful experiment, the signal-to-noise ratio can again provide an estimate of the cost savings associated with instituting the improvements. Whether a smaller-the-better characteristic or a larger-the-better response, each 3-decibel increase in η reduces the cost of quality by 50%. We restate the relationship in the space below:

$$\text{Cost}_{\text{new}} = \text{Cost}_{\text{existing}} \left| \frac{1}{2} \right|^{\frac{\eta_{\text{new}} - \eta_{\text{existing}}}{3}}$$

$$\text{Cost Savings} = \text{Cost}_{\text{existing}} - \text{Cost}_{\text{new}}$$

18.3 WIRE CONNECTOR ASSEMBLY CASE STUDY

Problem: A wire connector assembly has exhibited reliability problems in the field. The wires become loose and separate from the assembly causing a break in the electrical contact. The resulting electrical failures lead to machinery shutdown and contribute to customer dissatisfaction. With various problem-solving tools, the connector has been identified as the source of the problem. Furthermore, the inability to tighten the hold-down screws sufficiently has resulted in the wires' becoming disconnected with a minimum of force. A study has been initiated to determine if an improved design, better materials, or a combination of both can lead to a product that will increase the amount of force required to pull a wire cable out of the connector assembly.

Objective: Maximize the pull force required for disconnecting a wire cable from the connector assembly. Experiment design and data are shown in Figure 18-8.

Since the Interactions A × B and B × C require four degrees of freedom each, both will need to be assigned to two columns in accordance with an appropriate

Figure 18-8 Experiment Design and Data
y = pull force (pounds)

	1	2	3	4	5	6	7	8	9	10	11	12	13	pull force (pounds)			
			A × B	A × B				B × C			B × C			M_1		M_2	
Run#	A	B	B	B	C	D	E	C	F	G	C	H	I	N_1	N_2	N_1	N_2
1	1	1	1	1	1	1	1	1	1	1	1	1	1	5.7	6.2	5.5	6.0
2	1	1	1	1	2	2	2	2	2	2	2	2	2	6.1	6.0	5.8	6.0
3	1	1	1	1	3	3	3	3	3	3	3	3	3	7.5	7.0	7.5	7.0
4	1	2	2	2	1	1	1	2	2	2	3	3	3	4.2	3.0	4.5	4.0
5	1	2	2	2	2	2	2	3	3	3	1	1	1	10.0	10.0	11.0	11.2
6	1	2	2	2	3	3	3	1	1	1	2	2	2	6.1	6.0	6.0	5.5
7	1	3	3	3	1	1	1	3	3	3	2	2	2	6.6	6.0	7.0	6.5
8	1	3	3	3	2	2	2	1	1	1	3	3	3	6.6	7.8	6.5	7.0
9	1	3	3	3	3	3	3	2	2	2	1	1	1	6.6	6.5	7.0	6.8
10	2	1	2	3	1	2	3	1	2	3	1	2	3	8.3	9.5	8.0	8.8
11	2	1	2	3	2	3	1	2	3	1	2	3	1	10.6	11.0	10.0	11.6
12	2	1	2	3	3	1	2	3	1	2	3	1	2	4.1	3.8	4.0	4.5
13	2	2	3	1	1	2	3	2	3	1	3	1	2	9.3	9.6	9.5	9.8
14	2	2	3	1	2	3	1	3	1	2	1	2	3	5.0	4.5	5.5	5.0
15	2	2	3	1	3	1	2	1	2	3	2	3	1	9.2	10.0	9.5	9.9
16	2	3	1	2	1	2	3	3	1	2	2	3	1	7.7	8.0	7.5	8.0
17	2	3	1	2	2	3	1	1	2	3	3	1	2	8.1	8.0	8.5	8.8
18	2	3	1	2	3	1	2	2	3	1	1	2	3	7.5	7.5	8.5	7.5
19	3	1	3	2	1	3	2	1	3	2	1	3	2	9.9	11.0	10.6	10.7
20	3	1	3	2	2	1	3	2	1	3	2	1	3	5.8	5.0	6.5	5.5
21	3	1	3	2	3	2	1	3	2	1	3	2	1	9.6	9.5	9.2	10.0
22	3	2	1	3	1	3	2	2	1	3	3	2	1	9.8	9.5	10.0	10.5
23	3	2	1	3	2	1	3	3	2	1	1	3	2	6.0	6.2	6.6	5.5
24	3	2	1	3	3	2	1	1	3	2	2	1	3	9.2	9.5	9.0	10.2
25	3	3	2	1	1	3	2	3	2	1	2	1	3	7.8	8.6	7.5	8.2
26	3	3	2	1	2	1	3	1	3	2	3	2	1	9.9	10.0	9.5	10.9
27	3	3	2	1	3	2	1	2	1	3	1	3	2	7.5	8.0	7.5	7.0

linear graph. Therefore, $A \times B$ can be assigned to columns 3 and 4, and $B \times C$ can be inserted into columns 8 and 11.

1. Determine the S/N for each row (experimental run).

$$\#1\ S/N = -10 \log \frac{1/5.7^2 + 1/6.2^2 + 1/5.5^2 + 1/6.0^2}{4} = 15.32 \text{ db}$$

$$\#2\ S/N = -10 \log \frac{1/6.1^2 + 1/6.0^2 + 1/5.8^2 + 1/6.0^2}{4} = 15.52 \text{ db}$$

. . . .

$$\#27\ S/N = -10 \log \frac{1/7.3^2 + 1/8.0^2 + 1/7.5^2 + 1/7.0^2}{4} = 17.41 \text{ db}$$

By adding a column containing the signal-to-noise ratio for each respective row, we will obtain the resulting experimental design matrix.

	1	2	3	4	5	6	7	8	9	10	11	12	13	pull force (pounds)				
			A ×	A ×				B ×			B ×			M_1		M_2		
Run#	A	B	B	B	C	D	E	C	F	G	C	H	I	N_1	N_2	N_1	N_2	S/N
1	1	1	1	1	1	1	1	1	1	1	1	1	1	5.7	6.2	5.5	6.0	15.32
2	1	1	1	1	2	2	2	2	2	2	2	2	2	6.1	6.0	5.8	6.0	15.52
3	1	1	1	1	3	3	3	3	3	3	3	3	3	7.5	7.0	7.5	7.0	17.19
4	1	2	2	2	1	1	1	2	2	2	3	3	3	4.2	3.0	4.5	4.0	11.55
5	1	2	2	2	2	2	2	3	3	3	1	1	1	10.0	10.0	11.0	11.2	20.43
6	1	2	2	2	3	3	3	1	1	1	2	2	2	6.1	6.0	6.0	5.5	15.40
7	1	3	3	3	1	1	1	3	3	3	2	2	2	6.6	6.0	7.0	6.5	16.25
8	1	3	3	3	2	2	2	1	1	1	3	3	3	6.6	7.8	6.5	7.0	16.81
9	1	3	3	3	3	3	3	2	2	2	1	1	1	6.6	6.5	7.0	6.8	16.54
10	2	1	2	3	1	2	3	1	2	3	1	2	3	8.3	9.5	8.0	8.8	18.69
11	2	1	2	3	2	3	1	2	3	1	2	3	1	10.6	11.0	10.0	11.6	20.63
12	2	1	2	3	3	1	2	3	1	2	3	1	2	4.1	3.8	4.0	4.5	12.21
13	2	2	3	1	1	2	3	2	3	1	3	1	2	9.3	9.6	9.5	9.8	19.60
14	2	2	3	1	2	3	1	3	1	2	1	2	3	5.0	4.5	5.5	5.0	13.91
15	2	2	3	1	3	1	2	1	2	3	2	3	1	9.2	10.0	9.5	9.9	19.68
16	2	3	1	2	1	2	3	3	1	2	2	3	1	7.7	8.0	7.5	8.0	17.83
17	2	3	1	2	2	3	1	1	2	3	3	1	2	8.1	8.0	8.5	8.8	18.41
18	2	3	1	2	3	1	2	2	3	1	1	2	3	7.5	7.5	8.5	7.5	17.75
19	3	1	3	2	1	3	2	1	3	2	1	3	2	9.9	11.0	10.6	10.7	20.45
20	3	1	3	2	2	1	3	2	1	3	2	1	3	5.8	5.0	6.5	5.5	15.00
21	3	1	3	2	3	2	1	3	2	1	3	2	1	9.6	9.5	9.2	10.0	19.61
22	3	2	1	3	1	3	2	2	1	3	3	2	1	9.8	9.5	10.0	10.5	19.94
23	3	2	1	3	2	1	3	3	2	1	1	3	2	6.0	6.2	6.6	5.5	15.61
24	3	2	1	3	3	2	1	1	3	2	2	1	3	9.2	9.5	9.0	10.2	19.50
25	3	3	2	1	1	3	2	3	2	1	2	1	3	7.8	8.6	7.5	8.2	18.05
26	3	3	2	1	2	1	3	1	3	2	3	2	1	9.9	10.0	9.5	10.9	20.03
27	3	3	2	1	3	2	1	2	1	3	1	3	2	7.5	8.0	7.5	7.0	17.41

2. Calculate the average S/N for each factor and interaction level and develop a response table.

For factor A,

$$\overline{A}_1 = \frac{15.32+15.52+17.19+11.55+20.43+15.40+16.25+16.82+16.54}{9}$$

$$\overline{A}_1 = 16.11 \text{ (smallest)}$$

$$\overline{A}_2 = \frac{18.69+20.63+12.21+19.60+13.91+19.68+17.83+18.41+17.75}{9}$$

$$\overline{A}_2 = 17.63$$

$$\overline{A}_3 = \frac{20.45+15.00+19.61+19.94+15.61+19.50+18.05+20.03+17.41}{9}$$

$$\overline{A}_3 = 18.40 \text{ (largest)}$$

$$\text{Effect of A} = |\overline{A}_3 - \overline{A}_1| = |18.40 - 16.11| = 2.29 \text{ db}$$

For factor B,

$$\overline{B}_1 = \frac{15.32+15.52+17.19+18.69+20.63+12.21+20.45+15.00+19.61}{9}$$

$$\overline{B}_1 = 17.18 \text{ (smallest)}$$

$$\overline{B}_2 = \frac{11.55+20.43+15.40+19.60+13.91+19.68+19.94+15.61+19.50}{9}$$

$$\overline{B}_2 = 17.29$$

$$\overline{B}_3 = \frac{16.25+16.81+16.54+17.83+18.41+17.75+18.05+20.03+17.41}{9}$$

$$\overline{B}_3 = 17.68 \text{ (largest)}$$

$$\text{Effect of B} = |\overline{B}_3 - \overline{B}_1| = |17.68 - 17.18| = .22 \text{ db}$$

The average S/N for the remaining factors and interactions and their effect are calculated in the same fashion and will produce the following S/N response table.

S/N Response Table

	A	B	A × B_1	A × B_2	C	D	E	B × C_1	F
Level 1	16.11	17.18	17.45	17.41	17.52	15.93	16.96	18.25	15.98
Level 2	17.63	17.29	17.16	17.94	17.37	18.38	17.87	17.11	17.08
Level 3	18.40	17.68	17.54	17.35	17.25	17.84	17.32	16.79	19.09
Delta	2.29	.50	.38	.59	.27	2.45	.91	1.46	3.11

	G	B × C_2	H	I
Level 1	17.64	17.35	17.23	18.89
Level 2	16.39	17.54	17.46	16.76
Level 3	18.11	17.26	17.46	16.50
Delta	1.72	.28	.23	2.39

3. Based on the average S/N computed for each factor and interaction level, construct S/N response graphs (Figure 18-9).

4. Analyze the S/N response table and S/N response graphs.

S/N Response Table

	A	B	A × B_1	A × B_2	C	D	E	B × C_1	F
Level 1	16.11	17.18	17.45	17.41	17.52	15.93	16.96	**18.25**	15.98
Level 2	17.63	17.29	17.16	17.94	17.37	**18.38**	17.87	17.11	17.08
Level 3	**18.40**	17.68	17.54	17.35	17.25	17.84	17.32	16.79	**19.09**
Delta	**2.29**	.50	.38	.59	.27	**2.45**	.91	**1.46**	**3.11**

	G	B × C_2	H	I
Level 1	17.64	17.35	17.23	**18.89**
Level 2	16.39	17.54	17.46	16.76
Level 3	**18.11**	17.26	17.46	16.50
Delta	**1.72**	.28	.23	**2.39**

Legend: Strong effects in bold.
Values for recommended levels in bold.

Figure 18-9 S/N Response Graphs

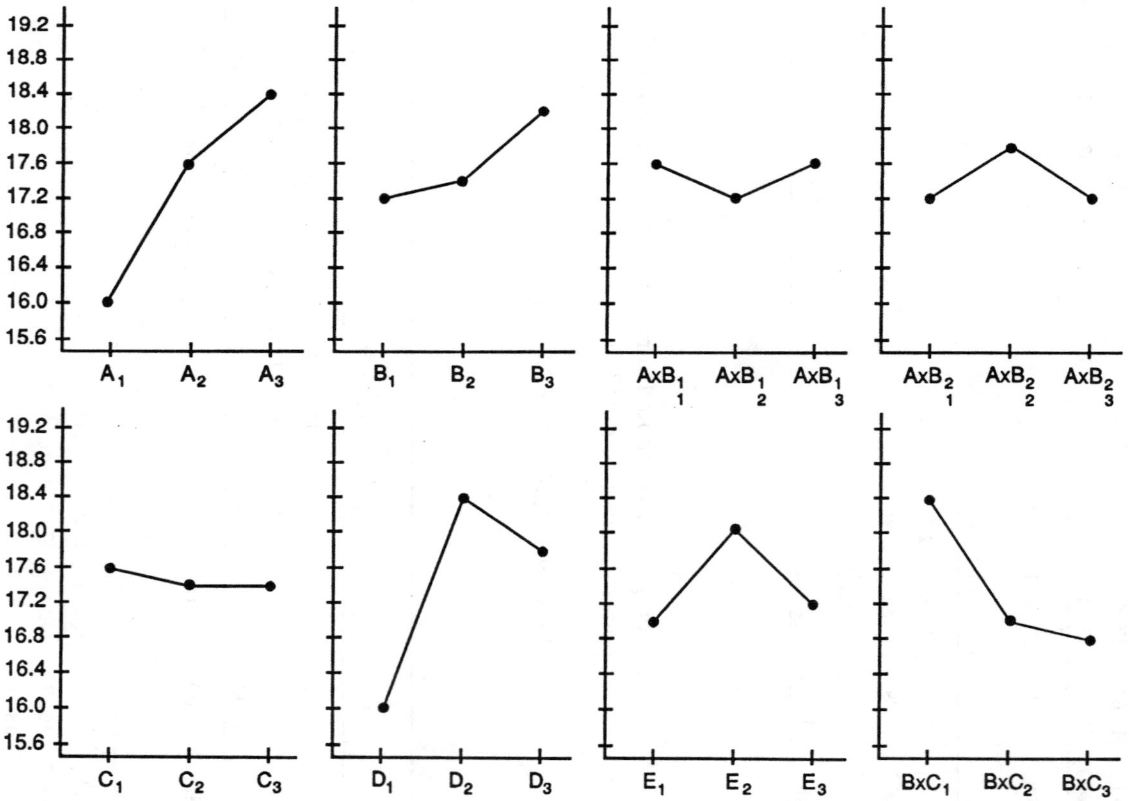

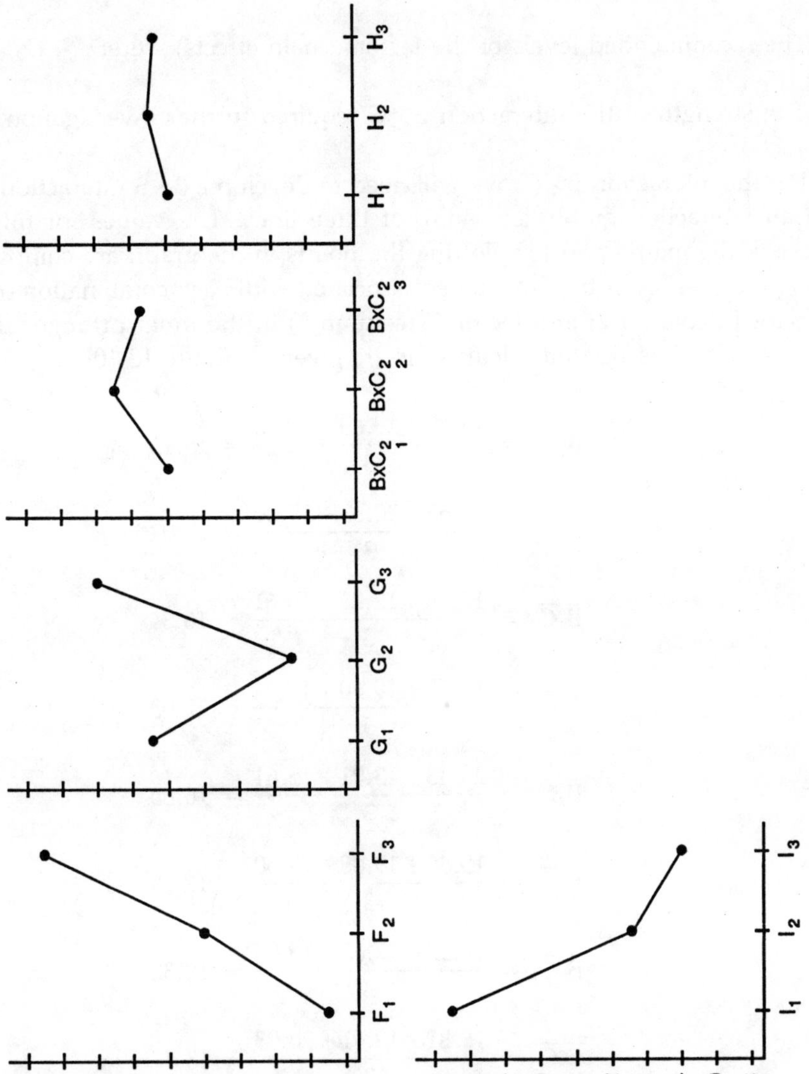
19.2
18.8
18.4
18.0
17.6
17.2
16.8
16.4
16.0
15.6
F1
F2
F3
G1
G2
G3
BxC2 1
BxC2 2
BxC2 3
H1
H2
H3
I1
I2
I3

Since the difference between the deltas for $B \times C_1$, and factor E was greater ($1.46 - .91 = .55$) than the differences between factor G and $B \times C_1$, ($1.72 - 1.46 = .26$) and between factor E and $A \times B_2$ ($.91 - .59 = .32$), it was ruled the logical breaking point. Therefore, the strong effects were: A, D, $B \times C$, F, G, and I.

The recommended levels of the factors (main effects) were: A_3, D_2, F_3, G_3, and I_1.

The strength of the interaction $B \times C$ required further investigation of that interaction.

For the interaction $B \times C$, we will need to develop a 3×3 interaction matrix and an interaction graph consisting of three lines. The values for filling the blocks in the matrix and for plotting the points in the graph are computed by taking the average of the S/N values associated with each combination of levels of factor B (column 2) and factor C (column 5) in the inner orthogonal array. The values and associated calculations are given in Figure 18-10.

$$\overline{B}_1\overline{C}_1 = \frac{15.32 + 18.69 + 20.45}{3} = 18.15$$

$$\overline{B}_1\overline{C}_2 = \frac{15.52 + 20.63 + 15.00}{3} = 17.02$$

$$\overline{B}_1\overline{C}_3 = \frac{17.19 + 12.21 + 19.61}{3} = 16.34$$

$$\overline{B}_2\overline{C}_1 = \frac{11.55 + 19.60 + 19.94}{3} = 17.03$$

$$\overline{B}_2\overline{C}_2 = \frac{20.43 + 13.91 + 15.61}{3} = 16.65$$

$$\overline{B}_2\overline{C}_3 = \frac{15.40 + 19.68 + 19.50}{3} = 18.19$$

$$\overline{B}_3\overline{C}_1 = \frac{16.25 + 17.83 + 18.05}{3} = 17.38$$

$$\overline{B}_3\overline{C}_2 = \frac{16.81 + 18.41 + 20.03}{3} = 18.42$$

$$\overline{B}_3\overline{C}_3 = \frac{16.54 + 17.75 + 17.41}{3} = 17.23$$

In the interaction graph, the intersection of all three lines at several locations reveals some strong interacting between the two factors. Neither factor B nor

Figure 18-10 B x C Interaction Analysis

B x C Interaction Matrix

	C_1	C_2	C_3
B_1	18.15	17.02	16.34
B_2	17.03	16.65	18.19
B_3	17.38	18.42	17.23

B×C Interaction Graph

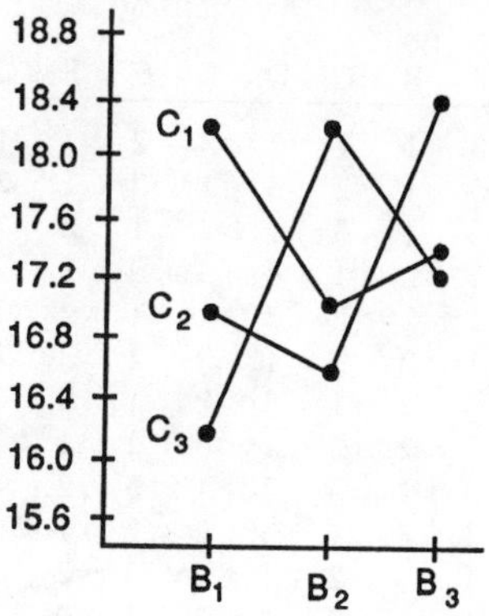

factor C was strong effects by themselves. Therefore, the wisest decision would be to select both factors based on the highest point on the interaction graph, which is B_3C_2. From the interaction matrix, the average S/N for that combination is 18.42 decibels.

Therefore, the recommended levels would be: A_3, B_3, C_2, D_2, F_3, G_3, and I_1.

Factor E is a mild effect, and we would prefer E_2, unless there was a dramatic cost differential between it and the other levels. Factor H is a very weak effect, and we can let cost and convenience determine the setting.

Our next focus of the analysis is on the impact of the noise factors. By totaling the columns of the outer array and obtaining an average result, we can compare the relative influence of each combination of noise factors.

	1	2	3	4	5	6	7	8	9	10	11	12	13	pull force (pounds) M₁		M₂	
Run#	A	B	A × B	A × B	C	D	E	B × C	F	G	B × C	H	I	N_1	N_2	N_1	N_2
1	1	1	1	1	1	1	1	1	1	1	1	1	1	5.7	6.2	5.5	6.0
2	1	1	1	1	2	2	2	2	2	2	2	2	2	6.1	6.0	5.8	6.0
3	1	1	1	1	3	3	3	3	3	3	3	3	3	7.5	7.0	7.5	7.0
4	1	2	2	2	1	1	1	2	2	2	3	3	3	4.2	3.0	4.5	4.0
5	1	2	2	2	2	2	2	3	3	3	1	1	1	10.0	10.0	11.0	11.2
6	1	2	2	2	3	3	3	1	1	1	2	2	2	6.1	6.0	6.0	5.5
7	1	3	3	3	1	1	1	3	3	3	2	2	2	6.6	6.0	7.0	6.5
8	1	3	3	3	2	2	2	1	1	1	3	3	3	6.6	7.8	6.5	7.0
9	1	3	3	3	3	3	3	2	2	2	1	1	1	6.6	6.5	7.0	6.8
10	2	1	2	3	1	2	3	1	2	3	1	2	3	8.3	9.5	8.0	8.8
11	2	1	2	3	2	3	1	2	3	1	2	3	1	10.6	11.0	10.0	11.6
12	2	1	2	3	3	1	2	3	1	2	3	1	2	4.1	3.8	4.0	4.5

	1	2	3	4	5	6	7	8	9	10	11	12	13	pull force (pounds)			
			A ×	A ×				B ×			B ×			M_1		M_2	
Run#	A	B	B	B	C	D	E	C	F	G	C	H	I	N_1	N_2	N_1	N_2
13	2	2	3	1	1	2	3	2	3	1	3	1	2	9.3	9.6	9.5	9.8
14	2	2	3	1	2	3	1	3	1	2	1	2	3	5.0	4.5	5.5	5.0
15	2	2	3	1	3	1	2	1	2	3	2	3	1	9.2	10.0	9.5	9.9
16	2	3	1	2	1	2	3	3	1	2	2	3	1	7.7	8.0	7.5	8.0
17	2	3	1	2	2	3	1	1	2	3	3	1	2	8.1	8.0	8.5	8.8
18	2	3	1	2	3	1	2	2	3	1	1	2	3	7.5	7.5	8.5	7.5
19	3	1	3	2	1	3	2	1	3	2	1	3	2	9.9	11.0	10.6	10.7
20	3	1	3	2	2	1	3	2	1	3	2	1	3	5.8	5.0	6.5	5.5
21	3	1	3	2	3	2	1	3	2	1	3	2	1	9.6	9.5	9.2	10.0
22	3	2	1	3	1	3	2	2	1	3	3	2	1	9.8	9.5	10.0	10.5
23	3	2	1	3	2	1	3	3	2	1	1	3	2	6.0	6.2	6.6	5.5
24	3	2	1	3	3	2	1	1	3	2	2	1	3	9.2	9.5	9.0	10.2
25	3	3	2	1	1	3	2	3	2	1	2	1	3	7.8	8.6	7.5	8.2
26	3	3	2	1	2	1	3	1	3	2	3	2	1	9.9	10.0	9.5	10.9
27	3	3	2	1	3	2	1	2	1	3	1	3	2	7.5	8.0	7.5	7.0
								Totals:						204.5	207.7	208.2	212.4
								Averages:						7.57	7.69	7.71	7.87

In comparing these averages of the pull force for each combination of noise factors, there does not appear to be a consistently strong impact made by any combination of the noise factors in this particular study. If there had been, we might have wanted to use this information for considering possible actions to regulate these influences. In addition, we might have wanted to consider the relative impact on the results of the confirmation run.

5. Compute an estimate of the predicted signal-to-noise ratio based on the selected levels of the strong effects.

From our analysis, the strong effects and elements to be included into the prediction equation are: A, B×C, D, F, G, and I.

The prediction equation then becomes:

$$\hat{\eta} = \overline{T} + (\overline{A}_3 - \overline{T}) + [(\overline{B_3C_2} - \overline{T}) - (\overline{B}_3 - \overline{T}) - (\overline{C}_2 - \overline{T})] + (\overline{D}_2 - \overline{T})$$
$$+ (\overline{F}_3 - \overline{T}) + (\overline{G}_3 - \overline{T}) + (\overline{I}_1 - \overline{T}).$$

By combining like terms, the equation reduces to:

$$\hat{\eta} = \overline{A}_3 + \overline{B_3C_2} - \overline{B}_3 - \overline{C}_2 + \overline{D}_2 + \overline{F}_3 + \overline{G}_3 + \overline{I}_1 - 3 \times \overline{T}.$$

Solving for $\overline{T}$,

$$\overline{T} = \sum_{i=1}^{n} \frac{\eta i}{n} = \frac{15.32 + 15.52 + \ . \ . \ . \ + 17.41}{} = 17.38.$$

Substituting values from the response table and interaction matrix,

$$\hat{\eta} = 8.04 \quad + 18.42 - 17.68 - 17.37 + 18.38 + 19.09 + 18.11$$
$$+ 18.89 - 3 \times 17.38$$
$$\hat{\eta} = 23.74 \text{ db}$$

6. Conduct a confirmation run and compare the actual results to the predicted results.

Confirmation Results		Previous Results	
12.3	12.4	6.0	9.5
12.5	11.5	9.5	6.0
11.5	14.0	9.5	6.0
12.0	13.5	8.0	11.5
13.2	14.0	7.0	9.5
12.5	13.8	6.0	9.5
12.8	12.5	11.5	8.0
13.0	13.0	9.5	7.0
13.5	12.2	7.0	7.0
13.5	13.0	8.0	8.0
S/N = 22.13 db		S/N = 17.74 db	
Avg = 12.84 lbs		Avg = 8.20 lbs	

The confirmation results were not quite as good as the predicted value. However, as evidenced from historical data (S/N = 17.74 db), this result is considerably better than existing production efforts. Therefore, the recommended settings should be implemented. For additional improvement, the experimentation team should return to the planning phase and study the possible reasons why the confirmation was not as good as predicted.

In the confirmation run, the data average was 12.84 pounds. If we analyze the predicted results in greater detail, we can also obtain an idea of what the actual values would need to be to achieve an S/N of 23.74 decibels.

$$S/N = 23.74 = -10 \log \sum_{i=1}^{n} \frac{1/y_i^2}{n}$$

If we were to assume that each measurement was the same,

$$23.74 = -10 \log 1/y^2$$

Then,

$$y = 15.38 \text{ pounds}$$

Therefore, for the confirmation to come close to the predicted results, the validation data would need to be in the range of 15 to 16 pounds. This additional insight also tells the experimentation team what they can gain from actually achieving the predicted results.

Based on the confirmation results and historical data, we can also obtain an estimate of the cost savings from implementing the recommended settings.

Let's say that per unit quality costs are $5.12 (based on rework, scrap, and efforts spent responding to dissatisfied customers divided by total units produced). Then,

$$\text{Cost}_{\text{new}} = \text{Cost}_{\text{existing}} \left| \frac{1}{2} \right|^{\frac{\eta_{\text{new}} - \eta_{\text{existing}}}{3}}$$

$$\text{Cost}_{\text{new}} = \text{Cost}_{\text{existing}} \left| \frac{1}{2} \right|^{\frac{22.13 - 17.74}{3}}$$

$$\text{Cost}_{\text{new}} = 5.12 \left| \frac{1}{2} \right|^{4.39/3}$$

$$\text{Cost}_{\text{new}} = \$1.86$$

$$\text{Cost Savings} = \text{Cost}_{\text{existing}} - \text{Cost}_{\text{new}}$$

$$\text{Cost Savings} = 5.12 - 1.86 = \$3.26/\text{unit}$$

If annual production is 10,000 units,

$$\text{Annual savings} = 3.26 \times 10{,}000 = \$326{,}000$$

It should be noted that this is only an estimate. However, the actual quality costs probably contain hidden expenses not accounted for in determining existing costs. Therefore, the calculation of annual savings will more likely be a conservative estimate.

Notes

1. *Introduction to Qualify Engineering*, p. 3-1.

Chapter 19

ANALYSIS: NOMINAL-THE-BEST

19.1 CONCEPTS

In performing analysis in the previous two sections on the smaller-the-better and larger-the-better quality characteristics, significant factors and optimum levels were determined solely by the signal-to-noise ratios. However, for a nominal-the-best quality characteristic, a different approach is required. To help you understand this approach, we must consider the classification of control factors as four categories.

Let's think of the resulting values from an experiment as being described by a normal (bell-shaped) curve. The center of the curve would represent the mean value, and the width of the curve would signify the amount of variability. In Figure 19-1, we have drawn such curves to represent the distribution of results produced with each level or setting of a control factor. In the upper left diagram, the two curves are centered around the same point. However, the curve or spread of the data for the second level is much wider. We can classify these factors as those that affect variation without affecting the mean and call them Type I factors.

In the upper right-hand graph, we have the Type II factor for which a change in the level results in a change in the mean or the average response value. As we note in the graph, both curves have the same spread, but values for level 2 are centered to the right of the values for level 1.

The third type, which is depicted in the lower left-hand diagram, shows both the centering and the width of the curves to be different. This represents a factor in which a change in levels affects the variability within the experiment results and also moves the overall average of the resulting data. We can call this type of control factor Type III.

In the lower right-hand portion of the figure, the two curves for level one and level two overlap each other. There is no difference in the spread of the experimental results or the overall average. This implies that the factor has no effect on either the process variability or the mean of the data. We can refer to this type of factor as a Type IV control factor.

Figure 19-1 Types of Control Factors

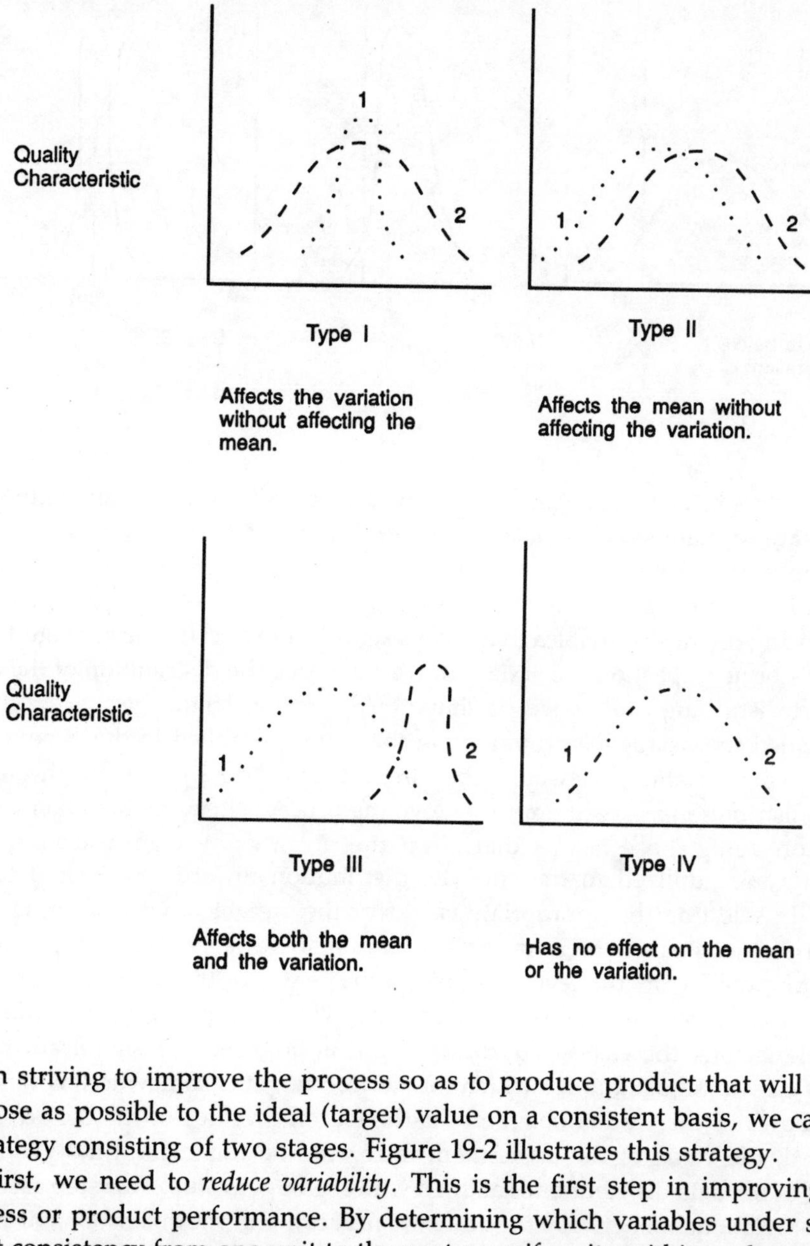
Quality Characteristic
1
2
Type I
Affects the variation without affecting the mean.
1
2
Type II
Affects the mean without affecting the variation.
Quality Characteristic
1
2
Type III
Affects both the mean and the variation.
1
2
Type IV
Has no effect on the mean or the variation.

In striving to improve the process so as to produce product that will come as close as possible to the ideal (target) value on a consistent basis, we can set a strategy consisting of two stages. Figure 19-2 illustrates this strategy.

First, we need to *reduce variability.* This is the first step in improving the process or product performance. By determining which variables under study affect consistency from one unit to the next or uniformity within each product, we have ascertained the knowledge to guide us in reducing variability within the process and ultimately between products. This new insight directs us toward

Figure 19-2 Nominal-the-Best Optimization Strategy

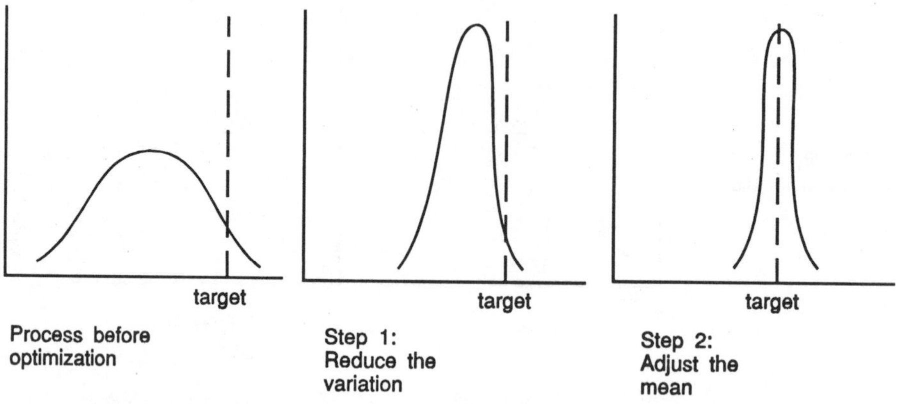

which factors have a significant impact on variability. Besides focusing attention on the appropriate factors, this information can also tell us which factor levels or settings will give us the least variability and will be least affected by noise.

Second, after reducing the spread of the data, we need to *adjust the mean*. By focusing on those variables that have a significant effect on the average result but little or no impact on the variation, we can move the distribution of the data without disturbing the spread or shape of the results. Since we have already ascertained the best levels from among the settings studied in the experiment for reducing variation, we want to be careful that we do not increase the width of the distribution as we attempt to move the process closer to the target value. Therefore, only those factors that affect the mean or average result and not variability are utilized for moving the distribution toward the desired target value. In selecting the appropriate values of the variables, we shall base individual decisions on whether a factor is continuously variable or discrete in nature. For a discrete factor, the level that brings the center of the distribution closest to the desired value would be the most logical choice. Concerning continuously variable factors, the easiest approach would be to select *one* significant factor that is easy to adjust and for which the desired target is somewhere within the boundaries of the results obtained for the extreme values of the factor. Once selected, the value of the adjustment factor can be tuned until the projected center of the data distribution is aligned with the target value. This step assumes a linear relationship between the adjustment factor and the quality characteristic and reinforces the importance of using engineering knowledge in the selection of factors to be incorporated into the experiment.

By looking at an example, we can see why this approach is quite logical. Let's say that we are building yardsticks. The length is a nominal-the-best characteristic with a target of 36.0 inches. If the current process was producing lengths from 24 inches to 42 inches with an average dimension of 33 inches, merely changing control settings to raise the average up to the target value would not solve the problem. However, if we determined those factors which caused the variation to be so great, we could ascertain settings for these parameters to reduce the variability from one yardstick to the next. Let's say that by this selection process we are able to reduce the process variability so that the process now would be capable of producing units with only a .25 inch difference from the shortest to longest unit. Then our adjustment of the process to increase the mean from 33 inches to 36 inches makes more sense and could be more easily achieved.

Based on the above strategy, identifying each control factor as one of the four types of factors discussed is essential to improving or refining the process. The factors that affect variation only (Type I) and those that affect both variation and the mean (Type III) are identified first. The levels that reduce variation the most are selected. Then, the factors that affect the mean only (Type II) are used to adjust the process toward the target value. Settings for the factors that have a significant effect neither on variation nor on the mean are selected on the basis of cost reduction.

19.1.1 Nominal-the-Best Equations

In order to assign the factors being investigated to the appropriate classification type, we must determine the magnitude by which each factor contributes to process variation and affects the average response results. For determining the impact on process variation, we must calculate the signal-to-noise ratio. The effect on the average response can be determined by computing the mean or average result for each experimental run.

19.1.1.1 Signal-to-Noise Ratio

To facilitate your understanding of the calculations for the signal-to-noise ratio for a nominal-the-best quality characteristic, let's review the definitions of a few terms and state some essential equations.

T = Sum of the data (experimental results)

n = number of data points

Sm = Sum of the squares of the mean

Ve = Experimental Variance

ηe = signal-to-noise ratio

1. T: The sum of the data is simply the sum of all the values associated with the experiment data points obtained.

$$T = \sum_{i=1}^{n} y_i$$

2. Sm: Typically, the easiest way of calculating Sm is by squaring the sum of the data and dividing by the number of data points.

$$Sm = n\,(\bar{y})^2 = \frac{T^2}{n}$$

3. Ve: The experimental variance is equal to the sum of the squares of the difference between each value and the experimental mean divided by the number of pieces of data minus one. A simpler calculation is to take the difference between the sum of the squares of all of the data points and the sum of the squares of the mean and divide the difference by $n - 1$.

$$Ve = \sum_{i=1}^{n} \frac{(y_i - \bar{y}^2)}{n - 1} = \frac{(y_1^2 + y_2^2 + \ldots + y_n^2) - Sm}{n - 1}$$

4. η: The signal-to-noise ratio (eta) is then a logarithmic function of the variability in relation to the mean where Sm − Ve reflects the square of the true mean and Ve represents the variability around the mean. Since this is a logarithmic base 10 function, the resulting units are in decibels.

$$\eta = -10 \log \left| \frac{1}{n} \frac{(Sm - Ve)}{Ve} \right|$$

In some rare instances, the quality characteristic may be defined such that the response values may be negative as well as positive. Because the above equation for signal-to-noise considers variability in relation to the percent change in the mean, average values approaching zero tend to reduce the meaning of these calculations. Therefore, we must consider variability in terms of an absolute reference. A more meaningful equation for eta in these situations is as follows:

$$\eta = -10 \log Ve.$$

19.1.1.2 Mean

The calculation of the mean ($\bar{y} = \sum_{i=1}^{n} \frac{y_i}{n}$) is straightforward. However, there can be special cases in which $\bar{y}$ does not provide an effective indication of the typical response value. For example, observe the following results:

$$10 \quad 8 \quad 16 \quad 460 \quad 6.$$

If we simply used $\bar{y}$, we would conclude that the typical response is around 100. However, this is not the case. As a matter of fact, the mean is 100, and the median is 10. The reason why each value is so far from the mean and the mean and median are so different from each other is because of the overriding effect of the fourth data point. Extreme values such as the 460 in this example are called outliers and can have a strong effect on the mean of a sample. As illustrated in this case, an outlier can result in erroneous conclusions about the data if the analysis is based on the mean.

Although this example may appear extreme at first glance, this type of situation tends to appear more frequently in research and development applications. In electronic design for example, one prototype (one experimental run) might result in an output frequency (output response) of 10 megahertz (10×10^6) while another produces 30 gigahertz (30×10^9). With values varying to this degree, y would be ineffective in guiding the experimenter to adjusting the process to the desired target value. It would be more effective to use a logarithmic function in these particular situations. Dr. Taguchi has selected Sm db, where

$$\text{Sm db} = 10 \log \text{Sm},$$

as a more effective measure of the sensitiveness of an experimental run to the target value.

In the above example of five pieces of data, the calculation would be as follows:

$$\text{Sm} = \frac{T^2}{n} = \frac{(10 + 8 + 16 + 460 + 6)^2}{5} = \frac{250000}{5} = 50000$$

$$\text{Sm db} = 10 \log \text{Sm} = 10 \log 50000 = 46.99 \text{ decibels}$$

As noted in the example, since the formula is a base 10 logarithmic function like the signal-to-noise ratio, the resulting units are also in decibels.

19.2 YARDSTICK CASE STUDY

After using the manufacture of yardsticks to illustrate the nominal-the-best optimization strategy, it seems fitting to use a related hypothetical case to explain the calculations and analysis that accompany the study of a nominal-the-best characteristic.

Problem: The yardsticks produced at the Three Yarder Yardstick Company have to be 100% inspected. Numerous yardsticks have to be filed down and many others have to be scrapped because they are too short. A sample from the final slicing area showed an average length of 35.20 inches with a standard deviation of .75 inches.

Objective: Reduce yardstick length variability and increase consistent lengths closer to 36.00 inches.

Quality Characteristic:	Target Value:	
Yardstick length	36.00 inches	
Control Factors:	Level 1	Level 2
Blade metal	carbon steel	tungsten steel
Saw rpm	low	high
Wood kiln time	1 month	3 months
Motor horsepower	2 hp	3 hp
Saw fence angle	0 degrees	12 degrees
Operator	Bill	John
Interaction:		
blade metal × saw rpm		
Noise Factor:	Level 1	Level 2
Wood source	northern	southern
Blade age	new	20,000 units

Experimental Matrix: Based on seven degrees of freedom determined from the number of the control factors and their corresponding number of levels, an L_8 orthogonal array was selected for the inner array. Since the noise factors required two degrees of freedom, the outer array becomes an L_4 consisting of four columns. The following experimental matrix with a total of 32 experimental units (8 rows × 4 columns) resulted.

Run#	A	B	A × B	C	D	E	F	M_1N_1	M_1N_2	M_2N_1	M_2N_2
1	1	1	1	1	1	1	1	35.675	36.42	34.805	35.69
2	1	1	1	2	2	2	2	35.72	35.695	35.80	36.76
3	1	2	2	1	1	2	2	35.83	36.275	36.13	35.145
4	1	2	2	2	2	1	1	35.655	35.025	36.22	35.57
5	2	1	2	1	2	1	2	35.805	36.47	35.22	34.765
6	2	1	2	2	1	2	1	36.68	36.115	36.78	36.995
7	2	2	1	1	2	2	1	36.87	36.255	36.985	36.35
8	2	2	1	2	1	1	2	35.54	35.255	35.24	36.125

Calculations:

1. Determine the mean for each row (experimental run).

$$\#1\ \bar{y}_1 = \frac{35.675 + 36.42 + 34.805 + 35.69}{4} = 35.6475$$

$$\#2\ \bar{y}_2 = \frac{35.72 + 35.695 + 35.80 + 36.76}{4} = 35.99375$$

. . . .

$$\#8\ \bar{y}_8 = \frac{35.54 + 35.255 + 35.24 + 36.125}{4} = 35.54$$

2. Determine the signal-to-noise ratio for each row (experimental run).

$$\#1\ \text{Sm} = \frac{(35.675 + 36.42 + 34.805 + 35.69)^2}{4} = 5082.977$$

$$\text{Ve} = \frac{(35.675^2 + 36.42^2 + 34.805^2 + 35.69^2) - 5082.977}{4 - 1} = .436$$

$$\eta_1 = 10 \log \left| \frac{1}{4} \frac{(5082.977 - .436)}{.436} \right| = 34.645$$

$$\#2\ \text{Sm} = \frac{(35.72 + 35.695 + 35.8 + 36.76)^2}{4} = 5182.200$$

$$\text{Ve} = \frac{(35.72^2 + 35.695^2 + 35.8^2 + 36.76^2) - 5182.200}{4 - 1} = .263$$

$$\eta_2 = 10 \log \left| \frac{1}{4} \frac{(5182.200 - .263)}{.263} \right| = 36.924$$

. . . .

$$\#8 \text{ Sm} = \frac{(35.54 + 35.255 + 35.24 + 36.125)^2}{4} = 5052.366$$

$$\text{Ve} = \frac{(35.54^2 + 35.255^2 + 35.24^2 + 36.125^2) - 5052.366}{4 - 1} = .171$$

$$\eta_8 = 10 \log \left| \frac{1}{4} \frac{(5052.366 - .171)}{.171} \right| = 38.684$$

After completing the calculations, we can set up columns for $\bar{y}$ and η alongside the experimental matrix and input the corresponding values for each set of experimental runs as shown below.

Run#	A	B	A × B	C	D	E	F	$\bar{y}$	n
1	1	1	1	1	1	1	1	35.648	34.645
2	1	1	1	2	2	2	2	35.994	36.924
3	1	2	2	1	1	2	2	35.595	31.164
4	1	2	2	2	2	1	1	35.618	37.249
5	2	1	2	1	2	1	2	35.565	33.656
6	2	1	2	2	1	2	1	36.643	39.787
7	2	2	1	1	2	2	1	36.615	40.002
8	2	2	1	2	1	1	2	35.540	38.684

3a. Calculate the average signal-to-noise ratio for each control factor level and develop a S/N response table. This is performed by selecting all values of eta at each factor level, taking the sum, and dividing by the number of values at each level. The absolute difference between the two averages is the effect of the factor.

For example: The associated values of eta for A would match those experimental runs at which A was set at level 1 as indicated in bold type.

Run#	A	B	A × B	C	D	E	F	$\bar{y}$	n
1	**1**	1	1	1	1	1	1	35.648	**34.645**
2	**1**	1	1	2	2	2	2	35.994	**36.924**
3	**1**	2	2	1	1	2	2	35.595	**31.164**
4	**1**	2	2	2	2	1	1	35.618	**37.249**
5	2	1	2	1	2	1	2	35.565	33.656
6	2	1	2	2	1	2	1	36.643	39.787
7	2	2	1	1	2	2	1	36.615	40.002
8	2	2	1	2	1	1	2	35.540	38.684

Then,

$$\overline{A}_1 = \frac{34.645 + 36.924 + 31.164 + 37.249}{4} = 34.996.$$

By the same procedures,

$$\overline{A}_2 = \frac{33.656 + 39.787 + 40.002 + 38.684}{4} = 38.032$$

$$\text{Effect of A} = |\overline{A}_1 - \overline{A}_2| = |34.996 - 38.032| = 3.036$$

Similarly,

$$\overline{B}_1 = \frac{34.645 + 36.924 + 33.656 + 39.787}{4} = 36.253$$

$$\overline{B}_2 = \frac{31.164 + 37.249 + 40.002 + 38.684}{4} = 36.775$$

$$\text{Effect of B} = |\overline{B}_1 - \overline{B}_2| = |36.253 - 36.775| = .522$$

By continuing in this fashion through $\overline{F}_1$ and $\overline{F}_2$, the following response table would be generated:

Signal-to-Noise Ratio

Response Table

	A	B	A × B	C	D	E	F
Level 1	34.996	36.253	37.564	34.867	36.070	36.059	37.921
Level 2	38.032	36.775	35.464	38.161	36.958	36.969	35.107
Delta	3.036	.522	2.100	3.294	.888	.910	2.814

3b. Based on the average signal-to-noise ratio computed for each factor level, construct S/N response graphs (Figure 19-3).

4. Analyze the S/N response table and S/N response graphs.

Several approaches can be taken to determine which factors are most significant for reducing variation. In analyzing the table, the technique is to select those factors displaying the greatest effect (change in the response value from one factor setting to the next). The rule of thumb is to select approximately half of the factors studied. The exact breaking point between which factors are to be

Figure 19-3 S/N Response Graphs

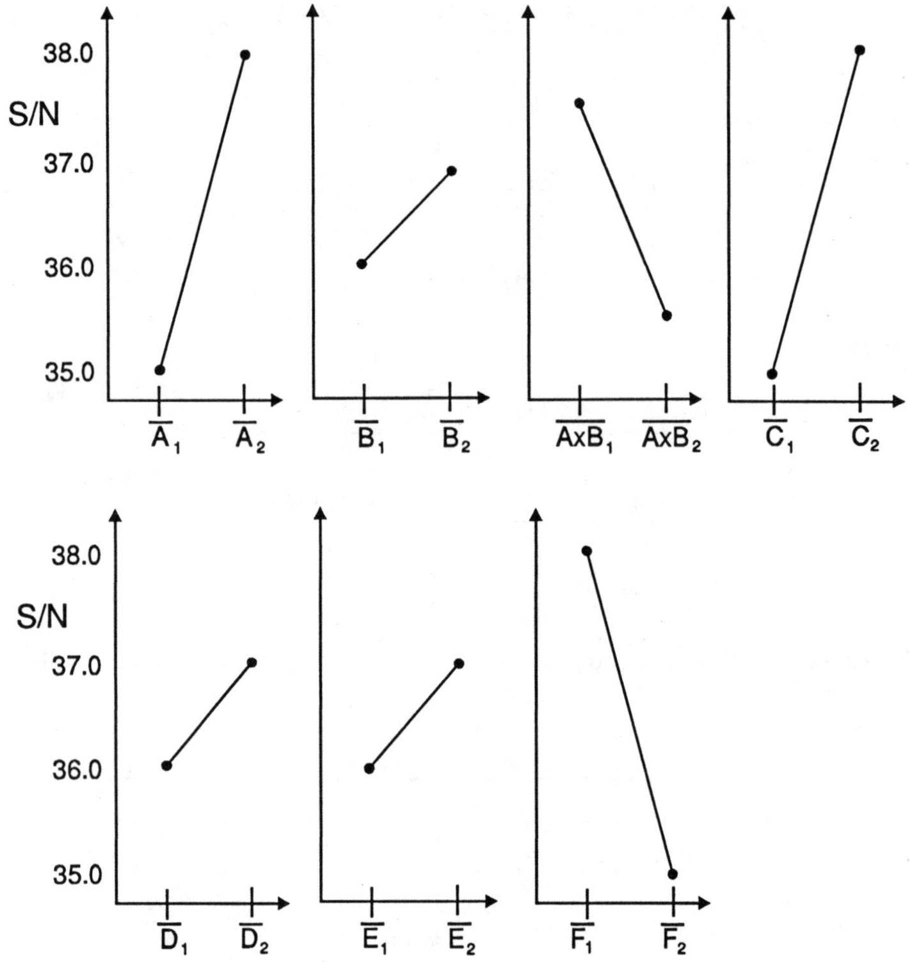

included and which are not to be considered is based on the relative difference from one effect to another.

Signal-to-Noise Ratio

Response Table

	A	B	A × B	C	D	E	F
Level 1	34.996	36.253	37.564	34.867	36.070	36.059	37.921
Level 2	38.032	36.775	35.464	38.161	36.958	36.969	35.107
Delta	**3.036**	.522	**2.100**	**3.294**	.888	.910	**2.814**

In the yardstick example, factor C (wood kiln time) had the greatest effect at 3.294. Next were factor A (blade metal) and factor F (operator) at 3.036 and 2.814, respectively. We are now near the midpoint of separating the strong effects from the other effects. The difference between the effect of F and the effect of the interaction A × B is .714 (2.814 − 2.100). The difference between the effect of A × B and E is 1.190 (2.100 − .910). Since 1.190 is greater, this is the logical breaking point. Therefore, the interaction A × B should be regarded as having a strong effect, and the main effect E and subsequent weaker effects should not be regarded as being significant.

Since the higher signal-to-noise ratio means the greatest robustness and the least variability, we will want to choose the level with the largest value in each case. Therefore, we will select A_2, C_2, and F_1.

The same determinations can be made with the response graphs. By comparing the relative slopes for each of the factors, we also observe that C, A, F, and A × B are the strongest effects in order of importance. By choosing the highest point on each graph of the strong effects, we again select C_2, A_2, and F_1.

With regard to the interaction A × B, we will need to study this effect further. To analyze the interaction, we will need to construct a matrix of the average results for each combination of settings of the two factors in the interaction. In this case, it is a 2 × 2 matrix. A corresponding interaction response graph should also be drawn.

The calculations for the matrix are given in Figure 19-4.

As illustrated by the interaction graph, the crossing over of the two lines indicates a strong interaction. Both the interaction matrix and the response graph indicate that A_2B_2 is the best combination of the two factors. We had previously

Figure 19-4 A × B Interaction Analysis

$$\overline{A_1B_1} = \frac{34.645 + 36.924}{2} = 35.785$$

$$\overline{A_1B_2} = \frac{31.164 + 37.249}{2} = 34.207$$

$$\overline{A_2B_1} = \frac{33.656 + 39.787}{2} = 36.722$$

$$\overline{A_2B_2} = \frac{40.002 + 38.684}{2} = 39.343$$

Figure 19-4 A × B Interaction Analysis (*cont'd.*)

Run#	A	B	A × B	C	D	E	F	$\bar{y}$	η
1	**1**	**1**	1	1	1	1	1	35.648	**34.645**
2	**1**	**1**	1	2	2	2	2	35.994	**36.924**
3	1	2	2	1	1	2	2	35.595	31.164
4	1	2	2	2	2	1	1	35.618	37.249
5	**2**	1	2	1	2	1	2	35.565	**33.656**
6	**2**	1	2	2	1	2	1	36.643	**39.787**
7	2	2	1	1	2	2	1	36.615	40.002
8	2	2	1	2	1	1	2	35.540	38.684

	B_1	B_2
A_1	35.785	34.207
A_2	36.722	39.343

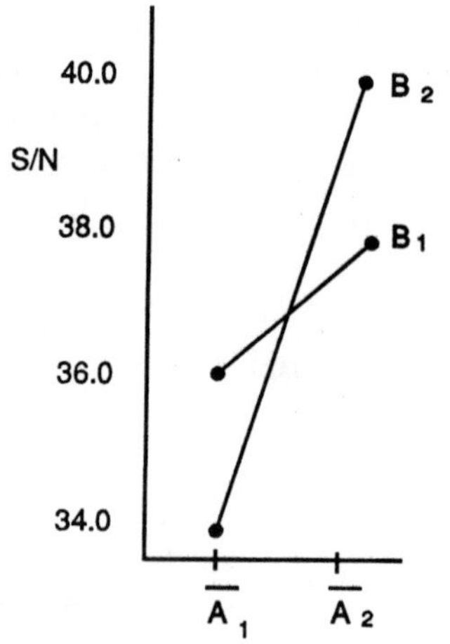

determined that A was a significant factor with A_2 as the best level. Thus, the analysis of the interaction reinforces the selection of A_2. Although factor B by itself did not have a major impact, it does have a strong effect in combination with factor A. Therefore, B_2 should be selected as well.

It should be noted that there will *never* be a conflict between the optimal level indicated from studying a main effect graph and from analyzing an interaction matrix or response graph. In other words, if analysis of a strong main effect indicates one particular level as being best, the graph of an interaction encompassing that same factor will recommend that same level. The reason is that the values such as $\overline{A_2B_2}$ are a culmination of the effects of each of the two factors and the interaction between them. The optimal level or levels of the effects will be reflected in the best combination of these factors.

5a. Calculate the average value of $\bar{y}$ for each control factor level and develop a means response table. Similarly to the procedures performed in step 3a, select all values of $\bar{y}$ at each factor level, take the sum, and divide by the number of values at each level. The absolute difference between the two values is the effect of the factor on the mean.

For example: The associated values of $\bar{y}$ for A_1 would match those experimental runs at which A was set at level 1 as indicated in bold type.

Run#	A	B	A × B	C	D	E	F	$\bar{y}$	η
1	1	1	1	1	1	1	1	**35.648**	34.645
2	1	1	1	2	2	2	2	**35.994**	36.924
3	1	2	2	1	1	2	2	**35.595**	31.164
4	1	2	2	2	2	1	1	**35.618**	37.249
5	2	1	2	1	2	1	2	35.565	33.656
6	2	1	2	2	1	2	1	36.643	39.787
7	2	2	1	1	2	2	1	36.615	40.002
8	2	2	1	2	1	1	2	35.540	38.684

Then,

$$A_1 = \frac{35.648 + 35.994 + 35.595 + 35.618}{4} = 35.714.$$

By the same procedures,

$$A_2 = \frac{35.565 + 36.643 + 36.615 + 35.540}{4} = 36.091$$

$$\text{Effect of A} = |\bar{A}_1 - \bar{A}_2| = |35.714 - 36.091| = .377$$

Similarly,

$$\bar{B}_1 = \frac{35.648 + 35.994 + 35.565 + 36.643}{4} = 35.963$$

$$\bar{B}_2 = \frac{35.595 + 35.618 + 36.615 + 35.540}{4} = 35.842$$

$$\text{Effect of B} = |\bar{B}_1 - \bar{B}_2| = |35.963 - 35.842| = .121$$

By continuing in this fashion through $\bar{F}_1$ and $\bar{F}_2$, the following response table would be generated:

Means

Response Table

	A	B	A × B	C	D	E	F
Level 1	35.714	35.963	35.949	35.856	35.857	35.593	36.131
Level 2	36.091	35.842	35.855	35.949	35.948	36.212	35.674
Delta	.377	.121	.094	.093	.091	.619	.457

5b. Based on the average $\bar{y}$ computed for each factor level, construct means response graphs (Figure 19-5).

6. Analyze the means response table and means response graphs.

The same techniques used for determining the most important factors for reducing variation can be used here for identifying those factors that have a strong effect on the mean. Again, the rule of thumb is selecting roughly half of the factors being investigated. The exact breaking point can be ascertained by

Figure 19-5 Means Response Graphs

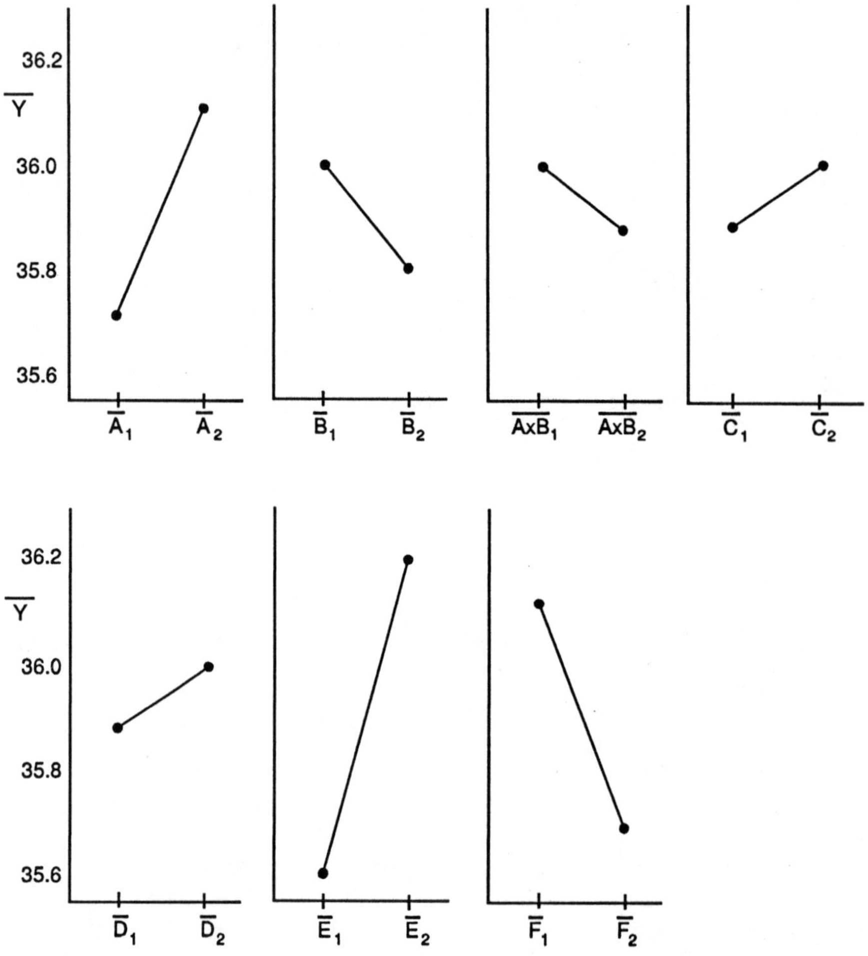

either finding a logical break between the effects in the response table or visually finding the greatest change in slopes from the response graphs.

Means

Response Table

	A	B	A × B	C	D	E	F
Level 1	35.714	35.963	35.949	35.856	35.857	35.593	36.131
Level 2	36.091	35.842	35.855	35.949	35.948	36.212	35.674
Delta	**.377**	.121	.094	.093	.091	**.619**	**.457**

From the yardstick means response table, factor E has the greatest effect at .619. This is followed by F at .457 and A at .377. Factor B is the next strongest at .121, but the difference between its effect and the effect of A is .256 (3.77 – .121) while the drop to the next strongest effect is only .027 (.121 – .094). Therefore, we stop at factor A. Since the interaction A × B was not included among the strong effects to the means, there will not be a need to construct an interaction matrix or response graph as we did in studying the signal-to-noise ratios.

In selecting the optimal factor levels, those factors that affect both variation and the mean have already been set at the best level for reducing variation. This approach means thinking again in terms of our two-step strategy of reducing variation and then moving the process to the target value. Both factor A and factor F fall into this category. Since factor E is the sole factor that affects only the mean, it is the adjustment factor.

Signal-to-Noise Ratio

Response Table

	A	B	A × B	C	D	E	F
Level 1	34.996	36.253	37.564	34.867	36.070	36.059	37.921
Level 2	38.032	36.775	35.464	38.161	36.958	36.969	35.107
Delta	**3.036**	.522	**2.100**	**3.294**	.888	.910	**2.814**

Means

Response Table

	A	B	A × B	C	D	E	F
Level 1	35.714	35.963	35.949	35.856	35.857	35.593	36.131
Level 2	36.091	35.842	35.855	35.949	35.948	36.212	35.674
Delta	**.377**	.121	.094	.093	.091	**.619**	**.457**

Since factor D has a strong effect on neither variation nor the mean, the less expensive level would be chosen. For factor D (motor horsepower), the smaller (cheaper) motor may be the preferred choice.

7. Compute an estimate of the predicted response based on the selected levels of the strong effects.

There are actually two predictions that can be generated. One is for the signal-to-noise ratio. The purpose of this is to obtain:

1. a relative measure of robustness
2. an estimate of the reduced process variation
3. a projection of the cost savings from improving the process

Since A, A × B, and F are the factors with a strong effect on variation, the S/N prediction equation becomes:

$$\hat{\eta} = \overline{T} + (\overline{A}_2 - \overline{T}) + [(\overline{A_2B_2} - \overline{T}) - (\overline{A}_2 - \overline{T}) - (\overline{B}_2 - \overline{T})] + (\overline{C}_2 - \overline{T}) + (\overline{F}_1 - \overline{T}).$$

This reduces to:

$$\hat{\eta} = \overline{A_2B_2} - \overline{B}_2 + \overline{C}_2 + \overline{F}_1 - \overline{T}$$

$$\hat{\eta} = 39.343 - 36.775 + 38.161 + 37.921 - 36.514$$

$$\hat{\eta} = 42.136 \text{ decibels}$$

Given the equation below we can estimate the new process variability based on the existing process information.

$$\sigma^2_{new} = \left|\frac{1}{2}\right|^{\frac{x}{3}} \sigma^2_{existing} \text{ where } x = \eta_{new} - \eta_{existing}$$

If historical data resulted in $\eta_{existing} = 36.136$ db, we could estimate the new process variability and calculate the associate standard deviation as follows:

$$\sigma^2_{new} = \left|\frac{1}{2}\right|^{\frac{42.136 - 36.136}{3}} \times .75^2 = .140625$$

$$\sigma_{new} = .375.$$

Although we will not prove the relationship between cost and S/N here, Dr. Taguchi proposes that a 3-decibel increase in the signal-to-noise ratio is equivalent to a 50% reduction in quality costs. The relationship is mathematically shown as:

$$\text{Cost}_{\text{new}} = \text{Cost}_{\text{existing}} \left| \frac{1}{2} \right|^{\frac{\eta_{\text{new}} - \eta_{\text{existing}}}{3}}$$

If existing quality costs such as scrape and rework amounted to $80,000 and η_{existing} was estimated at 36.136, we could project the cost savings as follows:

$$\text{Cost}_{\text{new}} = 80{,}000 \left| \frac{1}{2} \right|^{\frac{42.136 - 36.136}{3}}$$

$$\text{Cost}_{\text{new}} = 80{,}000 \times \frac{1}{4} = 20{,}000$$

$$\text{Cost savings} = 80{,}000 - 20{,}000 = \$60{,}000$$

The second prediction is for the average response. Since levels for those factors that affect both variability and the mean are determined by the level resulting in the least variation, the prediction equation provides us with the tool for:

1. selecting the appropriate levels of those discrete factors that affect the mean only (ex. material A or B)
2. determining the amount of change required in the adjustment factors, which by definition are continuously variable.

Since A, E, and F are the factors with a strong effect on the mean, the mean prediction equation becomes:

$$\hat{\mu} = \overline{T} + (\overline{A}_2 - \overline{T}) + (\overline{E}_? - \overline{T}) + (\overline{F}_1 - \overline{T}).$$

This reduces to:

$$\hat{\mu} = \overline{A}_2 + \overline{E}_? + \overline{F}_1 - 2 \times \overline{T}.$$

Then,

$$\hat{\mu} = 36.091 + \overline{E}_? + 36.131 - 2 \times 35.902$$

$$\hat{\mu} = \overline{E}_? + .418$$

Since our target is 36.000,

$$36.000 = \bar{E} + .418$$

$$\bar{E} = 35.592$$

The average response for E at level 1 (0 degree angle) is 35.593. Therefore, E should be chosen for moving the response distribution to the target value. Although in this case a specific level was selected, other experiments may require the selection of a value of the adjustment factor which is between experimental settings. If the factor has a linear effect on the response variable, a simple interpolation based on the results obtained at each level of the factor and the target can ascertain the required adjustment setting. This is not feasible in a nonlinear relationship.

$$\text{adjustment factor setting} = \text{level}_{\text{low}} + (\text{level}_{\text{high}} - \text{level}_{\text{low}}) \times \frac{(\text{target} - \text{response}_{\text{low}})}{(\text{response}_{\text{high}} - \text{response}_{\text{low}})}$$

Numerous special process runs at which other strong factors are fixed while the adjustment factor is being fine-tuned might be required. This difficulty is why careful selection and defining of factors in the planning stage is so critical to the rest of the experiment.

8. Perform the confirmation run and compare the actual results with the predicted results.

η and $\bar{y}$ are computed based on all the data obtained in the confirmation run. If 20 units are produced, then each of the 20 corresponding responses are included in determining the confirmation $\bar{y}$ and n.

$$\bar{y}_{\text{confirm}} = \frac{(y_1 + \ldots + y_{20})}{20}$$

$$\eta_{\text{confirm}} = -10 \log \left| \frac{1}{20} \frac{(Sm - Ve)}{Ve} \right|$$

Whether the confirmation is a success or not will depend on:

1. the relative improvement from the existing process results, and
2. your engineering expertise in deciding if the results are sufficiently close to the predicted value for both $\bar{y}$ and η ($\hat{\mu}$ and $\hat{\eta}$, respectively).

19.3 MODEM SUBCIRCUIT CASE STUDY

Objective: Design subcircuit that will produce center frequency of 35.75 megahertz.

Quality Characteristic
Specification: Center Frequency 35.75 MHz

Control Factors:		LEVEL 1	LEVEL 2	LEVEL 3
A.	VC1	1N5148	1N548A MODERATE	------------------------
B.	C2	10pf, ± 15%/C°	15pf, ± 15%/C°	15pf, ± 30ppm/C°
C.	L2	1.0 μh	1.2 μh	1.5 μh
D.	C4	10pf, ± 15%/C°	15pf, ± 15%/C°	15pf, ± 30ppm/C°
E.	C6	39pf	47pf	56pf
F.	C7	82pf	100pf	120pf
G.	L3	1.5 μh	1.8 μh	2.2 μh
H.	C1	15pf	18pf	22pf

Noise Factors:

(M)	Temperature—3 Levels	70°C/25°C/ – 10°C
(N)	Electrostatic Noise—2 Levels	low/high

Experimental Matrix:

MODEM SUBCIRCUIT

									M1		M2		M3	
Run	A	B	C	D	E	F	G	H	N1	N2	N1	N2	N1	N2
1	1	1	1	1	1	1	1	1	34.10	32.95	35.65	35.05	39.30	40.20
2	1	1	2	2	2	2	2	2	35.00	34.35	35.75	35.40	36.50	36.80
3	1	1	3	3	3	3	3	3	35.00	34.50	36.30	36.55	37.60	38.50
4	1	2	1	1	2	2	3	3	34.60	33.95	35.55	35.15	36.50	37.15
5	1	2	2	2	3	3	1	1	32.70	31.45	35.55	34.80	38.55	39.60
6	1	2	3	3	1	1	2	2	34.15	33.35	36.00	36.50	37.85	38.70
7	1	3	1	2	1	3	2	3	32.00	30.75	35.25	34.50	38.65	40.45
8	1	3	2	3	2	1	3	1	32.00	30.75	35.15	34.40	38.50	39.50
9	1	3	3	1	3	2	1	2	33.45	32.30	35.70	35.00	38.00	38.80
10	2	1	1	3	3	2	2	1	35.35	35.00	35.70	35.50	36.05	35.65
11	2	1	2	1	1	3	3	2	33.75	32.30	35.80	36.20	37.90	38.80
12	2	1	3	2	2	1	1	3	34.50	33.85	36.25	36.50	38.00	39.10

MODEM SUBCIRCUIT *cont'd.*

									M1		M2		M3	
Run	A	B	C	D	E	F	G	H	N1	N2	N1	N2	N1	N2
13	2	2	1	2	3	1	3	2	33.10	32.15	35.50	34.90	37.95	39.05
14	2	2	2	3	1	2	1	3	35.60	35.45	35.55	35.40	35.50	35.60
15	2	2	3	1	2	3	2	1	33.20	32.10	36.00	36.70	38.95	39.85
16	2	3	1	3	2	3	1	2	32.50	31.55	35.25	34.65	38.10	39.10
17	2	3	2	1	3	1	2	3	33.50	32.70	35.20	34.70	37.05	37.85
18	2	3	3	2	1	2	3	1	33.25	32.10	35.70	35.00	38.20	38.65

Calculations:

1. Determine the mean for each row (experimental run).

2. Determine the signal-to-noise ratio for each row (experimental run).

MODEM SUBCIRCUIT

									M1		M2		M3			
Run	A	B	C	D	E	F	G	H	N1	N2	N1	N2	N1	N2	$\bar{Y}$	S/N
1	1	1	1	1	1	1	1	1	34.10	32.95	35.65	35.05	39.30	40.20	36.21	21.91
2	1	1	2	2	2	2	2	2	35.00	34.35	35.75	35.40	36.50	36.80	35.63	31.76
3	1	1	3	3	3	3	3	3	35.00	34.50	36.30	36.55	37.60	38.50	36.41	27.62
4	1	2	1	1	2	2	3	3	34.60	33.95	35.55	35.15	36.50	37.15	35.48	29.50
5	1	2	2	2	3	3	1	1	32.70	31.45	35.55	34.80	38.55	39.60	35.44	20.91
6	1	2	3	3	1	1	2	2	34.15	33.35	36.00	36.50	37.85	38.70	36.09	24.84
7	1	3	1	2	1	3	2	3	32.00	30.75	35.25	34.50	38.65	40.45	35.27	19.48
8	1	3	2	3	2	1	3	1	32.00	30.75	35.15	34.40	38.50	39.50	35.05	20.10
9	1	3	3	1	3	2	1	2	33.45	32.30	35.70	35.00	38.00	38.80	35.54	22.97
10	2	1	1	3	3	2	2	1	35.35	35.00	35.70	35.50	36.05	35.65	35.54	40.03
11	2	1	2	1	1	3	3	2	33.75	32.30	35.80	36.20	37.90	38.80	35.79	23.29
12	2	1	3	2	2	1	1	3	34.50	33.85	36.25	36.50	38.00	39.10	36.37	25.19
13	2	2	1	2	3	1	3	2	33.10	32.15	35.50	34.90	37.95	39.05	35.44	22.42
14	2	2	2	3	1	2	1	3	35.60	35.45	35.55	35.40	35.50	35.60	35.52	52.77
15	2	2	3	1	2	3	2	1	33.20	32.10	36.00	36.70	38.95	39.85	36.13	21.43
16	2	3	1	3	2	3	1	2	32.50	31.55	35.25	34.65	38.10	39.10	35.19	21.43
17	2	3	2	1	3	1	2	3	33.50	32.70	35.20	34.70	37.05	37.85	35.17	24.94
18	2	3	3	2	1	2	3	1	33.25	32.10	35.70	35.00	38.20	38.65	35.48	22.66

3a. Calculate the average signal-to-noise ratio for each control factor and construct a S/N response table.

RESPONSE TABLE—S/N

Level	A	B	C	D	E	F	G	H
1	24.34	28.30	25.80	24.01	27.49	23.23	27.53	24.51
2	28.24	28.65	28.96	23.74	24.90	33.28	27.08	24.45
3		21.93	24.12	31.13	26.48	22.36	24.77	29.92
	3.90	6.72	4.84	7.39	2.59	10.92	3.26	5.47

When more than two levels for a factor occur as in this example, the effect of each factor is calculated based on the difference between the highest S/N and the lowest S/N. As demonstrated in this study, the extreme values may come from levels 1 and 2 or any combination composed from 1, 2, and 3.

3b. Based on the average signal-to-noise ratio computed for each factor level, construct S/N response graphs (Figure 19-6).

4. Analyze the S/N response table and S/N response graph.

RESPONSE TABLE—S/N

Level	A	B	C	D	E	F	G	H
1	24.34	28.30	25.80	24.01	27.49	23.23	27.53	24.51
2	28.24	28.65	28.96	23.74	24.90	33.28	27.08	24.45
3		21.93	24.12	31.13	26.48	22.36	24.77	29.92
	3.90	**6.72**	4.84	**7.39**	2.59	**10.92**	3.26	5.47

Strong Effects

Since the L_{18} orthogonal array has the unique capability of a built-in interaction between columns 1 and 2, we need to construct an interaction matrix and draw an interaction response graph as well (Figure 19-7).

Based on the S/N response table and response graphs for the main effects, factors F, D, and B were the strong effects. F_2 was the best level for factor F. D_3 was the best setting for factor D. Based on the S/N main effects only, either level 1 or level 2 was acceptable for factor B. In studying the interaction between A and B, the impact of A at level 2 and B at level 2 resulted in the highest signal-

Figure 19-6 S/N Response Graphs

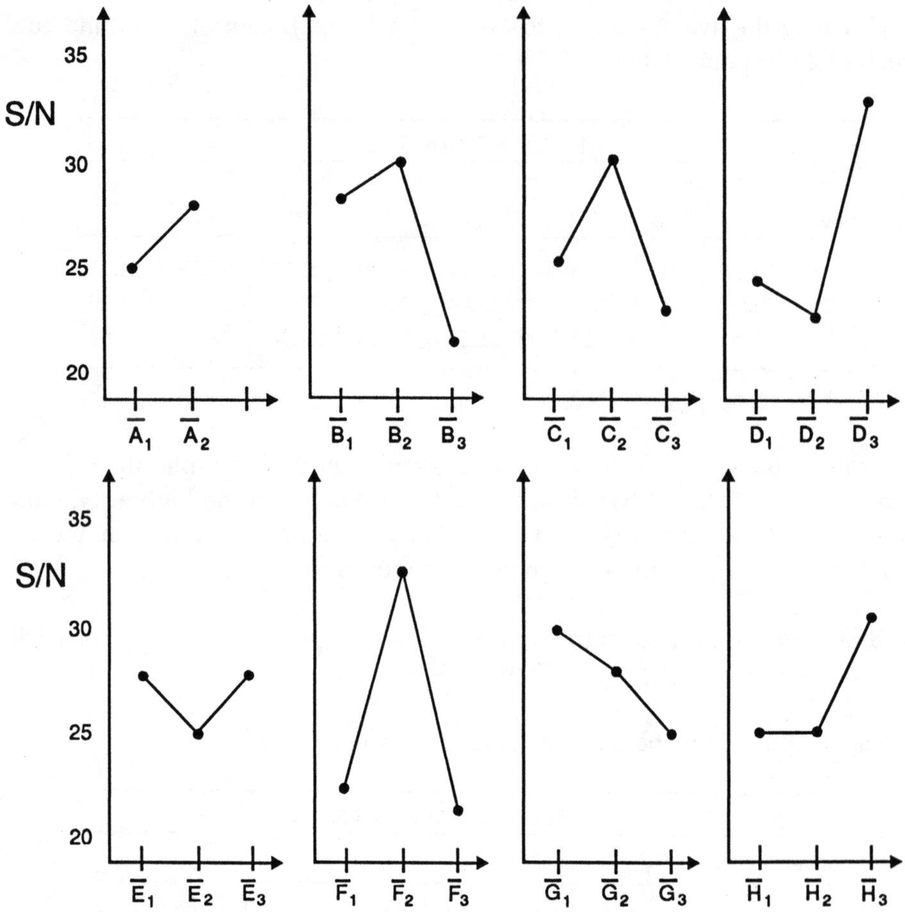

Figure 19-7 A × B Interaction S/N Analysis

	$\bar{B}_1$	$\bar{B}_2$	$\bar{B}_3$
$\bar{A}_1$	27.10	25.08	20.85
$\bar{A}_2$	29.50	32.21	23.01

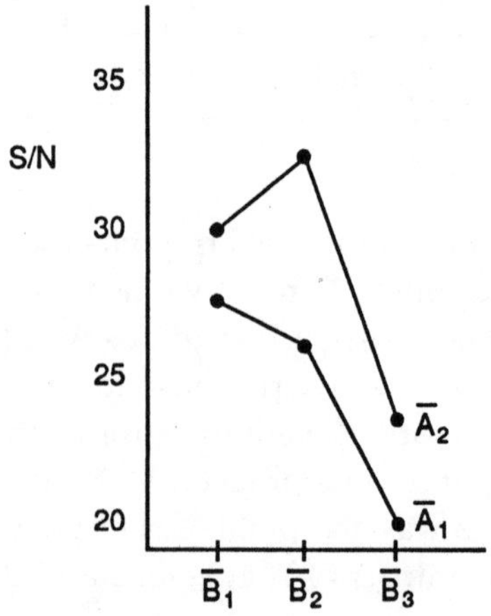

to-noise ratio among the combinations of A and B. Therefore for reducing variability, the strong effects and their recommended levels are:

$$F_2, D_3, B_2, \text{ and } A_2B_2.$$

5a. Calculate the average value of $\overline{y}$ for each control factor and construct a means response table.

Means Response Table

Level	A	B	C	D	E	F	G	H
1	35.68	35.99	35.52	35.72	35.73	35.72	35.71	35.64
2	35.63	35.68	35.43	35.61	35.64	35.53	35.64	35.61
3		35.28	36.00	35.63	35.59	35.71	35.61	35.70
	.05	.71	.57	.11	.14	.19	.10	.09

5b. Based on the average $\overline{y}$ computed for each factor level, construct means response graphs (Figure 19-8).

6. Analyze the means response table and means response graphs.

Means Response Table

Level	A	B	C	D	E	F	G	H
1	35.68	35.99	35.52	35.72	35.73	35.72	35.71	35.64
2	35.63	35.68	35.43	35.61	35.64	35.53	35.64	35.61
3		35.28	36.00	35.63	35.59	35.71	35.61	35.70
	.05	**.71**	**.57**	.11	.14	.19	.10	.09

Strong Effects

Just as we constructed a S/N response matrix and drew a S/N response graph for the interaction between A and B, we need to likewise develop a response matrix and response graph to study the effect of $A \times B$ on the mean as well (Figure 19-9).

Based on the means response table and the means response graphs for the main effects, factors B and C were the strongest effects. From our S/N analysis, we determined that B_2 was the best level for reducing variation. Therefore, C will be our adjustment factor.

Figure 19-8 Means Response Graphs

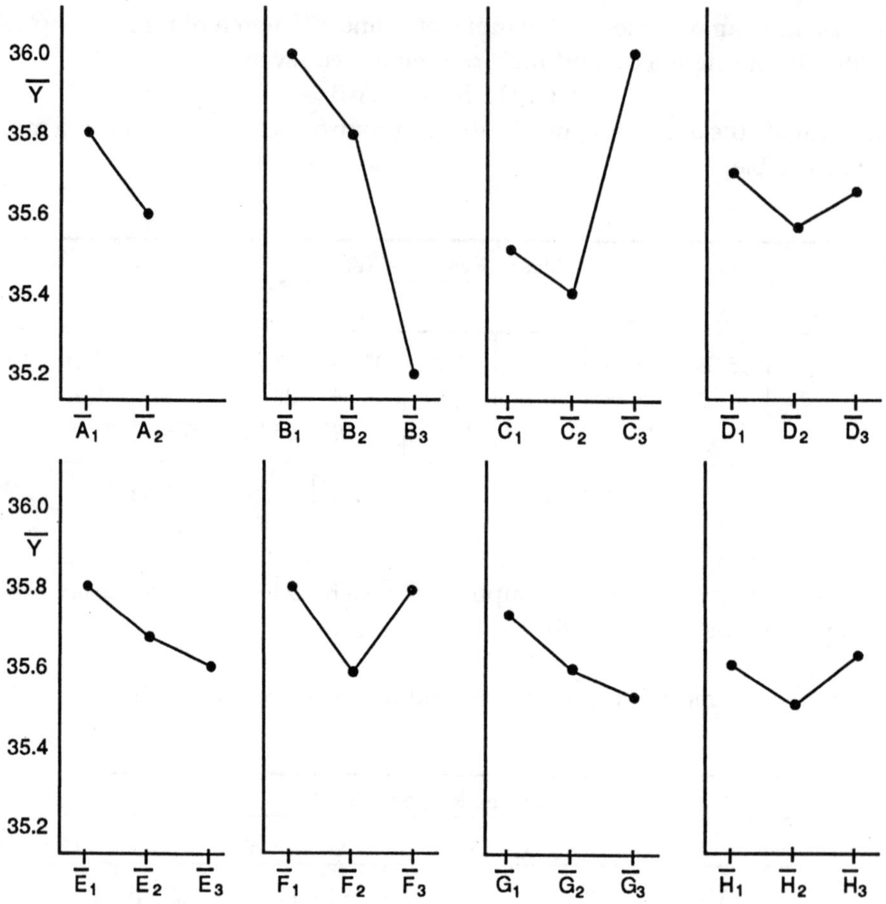

Figure 19-9 A × B Interaction Means Analysis

	$\overline{B}_1$	$\overline{B}_2$	$\overline{B}_3$
$\overline{A}_1$	36.08	35.67	35.29
$\overline{A}_2$	35.90	35.70	35.28

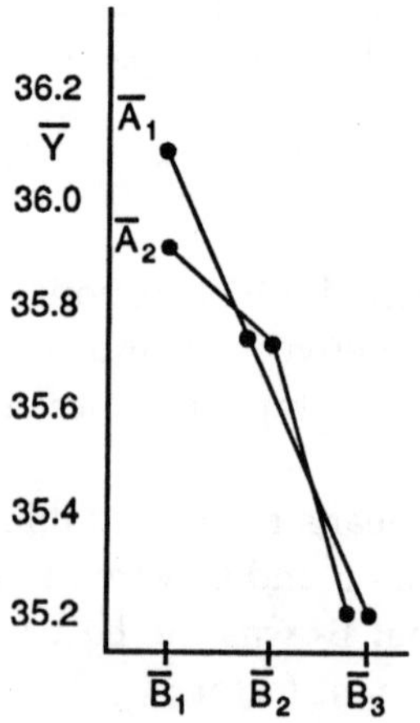

7. Compute an estimate of the predicted response based on the selected levels of the strong effects for $\hat{\eta}$ and $\hat{\mu}$.

For S/N:

$$\hat{\eta} = \overline{T} + (\overline{B}_2 - \overline{T}) + [(\overline{A_2B_2} - \overline{T}) - (\overline{A}_2 - \overline{T}) - (\overline{B}_2 - \overline{T})]$$
$$+ (\overline{D}_3 - \overline{T}) + (\overline{F}_2 - \overline{T})$$

$$\hat{\eta} = \overline{A_2B_2} - \overline{A}_2 + \overline{D}_3 + \overline{F}_2 - \overline{T}$$

$$\hat{\eta} = 32.21 - 28.24 + 31.13 + 33.28 - 26.29$$

$$\hat{\eta} = 42.09 \text{ decibels}$$

For $\overline{y}$:

$$\hat{\mu} = \overline{T} + (\overline{B}_2 - \overline{T}) + (\overline{C}_? - \overline{T})$$
$$\hat{\mu} = \overline{B}_2 + \overline{C}_? - \overline{T}$$
$$\hat{\mu} = 35.68 + C_? - 35.65$$

$$\text{Target} = 35.75 \text{ megahertz}$$

$$35.75 = 35.68 + C_? - 35.65$$

$$C_? = 35.72 \text{ megahertz}$$

Therefore, C must be adjusted between level 2 (1.2 μh) and level 3 (1.5 μh).

The optimal conditions are: A_2, B_2, D_3, F_2, with C between levels 2 and 3. E, G, and H are selected based on cost.

If cost differences are negligible, the preferred levels are: E_1, G_1, H_3 (based on highest S/N).

The predicted results *should always* be compared to the results of the confirmation run!

Chapter 20

ANALYSIS: DYNAMIC CHARACTERISTICS

In the cases of the smaller-the-better, larger-the-better, and nominal-the-best quality characteristics, we viewed a system, whether it was a design or a manufacturing process, as composed of a signal and a resulting output that could be affected by noise. This noise was defined as variation, and our goal was to maximize the strength of the signal in relation to minimizing the effect of the noise. This type of perspective is similar to the application of the signal-to-noise ratio concept to dynamic characteristics.

With a dynamic characteristic, we can again think of the strength of the signal having a direct effect on the results that we are trying to attain. We can also consider the deviations from the desired results as being a consequence of the effect of induced error.

$$\eta = \frac{\text{signal strength}}{\text{effect of error}}$$

We can picture the signal strength as reflecting the sensitiveness of the output to changes in the design or process inputs. If we think of a linear graph, we can relate to the slope of the line as a measure of sensitivity. The effect of error is the resulting variability. From this conclusion we can rewrite the signal-to-noise equation as:

$$\eta = \frac{\beta^2}{\sigma^2} .$$

20.1 APPLICATIONS

Earlier, we gave examples of dynamic quality characteristics in the planning phase of the book. However, it may be helpful to review the primary applications for dynamic systems and subsequent examples of quality characteristics.

20.1.1 Measurement Systems

One common and effective application of dynamic characteristics is to measurement systems. Often, we make measurements and produce deductions based on these bits of information without fully understanding the ability of the system to provide accurate information. For example, if we were to weigh produce at a grocery store and be charged based on the reading on the scale, we would expect that reading to be accurate. If we had selected a pound of grapes, we would expect the scale to read 1 pound. On the same scale, we would also expect 10 pounds of sweet potatoes to register as 10 pounds. Different items of the same weight should read the same value as well. Therefore, a robust measurement system would:

1. provide consistent measurements for the same inputs, and
2. continue to give accurate readings as the input values change.

We can think of the signal-to-noise ratio for a measurement system as:

$$\eta = \frac{(\text{sensitivity per unit input})^2}{(\text{measurement error})^2} \quad 1$$

20.1.2 Manufacturing Systems

Within a production process, we think of taking a specific input and converting it to a corresponding output. As the inputs change, the resulting outputs change by a predictable amount. We can think of a copying machine as an example. Each sheet of paper that is to be copied is an input. Each page will have a corresponding output or copy, which is expected to be similar to the original. To help us more fully understand this relationship, we need to define the resulting output as a functional consequence of the system. From the copying machine, we can think of the darkness or thickness of the lines as the input. The resulting darkness or thickness of the lines on the copy is the output. We would expect the thin or light lines on the original to reappear on the copy as thin or light also. Bold characters on the original would be expected to be transferred over as thick and dark reproductions. From this analogy, as the original signal increases (darker) or decreases (lighter or thinner), the output correspondingly changes. So if we consider a manufacturing process as a dynamic system, we would be concerned with:

1. the sensitivity of the process in converting the input signal into an output, and

2. the robustness of the process in attaining an anticipated output for a specific input signal.

The corresponding signal-to-noise ratio can be conceived as follows:

$$\eta = \frac{(\text{sensitivity per unit of input signal})^2}{(\text{output variability})}$$

20.1.3 Design Systems

As with manufacturing systems, the concept of dynamic chȧracteristics as applied to product design is to relate specific design factors to the functional output of the product. This method is considerably more efficient and conducive to obtaining new knowledge and advancing design capability than the static nominal-the-best characteristic. For the nominal-the-best case, we have the ability to determine the best settings for one specific result. Using a dynamic perspective allows us to determine the optimum values to achieve not one but a complete set of desired results. For example, instead of thinking of circuit design requirements in terms of a specific output value such as an ideal turn-on voltage value, we can envision a system which can assure multiple output voltages depending on the corresponding input signal. Therefore in considering a design as a dynamic system, the most important considerations are:

1. the sensitivity of the design in transforming the input signal into an output, and
2. the robustness of the design in attaining a desired output for a specific input signal.

20.2 CRITERIA

In examining the factors under consideration in a dynamic characteristic study, we must use a different perspective or criterion for determining which factors are significant and which levels should be selected for optimization. To facilitate this frame of reference, we need to think of the relationship between the characteristic of interest (output) and the factors under study (inputs) as a mathematical model.

$$y = \beta\, M,$$

where M is the input signal and β is slope of the response line.[2]

In comparing the ideal function above with the actual results, we must evaluate each of the factors under investigation as to its impact on the relationship between the input signal and the resulting output. This appraisal must be made on the basis of three criteria:

1. sensitivity
2. linearity
3. variability[3]

20.2.1 Sensitivity

Sensitivity refers to the amount of change in the resulting output based on changes in the input signal. Graphically, this relates to the slope of the line that represents the relationship between the two (Figure 20-1). Ideally, you would prefer the factor that would contribute to the higher slope (greater sensitivity). This is particularly true in manufacturing and design applications where the smallest change in the input signal for a desired adjustment in the output of interest would be preferred. For example, in an electronic assembly autoinsertion operation, component placement is a result of handling arm zero reference location. To make a required placement location change, it would be preferable to make the adjustment (output) with the smallest input possible. Therefore, you would select those factor levels with the greatest sensitivity.

In measurement systems, the objective is different. Since the desired result is to duplicate the actual value, your goal is to achieve a slope of 1, or a 45° angle to the origin.

20.2.2 Linearity

In dealing with the measurable characteristics—smaller-the-better, larger-the-better, and nominal-the-best—linearity was only a major concern as it affected the adjustment factor in the case of the nominal-the-best characteristic. Linearity

Figure 20-1 Sensitivity

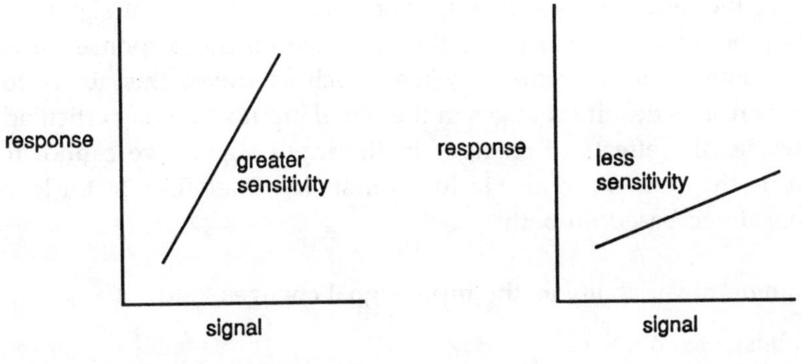

Figure 20-2 Linearity

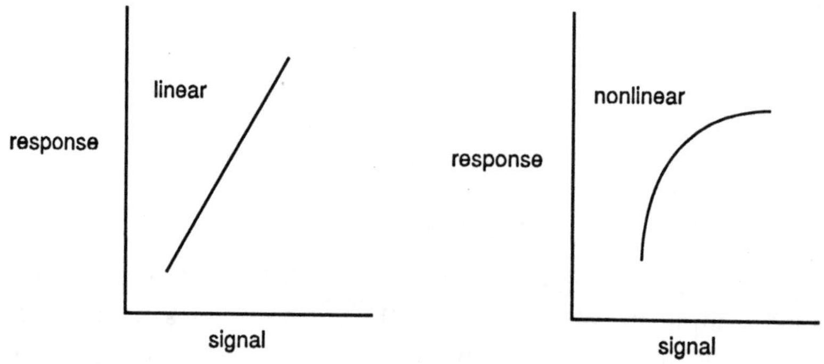

as defined here means that the output response is directly proportional to the input signal.

With dynamic characteristics, linearity is considerably more important and is a consideration for any of the factors being studied. The purpose for selecting factor levels that produce good linearity is that it simplifies the relationship between the output response and the input signal. As a linearly proportional relationship occurs between the two, it is easier to understand and to make the necessary adjustments to the input signal for producing desired outputs (Figure 20-2).

20.2.3 Variability

As with the other types of quality characteristics studied, variability in the responses from one result to another is a major concern. With dynamic characteristics, this consideration takes on an additional dimension. Not only are we concerned with variability around a specific target, but we must consider variability along the entire response line (Figure 20-3).

This difference means that we must select those factor levels that not only produce the results closest to a specific result for one input signal, but consistently produce results closest to the projected output response for each input signal value. In measurement systems such as scales, this ability to produce accurate results despite changes in the actual input values is particularly crucial.

Besides the effects of changes in the input signal, we cannot forget that noises to the system can also induce variability. Therefore, factor levels should be considered based on both:

1. minimum variability as the input signal changes, and
2. robustness to noise.

Figure 20-3 Variability

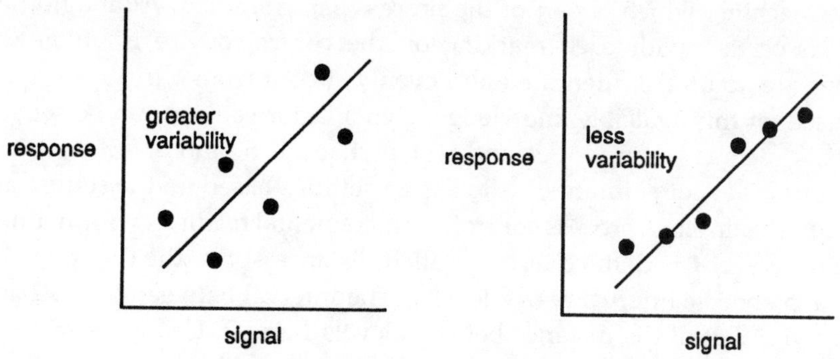

20.3 SIGNAL FACTOR CLASSIFICATIONS

Now that we have discussed the criteria for determining which factors are significant and which levels should be selected, it would be most appropriate at this time to identify the different types of signal factors with which we may become involved. This is important because the techniques and calculations associated with dynamic characteristic analysis change for different types of signal factors.

20.3.1 True Value Known

The ideal situation is when the true value of the signal factor is known. For one, it is easy to obtain an understanding of the linear effects. A simple plot of the response versus the actual signal factor values can provide a convenient visual analysis of the effect. Any nonlinear effect can then be combined with either measurement error (measurement systems) or variability (manufacturing and design systems), depending on the application.

The most frequent occurrence of knowing the true value is in the application of measurement systems. In a study of scales for example, standard weights would be used for the different signal factor levels. Known signal values can be seen in design systems as well. In the development of certain electronic tuning circuits, the objective is to create a design in which the circuit produces an impedence of the same value as the input resistor. As the input resistor changes, the equivalent circuit value is supposed to go to the same value as well. In manufacturing systems, it is not as likely for the true value of the signal factor to be known.

20.3.2 Intervals between Factor Levels Known

In many manufacturing systems, the actual value of the signal factor is unknown, but the difference or spread between signal factor settings is obtainable and easily understood. For example, a signal factor may be set or adjusted by a knob on the machine, which is part of the process being studied. Although the exact value associated with each marking on the control device is unknown, the settings are accurately identified and evenly spaced from 1 to 10.

Based on this available knowledge, signal factor settings can be set at equal intervals such as settings 1, 3, and 5 or perhaps 1, 5, and 9. An alternative to setting levels at equal intervals is to assign settings based on the setting interval ratios. For example, a process control has incremental readings with an unknown 0 setting. Level 1 is defined as a specified distance above the 0 setting. Level 2 is set at a specific interval above level 1. The interval between levels 2 and 3 is made twice that of the distance between levels 1 and 2. Using the same setting range as before, viable settings could be 1, 4 and 10 for levels 1, 2, and 3, respectively. A good generic example in which both approaches could be used is the heating controls on an oven.

20.3.3 Factor Level Ratios Known

Another situation in which the true value of the signal factor is unknown, but pertinent signal information exists, is where the settings for each level can be defined in terms of relative ratios. A chemical process can perhaps provide the best example and is probably one of the most likely sources where this type of signal factor would appear. Let's say that a solution being used has an unknown percentage of a particular ingredient. By diluting samples of the solution with the equal portions of water, we can produce various levels for the chemical process signal factor in which each of the levels is a percentage of the strength of the previous level. For example, level 1 is at a given strength. Level 2 is 50% of the strength of level 1 (original solution diluted once). Level 3 is 25% of the strength of level 1 or 50% the strength of level 2 (level 2 solution diluted once). Additional examples include other chemical type applications such as pharmaceutical, petrochemical, and pesticides.

20.3.4 Factor Level Values Vague

In the previous three cases, either the actual value was known or the levels could be ascertained so that we could conveniently graph the relationship between the input signal levels and the resulting system output values. Next are those situations in which the settings for the signal factor are so imprecise that we cannot study the linear relationship between the signal factor and the output. Since we could look directly at the linear portion of the effect when the signal settings were clearer, nonlinear effects could be pooled with error. However, that is not the situation when the signal values are vague. The total variation must be handled in a different manner. The way in which this is carried out will depend on whether the signal factor values are simply unascertainable, the signal values are inaccurate, or the different signal settings are vague but have additivity.

When the signal factors are unascertainable, the effect of the signal on the output response is assumed linear and nonlinearity is not considered. An example in which the signal factor values cannot be determined is a metal casting operation where the signal factor is defined as metal. The associated levels could be brass, aluminum, and tin.

In other situations, the values for the signal settings may be obtainable, but inaccuracies in measurement make a study of the linear relationship between signal and output response difficult. Any nonlinear effects that are detected may be the result of actual nonlinearity or may be due to inaccuracy in reading the signal factor values. In these cases, we can still estimate the linear effect, but any nonlinear effect should be kept separate from the determined error.

If it is known that the signal factor has additivity, the difference between the actual response when the levels are combined and the predicted results should be used as the estimate of error. For example, signal #1 produces a response of x_1, and signal #2 produces a response of x_2. If we were to assume additivity, we would expect the combined signal of #1 + #2 to result in a response of $x_1 + x_2$. Let's say that experimental runs are actually conducted at the combined signal. If the resulting response is $x_1 + x_2 + x_3$, the difference, x_3, is the estimate of error.

20.4 SIGNAL-TO-NOISE RATIO EQUATIONS

Just as a signal factor can be defined in terms of one of several classifications, different signal-to-noise ratio equations are available depending on the circumstances related to the input signal values and the resulting response data. In defining the different classifications of signal factors, we used the understanding of signal factor values and its impact on studying nonlinear effects as the primary criterion.

Now, we would like to discuss the alternate dynamic characteristic equations and when each is to be applied. Before proceeding further, let's define a few essential terms.

y = response value (output data)

β = slope of the line

M = signal factor value

r_o = number of pieces of data for each signal factor level

k = number of signal factor levels

A comparison of the alternate equations is given in Figure 20-4.

20.4.1 Zero Point Proportional Equation

When the relationship between the signal factor and the output response is such that the response line passes through the origin when drawn on a linear graph, the zero point proportional equation is appropriate. This equation assumes that when the signal factor is zero, the resulting response should also be zero. A typical example would be a bathroom scale. When no one is on the scale, the display should read zero.

The most obvious application of the zero point proportional equation is when the signal factor values are known. Measurement systems adjustable to zero fall into this category. This approach is also appropriate for manufacturing and design systems in which the signal can have a value of zero and the range of levels is fairly narrow and close to zero.

A second application of the zero point proportional equation is when the factor level ratios are known. This application is appropriate if the ratio of the relative settings can be accurately determined. For example, bath #1 has x% contamination or residue. By adding an equal amount of clean water, bath #2 has $x/2$% contamination or residue. By adding an additional equal quantity, bath #3 has $x/4$% contamination or residue. If each of these relative percentages can be accurately achieved, the zero point proportional equation can be used.

A third situation in which zero point is appropriate is when the signal factor actual values are unknown, but a plot of the line describing the relationship between the signal factor levels and the output response extends through the origin. The application assumes that the relationship is linear.

20.4.2 Reference Point Proportional Equation

Similar in application to zero point, the reference point proportional equation would apply where the line describing the relationship between the signal and output response either does not pass through the origin or would not be expected to pass through it. This situation would encompass signal factors with known values in which the settings are spread very wide apart or where all signal values are far away from zero. If in doubt between using zero point or reference point, plot the response as a function of the signal factor values on a linear graph and see if the y-intercept passes through the origin. If it does, use zero point instead. A measurement example of a reference point application is a tractor trailer weigh station on an interstate highway.

Figure 20-4 Signal-to-Noise Ratio Classifications

Zero Point Proportional	Reference Point Proportional	Linear Equation	Slope Calibration	No Calibration
Signal factor true values known: Response line passes through origin.	Signal factor true values known, wide range, far from zero: Response line does *not* pass through origin.	Signal factor true values known: All other cases where response line does *not* pass through origin.	Signal factor true values known: measurement systems, zero point proportional equation used.	Signal factor true values known: measurement systems, zero point proportional equation used, response line slope = 1.
	Signal factor true values unknown, intervals between factor levels known: data can be calibrated to a known standard.	Signal factor true values unknown, intervals between factor levels known: data *cannot* be calibrated to a known standard.		
Signal factor true values unknown, factor level ratios known: output response line passes through the origin.		Signal factor true values unknown, factor level ratios known: output response line does *not* pass through the origin.		
Signal factor true values vague or unknown: Response line passes through origin.		Signal factor true values vague or unknown: Response line does *not* pass through origin.		
		Signal factor values not accurate.		
		Signal factor true values vague or unknown, but exhibit additivity.		

A second type of signal factor for which this equation would apply is when the actual signal values are unknown, but the intervals between signal factor settings are known. If the data can be calibrated to a known standard, the reference point equation can be used. An example is oven controls. If one of the settings can be calibrated to a specific temperature, then use the reference point proportional equation. If this is not possible, then an alternative equation must be used.

20.4.3 Linear Equation

The linear equation is based on the least squares fit equation and can be applied to the various signal factor situations where zero point and reference point equations are not appropriate. When the signal values are known, zero point and reference point should be considered first. But if neither is appropriate, the linear equation model can be used. An example would be a situation in which the signal values are close together and the output response as a function of the signal does not intercept the y-axis at the origin.

In other cases where either zero point or reference point cannot be used, the linear equation is also an alternative. When the signal value is unknown, but the intervals between levels are understood, reference point is typically the first choice. However, reference point requires that the data be calibrated to a defined reference value. If this is not possible, then the linear equation should be used. When the signal value is unknown, but the factor level ratios are defined, zero point is typically the first choice. If the output response line does not intercept the y-axis at the origin, then the linear equation is the proper alternative.

When the signal factor values are vague or difficult to quantify, the linear equation should again be used in place of a proportional equation when the output response line will not or does not appear to pass through the origin. The error (S_e) is calculated by subtracting the variation within the signal factor (S_M) from the total variation (S_T), where:

$$y_t = \sum_{j=1}^{r_o} y_j \qquad y_t = \text{sum of the data for a specific signal factor level,}$$

and

$$S_M = \sum_{i=1}^{k} y_{t_i}^2/r_o - \left|\left(\sum_{i=1}^{k} y_{t_i}\right)^2 /r_o k\right.$$

and

$$S_e = S_T - S_M.$$

Then,

$$V_M = S_M/(k - 1)$$

and

$$V_e = S_e/(kr_o - 3).$$

A linear relationship is assumed. The other calculations for the linear equation approach that are described in Section 20.7 still apply, except that V_M is used in the S/N equation instead of S_β.

When accuracy arises as a problem for the values of the signal factor, the linear equations as described above and in Section 20.7 can still apply. However, the nonlinearity effect should be treated separately and not combined with error. If the signal factor values are vague but exhibit the characteristic of additivity, error can be determined by comparing the data obtained with each individual signal (A and B) with the results obtained with a combined signal (A + B). The remainder of the calculations can be performed using the appropriate linear equation formulas.

20.4.4 Slope Calibration

In measurement systems, the ideal situation in many cases is for the slope of the output response line to equal 1. In other words, if the signal is 50, the expected response should be 50. If the signal increases to 200, the response should increase to the same value. To achieve this relationship, calibration of the slope may be required after conducting zero point calibration. If bathroom scales tended to underestimate weight by increased amounts as the person on the scale became bigger, slope calibration might be desired.

20.4.5 No Calibration

Just as slope calibration might be required in some measurement systems, in other cases the data may indicate that the slope of the output response line appears actually to equal 1 or to be very close to it. In these cases, we may not feel that slope calibration is worth the effort and we would then make the assumption that the slope is in fact equal to 1.

20.5 ZERO POINT PROPORTIONAL EQUATION

As mentioned previously, zero point can be used where the signal values are known and the output response line passes through the origin. Therefore, it would be advisable at the onset of the analysis to plot the signal factor values against the data and draw a line through the approximate center of the results for each signal factor setting and see if it appears to pass through the origin. If not, another type of S/N equation may be more appropriate.

Now we will proceed through the calculations, explaining each equation as we go. To facilitate the understanding of the steps involved, a simple example (Figure 20-5) will accompany our discussion.

The ideal equation is:

$$y = \beta M.$$

However, the real world consists of variation, and the more realistic equation is:

$$y_{ij} = \beta M_i + e_{ij},$$

where

$$i = 1, 2, \ldots, k$$

and

$$j = 1, 2, \ldots, r_o.$$

Figure 20-5 Zero Point Proportional Equation Example

Quality Characteristic: weight

		M_1 = 59 lbs		M_2 = 120 lbs		M_3 = 174 lbs	
Run#	Repetition#	N_1	N_2	N_1	N_2	N_1	N_2
1	1	61	62	118	120	174	171
	2	58	59	122	130	176	178
	3	60	61	127	128	173	175
	4	57	62	125	128	175	178
2	1	57	58	120	126	171	172
	2	59	59	119	123	172	174
	3	61	62	120	124	174	178
	4	57	55	116	119	172	174

The objective is to determine the key control factors and best settings of these factors such that accurate data will be produced for different input weights (signal) despite the effect of extraneous factors (noise). This goal requires the calculation of the dynamic signal-to-noise ratio for each experimental run (inner array row). But to determine S/N, we must first separate the data into its signal and noise components.

Let's calculate S/N for run #1.

1. Determine r:

$$r = r_o (M_1^2 + M_2^2 + \ldots + M_k^2)$$

$$r = 8 (59^2 + 120^2 + 174^2)$$

Note: $r_0 = 8$ for experimental run #1 and 8 for experimental run #2 as well, consisting of 4 at N_1 and 4 at N_2 (4 + 4 each). For all following runs in a balanced experiment, r_o would be the same value.

$$r = 385{,}256$$

2. Calculate the slope β:

$$\beta = \frac{1}{r} (M_1 y_1 + M_2 y_2 + \ldots + M_k y_k)$$

$$\beta = \frac{59 \times (61 + 62 + \ldots + 62) + 120 \times (118 + 120 + \ldots + 128) + 174(174 + \ldots)}{385{,}256}$$

$$\beta = 391{,}680/385{,}256 = 1.02$$

3. Determine the total sum of squares:

$$S_T = y_{11}^2 + y_{12}^2 + \ldots + y_{kr_o}^2$$

$$S_T = 61^2 + 62^2 + \ldots + 178^2$$

$$S_T = 398{,}494$$

4. Determine the variation caused by linear effect:

$$S_\beta = \frac{1}{r} (M_1 y_1 + M_2 y_2 + \ldots + M_k y_k)^2$$

$$S_\beta = [59 \times (61 + 62 + \ldots + 62) + 120 \times (118 + 120 + \ldots + 128) + 174(174 + \ldots)]^2 / 385{,}256$$

$$S_\beta = 398{,}211.12$$

5. Calculate the variation associated with error and nonlinearity:

$$S_e = S_T - S_\beta$$

$$S_e = 398{,}494 - 398{,}211.12 = 282.88$$

6. Calculate the error variance:

$$V_e = \frac{1}{kr_o - 1} S_e$$

$$V_e = \frac{282.88}{3 \times 8 - 1} = 12.30$$

7. Calculate S/N:

$$\eta = 10 \log \frac{1}{r} \frac{(S_\beta - V_e)}{V_e}$$

$$\eta = 10 \log \frac{1}{385{,}256} \frac{(398{,}211.12 - 12.30)}{12.30}$$

$$\eta = 10 \log .0840321 = -10.76$$

8. Derive the S/N for the remaining experimental runs in the same manner.
9. Determine the factors with the strongest effects and the best levels using the S/N response table and response graphs and following the procedures described in the previous chapters for S/N analysis.

In measurement systems and certain cases of manufacturing and design systems, a slope of 1 ($\beta = 1$) is desired. If after zero point calibration the slope is not equal to or approximately 1, we can use slope calibration to get closer to the desired result. β is computed using the standard equation for the slope (step 2). Adjustments would then be made using the equation below:

$$M = \frac{y'}{\beta},$$

where y' is the actual measurement.

20.6 REFERENCE POINT PROPORTIONAL EQUATION

As explained in Section 20.4.2, reference point is appropriate when the signal values are known and the response line does not pass through the origin or when the signal values are unknown, but the intervals between signal levels are known and the data can be calibrated to a known standard. The following is an example of known intervals between signal values and will be used to help explain the computations for the reference point proportional equation technique. If it had been an example of the first case, a plot of the signal values against the data values would have been performed to check to see if in fact the response line did not pass through the origin.

Case Example: In a baking operation, the oven temperatures are adjusted using knob controls. The temperatures are not marked on the dials, but incremental markings appear on the face of each dial from low to high with 2 through 10 as the numbers in between (Figure 20-6).

Once again, the analysis will require the calculation of the signal-to-noise ratio for each experimental run. Upon completion of the calculations, a response table and response charts can be used to determine the strongest effects and the best levels. For the purpose of this chapter, we will again stop with the calculation of S/N for one experimental run.

The following are some new terms not previously defined in the zero point example.

Figure 20-6 Reference Point Proportional Equation Example

Quality Characteristic: temperature, degrees Fahrenheit

		$M_1 = 2$		$M_2 = 6$		$M_3 = 10$	
Run#	Repetition#	N_1	N_2	N_1	N_2	N_1	N_2
1	1	235	210	275	250	317	295
	2	242	236	292	282	339	328
	3	241	235	287	277	340	334
	4	235	225	290	278	330	322
	5	233	225	288	275	338	332
	6	228	215	280	270	330	324
2	1	228	217	275	272	325	315
	2	225	214	278	265	329	320
	3	233	230	285	270	337	333
	4	220	202	274	265	326	322
	5	223	203	283	269	331	329
	6	224	216	276	272	330	326

M_s = Reference standard

$\bar{y}_s$ = Average from reference standard data

The ideal reference point proportional equation is:

$$y - \bar{y}_s = \beta (M - M_s).$$

Now, let's calculate S/N for experimental run #1.

Before determining the slope or any of the other values required in the calculation of S/N, we need to pre-treat the raw data as follows:

1. Calculate the reference standard average:

$$\bar{y}_s = \frac{(y_1 + y_2 + \ldots + y_j)}{r_o}$$

$$\bar{y}_s(\#1) = \frac{(235 + 210 + \ldots + 215)}{12}$$

$$\bar{y}_s(\#1) = 230$$

$$\bar{y}_s = \frac{(y_1 + y_2 + \ldots + y_j)}{r_o}$$

$$\bar{y}_s(\#2) = \frac{(228 + 217 + \ldots + 216)}{12}$$

$$\bar{y}\,(\#2) = 220$$

2. Subtract the appropriate value of $\bar{y}$ from each piece of raw data. Also, subtract 2 (M_1) from each signal factor setting ($M_s = M_1$). See Figure 20-7.

3. Determine r:

$$r = r_o\,[(M_1 - M_s)^2 + (M_2 - M_s)^2 + \ldots + (M_k - M_s)^2]$$

$$r = 12\,[(2 - 2)^2 + (6 - 2)^2 + (10 - 2)^2]$$

Note: $r_o = 12$ for experimental run #1 and 12 for experimental run #2 as well, consisting of 6 at N_1 and 6 at N_2 (6 + 6 each).

$$r = 960$$

Figure 20-7 Reference Point Proportional Equation Modified Data

		$M_1 - M_s = 0$		$M_2 - M_s = 4$		$M_3 - M_s = 8$	
Run#	Repetition#	N_1	N_2	N_1	N_2	N_1	N_2
1	1	5	−20	45	20	87	65
	2	12	6	62	52	109	98
	3	11	5	57	47	110	104
	4	5	−5	60	48	100	92
	5	3	−5	58	45	108	102
	6	−2	−15	50	40	100	94
2	1	8	−3	55	52	105	95
	2	5	−5	58	45	109	100
	3	13	9	65	50	117	113
	4	0	−18	54	45	106	102
	5	3	−17	63	49	111	109
	6	4	−4	56	52	110	106

4. Compute the total adjusted sum for each signal factor setting.

$$y_k = \sum_{j=1}^{r_o} (y_j - \bar{y}_s)$$

$$y_1 = 5 - 20 + \ldots - 15 = 0$$

Note: It is not necessary for $\bar{y}_s$ to be exactly equal to $\Sigma y_1/r_o$ so that $y_1 = 0$. Although this is the case with experimental run #1, y_1 for experimental run #2 is equal to minus 5.

$$y_2 = 45 + 20 + \ldots + 40 = 584$$

$$y_3 = 87 + 65 + \ldots + 94 = 1169$$

5. Calculate the slope β:

$$\beta = \frac{1}{r} [y_1 (M_1 - M_s) + y_2 (M_2 - M_s) + \ldots + y_k(M_k - M_s)]$$

$$\beta = \frac{0 \times (0 - 0) + 584 \times (6 - 2) + 1169 \times (10 - 2)}{960}$$

$$\beta = 11{,}688/960 = 12.175$$

6. Determine the total sum of squares:

$$S_T = \sum_{i=1}^{k} \sum_{j=1}^{r_0} (y_{ij} - \bar{y}_s)^2$$

$$S_T = (5)^2 + (-20)^2 + \dots + (94)^2$$

$$S_T = 146{,}451$$

7. Determine the variation caused by the linear effect:

$$S_\beta = \frac{1}{r} [y_1 (M_1 - M_s) + y_2 (M_2 - M_s) + \dots + y_k (M_k - M_s)]^2$$

$$S_\beta = \frac{[0 \times (2 - 2) + 584 \times (6 - 2) + 1169 \times (10 - 2)]^2}{960}$$

$$S_\beta = 142{,}301.4$$

8. Calculate the variation associated with error and nonlinearity:

$$S_e = S_T - S_\beta$$

$$S_e = 146{,}451 - 142{,}301.4 = 4{,}149.6$$

9. Calculate the error variance:

$$V_e = \frac{1}{kr_o - 1} S_e$$

$$V_e = \frac{4{,}149.6}{3 \times 12 - 1} = 118.56$$

10. Calculate S/N:

$$\eta = 10 \log \frac{1}{r} \frac{(S_\beta - V_e)}{V_e}$$

$$\eta = 10 \log \frac{1}{960} \frac{(142{,}301.40 - 118.56)}{118.56}$$

$$\eta = 10 \log 1.2492166 = .9664$$

11. Derive the S/N for each of the other experimental runs in the same manner.

12. After computing the other S/N ratios, determine the factors with the strongest effects and the best levels using the S/N response table and response graphs and following the procedures described in the previous chapters for S/N analysis.

20.7 LINEAR EQUATION

If neither the zero point proportional equation nor the reference point proportional equation is appropriate, then the linear equation is the next logical choice. Although we could introduce numerous examples to demonstrate the procedures for using the linear equation, we will use an example in which the signal values are unknown, but the ratios between intervals are known. Because it does not appear that the response line would pass through the origin, the linear equation approach should be selected over the zero point proportional equation method.

Case Example: In a specialized metal stripping operation, sulfuric acid of unknown concentration is used. Depending on the depth of the required etches, the plates may be dipped into one of three baths of relatively different levels of concentration (Figure 20-8). The levels are based on mixing equal amounts of acid and tap water. The results are:

bath 1—1 volume acid, 1 volume water
bath 2—1 volume acid, 2 volumes water
bath 3—1 volume acid, 4 volumes water

Figure 20-8 Linear Equation Example

Quality Characteristic: grams—metal etched

		$M_1 = x$		$M_2 = x/2$		$M_3 = x/4$	
Run#	Repetition#	N_1	N_2	N_1	N_2	N_1	N_2
1	1	2.39	2.29	1.47	1.33	0.44	0.28
	2	2.40	2.30	1.33	1.25	0.25	0.22
	3	2.41	2.16	1.25	1.05	0.23	0.04
2	1	2.63	2.46	1.48	1.41	0.39	0.32
	2	2.63	2.45	1.38	1.24	0.25	0.18
	3	2.71	2.69	1.74	1.54	0.65	0.47
3	1	2.45	2.33	1.35	1.25	0.35	0.21
	2	2.40	2.25	1.35	1.18	0.24	0.05
	3	2.29	2.15	1.16	1.05	0.20	0.01

The general linear equation can be stated as:

$$y = m + \beta\,(M - \overline{M}) + e,$$

where

$$m = \overline{y}$$

and

$$e = \text{error}.$$

Now, let's go through the linear equation calculations using experimental run #1 to illustrate the procedures.

1. Determine r:

$$\overline{M} = (M_1 + M_2 + M_3)/3$$

$$\overline{M} = (1 + 1/2 + 1/4)/3 = 7/12$$

$$r = r_o\,[(M_1 - \overline{M})^2 + (M_2 - \overline{M})^2 + \ldots + (M_k - \overline{M})^2]$$

$$r = 6\,[(1 - 7/12]^2 + 1/2 - 7/12)^2 + (1/4 - 7/12)^2]$$

$$r = 1.75$$

2. Calculate the slope β:

$$y_1 = 2.39 + 2.29 + \ldots + 2.16 = 13.95$$

$$y_2 = 1.47 + 1.33 + \ldots + 1.05 = 7.68$$

$$y_3 = 0.44 + 0.28 + \ldots + 0.04 = 1.46$$

$$\beta = \frac{1}{r}\,[y_1\,(M_1 - \overline{M}) + y_2\,(M_2 - \overline{M}) + \ldots + y_k\,(M_k - \overline{M})]$$

$$\beta = \frac{13.95 \times (1 - 7/12) + 7.68 \times (1/2 - 7/12) + 1.46 \times (1/4 - 7/12)}{1.75}$$

$$\beta = 2.677619$$

3. Determine the total sum of squares:

$$S_T = y_{11}^2 + y_{12}^2 + \dots + y_{kr_o}^2 - \frac{\left(\sum_{i=1}^{k}\sum_{j=1}^{r_o} y_{ij}\right)^2}{kr_o}$$

$$S_T = 2.39^2 + 2.29^2 + \dots + 0.04^2 - \frac{(2.39 + 2.29 + \dots + 0.04)^2}{3 \times 6}$$

$$S_T = 13.224161$$

4. Determine the variation caused by the linear effect:

$$S_\beta = \frac{1}{r}[\, y_1 (M_1 - \overline{M}) + y_2 (M_2 - \overline{M}) + \dots + y_k (M_k - \overline{M})]^2$$

$$S_\beta = \frac{[13.95 \times (1 - 7/12) + 7.68 \times (1/2 - 7/12) + 1.46 \times (1/4 - 7/12)]^2}{1.75}$$

$$S_\beta = 12.546877$$

5. Calculate the variation associated with error and nonlinearity:

$$S_e = S_T - S_\beta$$

$$S_e = 13.224161 - 12.546877 = .677284$$

6. Calculate the error variance:

$$V_e = \frac{1}{kr_o - 2} S_e$$

$$V_e = \frac{.677284}{3 \times 6 - 2} = .042330$$

7. Calculate S/N:

$$\eta = 10 \log \frac{1}{r} \frac{(S_\beta - V_e)}{V_e}$$

$$\eta = 10 \log \frac{1}{1.75} \frac{(12.546877 - .042330)}{.042330}$$

$$\eta = 10 \log 168.80358 = 22.27 \text{ db}$$

8. Derive the S/N for each of the other experimental runs in the same manner.

9. After computing the other S/N ratios, determine the factors with the strongest effects and the best levels using the S/N response table and response graphs and following the procedures described in the previous chapters for S/N analysis.

20.8 CIRCUIT DESIGN EXAMPLE

Up to this point, we have:

discussed the applications of dynamic characteristic analysis,

explained the criteria for identifying strong effects,

defined the signal factor types, and

described the different analysis techniques including the use of examples to explain the use of the equations.

However, we have not gone beyond the determination of the signal-to-noise ratios. The following example, based on an actual circuit design study, will go from raw data to identification of strong effects and selection of best settings including the calculation of essential terms (see Figure 20-9, Figure 20-10).

1. In this particular study, the signal factor values are known. Since the expected result should be 0 ohms when the signal is also 0 ohms, the appropriate tool is the zero point proportional equation. Therefore, we will use the equations from Section 20.5 to determine the signal-to-noise ratios (Figure 20-11).

2. After determining S/N for each row, a S/N response table can be generated (Figure 20-12). Strong effects are determined by the relative difference in levels. Optimal levels are selected based on the higher S/N. The optimal settings are: A1, D2, E2, G2.

Based on the S/N computed for each of the strong effects and the experiment average, a predicted S/N can be determined which will be compared to the S/N calculated from the actual confirmation results.

3. In the confirmation run, the signal factor should be set at various values within the desired range of use. Besides comparing the predicted and actual signal-to-noise ratios, we can also look at the reduction in measurement error (process or design system error, if appropriate). After obtaining the new data, the difference (error) between the resulting value and actual or expected value should be computed for each point.

Figure 20-9 Circuit Diagram

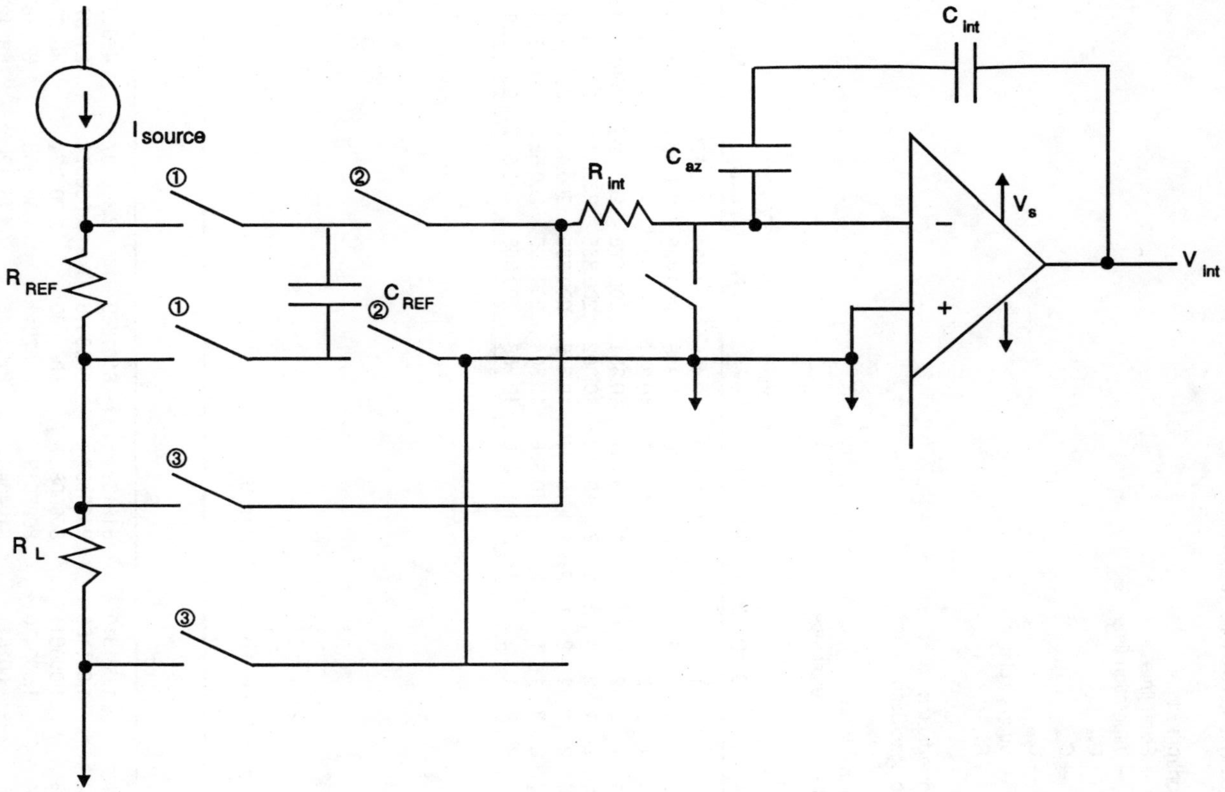

Figure 20-10 Circuit Design Study

Quality Characteristic: resistance

Control factors:
A — Fixed time
B — Integration time
C — C_{int}
D — C_{az}
E — C_{ref}
F — Supply voltage
G — R_{int}

Noise factor:
No scan/Scan

Signal factor:
M — Input resistance

Run #	A	B	C	D	E	F	G	M_1 = 10 ohms N_1	N_2	M_2 = 200 ohms N_1	N_2	M_3 = 2000 ohms N_1	N_2
1	1	1	1	1	1	1	1	10.425	10.495	200.454	200.579	2001.655	2003.531
2	1	1	1	2	2	2	2	10.366	10.368	200.452	200.685	2001.754	2002.800
3	1	2	2	1	1	2	2	10.286	10.334	200.383	200.599	2002.055	2000.313
4	1	2	2	2	2	1	1	10.291	10.331	200.378	200.596	2001.700	2000.102
5	2	1	2	1	2	1	2	10.266	10.302	200.355	200.444	2001.598	2004.426
6	2	1	2	2	1	2	1	10.293	10.318	200.395	200.484	2001.738	2004.797
7	2	2	1	1	2	2	1	10.306	10.304	200.395	200.555	2001.738	2004.676
8	2	2	1	2	1	1	2	10.280	10.288	200.355	200.516	2001.598	2004.305

Figure 20-11 Circuit Design Study

Run #	β	S_T	S_β	S_e	V_e	η
1	1.001310	8101391	8101389	2.300387	.460077	3.38
2	1.001156	8098897	8098896	1.056871	.211374	6.76
3	1.000611	8090082	8090080	2.001374	.400274	3.98
4	1.000470	8087813	8087811	1.800936	.360187	4.44
5	1.001511	8104649	8104645	4.167136	.833427	0.80
6	1.001640	8106730	8106725	4.875348	.975069	0.12
7	1.001611	8106273	8106269	4.542778	.908555	0.43
8	1.001483	8104193	8104189	3.860827	.772165	1.14

Figure 20-12 S/N Response Table

	A	B	C	D	E	F	G
Level 1	4.64	2.77	2.93	2.15	2.16	2.44	2.09
Level 2	0.62	2.50	2.34	3.12	3.11	2.82	3.17
	4.02	.27	.59	**.97**	**.95**	.38	**1.08**

Then,

$$S_e = \sum_{i=1}^{n} (\text{error}_i)^2$$

and

$$V_e = \frac{S_e}{n},$$

then,

$$s = \sqrt{V_e},$$

where n = number of data points excluding 0.

The new standard deviation can be compared with the standard deviation prior to the study. This will give a relative measure of the improvement gained from the new design values (process settings).

A new linear coefficient, β, can be calculated from the confirmation run as well. Slope calibration can be performed based on the following equation:

$$M = \frac{y'}{\beta},$$

where

y' = actual data (measurement)
M = adjusted sample.

Notes

1. *Quality Engineering: Dynamic Characteristics and Measurement Engineering,* p. 1-2.
2. Ibid., p. 5-2.
3. Ibid., p. 2-1.

Chapter 21

SPECIAL DESIGN TECHNIQUES

In the previous chapters, we discussed the design and analysis of experiments in which all factors could be defined independent of each other and each factor consisted of the same number of levels. We also often worked with a list of factors that conveniently fitted into a fairly small experimental matrix. However, in the real world, this situation does not always happen. With unequal factor levels, it is frequently impossible to even try to force each factor to have the same number of levels. On many occasions, the number of factors or degrees of freedom may be just one more than allowed by the orthogonal array that you like to use.

The purpose of this chapter is to provide an explanation of techniques that will provide methods for addressing these concerns. Specifically, we will discuss techniques that will:

1. incorporate factors of different levels into the same experiment;
2. handle situations in which levels of one factor are dependent on levels of another; and
3. modify the factor levels to reduce the size of the experiment.

21.1 MULTILEVEL ARRANGEMENTS

The application of this technique is for handling factors that have considerably more levels than the rest of the factors under study. Specific applications include four-level and eight-level factors that need to be fitted into 2^n type orthogonal arrays, such as the L_8 and the L_{16}, with other factors consisting of only two levels each. This technique also applies to nine-level factors that can be incorporated into 3^n type orthogonal arrays, such as the L_{27} and the L_{54}, with other factors that are composed of three levels.

21.1.1 Four-Level Factor

In an electronic design study, the following factors and levels are to be incorporated into an experimental design:

Fixed time: 8.2, 16.4, 32.8, 65.5 ms

C_{int}: .1, .2 μf

C_{ref}: .1, .2 μf

V_{supply}: −5.0, −7.0 v.

R_{int}: 125k, 250k ohms

Step 1: Count the degrees of freedom required for the factors (and interactions) under investigation.

$$\begin{array}{lcr} \text{4-level factor : df} & = & 3 \\ \text{2-level factors: df} & = 4 \times 1 = & 4 \\ \hline \text{Total df} & = & 7\text{ df} \end{array}$$

Step 2: Choose the orthogonal array that will accommodate the total number of degrees of freedom required.

$$L_8\ (2^7)\text{: degrees of freedom} = 7 \times (2 - 1) = 7\text{ df}$$

Step 3: Since the four-level factor requires three degrees of freedom, we will need to determine the appropriate three columns to which to assign this factor. From a linear graph of the orthogonal array selected in step 2, select two dots and their joining line segment. In the case of an L_8, the choice can be made between two different linear graph shapes.

From the linear graph shown on the left in Figure 21-1, we choose the two points and connecting line associated with columns 1, 2, and 3 of the orthogonal array L_8 (2^7).

Step 4: Next, select any two of the columns from step 3. These will be used to map the four levels to the appropriate experimental runs (rows). Four distinct combinations (levels) can be identified from the combinations of 1's and 2's from columns 1 and 2 without having to consider the third column.

Figure 21-1 L_8 (2^7) Orthogonal Array Linear Graphs

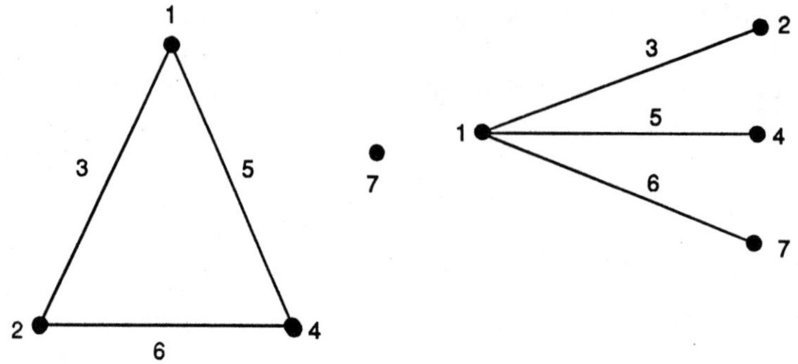

Identify the two columns in the orthogonal array below (columns one and two).

L_8 (2^7)

No.	1	2	3	4	5	6	7
1	**1**	**1**	1	1	1	1	1
2	**1**	**1**	1	2	2	2	2
3	**1**	**2**	2	1	1	2	2
4	**1**	**2**	2	2	2	1	1
5	**2**	**1**	2	1	2	1	2
6	**2**	**1**	2	2	1	2	1
7	**2**	**2**	1	1	2	2	1
8	**2**	**2**	1	2	1	1	2

Determine the mapping sequence for assigning the values of the four-level factor.

Column Levels		
1	2	Map to
1	1	1
1	1	1
1	2	2
1	2	2
2	1	3
2	1	3
2	2	4
2	2	4

Step 5: Replace the columns identified in step 3 with the new modified four-level column. The four levels of fixed time correspond to the four combinations in columns 1 and 2.

Step 6: Assign the two-level factors to the remaining columns.

Standard L_8

Run#	1	2	3	Modified	4	5	6	7
1	1	1	1	1	1	1	1	1
2	1	1	1	1	2	2	2	2
3	1	2	2	2	1	1	2	2
4	1	2	2	2	2	2	1	1
5	2	1	2	3	1	2	1	2
6	2	1	2	3	2	1	2	1
7	2	2	1	4	1	2	2	1
8	2	2	1	4	2	1	1	2

Modified L_8

Run#	Fixed time	C_{int}	C_{ref}	V_{supply}	R_{int}
1	1	1	1	1	1
2	1	2	2	2	2
3	2	1	1	2	2
4	2	2	2	1	1
5	3	1	2	1	2
6	3	2	1	2	1
7	4	1	2	2	1
8	4	2	1	1	2

21.1.2 Eight-Level Factor

In a surface mount process experiment, various factors are to be studied including eight wave profiles. The factors and levels of interest are as follows:

Wave profile: I, II, III, IV, V, VI, VII, VIII

Solder paste volume: low, high

Solder paste vendor: Supplier A, Supplier B

Pad design: IPC, JCN

Squeegee speed: 30, 60 (dial settings)

Squeegee pressure: 4, 6 kg.

Squeegee swivel: 3, 7 (dial settings)

Reflow temperature: low, high

Step 1: Count the degrees of freedom required for the factors (and interactions) under investigation.

$$\begin{aligned} \text{8-level factor : df} &= & 7 \\ \text{2-level factors: df} &= 7 \times 1 = & 7 \\ \hline \text{Total df} &= & 14 \text{ df} \end{aligned}$$

Step 2: Choose the orthogonal array that will accommodate the total number of degrees of freedom required.

$$L_{16}\ (2^{15})\text{: degrees of freedom} = 15 \times (2 - 1) = 15 \text{ df}$$

Step 3: Since the eight-level factor requires seven degrees of freedom, we will need to determine the appropriate seven columns to assign this factor. From a linear graph of the orthogonal array chosen in step 2, select a closed triangle. In the case of an L_{16}, the choice can be made between three different linear graph shapes (Figure 21-2).

Step 4: In the triangle identified from the selected linear graph, draw a line from one dot (apex) to the opposing line (base). Using the L_{16} (2^{15}) Interactions between Two Columns Table, determine the column associated with the newly constructed line (Figure 21-3).

Figure 21-2 L_{16} (2^{15}) Orthogonal Array Linear Graphs

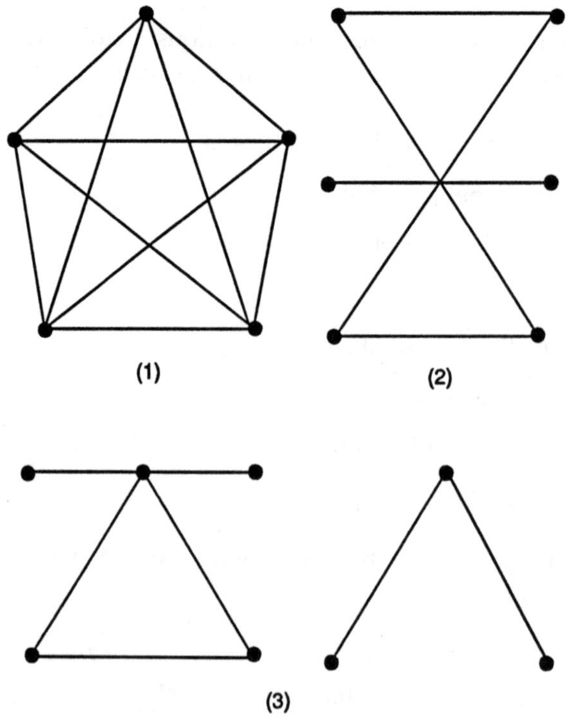

Figure 21-3 L_{16} (2^{15}) **Eight-Level Factor Column Assignments**

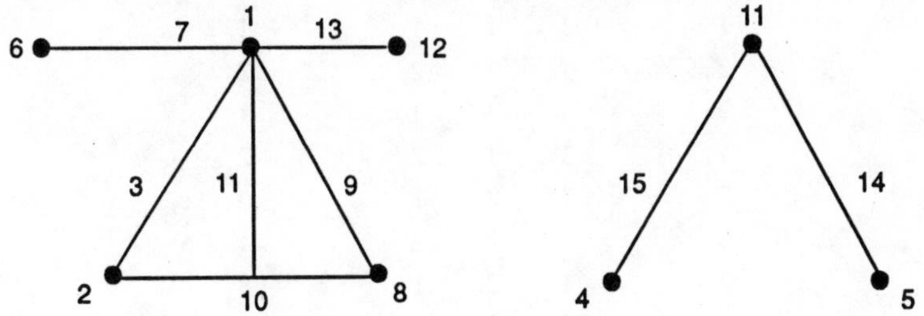

L_{16} (2^{15}) Interactions between Two Columns

	1	2	3	4	5	6	7	8	9	**10**	11	12	13	14	15
	(1)	3	2	5	4	7	6	9	8	**11**	10	13	12	15	14
		(2)	1	6	7	4	5	10	11	8	9	14	15	12	13
			(3)	7	6	5	4	11	10	9	8	15	14	13	12
				(4)	1	2	3	12	13	14	15	8	9	10	11
					(5)	3	2	13	12	15	14	9	8	11	10
						(6)	1	14	15	12	13	10	11	8	9
							(7)	15	14	13	12	11	10	9	8
								(8)	1	2	3	4	5	6	7
									(9)	3	2	5	4	7	6
										(10)	1	6	7	4	5
											(11)	7	6	5	4
												(12)	1	2	3
													(13)	3	2
														(14)	1

Let's choose Linear Graph III-1 (Appendix B) for making column assignments. From the closed triangle in Figure 21-3, six of the required seven column assignments are given. By selecting column 1 as the apex and column 10 as the opposing base, Figure 21-3 identifies column 11 as the corresponding assignment for the new line.

Step 5: Identify the columns associated with the dots (corners) of the triangle. Develop a mapping sequence based on the combinations of level settings for these three columns.

Run #	Column Levels 1	2	8	Map to
1	1	1	1	1
2	1	1	2	2
3	1	1	1	1
4	1	1	2	2
5	1	2	1	3
6	1	2	2	4
7	1	2	1	3
8	1	2	2	4
9	2	1	1	5
10	2	1	2	6
11	2	1	1	5
12	2	1	2	6
13	2	2	1	7
14	2	2	2	8
15	2	2	1	7
16	2	2	2	8

Three columns are essential for mapping the eight levels. The number of combinations of factor settings available is based on the number of columns and the number of levels within each selected column. Mathematically, this can be written as $\text{Levels}^{\text{columns}}$. Therefore, three columns are needed in an L_{16} to produce 8 combinations ($2^3 = 8$).

Step 6: Replace the columns identified in steps 3 and 4 with the new modified column. The eight levels of wave profile correspond to the eight combinations of columns 1, 2, and 8.

Standard L_{16}

Run#	1	2	8	Modified	3	4	5	6	7	9	10	11	12	13	14	15
1	1	1	1	1	1	1	1	1	1	1	1	1	1	1	1	1
2	1	1	2	2	1	1	1	1	1	2	2	2	2	2	2	2
3	1	1	1	1	1	2	2	2	2	1	1	1	2	1	2	2
4	1	1	2	2	1	2	2	2	2	2	2	2	1	1	1	1

Standard L_{16} *cont'd.*

Run#	1	2	8	Modified	3	4	5	6	7	9	10	11	12	13	14	15
5	1	2	1	3	2	1	1	2	2	1	2	2	1	1	2	2
6	1	2	2	4	2	1	1	2	2	2	1	1	2	2	1	1
7	1	2	1	3	2	2	2	1	1	1	2	2	2	2	1	1
8	1	2	2	4	2	2	2	1	1	2	1	1	1	1	2	2
9	2	1	1	5	2	1	2	1	2	2	1	2	1	2	1	2
10	2	1	2	6	2	1	2	1	2	1	2	1	2	1	2	1
11	2	1	1	5	2	2	1	2	1	2	1	2	2	1	2	1
12	2	1	2	6	2	2	1	2	1	1	2	1	1	2	1	2
13	2	2	1	7	1	1	2	2	1	2	2	1	1	2	2	1
14	2	2	2	8	1	1	2	2	1	1	1	2	2	1	1	2
15	2	2	1	7	1	2	1	1	2	2	2	1	2	1	1	2
16	2	2	2	8	1	2	1	1	2	1	1	2	1	2	2	1

Step 7: Assign the two-level factors to the remaining columns.

Modified L_{16}

Run#	wave profile	paste volume 4	paste vendor 5	pad 6	sq. speed 7	sq. pressure 12	sq. swivel 13	reflow temp 14	error 15
1	1	1	1	1	1	1	1	1	1
2	2	1	1	1	1	2	2	2	2
3	1	2	2	2	2	2	2	2	2
4	2	2	2	2	2	1	1	1	1
5	3	1	1	2	2	1	1	2	2
6	4	1	1	2	2	2	2	1	1
7	3	2	2	1	1	2	2	1	1
8	4	2	2	1	1	1	1	2	2
9	5	1	2	1	2	1	2	1	2
10	6	1	2	1	2	2	1	2	1
11	5	2	1	2	1	2	1	2	1
12	6	2	1	2	1	1	2	1	2
13	7	1	2	2	1	1	2	2	1
14	8	1	2	2	1	2	1	1	2
15	7	2	1	1	2	2	1	1	2
16	8	2	1	1	2	1	2	2	1

This is just one of several alternate designs that could be developed based on the preceding steps and the factors and levels to be studied. You may have chosen a different linear graph and modified entirely different columns. These designs would be equally correct to use.

21.1.3 Other Applications

Using the multilevel techniques, a nine-level factor can be fitted into an L_{27}. A six-level factor can be designed into the first two columns of the L_{18}. Multilevel arrangements are appropriate wherever the factor levels can be tied to a set of columns grouped together in a linear graph. On the other hand, if an appropriate linear graph is not available, multilevel techniques cannot be applied to that orthogonal array. Therefore this tool cannot be applied to an L_{12}, which has no linear graph. Since the L_{18} linear graph consists of a single line between the first two columns, only six-level factors as mentioned above can be incorporated. If a nine-level factor must be designed into the experiment, you must go up to at least an L_{27}.

Although we have demonstrated how to incorporate four-, six-, eight-, and nine-level factors into an orthogonal array, we have yet to deal with odd numbers of levels such as five or seven. This situation will be addressed in describing the next special design technique in Section 21.2.

21.1.4 Interactions Involving Multilevel Factors

Besides being able to study a multilevel factor as a main effect, we can also investigate the influence of interactions between it and other factors within the experiment. There is, however, a price to pay in terms of degrees of freedom. For the interaction of a four-level factor and a two-level factor in an $L_2{}^n$, three degrees of freedom,

$$(4 - 1) \times (2 - 1) = 3 \text{ df},$$

are required. Therefore, three columns of the orthogonal array must be set aside for the interaction in addition to the columns already reserved for the four-level factor (three columns) and the two-level factor (one column) as individual effects. As with an interaction between a pair of two-level factors, we would need to develop a matrix (2 by 4 in this case) and construct an interaction graph to obtain a clear picture of the exact relationship. We may find a substantial interaction effect throughout the region studied, in only a segment of the area investigated, or not at all. If the effect is significant, the interaction will need to be considered in constructing the prediction equation.

Interactions involving larger multilevel factors can be incorporated as well, but at a cost of even more degrees of freedom. For an eight-level factor, a two-level factor, and their interaction, we would need at least an L_{16} just to study the two together:

$$\begin{aligned}
\text{8-level factor: df} &= 8 - 1 &&= 7 \\
\text{2-level factor: df} &= 2 - 1 &&= 1 \\
\text{interaction: df} &= (8 - 1) \times (2 - 1) &&= 7 \\
\hline
&\text{Total df} &&= 15 \text{ df}
\end{aligned}$$

An L_{32} or larger orthogonal array would be required to study additional effects. An interaction involving a nine-level factor and a three-level factor would require a total of 26 degrees of freedom including the amount that would be needed by the two main effects themselves.

The point of this discussion is to inform you of the capability of studying interactions involving multilevel factors. However, for the sake of experiment efficiency and cost, caution should be taken. Careful consideration should go into the defining of factors potentially consisting of many levels so that multilevel interactions can be avoided as often as possible.

21.2 DUMMY TREATMENT

With the selection of an $L_3{}^n$ series orthogonal array, a balanced experiment requires the defining of three levels (or multiples of three levels—multilevel arrangements) for each factor. However, it is not uncommon in the design of experiments comprising three levels that one or two of the factors is restricted to just two levels. In the use of multilevel arrangements, the additional number of levels may not exactly match one of the special cases covered by multilevel arrangements. For example, we wish to add a five-level factor to an L_{18} instead of six levels, a six- or seven-level factor to an L_{16} or L_{32} instead of eight levels, or seven or eight levels to an L_{27} instead of nine levels. The purpose of dummy treatment is to provide a technique for assigning additional levels so that the experimental design will remain balanced.

21.2.1 Treating Two-Level Factors in $L_3{}^n$ Orthogonal Arrays

To balance the $L_3{}^n$ orthogonal array, each of the factors must be defined in terms of three levels. Since we either cannot or prefer not to define three different levels, we must repeat one of the existing two levels. The rule of thumb is to repeat that level for which you have the least current understanding. For example, one of the variables under study is the type of fixture. One level is defined as the existing fixture. The second level is defined as the new fixture. Since less is obviously known about the second one, level 2 is repeated as level 3. In the analysis, the results of levels 2 and 3 are combined and compared against level 1.

An experimentation team defined the following factors and corresponding settings.

	low	medium	high
Stencil	existing	new	
Squeegee velocity	20 mm/s	35 mm/s	50 mm/s
Squeegee pressure	110	135	150
Solder volume	low	moderate	high

Step 1: Count the degrees of freedom required for the factors (and interactions) under investigation.

$$\begin{aligned} \text{3-level factors: df} &= 3 \times 2 = 6 \\ \text{2-level factor: df} &= 1 \\ \text{dummy levels: df} &= 1 \\ \hline \text{Total df} &= 8 \text{ df} \end{aligned}$$

Note that each dummy treatment costs one degree of freedom.

Step 2: Choose the orthogonal array that will accommodate the total number of degrees of freedom required:

$$L_9\ (3^4)\text{: degrees of freedom} = 4 \times (3 - 1) = 8 \text{ df}$$

Step 3: Select a column for the two-level factor from the orthogonal array below.

L_9 (3^4)

No.	1	2	3	4
1	1	1	1	1
2	1	2	2	2
3	1	3	3	3
4	2	1	2	3
5	2	2	3	1
6	2	3	1	2
7	3	1	3	2
8	3	2	1	3
9	3	3	2	1

Although stencil could have been assigned to any of the columns, column 1 was selected because it consisted of the fewest level changes from one experimental run to another and stencil was the most time consuming factor to change of the factors being studied.

Step 4: Select the level of the two-level factor at which you would like more information. Since less was known concerning the new stencil, the new stencil (level 2) was repeated as level 3, or 2′.

Step 5: Modify the levels in the column selected for the two-level factor so that the selected level is repeated.

Step 6: Assign the three-level factors to the remaining columns.

Exp. Run#	Stencil	Squeegee velocity	Squeegee pressure	Solder volume
1	1	1	1	1
2	1	2	2	2
3	1	3	3	3
4	2	1	2	3
5	2	2	3	1
6	2	3	1	2
7	2′	1	3	2
8	2′	2	1	3
9	2′	3	2	1

21.2.2 Combining Dummy Treatment with Multilevel Arrangements

Another capability that dummy treatment provides is the ability to treat factors that have several more levels than the rest of the factors under study, but does not exactly fit the special cases covered by multilevel arrangements. A three-phase strategy combining both of these techniques is:

1. determine the closest or most appropriate multilevel arrangement possibility and select the required orthogonal array,
2. use multilevel arrangements to modify the array,
3. use dummy treatment to fill in the vacant levels.

Suppose we wish to investigate the following factors.

6-level factor : A

2-level factors: B, C, D, E, F, G, H

Step 1: Since a six-level factor will not fit into an L_2 orthogonal array, determine the next greatest number of levels that would.

8 levels

Step 2: Count the degrees of freedom.

$$\begin{aligned} \text{8-level factor: df} &= & 7 \\ \text{2-level factors: df} &= 7 \times 1 = & 7 \\ \hline \text{Total df} &= & 14 \text{ df} \end{aligned}$$

Step 3: Choose the orthogonal array that will accommodate the total degrees of freedom required.

$$L_{16}\ (2^{15})\text{: degrees of freedom} = 15 \times (2 - 1) = 15 \text{ df}$$

L_{16} (2^{15})

No.	1	2	3	4	5	6	7	8	9	10	11	12	13	14	15
1	1	1	1	1	1	1	1	1	1	1	1	1	1	1	1
2	1	1	1	1	1	1	1	2	2	2	2	2	2	2	2
3	1	1	1	2	2	2	2	1	1	1	1	2	2	2	2
4	1	1	1	2	2	2	2	2	2	2	2	1	1	1	1
5	1	2	2	1	1	2	2	1	1	2	2	1	1	2	2
6	1	2	2	1	1	2	2	2	2	1	1	2	2	1	1
7	1	2	2	2	2	1	1	1	1	2	2	2	2	1	1
8	1	2	2	2	2	1	1	2	2	1	1	1	1	2	2
9	2	1	2	1	2	1	2	1	2	1	2	1	2	1	2
10	2	1	2	1	2	1	2	2	1	2	1	2	1	2	1
11	2	1	2	2	1	2	1	1	2	1	2	2	1	2	1
12	2	1	2	2	1	2	1	2	1	2	1	1	2	1	2
13	2	2	1	1	2	2	1	1	2	2	1	1	2	2	1
14	2	2	1	1	2	2	1	2	1	1	2	2	1	1	2
15	2	2	1	2	1	1	2	1	2	2	1	2	1	1	2
16	2	2	1	2	1	1	2	2	1	1	2	1	2	2	1

Step 4: Use multilevel arrangements to modify the orthogonal array (reference Section 21.1.2: Eight-Level Factor).

Modified L_{16}

Run#	Modified	4	5	6	7	12	13	14	15
1	1	1	1	1	1	1	1	1	1
2	2	1	1	1	1	2	2	2	2
3	1	2	2	2	2	2	2	2	2
4	2	2	2	2	2	1	1	1	1
5	3	1	1	2	2	1	1	2	2
6	4	1	1	2	2	2	2	1	1
7	3	2	2	1	1	2	2	1	1
8	4	2	2	1	1	1	1	2	2
9	5	1	2	1	2	1	2	1	2
10	6	1	2	1	2	2	1	2	1
11	5	2	1	2	1	2	1	2	1
12	6	2	1	2	1	1	2	1	2
13	7	1	2	2	1	1	2	2	1
14	8	1	2	2	1	2	1	1	2
15	7	2	1	1	2	2	1	1	2
16	8	2	1	1	2	1	2	2	1

Step 5: Count the number of spare levels of the multilevel factor. Fill the spare levels with those levels at which you would like more information. Since two levels are vacant, we can elect to repeat any two of the six previously defined levels. In this experiment, we selected level 1 and level 2.

Step 6: Assign the two-level factors B, C, D, E, F, G, and H to the remaining columns.

Solution

	A	B	C	D	E	F	G	H	e
Run#		4	5	6	7	12	13	14	15
1	1	1	1	1	1	1	1	1	1
2	2	1	1	1	1	2	2	2	2
3	1	2	2	2	2	2	2	2	2
4	2	2	2	2	2	1	1	1	1
5	3	1	1	2	2	1	1	2	2
6	4	1	1	2	2	2	2	1	1
7	3	2	2	1	1	2	2	1	1
8	4	2	2	1	1	1	1	2	2
9	5	1	2	1	2	1	2	1	2

Solution *cont'd.*

Run#	A	B 4	C 5	D 6	E 7	F 12	G 13	H 14	e 15
10	6	1	2	1	2	2	1	2	1
11	5	2	1	2	1	2	1	2	1
12	6	2	1	2	1	1	2	1	2
13	1′	1	2	2	1	1	2	2	1
14	2′	1	2	2	1	2	1	1	2
15	1′	2	1	1	2	2	1	1	2
16	2′	2	1	1	2	1	2	2	1

Since there was one more column available than the number of two-level factors to be assigned, a spare column was left over as an error column. Because we arbitrarily assigned the two-level factors from left to right, column 15 became the error column.

21.3 COMBINATION DESIGNS

Combination designs relate to the merging of two or more factors into one unified parameter. Combination designs can be useful in assigning a pair of two-level factors to an $L_3{}^n$ orthogonal array. Instead of using dummy treatment and requiring an additional two degrees of freedom, the two factors can be jointly assigned to the same column using up a total of only two degrees of freedom. This reduction can be particularly helpful in reducing the size of the experiment when a few degrees of freedom are the difference between using one orthogonal array and the next larger array. One restriction of the added efficiency is that interactions between either of the combined factors and other factors can no longer be incorporated into the orthogonal array.

For example, let's say that we wish to investigate twelve three-level factors and two two-level factors. If we were to use dummy treatment on the two two-level factors, the total required degrees of freedom would be 28 df.

	Dummy treatment	Combination design
3-level factors: df	$= 12 \times 2 = 24$	$13 \times 2 = 26$
2-level factors: df	$= 2 \times 1 = 2$	
dummy treatment: df	$= 2 \times 1 = 2$	
Total df	= 28 df	26 df

Since an L_{27} has only 26 degrees of freedom, we would have to go up to an L_{54}. By using the combination design technique, the two two-level factors become one three-level factor, the required degrees of freedom are reduced to 26, and the L_{27} can be used—reducing the required size of the experiment by half.

A second application of combination design is when not all levels of one factor are available for all levels of another factor. Although the primary application of this technique is with two two-level factors, we can apply an extension of this type of design to three or more factors. This move will allow us the ability to investigate numerous factors collectively which could not otherwise be studied and to determine the best combination of the combined factors. However, in the case of three or more individual components' having been merged together, the confounding effect prohibits analysis of each of the elements on an individual basis.

21.3.1 Two Two-Level Factors

Suppose we consider the following effects:

2-level factors:	A, B
3-level factors:	C, D, E

2-level factors:	df $= 2 \times 1 =$	2
3-level factors:	df $= 3 \times 2 =$	6
dummy treatment:	df $= 2 \times 1 =$	2
Total	df $=$	10 df

As shown in the degrees of freedom calculation, we would need to select the smallest L_{3n} orthogonal array which has at least 10 degrees of freedom. This is the L_{18}. The alternative is to use the combination design technique and consolidate A and B as one three-level factor. This choice would reduce the required degrees of freedom to 8 and enable us to use the L_9, which is half the size of the alternative orthogonal array. The appropriate steps for combination design are:

Step 1: List all possible combinations of the pair of two-level factors.

$A_1B_1 \quad (AB)_1$

$A_1B_2 \quad (AB)_2$

$A_2B_1 \quad (AB)_3$

$A_2B_2 \quad (AB)_4$

Step 2: Select the levels of the "combined" factor to be run in the experiment.

A_1B_1	$(AB)_1$	level 1
A_1B_2	$(AB)_2$	level 2
A_2B_1	$(AB)_3$	level 3
A_2B_2	$(AB)_4$	

As the price of reducing the required degrees of freedom, we will be unable to run the combination of A_2B_2 in the experiment.

Step 3: Assign each of the factors to a column in the orthogonal array.

$L_9\ (3^4)$

	C	D	E	(AB)
No.	1	2	3	4
1	1	1	1	1
2	1	2	2	2
3	1	3	3	3
4	2	1	2	3
5	2	2	3	1
6	2	3	1	2
7	3	1	3	2
8	3	2	1	3
9	3	3	2	1

Analysis of the regular three-level factors is performed in the traditional manner, but this is not true for the "combined" factors, which are no longer orthogonal. However, we can still obtain an estimate of the relative individual effects and select preferred levels for each of the two factors. Let's look at the following S/N response table.

level	C	D	E	(AB)				
1	10.0	12.0	11.0	9.5	A_1B_1	9.5	A_1B_1	9.5
2	15.0	12.5	12.0	13.0	A_1B_2	13.0		
3	10.0	10.5	12.0	12.5			A_2B_1	12.5
	5	2	1			3.5		3.0

C, D, and E were examined in a regular manner. For A, we must compare A_1B_1 and A_2B_1. For B, we must look at A_1B_1 and A_1B_2. From the study, the strongest effects were C, B, and A, in that order. The selected levels for these factors are: C_2, B_2, A_2.

21.3.2 Multiple Factors

In studying a surface mount assembly process, the experimentation team wished to investigate various stencil characteristics. However, not all levels for each stencil were available for each level of the other stencil factors.

Step 1: List the factors and levels to be studied.

A. Stencil Thickness	B. Stencil Hole Geometry (Hole/Pad Ratio)	C. Stencil Material
1. 6 mils	1. 78%	1. Brass
2. 8 mils	2. 100%	2. Stainless Steel
3. 10 mils		3. Nickel Plated

Step 2: Generate a list of all of the possible combinations of the factor levels identified in step 1.

$A_1B_1C_1$	$A_2B_1C_1$	$A_3B_1C_1$
$A_1B_1C_2$	$A_2B_1C_2$	$A_3B_1C_2$
$A_1B_1C_3$	$A_2B_1C_1$	$A_3B_1C_3$
$A_1B_2C_1$	$A_2B_2C_1$	$A_3B_2C_1$
$A_1B_2C_2$	$A_2B_2C_2$	$A_3B_2C_2$
$A_1B_2C_3$	$A_2B_2C_3$	$A_3B_2C_3$

Step 3: Identify the combinations of factor levels from step 2 that are available.

$A_1B_2C_1$	$A_3B_2C_1$
$A_2B_2C_1$	$A_3B_2C_2$
$A_3B_1C_1$	$A_3B_2C_3$

Step 4: Redefine the available factor level combinations as one factor, with the number of levels corresponding to the number of available combinations.

$A_1B_2C_1$	$(ABC)_1$	level 1
$A_2B_2C_1$	$(ABC)_2$	level 2
$A_3B_1C_1$	$(ABC)_3$	level 3
$A_3B_2C_1$	$(ABC)_4$	level 4
$A_3B_2C_2$	$(ABC)_5$	level 5
$A_3B_2C_3$	$(ABC)_6$	level 6

Step 5: Use multilevel arrangements and dummy treatment to complete the designing of the experiment. In the analysis, the "combined" factor can be analyzed as a regular factor. However, confounding will not permit further analysis of the individual components of this "combined" factor.

21.4 SLIDING LEVELS

Interactions can have two major effects on an experiment. For one, the functional range of a factor can change as the values of those factors that have an interactive relationship with it vary. Although meaningful results can be produced within the initial factor boundaries, these optimal levels may no longer be capable of producing good product as the interacting factors change. This situation can produce catastrophic results in an experimental run and provide little additional insight into understanding the process/product being studied. Second, including the study of an interaction within an experiment costs degrees of freedom. The additional degrees of freedom result in larger orthogonal arrays and more experimental runs, which subsequently increases the cost of the experiment.

By understanding that an interaction may exist between two such factors that would produce a shift in the functional range of the first factor as the value of the second factor changes, we can modify the experiment ahead of time to reduce the potential danger. If we adjust values of the first factor as the level of the second factor changes, meaningful results can continue to be produced in the experiment. A second ramification is that by reducing the impact of changes in the second factor for different levels of the first factor, we have effectively minimized the effect of the interaction between the two factors. This consequence allows us to reduce the scale of the experiment since we no longer need to include the interaction as one of the effects under study. As a result, a smaller, more efficient, and cost effective experiment can be conducted.

21.4.1 Wavesolder Experiment

In a wavesolder study, the preheater settings and the conveyor speed were selected to be included within the experiment. The conveyor consisted of one belt while the heaters consisted of three sections with their own individual settings. Since the heat generated from the three heating sections tended to be additive, the levels for the preheater were defined in terms of the sum of the three temperatures. The standard operating boundaries for each of these two factors were:

	low	high
Preheater	350–370–380°F (1100 cumulative)	400–440–460°F (1300 cumulative)
Conveyor speed	5 ft/min	7 ft/min

However, the process engineer knows that excessive heat will be created at 390–420–440°F (1300) and 5 ft/min, which will damage the circuit board and the components. He also knows that the heater settings of 350–370–380°F (1100) and a conveyor speed of 7 ft/min will produce insufficient heat and result in poor solderability.

Step 1: Develop a matrix for determining feasible combinations of the two factors.

Conveyor Speed	Temperature Range
A_1 = 5 ft/min	350 – 380°F
	370 – 400°F
	380 – 420°F
	(1100) (1200)
A_2 = 6 ft/min	360 – 390°F
	390 – 420°F
	400 – 440°F
	(1150) (1250)
A_3 = 7 ft/min	380 – 400°F
	400 – 440°F
	420 – 460°F
	(1200) (1300)

Step 2: Set the levels for the second factor (temperature range) based on the functional range for each corresponding level of the first factor (conveyor speed). The levels of temperature (factor B) can be defined as:

B_1 = 50°F less than B_2

B_2 = median of the projected operating range

B_3 = 50°F greater than B_2

	B_1	B_2	B_3
A_1	1100	1150	1200
A_2	1150	1200	1250
A_3	1200	1250	1300

In the analysis of the experiment, we first determine the best level for conveyor speed (factor A) and then we select the best level for the preheaters (factor B). If the best levels were A_2 and B_3, then the appropriate levels would be 6 ft/min and 1250 (390–420–440°F).

21.4.2 Plastic Injection Molding Experiment

During the development of an experiment to study a plastic injection molding operation, concern was raised over the effect of the interaction between nozzle pressure and cure time. To complicate the matter, varying one of the two factors without considering the impact of the other could have drastic effects on the resulting product.

The functional boundaries for each factor are:

Nozzle Pressure	12000 psi	12500 psi
Cure Time	15 hrs	18 hrs

Step 1: Develop a matrix for determining feasible combinations of the two factors.

Nozzle Pressure	Cure Time
A_1 = 12000	15–17 hrs
A_2 = 12500	16–18 hrs

Step 2: Set the levels for the second factor (curve time) based on the functional range for each corresponding level of the first factor (nozzle pressure). The levels of cure time (factor B) can be defined as:

$$B_1 = 2 \text{ hrs less than } B_2$$

$$B_2 = 2 \text{ hrs greater than } B_1$$

	B_1	B_2
A_1	15 hrs	17 hrs
A_2	16 hrs	18 hrs

By defining the levels of cure time in this manner, the optimum cure time for each nozzle pressure setting is included within the ranges of B_1 and B_2. As previously discussed, we are thus saved from having to conduct experimental runs at factor level combinations that are known to produce undesired results.

21.5 NESTED FACTOR DESIGN

As we sometimes have to be reminded, not all experimental factors are equal. In some instances, the levels of some factors even dictate the actual definition of other factors. The term *nested factor* refers to these situations and can be defined as a factor whose levels are defined by the levels of another factor. In other words, the settings of the first factor are "nested" in the settings of the second one. Several factors as well as a single variable may be nested into another factor. The purpose of nested factor design is to address these occasions. The best way to explain the appropriate steps is through an example.

An experiment was conducted to determine the best methods and settings for a surface mount technology operation. The engineers were interested in determining whether to use an infrared or vapor phase system. However, in comparing the two machines, the list of control factors that would describe the infrared machine was different from the group of factors associated with the vapor phase unit. Some factors, such as heat rate increase and assembly material, were common to each. Other factors were *nested* within the factor of machine type (infrared or vapor phase).

The following is a list of the factors under consideration:

Machine type: Vapor Phase, Infrared

Heat rate increase: 2°C/sec, 4°C/sec

Pwb supplier: Aone, Brand X

Nested Factors:

Vapor Phase— Vapor temperature: 200°C, 215°C
Fluid: low boiling temp, high boiling temp

Infrared — Equilibrium temperature: 130°C, 160°C
Atmosphere: air, nitrogen

Step 1: Determine the degrees of freedom and select the appropriate orthogonal array. In addition to considering the degrees of freedom associated with each factor (no. levels − 1), we need to consider the tie between the nested factor and its primary factor. Since the nested factor extends from the definition of the primary factor, we may appropriately refer to machine type as the axial factor.[1] The additional degrees of freedom of the nesting are: (no. of levels: axial factor −1) × (no. of levels: nested factor −1).

Total degrees of freedom required:

Axial factor:	2 − 1	= 1
Regular factors:	2 × (2 − 1)	= 2
Nested factors:	2 × (2 − 1)	= 2
Axial-Nesting:	2 × (2 − 1)(2 − 1)	= 2
	Total df	= 7 df

L_8 degrees of freedom = 7 × (2 − 1) = 7 df

Step 2: Construct a linear graph of the axial factor and its corresponding nested factors (Figure 21-4). To simplify the graph, designate each factor by a corresponding letter.

A: Machine type

Vapor Phase— B′: Vapor temperature
C′: Fluid

Infrared — B″: Equilibrium temperature
C″: Atmosphere

D: Heat rate increase

E: Pwb supplier

Step 3: Select the most appropriate standard linear graph based on the graph from step 2.

Since only two nested factors are involved, we could have selected either standard linear graph in Figure 21-5. If, on the other hand, we had defined three nested factors, we would have had to use the graph on the right.

Figure 21-4 Linear Graph of Axial Factor and Nested Factors

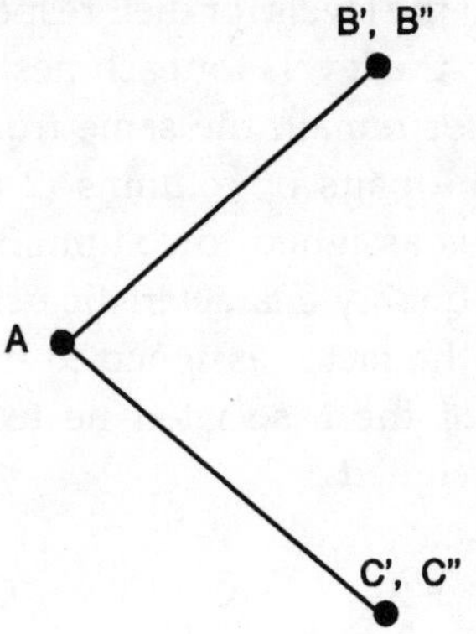

Step 4: Assign the factors from the linear graph to the corresponding columns in the orthogonal array.

No.	A 1	B',B" 2	3	C',C" 4	5	D 6	E 7
1	1	1	1	1	1	1	1
2	1	1	1	2	2	2	2
3	1	2	2	1	1	2	2
4	1	2	2	2	2	1	1
5	2	1	2	1	2	1	2
6	2	1	2	2	1	2	1
7	2	2	1	1	2	2	1
8	2	2	1	2	1	1	2

Figure 21-5 L_8 (2^7) Linear Graphs

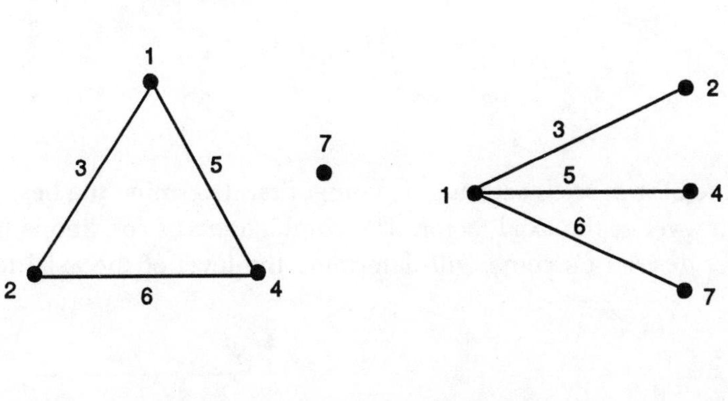

Although it would be tempting to assign additional factors to columns 3 and 5, we should not do so. Let's closely examine these two columns and compare the levels for each experimental run with the levels for their respective nested factors. As illustrated in the following table, the levels for each nested (axial) factor and the adjacent column either change or remain the same from one experimental run to another. This means that the pairs of columns (2 and 3, 4 and 5) are confounded together. If a factor was assigned to column 3 or 5, we could not be sure whether any change in the quality characteristic being measured was a result of the change in the level of the factor assigned to the column or due to a concurrent change in the level of the associated nested factor. Therefore, columns 3 and 5 must remain unassigned.[2]

Experimental Run #	A 1	B′,B″ 2	F′,F″ 3	C′,C″ 4	G′,G″ 5	D 6	E 7
1	1	1 B′	F′1	1 C′	G′1	1	1
2	1	1 B′	F′1	2 C′	G′2	2	2
3	1	2 B′	F′2	1 C′	G′1	2	2
4	1	2 B′	F′2	2 C′	G′2	1	1
5	2	1 B″	F″2	1 C″	G″2	1	2
6	2	1 B″	F″2	2 C″	G″1	2	1
7	2	2 B″	F″1	1 C″	G″2	2	1
8	2	2 B″	F″1	2 C″	G″1	1	2

Since columns 3 and 5 must remain unassigned, the orthogonal array can be reduced to the following:

Experimental Run #	A 1	B′,B″ 2	C′,C″ 4	D 6	E 7
1	1	1	1	1	1
2	1	1	2	2	2
3	1	2	1	2	2
4	1	2	2	1	1
5	2	1	1	1	2
6	2	1	2	2	1
7	2	2	1	2	1
8	2	2	2	1	2

To select the best process settings, we must first determine the best conditions under each level of the axial factor. The combination of conditions that results in the most desired outcome will determine the level of the axial factor to be chosen. Then we can determine the best levels of the other factors and develop a complete prediction equation.

Let's say that in the previous design, the response of interest was a smaller-the-better quality characteristic. Also, the study included noise factors and a resulting outer array. Based on the experimental data, the following S/N ratios were calculated for each experimental run.

Experimental Run #	A 1	B′,B″ 2	C′,C″ 4	D 6	E 7	S/N Ratio
1	1	1	1	1	1	23.85
2	1	1	2	2	2	20.68
3	1	2	1	2	2	22.55
4	1	2	2	1	1	25.33
5	2	1	1	1	2	24.23
6	2	1	2	2	1	27.06
7	2	2	1	2	1	25.43
8	2	2	2	1	2	22.25

To generate the response table, we must determine the average response for each factor level. This also means that we must calculate the average response for each nested factor level as well.

$$B'_1 = \frac{23.85 + 20.68}{2} = 22.265 \text{ db}$$

$$B'_2 = \frac{22.55 + 25.33}{2} = 23.940 \text{ db}$$

The other nested factor levels can be determined in the same manner. The S/N response table from the preceding data is:

S/N Response Table

level	A	B′	B″	C′	C″	D	E
1	23.1025	22.2650	25.6450	23.2000	24.8300	23.9150	25.4175
2	24.7425	23.9400	23.8400	23.0050	24.6550	23.9300	22.4275
	1.640	**1.675**	**1.805**	.195	.175	.015	**2.990**

In analyzing the table, B′ is significant for the vapor phase machine with level 2 being the best setting, and B″ is significant for the infrared unit with level 1 as the preferred level.

The predicted S/N for the vapor phase machine is equal to the average S/N for the vapor phase experimental runs plus the effect of each of its strong nested factors. In this example, only one nested factor was strong. The resulting predicted value can be computed as follows:

$$\hat{\eta} = \overline{A}_1 + (\overline{B'}_2 - \overline{A}_1)$$

$$= 23.1025 + (23.9400 - 23.1025) = 23.94 \text{ db}$$

The predicted S/N for the infrared unit can be determined in a similar manner. The result is:

$$\hat{\eta} = \overline{A}_2 + (\overline{B''}_1 - \overline{A}_2)$$

$$= 24.7425 + (25.6450 - 24.7425) = 25.645 \text{ db}$$

From comparing the two results, we can conclude that the infrared machine (A_2) should be preferred over the vapor phase system (A_1). Next, we need to calculate the overall prediction. The response table reveals that factor E has a strong effect, and it should therefore be added to the equation along with the combined nested effect contributed by factors A and B″ (infrared machine and equilibrium temperature, respectively). The prediction equation then becomes:

$$\hat{\eta} = \overline{T} + (\overline{A_2B''}_1 - \overline{T}) + (\overline{E}_1 - \overline{T}),$$

where

$$\overline{T} = (23.85 + \ldots + 22.25)/8 = 23.9225$$

$$\hat{\eta} = \overline{A_2B''}_1 + \overline{E}_1 - \overline{T}$$

$$\hat{\eta} = 25.645 + 25.4175 - 23.9225 = 27.14 \text{ db}$$

If the experiment had consisted of an inner orthogonal array only, we would have performed the same procedures for the average response and determined an optimal $\hat{\mu}$ instead.

Although we only investigated main effects in the example, we could have also incorporated interactions between unnested factors. However, the consideration of interactions between two nested factors or between a nested factor and one that is unnested is discouraged for several reasons. If in the previous example we had considered the interaction between nested factors B and C, the interaction column would have been column 6. To study the interaction, we would have to look separately at B′ with C′ and B″ with C″. This process would make the calculations more tedious and inject potential confusion. Since the first four rows now have to be analyzed separately from the last four rows of the array, we now have the same situation between columns 6 and 7 as we have with columns 2 and 3 as well as with columns 4 and 5, wherein the latter column in each pair must remain unassigned. Therefore, we have reduced the efficiency of the orthogonal array. If indeed a potentially strong interaction exists, sliding levels or redefining of the factors would result in a more efficient design.

21.6 IDLE COLUMN METHOD

Another technique that can be helpful for treating experimental designs with a mix of different levels is the idle column method. This method is most frequently used when the study involves a set of predominately two-level factors interspersed with several three-level factors. The technique can also be helpful with the insertion of four-level and seven-level factors into $L_2{}^n$ orthogonal arrays and seven-level variables into $L_2{}^n$ orthogonal arrays. Although multilevel arrangements and dummy treatment can serve the same purpose, the idle column method creates more efficient designs when more than one factor must be specially treated.

For example, let's consider a study involving six two-level factors and four three-level factors. Multilevel arrangements (defining the three-level factors as four-level variables) with dummy treatment would require:

$$\begin{aligned} \text{two-level factors df} &= 6 \times 1 = 6 \\ \text{three-level factors df} &= 4 \times 2 = 8 \\ \text{dummy treatment df} &= 4 \times 1 = 4 \\ \hline \text{Total df} &= 18 \text{ df} \end{aligned}$$

This treatment would require an L_{32}.

Pure dummy treatment (defining the two-level factors as three-level variables) would require:

$$\begin{aligned} \text{three-level factors df} &= 4 \times 2 = 8 \\ \text{two-level factors df} &= 6 \times 1 = 6 \\ \text{dummy treatment df} &= 6 \times 1 = 6 \\ \hline \text{Total df} &= 20 \text{ df} \end{aligned}$$

This approach would call for an L_{27}.

The idle column method would require:

$$\begin{aligned} \text{two-level factors df} &= 6 \times 1 = \ \ 6 \\ \text{idle column df} &= \qquad\quad\ \ 1 \\ \text{three-level factors df} &= \underline{4 \times 2 = \ \ 8} \\ \text{Total df} &= \qquad\ 15 \text{ df} \end{aligned}$$

This method would require only an L_{16}, which is the most efficient of the three alternatives under consideration.

In constructing the linear graphs and designing the experiment, the approach is very similar to the nested factor design. Instead of the axial factor, an unassigned column is used as the converging point. Then each of the three-level factors is assigned to two columns associated with a point and the line connecting it to the idle column, much like each of the nested factors.

Let's demonstrate the idle column technique through the following generic example:

two-level factors: A, B, C, D

three-level factors: E, F, G, H, I

Step 1: Determine the degrees of freedom and select the appropriate orthogonal array.

$$\begin{aligned} \text{two-level factors df} &= 4 \times 1 = \ \ 4 \\ \text{idle column df} &= \qquad\quad\ \ 1 \\ \text{three-level factors df} &= \underline{5 \times 2 = 10} \\ \text{Total df} &= 15 \text{ df} \\ L_{16}\ (2^{15}) \text{ df} &= 15 \times (2-1) = 15 \text{ df} \end{aligned}$$

Therefore, the L_{16} is the appropriate orthogonal array.

Step 2: Construct a linear graph (Figure 21-6) with a dot or circle representing the idle column connected to each three-level factor by a line.

Figure 21-6 Idle Column Linear Graph

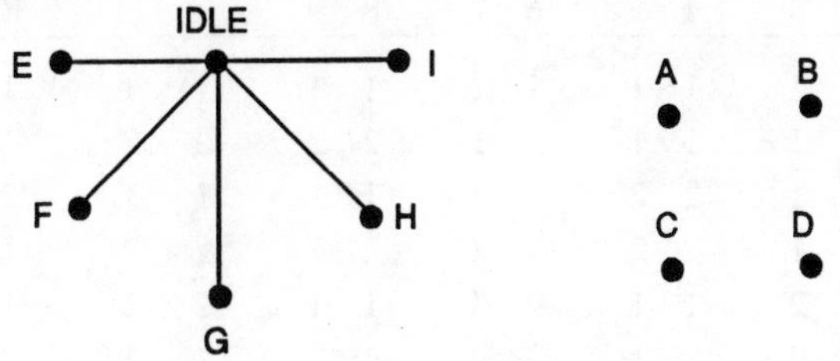

Step 3: Draw a circle or oval around the point and adjoining line representing each three-level factor.

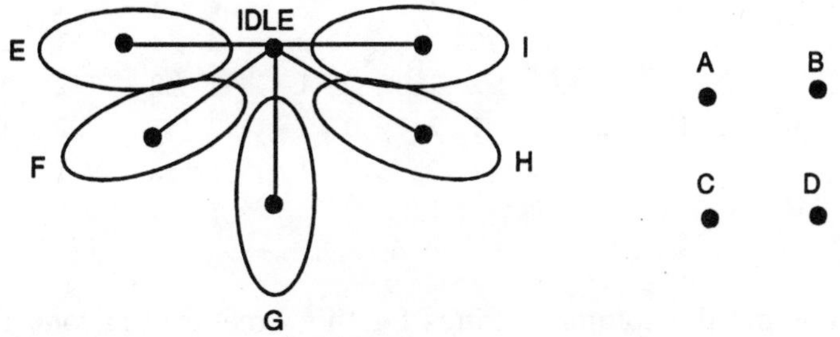

Step 4: Select the most appropriate standard linear graph based on the graph from step 2.

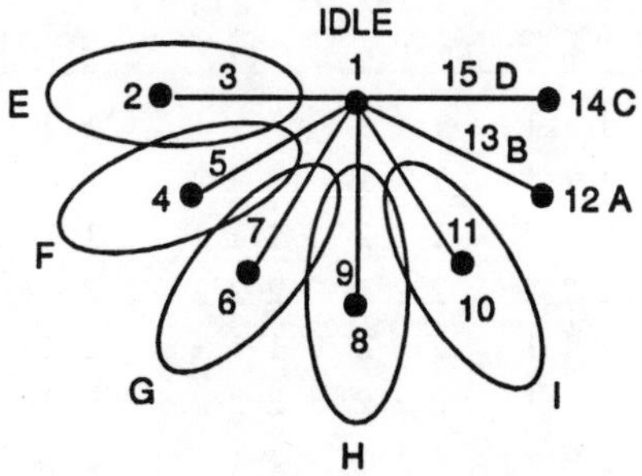

Step 5: Assign the factors from the linear graph to the corresponding columns in the orthogonal array.

L16 (2^{15})

No.	IDLE	E		F		G		H		I		A	B	C	D
	1	2	3	4	5	6	7	8	9	10	11	12	13	14	15
1	1	1	1	1	1	1	1	1	1	1	1	1	1	1	1
2	1	1	1	1	1	1	1	2	2	2	2	2	2	2	2
3	1	1	1	2	2	2	2	1	1	1	1	2	2	2	2
4	1	1	1	2	2	2	2	2	2	2	2	1	1	1	1
5	1	2	2	1	1	2	2	1	1	2	2	1	1	2	2
6	1	2	2	1	1	2	2	2	2	1	1	2	2	1	1
7	1	2	2	2	2	1	1	1	1	2	2	2	2	1	1
8	1	2	2	2	2	1	1	2	2	1	1	1	1	2	2
9	2	1	2	1	2	1	2	1	2	1	2	1	2	1	2
10	2	1	2	1	2	1	2	2	1	2	1	2	1	2	1
11	2	1	2	2	1	2	1	1	2	1	2	2	1	2	1
12	2	1	2	2	1	1	1	2	1	2	1	1	2	1	2
13	2	2	1	1	2	2	1	1	2	2	1	1	2	2	1
14	2	2	1	1	2	2	1	2	1	1	2	2	1	1	2
15	2	2	1	2	1	1	2	1	2	2	1	2	1	1	2
16	2	2	1	2	1	1	2	2	1	1	2	1	2	2	1

Step 6: Redefine the column settings for the three-level factors. Use dummy treatment on the fourth level.

L16 (2^{15})

Run #	IDLE	E	F	G	H	I	A	B	C	D
	1	2, 3	4, 5	6, 7	8, 9	10, 11	12	13	14	15
1	1	1 1 1	1 1 1	1 1 1	1 1 1	1 1 1	1	1	1	1
2	1	1 1 1	1 1 1	1 1 1	2 2 2	2 2 2	2	2	2	2
3	1	1 1 1	2 2 2	2 2 2	1 1 1	1 1 1	2	2	2	2
4	1	1 1 1	2 2 2	2 2 2	2 2 2	2 2 2	1	1	1	1
5	1	2 2 2	1 1 1	2 2 2	1 1 1	2 2 2	1	1	2	2
6	1	2 2 2	1 1 1	2 2 2	2 2 2	1 1 1	2	2	1	1
7	1	2 2 2	2 2 2	1 1 1	1 1 1	2 2 2	2	2	1	1
8	1	2 2 2	2 2 2	1 1 1	2 2 2	1 1 1	1	1	2	2
9	2	1 2 3	1 2 3	1 2 3	1 2 3	1 2 3	1	2	1	2
10	2	1 2 3	1 2 3	1 2 3	2 1 3′	2 1 2′	2	1	2	1
11	2	1 2 3	2 1 2′	2 1 1′	1 2 3	1 2 3	2	1	2	1
12	2	1 2 3	2 1 2′	2 1 1′	2 1 3′	2 1 2′	1	2	1	2

$L_{16}\ (2^{15})$

Run #	IDLE	E	F	G	H	I	A	B	C	D
	1	2, 3	4, 5	6, 7	8, 9	10, 11	12	13	14	15
13	2	2 1 1′	1 2 3	2 1 1′	1 2 3	2 1 2′	1	2	2	1
14	2	2 1 1′	1 2 3	2 1 1′	2 1 3′	1 2 3	2	1	1	2
15	2	2 1 1′	2 1 2′	1 2 3	1 2 3	2 1 2′	2	1	1	2
16	2	2 1 1′	2 1 2′	1 2 3	2 1 3′	1 2 3	1	2	2	1

Now that we have designed an experiment using the idle column method, let's perform the analysis. We will use the same experimental design and will analyze the signal-to-noise ratios calculated from the raw data. If we were looking at raw data instead, the same procedures would apply.

$L_{16}\ (2^{15})$

Run #	IDLE	E	F	G	H	I	A	B	C	D	S/N
	1	2, 3	4, 5	6, 7	8, 9	10, 11	12	13	14	15	Ratio
1	1	1 1 1	1 1 1	1 1 1	1 1 1	1 1 1	1	1	1	1	15.64
2	1	1 1 1	1 1 1	1 1 1	2 2 2	2 2 2	2	2	2	2	18.86
3	1	1 1 1	2 2 2	2 2 2	1 1 1	1 1 1	2	2	2	2	15.00
4	1	1 1 1	2 2 2	2 2 2	2 2 2	2 2 2	1	1	1	1	22.07
5	1	2 2 2	1 1 1	2 2 2	1 1 1	2 2 2	1	1	2	2	19.65
6	1	2 2 2	1 1 1	2 2 2	2 2 2	1 1 1	2	2	1	1	23.11
7	1	2 2 2	2 2 2	1 1 1	1 1 1	2 2 2	2	2	1	1	22.27
8	1	2 2 2	2 2 2	1 1 1	2 2 2	1 1 1	1	1	2	2	22.97
9	2	1 2 3	1 2 3	1 2 3	1 2 3	1 2 3	1	2	1	2	20.28
10	2	1 2 3	1 2 3	1 2 3	2 1 3′	2 1 2′	2	1	2	1	25.61
11	2	1 2 3	2 1 2′	2 1 1′	1 2 3	1 2 3	2	1	2	1	20.91
12	2	1 2 3	2 1 2′	2 1 1′	2 1 3′	2 1 2′	1	2	1	2	23.07
13	2	2 1 1′	1 2 3	2 1 1′	1 2 3	2 1 2′	1	2	2	1	19.35
14	2	2 1 1′	1 2 3	2 1 1′	2 1 3′	1 2 3	2	1	1	2	12.90
15	2	2 1 1′	2 1 2′	1 2 3	1 2 3	2 1 2′	2	1	1	2	19.25
16	2	2 1 1′	2 1 2′	1 2 3	2 1 3′	1 2 3	1	2	2	1	18.75

From the computations for each experimental run, we will want to construct three sets of response tables. These individual tables represent:

1. average response or S/N for the two levels of each of the three-level factors when the idle column is at level 1

2. average response or S/N for the two levels of each of the three-level factors when the idle column is at level 2

3. average response or S/N for the two levels of the idle column and the two-level factors

S/N Response Table

level	E	F	G	H	I
Idle	E_1 17.8925	F_1 19.3150	G_1 19.9350	H_1 18.1400	I_1 19.1800
Column 1	**E_2 22.0000**	**F_2 20.5775**	G_2 19.9575	**H_2 21.7525**	**I_2 20.7125**
	4.1075	**1.2625**	0.0225	**3.6125**	**1.5325**

S/N Response Table

level	E	F	G	H	I
Idle	**E_3 22.4675**	F_3 19.5350	**G_3 20.9725**	H_3 19.9475	I_3 18.2100
Column 2	E_1' 17.5625	F_2' 20.4950	G_1' 19.0575	H_3' 20.0825	**I_2' 21.8200**
	4.9050	0.960	**1.9150**	0.1350	**3.6100**

S/N Response Table

level	idle column	A	B	C	D
1	19.94625	20.22250	19.87500	19.823750	**20.96375**
2	20.01500	19.73875	20.08625	20.137500	18.99750
	0.06875	0.48375	0.21125	0.313750	**1.96625**

Next, we need to identify the strong effects. Similarly to previous analyses, we can initially compare the differences between levels within each of the tables and look for a logical break that will separate the significant and nonsignificant factors into approximately two equal groups. The factors identified as the strongest effects and the corresponding recommended levels are:

$$E_2,\ F_2,\ H_2,\ I_2,\ E_3,\ G_3,\ D_1.$$

E_2 was obtained from experiments with the idle column at level 1, whereas E_3 was the best level during runs with the idle column at level 2. To compare the levels, we must make some adjustments based on the average result for the common level, which for factor E is level 1.

$$\overline{E}_{1adj} = \frac{\overline{E}_1 + \overline{E}_1'}{2} = \frac{17.8925 + 17.5625}{2} = 17.7275$$

This value is used to determine the amount that we need to adjust the other two levels.

$$\bar{E}_{1adj} - \bar{E}_1 = 17.7275 - 17.8925 = -.165$$

$$\bar{E}_{1adj} - \bar{E}_1' = 17.7275 - 17.5625 = .165$$

We can then adjust $\bar{E}_2$ and $\bar{E}_3$.

$$\bar{E}_{2adj} = 22.0000 - .165 = 22.1650$$

$$\bar{E}_{3adj} = 22.4675 + .165 = 22.6325$$

For relative comparisons, we have:

$$\bar{E}_{1adj} = 17.7275$$

$$\bar{E}_{2adj} = 22.1650$$

$$\mathbf{\bar{E}_{3adj} = 22.6325}$$

From these values, we see that E_3 is the best of the three alternatives.

If we were to make similar adjustments to the other treated factors using the same procedures, we could develop a combined response table that reflects the relative comparisons among each of the three levels for each of the three level factors. We could also compare the relative strength of all of the factors under study.

Adjusted S/N Response Table

level	E	F	G	H	I
1	17.7275	19.27375	19.49625	18.174375	19.73375
2	22.1650	**20.53625**	19.51875	**21.786875**	**21.26625**
3	**22.6325**	19.57625	**21.41125**	19.980625	17.65625
	4.90500	1.26250	1.91500	3.612500	3.61000

S/N Response Table

level	idle column	A	B	C	D
1	19.94625	20.22250	19.87500	19.823750	**20.96375**
2	20.01500	19.73875	20.08625	20.137500	18.99750
	0.06875	0.48375	0.21125	0.313750	1.96625

Since the dummy treated level for factor H was level 3 and both were run at idle column level 2, adjustments for factor H have to be made differently. In this case, we would use the difference between the average response for the two levels of the idle column to make the adjustments.

$$\frac{\text{Idle Column}_1 + \text{Idle Column}_2}{2} = \frac{19.94625 + 20.01500}{2}$$

$$= 19.980625$$

$$\text{Idle Column Adjustment}_1 = 19.980625 - 19.94625 = .034375$$

$$\text{Idle Column Adjustment}_2 = 19.980625 - 20.01500 = -.034375$$

$$\overline{H}_1 \text{ adjusted} = 18.1400 + .034375 = 18.174375$$

$$\overline{H}_2 \text{ adjusted} = 21.7525 + .034375 = 21.786875$$

$$\overline{H}_3 \text{ adjusted} = \frac{19.9475 + 20.0825}{2} - .034375 = 19.980625$$

Although the study included examples of dummy treating all three levels, we recommend that the experiment be designed so that the level being treated and its treated counterpart be assigned to separate idle column levels. This precaution insures that we consistently use the same analysis techniques from factor to factor.

From the combined response table, we see that the strongest effects were E, H, and I with F, G, and D moderately strong. Based on values from the table, we would make the following recommendations:

Strongly recommended	Mildly recommended
E_3	F_2
H_2	G_3
I_2	D_1

These conclusions are consistent with the analysis performed with the three separate response charts. You could analyze the data with either the three response tables or the single combined table, or perform both and compare the results to insure consistency. As with all of the previous analyses, the prediction equation is based on the strong effects only.

Since the idle column method is alike in structure to nested factor design, we could have investigated interactions with the same reservations. Although interactions between the two-level factors could be inserted without adding complexity to the experiment analysis, an interaction between three-level factors or between a two-level factor and a three-level factor presents the same problems as with the nested factors in nested factor design. Therefore, they are equally discouraged in the idle column method.

Notes

1. Wu, Yuin, and Dr. Willie Hobbs Moore, *Quality Engineering, Product & Process Design Optimization*, p. 280.
2. Ibid., p. 282.

Chapter 22

MULTIPLE CHARACTERISTICS

It would not be uncommon for the experimentation team to be concerned with more than one care-about. There may in fact be numerous functions or physical concerns related to the resulting product that the team must consider. Regardless of the specific problem-solving strategy, a study could not be considered a success if improving one particular quality characteristic led to serious degradation of the other critical quality characteristics.

Although you should not disregard other characteristics and direct your efforts only on your primary focus, analysis and product/process optimization could become extremely cumbersome if too many quality characteristics were considered. Attempting to optimize 30 to 40 prediction equations simultaneously would be extremely frustrating if not futile. In such a situation, improving one equation would likely lead to the degradation of others.

How do we reduce the number of critical quality characteristics to a manageable level? In Chapter 3, we discussed some of the tools that can be used to identify the appropriate primary quality characteristic. If numerous concerns exist, these same techniques can be used to narrow the list down to a manageable few.

The process flow diagram can help focus the attention of the experiment. If the various characteristics are associated with different points along the process, the solution may be to divide the experiment into smaller studies, each of which incorporates the appropriate quality characteristics.

Pareto analysis can help identify the most critical characteristics so that effort is not wasted on the less important ones. Based either on a clear division in quality costs between the most important and the less significant characteristics or on a judgmental rule defined by the experimentation team, the significant few can be sorted from the trivial many.

Another pitfall that can lead to multiple characteristics is addressing the symptoms instead of the problem. Many symptoms may accompany only one problem. Too many characteristics may be a signal that symptoms are being addressed instead of the actual problem. The use of cause and effect diagrams can save the team from falling into this trap.

Similar to misdirection of effort toward the symptoms, the quality characteristics are often defined in terms of dimensions. A more efficient definition of the resulting quality would be as a form of energy. For example, a part coming out of a plastic injection mold may have many dimensions. If we were to assign each dimension a quality characteristic, measurement could be extremely time consuming. The ensuing analysis would likely be very cumbersome, and the overall best settings for all dimensions would be difficult to ascertain. A more efficient approach might be to define quality in terms of back pressure. If the back pressure is too low, insufficient material is released into the mold, and resulting dimensions are less than desired. If back pressure is too much, excess material is injected resulting in undesired flash.

A second approach to handling the plastic injection mold process is to define the dimensions of the molded part as a single dynamic characteristic. Each critical dimension within the mold cavity would be a separate signal factor level. Measurements from experiment samples would be taken for each dimension defined as a signal factor level. Recommended levels would be based on the highest signal-to-noise levels, which reflect the overall ability of the process to duplicate the dimensions of the cavity.

The purpose of reviewing these techniques and approaches is not to insinuate that we can always reduce our care-abouts to one encompassing quality characteristic. Instead, the purpose is to narrow the list to a more manageable number. Once the list has been reduced to only a few characteristics, tradeoffs between conflicting optimal factor levels for different quality characteristics become more manageable.

22.1 MEASURABLE CHARACTERISTICS

If we were to view all of the outputs of interest as continuously measurable, the characteristics could be still further categorized into smaller-the-better, larger-the-better, and nominal-the-best. A study involving two or more of these care-abouts could result in multiple combinations of these three types of characteristics. Let's first look at situations in which all of the characteristics fall within the same category.

If all of the quality outputs are defined in terms of smaller-the-better or larger-the-better characteristics, we might deduce that we could simply add the measurement or readings for each of the characteristics for each individual data point. Analysis could then be performed based on these cumulative values. If one characteristic was considered more important than another, associated weighting factors could be introduced. For example, the first data point for experimental run #1 has values of 5.2 (quality characteristic #1) and 2.5 (quality characteristic #2). If characteristic #1 is considered twice as important as the second measurement, the cumulative result becomes 12.9 (2 × 5.2 + 2.5). Although addressing the mean results, this simplistic approach ignores the individual variability associated with each quality characteristic.

Looking at two nominal-the-best characteristics makes the inadequacy of this approach clearer. Let's look at the individual distributions of the two characteristics in Figure 22-1. As we remember from earlier chapters, the objective in optimizing a nominal-the-best characteristic is first to reduce variation and then to move the distribution to the target value using adjustment factors. As reflected in the combined distribution, the spread of the totals is not normally distributed. This irregularity clouds the picture of how selecting combined optimal settings impacts the reduction in variability. What about adjustment factors for moving the abnormal distribution toward the combined target value? In the illustration, both characteristics were weighted equally. Where different weighting scales are used and more than two nominal-the-best characteristics are involved, optimization of the process by using this approach can become even more confusing.

A clearer approach would be to analyze the quality characteristics individually and to evaluate tradeoffs when conflicting optimal settings arise from one characteristic to another. This approach resolves the dilemma of trying to reduce variability around an abnormal distribution. For nominal-the-best characteristics, it also averts the confusion of adjusting multiple adjustment factors simultaneously to reach some combined target of undefinable units. However, in the advent of numerous measurable quality characteristics, even this method could become cumbersome if it were the sole technique used.

In concert with the individual approach, the use of the signal-to-noise ratio can allow us to look cumulatively at all of the continuous quality characteristics. S/N can be calculated for each characteristic for each experimental run. Different

Figure 22-1 Nominal-the-Best Distributions Combining Raw Data

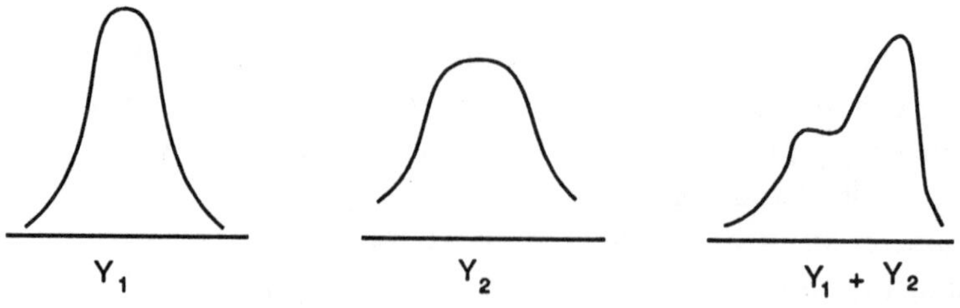

weights can be placed on the individual signal-to-noise ratios based on the team's evaluation of the relative importance of each quality characteristic. Then, the combined S/N can be determined for each run.

If we can think of the signal-to-noise ratio as a function of the square of the effect of the mean (signal) and the variability (error)

$$S/N = \frac{\text{signal strength}}{\text{effect of error}} = 10 \log \frac{\mu^2}{\sigma^2}$$

within the process or product, a viable method for weighting can be based on the relative importance of a one-decibel change for each characteristic. For smaller-the-better and larger-the-better characteristics, we can look at the mean square deviation. Alternatively, we can consider the difference in the square of the average results that a one-decibel change makes in one characteristic and weigh its importance to the impact resulting from a one-decibel change in the next characteristic. For nominal-the-best characteristics, we can consider the effect just on the variation resulting from a one-decibel change. We can then use individual adjustment factors for adjusting toward the target value for each respective quality characteristic.

22.1.1 Measurable Characteristic Example

For a double-sided SMT electronic assembly operation, solder paste is screened onto the pads on the top side of the circuit board for placement of components. Glue is applied to the bottom side for attaching electronic components. Prior to entering the infrared reflow stage, solder paste screening on the top side is checked by weighing the assemblies and measuring solder paste height. In addition, a pull force test is performed on designated component locations on the bottomside of the circuit board to check glue adhesion. (See Figures 22-2, 22-3, and 22-4.)

solder paste mass—nominal-the-best
target value = 4.2 grams
y_1 = solder paste mass

solder paste height—nominal-the-best
target value = 10 mils
y_2 = solder paste height

glue torque—larger-the-better (inch-ounces)
y_3 = glue torque

Figure 22-2 Double-Sided SMT Assembly Experiment: Raw Data

Experimental Run#	A	B	A × B	C	D	E	F	Solder Paste Mass M_1 N_1	M_1 N_2	M_2 N_1	M_2 N_2	Solder Paste Height M_1 N_1	M_1 N_2	M_2 N_1	M_2 N_2
1	1	1	1	1	1	1	1	4.15	3.42	3.95	3.80	11.00	10.62	8.85	11.00
2	1	1	1	2	2	2	2	4.13	4.46	4.13	3.33	9.23	9.56	9.23	7.73
3	1	2	2	1	1	2	2	3.15	3.12	2.97	2.02	11.28	11.58	9.13	9.78
4	1	2	2	2	2	1	1	2.99	2.29	2.63	2.64	11.15	10.80	11.15	11.15
5	2	1	2	1	2	1	2	4.22	4.52	4.87	4.07	11.97	11.92	12.27	10.77
6	2	1	2	2	1	2	1	5.74	6.73	6.53	6.38	8.90	9.55	7.05	9.20
7	2	2	1	1	2	2	1	4.72	5.70	5.35	5.35	13.19	13.84	13.49	13.49
8	2	2	1	2	1	1	2	3.27	3.57	4.07	3.12	5.72	5.67	3.87	4.52

Experimental Run #	A	B	A × B	C	D	E	F	Glue Torque M_1 N_1	M_1 N_2	M_2 N_1	M_2 N_2
1	1	1	1	1	1	1	1	15.90	12.95	11.60	13.55
2	1	1	1	2	2	2	2	15.33	13.66	13.50	10.70
3	1	2	2	1	1	2	2	15.02	13.29	10.74	10.39
4	1	2	2	2	2	1	1	16.55	13.60	14.70	14.20
5	2	1	2	1	2	1	2	19.35	19.70	20.80	18.00
6	2	1	2	2	1	2	1	18.48	20.11	17.46	19.41
7	2	2	1	1	2	2	1	20.95	22.58	22.38	21.88
8	2	2	1	2	1	1	2	12.92	13.27	11.92	11.57

Figure 22-3 Double-Sided SMT Assembly Experiment: Computations

Experimental Run #	A	B	A × B	C	D	E	F	Solder Paste Mass $\bar{y}_1$	Solder Paste Mass η	Solder Paste Height $\bar{y}_2$	Solder Paste Height η	Glue Torque $\bar{y}_3$	Glue Torque η
1	1	1	1	1	1	1	1	3.83	21.87	10.3675	20.07	13.50	22.44
2	1	1	1	2	2	2	2	4.0125	18.41	8.9375	20.74	13.2975	22.25
3	1	2	2	1	1	2	2	2.815	14.37	10.4425	18.95	12.36	21.54
4	1	2	2	2	2	1	1	2.6375	19.29	11.0625	36.02	14.7625	23.32
5	2	1	2	1	2	1	2	4.42	21.93	11.7325	24.99	19.4625	25.75
6	2	1	2	2	1	2	1	6.345	23.41	8.675	17.80	18.865	25.48
7	2	2	1	1	2	2	1	5.28	22.23	13.5025	34.12	21.9475	26.82
8	2	2	1	2	1	1	2	3.5075	18.44	4.945	14.70	12.42	21.84

Figure 22-4 Double-Sided SMT Assembly Experiment: Response Tables

Mass—S/N

Level	A	B	A × B	C	D	E	F
1	18.485	21.405	20.238	20.100	19.523	20.383	21.700
2	21.503	18.583	19.750	19.888	20.465	19.605	18.288
	3.018	**2.822**	0.488	0.212	0.942	0.778	**3.412**

Mass—y_1

Level	A	B	A × B	C	D	E	F
1	3.324	4.652	4.158	4.086	4.124	3.599	4.523
2	4.888	3.560	4.054	4.126	4.088	4.613	3.689
	1.564	**1.092**	0.104	0.040	0.036	**1.014**	**0.834**

Height—S/N

Level	A	B	A × B	C	D	E	F
1	23.945	20.901	22.409	24.533	17.881	23.947	27.003
2	22.904	25.949	24.441	22.316	28.968	22.903	19.847
	1.041	**5.048**	2.032	2.217	**11.087**	1.044	**7.156**

Height—y_2

Level	A	B	A × B	C	D	E	F
1	10.203	9.928	9.438	11.511	8.608	9.527	10.902
2	9.714	9.988	10.478	8.405	11.309	10.389	9.014
	0.489	0.060	1.040	**3.106**	**2.701**	0.862	**1.888**

Glue Torque—S/N

Level	A	B	A × B	C	D	E	F
1	22.389	23.980	23.338	24.139	22.827	23.338	24.515
2	24.973	23.382	24.024	23.223	24.535	24.024	22.847
	2.584	0.598	0.686	0.916	**1.708**	0.686	**1.668**

For reducing mass variation, the optimal settings for the strong effects are: A_2, B_1, F_1.

The adjustment factor is: E.

For reducing height variation, the optimal settings for the strong effects are: B_2, D_2, F_1.

The adjustment factor is: C.

For glue torque, the optimal settings for the strong effects are: A_2, D_2, F_1.

Based on these deductions, A_2, D_2, and F_1 would be recommended levels for improving robustness. Factors E and C would be adjustment factors for solder paste mass and solder paste height, respectively.

Factor B has a strong effect on both solder paste mass and height. However, conflicting optimal levels require additional study. If we compare the effect of factor B on the quality characteristics, we observe a 2.822 decibel change in the mass S/N and a 5.048 decibel effect on height. If our engineering knowledge tells us that each is of relatively the same importance, then our choice should be B_2, since

1. B has a greater impact on solder paste height, and
2. level 2 has the higher signal-to-noise ratio.

If we were to consider mass and height as having different levels of importance, we can also compare the effect of the different levels of factor B on the resulting variation for each quality characteristic.

Let's use the equation, $S/N = 10 \log \frac{\mu^2}{\sigma_2}$, and estimate the variation associated with each level for both characteristics. We will insert the values from the response table for S/N. The target values will be used for μ since we would expect that the adjustment factor(s) would allow us to approach or reach the desired value.

Mass	Height
level 1	level 1
$21.405 = 10 \log \frac{4.2^2}{\sigma^2}$	$20.901 = 10 \log \frac{10^2}{\sigma^2}$
$\sigma^2 = .1276$	$\sigma^2 = .8126$
$\sigma = .3573$	$\sigma = .9015$
level 2	level 2
$18.583 = 10 \log \frac{4.2^2}{\sigma^2}$	$25.949 = 10 \log \frac{10^2}{\sigma^2}$

$\sigma^2 = .2445$ $\qquad\qquad$ $\sigma^2 = .2542$

$\sigma = .4944$ $\qquad\qquad$ $\sigma = .5041$

Based on these estimations, the selection of the desired level for factor B would be based on whether reducing mass variation from .2445 to .1276 or decreasing height variability from .8126 to .2542 is the more desired result.

22.2 ATTRIBUTE CHARACTERISTICS

Just as there can be multiple continuously measurable quality characteristics, numerous attribute characteristics can exist. Many of these attribute responses are types of defects or rejects. Within the context of the definition of the defect or reject, different degrees of badness or goodness often differentiate the various classifications within which experiment results can be grouped. Depending on the experiment objectives, the purpose of the analysis may be either to maximize the number of units within a very good category or to minimize the quantity associated with a very bad classification. In dealing with a number of attribute characteristics, we could be maximizing numerous desired categories, minimizing several undesired classifications, or even attempting a combination of the two. The question is how do we reach decisions on determining optimal product values or process settings based on a potentially wide assortment of attribute characteristics and classifications?

Many types of rejects or defects can often be consolidated within one broad grouping. Specific results can then be classified according to the degree of badness. This ability can greatly reduce the number of potential characteristics and simplify the analysis. But even if the classifications can be similarly defined, the relative weight of badness or goodness between different characteristics may not be the same. Therefore, caution should be taken in grouping similar attribute characteristics.

At other times, attribute characteristics may not be similarly grouped at all. If we were to review a cheese packaging operation, we might evaluate the box or plastic wrap in terms of good, marginally acceptable, and totally unacceptable. The color of the cheese might also be a concern, but the corresponding categories of too light, slightly light, yellow, slightly dark, and too dark are completely different and unrelated categories.

Now that we have pointed out some of the major concerns, let's identify the steps for analyzing multiple attribute characteristics. After determining whether we wish to maximize or minimize specific classifications, we need to group the attribute characteristics according to similar category definitions. Next, we need to ascertain or estimate the cost associated with a unit belonging to a particular category that is being minimized or maximized. In the case of minimizing the frequency of undesirable categories, the cost may be associated with scrap or rework. In the event of a desired category, the value may be the amount saved by not having to perform rework or refinishing. Characteristics with the same relative cost can be grouped together.

Characteristics with different worth can also be combined with other concerns, but weighting factors must be incorporated. For example, the rework cost associated with characteristics A and B when a unit is severly bad is $10 each. The rework cost for characteristic C when a unit is severely bad is $15. To analyze a composite of the three characteristics, we would add together the frequency of occurrence within each similar category for A and B. We would also add the frequency of occurrence for C, but the numbers would be multiplied by the factor of 1.5.

For characteristics with unique or completely different categories, we would still want to obtain an estimate of the cost or value of a unit associated with the classification of greatest interest. We could then determine a weighting factor based on the ratio of the costs associated with the unique characteristic and the characteristic being used as the basis for determining any other weighting factors.

22.2.1 Attribute Characteristic Example

In a cheese packaging operation, the following quality characteristics and associated classifications were defined:

Characteristic			
package condition	acceptable	minor flaws	**major flaws**
package seal	sealed	loose seal	**unsealed**
label condition	acceptable	minor flaws	**major flaws**
label printing	clear	slight distortion	**major distortion**
cheese color	too light	**acceptable**	too dark

1. The team identified the specific categories which they wished to minimize or maximize (in boldface). The objectives were to maximize acceptable cheese color while minimizing major flaws and distortion associated with the other characteristics.

2. The team next estimated the cost of rework or scrap associated with units classified within the four undesirable categories and the additional cost prevented by acceptable cheese color.

Characteristic	Primary classification	Unit cost
package condition	major flaws	$.10
package seal	unsealed	.02
label condition	major flaws	.04
label printing	major distortion	.04
cheese color	acceptable	.20

Because the cost of poor label condition and label printing are approximately the same, the frequency of occurrence for both could be directly combined. Since the classification of unsealed packages has the lowest cost of quality, an easier approach would be to use unsealed packages as the base for determining the weighting of the other classifications. Then the frequency of occurrence for all of the characteristics could be combined based on their relative weight.

Characteristic	Primary classification	Relative weight
package condition	major flaws	5
package seal	unsealed	1
label condition	major flaws	2
label printing	major distortion	2
cheese color	acceptable	10

The experiment was conducted, and the resulting packages of cheese were inspected with the results shown in Figure 22-5. The experimental design consisted of an L_8 with 25 repetitions for each experimental run.

Figure 22-5 Cheese Packaging Experiment

Experimental Run #	A	B	A × B	C	D	E	F	package condition: acceptable	package condition: minor flaws	package condition: major flaws	package seal: seal	package seal: loose seal	package seal: no seal
1	1	1	1	1	1	1	1	3	8	14	2	10	13
2	1	1	1	2	2	2	2	5	10	10	4	7	14
3	1	2	2	1	1	2	2	13	7	5	14	7	4
4	1	2	2	2	2	1	1	18	5	2	21	3	1
5	2	1	2	1	2	1	2	14	8	3	11	9	5
6	2	1	2	2	1	2	1	9	9	7	11	9	5
7	2	2	1	1	2	2	1	24	1	0	15	5	5
8	2	2	1	2	1	1	2	22	3	0	21	3	1

Figure 22-5 Continued

Experimental Run #	A	B	A × B	C	D	E	F	label condition: acceptable	minor flaws	major flaws	label printing: clear	slight distort	major distort
1	1	1	1	1	1	1	1	7	9	9	16	5	4
2	1	1	1	2	2	2	2	12	9	4	2	8	15
3	1	2	2	1	1	2	2	5	10	10	7	10	8
4	1	2	2	2	2	1	1	19	1	5	10	3	12
5	2	1	2	1	2	1	2	12	7	6	5	10	10
6	2	1	2	2	1	2	1	20	5	0	8	9	8
7	2	2	1	1	2	2	1	12	7	6	9	6	10
8	2	2	1	2	1	1	2	18	5	2	7	8	10

Experimental Run#	A	B	A × B	C	D	E	F	cheese color: too light	acceptable	too dark	**undesired**
1	1	1	1	1	1	1	1	4	21	0	4
2	1	1	1	2	2	2	2	2	23	0	2
3	1	2	2	1	1	2	2	1	23	1	2
4	1	2	2	2	2	1	1	3	19	3	6
5	2	1	2	1	2	1	2	0	25	0	0
6	2	1	2	2	1	2	1	2	20	3	5
7	2	2	1	1	2	2	1	4	20	1	5
8	2	2	1	2	1	1	2	0	23	2	2

Based on the relative weighting for each characteristic, we can combine the adjusted values associated with each category that we desire to minimize. Although our objective with cheese color is to maximize the acceptable category, it would not make sense to add a quantity of desired results to the number of undesirable results. Instead, we will determine the number of undesirable results associated with cheese color, adjust the values based on relative weighting, and add these values to the other undesirable results for each corresponding experimental run.

For example, the composite total for experimental run #1 is:

$$5 \times 14 + 1 \times 13 + 2 \times 9 + 2 \times 4 + 10 \times 4 = 149$$

If we follow the same set of calculations for each experimental run, we will obtain a measure of the relative total impact for the other seven runs as well. These value are shown in Figure 22-6.

Figure 22-6 Cheese Packaging Experiment: Composite Data

Experimental Run#	A	B	A × B	C	D	E	F	composite data
1	1	1	1	1	1	1	1	149
2	1	1	1	2	2	2	2	122
3	1	2	2	1	1	2	2	85
4	1	2	2	2	2	1	1	105
5	2	1	2	1	2	1	2	52
6	2	1	2	2	1	2	1	106
7	2	2	1	1	2	2	1	87
8	2	2	1	2	1	1	2	45

From the composite values, we can generate a composite response table (Figure 22-7) reflecting the relative overall effect of each factor level. Based on the analysis from this table, optimal factor levels can be selected for the overall good of the process or product.

From the composite response table in Figure 22-7, we see that the strong effects are: A, B, F.

The mild effects are: A × B, E.

Factors with little overall impact are: C, D.

The optimal settings are:

strongly recommended—A_2, B_2, F_2

mildly recommended—E_1

Since the main effects of A and B are much stronger than their interaction, the best level for each main effect will override any alternative combinations suggested by the interaction.

One might suggest generating individual response tables for each quality characteristic and using the composite table only for those cases in which there are conflicting optimal levels for the strong effect. This suggestion may come

Figure 22-7 Cheese Packaging Experiment: Composite Response Table

Level	A	B	A × B	C	D	E	F
1	115.25	107.25	100.75	93.25	96.25	87.75	111.75
2	72.50	80.50	87.00	94.50	91.50	100.00	76.00
	42.75	**26.75**	13.75	1.25	4.75	12.25	**35.75**

from the fear that insignificant effects might dilute one significant level to the point that its impact is hidden. Although this approach will give good answers, it can be tedious and the composite approach is recommended. First, the concern for masking significant factors when using the composite table alone is invalid. Strong effects will remain obvious. Second, the method demonstrated above is less time consuming. Third, it has the additional advantage of incorporating relative costs into the decision making process.

22.3 MEASURABLE AND ATTRIBUTE CHARACTERISTICS

In dealing with a number of measurable quality characteristics, we discussed the direct or weighted combining of signal-to-noise ratios as one technique for analyzing multiple characteristics. We also showed that we could make direct one-on-one comparisons based on resulting variability. With an assortment of attribute characteristics, we demonstrated how dissimilar data could be combined into composite results based on relative quality costs. The question now is how do we treat situations when we encounter an assortment of measurable and attribute quality characteristics.

When a variety of quality characteristics have been defined and related data have been gathered, we can consider dividing the responses into two groups, continuously measurable and attribute. Within the continuously measurable group, we will want to calculate the signal-to-noise ratio for each experimental run for each quality characteristic. Signal-to-noise ratios can be combined using relative weighting based on the experimentation team's engineering knowledge of the product and/or process and the customers' desired results. This approach is fairly straightforward when dealing with all smaller-the-better or larger-the-better characteristics. As demonstrated in Section 22.1.1, we can do the same thing with nominal-the-best by assuming adjustment to the target value. However, with mixed measurable characteristics, the one-to-one comparison is the most appropriate technique when conflicting optimal levels arise in a factor significant to more than one characteristic. For the attribute characteristics, the most efficient strategy is to determine cost estimates and calculate composite responses as shown in Section 22.2.1. Then the optimal settings can be determined collectively for the entire group of attribute characteristics.

For comparisons between a measurable characteristic and an attribute response, we must make a direct comparison. A response table needs to be constructed for every quality characteristic for which data is being collected. We can then identify the strong effects and the associated best levels. Each response table is then reviewed to identify any conflicts in the selection of optimal levels. Only for instances of dissension between optimal factor levels do we need to make head-to-head comparisons.

The manner in which we make these comparisons depends on the types of measurable quality characteristics involved. The approach for relating the effect on a nominal-the-best characteristic is different from the analogy that would be used with a smaller-the-best response. The thought process related to a larger-the-better characteristic would be very similar to the smaller-the-better, since both signal-to-noise ratios relate to simultaneously reducing variation and increasing or reducing the typical response depending on which type characteristic that we are concerned with. However, even with these similarities, the way that we relate changes in the response for each in relation to attribute results is still somewhat different. To obtain a thorough understanding of how to handle each situation, we will step through the analysis of an example for each of the three possible cases.

22.3.1 Nominal-the-Best and Attribute Characteristics

A specific control factor was found to have a strong effect on both a nominal-the-best characteristic and an attribute characteristic. The average responses for the different levels of the factor for each characteristic were as follows:

	cheese weight (S/N)	unsealed packages
level 1	18.58 db	8
level 2	24.32 db	10
level 3	25.96 db	28

The number of unsealed units has no relative meaning by itself. Therefore, we need to translate this number into the percentage of packages unsealed. If the number of repetitions (packages produced) per experimental run was 80, the percent of unsealed packages would be as follows:

	percent unsealed packages
level 1	10.0%
level 2	12.5%
level 3	35.0%

To transform the signal-to-noise ratio into a form we can more easily relate to goodness and badness, we can use the formula in Section 22.1. This approach will at least allow us to compare the difference in variability for the measurable characteristic to the percentage of undesirable product within the category of interest for the attribute characteristic for each factor level. If our target value for cheese weight is 20 ounces, the estimate of the variability associated with each level of the factor being studied will be as follows:

$$\text{level 1} \quad S/N = 18.58 = 10 \log \frac{20^2}{\sigma_2} \quad \sigma^2 = 5.5470$$

$$\text{level 2} \quad S/N = 24.32 = 10 \log \frac{20^2}{\sigma_2} \quad \sigma^2 = 1.4793$$

$$\text{level 3} \quad S/N = 25.96 = 10 \log \frac{20^2}{\sigma_2} \quad \sigma^2 = 1.0141$$

Based on these two sets of conversions, we now have two sets of information to compare and make decisions upon. If we had been given specifications, we could take this analysis further and determine the projected process capability as well.

	cheese weight	unsealed packages
level 1	5.5470	10.0%
level 2	1.4793	12.5%
level 3	1.0141	35.0%

In this particular example, it would appear that level 2 is the best compromise between level 3 (with less weight variation, but a much greater rate of unsealed packages) and level 1 (with a slightly smaller quantity of unsealed packages, but considerably greater weight variability). For other cases, the solution may not be so obvious. However, the purpose of these procedures is to convert the information into a form that facilitates sound engineering judgment.

22.3.2 Smaller-the-Better and Attribute Characteristics

In a wavesolder operation, two of the concerns were circuit board warpage and contamination. The contamination is related to residue remaining on the circuit board after soldering and passing through a water rinsing chamber. Warpage is based on judgmental evaluation, and each assembly is rated among no noticeable warpage, slight warpage, and severe warpage. Contamination is evaluated by a tester and is measured in micrograms per square inch. For one particular factor that has a strong effect on both, the preferred level for each quality characteristic is different. The specific values are as follows:

	contamination (S/N)	severe warpage
level 1	−3.98 decibels	10
level 2	−6.77 decibels	6
level 3	−17.27 decibels	3

The severity of warpage will have a more relevant meaning if we convert the number of instances into the rate of occurrence. If the number of assemblies built per experimental run is 50, the rate of severe warpage for each level of the factor under discussion is as follows:

	rate of severe warpage
level 1	20%
level 2	12%
level 3	6%

It would also be helpful if we could convert the signal-to-noise ratios into a form that is easier for making comparisons to the rate of severe warpage. The equation for S/N for the smaller-the-better quality characteristic is:

$$\eta = -10 \log \frac{1}{n} \sum_{i=1}^{n} y_i^2$$

If we insert the value for the signal-to-noise ratio for each level into the equation, we can calculate an average response for y, which can then be used to make comparisons against severe warpage. Keep in mind that this is only an estimation for making comparisons between different quality characteristics. When actual data are collected, variation will exist from one response to another instead of each value's being the same. Since the mean square deviation for a smaller-the-better characteristic can be thought of as the sum of the square of the average response and the variation between the responses,

$$\text{MSD} = \bar{y}^2 + \sigma^2,$$

this derived estimate will result in a larger value than would be expected when each response is different.

level 1 $\quad -3.98 = -10 \log \frac{4y^2}{4} \quad y = 1.58 \text{ micrograms/in}^2$

$(n = 4)$

level 2 $\quad -6.77 = -10 \log \frac{4y^2}{4} \quad y = 2.18$ micrograms/in^2

$(n = 4)$

level 3 $\quad -17.27 = -10 \log \frac{4y^2}{4} \quad y = 7.30$ micrograms/in^2

$(n = 4)$

After making these transformations, we can now more easily relate the effect of each level on each of the two quality characteristics.

	contamination	rate of severe warpage
level 1	1.58 micrograms/in^2	20%
level 2	2.18 micrograms/in^2	12%
level 3	7.30 micrograms/in^2	6%

Depending on the relative importance of the given levels of contamination and the frequency of severe circuit board warpage, the team may select any one of the three levels. However, the data have at least been converted into more suitable forms for making comparisons and for facilitating decisions.

22.3.3 Larger-the-Better and Attribute Characteristics

For a given connector assembly, the experimentation team was concerned with multiple quality characteristics including the pull force that the connector could withstand and flash along the edges, which could prohibit insertion into a holding rack. For one particular factor under study, the optimal level for maximizing pull force was different from the level that resulted in the least number of occurrences of rejects due to flash. The average responses for each factor level for both characteristics were as follows:

	pull force (S/N)	unacceptable flash
level 1	16.40 db	15
level 2	19.91 db	5
level 3	17.73 db	2

Once again, we will need to convert the number of units rejected into a percentage. If a total of 40 units were assembled and tested for each experimental run, the resulting reject rates would be as follows:

	flash reject rate
level 1	37.5%
level 2	12.5%
level 3	5.0%

We will also want to convert the signal-to-noise ratios into terms that are more conducive for making comparative decisions. The equation for S/N for the larger-the-better quality characteristic is:

$$\eta = -10 \log \frac{1}{n} \sum_{i=1}^{n} \frac{1}{\mathbf{y}_i^2}$$

If we insert S/N into the equation, we can calculate an average response for y which can then be used to make comparisons against the flash reject rate. Again, we are only making an estimate for the purpose of comparing to a different type of quality characteristic, and we are not considering the variation between responses.

level 1 $\quad 16.40 = -10 \log \frac{1}{10} \frac{10}{y^2} \quad y = 6.61$ pounds

level 2 $\quad 19.91 = -10 \log \frac{1}{10} \frac{10}{y^2} \quad y = 9.90$ pounds

level 3 $\quad 17.73 = -10 \log \frac{1}{10} \frac{10}{y^2} \quad y = 7.70$ pounds

After making these transformations, we now have two sets of information which can be more easily compared for reaching the best overall quality.

	flash reject rate	estimated average pull force
level 1	37.5%	6.61 pounds
level 2	12.5%	9.90 pounds
level 3	5.0%	7.70 pounds

Depending on the relative importance of flash and pull force, the team will select either level 2 or level 3. But once again, the data has been converted into a more suitable form for facilitating decisions.

22.4 OPERATING WINDOW

A unique and special case of multiple characteristics that has proven extremely beneficial is the operating window. The operating window applies to a situation in which a smaller-the-better characteristic and a related larger-the-better characteristic are involved. Both responses are defined in terms of the same type of measurement units. The objective of the experiment is to minimize the measurement in terms of the smaller-the-better characteristic while maximizing the value as related to the larger-the-better characteristic.

The classic example of operating window is in the copier machine industry. The smaller-the-better characteristic is related to the spring force required to feed one piece of paper. If the force is insufficient, no paper is fed into the machine. The larger-the-better characteristic concerns the spring force that would cause more than one sheet at a time to be fed into the copying machine. If too much force is applied, more than one sheet is fed at a time, and a paper jam results. The goal behind the operating window is to increase the "window" within which the operation can perform efficiently. In this particular case, the objective is to minimize the amount of force required to feed one sheet of paper while at the same time increasing the amount of force which would result in feeding more than one piece and causing a paper jam.[1]

22.4.1 Wavesolder Example

In wavesolder operations, energy in the form of heat is required to form a molten tin-lead bond between the lead of a component and the pad on the printed circuit board. To provide this medium, the circuit board itself must have a certain amount of heat or energy, measured as top side board temperature. If this temperature is too low, insufficient energy results in solder voids. On the other hand, a too high temperature can cause too much energy and result in solder bridges, which is another undesired result. The objective within the context of an "operating window" is to widen the range within which the top side board temperature produces good solder joints without creating solder voids or solder bridges.

Quality characteristics:

1. y_1: top side board temperature at which solder voids start (smaller-the-better)
2. y_2: top side board temperature at which solder bridges begin (larger-the-better)

Control factors:	Level 1	Level 2
A. Pwb finish	hot air level	bare copper
B. Solder mask	liquid photoimageable	dry film
C. Pwb thickness	.062 inches	.090 inches
D. Plated thru hold size	.033 inches	.039 inches
E. Flux air knife pressure	40 psi	60 psi
F. Flux air knife angle	0 degrees	45 degrees
G. Flux wave height	low	high
H. Solder wave height	low	high
I. Flux composition	low solids	medium solids
J. Pad size	small	large
K. Solder pump size	55%	80%
L. Flux density	.86 grams/ml	.87 grams/ml
M. Solder temperature	460 degrees F	500 degrees F
N. Solder waves	single	dual
O. Pwb orientation	0 degrees	45 degrees

Noise factor:	Levels
X. Pwb wavesolder carriers	5 carriers

Experimentation strategy: Conveyor speed and preheaters are regulated to achieve specific top side board temperatures. For each experimental run, circuit board assemblies are fed through the process as temperatures are raised and lowered. The points at which solder voids and bridges begin to be created are recorded as y_1 and y_2, respectively.

Analysis steps: The following three steps apply to the row data in Figure 22-8.

1. Match each piece of data with the appropriate experimental run.

2. Calculate the signal-to-noise ratio for solder voids (smaller-the-better equation) and the signal-to-noise ratio for solder bridges (larger-the-better equation).

3. Combine the two signal-to-noise ratios together for each experimental run as illustrated in Figure 22-9.

Figure 22-8 Wavesolder "Operating Window" Orthogonal Array: Raw Data

Experimental Run#	A	B	C	D	E	F	G	H	I	J	K	L	M	N	O	y_1 smaller-the-better				
																X_1	X_2	X_3	X_4	X_5
1	1	1	1	1	1	1	1	1	1	1	1	1	1	1	1	247	245	242	245	240
2	1	1	1	1	1	1	1	2	2	2	2	2	2	2	2	235	232	230	232	230
3	1	1	1	2	2	2	2	1	1	1	1	2	2	2	2	229	223	220	225	220
4	1	1	1	2	2	2	2	2	2	2	2	1	1	1	1	234	230	235	233	228
5	1	2	2	1	1	2	2	1	1	2	2	1	1	2	2	242	235	234	235	230
6	1	2	2	1	1	2	2	2	2	1	1	2	2	1	1	242	230	238	234	237
7	1	2	2	2	2	1	1	1	1	2	2	2	2	1	1	237	234	235	230	232
8	1	2	2	2	2	1	1	2	2	1	1	1	1	2	2	238	235	236	235	230
9	2	1	2	1	2	1	2	1	2	1	2	1	2	1	2	241	240	235	240	235
10	2	1	2	1	2	1	2	2	1	2	1	2	1	2	1	230	225	222	215	215
11	2	1	2	2	1	2	1	1	2	1	2	2	1	2	1	224	220	215	212	212
12	2	1	2	2	1	2	1	2	1	2	1	1	2	1	2	231	230	228	228	226
13	2	2	1	1	2	2	1	1	2	2	1	1	2	2	1	239	235	235	230	235
14	2	2	1	1	2	2	1	2	1	1	2	2	1	1	2	239	235	238	235	230
15	2	2	1	2	1	1	2	1	2	2	1	2	1	1	2	223	220	215	218	218
16	2	2	1	2	1	1	2	2	1	1	2	1	2	2	1	222	220	215	224	218

Experimental Run#	A	B	C	D	E	F	G	H	I	J	K	L	M	N	O	y_2 larger-the-better				
																X_1	X_2	X_3	X_4	X_5
1	1	1	1	1	1	1	1	1	1	1	1	1	1	1	1	253	260	265	265	250
2	1	1	1	1	1	1	1	2	2	2	2	2	2	2	2	231	235	238	238	240
3	1	1	1	2	2	2	2	1	1	1	1	2	2	2	2	273	280	290	280	275
4	1	1	1	2	2	2	2	2	2	2	2	1	1	1	1	222	230	235	230	228
5	1	2	2	1	1	2	2	1	1	2	2	1	1	2	2	228	235	234	235	230
6	1	2	2	1	1	2	2	2	2	1	1	2	2	1	1	252	260	258	264	257
7	1	2	2	2	2	1	1	1	1	2	2	2	2	1	1	248	255	245	260	252
8	1	2	2	2	2	1	1	2	2	1	1	1	1	2	2	234	240	246	235	240
9	2	1	2	1	2	1	2	1	2	1	2	1	2	1	2	270	275	285	270	275
10	2	1	2	1	2	1	2	2	1	2	1	2	1	2	1	215	225	222	215	225
11	2	1	2	2	1	2	1	1	2	1	2	2	1	2	1	261	268	265	262	272
12	2	1	2	2	1	2	1	2	1	2	1	1	2	1	2	225	230	238	228	236
13	2	2	1	1	2	2	1	1	2	2	1	1	2	2	1	235	235	235	240	245
14	2	2	1	1	2	2	1	2	1	1	2	2	1	1	2	235	235	238	245	250
15	2	2	1	2	1	1	2	1	2	2	1	2	1	1	2	245	255	265	238	258
16	2	2	1	2	1	1	2	2	1	1	2	1	2	2	1	255	260	265	244	268

4. Generate a response table for the combined signal-to-noise ratios (Figure 22-10).

5. Identify the strong effects and optimal levels.

If we look for a logical breaking point between the strong and mild-to-weak effects so that close to half of the factors are included in the significant category, we would select factors

A, B, D, E, G, H, J, and L.

Figure 22-9 Wavesolder "Operating Window" Orthogonal Array: Signal-to-Noise Ratios

Experimental Run#	A	B	C	D	E	F	G	H	I	J	K	L	M	N	O	S-T-B	L-T-B	SUM
1	1	1	1	1	1	1	1	1	1	1	1	1	1	1	1	−47.7411	42.0694	−5.6717
2	1	1	1	1	1	1	1	2	2	2	2	2	2	2	2	−47.3025	41.2131	−6.0894
3	1	1	1	2	2	2	2	1	1	1	1	2	2	2	2	−46.9827	42.7195	−4.2632
4	1	1	1	2	2	2	2	2	2	2	2	1	1	1	1	−47.3103	40.9662	−6.3441
5	1	2	2	1	1	2	2	1	1	2	2	1	1	2	2	−47.4299	41.1072	−6.3227
6	1	2	2	1	1	2	2	2	2	1	1	2	2	1	1	−47.4669	42.0108	−5.4561
7	1	2	2	2	2	1	1	1	1	2	2	2	2	1	1	−47.3699	41.7888	−5.5811
8	1	2	2	2	2	1	1	2	2	1	1	1	1	2	2	−47.4145	41.3236	−6.0909
9	2	1	2	1	2	1	2	1	2	1	2	1	2	1	2	−47.5394	42.5482	−4.9912
10	2	1	2	1	2	1	2	2	1	2	1	2	1	2	1	−46.9065	40.5918	−6.3147
11	2	1	2	2	1	2	1	1	2	1	2	2	1	2	1	−46.7152	42.2103	−4.5049
12	2	1	2	2	1	2	1	2	1	2	1	1	2	1	2	−47.1818	41.0161	−6.1657
13	2	2	1	1	2	2	1	1	2	2	1	1	2	2	1	−47.4146	41.2484	−6.1662
14	2	2	1	1	2	2	1	2	1	1	2	2	1	1	2	−47.4369	41.3236	−6.1133
15	2	2	1	2	1	1	2	1	2	2	1	2	1	1	2	−46.8016	41.7433	−5.0583
16	2	2	1	2	1	1	2	2	1	1	2	1	2	2	1	−46.8414	41.9387	−4.9027

Figure 22-10 Wavesolder "Operating Window": S/N Response Table

level	A	B	C	D	E	F	G	H
1	−5.7274	−5.5431	−5.5761	−5.8907	−5.5214	−5.5875	−5.7979	−5.1123
2	−5.5271	−5.7114	−5.6784	−5.3639	−5.7331	−5.6670	−5.4566	−5.9412
	.2003	**.1683**	.1023	**.5268**	**.2117**	.0795	**.3413**	**.8289**

level	I	J	K	L	M	N	O
1	−5.6669	−5.2493	−5.6484	−5.8319	−5.5425	−5.6727	−5.6177
2	−5.5876	−6.0053	−5.6062	−5.4226	−5.4520	−5.5818	−5.6368
	.0793	**.7560**	.0422	**.4093**	.0905	.0909	.0191

The optimal levels for these factors (highest combined S/N) are:

$$A_2, B_1, D_2, E_1, G_2, H_1, J_1, L_2.$$

6. Construct the prediction equation and compute the estimated results with the optimal settings.

The prediction equation could be set up based on the sum of the two signal-to-noise ratios or as two individual prediction equations. The advantage of an equation for each characteristic is that comparison of the confirmation results to the predicted results is easier. On the other hand, some factors may have a strong effect on one of the two characteristics without having a significant impact on the "operating window." This tendency could lead to an underestimation of the individual response. Data from the confirmation run would appear to reflect that a major effect was missing from the prediction equation when in fact the key factors had been properly identified. The suggested approach is to compute the prediction both ways, but to rely more heavily on the combined S/N equation.

Notes

1. *Introduction to Quality Engineering,* Version 2.1, pp. 5:61–62.

Chapter 23

MISSING AND INFEASIBLE DATA

The strength of the orthogonal array experimental design and the resulting efficiency from being able to study many effects with a relative few experimental runs stem from a balanced design. The orthogonality within the array means that there are an equal number of data points for each level of each factor as for each level of all of the other factors under consideration. For parameter design, this means that there is an equal number of data points for each column of the outer array as well as a consistent quantity of readings or measurements for each row of the inner array. If a dynamic characteristic is involved, there is also an equal number of data points for each signal factor value.

In the real world, it is not always possible to obtain data for each of the experimental settings. For one reason or another, the data may become lost or were never available. Perhaps a specific sample was lost, or maybe a data sheet has been misplaced. Another reason for missing data is that the specific experimental run was never conducted. Perhaps the study involved specially built prototypes, and an insufficient quantity was produced. For example, an experimentation team is investigating solderability of several prototype circuit boards. The experiment will consist of an L_{18} inner array and a two-level compounded noise factor. Since there are two prototypes (level 1 and level 2), the experiment will require 18 pieces of each type. In the purchase of circuit boards, the largest portion of the cost is in the setup tooling. Therefore, the first unit actually costs more than the other seventeen put together. If our resulting quantity for one of the prototypes was only seventeen, it would therefore be very expensive just to order one additional unit. As a matter of fact, it is quite doubtful that we would either order or obtain approval to order the one additional unit. Thus, we would have to deal with a missing piece of data.

A second type of situation for which data are not available is when the combination of factors is so poor that product cannot be produced at all. For example, in a plastic mold injection process, our quality characteristic is a critical dimension. A specific combination of factors is so poor that the process is unable to produce a part. Therefore, we have nothing to measure and no data. Here, instead of a piece of data or unit being actually missing, we have an infeasible experimental run and hence an infeasible data point.

In both cases, the result is an unbalanced experiment. Neither can be effectively analyzed in the present state. With this situation in mind, the objective of this chapter is to provide techniques for producing estimates for the missing data points and infeasible experimental runs so that the experiment can be effectively analyzed.

23.1 MISSING DATA

In missing data situations (Figure 23-1), a specific data point is missing. So all that has to be replaced typically is one data point. To restore orthogonality, we must replace the missing data point with an estimate of what the data would be expected to resemble. Since the purpose of performing an experiment is to determine the strong effects, we need to obtain an estimate that adequately reflects these influences.

23.1.1 Estimation Techniques

One effective method is an iterative approach based on the estimated effects of the strong factors (and interactions) at the particular level settings for that experimental run in which the data are missing (Figure 23-2). For the first estimate of the missing data point, substitute the average value of the existing data within that same column of the outer array. Then develop a means response chart based on the column of interest alone. Based on the strong effects for that particular noise factor setting or noise factor combination, calculate an estimate for the resulting response. Substitute this estimate for the missing data, recom-

Figure 23-1 Missing Data Illustration

	$L_8\ (2^7)$								
Experimental Run #	1	2	3	4	5	6	7	N_1	N_2
1	1	1	1	1	1	1	1	y_{11}	y_{12}
2	1	1	1	2	2	2	2	y_{21}	y_{22}
3	1	2	2	1	1	2	2	y_{31}	y_{32}
4	1	2	2	2	2	1	1	y_{41}	y_{42}
5	2	1	2	1	2	1	2	y_{51}	missing
6	2	1	2	2	1	2	1	y_{61}	y_{62}
7	2	2	1	1	2	2	1	y_{71}	y_{72}
8	2	2	1	2	1	1	2	y_{81}	y_{82}

pute the values for the response table, reexamine the strong effects, and obtain a new estimate of the response. This approach should be continued until the missing data estimate converges around a particular value. This usually only takes three or four iterations.

Figure 23-2 Missing Data: Iterative Approach

1. Calculate the mean of the existing data for the appropriate column. Use this as the initial estimate for the missing data point.
2. Construct a means response table using data only from the appropriate column.
3. Identify the strong effects.
4. Compute an estimate of the missing response based on the levels of the strong effects for the missing data point.
5. Has the estimate of the missing data point converged around a specific value?
   a. If yes, perform analysis of the experiment using the last estimate for the missing data point.
   b. If no, go to Step 2.

A similar approach is to apply the iterative technique to the signal-to-noise ratio. This application would certainly be appropriate if data were missing for the entire row of the experiment matrix. However, if only one point is missing, this approach ignores the available data. By focusing on the noise level or noise factor combinations for which the data point is missing, you are addressing the interactions between the control factors and the noise factors at the relevant noise factor settings. This approach gives you a more meaningful estimate of what exactly is missing.

This estimation technique can be used for replacing more than one missing data point. The difference is that there will be one prediction equation for each missing data point. In the event that all data points for a specific row of the matrix are missing, it would be more appropriate to use the signal-to-noise ratio to estimate the effect of the unknown data points. Where a nominal-the-best quality characteristic is involved, and an entire row of data is missing, both mean and S/N estimates are required.

However, be careful not to abuse the use of estimation techniques. The more data points that are missing, the less reliable each estimate will be. The best solution is to obtain the necessary resources to run any incompleted experimental runs so that actual data can replace any missing data points.

23.1.2 Missing Data Example

$L_8\ (2^7)$

Experimental Run #	A 1	B 2	A×B 3	C 4	D 5	E 6	F 7	N_1	N_2
1	1	1	1	1	1	1	1	16	20
2	1	1	1	2	2	2	2	17	18
3	1	2	2	1	1	2	2	23	25
4	1	2	2	2	2	1	1	24	28
5	2	1	2	1	2	1	2	23	26
6	2	1	2	2	1	2	1	18	18
7	2	2	1	1	2	2	1	missing	16
8	2	2	1	2	1	1	2	21	24

1. Calculate the mean of the existing data for the appropriate column. Use this as the initial estimate for the missing data point.

$$y_{\text{missing}} = \frac{16 + 17 + \ldots + 21}{7} = \frac{142}{7} = 20.29$$

2. Construct a means response table using data only from the appropriate column.

$L_8\ (2^7)$

Experimental Run #	A 1	B 2	A × B 3	C 4	D 5	E 6	F 7	N_1	N_2
1	1	1	1	1	1	1	1	16	20
2	1	1	1	2	2	2	2	17	18
3	1	2	2	1	1	2	2	23	25
4	1	2	2	2	2	1	1	24	28
5	2	1	2	1	2	1	2	23	26
6	2	1	2	2	1	2	1	18	18
7	2	2	1	1	2	2	1	**20.29**	16
8	2	2	1	2	1	1	2	21	24

Means Response Table

Level	A	B	A × B	C	D	E	F
1	20.0000	18.5000	18.5725	20.5725	19.5000	21.0000	19.5725
2	20.5725	22.0725	22.0000	20.0000	21.0725	19.5725	21.0000
	.5725	**3.5725**	**3.4275**	.5725	**1.5725**	**1.4275**	**1.4275**

3. Identify the strong effects.

$$B,\ A \times B,\ D,\ E,\ F$$

If in doubt whether a factor is a strong or mild effect, include it, because the use of the mean for predicting the missing values will tend to underestimate the strength of the truly strong effects. Thus, factors and interactions that appear marginally important may be actually stronger. As the iteration process continues, the estimates of the strong effects will increase in value while the estimates of the weak effects will decrease.

4. Compute an estimate of the missing response based on the levels of the strong effects for the missing data point.

$$y_{\text{missing}} = \bar{T} + (\bar{B}_2 - \bar{T}) + [(\bar{A}_2\bar{B}_2 - \bar{T}) - (\bar{A}_2 - T) - (\bar{B}_2 - T) + (\bar{D}_2 - \bar{T}) + (\bar{E}_2 - \bar{T}) + (\bar{F}_1 - \bar{T})$$

$$y_{\text{missing}} = \bar{A}_2\bar{B}_2 - \bar{A}_2 + \bar{D}_2 + \bar{E}_2 + \bar{F}_1 - 2 \times \bar{T},$$

where

$$\bar{A}_2\bar{B}_2 = \frac{20.29 + 21}{2} = 20.645$$

$$y_{\text{missing}} = 20.645 - 20.5725 + 21.0725 + 19.5725 + 19.5725 - 2(20.28625)$$

$$y_{\text{missing}} = 19.7175$$

5. Has the estimate of the missing data point converged around a specific value?

a. If yes, perform analysis of the experiment using the last estimate for the missing data point.

b. If no, go to Step 2. Repeat Steps 2–5 using the new estimate for the missing data point.

Second Iteration:

$L_8\ (2^7)$

Experimental Run #	A 1	B 2	A × B 3	C 4	D 5	E 6	F 7	N_1	N_2
1	1	1	1	1	1	1	1	16	20
2	1	1	1	2	2	2	2	17	18
3	1	2	2	1	1	2	2	23	25
4	1	2	2	2	2	1	1	24	28
5	2	1	2	1	2	1	2	23	26
6	2	1	2	2	1	2	1	18	18
7	2	2	1	1	2	2	1	**19.7175**	16
8	2	2	1	2	1	1	2	21	24

Means Response Table

Level	A	B	A × B	C	D	E	F
1	20.0000	18.5000	18.4294	20.4294	19.5000	21.0000	19.4294
2	20.4294	21.9294	22.0000	20.0000	20.9294	19.4294	21.0000
	.4294	**3.4294**	**3.5706**	.4294	1.4294	**1.5706**	**1.5706**

In comparing the relative strength of the effects between iteration #1 and iteration #2, the interaction A × B, factor E, and factor F grew while the other effects decreased in importance. This result suggests that A × B, E, and F are the truly strong effects, whereas the other effects have a lesser influence. Therefore, the prediction equation should contain only these three effects.

Therefore,

$$y_{\text{missing}} = \overline{T} + [(\overline{A_2B_2} - \overline{T}) - (\overline{A}_2 - T) - (\overline{B}_2 - T)] + (\overline{E}_2 - \overline{T}) + (\overline{F}_1 - \overline{T})$$

$$y_{\text{missing}} = \overline{A_2B_2} - \overline{A}_2 - \overline{B}_2 + \overline{E}_2 + \overline{F}_1,$$

where

$$\overline{A_2B_2} = \frac{19.7175 + 21}{2} = 20.3588$$

$$y_{\text{missing}} = 20.3588 - 20.4294 - 21.9294 + 19.4294 + 19.4294$$

$$y_{\text{missing}} = 16.8588$$

Third Iteration:

Means Response Table

Level	A	B	A × B	C	D	E	F
1	20.0000	18.5000	17.7147	19.7147	19.5000	21.0000	18.7147
2	19.7147	21.2147	22.0000	20.0000	20.2147	18.7147	21.0000
	.2853	2.7147	4.2853	.2853	.7147	2.2853	2.2853

In comparing the second and third iterations, we again see the effects of A×B, E, and F increase while the other effects continue to lessen in magnitude. Therefore, we will incorporate the same effects in the prediction equation as used in the previous iteration.

$$y_{\text{missing}} = \overline{T} + [(\overline{A_2B_2} - \overline{T}) - (\overline{A}_2 - \overline{T}) - (\overline{B}_2 - \overline{T})] + (\overline{E}_2 - \overline{T}) + (\overline{F}_1 - \overline{T})$$

$$y_{\text{missing}} = \overline{A_2B_2} - \overline{A}_2 - \overline{B}_2 + \overline{E}_2 + \overline{F}_1,$$

where

$$\overline{A_2B_2} = \frac{16.8588 + 21}{2} = 18.9294$$

$$y_{\text{missing}} = 18.9294 - 19.7147 - 21.2147 + 18.7147 + 18.7147$$

$$y_{\text{missing}} = 15.4294$$

Fourth Iteration: $y_{\text{missing}} = 14.7147$

Fifth Iteration: $y_{\text{missing}} = 14.3573$

Sixth Iteration: $y_{\text{missing}} = 14.1787$

Seventh Iteration: $y_{\text{missing}} = 14.0894$

Although we carried the estimations out to seven iterations, we could have stopped earlier depending on the number of significant decimal places required. In our example, actual data readings were in whole numbers. For consistency, we could round off the missing data estimate to the nearest whole number. Since the difference between the fourth and fifth iterations was less than .5 (14.7147 − 14.3573 = .3574), and the fifth estimate was 14.3573, we should recognize that additional iterations would not change the rounded-off value of the estimated value of the missing data point, which would remain at 14. Therefore, five iterations would have been sufficient in this case. If in doubt where to stop, there is no penalty for performing additional iterations.

23.2 INFEASIBLE DATA

When the control factors are so defined that catastrophic failure results in no producible part or in unmeasurable results, we must develop an estimate for this result so that this effect can be reflected in the analysis. Simply to calculate an average based on the surrounding data would be misleading in that it would underestimate the impact of the factors at the settings of this particular experimental run. Therefore, the estimate must reflect a condition that is worse than any of the results we were able to obtain.

An infeasible condition usually means that the experimental run will not produce measurable results for the stated control factor settings regardless of changes in the noise factor settings. Therefore, the entire row of data is typically empty. Since the extremely adverse condition reflects excessive process variation, we would expect the signal-to-noise ratio for that experimental run to be extremely low. By approximating an appropriate S/N for this experimental run, we can include consideration of the effects culminating in these unsatisfactory results into the analysis.

Figure 23-3 Infeasible Data Illustration

Experimental Run #	$L_8(2^7)$								
	1	2	3	4	5	6	7	N_1	N_2
1	1	1	1	1	1	1	1	y_{11}	y_{12}
2	1	1	1	2	2	2	2	y_{21}	y_{22}
3	1	2	2	1	1	2	2	y_{31}	y_{32}
4	1	2	2	2	2	1	1	y_{41}	y_{42}
5	2	1	2	1	2	1	2	infeasible	
6	2	1	2	2	1	2	1	y_{61}	y_{62}
7	2	2	1	1	2	2	1	y_{71}	y_{72}
8	2	2	1	2	1	1	2	y_{81}	y_{82}

23.2.1 Smaller-the-Better Characteristic

For the smaller-the-better quality characteristic in parameter design, the strongest effects are ascertained by the influence on the signal-to-noise ratio. Those levels that result in the highest S/N indicate the most desired conditions and are chosen. The levels that result in the lowest S/N reflect the worst conditions. Since an infeasible condition signifies a combination of factor settings worse than any of the combinations for which there is a measurable result, the S/N for an infeasible condition should be even lower. In assigning a value to the infeasible condition, we clearly want to reflect that this run is significantly worse than other combinations of factors. At the same time, we do not want to underestimate the S/N for this set of experimental conditions and mask the effects of the factors under study at other levels. Three decibels typically represents a significant difference in signal-to-noise ratios, but is not such a large difference as to override the signal-to-noise ratios for the other experimental runs. Therefore, we can usually achieve an effective representation of the infeasible experimental run by identifying the lowest calculated S/N, subtracting 3, and assigning this value to the appropriate row of the experimental design.

Although the estimation is derived simply, it does require calculation of the signal-to-noise ratio for those experimental runs without infeasible data points. This calculation in turn requires an outer array within the experimental design structure. If no noise factors were defined in the planning phase, repetitions should be performed for each experimental run, and the signal-to-noise ratio can then be calculated from this set of data.

After calculating the signal-to-noise ratios for the experimental runs in which data were obtainable, we identify the run with the lowest S/N. From Figure 23-4, we observe that experimental run #8 has the lowest S/N at −35.58. We can then estimate the signal-to-noise ratio for experimental run #7 as follows:

$$S/N_{\#7} = -35.58 - 3.00 = -38.58 \text{ db}$$

After inserting this value into row 7 of the matrix, we can generate the S/N response table and analyze the table in the regular manner.

In the event that two or more repetitions are unattainable due to scheduling impossibilities, lack of sufficient material, or other constraints, a second estimation method is available. Although less desirable than the previous type of estimation, it does at least provide a consistent method for obtaining an estimate that can reflect the strength of the factor levels resulting in the infeasible run without completely overriding the effect of other factor levels.

The method requires scanning the raw data and identifying the highest value. An adjustment value is then computed based on the difference between the

Figure 23-4 Infeasible Data: Smaller-the-Better

	$L_8\ (2^7)$											M₁		M₂		
Experimental Run#	1	2	3	4	5	6	7	8	9	10	11	N_1	N_2	N_1	N_2	S/N
1	1	1	1	1	1	1	1	1	1	1	1	37.21	40.81	44.65	53.41	−32.95
2	1	1	1	1	1	2	2	2	2	2	2	33.81	38.17	40.57	49.21	−32.22
3	1	1	2	2	2	1	1	1	2	2	2	32.64	37.24	39.16	47.75	−31.95
4	1	2	1	2	2	1	2	2	1	1	2	34.24	39.46	41.08	50.34	−32.40
5	1	2	2	1	2	2	1	2	1	2	1	44.89	49.24	53.86	64.44	−34.58
6	1	2	2	2	1	2	2	1	2	1	1	42.25	46.34	50.70	60.65	−34.06
7	2	1	2	2	1	1	2	2	1	2	1		**infeasible data**			
8	2	1	2	1	2	2	2	1	1	1	2	46.24	58.06	55.48	76.64	**−35.58**
9	2	1	1	2	2	2	1	2	2	1	1	38.29	42.11	45.94	55.03	−33.21
10	2	2	2	1	1	1	1	2	2	1	2	46.26	50.72	55.51	66.39	−34.84
11	2	2	1	2	1	2	1	1	1	2	2	48.61	52.25	58.33	69.11	−35.21
12	2	2	1	1	2	1	2	1	2	2	1	47.04	54.90	56.44	69.59	−35.20

highest value and the average of the data from the feasible experimental runs. The value for the infeasible data point is then estimated by dividing the adjustment value by 3 and adding the result to the highest response.

$$\text{Infeasible data point} = y_{max} + \frac{(y_{max} - \overline{T})}{3}$$

For example in Figure 23-5, we see an experiment in which multiple repetitions could not be run, but an infeasible experimental run was experienced. The estimated value for the raw data for the infeasible data point is determined as follows:

$$y_{max} = 76.64$$

$$\overline{T} = \frac{53.41 + 33.81 + \ldots + 69.59}{11} = \frac{511}{11} = 50.09$$

$$\text{infeasible data point} = 76.64 + \frac{(76.64 - 50.09)}{3} = 85.49$$

The estimate can now be placed in the appropriate row of the response column. The response table and response graph can then be generated, and marginal analysis can be performed following the standard guidelines.

Figure 23-5 Infeasible Data: Smaller-the-Better

	L_{12} (2^{11})											
Experimental Run #	1	2	3	4	5	6	7	8	9	10	11	y
1	1	1	1	1	1	1	1	1	1	1	1	53.41
2	1	1	1	1	1	2	2	2	2	2	2	33.81
3	1	1	2	2	2	1	1	1	2	2	2	32.64
4	1	2	1	2	2	1	2	2	1	1	2	39.46
5	1	2	2	1	2	2	1	2	1	2	1	49.24
6	1	2	2	2	1	2	2	1	2	1	1	46.34
7	2	1	2	2	1	1	2	2	1	2	1	**infeasible**
8	2	1	2	1	2	2	2	1	1	1	2	**76.64**
9	2	1	1	2	2	2	1	2	2	1	1	42.11
10	2	2	2	1	1	1	1	2	2	1	2	55.51
11	2	2	1	2	1	2	1	1	1	2	2	52.25
12	2	2	1	1	2	1	2	1	2	2	1	69.59

23.2.2 Larger-the-Better Characteristic

Treatment of infeasible data for larger-the-better quality characteristics is similar to the method used for smaller-the-better characteristics. Since the strongest effects for both types of characteristics can be determined solely by calculating and analyzing the signal-to-noise ratios, the same techniques can apply in each case. The only difference is in the equations to compute the signal-to-noise ratio.

Again, an infeasible condition signifies a combination of factor settings worse than any of the combinations for which there is a measurable result. We would expect the results if obtainable to be smaller since this is a larger-the-better characteristic. Accordingly, the S/N for the infeasible condition should be lower than that of the feasible runs. Using the same considerations that guided us in handling smaller-the-better instances of infeasible data, we can again obtain an estimate for the infeasible experimental run by identifying the lowest calculated S/N, subtracting 3, and assigning this value to the appropriate row of the experimental design.

As with the previous type of quality characteristic, the signal-to-noise ratio must be determined for all those experimental runs not containing infeasible data points. Again, the experimental design structure must contain an outer array consisting of either noise factors or repetitions to use this particular technique for handling infeasible data.

In Figure 23-6, we have an infeasible data condition. After calculating S/N for each experimental run for which data were obtainable, we identify the run with the lowest resulting value. In scanning the calculations, we observe that

Figure 23-6 Infeasible Data: Larger-the-Better

Experimental Run#	L_{12} (2^{11}) 1	2	3	4	5	6	7	8	9	10	11	N_1	N_2	N_3	N_4	S/N
1	1	1	1	1	1	1	1	1	1	1	1	21.89	18.19	19.29	15.59	24.29
2	1	1	1	1	1	2	2	2	2	2	2	22.79	19.09	17.79	19.09	24.80
3	1	1	2	2	2	1	1	1	2	2	2	20.24	20.19	17.64	17.59	24.88
4	1	2	1	2	2	1	2	2	1	1	2	23.96	20.21	16.36	17.61	24.88
5	1	2	2	1	2	2	1	2	1	2	1		**infeasible data**			
6	1	2	2	2	1	2	2	1	2	1	1	15.84	15.79	10.84	15.79	22.90
7	2	1	2	2	1	1	2	2	1	2	1	16.57	16.52	8.97	13.92	**22.06**
8	2	1	2	1	2	2	2	1	1	1	2	16.00	16.00	11.00	16.00	23.01
9	2	1	1	2	2	2	1	2	2	1	1	16.16	12.41	16.16	12.41	22.87
10	2	2	2	1	1	1	1	2	2	1	2	18.89	18.89	16.29	16.29	24.83
11	2	2	1	2	1	2	1	1	1	2	2	20.05	16.30	20.05	16.30	25.05
12	2	2	1	1	2	1	2	1	2	2	1	19.00	15.30	11.40	12.70	22.81

experimental run #7 has the lowest S/N at 22.06. We can then estimate the signal-to-noise ratio for experimental run #5 as follows:

$$S/N_{\#5} = 22.06 - 3.00 = 19.06 \text{ db}$$

After inserting this value into row 5 of the matrix, we can generate the S/N response table and analyze the effects in the regular manner.

As described in the smaller-the-better section, an alternative estimation method can be used for handling raw data when two or more repetitions are unavailable. Again, this is less desirable than subtracting 3 decibels from the smallest S/N, but it does at least provide a consistent method for dealing with experimental runs for which data cannot be obtained. As mentioned previously, the key is to provide an estimate that can reflect the strength of the factor level combination resulting in the infeasible run without completely overriding the impact of other experimental runs.

For a larger-the-better characteristic, the first step is to identify the lowest response from the collection of raw data. The adjustment value is then computed based on the difference between the average response from the feasible experimental runs and the lowest response. The value for the infeasible data point is then estimated by dividing the adjustment value by 3 and subtracting this quotient from the lowest response.

$$\text{Infeasible data point} = y_{\min} - \frac{(\overline{T} - y_{\min})}{3}$$

Figure 23-7 Infeasible Data: Larger-the-Better

L_{12} (2^{11})

Experimental Run #	1	2	3	4	5	6	7	8	9	10	11	Response
1	1	1	1	1	1	1	1	1	1	1	1	15.59
2	1	1	1	1	1	2	2	2	2	2	2	19.09
3	1	1	2	2	2	1	1	1	2	2	2	17.59
4	1	2	1	2	2	1	2	2	1	1	2	17.61
5	1	2	2	1	2	2	1	2	1	2	1	16.45
6	1	2	2	2	1	2	2	1	2	1	1	15.79
7	2	1	2	2	1	1	2	2	1	2	1	13.92
8	2	1	2	1	2	2	2	1	1	1	2	16.00
9	2	1	1	2	2	2	1	2	2	1	1	**infeasible**
10	2	2	2	1	1	1	1	2	2	1	2	16.29
11	2	2	1	2	1	2	1	1	1	2	2	16.30
12	2	2	1	1	2	1	2	1	2	2	1	**12.70**

For example in Figure 23-7, we see an experiment in which multiple repetitions could not be run, and an infeasible experimental run was experienced. The estimated value for the raw data is determined as follows:

$$y_{\min} = 12.70$$

$$\overline{T} = \frac{15.59 + 19.09 + \ldots + 12.70}{11} = \frac{177.33}{11} = 16.12$$

$$\text{infeasible data point} = 12.70 - \frac{(16.12 - 12.70)}{3} = 11.56$$

The estimate can now be placed in the ninth row of the response column. The response table and response graph can then be generated, and marginal analysis can be performed following the standard guidelines.

23.2.3 Nominal-the-Best Characteristic

Treatment of infeasible experimental runs is more complicated when a nominal-the-best quality characteristic is involved. Under the previous two types of situations, all determinations of strong effects and optimal levels could be determined strictly based on the signal-to-noise ratio. Even when the lack of repetitions prohibited us from calculating the signal-to-noise ratios, we still knew whether an increase in the raw data (smaller-the-better) or a decrease (larger-the-better) represented a worse case situation. However, in the case of the nominal-the-best characteristic, these determinations are not as simple or clear-cut. For one, we must be interested in the mean response for each experimental run as well as the signal-to-noise ratio. In addition, a worse case condition could either be smaller or greater than the nominal or target value.

In addressing the signal-to-noise ratio, we can still use

$$S/N_{\text{infeasible}} = S/N_{\min} - 3$$

to obtain an estimate for the infeasible experimental run to study changes in variability. To obtain an estimate of $\bar{y}$ to study changes in the mean requires engineering knowledge. If the quality characteristic has been effectively defined in terms of some form or measure of energy, we can ask if the reason for no data is too much energy or not enough energy. If sufficient energy was not available to obtain measurable results, an equation similar to the one for larger-the-better infeasible data,

$$\text{infeasible mean} = \bar{y}_{\min} - \frac{(\bar{T} - \bar{y}_{\min})}{3},$$

where

$$\bar{T} = \text{average of } \bar{y} \text{ for the feasible runs,}$$

can be used to estimate the average response for the infeasible experimental run. If, on the other hand, too much energy was present, we can use an equation closely resembling the approximation for smaller-the-better infeasible data to estimate the mean for the unobtainable data set.

$$\text{infeasible mean} = \bar{y}_{\max} + \frac{(\bar{y}_{\max} - \bar{T})}{3}$$

If existing engineering knowledge is insufficient to make a determination either way, an additional experimental run with the factors set at slightly more conservative levels can be used to ascertain which equation to use to estimate the mean response for the infeasible run. Factor settings for which the orthogonal array calls for low levels can be slightly increased, and required high levels can be adjusted downward. Discrete factors and those that appear to have minimal influence based on the other experimental runs can be set at their originally defined settings.

23.3 IDEAL DATA, INFEASIBLE CALCULATIONS

Besides experimental conditions being too bad to obtain measurable results, data in the application of nominal-the-best criteria could be so good that the calculations to perform S/N analysis could not be performed. Let's say that for a specific experimental run, we have an outer array composed of four columns with one measurement each. The resulting four measurements for that experimental run are 25.00 each. If we try to calculate S/N for this data, we find that Ve = 0.

$$\text{Sm} = \frac{(25.00 + 25.00 + 25.00 + 25.00)^2}{4} = 2500.00$$

$$\text{Ve} = \frac{25.00^2 + 25.00^2 + 25.00^2 + 25.00^2 - 2500.00}{4 - 1} = 0.$$

Since

$$\eta = 10 \log \frac{\text{Sm} - \text{Ve}}{n\,(\text{Ve})},$$

the signal-to-noise ratio is indeterminable. Therefore, we must obtain a measure of the S/N in another way. Just as we estimated the variability within an infeasible run by adjusting the worst calculated S/N, we can similarly identify the best calculated S/N and add 3 to obtain an estimate for the indeterminate S/N.

$$\text{S/N}_{\text{indeterminate}} = \text{S/N}_{\text{max}} + 3 \text{ db}.$$

Bibliography

American Society for Quality Control, Statistics Division, *Glossary and Tables for Statistical Quality Control*, 2nd ed. Milwaukee, American Society for Quality Control, 1983.

Broadwater, John. "Cracked Ceramic Surface Mount Capacitors." (unpublished paper).

Ealey, Lance A. *Quality by Design*. Dearborn, MI: ASI Press, 1988.

Farago, Francis T., *Handbook of Dimensional Measurement*, 2nd ed. New York: Industrial Press Inc., 1982.

Grant, Eugene L., and Richard S. Leavenworth, *Statistical Quality Control*, 5th ed. New York: McGraw-Hill, 1980.

Handbook Committee, Western Electric Co., Inc. *Statistical Quality Control Handbook*, 2nd ed. Charlotte, NC: Delmar, 1985.

Horner, Stan. *Statistical Process Control*. Dallas: Texas Instruments, 1983.

Introduction to Quality Engineering. Dearborn, MI: American Supplier Institute, 1987.

Introduction to Quality Engineering. Version 2.1. 1989.

Ishikawa, Kaoru. *Guide to Quality Control*. Tokyo: Asian Productivity Organization, 1976.

Juran, Joseph M. *Juran on Quality Improvement*. New York: Juran Enterprises, 1981.

_______ *Quality Control Handbook*. 3rd ed. New York: McGraw-Hill Book Company, 1979.

Melder, Melissa, Wayne Murdock, Lisa Reagan, and Eric Schild. *Taguchi's Approach to Quality Engineering*, Volume I. 3rd Printing. Dallas: Texas Instruments, 1989.

Peace, Glen S. "The Quality Engineering Systems Controversy: The Taguchi Method and Statistical Process Control." n.p., *14th Annual Rocky Mountain Quality Conference*, 1990, p. 253–261.

_______ "Surface Mount Technology Statistical Applications." *42nd Annual Quality Congress Transactions*. n.p., American Society for Quality Control, 1988, pp. 500–507.

_______*Taguchi for Design Engineering*. Johnson City, TN: Texas Instruments, 1987.

Phadke, Madhav S. *Quality Engineering Using Robust Design*. Englewood Cliffs, NJ: Prentice Hall, 1989.

Quality Engineering: Dynamic Characteristics and Measurement Engineering. Dearborn, MI: American Supplier Institute, 1990.

RCA Color Television Owner's Manual. Indianapolis: Thomson Consumer Electronics, 1990.

Sarazen, J. Stephen. "The Tools of Quality Part II: Cause-and-Effect Diagrams." *Quality Progress.* July 1990, pp. 59–62.

Scholtes, Peter R. *The Team Handbook.* Madison, WI: Joiner Associates, 1988.

Taguchi, Genichi. *System of Experimental Design.* Tech Ed. Don Clausing. English translation by Louise Watanabe Tung. 2 vols. White Plains, NY: Kraus International Publications and Dearborn, MI: American Supplier Institute, 1987.

Taguchi, G., and S. Konishi. *Orthogonal Arrays and Linear Graphs.* Dearborn, MI: American Supplier Institute, 1987.

Taguchi, Shin. "Controlling Process for High Quality, Low Cost." *Eighth Symposium on Taguchi Methods.* Dearborn, MI: American Supplier Institute, 1990.

——— *"Dynamic System Optimization: An Introduction to Dynamic Characteristics."* Dearborn, MI: American Supplier Institute, no date.

Wu, Yuin. *Introduction to Dynamic Characteristics.* Dearborn, MI: American Supplier Institute, 1990.

Wu, Yuin, and Dr. Willie Hobbs Moore. *Quality Engineering: Product & Process Design Optimization.* Dearborn, MI: American Supplier Institute, 1986.

Appendices

Copied by permission of the American Supplier Institute, a nonprofit organization dedicated to improving the competitive position of U.S. industry.

Appendix A: Orthogonal Arrays

Appendix B: Linear Graphs

Appendix C: Interactions between Two Columns Tables

Appendix A: Orthogonal Arrays

$L_4 (2^3)$

No.	1	2	3
1	1	1	1
2	1	2	2
3	2	1	2
4	2	2	1

$L_8 (2^7)$

No.	1	2	3	4	5	6	7
1	1	1	1	1	1	1	1
2	1	1	1	2	2	2	2
3	1	2	2	1	1	2	2
4	1	2	2	2	2	1	1
5	2	1	2	1	2	1	2
6	2	1	2	2	1	2	1
7	2	2	1	1	2	2	1
8	2	2	1	2	1	1	2

L_{12} (2^{11})

No.	1	2	3	4	5	6	7	8	9	10	11
1	1	1	1	1	1	1	1	1	1	1	1
2	1	1	1	1	1	2	2	2	2	2	2
3	1	1	2	2	2	1	1	1	2	2	2
4	1	2	1	2	2	1	2	2	1	1	2
5	1	2	2	1	2	2	1	2	1	2	1
6	1	2	2	2	1	2	2	1	2	1	1
7	2	1	2	2	1	1	2	2	1	2	1
8	2	1	2	1	2	2	2	1	1	1	2
9	2	1	1	2	2	2	1	2	2	1	1
10	2	2	2	1	1	1	1	2	2	1	2
11	2	2	1	2	1	2	1	1	1	2	2
12	2	2	1	1	2	1	2	1	2	2	1

In the L_{12} (2^{11}) array, the effects of interactions are distributed fairly uniformly across all columns, prohibiting the study of interactions.

L_{16} (2^{15})

No.	1	2	3	4	5	6	7	8	9	10	11	12	13	14	15
1	1	1	1	1	1	1	1	1	1	1	1	1	1	1	1
2	1	1	1	1	1	1	1	2	2	2	2	2	2	2	2
3	1	1	1	2	2	2	2	1	1	1	1	2	2	2	2
4	1	1	1	2	2	2	2	2	2	2	2	1	1	1	1
5	1	2	2	1	1	2	2	1	1	2	2	1	1	2	2
6	1	2	2	1	1	2	2	2	2	1	1	2	2	1	1
7	1	2	2	2	2	1	1	1	1	2	2	2	2	1	1
8	1	2	2	2	2	1	1	2	2	1	1	1	1	2	2
9	2	1	2	1	2	1	2	1	2	1	2	1	2	1	2
10	2	1	2	1	2	1	2	2	1	2	1	2	1	2	1
11	2	1	2	2	1	2	1	1	2	1	2	2	1	2	1
12	2	1	2	2	1	2	1	2	1	2	1	1	2	1	2
13	2	2	1	1	2	2	1	1	2	2	1	1	2	2	1
14	2	2	1	1	2	2	1	2	1	1	2	2	1	1	2
15	2	2	1	2	1	1	2	1	2	2	1	2	1	1	2
16	2	2	1	2	1	1	2	2	1	1	2	1	2	2	1

L_{32} (2^{31})

No.	1	2	3	4	5	6	7	8	9	10	11	12	13	14	15	16	17	18	19	20	21	22	23	24	25	26	27	28	29	30	31
1	1	1	1	1	1	1	1	1	1	1	1	1	1	1	1	1	1	1	1	1	1	1	1	1	1	1	1	1	1	1	1
2	1	1	1	1	1	1	1	1	1	1	1	1	1	1	1	2	2	2	2	2	2	2	2	2	2	2	2	2	2	2	2
3	1	1	1	1	1	1	1	2	2	2	2	2	2	2	2	1	1	1	1	1	1	1	1	2	2	2	2	2	2	2	2
4	1	1	1	1	1	1	1	2	2	2	2	2	2	2	2	2	2	2	2	2	2	2	2	1	1	1	1	1	1	1	1
5	1	1	1	2	2	2	2	1	1	1	1	2	2	2	2	1	1	1	1	2	2	2	2	1	1	1	1	2	2	2	2
6	1	1	1	2	2	2	2	1	1	1	1	2	2	2	2	2	2	2	2	1	1	1	1	2	2	2	2	1	1	1	1
7	1	1	1	2	2	2	2	2	2	2	2	1	1	1	1	1	1	1	1	2	2	2	2	2	2	2	2	1	1	1	1
8	1	1	1	2	2	2	2	2	2	2	2	1	1	1	1	2	2	2	2	1	1	1	1	1	1	1	1	2	2	2	2
9	1	2	2	1	1	2	2	1	1	2	2	1	1	2	2	1	1	2	2	1	1	2	2	1	1	2	2	1	1	2	2
10	1	2	2	1	1	2	2	1	1	2	2	1	1	2	2	2	2	1	1	2	2	1	1	2	2	1	1	2	2	1	1
11	1	2	2	1	1	2	2	2	2	1	1	2	2	1	1	1	1	2	2	1	1	2	2	2	2	1	1	2	2	1	1
12	1	2	2	1	1	2	2	2	2	1	1	2	2	1	1	2	2	1	1	2	2	1	1	1	1	2	2	1	1	2	2
13	1	2	2	2	2	1	1	1	1	2	2	2	2	1	1	1	1	2	2	2	2	1	1	1	1	2	2	2	2	1	1
14	1	2	2	2	2	1	1	1	1	2	2	2	2	1	1	2	2	1	1	1	1	2	2	2	2	1	1	1	1	2	2

15	1	2	2	2	2	1	1	2	2	1	1	1	1	2	2	1	1	2	2	2	2	1	1	2	2	1	1	1	1	2	2
16	1	2	2	2	2	1	1	2	2	1	1	1	1	2	2	2	2	1	1	1	1	2	2	1	1	2	2	2	2	1	1
17	2	1	2	1	2	1	2	1	2	1	2	1	2	1	2	1	2	1	2	1	2	1	2	1	2	1	2	1	2	1	2
18	2	1	2	1	2	1	2	1	2	1	2	1	2	1	2	2	1	2	1	2	1	2	1	2	1	2	1	2	1	2	1
19	2	1	2	1	2	1	2	2	1	2	1	2	1	2	1	1	2	1	2	1	2	1	2	2	1	2	1	2	1	2	1
20	2	1	2	1	2	1	2	2	1	2	1	2	1	2	1	2	1	2	1	2	1	2	1	1	2	1	2	1	2	1	2
21	2	1	2	2	1	2	1	1	2	1	2	2	1	2	1	1	2	1	2	2	1	2	1	1	2	1	2	2	1	2	1
22	2	1	2	2	1	2	1	1	2	1	2	2	1	2	1	2	1	2	1	1	2	1	2	2	1	2	1	1	2	1	2
23	2	1	2	2	1	2	1	2	1	2	1	1	2	1	2	1	2	1	2	2	1	2	1	2	1	2	1	1	2	1	2
24	2	1	2	2	1	2	1	2	1	2	1	1	2	1	2	2	1	2	1	1	2	1	2	1	2	1	2	2	1	2	1
25	2	2	1	1	2	2	1	1	2	2	1	1	2	2	1	1	2	2	1	1	2	2	1	1	2	2	1	1	2	2	1
26	2	2	1	1	2	2	1	1	2	2	1	1	2	2	1	2	1	1	2	2	1	1	2	2	1	1	2	2	1	1	2
27	2	2	1	1	2	2	1	2	1	1	2	2	1	1	2	1	2	2	1	1	2	2	1	2	1	1	2	2	1	1	2
28	2	2	1	1	2	2	1	2	1	1	2	2	1	1	2	2	1	1	2	2	1	1	2	1	2	2	1	1	2	2	1
29	2	2	1	2	1	1	2	1	2	2	1	2	1	1	2	1	2	2	1	2	1	1	2	1	2	2	1	2	1	1	2
30	2	2	1	2	1	1	2	1	2	2	1	2	1	1	2	2	1	1	2	1	2	2	1	2	1	1	2	1	2	2	1
31	2	2	1	2	1	1	2	2	1	1	2	1	2	2	1	1	2	2	1	2	1	1	2	2	1	1	2	1	2	2	1
32	2	2	1	2	1	1	2	2	1	1	2	1	2	2	1	2	1	1	2	1	2	2	1	1	2	2	1	2	1	1	2

$L_{64}(2^{63})$

No.	1	2	3	4	5	6	7	8	9	10	11	12	13	14	15	16	17	18	19	20	21	22	23	24	25	26	27	28	29	30	31
1	1	1	1	1	1	1	1	1	1	1	1	1	1	1	1	1	1	1	1	1	1	1	1	1	1	1	1	1	1	1	1
2	1	1	1	1	1	1	1	1	1	1	1	1	1	1	1	1	1	1	1	1	1	1	1	1	1	1	1	1	1	1	1
3	1	1	1	1	1	1	1	1	1	1	1	1	1	1	1	2	2	2	2	2	2	2	2	2	2	2	2	2	2	2	2
4	1	1	1	1	1	1	1	1	1	1	1	1	1	1	1	2	2	2	2	2	2	2	2	2	2	2	2	2	2	2	2
5	1	1	1	1	1	1	1	2	2	2	2	2	2	2	2	1	1	1	1	1	1	1	1	2	2	2	2	2	2	2	2
6	1	1	1	1	1	1	1	2	2	2	2	2	2	2	2	1	1	1	1	1	1	1	1	2	2	2	2	2	2	2	2
7	1	1	1	1	1	1	1	2	2	2	2	2	2	2	2	2	2	2	2	2	2	2	2	1	1	1	1	1	1	1	1
8	1	1	1	1	1	1	1	2	2	2	2	2	2	2	2	2	2	2	2	2	2	2	2	1	1	1	1	1	1	1	1
9	1	1	1	2	2	2	2	1	1	1	1	2	2	2	2	1	1	1	1	2	2	2	2	1	1	1	1	2	2	2	2
10	1	1	1	2	2	2	2	1	1	1	1	2	2	2	2	1	1	1	1	2	2	2	2	1	1	1	1	2	2	2	2
11	1	1	1	2	2	2	2	1	1	1	1	2	2	2	2	2	2	2	2	1	1	1	1	2	2	2	2	1	1	1	1
12	1	1	1	2	2	2	2	1	1	1	1	2	2	2	2	2	2	2	2	1	1	1	1	2	2	2	2	1	1	1	1
13	1	1	1	2	2	2	2	2	2	2	2	1	1	1	1	1	1	1	1	2	2	2	2	2	2	2	2	1	1	1	1
14	1	1	1	2	2	2	2	2	2	2	2	1	1	1	1	1	1	1	1	2	2	2	2	2	2	2	2	1	1	1	1
15	1	1	1	2	2	2	2	2	2	2	2	1	1	1	1	2	2	2	2	1	1	1	1	1	1	1	1	2	2	2	2
16	1	1	1	2	2	2	2	2	2	2	2	1	1	1	1	2	2	2	2	1	1	1	1	1	1	1	1	2	2	2	2
17	1	2	2	1	1	2	2	1	1	2	2	1	1	2	2	1	1	2	2	1	1	2	2	1	1	2	2	1	1	2	2
18	1	2	2	1	1	2	2	1	1	2	2	1	1	2	2	1	1	2	2	1	1	2	2	1	1	2	2	1	1	2	2
19	1	2	2	1	1	2	2	1	1	2	2	1	1	2	2	2	2	1	1	2	2	1	1	2	2	1	1	2	2	1	1
20	1	2	2	1	1	2	2	1	1	2	2	1	1	2	2	2	2	1	1	2	2	1	1	2	2	1	1	2	2	1	1
21	1	2	2	1	1	2	2	2	2	1	1	2	2	1	1	1	1	2	2	1	1	2	2	2	2	1	1	2	2	1	1
22	1	2	2	1	1	2	2	2	2	1	1	2	2	1	1	1	1	2	2	1	1	2	2	2	2	1	1	2	2	1	1
23	1	2	2	1	1	2	2	2	2	1	1	2	2	1	1	2	2	1	1	2	2	1	1	1	1	2	2	1	1	2	2
24	1	2	2	1	1	2	2	2	2	1	1	2	2	1	1	2	2	1	1	2	2	1	1	1	1	2	2	1	1	2	2
25	1	2	2	2	2	1	1	1	1	2	2	2	2	1	1	1	1	2	2	2	2	1	1	1	1	2	2	2	2	1	1
26	1	2	2	2	2	1	1	1	1	2	2	2	2	1	1	1	1	2	2	2	2	1	1	1	1	2	2	2	2	1	1
27	1	2	2	2	2	1	1	1	1	2	2	2	2	1	1	2	2	1	1	1	1	2	2	2	2	1	1	1	1	2	2
28	1	2	2	2	2	1	1	1	1	2	2	2	2	1	1	2	2	1	1	1	1	2	2	2	2	1	1	1	1	2	2
29	1	2	2	2	2	1	1	2	2	1	1	1	1	2	2	1	1	2	2	2	2	1	1	2	2	1	1	1	1	2	2
30	1	2	2	2	2	1	1	2	2	1	1	1	1	2	2	1	1	2	2	2	2	1	1	2	2	1	1	1	1	2	2
31	1	2	2	2	2	1	1	2	2	1	1	1	1	2	2	2	2	1	1	1	1	2	2	1	1	2	2	2	2	1	1
32	1	2	2	2	2	1	1	2	2	1	1	1	1	2	2	2	2	1	1	1	1	2	2	1	1	2	2	2	2	1	1
33	2	1	2	1	2	1	2	1	2	1	2	1	2	1	2	1	2	1	2	1	2	1	2	1	2	1	2	1	2	1	2
34	2	1	2	1	2	1	2	1	2	1	2	1	2	1	2	1	2	1	2	1	2	1	2	1	2	1	2	1	2	1	2
35	2	1	2	1	2	1	2	1	2	1	2	1	2	1	2	2	1	2	1	2	1	2	1	2	1	2	1	2	1	2	1
36	2	1	2	1	2	1	2	1	2	1	2	1	2	1	2	2	1	2	1	2	1	2	1	2	1	2	1	2	1	2	1
37	2	1	2	1	2	1	2	2	1	2	1	2	1	2	1	1	2	1	2	1	2	1	2	2	1	2	1	2	1	2	1
38	2	1	2	1	2	1	2	2	1	2	1	2	1	2	1	1	2	1	2	1	2	1	2	2	1	2	1	2	1	2	1
39	2	1	2	1	2	1	2	2	1	2	1	2	1	2	1	2	1	2	1	2	1	2	1	1	2	1	2	1	2	1	2
40	2	1	2	1	2	1	2	2	1	2	1	2	1	2	1	2	1	2	1	2	1	2	1	1	2	1	2	1	2	1	2
41	2	1	2	2	1	2	1	1	2	1	2	2	1	2	1	1	2	1	2	2	1	2	1	1	2	1	2	2	1	2	1
42	2	1	2	2	1	2	1	1	2	1	2	2	1	2	1	1	2	1	2	2	1	2	1	1	2	1	2	2	1	2	1
43	2	1	2	2	1	2	1	1	2	1	2	2	1	2	1	2	1	2	1	1	2	1	2	2	1	2	1	1	2	1	2
44	2	1	2	2	1	2	1	1	2	1	2	2	1	2	1	2	1	2	1	1	2	1	2	2	1	2	1	1	2	1	2
45	2	1	2	2	1	2	1	2	1	2	1	1	2	1	2	1	2	1	2	2	1	2	1	2	1	2	1	1	2	1	2
46	2	1	2	2	1	2	1	2	1	2	1	1	2	1	2	1	2	1	2	2	1	2	1	2	1	2	1	1	2	1	2
47	2	1	2	2	1	2	1	2	1	2	1	1	2	1	2	2	1	2	1	1	2	1	2	1	2	1	2	2	1	2	1
48	2	1	2	2	1	2	1	2	1	2	1	1	2	1	2	2	1	2	1	1	2	1	2	1	2	1	2	2	1	2	1
49	2	2	1	1	2	2	1	1	2	2	1	1	2	2	1	1	2	2	1	1	2	2	1	1	2	2	1	1	2	2	1
50	2	2	1	1	2	2	1	1	2	2	1	1	2	2	1	1	2	2	1	1	2	2	1	1	2	2	1	1	2	2	1
51	2	2	1	1	2	2	1	1	2	2	1	1	2	2	1	2	1	1	2	2	1	1	2	2	1	1	2	2	1	1	2
52	2	2	1	1	2	2	1	1	2	2	1	1	2	2	1	2	1	1	2	2	1	1	2	2	1	1	2	2	1	1	2
53	2	2	1	1	2	2	1	2	1	1	2	2	1	1	2	1	2	2	1	1	2	2	1	2	1	1	2	2	1	1	2
54	2	2	1	1	2	2	1	2	1	1	2	2	1	1	2	1	2	2	1	1	2	2	1	2	1	1	2	2	1	1	2
55	2	2	1	1	2	2	1	2	1	1	2	2	1	1	2	2	1	1	2	2	1	1	2	1	2	2	1	1	2	2	1
56	2	2	1	1	2	2	1	2	1	1	2	2	1	1	2	2	1	1	2	2	1	1	2	1	2	2	1	1	2	2	1
57	2	2	1	2	1	1	2	1	2	2	1	2	1	1	2	1	2	2	1	2	1	1	2	1	2	2	1	2	1	1	2
58	2	2	1	2	1	1	2	1	2	2	1	2	1	1	2	1	2	2	1	2	1	1	2	1	2	2	1	2	1	1	2
59	2	2	1	2	1	1	2	1	2	2	1	2	1	1	2	2	1	1	2	1	2	2	1	2	1	1	2	1	2	2	1
60	2	2	1	2	1	1	2	1	2	2	1	2	1	1	2	2	1	1	2	1	2	2	1	2	1	1	2	1	2	2	1
61	2	2	1	2	1	1	2	2	1	1	2	1	2	2	1	1	2	2	1	2	1	1	2	2	1	1	2	1	2	2	1
62	2	2	1	2	1	1	2	2	1	1	2	1	2	2	1	1	2	2	1	2	1	1	2	2	1	1	2	1	2	2	1
63	2	2	1	2	1	1	2	2	1	1	2	1	2	2	1	2	1	1	2	1	2	2	1	1	2	2	1	2	1	1	2
64	2	2	1	2	1	1	2	2	1	1	2	1	2	2	1	2	1	1	2	1	2	2	1	1	2	2	1	2	1	1	2

$L_{64}\ (2^{63})$ *cont'd.*

32	33	34	35	36	37	38	39	40	41	42	43	44	45	46	47	48	49	50	51	52	53	54	55	56	57	58	59	60	61	62	63
1	1	1	1	1	1	1	1	1	1	1	1	1	1	1	1	1	1	1	1	1	1	1	1	1	1	1	1	1	1	1	1
2	2	2	2	2	2	2	2	2	2	2	2	2	2	2	2	2	2	2	2	2	2	2	2	2	2	2	2	2	2	2	2
1	1	1	1	1	1	1	1	1	1	1	1	1	1	1	1	2	2	2	2	2	2	2	2	2	2	2	2	2	2	2	2
2	2	2	2	2	2	2	2	2	2	2	2	2	2	2	2	1	1	1	1	1	1	1	1	1	1	1	1	1	1	1	1
1	1	1	1	1	1	1	1	2	2	2	2	2	2	2	2	1	1	1	1	1	1	1	1	2	2	2	2	2	2	2	2
2	2	2	2	2	2	2	2	1	1	1	1	1	1	1	1	2	2	2	2	2	2	2	2	1	1	1	1	1	1	1	1
1	1	1	1	1	1	1	1	2	2	2	2	2	2	2	2	2	2	2	2	2	2	2	2	1	1	1	1	1	1	1	1
2	2	2	2	2	2	2	2	1	1	1	1	1	1	1	1	1	1	1	1	1	1	1	1	2	2	2	2	2	2	2	2
1	1	1	1	2	2	2	2	1	1	1	1	2	2	2	2	1	1	1	1	2	2	2	2	1	1	1	1	2	2	2	2
2	2	2	2	1	1	1	1	2	2	2	2	1	1	1	1	2	2	2	2	1	1	1	1	2	2	2	2	1	1	1	1
1	1	1	1	2	2	2	2	1	1	1	1	2	2	2	2	2	2	2	2	1	1	1	1	2	2	2	2	1	1	1	1
2	2	2	2	1	1	1	1	2	2	2	2	1	1	1	1	1	1	1	1	2	2	2	2	1	1	1	1	2	2	2	2
1	1	1	1	2	2	2	2	2	2	2	2	1	1	1	1	1	1	1	1	2	2	2	2	2	2	2	2	1	1	1	1
2	2	2	2	1	1	1	1	1	1	1	1	2	2	2	2	2	2	2	2	1	1	1	1	1	1	1	1	2	2	2	2
1	1	1	1	2	2	2	2	2	2	2	2	1	1	1	1	2	2	2	2	1	1	1	1	1	1	1	1	2	2	2	2
2	2	2	2	1	1	1	1	1	1	1	1	2	2	2	2	1	1	1	1	2	2	2	2	2	2	2	2	1	1	1	1
1	1	2	2	1	1	2	2	1	1	2	2	1	1	2	2	1	1	2	2	1	1	2	2	1	1	2	2	1	1	2	2
2	2	1	1	2	2	1	1	2	2	1	1	2	2	1	1	2	2	1	1	2	2	1	1	2	2	1	1	2	2	1	1
1	1	2	2	1	1	2	2	1	1	2	2	1	1	2	2	2	2	1	1	2	2	1	1	2	2	1	1	2	2	1	1
2	2	1	1	2	2	1	1	2	2	1	1	2	2	1	1	1	1	2	2	1	1	2	2	1	1	2	2	1	1	2	2
1	1	2	2	1	1	2	2	2	2	1	1	2	2	1	1	1	1	2	2	1	1	2	2	2	2	1	1	2	2	1	1
2	2	1	1	2	2	1	1	1	1	2	2	1	1	2	2	2	2	1	1	2	2	1	1	1	1	2	2	1	1	2	2
1	1	2	2	1	1	2	2	2	2	1	1	2	2	1	1	2	2	1	1	2	2	1	1	1	1	2	2	1	1	2	2
2	2	1	1	2	2	1	1	1	1	2	2	1	1	2	2	1	1	2	2	1	1	2	2	2	2	1	1	2	2	1	1
1	1	2	2	2	2	1	1	1	1	2	2	2	2	1	1	1	1	2	2	2	2	1	1	1	1	2	2	2	2	1	1
2	2	1	1	1	1	2	2	2	2	1	1	1	1	2	2	2	2	1	1	1	1	2	2	2	2	1	1	1	1	2	2
1	1	2	2	2	2	1	1	1	1	2	2	2	2	1	1	2	2	1	1	1	1	2	2	2	2	1	1	1	1	2	2
2	2	1	1	1	1	2	2	2	2	1	1	1	1	2	2	1	1	2	2	2	2	1	1	1	1	2	2	2	2	1	1
1	1	2	2	2	2	1	1	2	2	1	1	1	1	2	2	1	1	2	2	2	2	1	1	2	2	1	1	1	1	2	2
2	2	1	1	1	1	2	2	1	1	2	2	2	2	1	1	2	2	1	1	1	1	2	2	1	1	2	2	2	2	1	1
1	1	2	2	2	2	1	1	2	2	1	1	1	1	2	2	2	2	1	1	1	1	2	2	1	1	2	2	2	2	1	1
2	2	1	1	1	1	2	2	1	1	2	2	2	2	1	1	1	1	2	2	2	2	1	1	2	2	1	1	1	1	2	2
1	2	1	2	1	2	1	2	1	2	1	2	1	2	1	2	1	2	1	2	1	2	1	2	1	2	1	2	1	2	1	2
2	1	2	1	2	1	2	1	2	1	2	1	2	1	2	1	2	1	2	1	2	1	2	1	2	1	2	1	2	1	2	1
1	2	1	2	1	2	1	2	1	2	1	2	1	2	1	2	2	1	2	1	2	1	2	1	2	1	2	1	2	1	2	1
2	1	2	1	2	1	2	1	2	1	2	1	2	1	2	1	1	2	1	2	1	2	1	2	1	2	1	2	1	2	1	2
1	2	1	2	1	2	1	2	2	1	2	1	2	1	2	1	1	2	1	2	1	2	1	2	2	1	2	1	2	1	2	1
2	1	2	1	2	1	2	1	1	2	1	2	1	2	1	2	2	1	2	1	2	1	2	1	1	2	1	2	1	2	1	2
1	2	1	2	1	2	1	2	2	1	2	1	2	1	2	1	2	1	2	1	2	1	2	1	1	2	1	2	1	2	1	2
2	1	2	1	2	1	2	1	1	2	1	2	1	2	1	2	1	2	1	2	1	2	1	2	2	1	2	1	2	1	2	1
1	2	1	2	2	1	2	1	1	2	1	2	2	1	2	1	1	2	1	2	2	1	2	1	1	2	1	2	2	1	2	1
2	1	2	1	1	2	1	2	2	1	2	1	1	2	1	2	2	1	2	1	1	2	1	2	2	1	2	1	1	2	1	2
1	2	1	2	2	1	2	1	1	2	1	2	2	1	2	1	2	1	2	1	1	2	1	2	2	1	2	1	1	2	1	2
2	1	2	1	1	2	1	2	2	1	2	1	1	2	1	2	1	2	1	2	2	1	2	1	1	2	1	2	2	1	2	1
1	2	1	2	2	1	2	1	2	1	2	1	1	2	1	2	1	2	1	2	2	1	2	1	2	1	2	1	1	2	1	2
2	1	2	1	1	2	1	2	1	2	1	2	2	1	2	1	2	1	2	1	1	2	1	2	1	2	1	2	2	1	2	1
1	2	1	2	2	1	2	1	2	1	2	1	1	2	1	2	2	1	2	1	1	2	1	2	1	2	1	2	2	1	2	1
2	1	2	1	1	2	1	2	1	2	1	2	2	1	2	1	1	2	1	2	2	1	2	1	2	1	2	1	1	2	1	2
1	2	2	1	1	2	2	1	1	2	2	1	1	2	2	1	1	2	2	1	1	2	2	1	1	2	2	1	1	2	2	1
2	1	1	2	2	1	1	2	2	1	1	2	2	1	1	2	2	1	1	2	2	1	1	2	2	1	1	2	2	1	1	2
1	2	2	1	1	2	2	1	1	2	2	1	1	2	2	1	2	1	1	2	2	1	1	2	2	1	1	2	2	1	1	2
2	1	1	2	2	1	1	2	2	1	1	2	2	1	1	2	1	2	2	1	1	2	2	1	1	2	2	1	1	2	2	1
1	2	2	1	1	2	2	1	2	1	1	2	2	1	1	2	1	2	2	1	1	2	2	1	2	1	1	2	2	1	1	2
2	1	1	2	2	1	1	2	1	2	2	1	1	2	2	1	2	1	1	2	2	1	1	2	1	2	2	1	1	2	2	1
1	2	2	1	1	2	2	1	2	1	1	2	2	1	1	2	2	1	1	2	2	1	1	2	1	2	2	1	1	2	2	1
2	1	1	2	2	1	1	2	1	2	2	1	1	2	2	1	1	2	2	1	1	2	2	1	2	1	1	2	2	1	1	2
1	2	2	1	2	1	1	2	1	2	2	1	2	1	1	2	1	2	2	1	2	1	1	2	1	2	2	1	2	1	1	2
2	1	1	2	1	2	2	1	2	1	1	2	1	2	2	1	2	1	1	2	1	2	2	1	2	1	1	2	1	2	2	1
1	2	2	1	2	1	1	2	1	2	2	1	2	1	1	2	2	1	1	2	1	2	2	1	2	1	1	2	1	2	2	1
2	1	1	2	1	2	2	1	2	1	1	2	1	2	2	1	1	2	2	1	2	1	1	2	1	2	2	1	2	1	1	2
1	2	2	1	2	1	1	2	2	1	1	2	1	2	2	1	1	2	2	1	2	1	1	2	2	1	1	2	1	2	2	1
2	1	1	2	1	2	2	1	1	2	2	1	2	1	1	2	2	1	1	2	1	2	2	1	1	2	2	1	2	1	1	2
1	2	2	1	2	1	1	2	2	1	1	2	1	2	2	1	2	1	1	2	1	2	2	1	1	2	2	1	2	1	1	2
2	1	1	2	1	2	2	1	1	2	2	1	2	1	1	2	1	2	2	1	2	1	1	2	2	1	1	2	1	2	2	1

$L_9\ (3^4)$

No.	1	2	3	4
1	1	1	1	1
2	1	2	2	2
3	1	3	3	3
4	2	1	2	3
5	2	2	3	1
6	2	3	1	2
7	3	1	3	2
8	3	2	1	3
9	3	3	2	1

$L_{18}\ (2^1 \times 3^7)$

No.	1	2	3	4	5	6	7	8
1	1	1	1	1	1	1	1	1
2	1	1	2	2	2	2	2	2
3	1	1	3	3	3	3	3	3
4	1	2	1	1	2	2	3	3
5	1	2	2	2	3	3	1	1
6	1	2	3	3	1	1	2	2
7	1	3	1	2	1	3	2	3
8	1	3	2	3	2	1	3	1
9	1	3	3	1	3	2	1	2
10	2	1	1	3	3	2	2	1
11	2	1	2	1	1	3	3	2
12	2	1	3	2	2	1	1	3
13	2	2	1	2	3	1	3	2
14	2	2	2	3	1	2	1	3
15	2	2	3	1	2	3	2	1
16	2	3	1	3	2	3	1	2
17	2	3	2	1	3	1	2	3
18	2	3	3	2	1	2	3	1

L_{27} (3^{13})

No.	1	2	3	4	5	6	7	8	9	10	11	12	13
1	1	1	1	1	1	1	1	1	1	1	1	1	1
2	1	1	1	1	2	2	2	2	2	2	2	2	2
3	1	1	1	1	3	3	3	3	3	3	3	3	3
4	1	2	2	2	1	1	1	2	2	2	3	3	3
5	1	2	2	2	2	2	2	3	3	3	1	1	1
6	1	2	2	2	3	3	3	1	1	1	2	2	2
7	1	3	3	3	1	1	1	3	3	3	2	2	2
8	1	3	3	3	2	2	2	1	1	1	3	3	3
9	1	3	3	3	3	3	3	2	2	2	1	1	1
10	2	1	2	3	1	2	3	1	2	3	1	2	3
11	2	1	2	3	2	3	1	2	3	1	2	3	1
12	2	1	2	3	3	1	2	3	1	2	3	1	2
13	2	2	3	1	1	2	3	2	3	1	3	1	2
14	2	2	3	1	2	3	1	3	1	2	1	2	3
15	2	2	3	1	3	1	2	1	2	3	2	3	1
16	2	3	1	2	1	2	3	3	1	2	2	3	1
17	2	3	1	2	2	3	1	1	2	3	3	1	2
18	2	3	1	2	3	1	2	2	3	1	1	2	3
19	3	1	3	2	1	3	2	1	3	2	1	3	2
20	3	1	3	2	2	1	3	2	1	3	2	1	3
21	3	1	3	2	3	2	1	3	2	1	3	2	1
22	3	2	1	3	1	3	2	2	1	3	3	2	1
23	3	2	1	3	2	1	3	3	2	1	1	3	2
24	3	2	1	3	3	2	1	1	3	2	2	1	3
25	3	3	2	1	1	3	2	3	2	1	2	1	3
26	3	3	2	1	2	1	3	1	3	2	3	2	1
27	3	3	2	1	3	2	1	2	1	3	1	3	2

$L_{54}\ (2^1 \times 3^{25})$

No.	1	2	3	4	5	6	7	8	9	10	11	12	13	14	15	16	17	18	19	20	21	22	23	24	25	26
1	1	1	1	1	1	1	1	1	1	1	1	1	1	1	1	1	1	1	1	1	1	1	1	1	1	1
2	1	1	1	1	1	1	1	1	2	2	2	2	2	2	2	2	2	2	2	2	2	2	2	2	2	2
3	1	1	1	1	1	1	1	1	3	3	3	3	3	3	3	3	3	3	3	3	3	3	3	3	3	3
4	1	1	2	2	2	2	2	2	1	1	1	1	1	1	2	3	2	3	2	3	2	3	2	3	2	3
5	1	1	2	2	2	2	2	2	2	2	2	2	2	2	3	1	3	1	3	1	3	1	3	1	3	1
6	1	1	2	2	2	2	2	2	3	3	3	3	3	3	1	2	1	2	1	2	1	2	1	2	1	2
7	1	1	3	3	3	3	3	3	1	1	1	1	1	1	3	2	3	2	3	2	3	2	3	2	3	2
8	1	1	3	3	3	3	3	3	2	2	2	2	2	2	1	3	1	3	1	3	1	3	1	3	1	3
9	1	1	3	3	3	3	3	3	3	3	3	3	3	3	2	1	2	1	2	1	2	1	2	1	2	1
10	1	2	1	1	2	2	3	3	1	1	2	2	3	3	1	1	1	1	2	3	2	3	3	2	3	2
11	1	2	1	1	2	2	3	3	2	2	3	3	1	1	2	2	2	2	3	1	3	1	1	3	1	3
12	1	2	1	1	2	2	3	3	3	3	1	1	2	2	3	3	3	3	1	2	1	2	2	1	2	1
13	1	2	2	2	3	3	1	1	1	1	2	2	3	3	2	3	2	3	3	2	3	2	1	1	1	1
14	1	2	2	2	3	3	1	1	2	2	3	3	1	1	3	1	3	1	1	3	1	3	2	2	2	2
15	1	2	2	2	3	3	1	1	3	3	1	1	2	2	1	2	1	2	2	1	2	1	3	3	3	3
16	1	2	3	3	1	1	2	2	1	1	2	2	3	3	3	2	3	2	1	1	1	1	2	3	2	3
17	1	2	3	3	1	1	2	2	2	2	3	3	1	1	1	3	1	3	2	2	2	2	3	1	3	1
18	1	2	3	3	1	1	2	2	3	3	1	1	2	2	2	1	2	1	3	3	3	3	1	2	1	2
19	1	3	1	2	1	3	2	3	1	2	1	3	2	3	1	1	2	3	1	1	3	2	2	3	3	2
20	1	3	1	2	1	3	2	3	2	3	2	1	3	1	2	2	3	1	2	2	1	3	3	1	1	3
21	1	3	1	2	1	3	2	3	3	1	3	2	1	2	3	3	1	2	3	3	2	1	1	2	2	1
22	1	3	2	3	2	1	3	1	1	2	1	3	2	3	2	3	3	2	2	3	1	1	3	2	1	1
23	1	3	2	3	2	1	3	1	2	3	2	1	3	1	3	1	1	3	3	1	2	2	1	3	2	2
24	1	3	2	3	2	1	3	1	3	1	3	2	1	2	1	2	2	1	1	2	3	3	2	1	3	3
25	1	3	3	1	3	2	1	2	1	2	1	3	2	3	3	2	1	1	3	2	2	3	1	1	2	3
26	1	3	3	1	3	2	1	2	2	3	2	1	3	1	1	3	2	2	1	3	3	1	2	2	3	1
27	1	3	3	1	3	2	1	2	3	1	3	2	1	2	2	1	3	3	2	1	1	2	3	3	1	2

L_{54} $(2^1 \times 3^{25})$ *cont'd.*

No.	1	2	3	4	5	6	7	8	9	10	11	12	13	14	15	16	17	18	19	20	21	22	23	24	25	26
28	2	1	1	3	3	2	2	1	1	3	3	2	2	1	1	1	3	2	3	2	2	3	2	3	1	1
29	2	1	1	3	3	2	2	1	2	1	1	3	3	2	2	2	1	3	1	3	3	1	3	1	2	2
30	2	1	1	3	3	2	2	1	3	2	2	1	1	3	3	3	2	1	2	1	1	2	1	2	3	3
31	2	1	2	1	1	3	3	2	1	3	3	2	2	1	2	3	1	1	1	1	3	2	3	2	2	3
32	2	1	2	1	1	3	3	2	2	1	1	3	3	2	3	1	2	2	2	2	1	3	1	3	3	1
33	2	1	2	1	1	3	3	2	3	2	2	1	1	3	1	2	3	3	3	3	2	1	2	1	1	2
34	2	1	3	2	2	1	1	3	1	3	3	2	2	1	3	2	2	3	2	3	1	1	1	1	3	2
35	2	1	3	2	2	1	1	3	2	1	1	3	3	2	1	3	3	1	3	1	2	2	2	2	1	3
36	2	1	3	2	2	1	1	3	3	2	2	1	1	3	2	1	1	2	1	2	3	3	3	3	2	1
37	2	2	1	2	3	1	3	2	1	2	3	1	3	2	1	1	2	3	3	2	1	1	3	2	2	3
38	2	2	1	2	3	1	3	2	2	3	1	2	1	3	2	2	3	1	1	3	2	2	1	3	3	1
39	2	2	1	2	3	1	3	2	3	1	2	3	2	1	3	3	1	2	2	1	3	3	2	1	1	2
40	2	2	2	3	1	2	1	3	1	2	3	1	3	2	2	3	3	2	1	1	2	3	1	1	3	2
41	2	2	2	3	1	2	1	3	2	3	1	2	1	3	3	1	1	3	2	2	3	1	2	2	1	3
42	2	2	2	3	1	2	1	3	3	1	2	3	2	1	1	2	2	1	3	3	1	2	3	3	2	1
43	2	2	3	1	2	3	2	1	1	2	3	1	3	2	3	2	1	1	2	3	3	2	2	3	1	1
44	2	2	3	1	2	3	2	1	2	3	1	2	1	3	1	3	2	2	3	1	1	3	3	1	2	2
45	2	2	3	1	2	3	2	1	3	1	2	3	2	1	2	1	3	3	1	2	2	1	1	2	3	3
46	2	3	1	3	2	3	1	2	1	3	2	3	1	2	1	1	3	2	2	3	3	2	1	1	2	3
47	2	3	1	3	2	3	1	2	2	1	3	1	2	3	2	2	1	3	3	1	1	3	2	2	3	1
48	2	3	1	3	2	3	1	2	3	2	1	2	3	1	3	3	2	1	1	2	2	1	3	3	1	2
49	2	3	2	1	3	1	2	3	1	3	2	3	1	2	2	3	1	1	3	2	1	1	2	3	3	2
50	2	3	2	1	3	1	2	3	2	1	3	1	2	3	3	1	2	2	1	3	2	2	3	1	1	3
51	2	3	2	1	3	1	2	3	3	2	1	2	3	1	1	2	3	3	2	1	3	3	1	2	2	1
52	2	3	3	2	1	2	3	1	1	3	2	3	1	2	3	2	2	3	1	1	2	3	3	2	1	1
53	2	3	3	2	1	2	3	1	2	1	3	1	2	3	1	3	3	1	2	2	3	1	1	3	2	2
54	2	3	3	2	1	2	3	1	3	2	1	2	3	1	2	1	1	2	3	3	1	2	2	1	3	3

$L_{81}\ (3^{40})$

No.	1	2	3	4	5	6	7	8	9	10	11	12	13	14	15	16	17	18	19	20	21	22	23	24	25	26	27	28	29	30	31	32	33	34	35	36	37	38	39	40
1	1	1	1	1	1	1	1	1	1	1	1	1	1	1	1	1	1	1	1	1	1	1	1	1	1	1	1	1	1	1	1	1	1	1	1	1	1	1	1	1
2	1	1	1	1	1	1	1	1	1	1	1	1	1	2	2	2	2	2	2	2	2	2	2	2	2	2	2	2	2	2	2	2	2	2	2	2	2	2	2	2
3	1	1	1	1	1	1	1	1	1	1	1	1	1	3	3	3	3	3	3	3	3	3	3	3	3	3	3	3	3	3	3	3	3	3	3	3	3	3	3	3
4	1	1	1	1	2	2	2	2	2	2	2	2	2	1	1	1	1	1	1	1	1	1	2	2	2	2	2	2	2	2	2	3	3	3	3	3	3	3	3	3
5	1	1	1	1	2	2	2	2	2	2	2	2	2	2	2	2	2	2	2	2	2	2	3	3	3	3	3	3	3	3	3	1	1	1	1	1	1	1	1	1
6	1	1	1	1	2	2	2	2	2	2	2	2	2	3	3	3	3	3	3	3	3	3	1	1	1	1	1	1	1	1	1	2	2	2	2	2	2	2	2	2
7	1	1	1	1	3	3	3	3	3	3	3	3	3	1	1	1	1	1	1	1	1	1	3	3	3	3	3	3	3	3	3	2	2	2	2	2	2	2	2	2
8	1	1	1	1	3	3	3	3	3	3	3	3	3	2	2	2	2	2	2	2	2	2	1	1	1	1	1	1	1	1	1	3	3	3	3	3	3	3	3	3
9	1	1	1	1	3	3	3	3	3	3	3	3	3	3	3	3	3	3	3	3	3	3	2	2	2	2	2	2	2	2	2	1	1	1	1	1	1	1	1	1
10	1	2	2	2	1	1	1	2	2	2	3	3	3	1	1	1	2	2	2	3	3	3	1	1	1	2	2	2	3	3	3	1	1	1	2	2	2	3	3	3
11	1	2	2	2	1	1	1	2	2	2	3	3	3	2	2	2	3	3	3	1	1	1	2	2	2	3	3	3	1	1	1	2	2	2	3	3	3	1	1	1
12	1	2	2	2	1	1	1	2	2	2	3	3	3	3	3	3	1	1	1	2	2	2	3	3	3	1	1	1	2	2	2	3	3	3	1	1	1	2	2	2
13	1	2	2	2	2	2	2	3	3	3	1	1	1	1	1	1	2	2	2	3	3	3	2	2	2	3	3	3	1	1	1	3	3	3	1	1	1	2	2	2
14	1	2	2	2	2	2	2	3	3	3	1	1	1	2	2	2	3	3	3	1	1	1	3	3	3	1	1	1	2	2	2	1	1	1	2	2	2	3	3	3
15	1	2	2	2	2	2	2	3	3	3	1	1	1	3	3	3	1	1	1	2	2	2	1	1	1	2	2	2	3	3	3	2	2	2	3	3	3	1	1	1
16	1	2	2	2	3	3	3	1	1	1	2	2	2	1	1	1	2	2	2	3	3	3	3	3	3	1	1	1	2	2	2	2	2	2	3	3	3	1	1	1
17	1	2	2	2	3	3	3	1	1	1	2	2	2	2	2	2	3	3	3	1	1	1	1	1	1	2	2	2	3	3	3	3	3	3	1	1	1	2	2	2
18	1	2	2	2	3	3	3	1	1	1	2	2	2	3	3	3	1	1	1	2	2	2	2	2	2	3	3	3	1	1	1	1	1	1	2	2	2	3	3	3
19	1	3	3	3	1	1	1	3	3	3	2	2	2	1	1	1	3	3	3	2	2	2	1	1	1	3	3	3	2	2	2	1	1	1	3	3	3	2	2	2
20	1	3	3	3	1	1	1	3	3	3	2	2	2	2	2	2	1	1	1	3	3	3	2	2	2	1	1	1	3	3	3	2	2	2	1	1	1	3	3	3
21	1	3	3	3	1	1	1	3	3	3	2	2	2	3	3	3	2	2	2	1	1	1	3	3	3	2	2	2	1	1	1	3	3	3	2	2	2	1	1	1

22	1	3	3	3	2	2	2	1	1	1	3	3	3	1	1	1	3	3	3	2	2	2	2	2	2	1	1	1	3	3	3	3	3	3	2	2	2	1	1	1
23	1	3	3	3	2	2	2	1	1	1	3	3	3	2	2	2	1	1	1	3	3	3	3	3	3	2	2	2	1	1	1	1	1	1	3	3	3	2	2	2
24	1	3	3	3	2	2	2	1	1	1	3	3	3	3	3	3	2	2	2	1	1	1	1	1	1	3	3	3	2	2	2	2	2	2	1	1	1	3	3	3
25	1	3	3	3	3	3	3	2	2	2	1	1	1	1	1	1	3	3	3	2	2	2	3	3	3	2	2	2	1	1	1	2	2	2	1	1	1	3	3	3
26	1	3	3	3	3	3	3	2	2	2	1	1	1	2	2	2	1	1	1	3	3	3	1	1	1	3	3	3	2	2	2	3	3	3	2	2	2	1	1	1
27	1	3	3	3	3	3	3	2	2	2	1	1	1	3	3	3	2	2	2	1	1	1	2	2	2	1	1	1	3	3	3	1	1	1	3	3	3	2	2	2
28	2	1	2	3	1	2	3	1	2	3	1	2	3	1	2	3	1	2	3	1	2	3	1	2	3	1	2	3	1	2	3	1	2	3	1	2	3	1	2	3
29	2	1	2	3	1	2	3	1	2	3	1	2	3	2	3	1	2	3	1	2	3	1	2	3	1	2	3	1	2	3	1	2	3	1	2	3	1	2	3	1
30	2	1	2	3	1	2	3	1	2	3	1	2	3	3	1	2	3	1	2	3	1	2	3	1	2	3	1	2	3	1	2	3	1	2	3	1	2	3	1	2
31	2	1	2	3	2	3	1	2	3	1	2	3	1	1	2	3	1	2	3	1	2	3	2	3	1	2	3	1	2	3	1	3	1	2	3	1	2	3	1	2
32	2	1	2	3	2	3	1	2	3	1	2	3	1	2	3	1	2	3	1	2	3	1	3	1	2	3	1	2	3	1	2	1	2	3	1	2	3	1	2	3
33	2	1	2	3	2	3	1	2	3	1	2	3	1	3	1	2	3	1	2	3	1	2	1	2	3	1	2	3	1	2	3	2	3	1	2	3	1	2	3	1
34	2	1	2	3	3	1	2	3	1	2	3	1	2	1	2	3	1	2	3	1	2	3	3	1	2	3	1	2	3	1	2	2	3	1	2	3	1	2	3	1
35	2	1	2	3	3	1	2	3	1	2	3	1	2	2	3	1	2	3	1	2	3	1	1	2	3	1	2	3	1	2	3	3	1	2	3	1	2	3	1	2
36	2	1	2	3	3	1	2	3	1	2	3	1	2	3	1	2	3	1	2	3	1	2	2	3	1	2	3	1	2	3	1	1	2	3	1	2	3	1	2	3
37	2	2	3	1	1	2	3	2	3	1	3	1	2	1	2	3	2	3	1	3	1	2	1	2	3	2	3	1	3	1	2	1	2	3	2	3	1	3	1	2
38	2	2	3	1	1	2	3	2	3	1	3	1	2	2	3	1	3	1	2	1	2	3	2	3	1	3	1	2	1	2	3	2	3	1	3	1	2	1	2	3
39	2	2	3	1	1	2	3	2	3	1	3	1	2	3	1	2	1	2	3	2	3	1	3	1	2	1	2	3	2	3	1	3	1	2	1	2	3	2	3	1
40	2	2	3	1	2	3	1	3	1	2	1	2	3	1	2	3	2	3	1	3	1	2	2	3	1	3	1	2	1	2	3	3	1	2	1	2	3	2	3	1
41	2	2	3	1	2	3	1	3	1	2	1	2	3	2	3	1	3	1	2	1	2	3	3	1	2	1	2	3	2	3	1	1	2	3	2	3	1	3	1	2
42	2	2	3	1	2	3	1	3	1	2	1	2	3	3	1	2	1	2	3	2	3	1	1	2	3	2	3	1	3	1	2	2	3	1	3	1	2	1	2	3

L_{81} (3^{40}) *cont'd.*

No.	1	2	3	4	5	6	7	8	9	10	11	12	13	14	15	16	17	18	19	20	21	22	23	24	25	26	27	28	29	30	31	32	33	34	35	36	37	38	39	40
43	2	2	3	1	3	1	2	1	2	3	2	3	1	1	2	3	2	3	1	3	1	2	3	1	2	1	2	3	2	3	1	2	3	1	3	1	2	1	2	3
44	2	2	3	1	3	1	2	1	2	3	2	3	1	2	3	1	3	1	2	1	2	3	1	2	3	2	3	1	3	1	2	3	1	2	1	2	3	2	3	1
45	2	2	3	1	3	1	2	1	2	3	2	3	1	3	1	2	1	2	3	2	3	1	2	3	1	3	1	2	1	2	3	1	2	3	2	3	1	3	1	2
46	2	3	1	2	1	2	3	3	1	2	2	3	1	1	2	3	3	1	2	2	3	1	1	2	3	3	1	2	2	3	1	1	2	3	3	1	2	2	3	1
47	2	3	1	2	1	2	3	3	1	2	2	3	1	2	3	1	1	2	3	3	1	2	2	3	1	1	2	3	3	1	2	2	3	1	1	2	3	3	1	2
48	2	3	1	2	1	2	3	3	1	2	2	3	1	3	1	2	2	3	1	1	2	3	3	1	2	2	3	1	1	2	3	3	1	2	2	3	1	1	2	3
49	2	3	1	2	2	3	1	1	2	3	3	1	2	1	2	3	3	1	2	2	3	1	2	3	1	1	2	3	3	1	2	3	1	2	2	3	1	1	2	3
50	2	3	1	2	2	3	1	1	2	3	3	1	2	2	3	1	1	2	3	3	1	2	3	1	2	2	3	1	1	2	3	1	2	3	3	1	2	2	3	1
51	2	3	1	2	2	3	1	1	2	3	3	1	2	3	1	2	2	3	1	1	2	3	1	2	3	3	1	2	2	3	1	2	3	1	1	2	3	3	1	2
52	2	3	1	2	3	1	2	2	3	1	1	2	3	1	2	3	3	1	2	2	3	1	3	1	2	2	3	1	1	2	3	2	3	1	1	2	3	3	1	2
53	2	3	1	2	3	1	2	2	3	1	1	2	3	2	3	1	1	2	3	3	1	2	1	2	3	3	1	2	2	3	1	3	1	2	2	3	1	1	2	3
54	2	3	1	2	3	1	2	2	3	1	1	2	3	3	1	2	2	3	1	1	2	3	2	3	1	1	2	3	3	1	2	1	2	3	3	1	2	2	3	1
55	3	1	3	2	1	3	2	1	3	2	1	3	2	1	3	2	1	3	2	1	3	2	1	3	2	1	3	2	1	3	2	1	3	2	1	3	2	1	3	2
56	3	1	3	2	1	3	2	1	3	2	1	3	2	2	1	3	2	1	3	2	1	3	2	1	3	2	1	3	2	1	3	2	1	3	2	1	3	2	1	3
57	3	1	3	2	1	3	2	1	3	2	1	3	2	3	2	1	3	2	1	3	2	1	3	2	1	3	2	1	3	2	1	3	2	1	3	2	1	3	2	1
58	3	1	3	2	2	1	3	2	1	3	2	1	3	1	3	2	1	3	2	1	3	2	2	1	3	2	1	3	2	1	3	3	2	1	3	2	1	3	2	1
59	3	1	3	2	2	1	3	2	1	3	2	1	3	2	1	3	2	1	3	2	1	3	3	2	1	3	2	1	3	2	1	1	3	2	1	3	2	1	3	2
60	3	1	3	2	2	1	3	2	1	3	2	1	3	3	2	1	3	2	1	3	2	1	1	3	2	1	3	2	1	3	2	2	1	3	2	1	3	2	1	3

61	3	1	3	2	3	2	1	3	2	1	3	2	1	1	3	2	1	3	2	1	3	2	3	2	1	3	2	1	3	2	1	2	1	3	2	1	3	2	1	3
62	3	1	3	2	3	2	1	3	2	1	3	2	1	2	1	3	2	1	3	2	1	3	1	3	2	1	3	2	1	3	2	3	2	1	3	2	1	3	2	1
63	3	1	3	2	3	2	1	3	2	1	3	2	1	3	2	1	3	2	1	3	2	1	2	1	3	2	1	3	2	1	3	1	3	2	1	3	2	1	3	2
64	3	2	1	3	1	3	2	2	1	3	3	2	1	1	3	2	2	1	3	3	2	1	1	3	2	2	1	3	3	2	1	1	3	2	2	1	3	3	2	1
65	3	2	1	3	1	3	2	2	1	3	3	2	1	2	1	3	3	2	1	1	3	2	2	1	3	3	2	1	1	3	2	2	1	3	3	2	1	1	3	2
66	3	2	1	3	1	3	2	2	1	3	3	2	1	3	2	1	1	3	2	2	1	3	3	2	1	1	3	2	2	1	3	3	2	1	1	3	2	2	1	3
67	3	2	1	3	2	1	3	3	2	1	1	3	2	1	3	2	2	1	3	3	2	1	2	1	3	3	2	1	1	3	2	3	2	1	1	3	2	2	1	3
68	3	2	1	3	2	1	3	3	2	1	1	3	2	2	1	3	3	2	1	1	3	2	3	2	1	1	3	2	2	1	3	1	3	2	2	1	3	3	2	1
69	3	2	1	3	2	1	3	3	2	1	1	3	2	3	2	1	1	3	2	2	1	3	1	3	2	2	1	3	3	2	1	2	1	3	3	2	1	1	3	2
70	3	2	1	3	3	2	1	1	3	2	2	1	3	1	3	2	2	1	3	3	2	1	3	2	1	1	3	2	2	1	3	2	1	3	3	2	1	1	3	2
71	3	2	1	3	3	2	1	1	3	2	2	1	3	2	1	3	3	2	1	1	3	2	1	3	2	2	1	3	3	2	1	3	2	1	1	3	2	2	1	3
72	3	2	1	3	3	2	1	1	3	2	2	1	3	3	2	1	1	3	2	2	1	3	2	1	3	3	2	1	1	3	2	1	3	2	2	1	3	3	2	1
73	3	3	2	1	1	3	2	3	2	1	2	1	3	1	3	2	3	2	1	2	1	3	1	3	2	3	2	1	2	1	3	1	3	2	3	2	1	2	1	3
74	3	3	2	1	1	3	2	3	2	1	2	1	3	2	1	3	1	3	2	3	2	1	2	1	3	1	3	2	3	2	1	2	1	3	1	3	2	3	2	1
75	3	3	2	1	1	3	2	3	2	1	2	1	3	3	2	1	2	1	3	1	3	2	3	2	1	2	1	3	1	3	2	3	2	1	2	1	3	1	3	2
76	3	3	2	1	2	1	3	1	3	2	3	2	1	1	3	2	3	2	1	2	1	3	2	1	3	1	3	2	3	2	1	3	2	1	2	1	3	1	3	2
77	3	3	2	1	2	1	3	1	3	2	3	2	1	2	1	3	1	3	2	3	2	1	3	2	1	2	1	3	1	3	2	1	3	2	3	2	1	2	1	3
78	3	3	2	1	2	1	3	1	3	2	3	2	1	3	2	1	2	1	3	1	3	2	1	3	2	3	2	1	2	1	3	2	1	3	1	3	2	3	2	1
79	3	3	2	1	3	2	1	2	1	3	1	3	2	1	3	2	3	2	1	2	1	3	3	2	1	2	1	3	1	3	2	2	1	3	1	3	2	3	2	1
80	3	3	2	1	3	2	1	2	1	3	1	3	2	2	1	3	1	3	2	3	2	1	1	3	2	3	2	1	2	1	3	3	2	1	2	1	3	1	3	2
81	3	3	2	1	3	2	1	2	1	3	1	3	2	3	2	1	2	1	3	1	3	2	2	1	3	1	3	2	3	2	1	1	3	2	3	2	1	2	1	3

L_{16} (4^5)

No.	1	2	3	4	5
1	1	1	1	1	1
2	1	2	2	2	2
3	1	3	3	3	3
4	1	4	4	4	4
5	2	1	2	3	4
6	2	2	1	4	3
7	2	3	4	1	2
8	2	4	3	2	1
9	3	1	3	4	2
10	3	2	4	3	1
11	3	3	1	2	4
12	3	4	2	1	3
13	4	1	4	2	3
14	4	2	3	1	4
15	4	3	2	4	1
16	4	4	1	3	2

L_{32} $(2^1 \times 4^9)$

No.	1	2	3	4	5	6	7	8	9	10
1	1	1	1	1	1	1	1	1	1	1
2	1	1	2	2	2	2	2	2	2	2
3	1	1	3	3	3	3	3	3	3	3
4	1	1	4	4	4	4	4	4	4	4
5	1	2	1	1	2	2	3	3	4	4
6	1	2	2	2	1	1	4	4	3	3
7	1	2	3	3	4	4	1	1	2	2
8	1	2	4	4	3	3	2	2	1	1
9	1	3	1	2	3	4	1	2	3	4
10	1	3	2	1	4	3	2	1	4	3
11	1	3	3	4	1	2	3	4	1	2
12	1	3	4	3	2	1	4	3	2	1
13	1	4	1	2	4	3	3	4	2	1
14	1	4	2	1	3	4	4	3	1	2
15	1	4	3	4	2	1	1	2	4	3
16	1	4	4	3	1	2	2	1	3	4
17	2	1	1	4	1	4	2	3	2	3
18	2	1	2	3	2	3	1	4	1	4
19	2	1	3	2	3	2	4	1	4	1
20	2	1	4	1	4	1	3	2	3	2
21	2	2	1	4	2	3	4	1	3	2
22	2	2	2	3	1	4	3	2	4	1
23	2	2	3	2	4	1	2	3	1	4
24	2	2	4	1	3	2	1	4	2	3
25	2	3	1	3	3	1	2	4	4	2
26	2	3	2	4	4	2	1	3	3	1
27	2	3	3	1	1	3	4	2	2	4
28	2	3	4	2	2	4	3	1	1	3
29	2	4	1	3	4	2	4	2	1	3
30	2	4	2	4	3	1	3	1	2	4
31	2	4	3	1	2	4	2	4	3	1
32	2	4	4	2	1	3	1	3	4	2

L_{64} (4^{21})

No.	1	2	3	4	5	6	7	8	9	10	11	12	13	14	15	16	17	18	19	20	21
1	1	1	1	1	1	1	1	1	1	1	1	1	1	1	1	1	1	1	1	1	1
2	1	1	1	1	1	2	2	2	2	2	2	2	2	2	2	2	2	2	2	2	2
3	1	1	1	1	1	3	3	3	3	3	3	3	3	3	3	3	3	3	3	3	3
4	1	1	1	1	1	4	4	4	4	4	4	4	4	4	4	4	4	4	4	4	4
5	1	2	2	2	2	1	1	1	1	2	2	2	2	3	3	3	3	4	4	4	4
6	1	2	2	2	2	2	2	2	2	1	1	1	1	4	4	4	4	3	3	3	3
7	1	2	2	2	2	3	3	3	3	4	4	4	4	1	1	1	1	2	2	2	2
8	1	2	2	2	2	4	4	4	4	3	3	3	3	2	2	2	2	1	1	1	1
9	1	3	3	3	3	1	1	1	1	3	3	3	3	4	4	4	4	2	2	2	2
10	1	3	3	3	3	2	2	2	2	4	4	4	4	3	3	3	3	1	1	1	1
11	1	3	3	3	3	3	3	3	3	1	1	1	1	2	2	2	2	4	4	4	4
12	1	3	3	3	3	4	4	4	4	2	2	2	2	1	1	1	1	3	3	3	3
13	1	4	4	4	4	1	1	1	1	4	4	4	4	2	2	2	2	3	3	3	3
14	1	4	4	4	4	2	2	2	2	3	3	3	3	1	1	1	1	4	4	4	4
15	1	4	4	4	4	3	3	3	3	2	2	2	2	4	4	4	4	1	1	1	1
16	1	4	4	4	4	4	4	4	4	1	1	1	1	3	3	3	3	2	2	2	2
17	2	1	2	3	4	1	2	3	4	1	2	3	4	1	2	3	4	1	2	3	4
18	2	1	2	3	4	2	1	4	3	2	1	4	3	2	1	4	3	2	1	4	3
19	2	1	2	3	4	3	4	1	2	3	4	1	2	3	4	1	2	3	4	1	2
20	2	1	2	3	4	4	3	2	1	4	3	2	1	4	3	2	1	4	3	2	1
21	2	2	1	4	3	1	2	3	4	2	1	4	3	3	4	1	2	4	3	2	1
22	2	2	1	4	3	2	1	4	3	1	2	3	4	4	3	2	1	3	4	1	2
23	2	2	1	4	3	3	4	1	2	4	3	2	1	1	2	3	4	2	1	4	3
24	2	2	1	4	3	4	3	2	1	3	4	1	2	2	1	4	3	1	2	3	4
25	2	3	4	1	2	1	2	3	4	3	4	1	2	4	3	2	1	2	1	4	3
26	2	3	4	1	2	2	1	4	3	4	3	2	1	3	4	1	2	1	2	3	4
27	2	3	4	1	2	3	4	1	2	1	2	3	4	2	1	4	3	4	3	2	1
28	2	3	4	1	2	4	3	2	1	2	1	4	3	1	2	3	4	3	4	1	2
29	2	4	3	2	1	1	2	3	4	4	3	2	1	2	1	4	3	3	4	1	2
30	2	4	3	2	1	2	1	4	3	3	4	1	2	1	2	3	4	4	3	2	1
31	2	4	3	2	1	3	4	1	2	2	1	4	3	4	3	2	1	1	2	3	4
32	2	4	3	2	1	4	3	2	1	1	2	3	4	3	4	1	2	2	1	4	3

$L_{64}(4^{21})$ *cont'd.*

No.	1	2	3	4	5	6	7	8	9	10	11	12	13	14	15	16	17	18	19	20	21
33	3	1	3	4	2	1	3	4	2	1	3	4	2	1	3	4	2	1	3	4	2
34	3	1	3	4	2	2	4	3	1	2	4	3	1	2	4	3	1	2	4	3	1
35	3	1	3	4	2	3	1	2	4	3	1	2	4	3	1	2	4	3	1	2	4
36	3	1	3	4	2	4	2	1	3	4	2	1	3	4	2	1	3	4	2	1	3
37	3	2	4	3	1	1	3	4	2	2	4	3	1	3	1	2	4	4	2	1	3
38	3	2	4	3	1	2	4	3	1	1	3	4	2	4	2	1	3	3	1	2	4
39	3	2	4	3	1	3	1	2	4	4	2	1	3	1	3	4	2	2	4	3	1
40	3	2	4	3	1	4	2	1	3	3	1	2	4	2	4	3	1	1	3	4	2
41	3	3	1	2	4	1	3	4	2	3	1	2	4	4	2	1	3	2	4	3	1
42	3	3	1	2	4	2	4	3	1	4	2	1	3	3	1	2	4	1	3	4	2
43	3	3	1	2	4	3	1	2	4	1	3	4	2	2	4	3	1	4	2	1	3
44	3	3	1	2	4	4	2	1	3	2	4	3	1	1	3	4	2	3	1	2	4
45	3	4	2	1	3	1	3	4	2	4	2	1	3	2	4	3	1	3	1	2	4
46	3	4	2	1	3	2	4	3	1	3	1	2	4	1	3	4	2	4	2	1	3
47	3	4	2	1	3	3	1	2	4	2	4	3	1	4	2	1	3	1	3	4	2
48	3	4	2	1	3	4	2	1	3	1	3	4	2	3	1	2	4	2	4	3	1
49	4	1	4	2	3	1	4	2	3	1	4	2	3	1	4	2	3	1	4	2	3
50	4	1	4	2	3	2	3	1	4	2	3	1	4	2	3	1	4	2	3	1	4
51	4	1	4	2	3	3	2	4	1	3	2	4	1	3	2	4	1	3	2	4	1
52	4	1	4	2	3	4	1	3	2	4	1	3	2	4	1	3	2	4	1	3	2
53	4	2	3	1	4	1	4	2	3	2	3	1	4	3	2	4	1	4	1	3	2
54	4	2	3	1	4	2	3	1	4	1	4	2	3	4	1	3	2	3	2	4	1
55	4	2	3	1	4	3	2	4	1	4	1	3	2	1	4	2	3	2	3	1	4
56	4	2	3	1	4	4	1	3	2	3	2	4	1	2	3	1	4	1	4	2	3
57	4	3	2	4	1	1	4	2	3	3	2	4	1	4	1	3	2	2	3	1	4
58	4	3	2	4	1	2	3	1	4	4	1	3	2	3	2	4	1	1	4	2	3
59	4	3	2	4	1	3	2	4	1	1	4	2	3	2	3	1	4	4	1	3	2
60	4	3	2	4	1	4	1	3	2	2	3	1	4	1	4	2	3	3	2	4	1
61	4	4	1	3	2	1	4	2	3	4	1	3	2	2	3	1	4	3	2	4	1
62	4	4	1	3	2	2	3	1	4	3	2	4	1	1	4	2	3	4	1	3	2
63	4	4	1	3	2	3	2	4	1	2	3	1	4	4	1	3	2	1	4	2	3
64	4	4	1	3	2	4	1	3	2	1	4	2	3	3	2	4	1	2	3	1	4

L_{25} (5^6)

No.	1	2	3	4	5	6
1	1	1	1	1	1	1
2	1	2	2	2	2	2
3	1	3	3	3	3	3
4	1	4	4	4	4	4
5	1	5	5	5	5	5
6	2	1	2	3	4	5
7	2	2	3	4	5	1
8	2	3	4	5	1	2
9	2	4	5	1	2	3
10	2	5	1	2	3	4
11	3	1	3	5	2	4
12	3	2	4	1	3	5
13	3	3	5	2	4	1
14	3	4	1	3	5	2
15	3	5	2	4	1	3
16	4	1	4	2	5	3
17	4	2	5	3	1	4
18	4	3	1	4	2	5
19	4	4	2	5	3	1
20	4	5	3	1	4	2
21	5	1	5	4	3	2
22	5	2	1	5	4	3
23	5	3	2	1	5	4
24	5	4	3	2	1	5
25	5	5	4	3	2	1

L_{50} ($2^1 \times 5^{11}$)

No.	1	2	3	4	5	6	7	8	9	10	11	12
1	1	1	1	1	1	1	1	1	1	1	1	1
2	1	1	2	2	2	2	2	2	2	2	2	2
3	1	1	3	3	3	3	3	3	3	3	3	3
4	1	1	4	4	4	4	4	4	4	4	4	4
5	1	1	5	5	5	5	5	5	5	5	5	5
6	1	2	1	2	3	4	5	1	2	3	4	5
7	1	2	2	3	4	5	1	2	3	4	5	1
8	1	2	3	4	5	1	2	3	4	5	1	2
9	1	2	4	5	1	2	3	4	5	1	2	3
10	1	2	5	1	2	3	4	5	1	2	3	4
11	1	3	1	3	5	2	4	4	1	3	5	2
12	1	3	2	4	1	3	5	5	2	4	1	3
13	1	3	3	5	2	4	1	1	3	5	2	4
14	1	3	4	1	3	5	2	2	4	1	3	5
15	1	3	5	2	4	1	3	3	5	2	4	1
16	1	4	1	4	2	5	3	5	3	1	4	2
17	1	4	2	5	3	1	4	1	4	2	5	3
18	1	4	3	1	4	2	5	2	5	3	1	4
19	1	4	4	2	5	3	1	3	1	4	2	5
20	1	4	5	3	1	4	2	4	2	5	3	1
21	1	5	1	5	4	3	2	4	3	2	1	5
22	1	5	2	1	5	4	3	5	4	3	2	1
23	1	5	3	2	1	5	4	1	5	4	3	2
24	1	5	4	3	2	1	5	2	1	5	4	3
25	1	5	5	4	3	2	1	3	2	1	5	4
26	2	1	1	1	4	5	4	3	2	5	2	3
27	2	1	2	2	5	1	5	4	3	1	3	4
28	2	1	3	3	1	2	1	5	4	2	4	5
29	2	1	4	4	2	3	2	1	5	3	5	1
30	2	1	5	5	3	4	3	2	1	4	1	2

L_{50} $(2^1 \times 5^{11})$ *cont'd.*

No.	1	2	3	4	5	6	7	8	9	10	11	12
31	2	2	1	2	1	3	3	2	4	5	5	4
32	2	2	2	3	2	4	4	3	5	1	1	5
33	2	2	3	4	3	5	5	4	1	2	2	1
34	2	2	4	5	4	1	1	5	2	3	3	2
35	2	2	5	1	5	2	2	1	3	4	4	3
36	2	3	1	3	3	1	2	5	5	4	2	4
37	2	3	2	4	4	2	3	1	1	5	3	5
38	2	3	3	5	5	3	4	2	2	1	4	1
39	2	3	4	1	1	4	5	3	3	2	5	2
40	2	3	5	2	2	5	1	4	4	3	1	3
41	2	4	1	4	5	4	1	2	5	2	3	3
42	2	4	2	5	1	5	2	3	1	3	4	4
43	2	4	3	1	2	1	3	4	2	4	5	5
44	2	4	4	2	3	2	4	5	3	5	1	1
45	2	4	5	3	4	3	5	1	4	1	2	2
46	2	5	1	5	2	2	5	3	4	4	3	1
47	2	5	2	1	3	3	1	4	5	5	4	2
48	2	5	3	2	4	4	2	5	1	1	5	3
49	2	5	4	3	5	5	3	1	2	2	1	4
50	2	5	5	4	1	1	4	2	3	3	2	5

Appendix B: Linear Graphs

Linear Graph for L_4 (2^3)

Linear Graphs for L_8 (2^7)

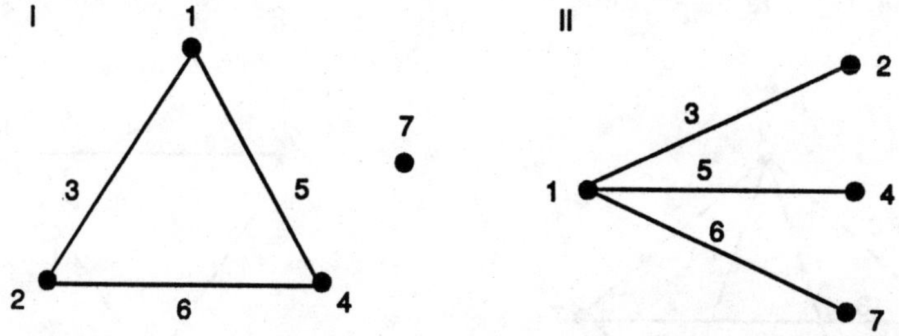

Linear Graphs for L_{16} (2^{15})

I

①

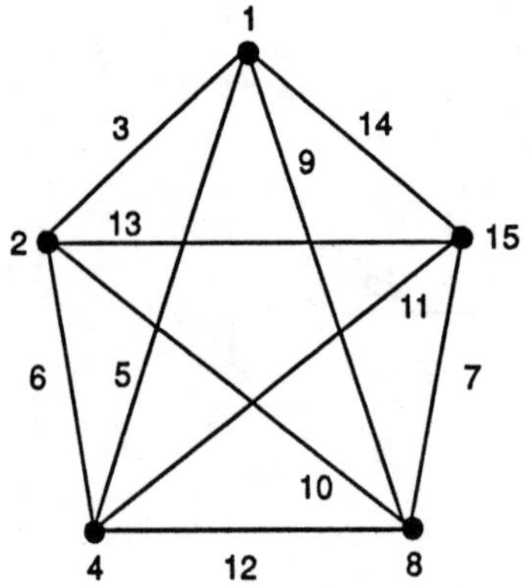

II

①

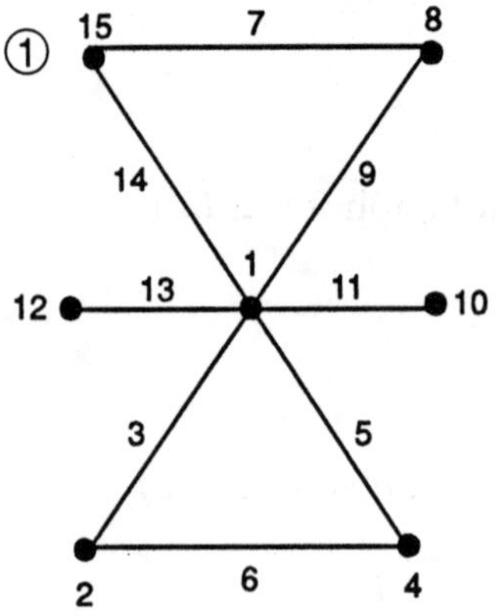

②

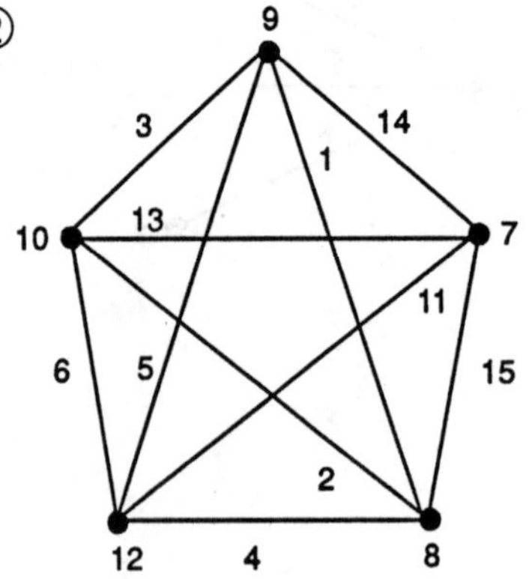

②

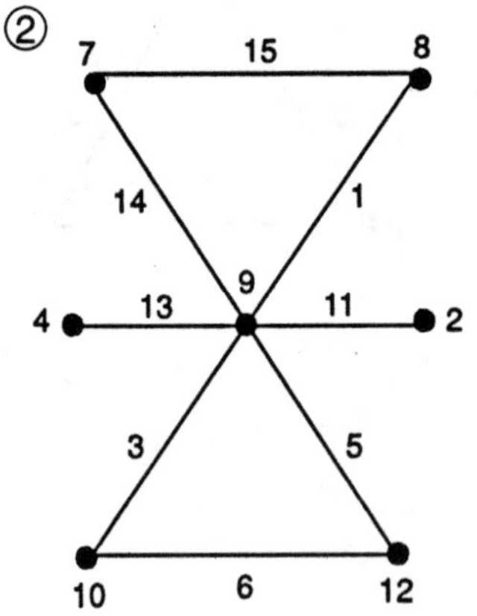

③

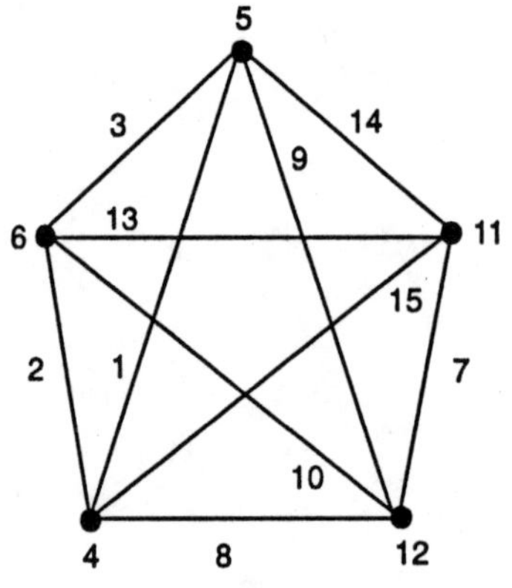

③

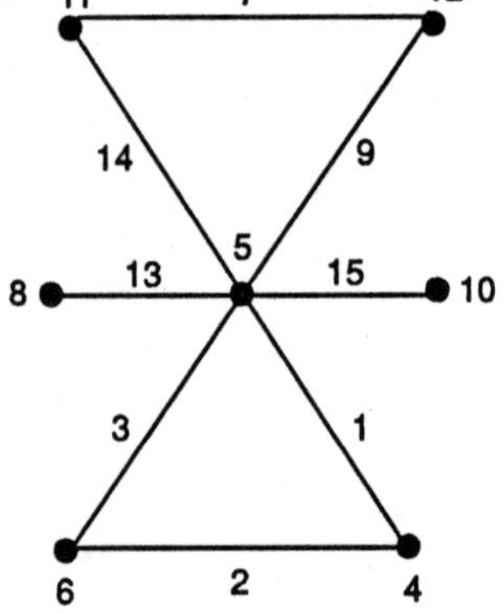

L_{16} (2^{15}) *cont'd.*

III

①

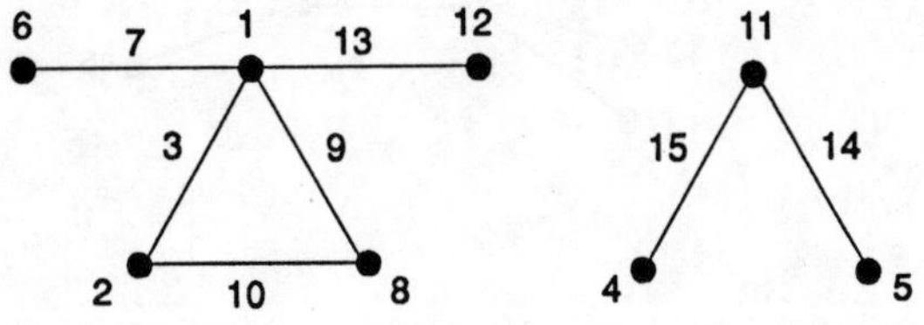

②

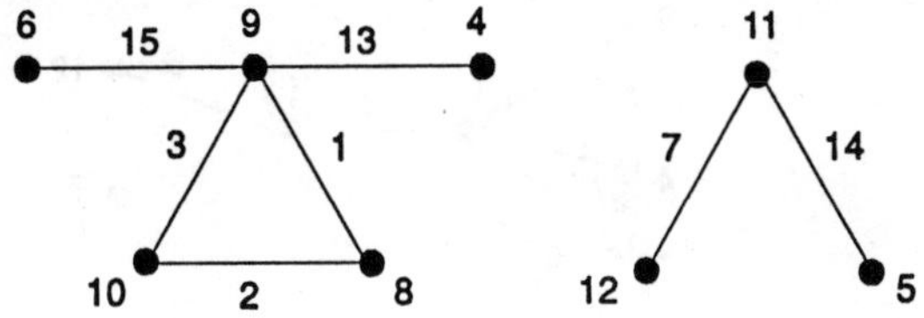

③

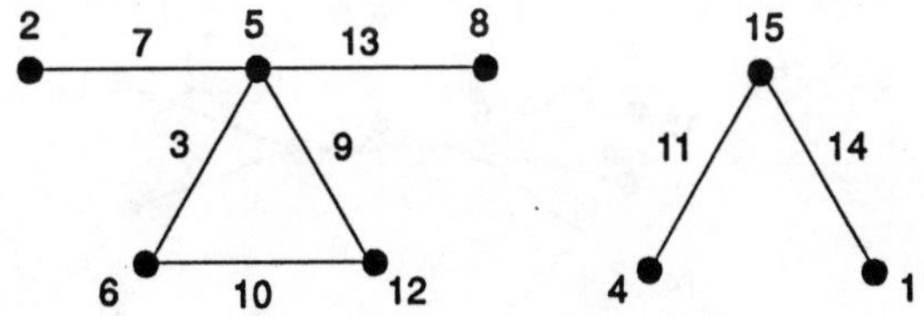

IV

①

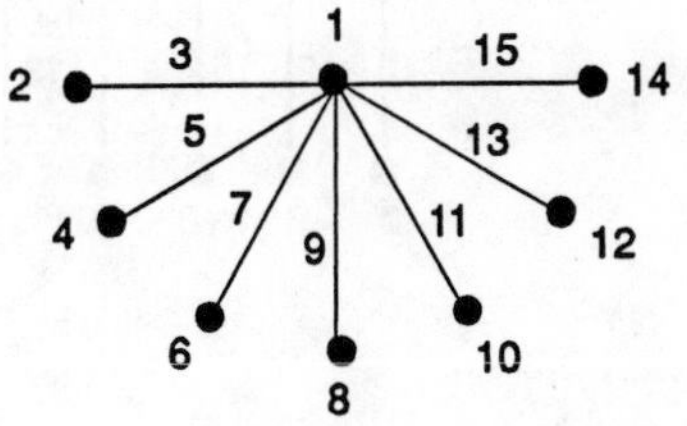

②

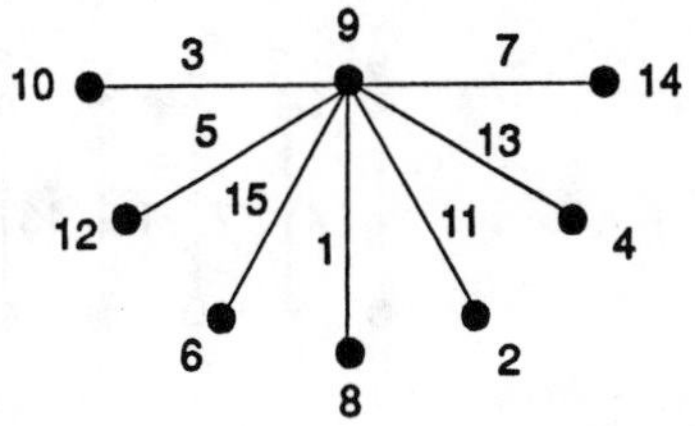

③

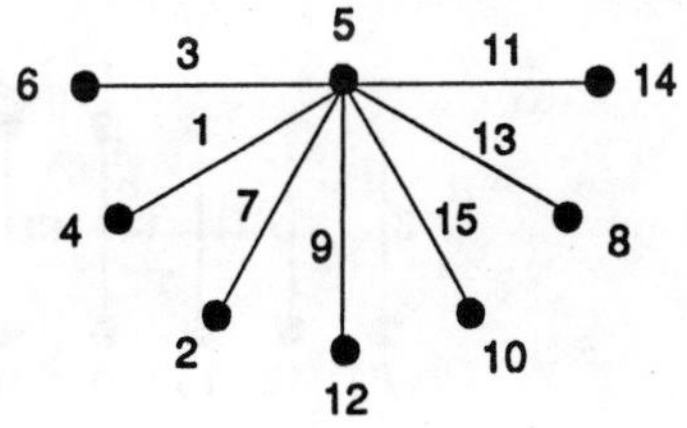

L_{16} (2^{15}) *cont'd.*

V

①

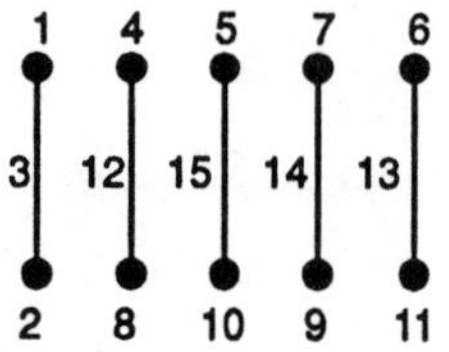

②

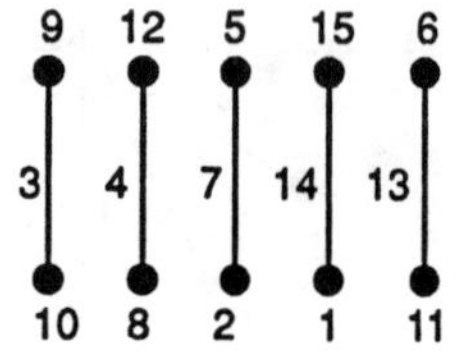

③

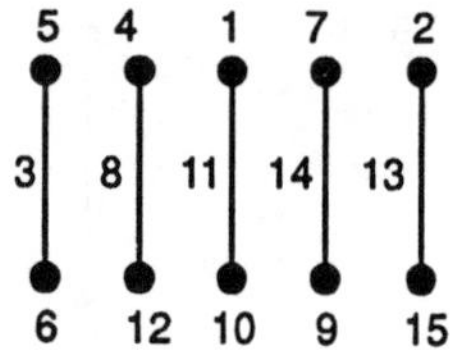

VI

①

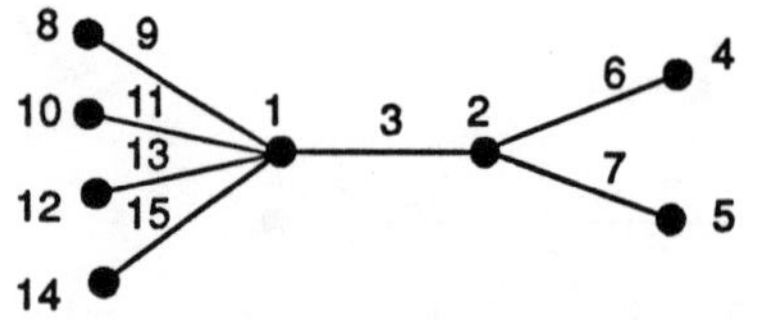

②

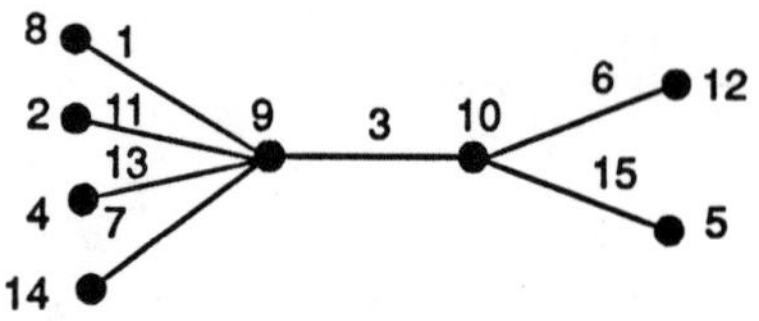

③

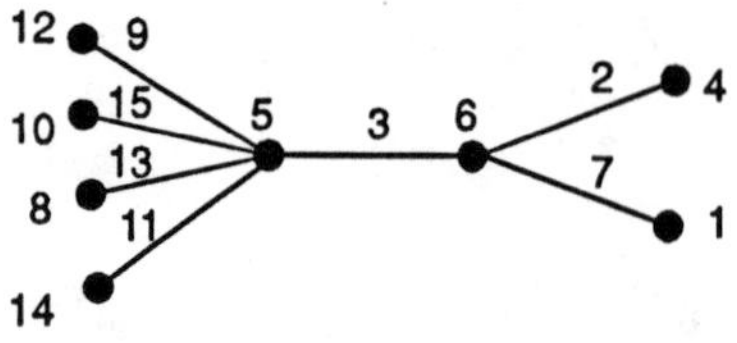

Linear Graphs for L_{32} (2^{31})

I

①

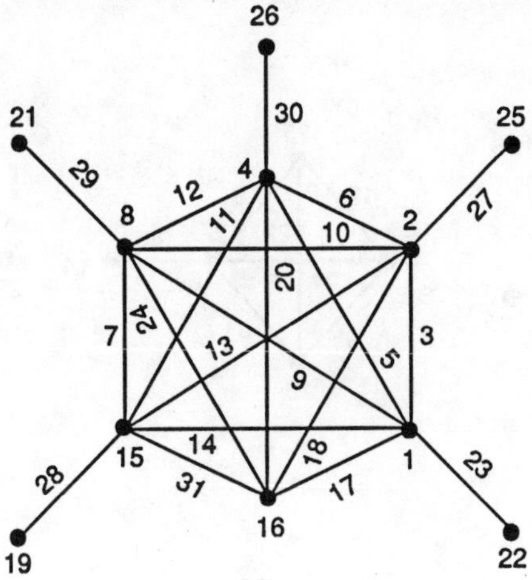

②

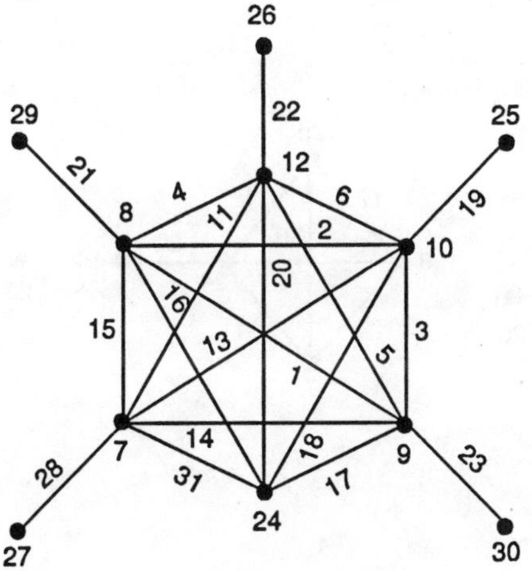

③

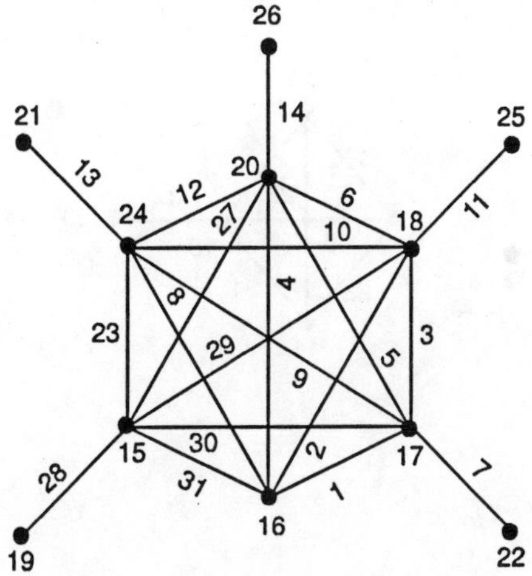

II

①

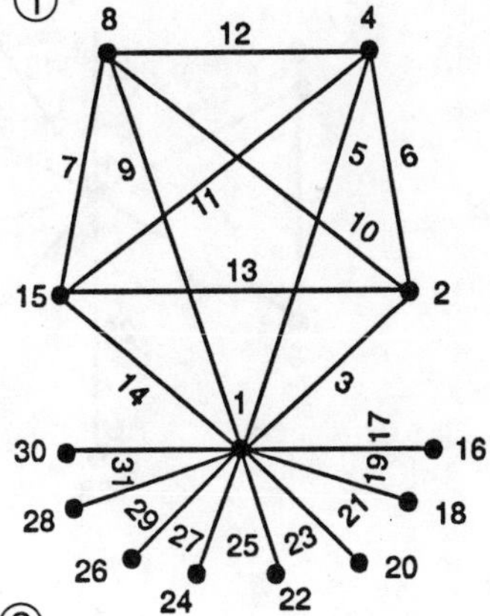

②

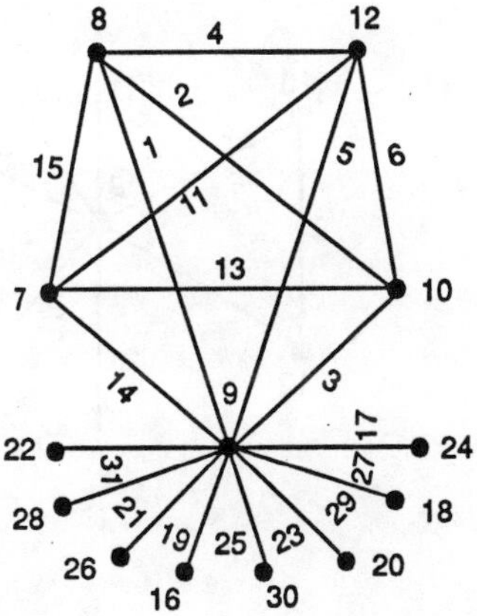

③

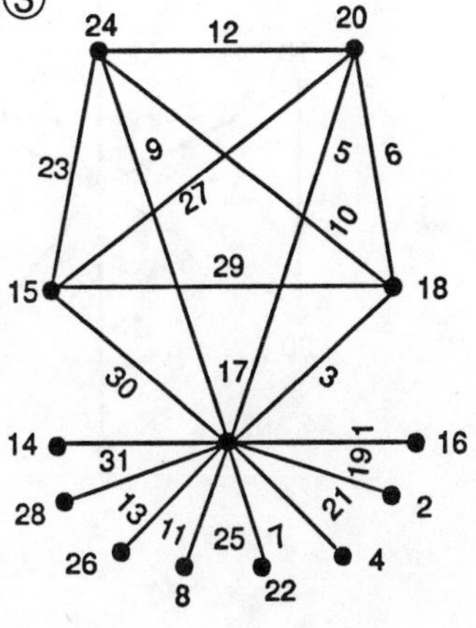

$L_{32}\ (2^{31})$ *cont'd.*

III

①

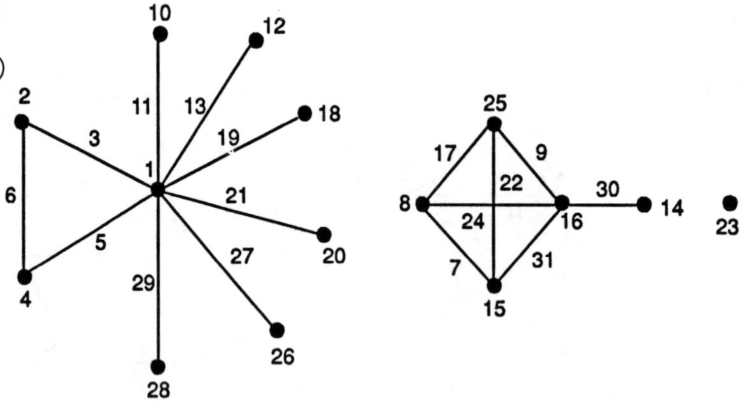

②

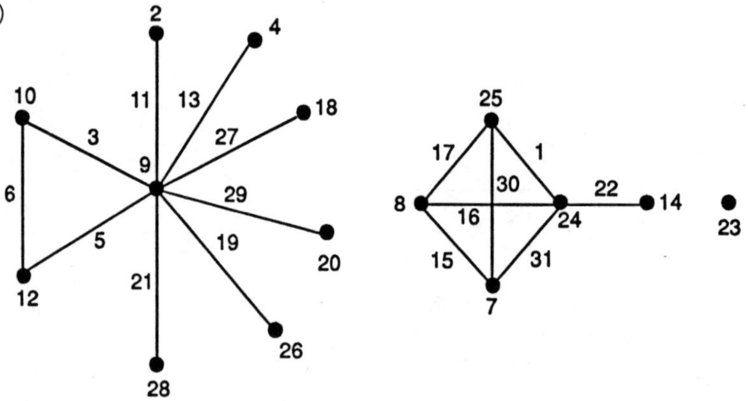

③

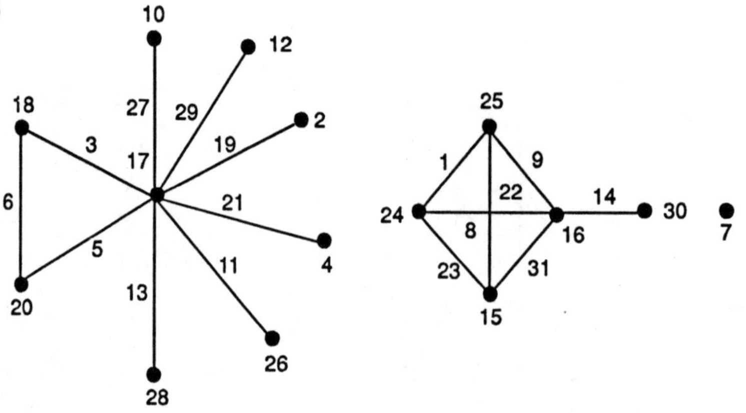

L_{32} (2^{31}) *cont'd.*

IV

①

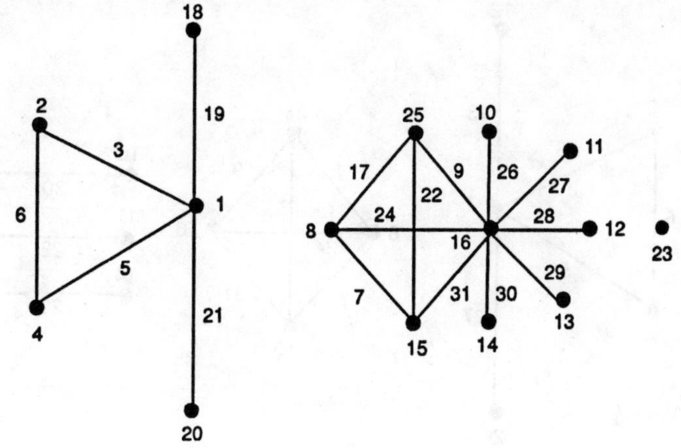

②

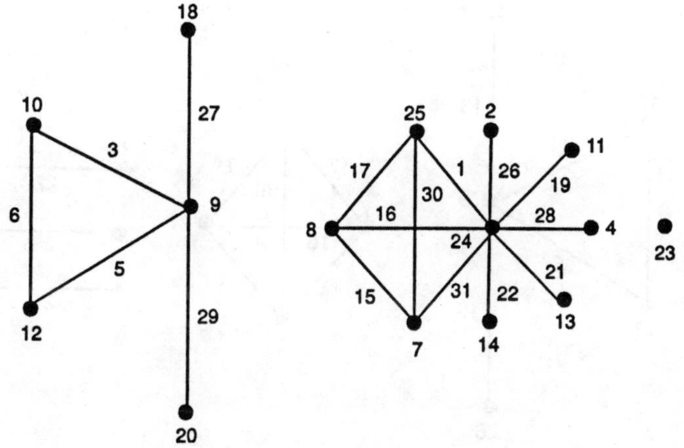

③

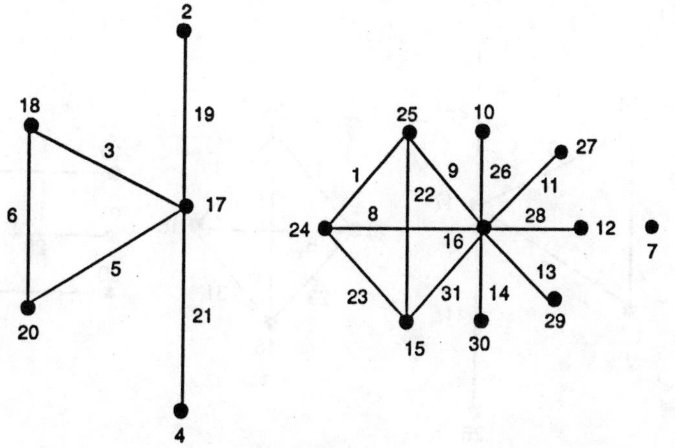

L_{32} (2^{31}) *cont'd.*

V

①

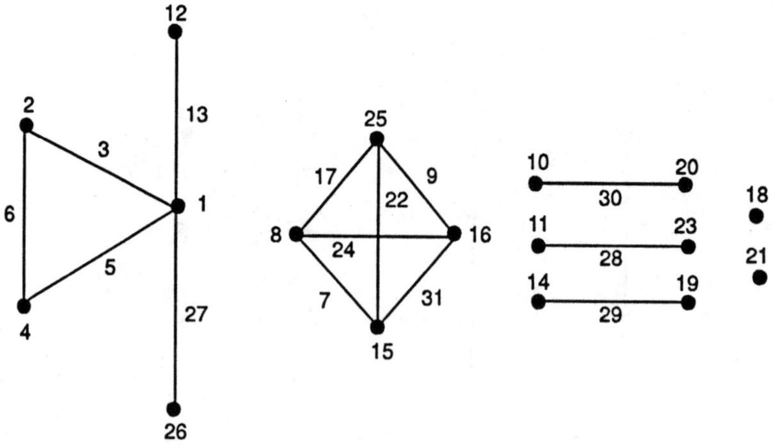

②

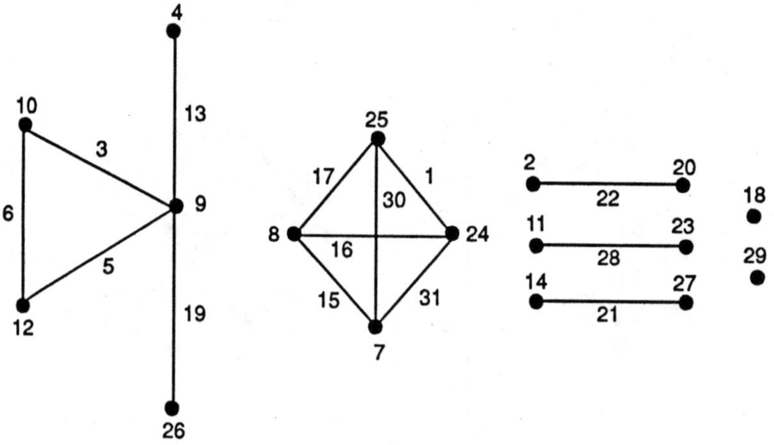

③

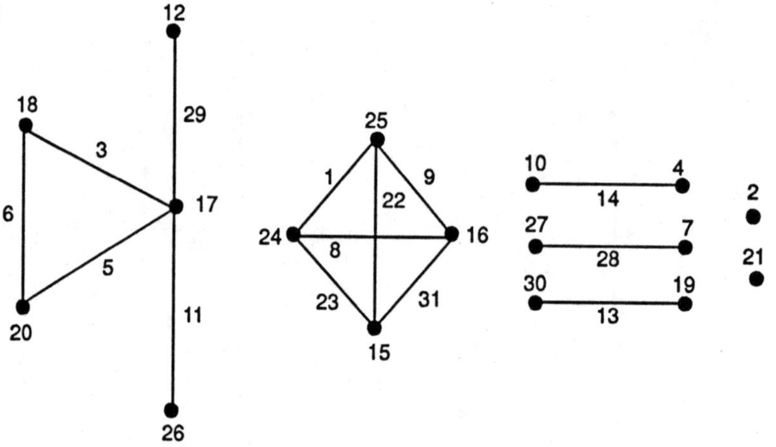

L_{32} (2^{31}) *cont'd.*

VI

①

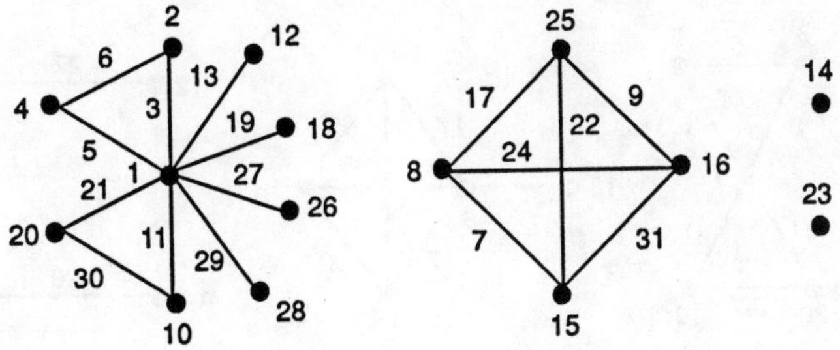

②

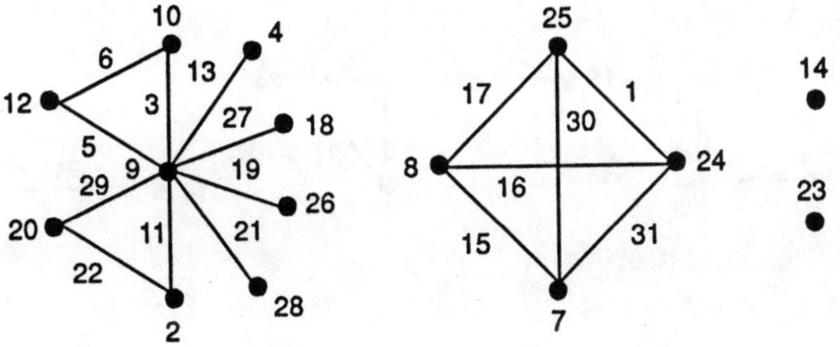

③

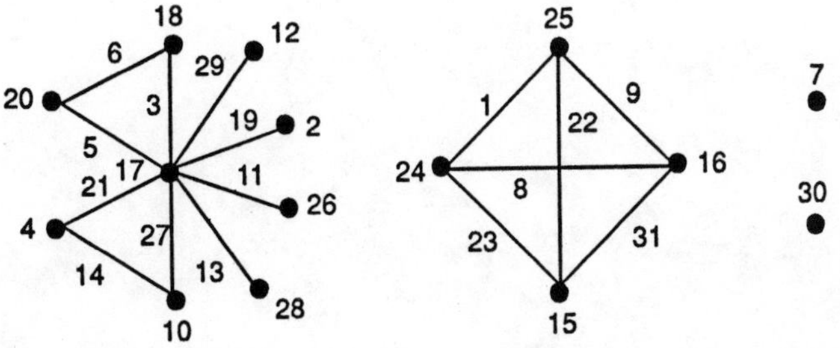

$L_{32}\ (2^{31})$ *cont'd.*

VII

①

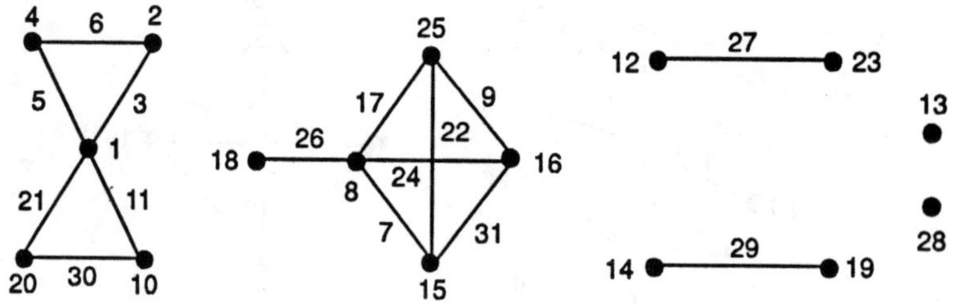

②

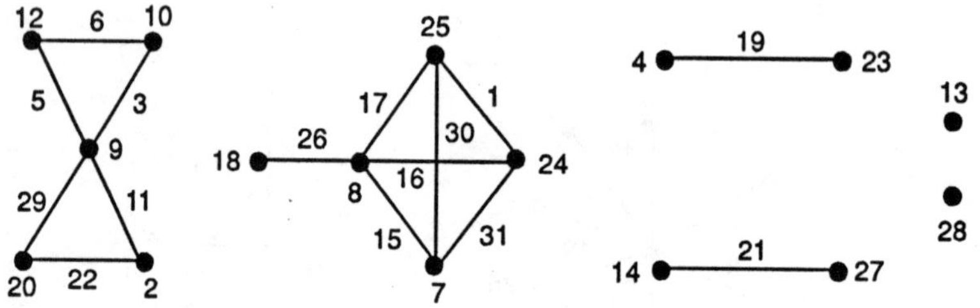

③

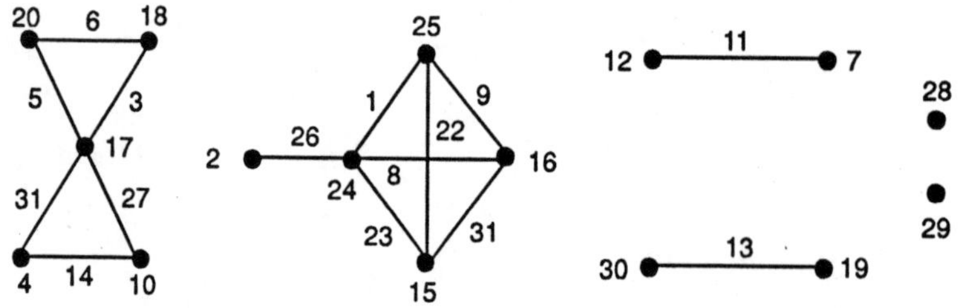

L_{32} (2^{31}) *cont'd.*

VIII

①

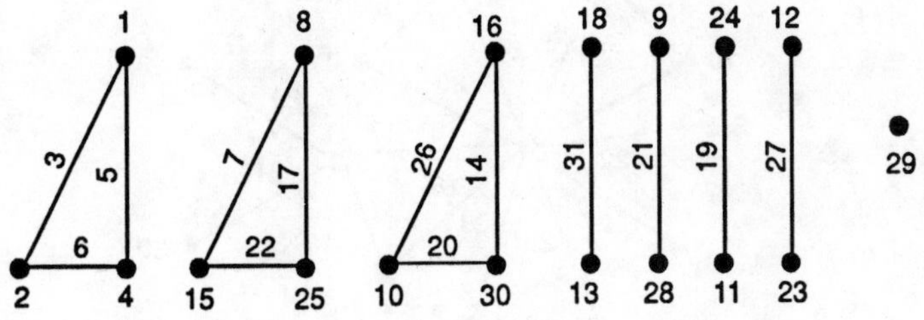

②

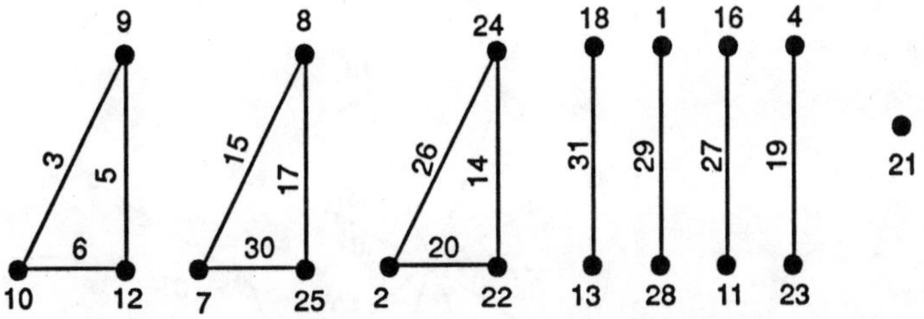

③

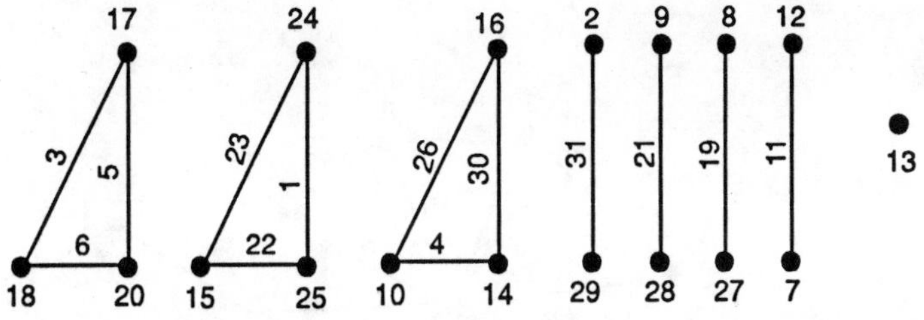

L_{32} (2^{31}) *cont'd.*

IX

①

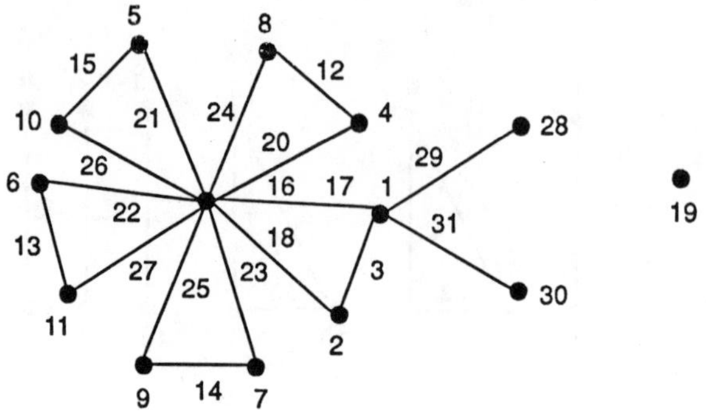

②

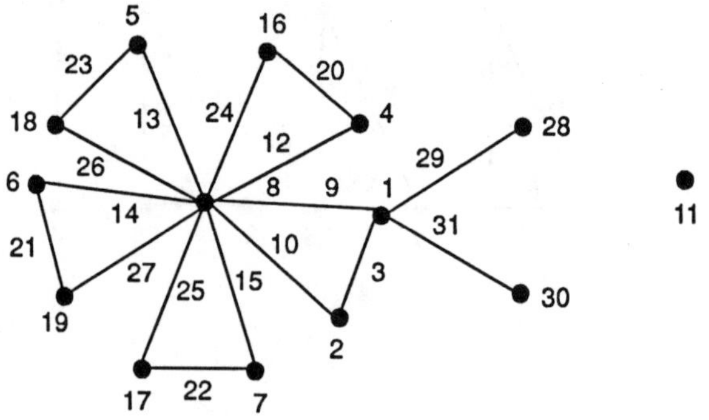

③

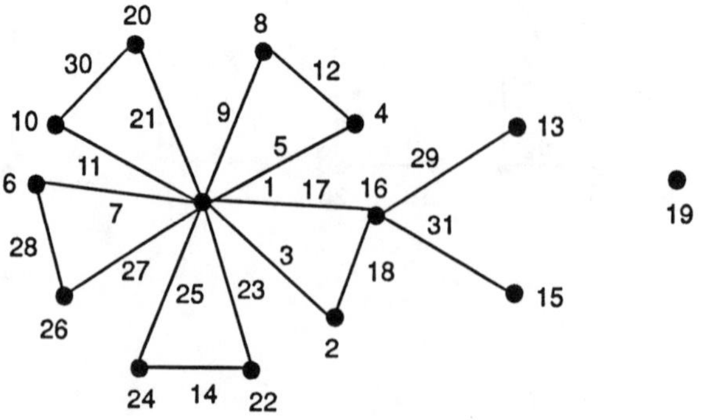

$L_{32}\ (2^{31})$ *cont'd.*

X

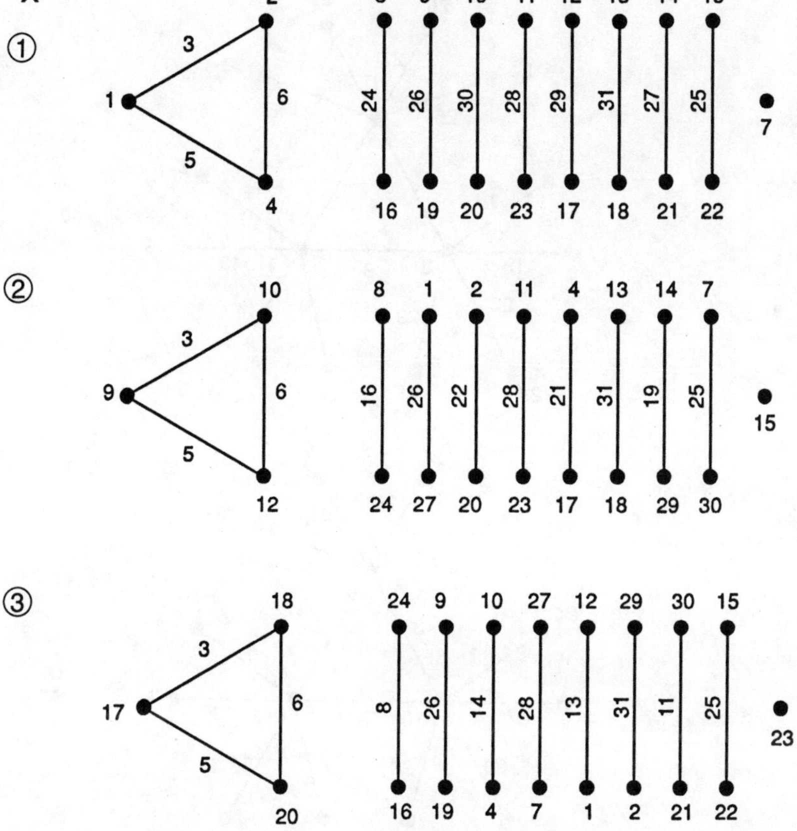

L_{32} (2^{31}) *cont'd.*

XI

①

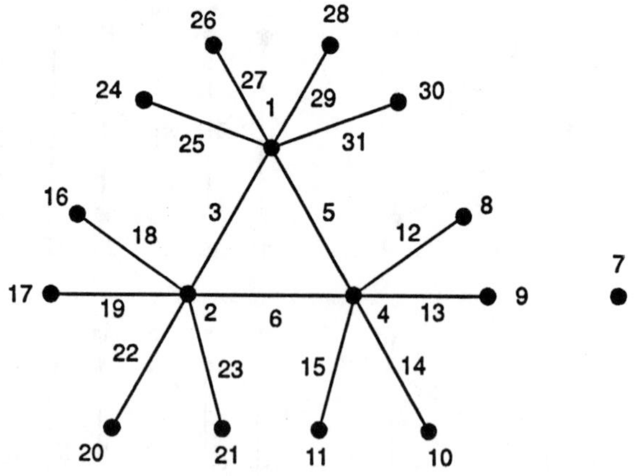

②

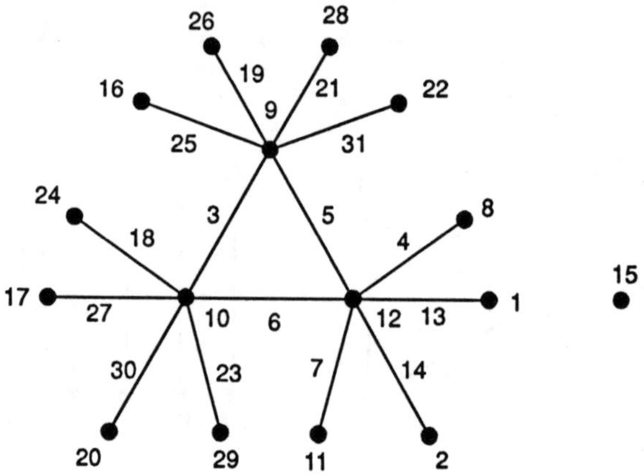

③

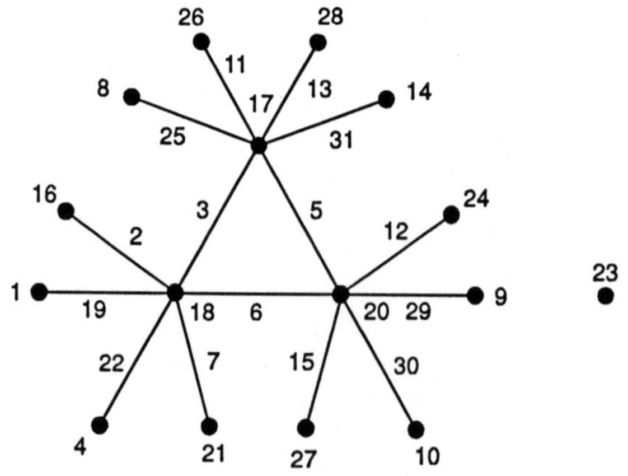

L_{32} (2^{31}) *cont'd.*

XII

①

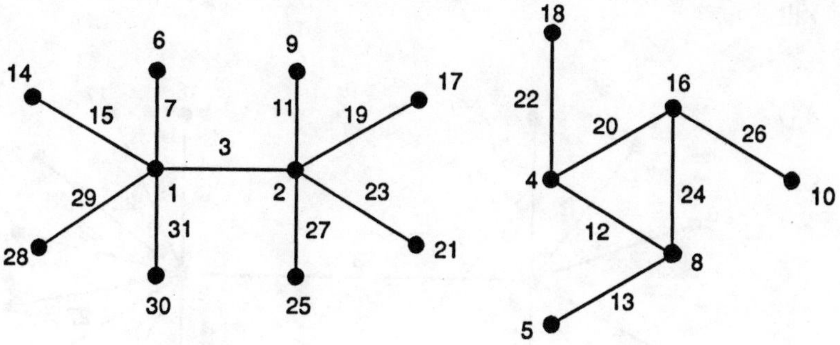

②

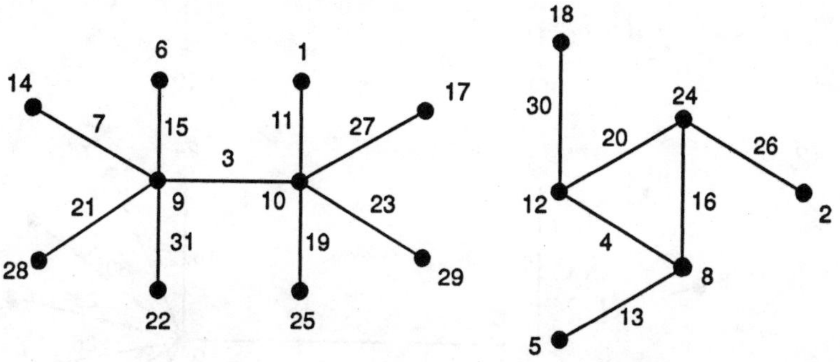

③

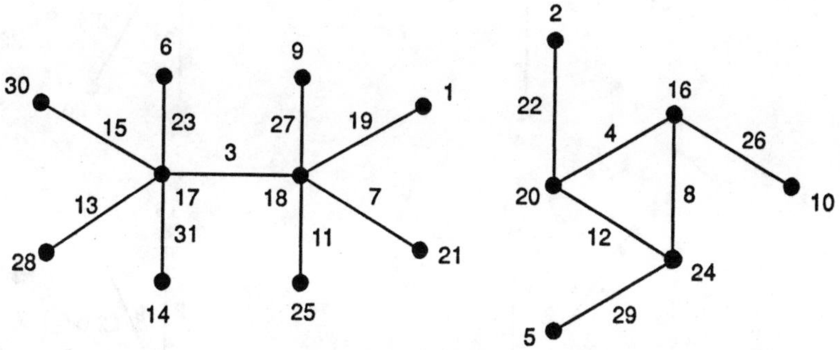

L_{32} (2^{31}) *cont'd.*

XIII

①

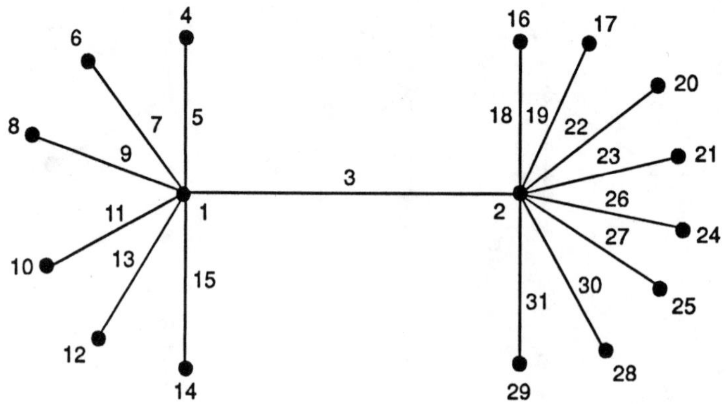

②

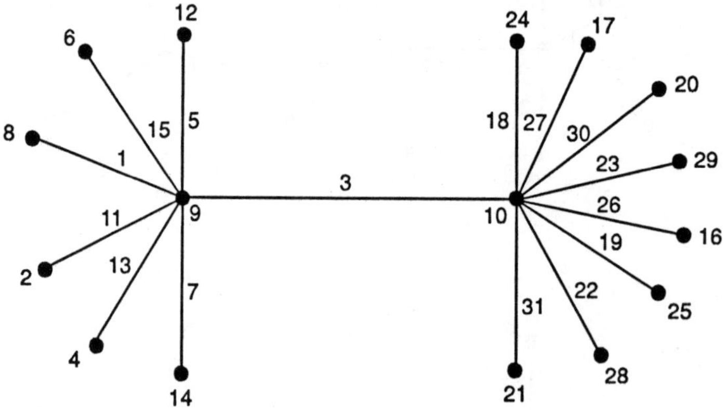

③

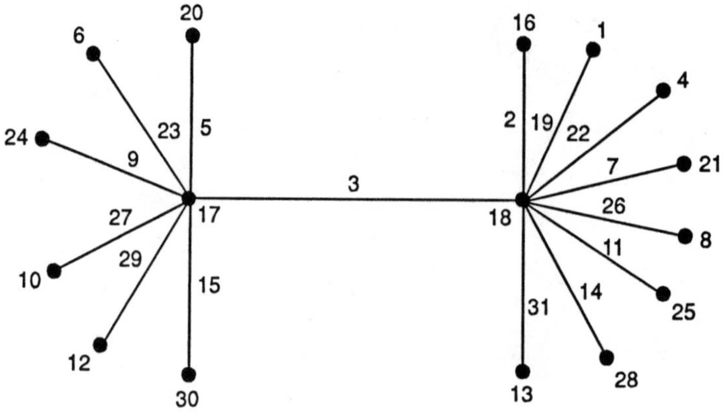

Linear Graphs for L_{64} (2^{63})

I

①

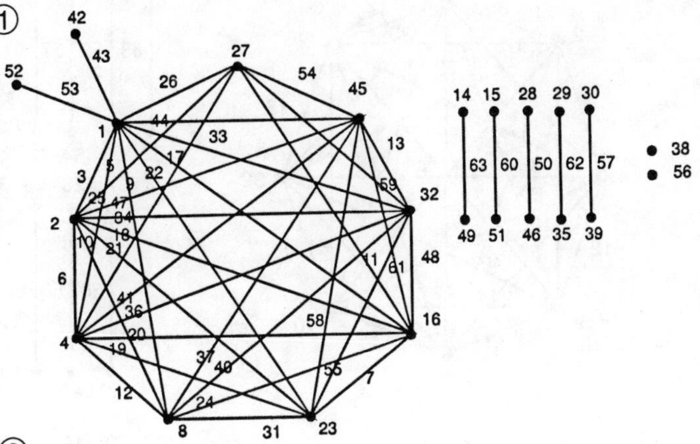

②

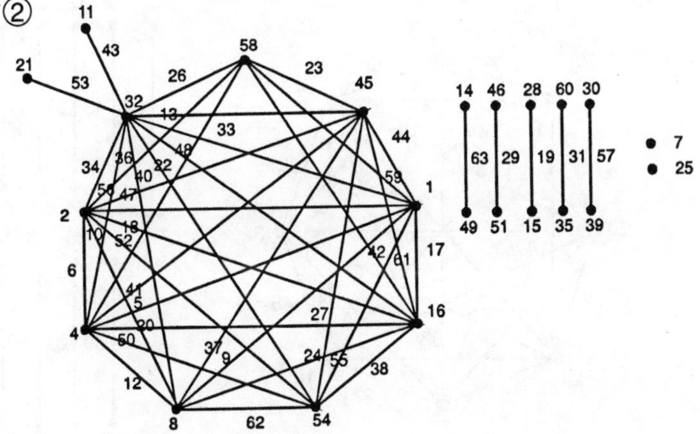

③

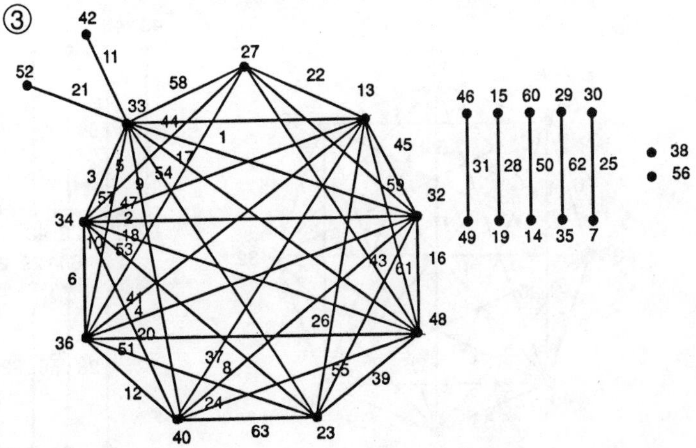

L$_{64}$ (2^{63}) *cont'd.*

II

①

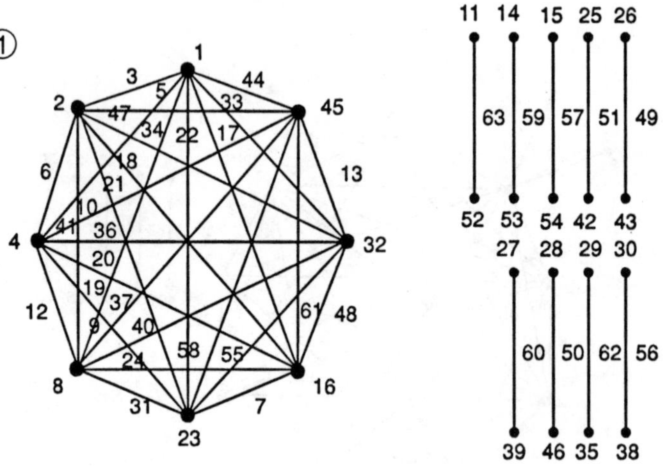

②

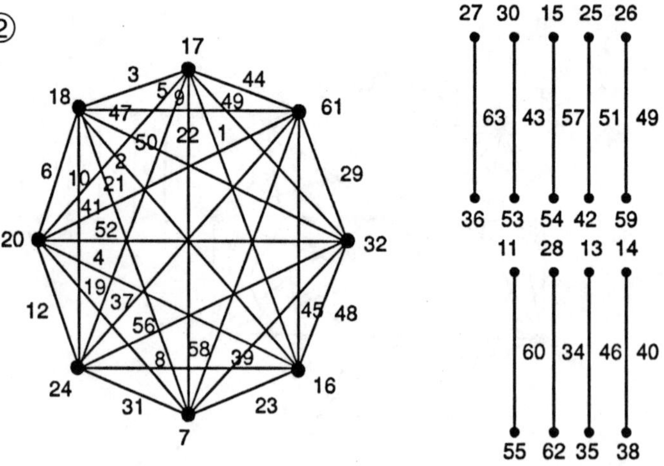

③

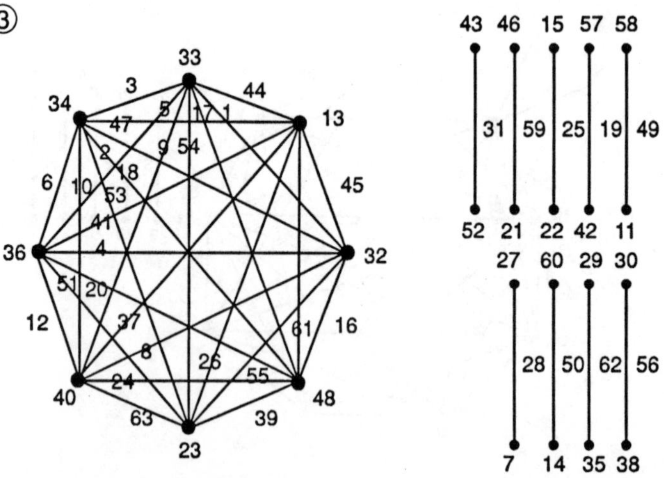

L_{64} (2^{63}) *cont'd.*

III

①

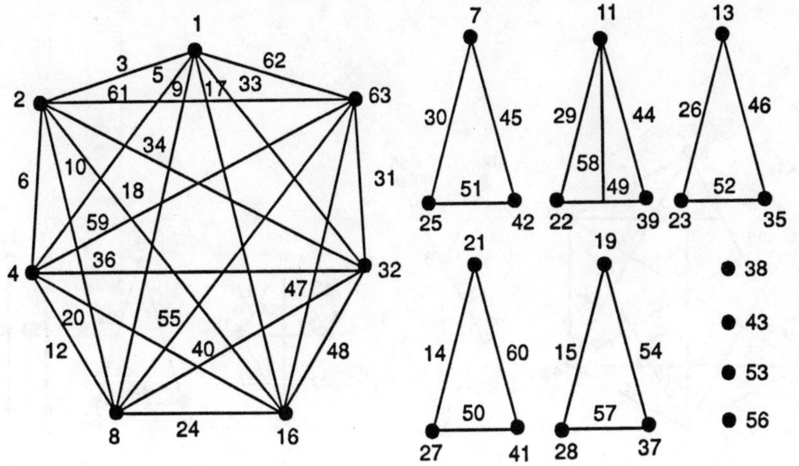

②

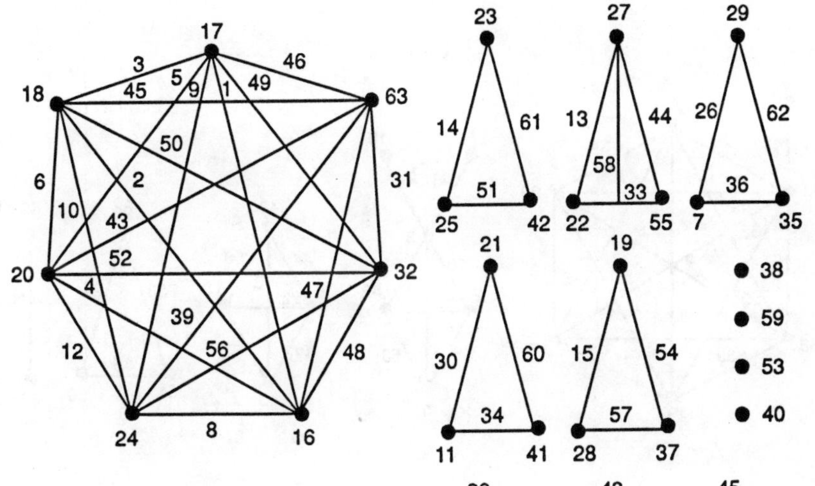

③

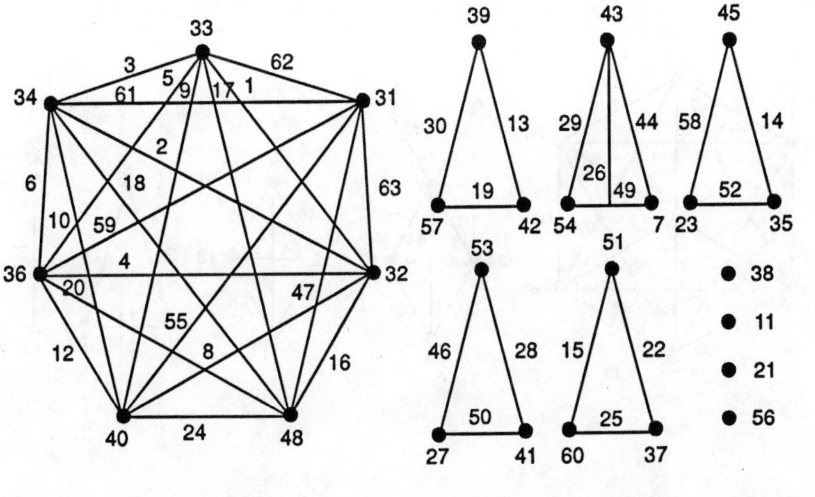

L_{64} (2^{63}) *cont'd.*

IV

①

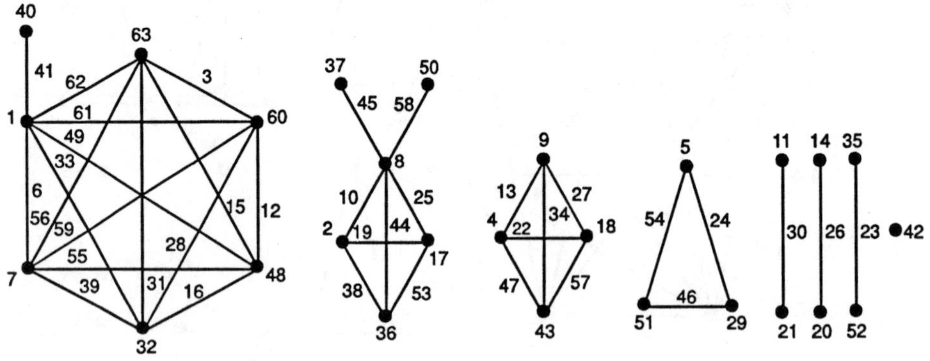

②

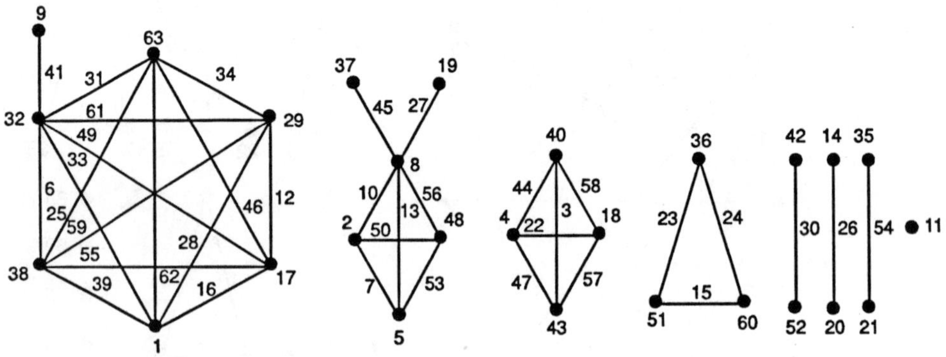

③

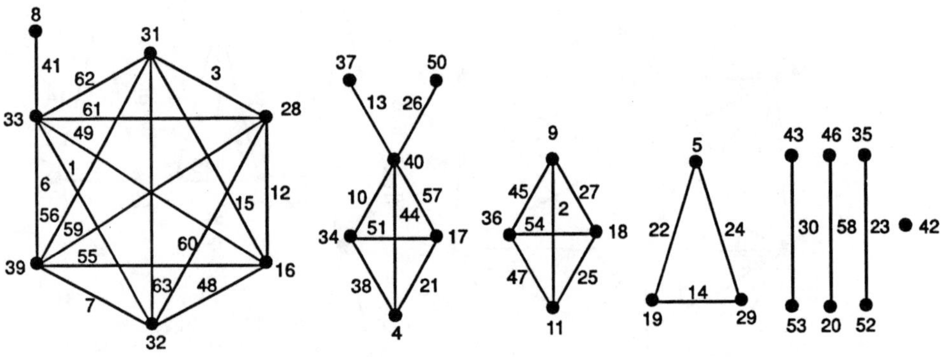

L_{64} (2^{63}) *cont'd.*

V

①

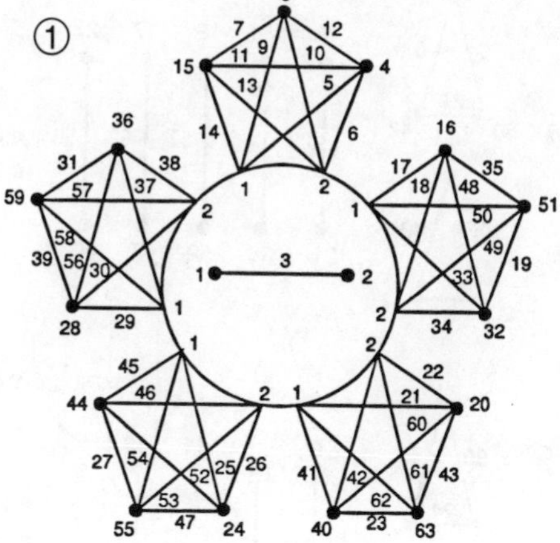

VI

①

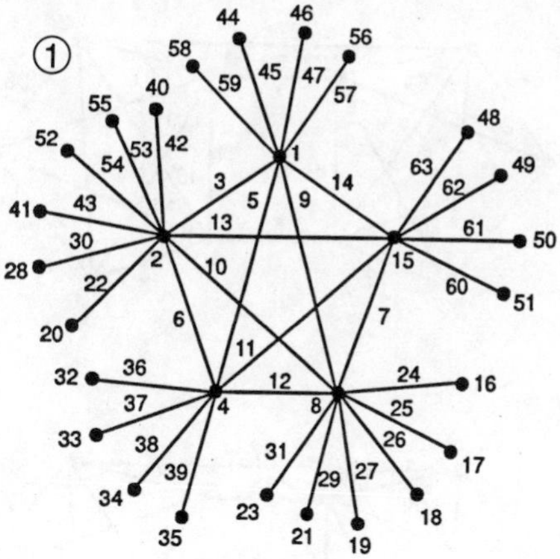

V

②

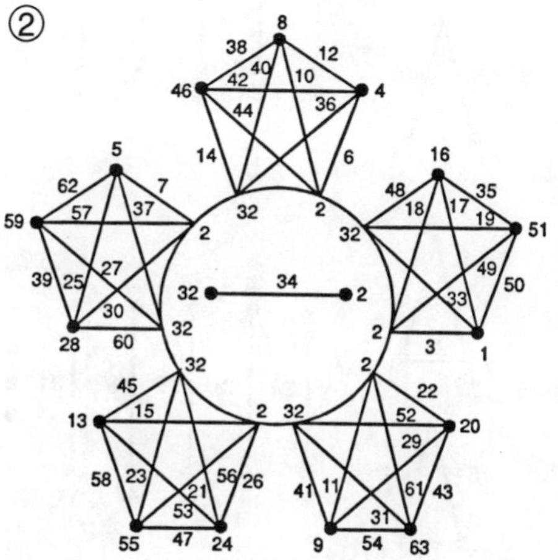

VI

②

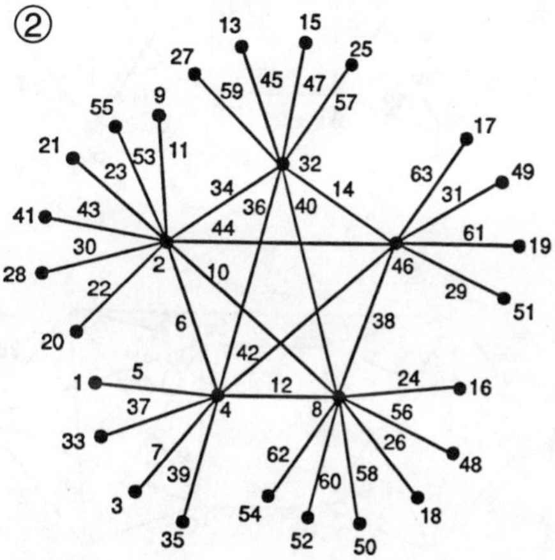

V

③

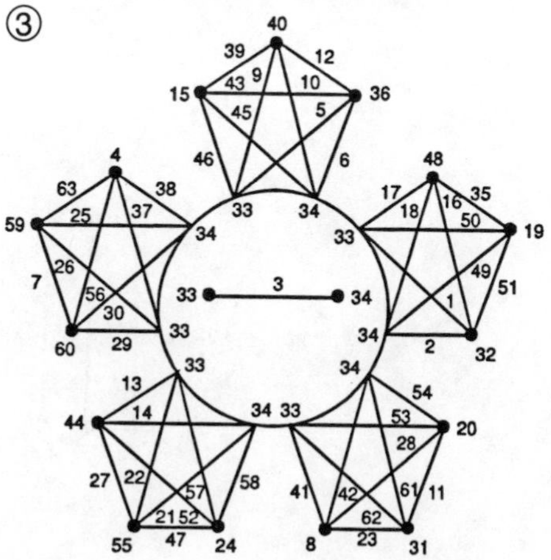

VI

③

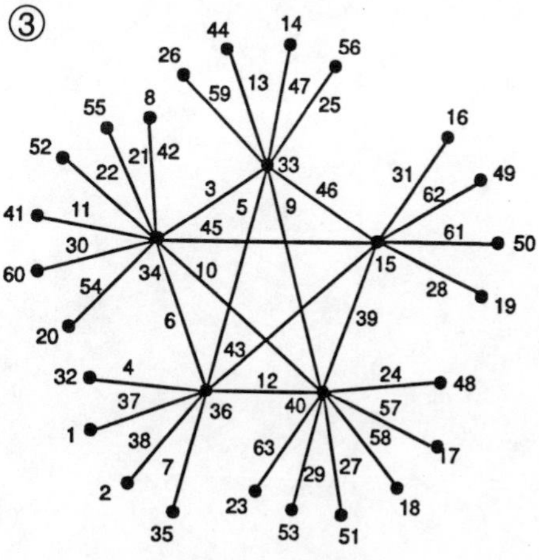

L_{64} (2^{63}) *cont'd.*

VII

①

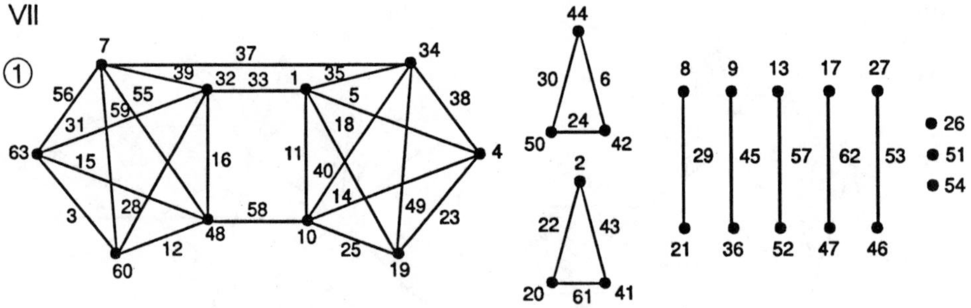

②

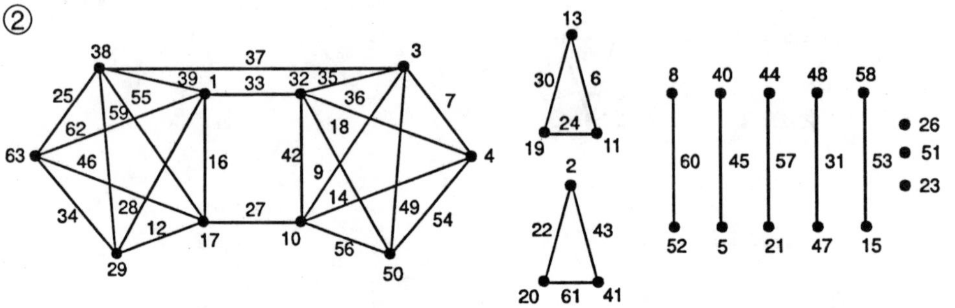

③

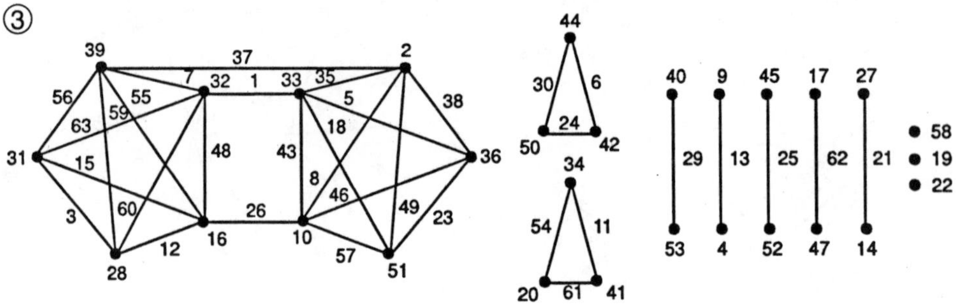

$L_{64}\ (2^{63})$ *cont'd.*

VIII

①

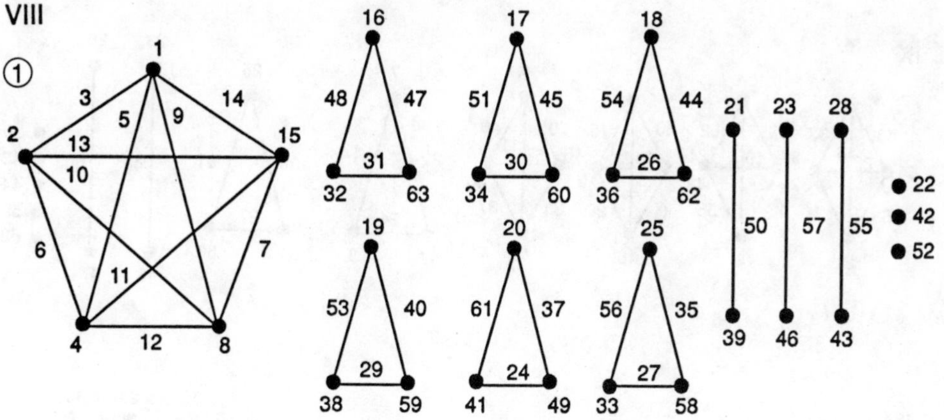

②

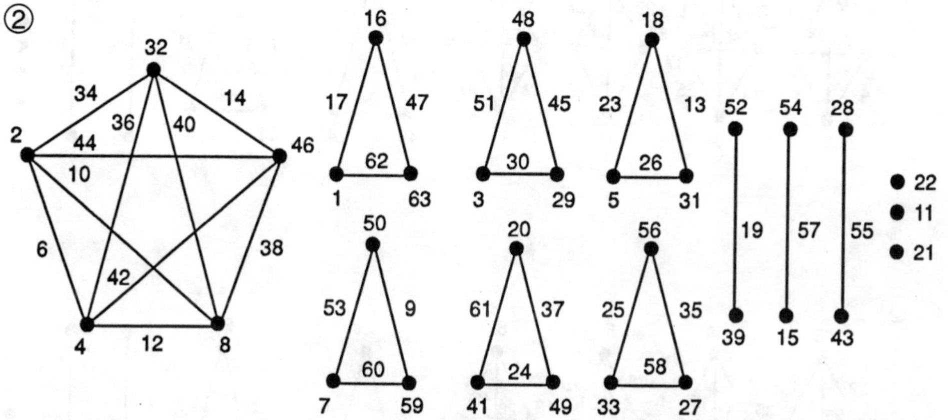

③

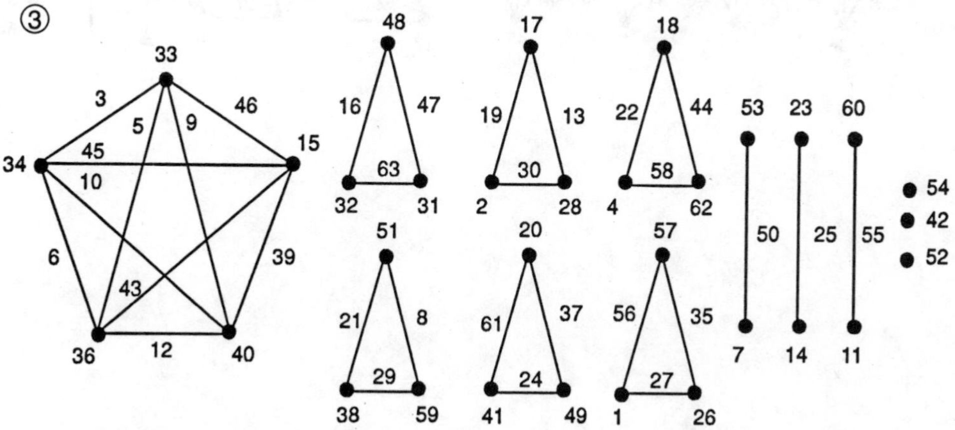

$L_{64}\ (2^{63})$ *cont'd.*

IX

①

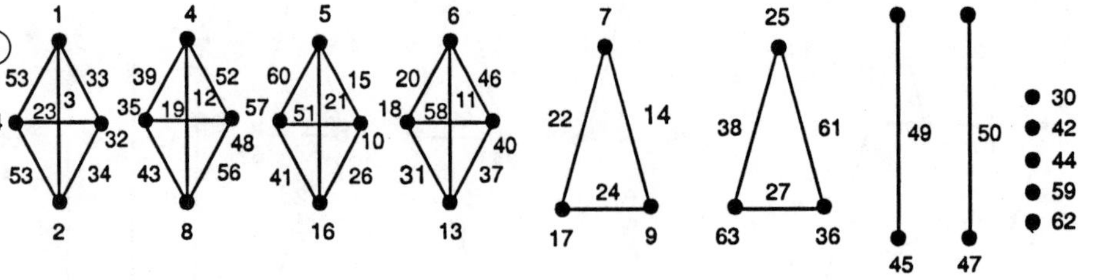

②

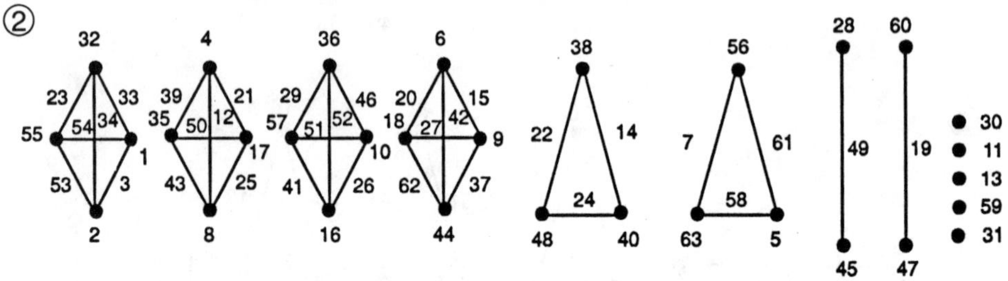

③

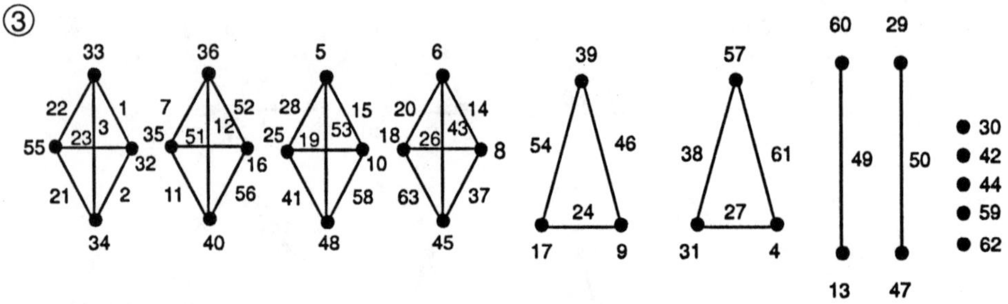

L_{64} (2^{63}) *cont'd.*

X

①

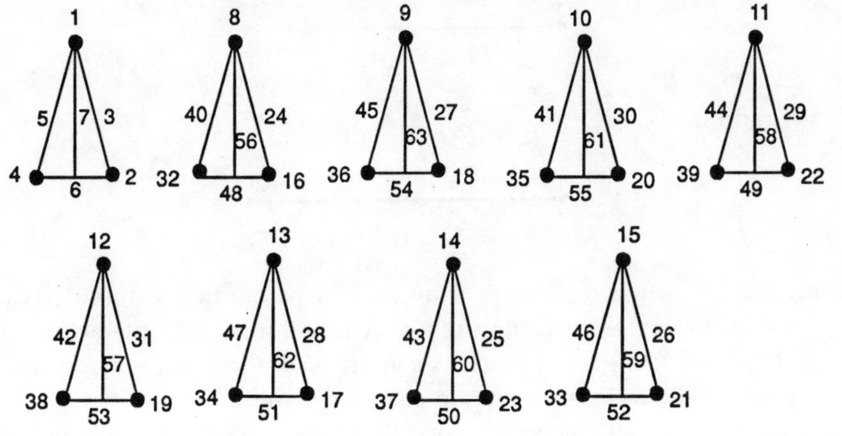

②

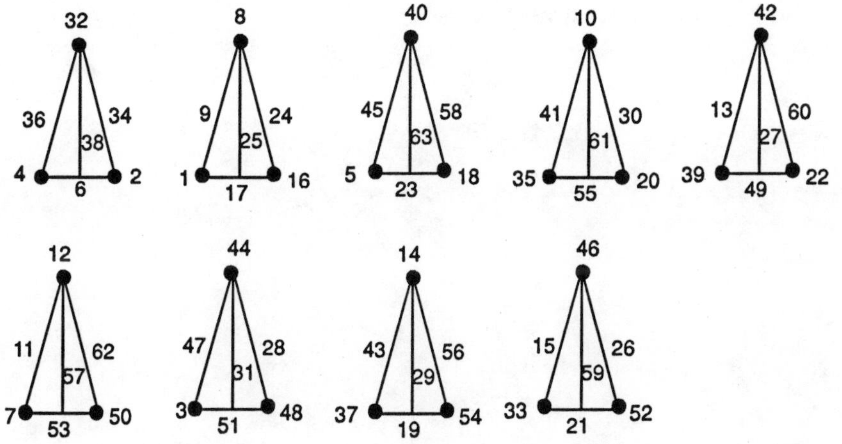

③

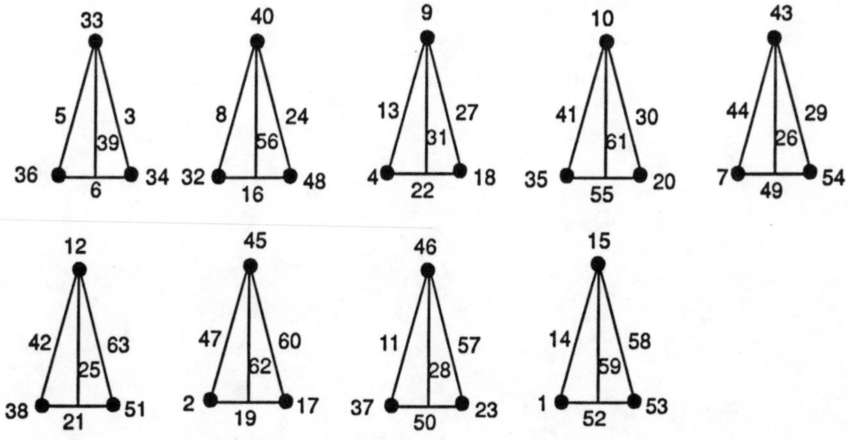

Linear Graph for L_9 (3^4)

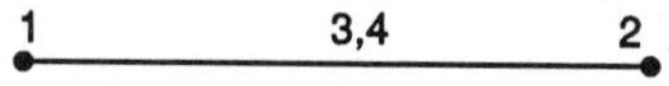

Linear Graph for L_{18} ($2^1 \times 3^7$)

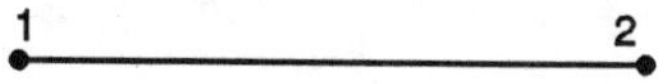

The interaction between columns 1 and 2 can be studied without having to assign the effect of the interaction to a specific column. The interaction can be studied by constructing a 2 × 5 matrix comprised of the average results for each combination of the factors residing in columns 1 and 2.

The effects of the interactions among the three-level columns are distributed fairly uniformly across all three-level columns, prohibiting the investigation of interactions among three-level factors.

Linear Graphs for L_{27} (3^{13})

I

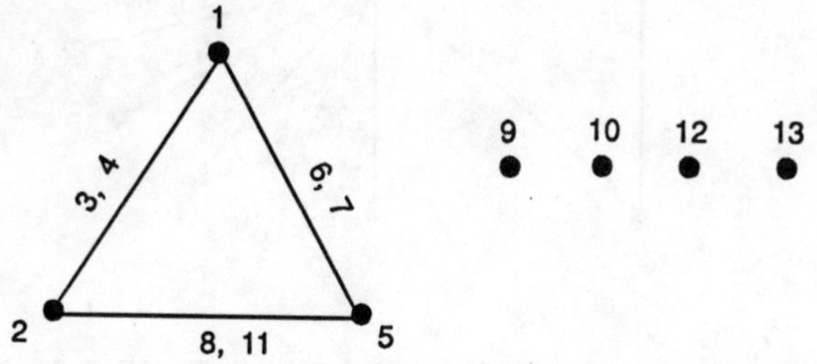

II

①

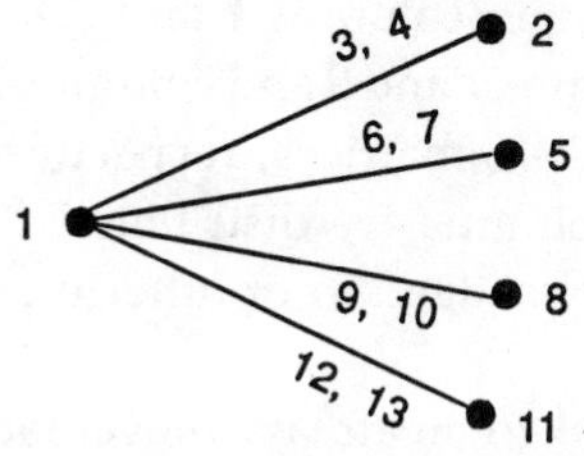

②

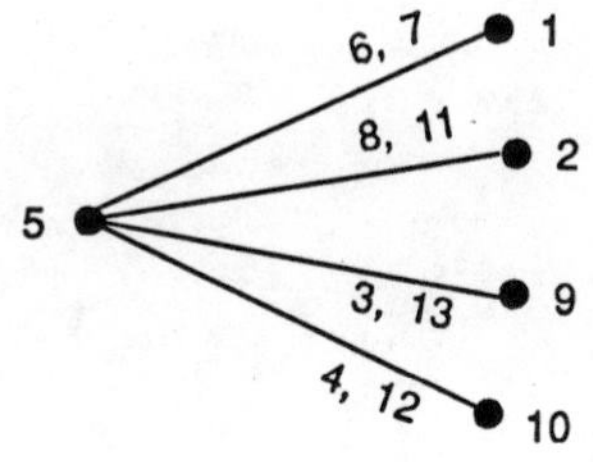

Linear Graph for L_{54} $(2^1 \times 3^{25})$

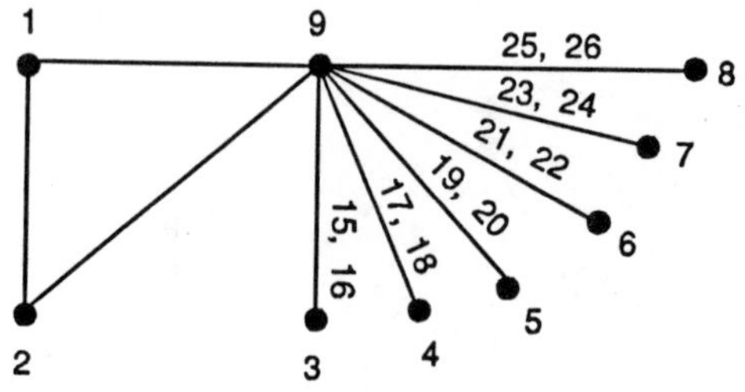

The interaction between columns 1 and 2 can be studied without having to assign the effect of the interaction to a specific column. The interaction can be studied by constructing a 2 × 3 matrix comprised of the average results for each combination of the factors residing in columns 1 and 2.

The interactions between columns 1 and 9 and columns 2 and 9 can be studied in the same manner (2 × 3 and 3 × 3 matrices, respectively). The effects of the interactions among these three columns are distributed fairly uniformly across columns 10–14, prohibiting the investigation of other interactions in these columns.

If columns 1 and 2 are merged to create a six-level factor (see Chapter 21), the interaction between this factor and column 9 can be studied by constructing a 6 × 3 matrix comprised of the average results for each combination of these two factors and leaving columns 10–14 idle.

Linear Graphs for L_{81} (3^{40})

I

①

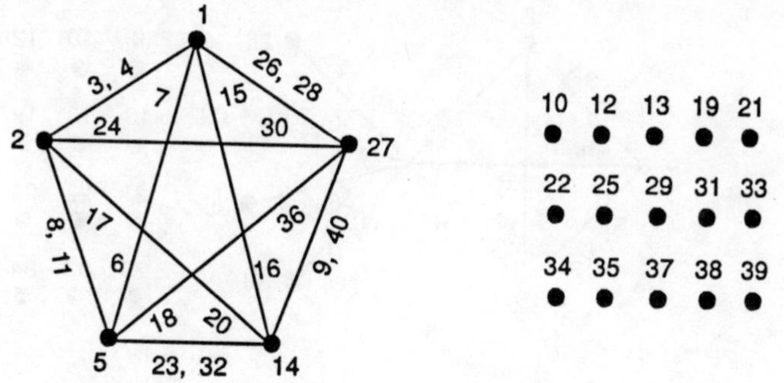

②

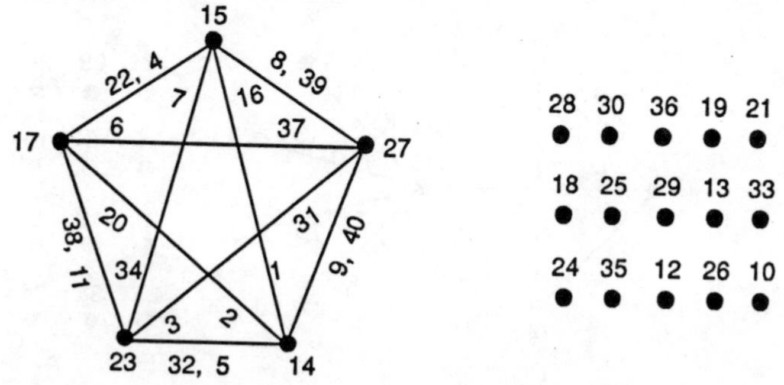

③

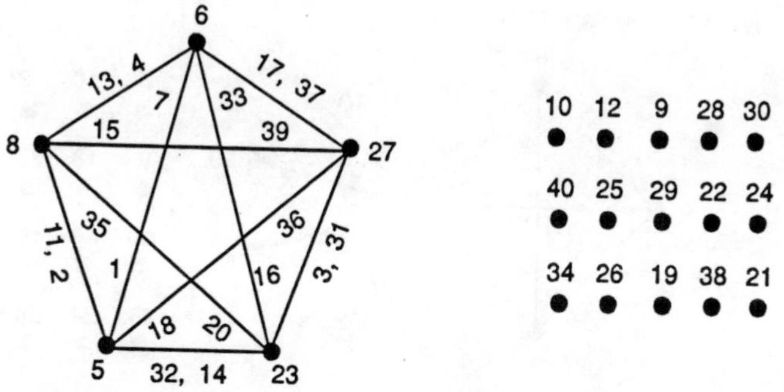

L_{81} (3^{40}) *cont'd.*

II

①

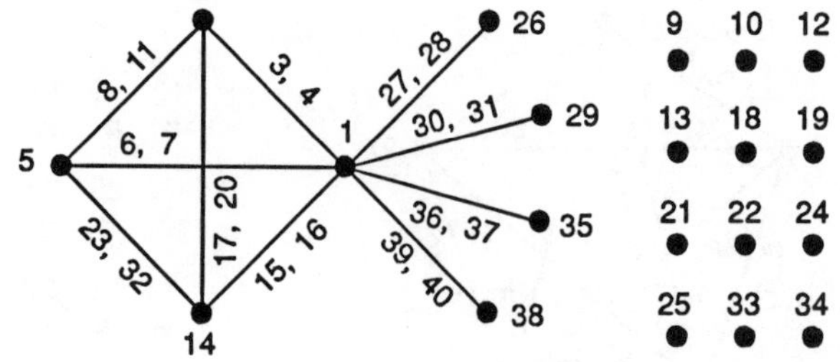

②

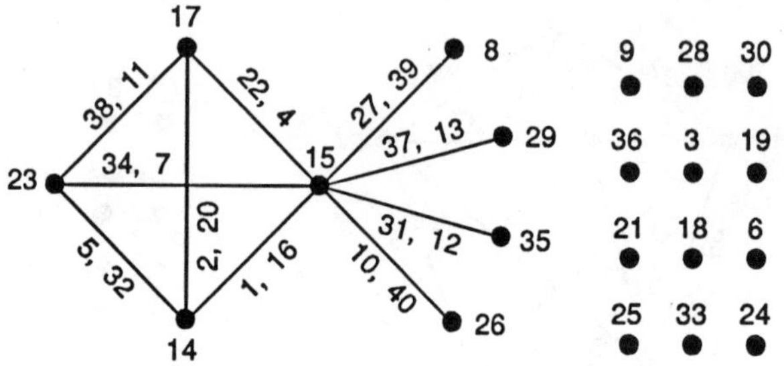

③

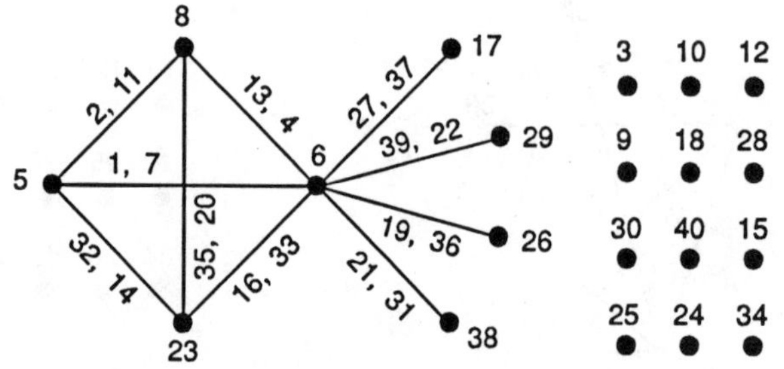

L_{81} (3^{40}) *cont'd.*

III

①

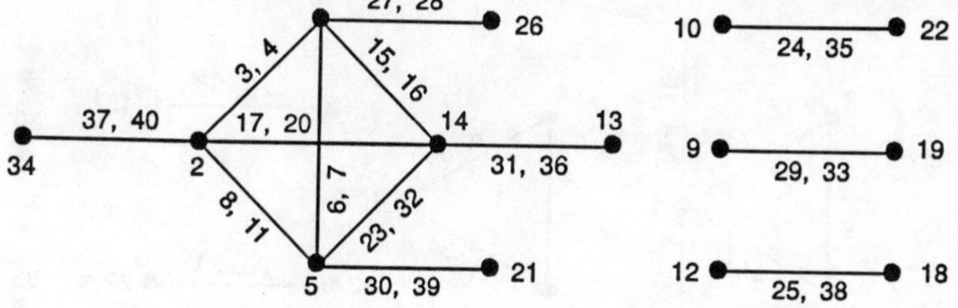

②

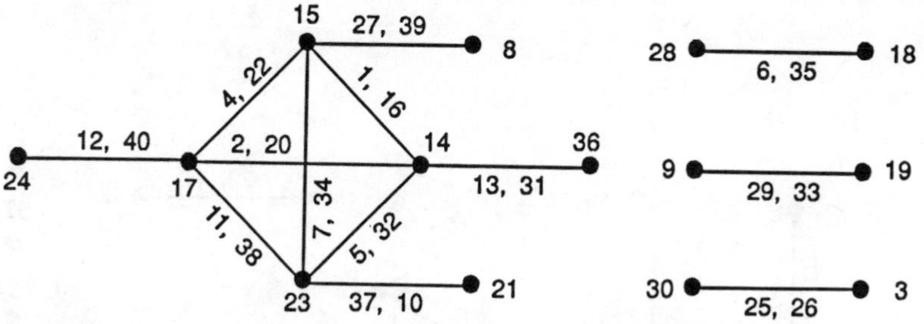

③

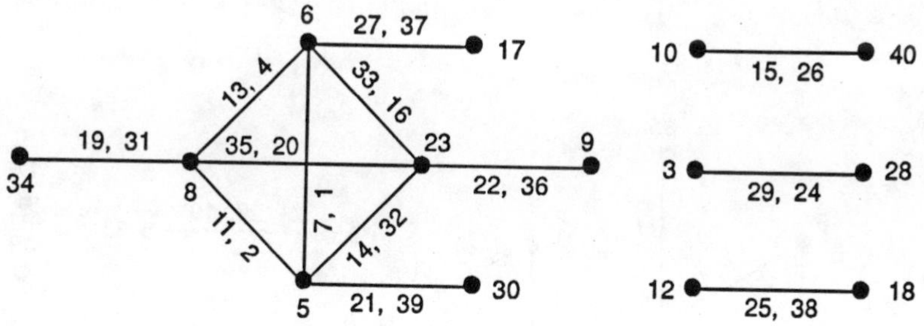

L_{81} (3^{40}) *cont'd.*

IV

①

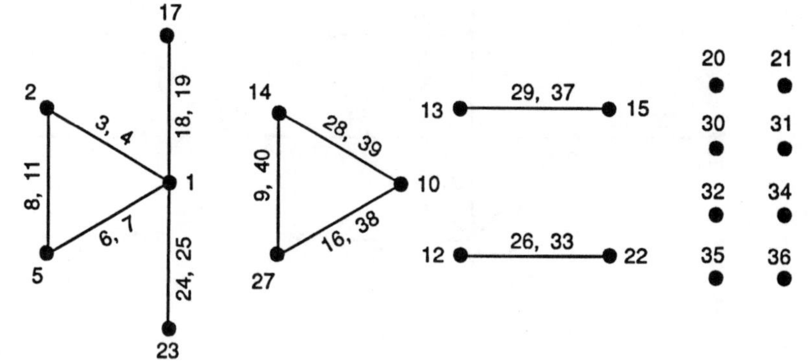

②

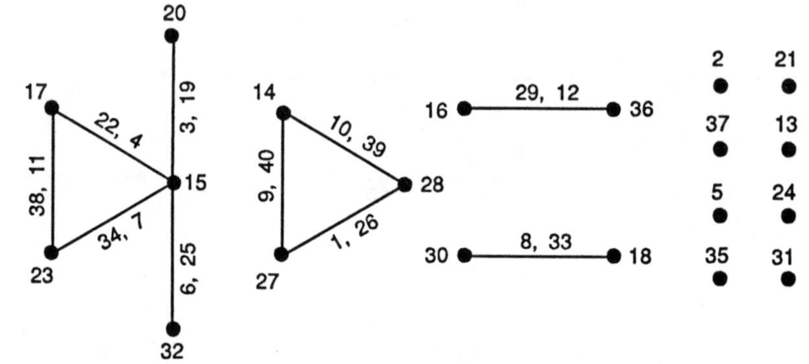

③

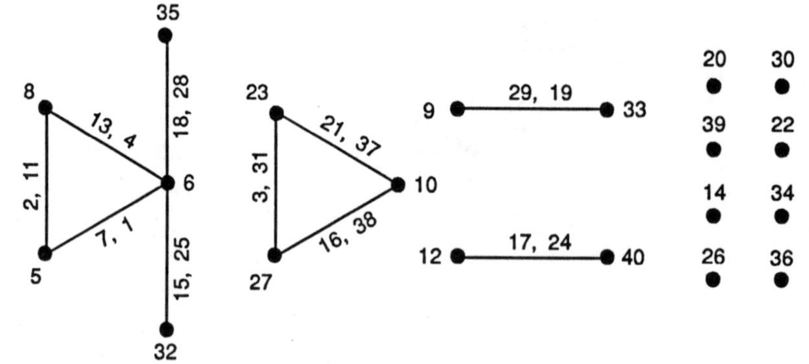

L$_{81}$ (3^{40}) *cont'd.*

V

①

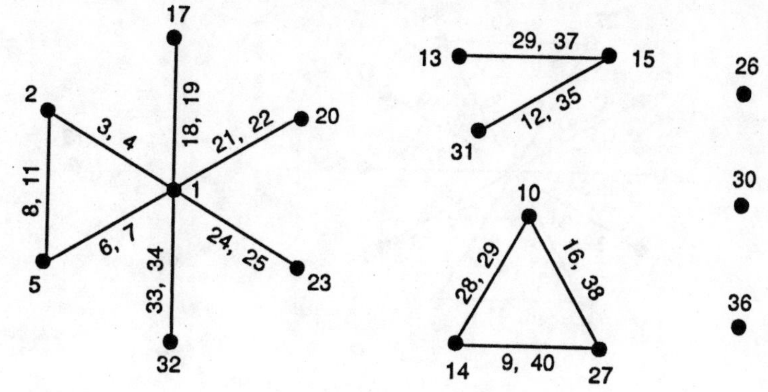

②

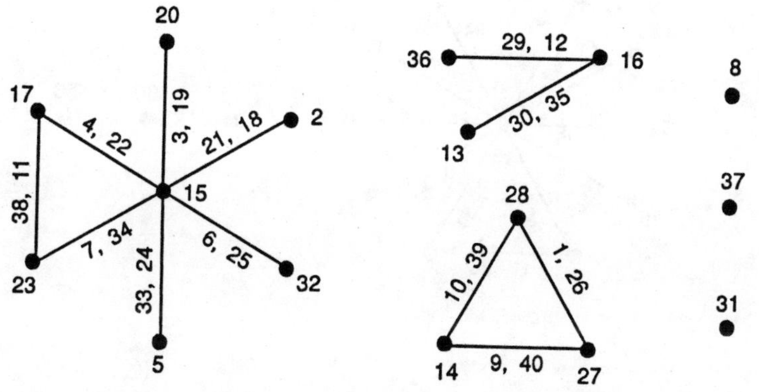

③

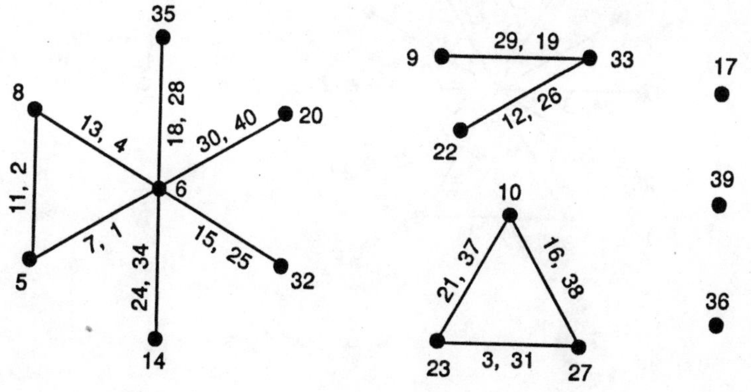

L_{81} (3^{40}) *cont'd.*

VI

①

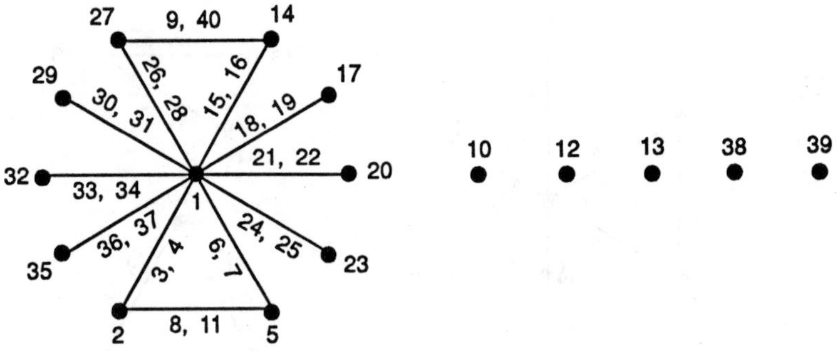

②

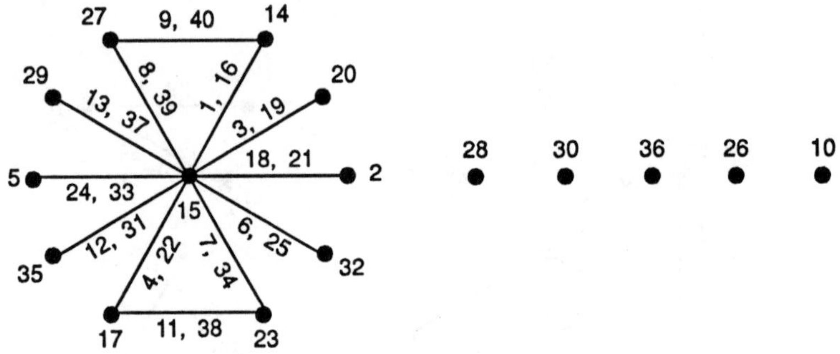

③

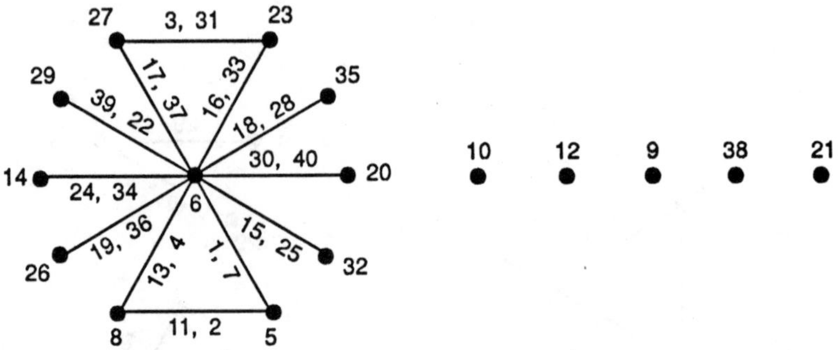

L_{81} (3^{40}) *cont'd.*

VII

①

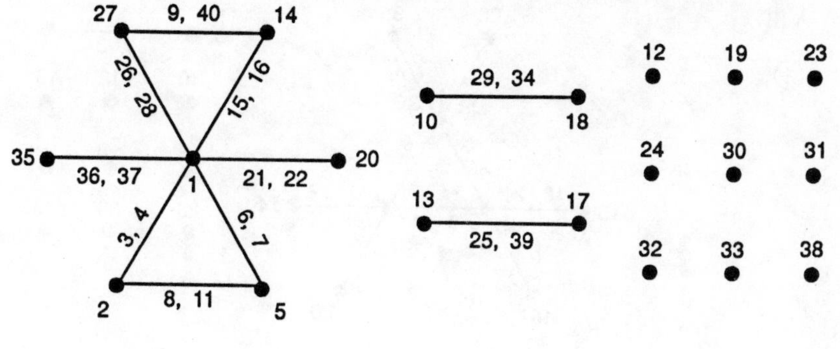

②

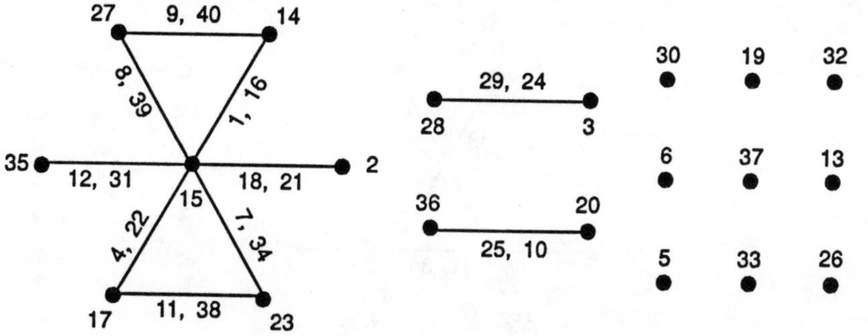

③

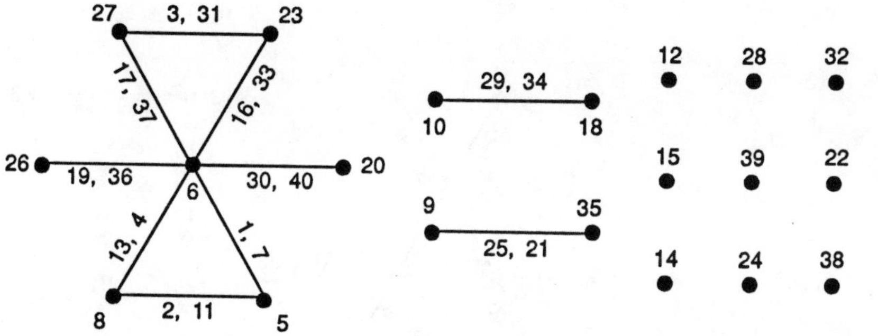

L$_{81}$ (3^{40}) *cont'd.*

VIII

①

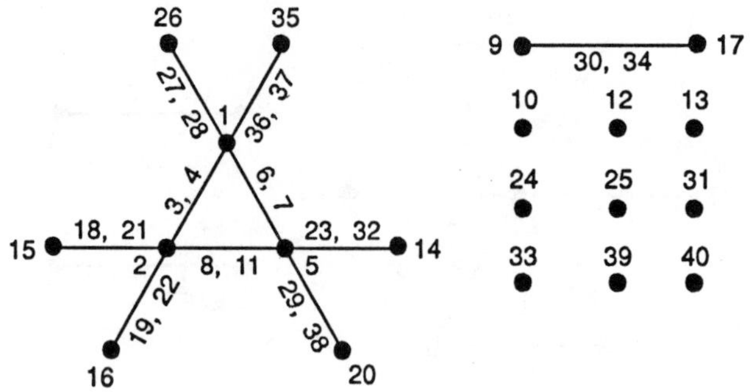

②

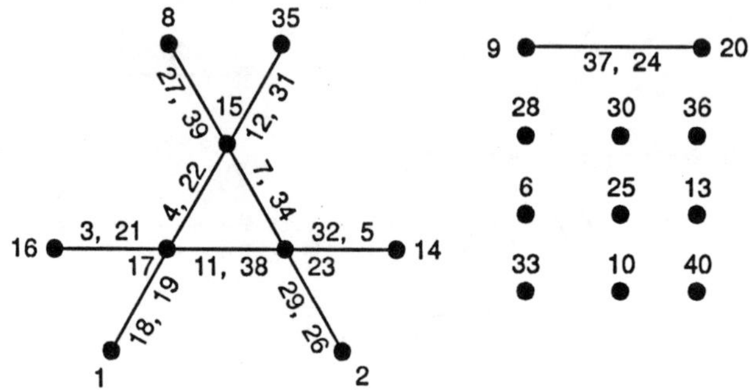

③

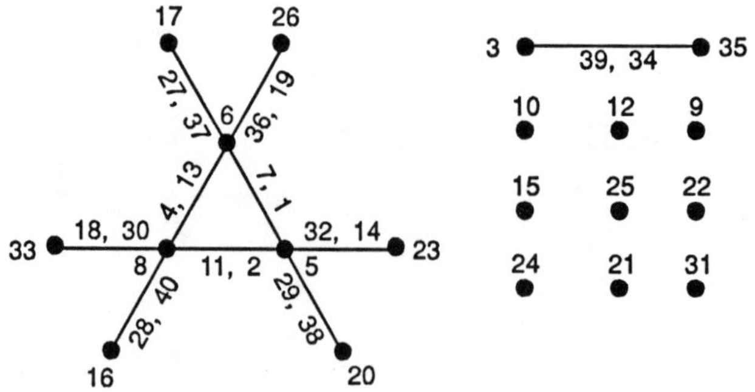

L_{81} (3^{40}) *cont'd.*

IX

①

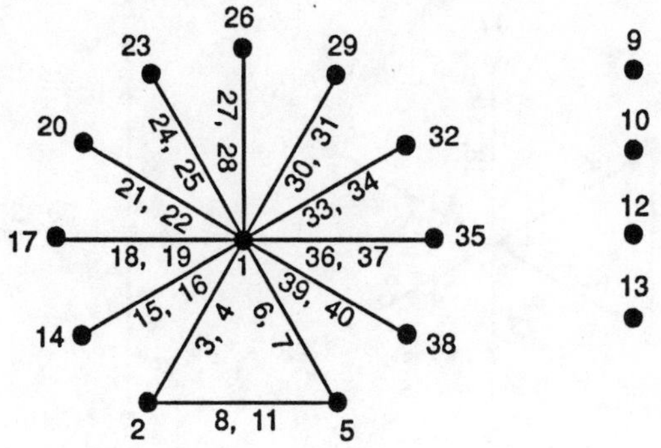

②

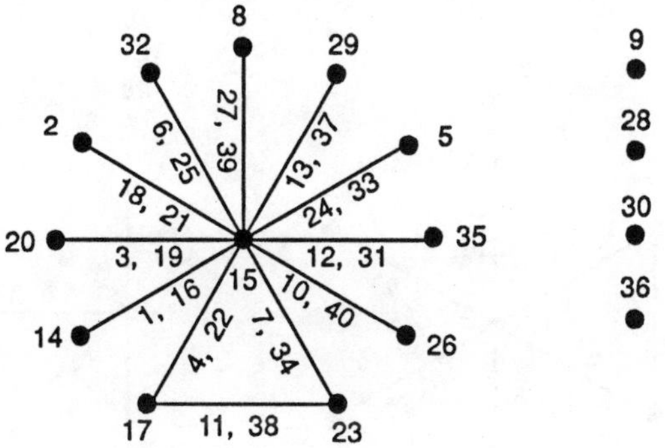

③

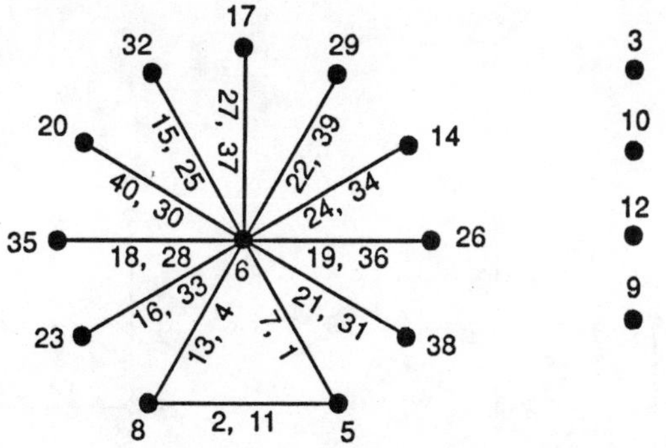

L_{81} (3^{40}) *cont'd.*

X

①

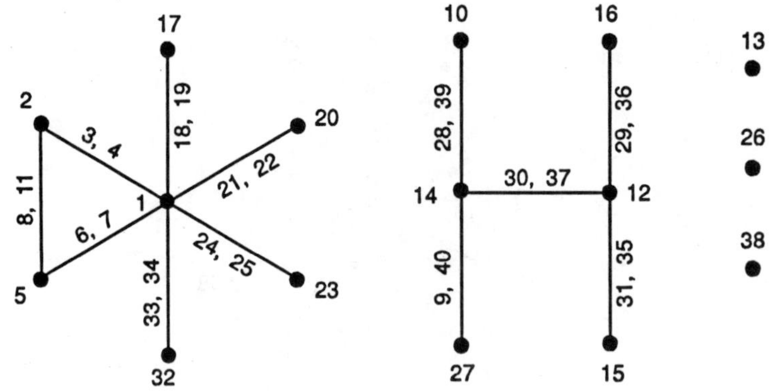

②

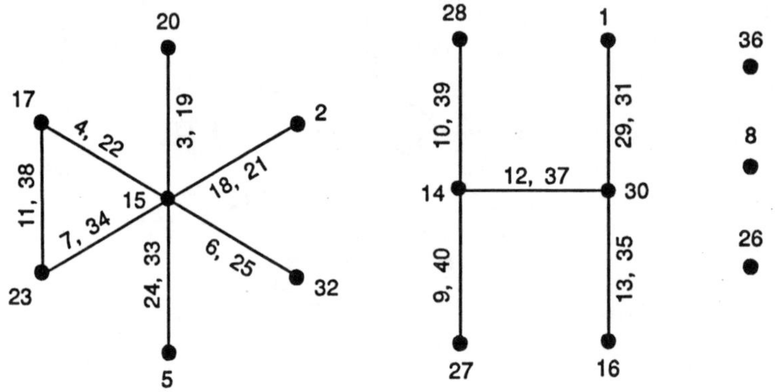

③

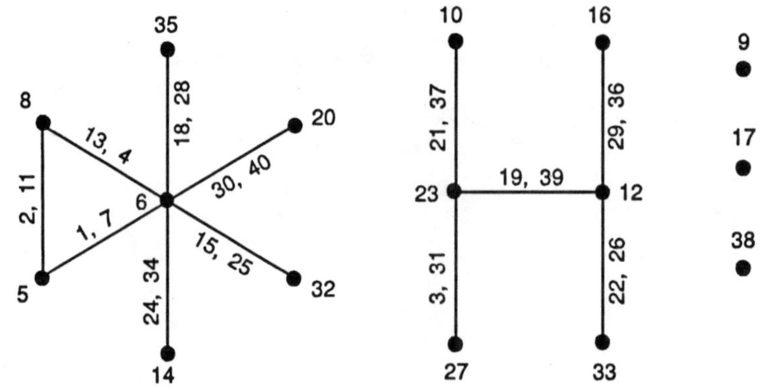

L_{81} (3^{40}) *cont'd.*

XI

①

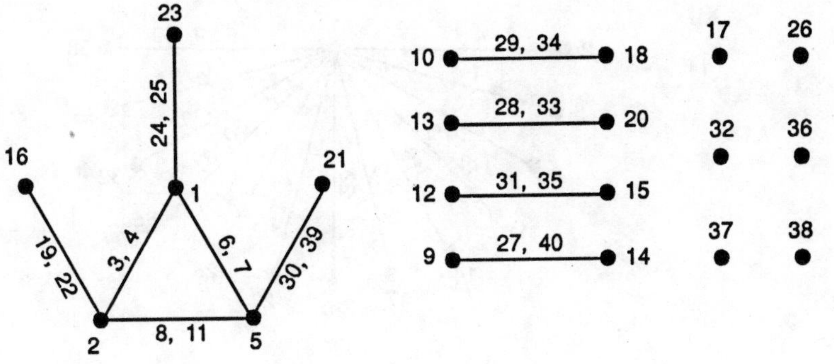

②

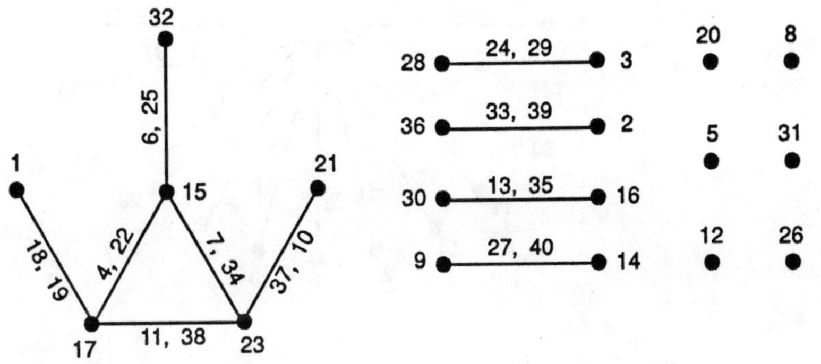

③

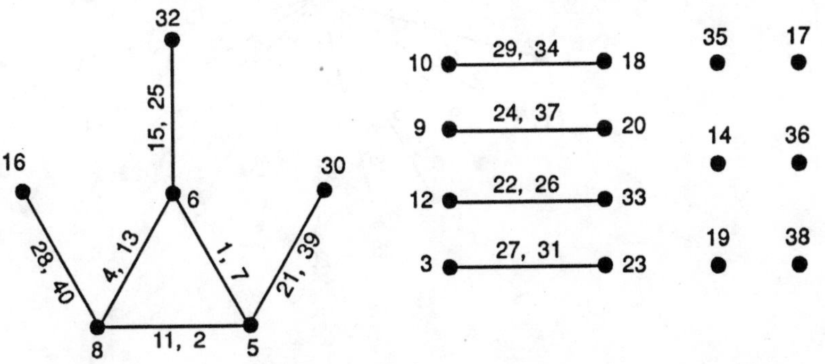

L_{81} (3^{40}) *cont'd.*

XII

①

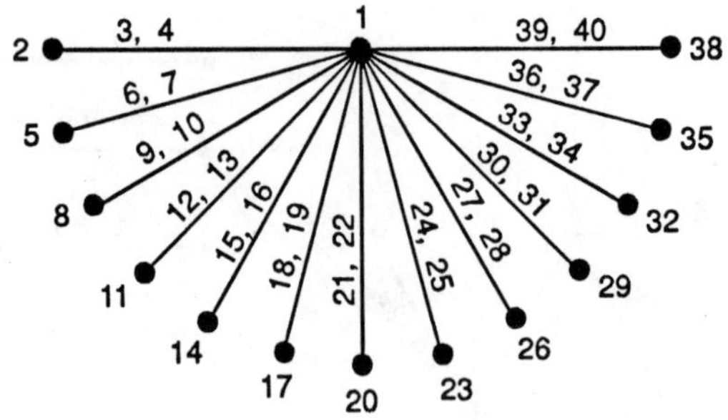

②

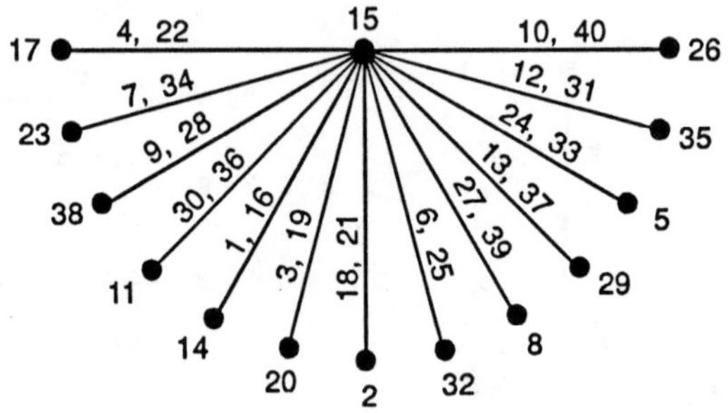

③

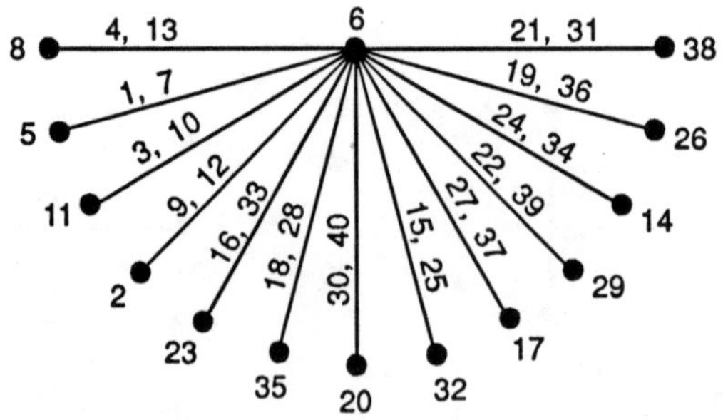

L_{81} (3^{40}) *cont'd.*

XIII

①

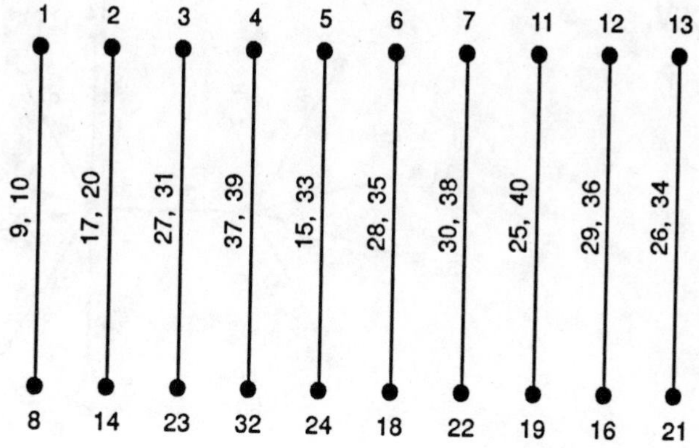

②

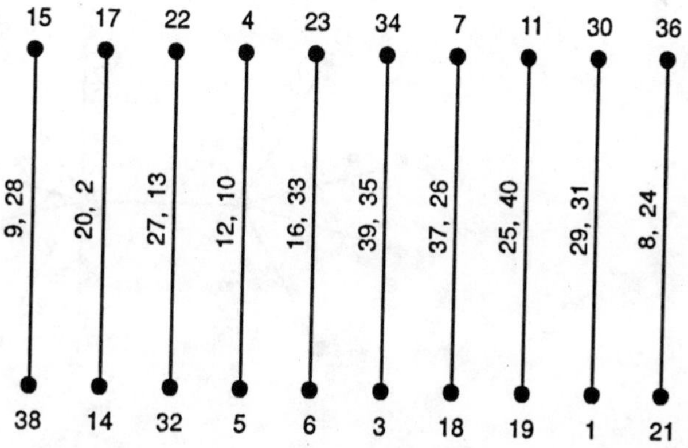

③

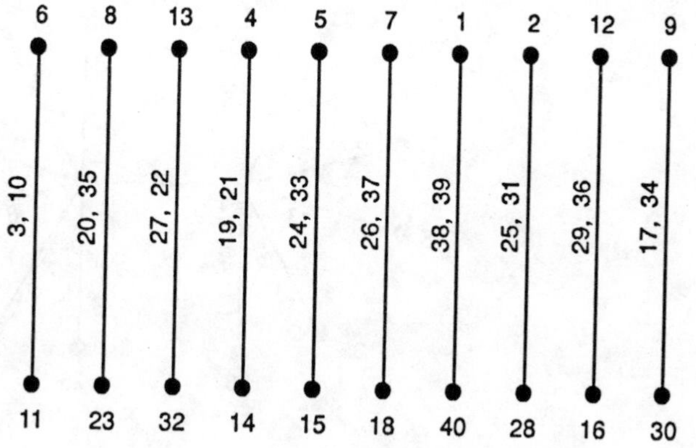

L_{81} (3^{40}) *cont'd.*

XIV

①

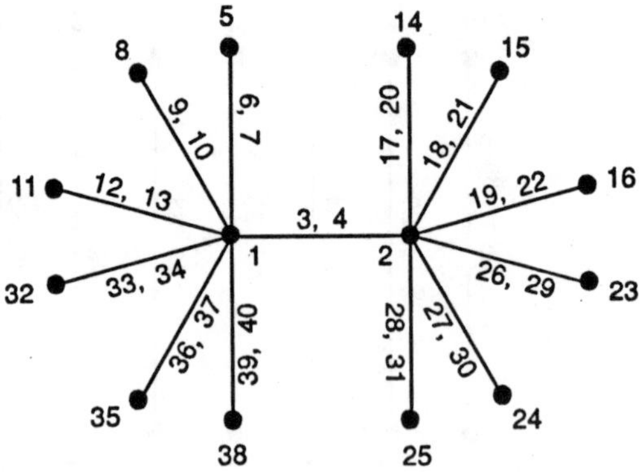

②

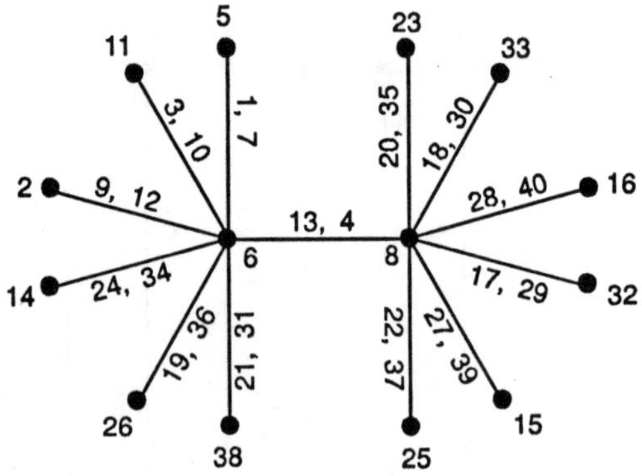

③

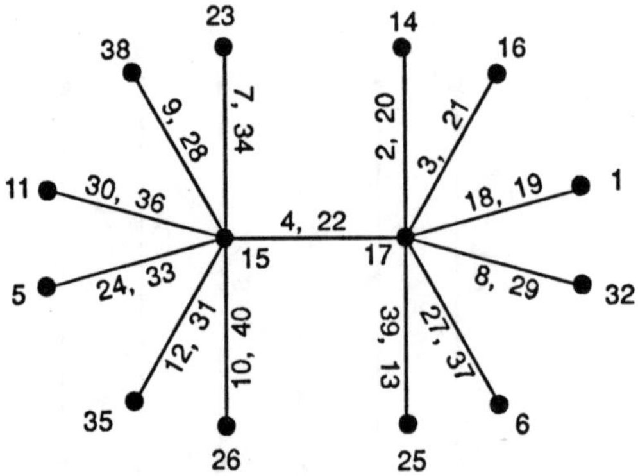

Linear Graph for L_{16} (4^5)

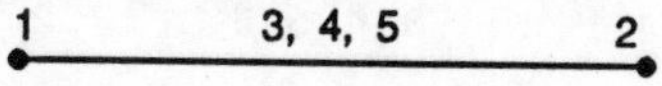

Linear Graph for L_{32} $(2^1 \times 4^9)$

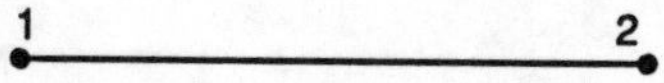

The interaction between columns 1 and 2 can be studied without having to assign the effect of the interaction to a specific column. The interaction can be studied by constructing a 2 × 4 matrix comprised of the average results for each combination of the factors residing in columns 1 and 2.

The effects of the interactions among the four-level columns are distributed fairly uniformly across all four-level columns, prohibiting the investigation of interactions among four-level factors.

Linear Graphs for L_{64} (4^{21})

I

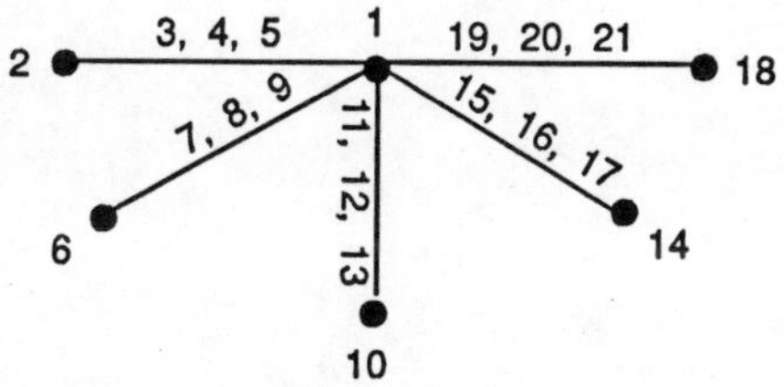

II

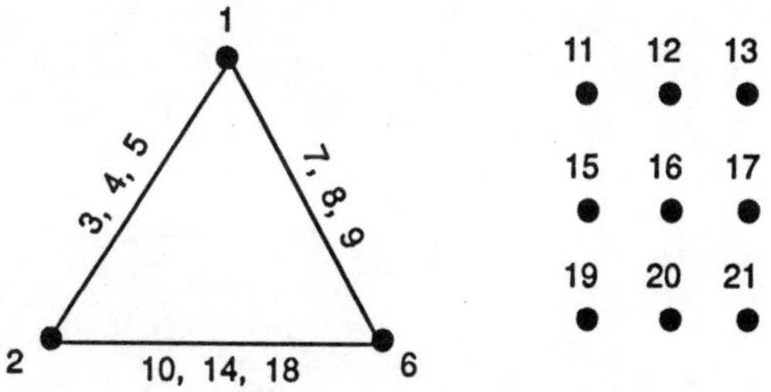

Linear Graph for L_{25} (5^6)

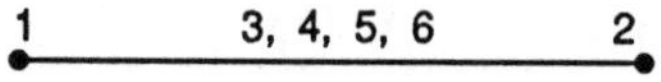

Linear Graph for L_{50} ($2^1 \times 5^{11}$)

The interaction between columns 1 and 2 can be studied without having to assign the effect of the interaction to a specific column. The interaction can be studied by constructing a 2 × 3 matrix comprised of the average results for each combination of the factors residing in columns 1 and 2.

The effects of the interactions among the five-level columns are distributed fairly uniformly across all five-level columns, prohibiting the investigation of interactions among five-level factors.

Appendix C: Interactions between Two Columns Tables

L_8 (2^7) Interactions between Two Columns

1	2	3	4	5	6	7
(1)	3	2	5	4	6	7
	(2)	1	6	7	4	5
		(3)	7	6	5	4
			(4)	1	2	3
				(5)	3	2
					(6)	1

L_{16} (2^{15}) Interactions between Two Columns

1	2	3	4	5	6	7	8	9	10	11	12	13	14	15
(1)	3	2	5	4	7	6	9	8	11	10	13	12	15	14
	(2)	1	6	7	4	5	10	11	8	9	14	15	12	13
		(3)	7	6	5	4	11	10	9	8	15	14	13	12
			(4)	1	2	3	12	13	14	15	8	9	10	11
				(5)	3	2	13	12	15	14	9	8	11	10
					(6)	1	14	15	12	13	10	11	8	9
						(7)	15	14	13	12	11	10	9	8
							(8)	1	2	3	4	5	6	7
								(9)	3	2	5	4	7	6
									(10)	1	6	7	4	5
										(11)	7	6	5	4
											(12)	1	2	3
												(13)	3	2
													(14)	1

L_{32} (2^{31}) Interactions between Two Columns

1	2	3	4	5	6	7	8	9	10	11	12	13	14	15	16	17	18	19	20	21	22	23	24	25	26	27	28	29	30	31
(1)	3	2	5	4	7	6	9	8	11	10	13	12	15	14	17	16	19	18	21	20	23	22	25	24	27	26	29	28	31	30
	(2)	1	6	7	4	5	10	11	8	9	14	15	12	13	18	19	16	17	22	23	20	21	26	27	24	25	30	31	28	29
		(3)	7	6	5	4	11	10	9	8	15	14	13	12	19	18	17	16	23	22	21	20	27	26	25	24	31	30	29	28
			(4)	1	2	3	12	13	14	15	8	9	10	11	20	21	22	23	16	17	18	19	28	29	30	31	24	25	26	27
				(5)	3	2	13	12	15	14	9	8	11	10	21	20	23	22	17	16	19	18	29	28	31	30	25	24	27	26
					(6)	1	14	15	12	13	10	11	8	9	22	23	20	21	18	19	16	17	30	31	28	29	26	27	24	25
						(7)	15	14	13	12	11	10	9	8	23	22	21	20	19	18	17	16	31	30	29	28	27	26	25	24
							(8)	1	2	3	4	5	6	7	24	25	26	27	28	29	30	31	16	17	18	19	20	21	22	23
								(9)	3	2	5	4	7	6	25	24	27	26	29	28	31	30	17	16	19	18	21	20	23	22
									(10)	1	6	7	4	5	26	27	24	25	30	31	28	29	18	19	16	17	22	23	20	21
										(11)	7	6	5	4	27	26	25	24	31	30	29	28	19	18	17	16	23	22	21	20
											(12)	1	2	3	28	29	30	31	24	25	26	27	20	21	22	23	16	17	18	19
												(13)	3	2	29	28	31	30	25	24	27	26	21	20	23	22	17	16	19	18
													(14)	1	30	31	28	29	26	27	24	25	22	23	20	21	18	19	16	17
														(15)	31	30	29	28	27	26	25	24	23	22	21	20	19	18	17	16
															(16)	1	2	3	4	5	6	7	8	9	10	11	12	13	14	15
																(17)	3	2	5	4	7	6	9	8	11	10	13	12	15	14
																	(18)	1	6	7	4	5	10	11	8	9	14	15	12	13
																		(19)	7	6	5	4	11	10	9	8	15	14	13	12
																			(20)	1	2	3	12	13	14	15	8	9	10	11
																				(21)	3	2	13	12	15	14	9	8	11	10
																					(22)	1	14	15	12	13	10	11	8	9
																						(23)	15	14	13	12	11	10	9	8
																							(24)	1	2	3	4	5	6	7
																								(25)	3	2	5	4	7	6
																									(26)	1	6	7	4	5
																										(27)	7	6	5	4
																											(28)	1	2	3
																												(29)	3	2
																													(30)	1

L_{27} (3^{13}) Interactions between Two Columns

1	2	3	4	5	6	7	8	9	10	11	12	13
(1)	3 4	2 4	2 3	6 7	5 7	5 6	9 10	8 10	8 9	12 13	11 13	11 12
	(2)	1 4	1 3	8 11	9 12	10 13	5 11	6 12	7 13	5 8	6 9	7 10
		(3)	1 2	9 13	10 11	8 12	7 12	5 13	6 11	6 10	7 8	5 9
			(4)	10 12	8 13	9 11	6 13	7 11	5 12	7 9	5 10	6 8
				(5)	1 7	1 6	2 11	3 13	4 12	2 8	4 10	3 9
					(6)	1 5	4 13	2 12	3 11	3 10	2 9	4 8
						(7)	3 12	4 11	2 13	4 9	3 8	2 10
							(8)	1 10	1 9	2 5	3 7	4 6
								(9)	1 8	4 7	2 6	3 5
									(10)	3 6	4 5	2 7
										(11)	1 13	1 12
											(12)	1 11

L_{64} (2^{63}) Interactions between Two Columns

1	2	3	4	5	6	7	8	9	10	11	12	13	14	15	16	17	18	19	20	21	22	23	24	25	26	27	28	29	30
(1)	3	2	5	4	7	6	9	8	11	10	13	12	15	14	17	16	19	18	21	20	23	22	25	24	27	26	29	28	31
	(2)	1	6	7	4	5	10	11	8	9	14	15	12	13	18	19	16	17	22	23	20	21	26	27	24	25	30	31	28
		(3)	7	6	5	4	11	10	9	8	15	14	13	12	19	18	17	16	23	22	21	20	27	26	25	24	31	30	29
			(4)	1	2	3	12	13	14	15	8	9	10	11	20	21	22	23	16	17	18	19	28	29	30	31	24	25	26
				(5)	3	2	13	12	15	14	9	8	11	10	21	20	23	22	17	16	19	18	29	28	31	30	25	24	27
					(6)	1	14	15	12	13	10	11	8	9	22	23	20	21	18	19	16	17	30	31	28	29	26	27	24
						(7)	15	14	13	12	11	10	9	8	23	22	21	20	19	18	17	16	31	30	29	28	27	26	25
							(8)	1	2	3	4	5	6	7	24	25	26	27	28	29	30	31	16	17	18	19	20	21	22
								(9)	3	2	5	4	7	6	25	24	27	26	29	28	31	30	17	16	19	18	21	20	23
									(10)	1	6	7	4	5	26	27	24	25	30	31	28	29	18	19	16	17	22	23	20
										(11)	7	6	5	4	27	26	25	24	31	30	29	28	19	18	17	16	23	22	21
											(12)	1	2	3	28	29	30	31	24	25	26	27	20	21	22	23	16	17	18
												(13)	3	2	29	28	31	30	25	24	27	26	21	20	23	22	17	16	19
													(14)	1	30	31	28	29	26	27	24	25	22	23	20	21	18	19	16
														(15)	31	30	29	28	27	26	25	24	23	22	21	20	19	18	17
															(16)	1	2	3	4	5	6	7	8	9	10	11	12	13	14
																(17)	3	2	5	4	7	6	9	8	11	10	13	12	15
																	(18)	1	6	7	4	5	10	11	8	9	14	15	12
																		(19)	7	6	5	4	11	10	9	8	15	14	13
																			(20)	1	2	3	12	13	14	15	8	9	10
																				(21)	3	2	13	12	15	14	9	8	11
																					(22)	1	14	15	12	13	10	11	8
																						(23)	15	14	13	12	11	10	9
																							(24)	1	2	3	4	5	6
																								(25)	3	2	5	4	7
																									(26)	1	6	7	4
																										(27)	7	6	5
																											(28)	1	2
																												(29)	3
																													(30)

	31	32	33	34	35	36	37	38	39	40	41	42	43	44	45	46	47	48	49	50	51	52	53	54	55	56	57	58	59	60	61	62	63
30	33	32	35	34	37	36	39	38	41	40	43	42	45	44	47	46	49	48	51	50	53	52	55	54	57	56	59	58	61	60	63	62
29	34	35	32	33	38	39	36	37	42	43	40	41	46	47	44	45	50	51	48	49	54	55	52	53	58	59	56	57	62	63	60	61
28	35	34	33	32	39	38	37	36	43	42	41	40	47	46	45	44	51	50	49	48	55	54	53	52	59	58	57	56	63	62	61	60
27	36	37	38	39	32	33	34	35	44	45	46	47	40	41	42	43	52	53	54	55	48	49	50	51	60	61	62	63	56	57	58	59
26	37	36	39	38	33	32	35	34	45	44	47	46	41	40	43	42	53	52	55	54	49	48	51	50	61	60	63	62	57	56	59	58
25	38	39	36	37	34	35	32	33	46	47	44	45	42	43	40	41	54	55	52	53	50	51	48	49	62	63	60	61	58	59	56	57
24	39	38	37	36	35	34	33	32	47	46	45	44	43	42	41	40	55	54	53	52	51	50	49	48	63	62	61	60	59	58	57	56
23	40	41	42	43	44	45	46	47	32	33	34	35	36	37	38	39	56	57	58	59	60	61	62	63	48	49	50	51	52	53	54	55
22	41	40	43	42	45	44	47	46	33	32	35	34	37	36	39	38	57	56	59	58	61	60	63	62	49	48	51	50	53	52	55	54
21	42	43	40	41	46	47	44	45	34	35	32	33	38	39	36	37	58	59	56	57	62	63	60	61	50	51	48	49	54	55	52	53
20	43	42	41	40	47	46	45	44	35	34	33	32	39	38	37	36	59	58	57	56	63	62	61	60	51	50	49	48	55	54	53	52
19	44	45	46	47	40	41	42	43	36	37	38	39	32	33	34	35	60	61	62	63	56	57	58	59	52	53	54	55	48	49	50	51
18	45	44	47	46	41	40	43	42	37	36	39	38	33	32	35	34	61	60	63	62	57	56	59	58	53	52	55	54	49	48	51	50
17	46	47	44	45	42	43	40	41	38	39	36	37	34	35	32	33	62	63	60	61	58	59	56	57	54	55	52	53	50	51	48	49
16	47	46	45	44	43	42	41	40	39	38	37	36	35	34	33	32	63	62	61	60	59	58	57	56	55	54	53	52	51	50	49	48
15	48	49	50	51	52	53	54	55	56	57	58	59	60	61	62	63	32	33	34	35	36	37	38	39	40	41	42	43	44	45	46	47
14	49	48	51	50	53	52	55	54	57	56	59	58	61	60	63	62	33	32	35	34	37	36	39	38	41	40	43	42	45	44	47	46
13	50	51	48	49	54	55	52	53	58	59	56	57	62	63	60	61	34	35	32	33	38	39	36	37	42	43	40	41	46	47	44	45
12	51	50	49	48	55	54	53	52	59	58	57	56	63	62	61	60	35	34	33	32	39	38	37	36	43	42	41	40	47	46	45	44
11	52	53	54	55	48	49	50	51	60	61	62	63	56	57	58	59	36	37	38	39	32	33	34	35	44	45	46	47	40	41	42	43
10	53	52	55	54	49	48	51	50	61	60	63	62	57	56	59	58	37	36	39	38	33	32	35	34	45	44	47	46	41	40	43	42
9	54	55	52	53	50	51	48	49	62	63	60	61	58	59	56	57	38	39	36	37	34	35	32	33	46	47	44	45	42	43	40	41
8	55	54	53	52	51	50	49	48	63	62	61	60	59	58	57	56	39	38	37	36	35	34	36	32	47	46	45	44	43	42	41	40
7	56	57	58	59	60	61	62	63	48	49	50	51	52	53	54	55	40	41	42	43	44	45	46	47	32	33	34	35	36	37	38	39
6	57	56	59	58	61	60	63	62	49	48	51	50	53	52	55	54	41	40	43	42	45	44	47	46	33	32	35	34	37	36	39	38
5	58	59	56	57	62	63	60	61	50	51	48	49	54	55	52	53	42	43	40	41	46	47	44	45	34	35	32	33	38	39	36	37
4	59	58	57	56	63	62	61	60	51	50	49	48	55	54	53	52	43	42	41	40	47	46	45	44	35	34	33	32	39	38	37	36
3	60	61	62	63	56	57	58	59	52	53	54	55	48	49	50	51	44	45	46	47	40	41	42	43	36	37	38	39	32	33	34	35
2	61	60	63	62	57	56	59	58	53	52	55	54	49	48	51	50	45	44	47	46	41	40	43	42	37	36	39	38	33	32	35	34
1	62	63	60	61	58	59	56	57	54	55	52	53	50	51	48	49	46	47	44	45	42	43	40	41	38	39	36	37	34	35	32	33
(31)		3	62	61	60	59	58	57	56	55	54	53	52	51	50	49	48	47	46	45	44	43	42	41	40	39	38	37	36	35	34	33	32
(32)			1	2	3	4	5	6	7	8	9	10	11	12	13	14	15	16	17	18	19	20	21	22	23	24	25	26	27	28	29	30	31
(33)				3	2	5	4	7	6	9	8	11	10	13	12	15	14	17	16	19	18	21	20	23	22	25	24	27	26	29	28	31	30
(34)					1	6	7	4	5	10	11	8	9	14	15	12	13	18	19	16	17	22	23	20	21	26	27	24	25	30	31	[illegible]	29
(35)						7	6	5	4	11	10	9	8	15	14	13	12	19	18	17	16	23	22	21	20	27	26	25	24	31	30	29	28
(36)							1	2	3	12	13	14	15	8	9	10	11	20	21	22	23	16	17	18	19	28	29	30	31	24	25	26	27
(37)								3	2	13	12	15	14	9	8	11	10	21	20	23	22	17	16	19	18	29	28	31	30	25	24	27	26
(38)									1	14	15	12	13	10	11	8	9	22	23	20	21	18	19	16	17	30	31	28	29	26	27	24	25
(39)										15	14	13	12	11	10	9	8	23	22	21	20	19	18	17	16	31	30	29	28	27	26	25	24
(40)											1	2	3	4	5	6	7	24	25	26	27	28	29	30	31	16	17	18	19	20	21	22	23
(41)												3	2	5	4	7	6	25	24	27	26	29	28	31	30	17	16	19	18	21	20	23	22
(42)													1	6	7	4	5	26	27	24	25	30	31	28	29	18	19	16	17	22	23	20	21
(43)														7	6	5	4	27	26	25	24	31	30	29	28	19	18	17	16	23	22	21	20
(44)															1	2	3	28	29	30	31	24	25	26	27	20	21	22	23	16	17	18	19
(45)																3	2	29	28	31	30	25	24	27	26	21	20	23	22	17	16	19	18
(46)																	1	30	31	28	29	26	27	24	25	22	23	20	21	18	19	16	17
(47)																		31	30	29	28	27	26	25	24	23	22	21	20	19	18	17	16
(48)																			1	2	3	4	5	6	7	8	9	10	11	12	13	14	15
(49)																				3	2	5	4	7	6	9	8	11	10	13	12	15	14
(50)																					1	6	7	4	5	10	11	8	9	14	15	12	13
(51)																						7	6	5	4	11	10	9	8	15	14	13	12
(52)																							1	2	3	12	13	14	15	8	9	10	11
(53)																								3	2	13	12	15	14	9	8	11	10
(54)																									1	14	15	12	13	10	11	8	9
(55)																										15	14	13	12	11	10	9	8
(56)																											1	2	3	4	5	6	7
(57)																												3	2	5	4	7	6
(58)																													1	6	7	4	5
(59)																														7	6	5	4
(60)																															1	2	3
(61)																																3	2
(62)																																	1

$L_{81}(3^{40})$ Interactions Between Two Columns

1	2	3	4	5	6	7	8	9	10	11	12	13	14	15	16	17	18	19	20
(1)	3	2	2	6	5	5	9	8	8	12	11	11	15	14	14	18	17	17	21
	4	4	3	7	7	6	10	10	9	13	13	12	16	16	15	19	19	18	22
	(2)	1	1	8	9	10	5	6	7	5	6	7	17	18	19	14	15	16	14
		4	3	11	12	13	11	12	13	8	9	10	20	21	22	20	21	22	17
		(3)	1	9	10	8	7	5	6	6	7	5	18	19	17	16	14	15	15
			2	13	11	12	12	13	11	10	8	9	22	20	21	21	22	20	19
			(4)	10	8	9	6	7	5	7	5	6	19	17	18	15	16	14	16
				12	13	11	13	11	12	9	10	8	21	22	20	22	20	21	18
				(5)	1	1	2	3	4	2	4	3	23	24	25	26	27	28	29
					7	6	11	13	12	8	10	9	32	33	34	35	36	37	38
					(6)	1	4	2	3	3	2	4	24	25	23	27	28	26	30
						5	13	12	11	10	9	8	34	32	33	37	35	36	40
						(7)	3	4	2	4	3	2	25	23	24	28	26	27	31
							12	11	13	9	8	10	33	34	32	36	37	35	39
							(8)	1	1	2	3	4	26	27	28	29	30	31	23
								10	9	5	7	6	38	39	40	32	33	34	35
								(9)	1	4	2	3	27	28	26	30	31	29	24
									8	7	6	5	40	38	39	34	32	33	37
									(10)	3	4	2	28	26	27	31	29	30	25
										6	5	7	39	40	38	33	34	32	36
										(11)	1	1	29	30	31	23	24	25	26
											13	12	35	36	37	38	39	40	32
											(12)	1	30	31	29	24	25	23	27
												11	37	35	36	40	38	39	34
												(13)	31	29	30	25	23	24	28
													36	37	35	39	40	38	33
													(14)	1	1	2	3	4	2
														16	15	20	22	21	17
														(15)	1	4	2	3	3
															14	22	21	20	19
															(16)	3	4	2	4
																21	20	22	18
																(17)	1	1	2
																	19	18	14
																	(18)	1	4
																		17	16
																		(19)	3
																			15

Row	21	22	23	24	25	26	27	28	29	30	31	32	33	34	35	36	37	38	39	40
(1)	20	20	24	23	23	27	26	26	30	29	29	33	32	32	36	35	35	39	38	38
	22	21	25	25	24	28	28	27	31	31	30	34	34	33	37	37	36	40	40	39
(2)	15	16	26	27	28	23	24	25	23	24	25	35	36	37	32	33	34	32	33	34
	18	19	29	30	31	29	30	31	26	27	28	38	39	40	38	39	40	35	36	37
(3)	16	14	27	28	26	25	23	24	24	25	23	36	37	35	34	32	33	33	34	32
	17	18	31	29	30	30	31	29	28	26	27	40	38	39	39	40	38	37	35	36
(4)	14	15	28	26	27	24	25	23	25	23	24	37	35	36	33	34	32	34	32	33
	19	17	30	31	29	31	29	30	27	28	26	39	40	38	40	38	39	36	37	35
(5)	30	31	14	15	16	17	18	19	20	21	22	14	15	16	17	18	19	20	21	22
	39	40	32	33	34	35	36	37	38	39	40	23	24	25	26	27	28	29	30	31
(6)	31	29	16	14	15	19	17	18	22	20	21	15	16	14	18	19	17	21	22	20
	38	39	33	34	32	36	37	35	39	40	38	25	23	24	28	26	27	31	29	30
(7)	29	30	15	16	14	18	19	17	21	22	20	16	14	15	19	17	18	22	20	21
	40	38	34	32	33	37	35	36	40	38	39	24	25	23	27	28	26	30	31	29
(8)	24	25	20	21	22	14	15	16	17	18	19	17	18	19	20	21	22	14	15	16
	36	37	35	36	37	38	39	40	32	33	34	29	30	31	23	24	25	26	27	28
(9)	25	23	22	20	21	16	14	15	19	17	18	18	19	17	21	22	20	15	16	14
	35	36	36	37	35	39	40	38	33	34	32	31	29	30	25	23	24	28	26	27
(10)	23	24	21	22	20	15	16	14	18	19	17	19	17	18	22	20	21	16	14	15
	37	35	37	35	36	40	38	39	34	32	33	30	31	29	24	25	23	27	28	26
(11)	27	28	17	18	19	20	21	22	14	15	16	20	21	22	14	15	16	17	18	19
	33	34	38	39	40	32	33	34	35	36	37	26	27	28	29	30	31	23	24	25
(12)	28	26	19	17	18	22	20	21	16	14	15	21	22	20	15	16	14	18	19	17
	32	33	39	40	38	33	34	32	36	37	35	28	26	27	31	29	30	25	23	24
(13)	26	27	18	19	17	21	22	20	15	16	14	22	20	21	16	14	15	19	17	18
	34	32	40	38	39	34	32	33	37	35	36	27	28	26	30	31	29	24	25	23
(14)	4	3	5	6	7	8	9	10	11	12	13	5	7	6	11	13	12	8	10	9
	19	18	32	34	33	38	40	39	35	37	36	23	25	24	29	31	30	26	28	27
(15)	2	4	7	5	6	10	8	9	13	11	12	6	5	7	12	11	13	9	8	10
	18	17	34	33	32	40	39	38	37	36	35	25	24	23	31	30	29	28	27	26
(16)	3	2	6	7	5	9	10	8	12	13	11	7	6	5	13	12	11	10	9	8
	17	19	33	32	34	39	38	40	36	35	37	24	23	25	30	29	31	27	26	28
(17)	3	4	11	12	13	5	6	7	8	9	10	8	10	9	5	7	6	11	13	12
	16	15	38	40	39	35	37	36	32	34	33	29	31	30	26	28	27	23	25	24
(18)	2	3	13	11	12	7	5	6	10	8	9	9	8	10	6	5	7	12	11	13
	15	14	40	39	38	37	36	35	34	33	32	31	30	29	28	27	26	25	24	23
(19)	4	2	12	13	11	6	7	5	9	10	8	10	9	8	7	6	5	13	12	11
	14	16	39	38	40	36	35	37	33	32	34	30	29	31	27	26	28	24	23	25

(20)	1	1	8	9	10	11	12	13	5	6	7	11	13	12	8	10	9	5	7	6
	22	21	35	37	36	32	34	33	38	40	39	26	28	27	23	25	24	29	31	30
(21)		1	10	8	9	13	11	12	7	5	6	12	11	13	9	8	10	6	5	7
		20	37	36	35	34	33	32	40	39	38	28	27	26	25	24	23	31	30	29
(22)			9	10	8	12	13	11	6	7	5	13	12	11	10	9	8	7	6	5
			36	35	37	33	32	34	39	38	40	27	26	28	24	23	25	30	29	31
(23)				1	1	2	3	4	2	4	3	5	6	7	8	9	10	11	12	13
				25	24	29	31	30	26	28	27	14	16	15	20	22	21	17	19	18
(24)					1	4	2	3	3	2	4	7	5	6	10	8	9	13	11	12
					23	31	30	29	28	27	26	16	15	14	22	21	20	19	18	17
(25)						3	4	2	4	3	2	6	7	5	9	10	8	12	13	11
						30	29	31	27	26	28	15	14	16	21	20	22	18	17	19
(26)							1	1	2	3	4	11	12	13	5	6	7	8	9	10
							28	27	23	25	24	20	22	21	17	19	18	14	16	15
(27)								1	4	2	3	13	11	12	7	5	6	10	8	9
								26	25	24	23	22	21	20	19	18	17	16	15	14
(28)									3	4	2	12	13	11	6	7	5	9	10	8
									24	23	25	21	20	22	18	17	19	15	14	16
(29)										1	1	8	9	10	11	12	13	5	6	7
										31	30	17	19	18	14	16	15	20	22	21
(30)											1	10	8	9	13	11	12	7	5	6
											29	19	18	17	16	15	14	22	21	20
(31)												9	10	8	12	13	11	6	7	5
												18	17	19	15	14	16	21	20	22
(32)													1	1	2	3	4	2	4	3
													34	33	38	40	39	35	37	36
(33)														1	4	2	3	3	2	4
														32	40	39	38	37	36	35
(34)															3	4	2	4	3	2
															39	38	40	36	35	37
(35)																1	1	2	3	4
																37	36	32	34	33
(36)																	1	4	2	3
																	35	34	33	32
(37)																		3	4	2
																		33	32	34
(38)																			1	1
																			40	39
(39)																				1
																				38

L_{64} (4^{21}) Interactions between Two Columns

	1	2	3	4	5	6	7	8	9	10	11	12	13	14	15	16	17	18	19	20	21
		3	2	2	2	7	6	6	6	11	10	10	10	15	14	14	14	19	18	18	18
(1)		4	4	3	3	8	8	7	7	12	12	11	11	16	16	15	15	20	20	19	19
		5	5	5	4	9	9	9	8	13	13	13	12	17	17	17	16	21	21	21	20
			1	1	1	10	11	12	13	6	7	8	9	6	7	8	9	6	7	8	9
(2)			4	3	3	14	15	16	17	14	15	16	17	10	11	12	13	10	11	12	13
			5	5	4	18	19	20	21	18	19	20	21	18	19	20	21	14	15	16	17
				1	1	11	10	13	12	7	6	9	8	8	9	6	7	9	8	7	6
(3)				2	2	16	17	14	15	17	16	15	14	13	12	11	10	12	13	10	11
				5	4	21	20	19	18	20	21	18	19	19	18	21	20	15	14	17	16
					1	12	13	10	11	8	9	6	7	9	8	7	6	7	6	9	8
(4)					2	17	16	15	14	15	14	17	16	11	10	13	12	13	12	11	10
					3	19	18	21	20	21	20	19	18	20	21	18	19	16	17	14	15
						13	12	11	10	9	8	7	6	7	6	9	8	8	9	6	7
(5)						15	14	17	16	16	17	14	15	12	13	10	11	11	10	13	12
						20	21	18	19	19	18	21	20	21	20	19	18	17	16	15	14
							1	1	1	2	3	4	5	2	5	3	4	2	4	5	3
(6)							8	7	7	14	16	17	15	10	13	11	12	10	12	13	11
							9	9	8	18	21	19	20	18	20	21	19	14	17	15	16
								1	1	3	2	5	4	5	2	4	3	4	2	3	5
(7)								6	6	17	15	14	16	12	11	13	10	13	11	10	12
								9	8	20	19	21	18	21	19	18	20	16	15	17	14
									1	4	5	2	3	3	4	2	5	5	3	2	4
(8)									6	15	17	16	14	13	10	12	11	11	13	12	10
									7	21	18	20	19	19	21	20	18	17	14	16	15
										5	4	3	2	4	3	5	2	3	5	4	2
(9)										16	14	15	17	11	12	10	13	12	10	11	13
										19	20	18	21	20	18	19	21	15	16	14	17
											1	1	1	2	4	5	3	2	5	3	4
(10)											12	11	11	6	8	9	7	6	9	7	8
											13	13	12	18	21	19	20	14	16	17	15
												1	1	4	2	3	5	5	2	4	3
(11)												10	10	9	7	6	8	8	7	9	6
												13	12	20	19	21	18	17	15	14	16
													1	5	3	2	4	3	4	2	5
(12)													10	7	9	8	6	9	6	8	7
													11	21	18	20	19	15	17	16	14
														3	5	4	2	4	3	5	2
(13)														8	6	7	9	7	8	6	9
														19	20	18	21	16	14	15	17
															1	1	1	2	3	4	5
(14)															16	15	15	6	8	9	7
															17	17	16	10	13	11	12
																1	1	3	2	5	4
(15)																14	14	9	7	6	8
																17	16	12	11	13	10
																	1	4	5	2	3
(16)																	14	7	9	8	6
																	15	13	10	12	11
																		5	4	3	2
(17)																		8	6	7	9
																		11	12	10	13
																			1	1	1
(18)																			20	19	19
																			21	21	20
																				1	1
(19)																				18	18
																				21	20
																					1
(20)																					18
																					19

Index

A

Accuracy, testing/measurement instrument, 58–62
Additivity, 45–46, 86
Analysis of variance (ANOVA), 9, 177
Analyzing experiment phase, 11, 12
AT&T, 2
Attribute analysis, classified
  case study, 264–72
  concepts of, 256–64
Attribute measurements, classified, 64–66
Attribute quality characteristics
  description of, 47–49, 51–53
  handling multiple, 407–12
  handling multiple measurable and, 412–17
  larger-the-better and, 416–17
  nominal-the-best and, 413–14
  smaller-the-better and, 414–16
Attribute run sheet, classified, 224–28

B

Bell Laboratories, 2
Between experiment error, 175, 176–77
Between product noise, 76, 77
Bias
  experimental error and, 175–78
  measurement, 63, 64–66
  randomization and, 178–80, 183–87
  repetition and, 180–81
  replication and, 182–83
Brainstorming
  description of, 24, 25–27
  selecting factors and, 70, 71–72

C

Calibration, 58–59
Case studies
  casing paint, 264–72
  control device, 249–55
  digital circuit, 240–49
  electronic circuit time out, 281–91
  modem subcircuit, 331–37
  randomization, 186–87
  white powder, 90–96
  wire connector assembly, 299–311
  yardstick, 318–30
Cause-and-effect diagrams
  selecting factors and, 71
  use of, 24, 36–39
Cause enumeration diagrams
  description of, 36, 38
  selecting factors and, 71

Classified attribute analysis
case study, 264–72
concepts of, 256–64
Classified attribute measurements, 64–66
Classified attribute run sheet, 224–28
Combination designs, 378–82
Conducting experiment phase
description of, 10, 11, 12
experimental run coordination, 219–20
experimental run sheets, 220–28
time constraints and other considerations, 228, 231–33
Continuous experiments, 97, 101–4
Control charts, measurement error, 59–62
Control factors, 77–78, 80–82
Costs
additional unit, 66
first unit, 66
total, 66–67
Customers, as part of experimentation team, 18

D

Data, infeasible
estimation for, 430
larger-the-better and, 433–35
nominal-the-best and, 435–37
reasons for, 423–24
smaller-the-better and, 431–33
Data, missing
estimation techniques, 424–25
example, 426–30
reasons for, 423–24
Data worksheet
design of, 197–98
information contained in, 191, 198
purpose of, 191, 197
surface mount, 199
wavesolder, 199
Degrees of freedom
calculating, 131–37
concept of, 129–31
for factors, 132
for interactions, 132–34
for orthogonal arrays, 134–37
Descriptive characteristics, 74
Design engineers, input from, 20
Design experiment phase, 10, 11
Design of Experiments (DOE), importance of, xvii–xviii
Design systems, dynamic characteristic analysis and, 340
Design techniques, special
combination designs, 378–82
dummy treatment, 373–78
idle column method, 391–99
multilevel arrangements, 364–73
nested factor designs, 385–91
sliding levels, 382–85
Dispersion analysis diagrams
description of, 36, 37
selecting factors and, 71
Documentation of experiment, 233–35
Dummy treatment, 373–78
Dynamic characteristic analysis
applications, 338–40
circuit design example, 360–63
design systems and, 340
linear equation and, 348–49, 357–60
linearity and, 341–42
manufacturing systems and, 339–40
measurement systems and, 339
reference point proportional equation and, 346, 348, 353–57
sensitivity and, 341
signal factors and, 343–45
signal-to-noise ratio equations and, 345–60
slope calibration and, 349
variability and, 342
zero point proportional equation and, 346, 350–52
Dynamic characteristic run sheet, 228, 229–30

Dynamic quality characteristics
  description of, 49–51, 53–54
  outer arrays and, 172–74

E

Equipment
  acquiring, 212–13
  scheduling, 217
  selecting, 210–11
Errors
  primary, 175, 176–77
  secondary, 175, 177–78
Experimental run coordination, 219–20
Experimental run sheets
  classified attribute, 224–28
  dynamic characteristic, 228, 229–30
  measurable characteristic, 220–24
  purpose of, 220
Experimentation team
  design engineers and, 20
  determining who can best impact the goal, 16–20
  establishing goals and, 14–16
  examples of possible members, 18, 21–22
  importance of, 12–14
  inspectors and, 19
  machine operators as members, 18–19
  process experts and, 19–20
  product/manufacturing engineers and, 19–20
  quality engineers/supervisors and, 20
  selecting a team leader, 21–22
  when to form, 14
Experiment design, comparisons, 9–10
Experiment phases
  analyzing phase, 11, 12
  conducting phase, 10, 11, 12
  design phase, 10, 11
  planning phase, 10, 11
Experiment preparation
  acquiring equipment, 212–13
  acquiring materials, 211–12
  identifying and randomizing test samples, 213–14
  inspection guidelines, 215–16
  scheduling equipment, 217
  screening materials, 213
  selecting equipment, 210–11
  selecting materials, 208–10
  test operators/inspectors, 214–15
Experiments
  continuous, 97, 101–4
  documentation of, 233–35
  focusing, 98, 107–10
  screening, 97–98, 104–7
  sequential, 98, 110–13
  single, 97, 98–100

F

Factors
  adjustment, 314, 327, 330
  assigning, to linear graphs, 141–42
  brainstorming and selecting, 70, 71–72
  cause-and-effect diagrams and selecting, 71
  classifying noise, 74–79
  control, 77–78, 80–82
  degrees of freedom for, 132
  generating a list of, 70–72
  interaction and, 85–90
  screening list of, 72–74
  signal, 343–45
  specifying noise, 82–85
  specifying parameter settings, 79–85
  use of the term, 70
Failure Mode and Effect Analysis (FMEA), use of, 41–44
Fault tree analysis, use of, 39–41

Fishbone diagrams, use of, 36–39
Fisher, R. A., 4, 115
Flip charts, use of, 26
Focusing experiments, 98, 107–10
Ford Motor Co., 2
Fractional factorials, use of, 10
Fuji Film, 2
Full factorial approach, 2, 9–10
Functional characteristics, 74
Functional variation, 3

G

Goal(s)
- establishing, 14–16
- examples of basic, 16
- importance of team members who understand, 16–17
- involvement of those affected by experiment, 17–18

Guide to Quality Control (Ishikara), 31

I

Idle column method, 391–99
Inner array, 167
Inner noise, 76
Inspection, guidelines for, 215–16
Inspectors. *See also* Test operator/inspector
- experiment preparation and, 214–15
- input from, 19

Interactions
- degrees of freedom for, 132–34
- description of, 85–90
- involving multilevel factors, 372–73
- orthogonal arrays and, 119–22

Ishikara, Kaoru, 31, 36
Ishikawa diagrams, use of, 24, 36–39

J

Juran, J. M., 31

L

Larger-the-better analysis, 292
- analysis techniques, 295–99
- case study, 299–311
- signal-to-noise ratio and, 294–95

Larger-the-better measurable quality characteristic, 47
- attribute quality characteristics and, 416–17
- infeasible data and, 433–35
- level average analysis and case study, 240–49

Level average analysis
- concept of, 236–40
- control device (smaller-the-better) case study, 249–55
- digital circuit (larger-the-better) case study, 240–49
- graphical method, 237–39
- tabular method, 236–37

Linear equation, 348–49, 357–60
Linear graphs
- assigning factors to, 141–42
- concepts, 138–40
- modified problems, examples of, 157–66
- modifying standard, 154–57
- orthogonal arrays and, 4–5
- standard, 142–46
- standard problems, examples of, 146–54

Linearity, dynamic characteristic analysis and, 341–42
Loss function, 3–4

M

Machine operators, input from, 18–19
Main effects, 115. *See also* Factors
Management, meeting with, 15
Management support
  how to obtain, 14–15
  importance of, 14, 16
Manufacturing supervisor, as part of experimentation team, 17
Manufacturing systems, dynamic characteristic analysis and, 339–40
Marketing personnel, as part of experimentation team, 17
Materials
  acquiring, 211–12
  screening, 213
  selecting, 208–10
Mean square deviation
  larger-the-better, 294–95
  smaller-the-better, 275
Measurable characteristic run sheet, 220–24
Measurable quality characteristics, 46–47
  handling multiple, 401–7
  handling multiple attribute and, 412–17
Measurement
  bias, 63, 64–66
  classified attribute, 64–66
  dynamic characteristic analysis and, 339
  environment, 63–64
  importance of, 55
  noise, 63–64
  planning, 56–57
  sampling requirements, 66–68
  testing/measurement instrument accuracy/repeatability, 58–62
  testing/measurement instrument availability, 57
  testing/measurement instrument resolution, 58
  test operator/inspector and, 62–63
Morinaga Pharmaceutical, 1
Morinaga Sieka, 2
Multilevel arrangements, 364
  combining dummy treatment with, 375–78
  for eight-level factors, 367–72
  for four-level factors, 365–67
  interactions involving, 372–73
  operating window, 418–22
  other applications, 372

N

Nested factor design, 385–91
Nippon Telephone and Telegraph Co., 2
Noise
  between product, 76, 77
  compounding, 82–83
  continuous, 84–85
  definition of, 78
  discrete, 82–84
  examples of, 75
  inner, 76
  measurement, 63–64
  outer, 76
  outer arrays and, 169–71
  specifying, 82–85
  use of the term, 8
Nominal-the-best analysis
  adjusting the mean, 314
  calculating the mean, 317
  concepts of, 312–15
  equations, 315–17
  modem subcircuit case study, 331–37
  reducing the variability, 313–14
  signal-to-noise ratio and, 315–16

Nominal-the-best analysis (*continued*)
  yardstick case study, 318–30
Nominal-the-best measurable quality characteristic, 46
  attribute quality characteristics and, 413–14
  infeasible data and, 435–37

O

Objectives, determining
  brainstorming and, 24, 25–27
  cause-and-effect diagrams and, 24, 36–39
  defining quality characteristic and, 44–54
  failure mode and effect analysis and, 41–44
  fault tree analysis and, 39–41
  methods for, 24–44
  Pareto charts and, 24, 27–31
  process flow diagrams and, 24, 31–36
  tips for, 23–24
Off-line quality control
  parameter design and, 8–9
  purpose of, 7
  system design and, 8
  tolerance design and, 9
Omega Transformation, 262–63
On-line quality control, 7
Operating window, 418–22
Orthogonal arrays
  advantages of, 4, 116–17
  analysis of, 119
  cost efficiency of, 117
  degrees of freedom for, 134–37
  development of, 4, 115
  disadvantage of, 118
  interactions and, 119–22
  levels of, 122–27
  linear graphs and, 4–5
  reproducibility of, 116–17
  terminology for, 118–19
  three-level, 125–27
  two-level, 123–25
  use of, 2, 4–5, 114–15
Orthogonality, defining, 115–16
Outer array
  dynamic characteristics and, 172–74
  noise factors and use of, 169–71
  no noise factors and, 167–68
  use of the term, 167
Outer noise, 76

P

Parameter design, off-line quality control and, 8–9
Pareto charts, use of, 24, 27–31
Pareto principle, 27, 400
Percentages, 261–62
Piece-to-piece variation, 77
Planning
  experiment phase, 10, 11
  measurement, 56–57
Prediction equation, 248, 261–62, 280, 298–99
Primary error, 175, 176–77
Process, robustness and, 5
Process experts, input from, 19–20
Process flow diagrams
  selecting factors and, 71
  use of, 24, 31–36, 400
Product, robustness and, 5
Product/manufacturing engineers, input from, 19–20
Production process classification diagrams
  description of, 36
  selecting factors and, 71

Q

Quality
  loss function and, 3–4

Quality (*continued*)
orthogonal arrays and linear graphs and, 4–5
robustness and, 5
Quality characteristics
attribute, 47–49, 51–53
comparison of, 51–54
defining, 44–54
dynamic, 49–51, 53–54
measurable, 46–47
tips for selecting, 44–46
Quality characteristics, handling multiple
attribute, 407–12
measurable, 401–7
measurable and attribute, 412–17
Pareto analysis and, 400
process flow diagrams and, 400
Quality Control Handbook (Juran), 31
Quality engineering
off-line quality control, 7–9
on-line quality control, 7
use of the term, 6
Quality engineers/supervisors, input from, 20

R

Randomization
case study using, 186–87
description of, 178–80
full versus partial, 183–86
Random noise, 2
Reference point proportional equation, 346, 348, 353–57
Repeatability, testing/measurement instrument, 58–62
Repetition, bias and, 180–81
Replication, bias and, 182–83
Resolution, testing/measurement instrument, 58
Response graphs, 244–46, 259–60, 278, 297–98
Robustness
definition of, 2, 5, 77
examples of, 77
quality and, 5
Run sheets. *See* Experimental run sheets

S

Sampling
factors that affect, 66–68
guidelines, 192–93
identification, 196–97
identifying and randomizing, 213–14
ordering, 197
preparation, 196
selection, 193–96
Screening experiments, 97–98, 104–7
Secondary error, 175, 177–78
Sensitivity, 58
dynamic characteristic analysis and, 341
Sequential experiments, 98, 110–13
Signal-to-noise (S/N) ratio
dynamic characteristic analysis and, 345–60
larger-the-better analysis and, 294–95
linear equation, 348–49, 357–60
nominal-the-best analysis and, 315–16
reference point proportional equation, 346, 348, 353–57
smaller-the-better analysis and, 274–76
zero point proportional equation, 346, 350–52
Single experiments, 97, 98–100
Sliding levels
description of, 89–90, 382
plastic injection molding experiment, 384–85
wavesolder experiment, 383–84
Slope calibration, 349
Smaller-the-better analysis, 273
analysis techniques, 276–81

Smaller-the-better analysis (*continued*)
- case study, 281–91
- signal-to-noise ratio and, 274–76

Smaller-the-better measurable quality characteristic, 47
- attribute quality characteristics and, 414–16
- infeasible data and, 431–33
- level average analysis and case study, 249–55

Surface mount data sheet, 199
System design, off-line quality control and, 8
System of Experimental Design (Taguchi), 262

T

Taguchi, Genichi, xvii, xix, 1, 262
Taguchi methods, historical background of, 12
Taylor Expansion Series, 4
Testing/measurement instrument
- accuracy/repeatability, 58–62
- availability, 57
- resolution, 58

Test operator/inspector
- bias and, 64–66
- experiment preparation and, 214–15
- proficiency of, 62–63

Test plan
- example of, 199, 202–7
- importance of, 189

Test plan sampling
- guidelines, 192–93
- identification, 196–97
- identifying and randomizing, 213–14
- ordering, 197
- preparation, 196
- selection, 193–96

Test plan structure
- analysis techniques, 191–92
- data worksheet, 191
- experiment description, 190
- experiment objectives, 189–90
- statement of purpose, 189
- testing/inspection procedures, 190–91

Time constraints, 228, 231–33
Tolerance design, off-line quality control and, 9
Toyota, 2

V

Variability, dynamic characteristic analysis and, 342
Variables. *See* Factors
Visual aids, use of, 65–66

W

Wavesolder data sheet, 199
Western Electric, 2
Within experiment error, 175, 177–78

X

Xerox, 2

Z

Zero point proportional equation, 346, 350–52